Primer curso de lengua española

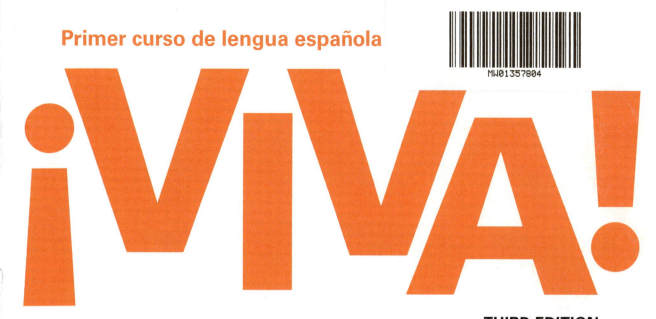

THIRD EDITION

José A. Blanco

Philip Redwine Donley, late
Austin Community College

Boston, Massachusetts

On the cover: folk dancers in
San Miguel de Allende, Mexico.

Publisher: José A. Blanco
President: Janet Dracksdorf
Editorial Development: Deborah Coffey, María Victoria Echeverri, Verónica Tejeda
Project Management: Maria Rosa Alcaraz, Cécile Engeln, Hillary Gospodarek,
Sharon Inglis, Sofía Pellón
Technology Production: Lauren Krolick, Jamie Kostecki, Paola Ríos Schaaf
Design: Robin Herr, Michelle Ingari, Jhoany Jiménez, Nick Ventullo
Production: Oscar Díez, Jennifer López, Fabián Montoya, Andrés Vanegas

© 2015 by Vista Higher Learning, Inc.

No part of this work may be reproduced or distributed in any form or by any means,
electronic or mechanical, including photocopying and recording, or by any information
storage or retrieval system without prior written permission from Vista Higher Learning,
500 Boylston Street, Suite 620, Boston, MA 02116-3736.

Student Text ISBN: 978-1-61857-994-2
Instructor's Annotated Edition ISBN: 978-1-61857-995-9
Library of Congress Control Number: 2013955856

2 3 4 5 6 7 8 9 TC 19 18 17 16 15 14

Printed in Canada.

Introduction

Welcome to **¡VIVA!, Third Edition**. This highly successful introductory Spanish program is designed to provide you with an active and rewarding learning experience. You are about to embark on an exciting adventure as you learn Spanish and explore the diverse cultures of the Spanish-speaking world.

New to the Third Edition

- A completely new **Fotonovela**, filmed in the Yucatan Peninsula and Mexico City that features engaging international characters and a captivating storyline. Photos from the **Fotonovela** open each lesson.
- Enhanced Supersite—groundbreaking technology with powerful course management tools and a simplified user experience
- Online chat activities for synchronous communication and oral practice
- An expanded Testing Program with new tests, plus vocabulary and grammar
- 4 new **Lectura** readings, plus Supersite audio-sync technology for all **Lectura** readings
- 6 new authentic TV Clips showcasing Spanish from diverse locations in the Spanish-speaking world
- iPad®-friendly access*—get Supersite and vText on the go!
- New realia—a new design for most of the **Español en vivo** realistic readings

Original Hallmark Features

- Fresh, user-friendly design and layout that support and facilitate language learning
- An easy-to-navigate, color-coded lesson organization
- An abundance of illustrations, photos, and charts specifically chosen to help you learn
- Integration of an appealing storyline video in each lesson, plus additional cultural videos
- Practical, high-frequency vocabulary for communicating in real-life situations
- Clear, concise grammar explanations that graphically highlight important concepts
- Guided activities practice vocabulary and grammar so that you feel confident communicating in Spanish
- Abundant opportunities to interact in communicative situations
- A process approach to reading, writing, and listening skills
- Presentation of important cultural aspects of the daily lives of Spanish speakers and coverage of the entire Spanish-speaking world
- A complete set of print and technology ancillaries to make learning Spanish easier

*Students must use a computer for audio recording and select presentations and tools that require Flash or Shockwave.

TABLE OF CONTENTS

	PREPARACIÓN	**ESCENAS**

Lección 1
Hola, ¿qué tal?

PREPARACIÓN
Basic greetings and farewells 2
Introductions 3
Courtesy expressions 3

ESCENAS
Fotonovela:
  Bienvenida, Marissa 6

Lección 2
Las clases

PREPARACIÓN
People and places at
  the university 24
Courses of study 24
Days of the week 25

ESCENAS
Fotonovela:
  ¿Qué estudias? 28

Lección 3
La familia

PREPARACIÓN
Family relationships 50
Professions 51

ESCENAS
Fotonovela:
  Un domingo en familia 54

Lección 4
El fin de semana

PREPARACIÓN
Pastimes 72
Places in the city 73

ESCENAS
Fotonovela:
  Fútbol, cenotes y mole 76

iv

TABLE OF CONTENTS

EXPLORACIÓN

Bajo la lupa:
Saludos y besos en los
países hispanos 8

Flash cultura:
Encuentros en la plaza 9

GRAMÁTICA

1.1 Nouns and articles 10
1.2 Numbers 0-30 12
1.3 Present tense of **ser** 14
1.4 Telling time 16

LECTURA

Lectura:
Teléfonos importantes
y direcciones electrónicas . . . 20

Bajo la lupa:
La elección de una
carrera universitaria 30

Flash cultura:
Los estudios 31

2.1 Present tense of regular
–ar verbs 32
2.2 Forming questions 34
2.3 The present tense
of **estar** 36
2.4 Numbers 31–100 38

Lectura:
UAE: La mejor
universidad de Europa 42

¡Vivan los países hispanos!
Estados Unidos y Canadá 45

Bajo la lupa:
¿Cómo te llamas? 56

Flash cultura:
La familia 57

3.1 Descriptive adjectives 58
3.2 Possessive adjectives 60
3.3 Present tense of regular
–er and **–ir** verbs 62
3.4 Present tense of **tener**
and **venir** 64

Lectura:
Las familias 68

Bajo la lupa:
Real Madrid y Barça:
rivalidad total 78

Flash cultura:
¡Fútbol en España! 79

4.1 The present tense of **ir** . . . 80
4.2 Stem-changing
verbs: e→ie, o→ue . . . 82
4.3 Stem-changing
verbs: e→i 84
4.4 Verbs with irregular
yo forms 86

Lectura:
Guía para el fin de semana . . . 90

¡Vivan los países hispanos!
México 93

v

TABLE OF CONTENTS

	PREPARACIÓN	ESCENAS
Lección 5 **Las vacaciones**	Words related to transportation and lodging .... 98 Days of the week, months, seasons, and weather expressions 99	**Fotonovela:** ¡Vamos a la playa! 102
Lección 6 **¡De compras!**	Shopping .... 120 Clothing and colors 121	**Fotonovela:** En el mercado 124
Lección 7 **La vida diaria**	Daily routine and personal hygiene .... 146 Sequencing expressions 147	**Fotonovela:** ¡Necesito arreglarme! 150
Lección 8 **¡A comer!**	Foods and meals .... 168 Adjectives that describe food .. 168	**Fotonovela:** Una cena... romántica 172

vi

TABLE OF CONTENTS

EXPLORACIÓN	GRAMÁTICA	LECTURA

Bajo la lupa:
El Camino Inca 104

Flash cultura:
¡Vacaciones en Perú! 105

5.1 Estar with conditions
and emotions 106

5.2 The present progressive . . 108

5.3 Comparing **ser** and
estar. 110

5.4 Direct object nouns
and pronouns 112

Lectura:
Turismo ecológico
en Puerto Rico 116

Bajo la lupa:
Los mercados al aire libre. . . 126

Flash cultura:
Comprar en los mercados . . 127

6.1 Numbers 101 and
higher 128

6.2 The preterite tense of
regular verbs. 130

6.3 Indirect object pronouns . . 132

6.4 Demonstrative adjectives
and pronouns 134

Lectura:
Corona 138

¡Vivan los países hispanos!
El Caribe 141

Bajo la lupa:
La siesta 152

Flash cultura:
Tapas para todos los días . . . 153

7.1 Reflexive verbs 154

7.2 Indefinite and
negative words 156

7.3 Preterite of **ser** and **ir** . . . 158

7.4 Gustar and verbs
like **gustar** 160

Lectura:
¡Una mañana desastrosa! . . . 164

Bajo la lupa:
Frutas y verduras
de América. 174

Flash cultura:
La comida latina 175

8.1 Preterite of
stem-changing verbs . . . 176

8.2 Double object pronouns . . 178

8.3 Saber and **conocer** 180

8.4 Comparatives and
superlatives. 182

Lectura:
Cinco estrellas para
El Palmito 186

¡Vivan los países hispanos!
Suramérica I 189

TABLE OF CONTENTS

	PREPARACIÓN	ESCENAS

Lección 9
Las celebraciones

	Celebrations 194
	Personal relationships
	   and the stages of life 195
		Fotonovela:
		   El Día de Muertos 198

Lección 10
En el consultorio

	Parts of the body 216
	Health and
	   medical conditions 217
		Fotonovela:
		   ¡Qué dolor! 220

Lección 11
El carro y la tecnología

	The car and its accessories . . . 240
	Computers and
	   electronic products 241
		Fotonovela:
		   En el taller 244

Lección 12
Hogar, dulce hogar

	The parts of a house;
	   household chores 260
	Table settings 260
		Fotonovela:
		   Los quehaceres 264

TABLE OF CONTENTS

EXPLORACIÓN	GRAMÁTICA	LECTURA

Bajo la lupa:
Semana Santa: vacaciones y tradición 200

Flash cultura:
Las fiestas 201

9.1 Irregular preterites 202
9.2 Verbs that change meaning in the preterite 204
9.3 Relative pronouns 206
9.4 ¿Qué? and ¿cuál? 208

Lectura:
Vida social 212

Bajo la lupa:
Servicios de salud 222

Flash cultura:
La salud 223

10.1 The imperfect tense 224
10.2 Constructions with se . . . 226
10.3 Adverbs 228

Lectura:
El consultorio 232

¡Vivan los países hispanos!
Suramérica II 235

Bajo la lupa:
Los cibercafés 246

Flash cultura:
Maravillas de la tecnología . . 247

11.1 The preterite and the imperfect 248
11.2 Por and para 250
11.3 Stressed possessive adjectives and pronouns 252

Lectura:
Tira cómica: *El celular*, Tute . . . 256

Bajo la lupa:
El patio central 256

Flash cultura:
La casa de Frida 257

12.1 Usted and ustedes commands 268
12.2 The present subjunctive 270
12.3 Subjunctive with verbs of will and influence 274

Lectura:
¡Bienvenidos a la Casa Colorada! 278

¡Vivan los países hispanos!
América Central I 281

ix

TABLE OF CONTENTS

	PREPARACIÓN	ESCENAS
Lección 13 **La naturaleza** 	The environment .... 286 Conservation 287	**Fotonovela:** Aventuras en la naturaleza .. 290
Lección 14 **En la ciudad** 	City life .... 306 Postal needs .... 306 Banking .... 307 Giving directions 307	**Fotonovela:** Corriendo por la ciudad 310
Lección 15 **El bienestar** 	Personal fitness and well-being............. 330 Nutrition 331	**Fotonovela:** Chichén Itzá 334
Lección 16 **El mundo del trabajo** 	Professions and the workplace........... 350 Job interviews 351	**Fotonovela:** La entrevista de trabajo 354

TABLE OF CONTENTS

EXPLORACIÓN	GRAMÁTICA	LECTURA

Bajo la lupa:
¡Los Andes se mueven! 292

Flash cultura:
Naturaleza en Costa Rica... 293

13.1 The subjunctive with verbs of emotion 294

13.2 The subjunctive with doubt, disbelief, and denial 296

13.3 The subjunctive with conjunctions 298

Lectura:
Dos fábulas 302

Bajo la lupa:
Paseando en metro 312

Flash cultura:
El metro del D.F. 313

14.1 The subjunctive in adjective clauses 314

14.2 Familiar (**tú**) commands ...316

14.3 **Nosotros/as** commands ..318

Lectura:
Esquina peligrosa,
Marco Denevi 322

¡Vivan los países hispanos!
América Central II 325

Bajo la lupa:
Spas naturales........... 336

Flash cultura:
¿Estrés? ¿Qué estrés? 337

15.1 Past participles used as adjectives 338

15.2 The present perfect 340

15.3 The past perfect 342

Lectura:
El viaje, Cristina Peri Rossi...346

Bajo la lupa:
Beneficios en los empleos ...356

Flash cultura:
El mundo del trabajo 357

16.1 The future tense 358

16.2 The conditional tense ... 360

16.3 The past subjunctive.... 362

Lectura:
Imaginación y destino,
Augusto Monterroso 366

¡Vivan los países hispanos!
España 369

xi

SUPERSITE

Supersite

Each section of your textbook comes with activities on the **¡VIVA!** Supersite, many of which are auto-graded for immediate feedback. Plus, the Supersite is iPad®-friendly*, so it can be accessed on the go!

PREPARACIÓN
- Vocabulary tutorials
- Image-based vocabulary activity with audio
- Listening activities
- Textbook activities
- Additional activities for extra practice
- Chat activities for conversational skill-building and oral practice
- Audio files for **Pronunciación**
- Record-compare practice

ESCENAS
- Streaming video of **Escenas** dramatic series, with instructor-managed options for subtitles and transcripts
- Textbook activities
- Additional activities for extra practice

EXPLORACIÓN
- Reading available online
- Streaming video of **Flash Cultura** series, with instructor-managed options for subtitles and transcripts
- Keywords and support for **Conexión Internet**
- Textbook activities
- Additional activities for extra practice

GRAMÁTICA
- Animated grammar tutorials
- Grammar presentations available online
- Textbook activities
- Additional activities for extra practice
- Chat activities for conversational skill-building and oral practice
- Streaming **TV Clip**, with instructor-managed options for subtitles and transcripts in Spanish and English
- Composition activity for the **Escribir** activity in **Ampliación**

LECTURA
- Audio-synced reading
- Additional reading
- Textbook activities
- Additional activities for extra practice

VOCABULARIO
- Vocabulary list with audio
- Flashcards with audio

¡VIVAN LOS PAÍSES HISPANOS!
- Interactive map
- Textbook activities
- Additional activities for extra practice
- Streaming video of **¡Vivan los países hispanos!** series, with instructor-managed options for subtitles and transcripts in Spanish and English

Plus!
- All textbook and lab audio MP3 files
- Communication center for instructor notifications and feedback
- Live Chat tool for video chat, audio chat, and instant messaging without leaving your browser
- WebSAM online Workbook, Video Manual and Lab Manual
- **v̂Text** online, interactive student edition with access to Supersite activities, audio, and video

Supersite features vary by access level. Visit **vistahigherlearning.com** to explore which Supersite level is right for you.
*Students must use a computer for audio recording and select presentations and tools that require Flash or Shockwave.

Icons and *Recursos* boxes

Icons Familiarize yourself with these icons that appear throughout ¡VIVA!

Additional practice on the Supersite, not included in the textbook, is indicated with this icon feature:

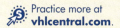

Recursos boxes let you know exactly which print and technology ancillaries you can use to reinforce and expand on every section of every lesson. They include page numbers when applicable.

xiii

¡VIVA! at-a-glance

Lesson Openers
outline the content and goals of each lesson.

Para empezar A series of questions on the lesson opener photo recycles the language you already know and previews the vocabulary you are about to learn.

Lesson organization Consistent, color-coded sections make navigating each lesson easy.

Supersite

Supersite resources are available for every section of the lesson at **vhlcentral.com**. Icons show you which textbook activities are also available online, and where additional practice activities are available. The description next to the (S) icon indicates what additional resources are available for each section: videos, recordings, tutorials, presentations, and more!

Supersite features vary by access level. Visit **vistahigherlearning.com** to explore which Supersite level is right for you.

Preparación
introduces vocabulary central to the lesson theme.

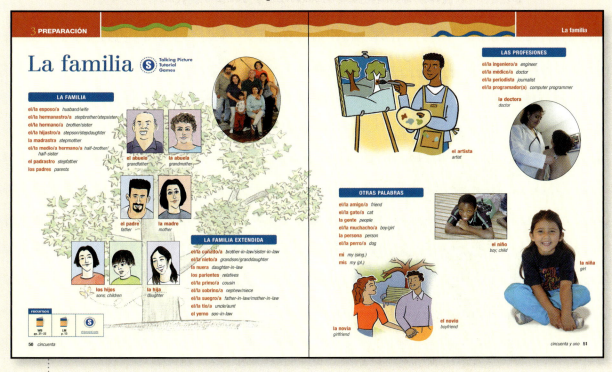

Art Dynamic photos and illustrations present high-frequency vocabulary.

Recursos These boxes let you know exactly which print and technology ancillaries you can use to reinforce and expand on every lesson.

Vocabulary Theme-related vocabulary appears in easy-to-reference Spanish/English lists.

Supersite
- Vocabulary tutorials and games
- Audio support for vocabulary presentation

Supersite features vary by access level. Visit vistahigherlearning.com to explore which Supersite level is right for you.

¡VIVA! at-a-glance

Preparación
practices vocabulary in stages.

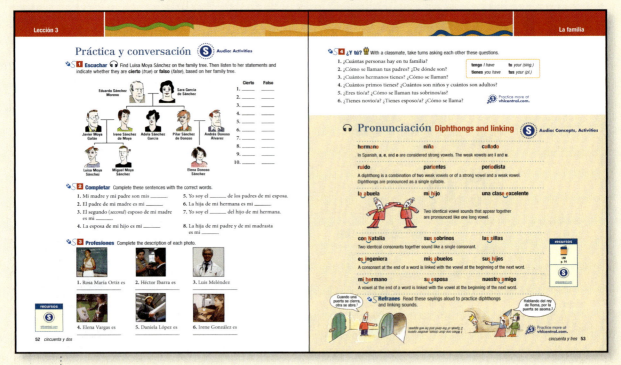

Práctica y conversación Practice always begins with listening activities that focus on vocabulary recognition and comprehension.

Practice continues with a page of guided and transitional activities that reinforce the new vocabulary in diverse formats.

Practice concludes with a variety of activities that get you using vocabulary creatively for self-expression in interactions with a partner, a small group, or the entire class.

Pronunciación explains the sounds and pronunciation of Spanish in **Lecciones 1-9**. **Ortografía** focuses on topics related to Spanish spelling in **Lecciones 10-16**.

Icons Icons provide a visual cue that indicates listening, Supersite, pair, and group activities.

Supersite

- Textbook activities
- Additional online-only practice activities
- Chat activities for conversational skill-building and oral practice

Supersite features vary by access level. Visit vistahigherlearning.com to explore which Supersite level is right for you.

xvi

¡VIVA! at-a-glance

Escenas tells the story of a group of students living and traveling in Mexico.

Personajes The characters who appear in the episode are shown at the top of the page.

Conversations Taken from the **Escenas** video, the conversations re-enter vocabulary from **Preparación**. They also preview structures from the upcoming **Gramática** section in context and in a comprehensible way.

Escenas video The photo-based **Escenas** conversations appear in the textbook's video program.

Expresiones útiles New words and expressions are organized by language function so you can focus on using them for real-life, practical purposes.

Actividades Guided exercises check your understanding and communicative activities allow you to react in a personalized way.

Supersite

- Streaming video of the **Escenas** episode
- Textbook activities
- Additional online-only practice activities

Supersite features vary by access level. Visit vistahigherlearning.com to explore which Supersite level is right for you.

xvii

¡VIVA! at-a-glance

Exploración
highlights engaging contemporary culture through readings and video.

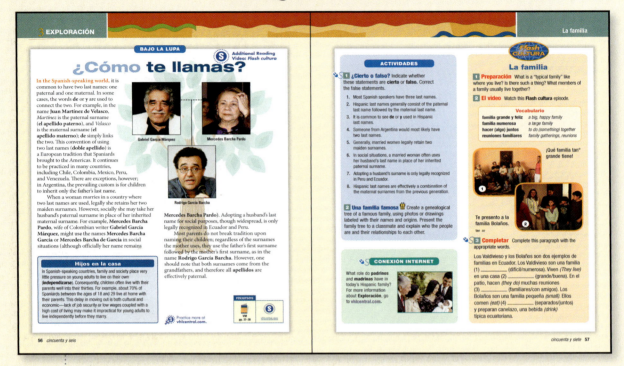

Feature article This focuses on a person, place, custom, event, or tradition in the Spanish-speaking world, with an emphasis on contemporary, day-to-day culture. Written in Spanish as of **Lección 7**, this feature also provides valuable reading practice.

Flash cultura The enormously successful video offers specially-shot content tied to the lesson theme. Previewing support and comprehension activities are integrated into the student text.

Supersite

- **Exploración** article
- Textbook activities
- Additional online-only practice
- **Conexión Internet** activity with questions and keywords related to lesson theme
- Streaming video of **Flash Cultura**

Supersite features vary by access level. Visit vistahigherlearning.com to explore which Supersite level is right for you.

Gramática
uses innovative design to support learning Spanish.

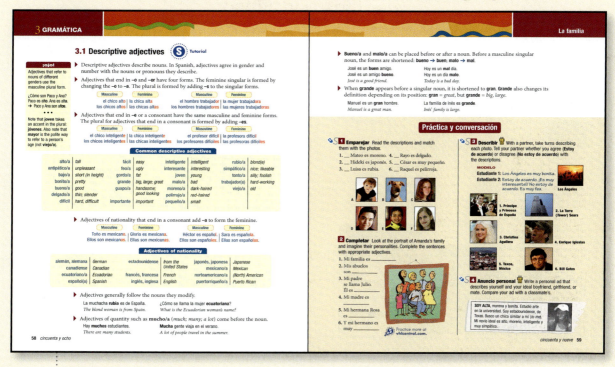

Explanations Written with the student in mind, **¡VIVA!'s** grammar explanations are known for their clarity. Images, charts, and diagrams support the text by illustrating language and calling out key grammatical structures, patterns, and vocabulary.

Video Photos from the **Escenas** video integrate it into the grammar explanations, providing a model and a real-life context for the structures you are studying.

Español en vivo Authentic documents, like advertisements and movie posters, highlight the new grammar point in a real-life context.

Supersite
- Animated grammar tutorials
- Textbook activities
- Additional online-only practice activities
- Chat activities for conversational skill-building and oral practice

Supersite features vary by access level. Visit **vistahigherlearning.com** to explore which Supersite level is right for you.

¡VIVA! at-a-glance

xix

¡VIVA! at-a-glance

Gramática
progresses from directed to communicative practice.

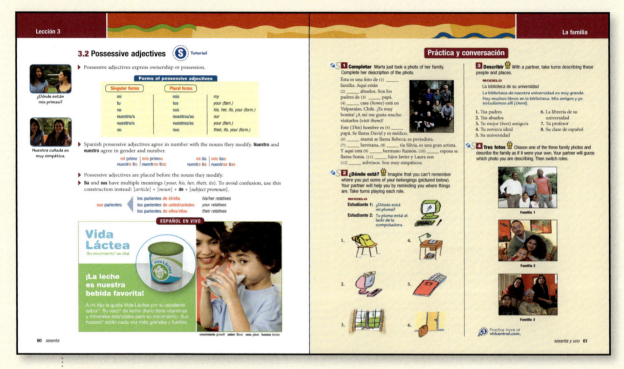

Guided practice *Práctica y conversación* begins with a wide range of guided exercises in contexts that combine current and previously learned vocabulary with each grammar point.

Open-ended practice *Práctica y conversación* ends with opportunities for personalized expression use the lesson's grammar and vocabulary. Activities take place with a partner, in small groups, or with the whole class.

Icons Mouse and Supersite icons let you know when content from the text is available online with auto-grading and when additional content is available.

Supersite

- Animated grammar tutorials
- Textbook activities
- Additional online-only practice activities
- Chat activities for conversational skill-building and oral practice

Supersite features vary by access level. Visit **vistahigherlearning.com** to explore which Supersite level is right for you.

Gramática
emphasizes listening, writing, and speaking in *Ampliación*.

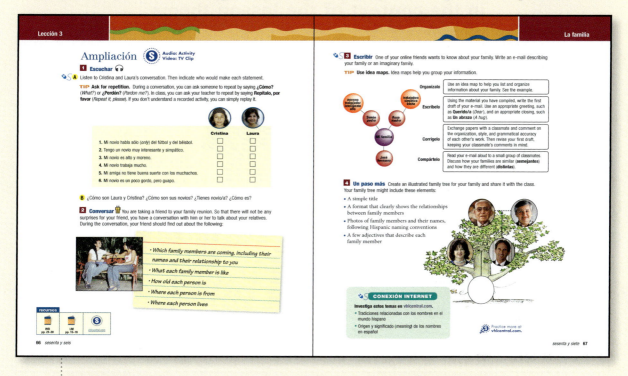

Escuchar A recorded conversation or narration develops your listening skills in Spanish and checks your understanding of what you heard. Valuable on-the-spot listening tips help you carry out the activity effectively.

Conversar Your oral communication skills are developed through realistic, practical role-plays and situations.

Escribir A writing topic and plan take you step-by-step through the writing process, including planning, writing a first draft, peer review, and correcting your work. Valuable on-the-spot writing strategies (tips) help you carry out the activity effectively.

Un paso más This project guides you to research and create a tangible product such as a brochure or a web page or else give a presentation about a certain topic.

Supersite

- Audio activity
- Streaming video of **TV Clip**
- **Conexión Internet** activity with questions and keywords related to lesson theme

Supersite features vary by access level. Visit vistahigherlearning.com to explore which Supersite level is right for you.

¡VIVA! at-a-glance

¡VIVA! at-a-glance

Lectura
supports the development of reading skills in the context of the lesson theme.

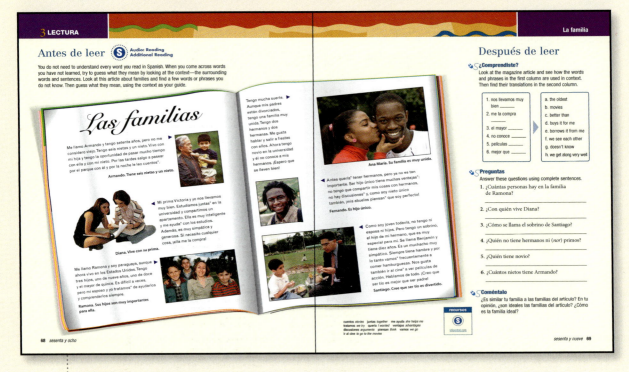

Antes de leer This feature presents helpful strategies and pre-reading activities to build your reading abilities in Spanish.

Readings The selections are specifically related to the lesson theme and recycle the vocabulary and grammar you have learned. **Lecciones 13–16** feature literary selections so you can experience reading works by well-known authors in Spanish.

Después de leer Exercises check your comprehension of the reading.

Coméntalo Activities encourage you to discuss the material in the reading from your own, personal perspective.

Supersite

- Audio-sync reading that highlights text as it is being read
- Textbook activities
- Additional online-only practice

Supersite features vary by access level. Visit vistahigherlearning.com to explore which Supersite level is right for you.

xxii

¡VIVA! at-a-glance

Vocabulario
summarizes the active vocabulary in each lesson.

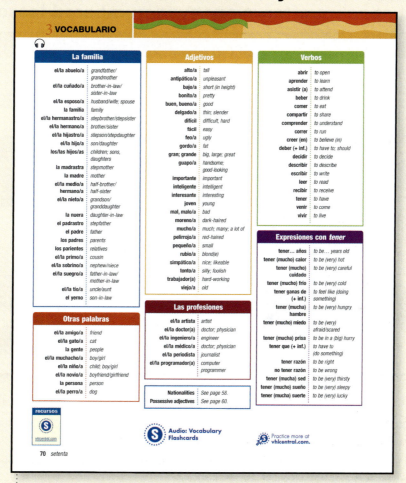

Vocabulario The end-of-lesson page lists the active vocabulary from this lesson. This is the vocabulary that may appear on quizzes or tests.

Supersite

- Audio for all vocabulary items
- Vocabulary flashcards with audio
- **Repaso** activities for practicing vocabulary, grammar, and oral language

Supersite features vary by access level. Visit vistahigherlearning.com to explore which Supersite level is right for you.

¡VIVA! at-a-glance

¡Vivan los países hispanos!
presents the countries of the Spanish-speaking world and appears after every even-numbered lesson.

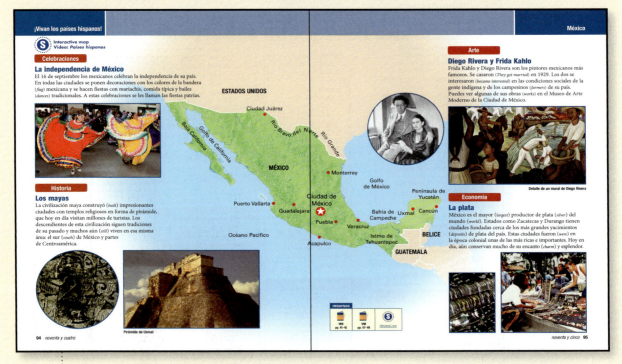

Maps These maps situate the country or region on its continent and highlight significant features.

Readings Short readings with eye-catching photos explore key facets of the location's culture, such as history, fine arts, food, celebrations, and traditions.

Video A video segment from the ¡Vivan los países hispanos! Video Program lets you experience the sights and sounds of each country featured in this section.

Opening and closing pages The opening page sets the scene for the section with a dramatic photo and statistics about the location. ¿Qué aprendiste? activities on the closing page connect what you've learned with your own experiences.

Supersite

- Interactive map
- Streaming video of the ¡Vivan los países hispanos! program
- Textbook activities
- Additional online-only practice activities
- **Conexión Internet** activity with questions and keywords related to lesson theme

Supersite features vary by access level. Visit vistahigherlearning.com to explore which Supersite level is right for you.

¡VIVA! at-a-glance

Consulta

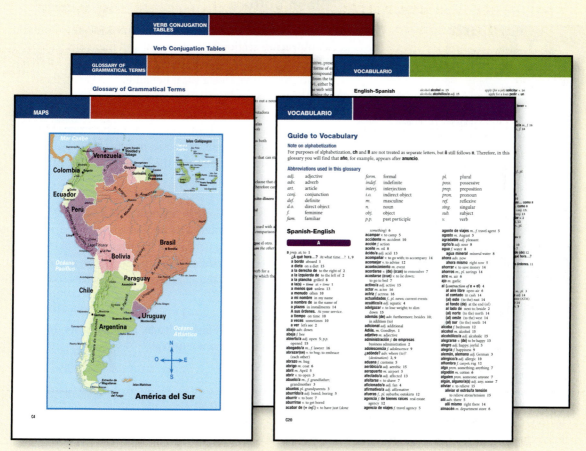

Consulta Find useful reference materials at the end of your textbook.

Maps Find one map for each of the Spanish speaking countries.

Glossary of Grammatical Terms A glossary that contains definitions, explanations and examples of all the grammar concepts covered in the textbook.

Verb Conjugation Tables Verb conjugation tables that show you how to conjugate every verb taught in ¡VIVA!

Vocabulary A comprehensive Spanish-English/English-Spanish vocabulary list that cross-references the lessons, and includes additional common words and expressions.

Supersite

- Reference materials available on the vText

Supersite features vary by access level. Visit vistahigherlearning.com to explore which Supersite level is right for you.

XXV

VIDEO PROGRAMS

VIDEO PROGRAMS

Flash cultura

The dynamic **Flash cultura** video is fully integrated into the **Exploración** section of each lesson and into your Video Manual. Shot in eight countries (US, Puerto Rico, Mexico, Spain, Argentina, Costa Rica, Ecuador, and Peru), these contemporary and engaging episodes expand on the lesson themes. Each episode is hosted by a correspondent from the featured country; the host provides valuable information about a tradition, event, resource, or other aspect of the country's culture and talks to the locals to get their opinions about the subject at hand.

The episodes are entirely in Spanish as of **Lección 7**, but all lessons feature real interviews in Spanish, exposing you to the diverse and authentic accents of the Spanish-speaking world. Support materials in the text, on the Supersite, and in the Video Manual make these interviews accessible so you get the most out of them.

We hope you enjoy **Flash cultura, ¡el programa donde aprender es toda una aventura!**

TV Clip

The **¡VIVA!** Supersite features an authentic TV Clip from the Spanish-speaking world for each lesson. Clip formats include commercials, news stories, and even a short film. These clips have been carefully chosen to be comprehensible for students learning Spanish, and are accompanied by activities and vocabulary lists to facilitate understanding. Developed by Spanish speakers for Spanish speakers, they offer another valuable window into the products, practices, and perspectives that are key to the cultures of the Spanish-speaking world. More importantly, though, these clips are a fun and motivating way to improve your Spanish!

Here are the countries represented in each lesson in **TV Clip**:

Lesson 1 US	Lesson 5 Mexico	Lesson 9 Argentina	Lesson 13 Argentina
Lesson 2 Chile	Lesson 6 Spain	Lesson 10 Spain	Lesson 14 Argentina
Lesson 3 Spain	Lesson 7 Argentina	Lesson 11 Colombia	Lesson 15 Uruguay
Lesson 4 Peru	Lesson 8 Colombia	Lesson 12 Spain	Lesson 16 El Salvador

VIDEO PROGRAMS

Escenas

Fully integrated with your textbook, the **Escenas** video contains sixteen episodes. The episodes present the adventures of the Díaz family, whose household includes two college-aged children and a visiting student from the U.S. Over the course of an academic year, Jimena, Felipe, Marissa, and their friends explore **el D.F.** and other parts of Mexico as they make plans for their future. Their adventures take them through some of the greatest natural and cultural treasures of the Spanish-speaking world, as well as the highs and lows of everyday life.

The **Escenas** section in each textbook lesson is actually an abbreviated version of the dramatic episode featured in the video. Therefore, each **Escenas** section can be done before you see the corresponding video episode, after it, or as a section that stands alone.

The cast

Here are the main characters you will meet when you watch the **Escenas** video:

 From Mexico, Jimena Díaz Velázquez

 From Argentina, Juan Carlos Rossi

 From Mexico, Felipe Díaz Velázquez

 From the U.S., Marissa Wagner

 From Mexico, María Eugenia (Maru) Castaño

 From Spain, Miguel Ángel Lagasca Martínez

xxvii

VIDEO PROGRAMS

In each dramatic segment, the characters interact using the vocabulary and grammar you are studying. As the storyline unfolds, the episodes combine new vocabulary and grammar with previously taught language. The **Resumen** segment serves to recap the plot as well as to emphasize the grammar and vocabulary you are studying.

VIDEO PROGRAMS

¡Vivan los países hispanos!

The **¡Vivan los países hispanos!** video is integrated with the **¡Vivan los países hispanos!** section in **¡VIVA!**. Each segment is 2–3 minutes long and consists of documentary footage from each of the countries featured. The images were specially chosen for interest level and visual appeal, while the all-Spanish narrations were carefully written to reflect the vocabulary and grammar covered in the textbook.

As you watch the video segments, you will experience a diversity of images and topics: cities, monuments, traditions, festivals, archaeological sites, geographical wonders, and more. You will be transported to each Spanish-speaking country, including the United States and Canada, thereby having the opportunity to expand your cultural perspectives with information directly related to the content of **¡VIVA!**.

xxix

ANCILLARIES

STUDENT ANCILLARIES

- **Student Activities Manual (Workbook/Video Manual/Lab Manual)**

The Workbook activities provide additional practice of the vocabulary and grammar in each textbook lesson and the information in the **¡Vivan los países hispanos!** sections. The Video Manual includes pre-, while-, and post-viewing activities for the **Escenas**, **¡Vivan los países hispanos!**, and the **Flash cultura** videos. The Lab Manual activities build listening comprehension, speaking, and pronunciation skills.

- **Lab Program MP3s**

The Lab Program MP3 audio files provide the recordings to be used in conjunction with the activities in the Lab Manual. These recordings are available on the **¡VIVA!** Supersite.

- **Textbook MP3s**

The Textbook MP3 files are the recordings for the listening activities in the **Preparación**, **Pronunciación**, and **Ampliación** sections in each lesson of the student text, as well as the active vocabulary in each end-of-lesson **Vocabulario** list. These recordings are available on the **¡VIVA!** Supersite.

- **WebSAM**

The WebSAM delivers the Workbook, Video Manual, and Lab Manual online.

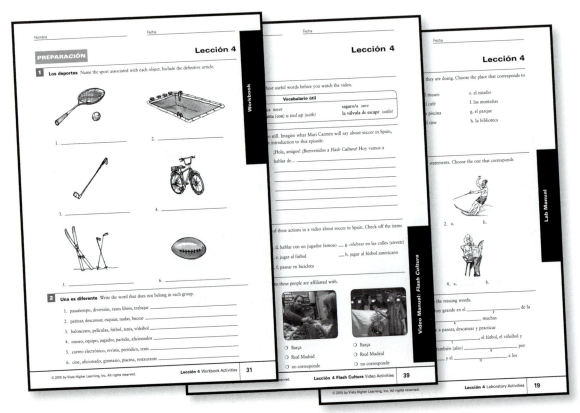

xxx

ACKNOWLEDGMENTS

We are grateful to the members of the Spanish-teaching community who reviewed the original manuscript and/or class-tested the materials. Their insights and detailed comments were invaluable to us as we created the First Edition.

¡VIVA!, Third Edition, has been informed by extensive reviews and ongoing input from both students and instructors using the Second Edition. Accordingly, we gratefully acknowledge those who shared their suggestions, recommendations, and ideas as we prepared this Third Edition.

We express our appreciation to the many instructors and hundreds of students using ¡VIVA! who completed our online reviews. Their comments and suggestions were instrumental in shaping the entire ¡VIVA!, Third Edition, program.

Reviewers

Regina Alderton
Frostburg State University

Aleta Anderson
Grand Rapids Community College

Sr. Antoine-Marie Baurier
Marymount College, Palos Verdes

John R. Boyst
Salem College

Man-Lih Chai
John Carroll University

Florence Dwyer
Thomas More College

Arcides Gonzales
California University of Pennsylvania

Krishauna Hines-Gaither
Salem College

Douglas A. Jackson
University of South Carolina Upstate

Dianne Jernigan
Madisonville Community College

Susan Kalt, Ph.D.
Roxbury Community College

Isidoro Kessel
Thomas Nelson Community College

Celeste Dolores Mann
Georgian Court University

Lori Merck
University of South Carolina Upstate

Deborah Neuman
Gaston College

Tim Owens
St. Clair County Community College

Kathryn Quinn-Sanchez
Georgian Court University

Dr. Jorge Salvo
Claflin University

Bryant Smith
Nicholls State University

Margaret M. Walker
Bryn Athyn College

Mac Williams
Coker College

Ho Sang Yoon
Salem College

1 Hola, ¿qué tal?

Communicative Goals

You will learn how to:
- use greetings, farewells, courtesy expressions, and numbers
- identify yourself and others
- tell time

PREPARACIÓN
pages 2–5
- Words related to meeting, greeting, and saying goodbye
- Courtesy expressions
- Pronouncing the Spanish alphabet

ESCENAS
pages 6–7
- Marissa arrives from the U.S. for a year abroad in Mexico City. She meets her Mexican hosts, the Díaz family, survives a practical joke, and settles in to unpack.

EXPLORACIÓN
pages 8–9
- Bajo la lupa: *Saludos y besos en los países hispanos*
- Flash cultura: *Encuentros en la plaza*

GRAMÁTICA
pages 10–19
- Nouns and articles
- Numbers 0–30
- Present tense of **ser**
- Telling time

LECTURA
pages 20–21
- Address book: *Información importante*

Para empezar

- Guess what the people in the photo are saying:
  a. Por favor.   b. Hola.   c. amigo
- Most likely they would also say:
  a. Gracias.   b. fiesta   c. Buenos días.

1 PREPARACIÓN

Hola, ¿qué tal?

Talking Picture Tutorial Games

SALUDOS Y DESPEDIDAS

Buenas noches. *Good evening; Good night.*
Buenas tardes. *Good afternoon.*
Hasta la vista. *See you later.*
Hasta pronto. *See you soon.*
Hasta mañana. *See you tomorrow.*

SEÑORA	Hola, señor Lara. ¿Cómo está usted?
SEÑOR	Muy bien, gracias. ¿Y usted, señora Salas?
SEÑORA	Bien, gracias.
SEÑOR	Hasta luego, señora Salas. Saludos al señor Salas.
SEÑORA	Adiós.

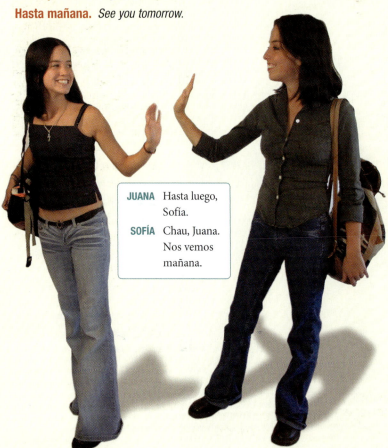

JUANA	Hasta luego, Sofía.
SOFÍA	Chau, Juana. Nos vemos mañana.

¿CÓMO ESTÁS?

¿Cómo estás? *(familiar) How are you?*
No muy bien. *Not very well.*
¿Qué pasa? *What's happening?; What's going on?*

CARLOS	¿Qué tal, Roberto?
ROBERTO	Regular. ¿Y tú?
CARLOS	Bien. ¿Qué hay de nuevo?
ROBERTO	Nada.

recursos

WB pp. 1–2
LM p. 1
vhlcentral.com

Hola, ¿qué tal?

PRESENTACIONES

¿Cómo se llama usted? *What's your name? (form.)*
¿Cómo te llamas (tú)? *What's your name? (fam.)*
Le presento a… *I would like to introduce you to (name). (form.)*
Te presento a… *I would like to introduce you to (name). (fam.)*
Éste es… *This is… (masculine)*
Ésta es… *This is… (feminine)*

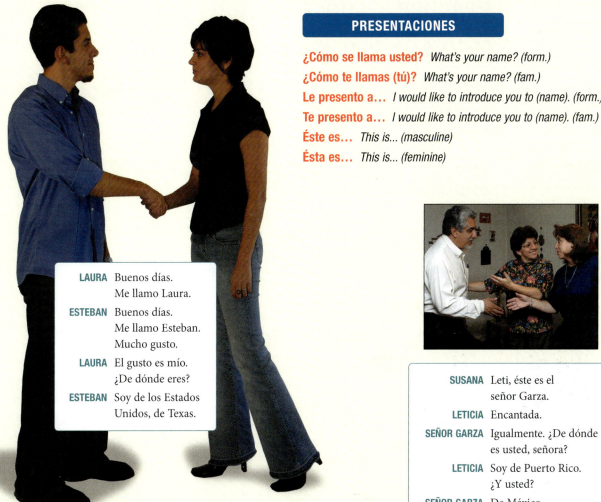

LAURA Buenos días. Me llamo Laura.
ESTEBAN Buenos días. Me llamo Esteban. Mucho gusto.
LAURA El gusto es mío. ¿De dónde eres?
ESTEBAN Soy de los Estados Unidos, de Texas.

SUSANA Leti, éste es el señor Garza.
LETICIA Encantada.
SEÑOR GARZA Igualmente. ¿De dónde es usted, señora?
LETICIA Soy de Puerto Rico. ¿Y usted?
SEÑOR GARZA De México.

EXPRESIONES DE CORTESÍA

Por favor. *Please.*
De nada. *You're welcome.*
No hay de qué. *You're welcome.*
Lo siento. *I'm sorry.*
Muchas gracias. *Thank you very much; Thanks a lot.*

tres **3**

Lección 1

Práctica y conversación

1 **¿Lógico o ilógico?** Listen to each conversation and indicate whether the conversation is logical or illogical.

	1.	2.	3.	4.	5.	6.
Lógico						
Ilógico						

> **¡ojo!**
> Look at these words:
> **señor (Sr.)** *Mr.; sir*
> **señora (Sra.)** *Mrs.; ma'am*
> **señorita (Srta.)** *Miss*
> Note that the abbreviations are capitalized, while the titles themselves are not.
>
> • • •
>
> There is no Spanish equivalent for the English title *Ms.*

2 **Una fiesta** Margarita is having an all-day party to celebrate her twentieth birthday. Listen to the conversations and indicate whether each guest is arriving (**Llega**) or leaving (**Sale**).

	Llega	Sale		Llega	Sale
1. Ramiro	_____	_____	4. Vicente	_____	_____
2. Sra. Sánchez	_____	_____	5. Profesor Lado	_____	_____
3. Luisa	_____	_____	6. Sr. Torres	_____	_____

3 **Sinónimos** For each expression, write a word or phrase that expresses a similar idea.

MODELO
¿Cómo estas? ¿Qué tal?

1. De nada. _____
2. Encantado. _____
3. Adiós. _____
4. Te presento a Antonio. _____
5. ¿Qué hay de nuevo? _____
6. Mucho gusto. _____

4 **Ordenar** With a classmate, put this scrambled conversation in order. Then act it out.

—Muy bien, gracias. Soy María Rosa.
—Soy de Ecuador. ¿Y tú?
—Mucho gusto, María Rosa.
—Hola. Me llamo Carlos. ¿Cómo estás?
—Soy de Argentina.
—Igualmente. ¿De dónde eres, Carlos?

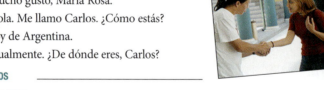

CARLOS _____
MARÍA ROSA _____
CARLOS _____
MARÍA ROSA _____
CARLOS _____
MARÍA ROSA _____

recursos
vhlcentral.com

4 *cuatro*

Hola, ¿qué tal?

 5 Conversaciones With a partner, make up a conversation in Spanish for each photo.

Practice more at vhlcentral.com.

Pronunciación The Spanish alphabet

Audio: Concepts, Activities

The Spanish and English alphabets are almost identical, with a few exceptions. For example, the Spanish letter **ñ** (**eñe**) doesn't occur in the English alphabet. Furthermore, the letters **k** (**ka**) and **w** (**doble v**) are used only in words of foreign origin. Examine the chart below to find other differences.

Letra	Nombre(s)	Ejemplo(s)	Letra	Nombre(s)	Ejemplo(s)
a	a	adiós	m	eme	mapa
b	be	bien, problema	n	ene	nacionalidad
c	ce	cosa, cero	ñ	eñe	mañana
ch	che	chico	o	o	once
d	de	diario, nada	p	pe	profesor
e	e	estudiante	q	cu	qué
f	efe	foto	r	ere	regular, señora
g	ge	gracias, Gerardo, regular	s	ese	señor
			t	te	tú
h	hache	hola	u	u	usted
i	i	igualmente	v	ve	vista, nuevo
j	jota	Javier	w	doble ve	walkman
k	ka, ca	kilómetro	x	equis	existir, México
l	ele	lápiz	y	i griega, ye	yo
ll	elle	llave	z	zeta, ceta	zona

¡LENGUA VIVA!
Note that **ch** and **ll** are digraphs, or two letters that together produce one sound. Conventionally they are considered part of the alphabet, but **ch** and **ll** do not have their own entries when placing words in alphabetical order, as in a glossary.

Refranes Read these sayings aloud.

Ver es creer.[1]

En boca cerrada no entran moscas.[2]

[1] Seeing is believing. [2] Silence is golden.

Practice more at vhlcentral.com.

recursos

LM p. 2

vhlcentral.com

cinco 5

ESCENAS

¡Bienvenida, Marissa! Video: *Fotonovela*

Marissa llega a México para pasar un año con la familia Díaz.

Expresiones útiles

Identifying yourself and others
¿Cómo se llama usted?
What's your name?
Yo soy Diego, el portero. Mucho gusto.
I'm Diego, the doorman. Nice to meet you.
¿Cómo te llamas?
What's your name?
Me llamo Marissa.
My name is Marissa.
¿Quién es…? / ¿Quiénes son…?
Who is…? / Who are…?
Es mi esposo. *He's my husband.*
Tú eres…, ¿verdad? / ¿cierto? / ¿no?
You are…, right?

Identifying objects
¿Qué hay en esta cosa?
What's in this thing?
Bueno, a ver, aquí hay tres cuadernos.
Well, let's see, here are three notebooks.
**Oye / Oiga, ¿cómo se dice *suitcase*
en español?**
Hey, how do you say suitcase *in Spanish?*
Se dice maleta. *You say maleta.*

Saying what time it is
¿Qué hora es? *What time is it?*
Es la una. / Son las dos.
It's one o'clock. / It's two o'clock.
Son las cuatro y veinticinco.
It's four twenty-five.

Polite expressions
Con permiso.
Pardon me; Excuse me.
(to request permission)
Perdón.
Pardon me; Excuse me. (to get someone's attention or excuse yourself)
¡Bienvenido/a! *Welcome!*

MARISSA ¿Usted es de Cuba?
SRA. DÍAZ Sí, de La Habana. Y Roberto es de Mérida. Tú eres de Wisconsin, ¿verdad?
MARISSA Sí, de Appleton, Wisconsin.

MARISSA ¿Quiénes son los dos chicos de las fotos? ¿Jimena y Felipe?
SRA. DÍAZ Sí. Ellos son estudiantes.

DON DIEGO Buenas tardes, señora. Señorita, bienvenida a la ciudad de México.
MARISSA ¡Muchas gracias!

MARISSA ¿Cómo se llama usted?
DON DIEGO Yo soy Diego. Mucho gusto.
MARISSA El gusto es mío, don Diego.

DON DIEGO ¿Cómo está usted hoy, señora Carolina?
SRA. DÍAZ Muy bien, gracias. ¿Y usted?
DON DIEGO Bien, gracias.

---

recursos

VM
pp. 1–2

vhlcentral.com

6 seis

Hola, ¿qué tal?

MARISSA SRA. DÍAZ DON DIEGO SR. DÍAZ FELIPE JIMENA

SRA. DÍAZ Ahí hay dos maletas. Son de Marissa.
DON DIEGO Con permiso.

SR. DÍAZ ¿Qué hora es?
FELIPE Son las cuatro y veinticinco.

SRA. DÍAZ Marissa, te presento a Roberto, mi esposo.
SR. DÍAZ Bienvenida, Marissa.
MARISSA Gracias, señor Díaz.

JIMENA ¿Qué hay en esta cosa?
MARISSA Bueno, a ver, hay tres cuadernos, un mapa... ¡Y un diccionario!
JIMENA ¿Cómo se dice mediodía en inglés?
FELIPE "*Noon*".

FELIPE Estás en México, ¿verdad?
MARISSA ¿Sí?
FELIPE Nosotros somos tu diccionario.

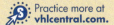

Practice more at **vhlcentral.com**.

Actividades

1 ¿Cierto o falso? Indicate if each statement is **cierto** or **falso**. Then correct the false statements.

1. La Sra. Díaz es de Caracas.
2. El Sr. Díaz es de Mérida.
3. Marissa es de Los Ángeles, California.
4. Jimena y Felipe son profesores.
5. Las dos maletas son de Jimena.

2 Completar Complete the conversation between Don Diego and Marissa.

DON DIEGO Buenos días, (1) _____.
MARISSA Buenos días, señor. ¿Cómo se (2) _____ usted?
DON DIEGO Yo me llamo Diego, ¿y (3) _____?
MARISSA Yo me llamo Marissa. (4) _____.
DON DIEGO (5) _____, señorita Marissa.

3 Preguntas Imagine that you are speaking with a traveler you just met at the airport. With a partner, create a conversation using these cues.

- Greet each other.
- Introduce yourselves.
- Ask how your partner is doing.
- Ask where your partner is from.
- Say goodbye.

EXPLORACIÓN

BAJO LA LUPA

S Additional Reading
Video: *Flash cultura*

Saludos y besos en los países hispanos

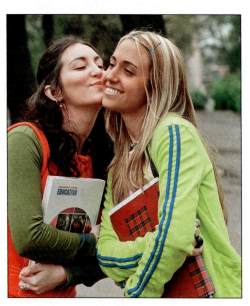

In Spanish-speaking countries, kissing on the cheek is a customary way to greet friends and family members. Even when people are introduced for the first time, it is common for them to kiss, particularly in non-business settings. Whereas North Americans maintain considerable personal space when greeting, Spaniards and Latin Americans tend to decrease their personal space and give one or two kisses (**besos**) on the cheek, sometimes accompanied by a handshake or a hug. In formal business settings, where associates do not know one another on a personal level, a simple handshake is appropriate.

Greeting someone with a **beso** varies according to gender and region. Men generally greet each other with a hug or warm handshake, with the exception of Argentina, where male friends and relatives lightly kiss on the cheek. Greetings between men and women, and between women, generally include kissing, but can differ depending on the country and context. In Spain, it is customary to give **dos besos**, starting with the right cheek first. In Latin American countries, including Mexico, Costa Rica, Colombia, and Chile, a greeting consists of a single "air kiss" on the right cheek. Peruvians also "air kiss," but strangers will simply shake hands. In Colombia, female acquaintances tend to simply pat each other on the right forearm or shoulder.

Tendencias

País	Beso	País	Beso
Argentina	💋	España	💋💋
Bolivia	💋	México	💋
Chile	💋	Paraguay	💋💋
Colombia	💋	Puerto Rico	💋
El Salvador	💋	Venezuela	💋/💋💋

Practice more at vhlcentral.com.

Hola, ¿qué tal?

ACTIVIDADES

1 **¿Cierto o falso?** Indicate whether these statements are true (**cierto**) or false (**falso**). Correct the false statements.

1. Hispanic people use less personal space when greeting than in the U.S.
2. Men never greet with a kiss in Spanish-speaking countries.
3. Shaking hands is not appropriate for a business setting in Latin America.
4. Spaniards greet with one kiss on the right cheek.
5. In Mexico, people greet with an "air kiss."
6. Gender can play a role in the type of greeting given.
7. If two women acquaintances meet in Colombia, they should exchange two kisses on the cheek.
8. In Peru, a man and a woman meeting for the first time would probably greet each other with an "air kiss."

2 **Saludos** Role-play these greetings with a partner. Include a verbal greeting as well as a kiss or handshake, as appropriate.

1. friends in Mexico
2. business associates at a conference in Chile

CONEXIÓN INTERNET

What is the Spanish custom of **el paseo**? For more information about **Exploración**, go to **vhlcentral.com**.

Encuentros en la plaza

1 **Preparación** Where do you usually meet? Are there public places where you get together? What do you do there?

2 **El video** Watch this **Flash cultura** episode.

Vocabulario
abrazo *hug*   plaza *square*

Today we are at the **Plaza de Mayo**.

People come to walk and get some fresh air…

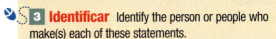

3 **Identificar** Identify the person or people who make(s) each of these statements.

1. ¿Cómo están ustedes?   a. Gonzalo
2. ¡Qué bueno verte!   b. Mariana
3. Mucho gusto, Mariana.   c. Mark
4. Hola.   d. Silvina

recursos

VM
pp. 33–34

vhlcentral.com

nueve 9

1 GRAMÁTICA

1.1 Nouns and articles

▶ Nouns identify people, places, animals, things. All Spanish nouns have gender (masculine or feminine) and number (singular or plural).

▶ The majority of the time, nouns referring to males are masculine and nouns referring to females are feminine.

Masculine		Feminine		Masculine		Feminine	
el hombre	the man	la mujer	the woman	el conductor	the driver	la conductora	the driver
el chico	the boy	la chica	the girl	el profesor	the teacher	la profesora	the teacher
el pasajero	the passenger	la pasajera	the passenger				

▶ Most nouns ending in **–o**, **–ma**, and **–s** are masculine. Most nouns ending in **–a**, **–ción**, and **–dad** are feminine.

Masculine		Feminine	
el cuaderno	the notebook	la cosa	the thing
el diario	the diary	la escuela	the school
el diccionario	the dictionary	la maleta	the suitcase
el número	the number	la mochila	the backpack
el video	the video	la palabra	the word
el problema	the problem	la lección	the lesson
el programa	the program	la conversación	the conversation
el autobús	the bus	la nacionalidad	the nationality
el país	the country	la comunidad	the community

¡ojo!
Video and **problema** are *cognates*—words that share similar spellings and meanings in Spanish and English. Recognizing cognates will help you determine the meaning of many Spanish words. Here are some other cognates: **el animal**, **el apartamento**, **la decisión**, **la música**, **el restaurante**.

▶ Some nouns have identical masculine and feminine forms. The definite article (**el** or **la**) indicates the gender of these words.

Masculine		Feminine	
el turista	the tourist	la turista	the tourist
el joven	the young man	la joven	the young woman
el estudiante	the student	la estudiante	the student

¡ojo!
El lápiz (*pencil*), **el mapa** (*map*), and **el día** (*day*) are masculine. **La mano** (*hand*) is feminine.

•••

In general, when a singular noun has an accent mark on the last syllable, the accent is dropped from the plural form:

la lecci**ó**n → las lecci**o**nes

el autob**ú**s → los autob**u**ses

Plural of nouns

▶ Nouns that end in a vowel form the plural by adding **–s**. Nouns that end in a consonant add **–es**. Nouns that end in **–z** change the **–z** to **–c**, then add **–es**.

SINGULAR	PLURAL	SINGULAR	PLURAL
el chico	los chicos	el país	los países
la palabra	las palabras	el lápiz	los lápices

▶ The masculine plural form may refer to a mixed-gender group.

1 pasajero + 2 pasajeras = 3 pasajeros

10 *diez*

Hola, ¿qué tal?

Spanish articles

Spanish has four forms that are equivalent to the English definite article *the*. Spanish also has four forms that are equivalent to the English indefinite article, which, according to context, may mean *a, an,* or *some*.

Spanish articles

Definite articles

MASCULINE		FEMININE	
el diccionario	the dictionary	la computadora	the computer
los diccionarios	the dictionaries	las computadoras	the computers

Indefinite articles

un pasajero	a (one) passenger	una fotografía	a (one) photograph
unos pasajeros	some passengers	unas fotografías	some photographs

¡ojo!

Feminine singular nouns that begin with **a-** or **ha-** require the masculine articles **el** and **un** to avoid repetition of the **a** sound:

el agua *water*
las aguas *waters*
un hacha *ax*
unas hachas *axes*

Práctica y conversación

Practice more at **vhlcentral.com**.

1 Singular y plural Make the singular words plural and the plural words singular.

1. el turista _____
2. las cosas _____
3. una mujer _____
4. la mochila _____
5. los países _____
6. el problema _____
7. unos hombres _____
8. el conductor _____
9. un pasajero _____
10. una mano _____

2 Identificar For each photo, provide the noun and its corresponding definite and indefinite articles.

MODELO
Las maletas, unas maletas.

1. _____   3. _____

2. _____   4. _____

3 Clasificar  With a partner, identify the photos in Spanish and supply the definite and indefinite articles. Then indicate whether the photos represent objects or persons.

¿Qué es/son? ¿Objeto(s) o persona(s)?

1. _____   2. _____   3. _____
_____   _____   _____

4. _____   5. _____   6. _____
_____   _____   _____

4 Charadas In groups, play a game of charades. Individually, think of two nouns for each charade—for example, a boy using a computer (**un chico**; **una computadora**). The first person to guess correctly acts out the next charade.

once 11

Lección 1

1.2 Numbers 0–30  Tutorial

Numbers 0–30

0 cero	4 cuatro	8 ocho	12 doce	16 dieciséis	20 veinte	24 veinticuatro	28 veintiocho
1 uno	5 cinco	9 nueve	13 trece	17 diecisiete	21 veintiuno	25 veinticinco	29 veintinueve
2 dos	6 seis	10 diez	14 catorce	18 dieciocho	22 veintidós	26 veintiséis	30 treinta
3 tres	7 siete	11 once	15 quince	19 diecinueve	23 veintitrés	27 veintisiete	

¡ojo!

Uno and **veintiuno** are used when counting (**uno, dos, tres…veinte, veintiuno, veintidós…**). They are also used after a noun, even if it is feminine (**la lección uno**).

▶ Before a masculine noun, **uno** shortens to **un**. Before a feminine noun, **uno** changes to **una**.

un hombre → veintiún hombres   una mujer → veintiuna mujeres

▶ To ask *how many*, use **¿Cuántos?** with a masculine noun and **¿Cuántas?** with a feminine one. **Hay** means both *there is* and *there are*. Use **¿Hay…?** to ask *Is/Are there…?* Use **no hay** to express *there is/are not*.

¿**Hay** chicas en la fotografía?
No, **no hay** chicas.
Are there girls in the picture?
No, there aren't any girls.

¿**Cuántos** chicos **hay**?
Hay cuatro.
How many guys are there?
There are four.

80 *ochenta*   **trabaja** *works*   **mejor** *better*   **Apoye** *Support*

12   doce

Práctica y conversación

1 Matemáticas Solve these math problems.

+ más − menos = es (singular) / son (plural)

MODELO 9 + 2 = Nueve más dos son once.

1. 3 + 10 = _____
2. 22 − 3 = _____
3. 4 + 8 = _____
4. 17 + 13 = _____
5. 22 + 1 = _____
6. 5 − 2 = _____
7. 11 + 12 = _____
8. 10 − 10 = _____
9. 3 + 14 = _____
10. 22 − 11 = _____

2 ¿Cuántos hay? Indicate how many people or things there are in each drawing.

MODELO
¿Cuántas maletas hay?
Hay cuatro maletas.

1. ¿Cuántos hombres hay?
_____
4. ¿Cuántas fotografías hay?
_____

2. ¿Cuántos chicos hay?
_____
5. ¿Cuántos turistas hay?
_____

3. ¿Cuántas conductoras hay?
_____
6. ¿Cuántas chicas hay?
_____

3 Describir With a classmate, answer these questions about the photo.

1. ¿Cuántas mujeres hay en la fotografía?
_____
2. ¿Cuántos hombres hay?
_____
3. ¿Cuántos jóvenes hay?
_____
4. ¿Cuántos libros (*books*) hay?
_____
5. ¿Cuántas personas hay?
_____
6. ¿Cuántos/as adultos/as (*adults*) hay?
_____

4 En la clase With a classmate, take turns asking and answering these questions about your classroom.

1. ¿Cuántos estudiantes hay?
2. ¿Cuántos profesores hay?
3. ¿Cuántos hombres hay?
4. ¿Cuántas mujeres hay?
5. ¿Hay una computadora?
6. ¿Hay fotografías?
7. ¿Cuántos mapas hay?
8. ¿Hay diccionarios?
9. ¿Hay cuadernos?
10. ¿Cuántas mochilas hay?
11. ¿Hay maletas?
12. ¿Hay chicos?

Practice more at vhlcentral.com.

Hola, ¿qué tal?

trece 13

Lección 1

1.3 Present tense of ser Tutorial

Subject pronouns

> ¡ojo!
>
> **Nosotros, vosotros,** and **ellos** refer to a group of males or to a group of males and females. **Nosotras, vosotras,** and **ellas** refer only to groups of females.
>
> • • •
>
> In Latin America, **ustedes** is used as the plural of both **tú** and **usted.** In Spain, **vosotros/as** is used as the plural of **tú. Usted** and **ustedes** are abbreviated as **Ud.** and **Uds.**

▸ In order to use verbs, you will need to learn about subject pronouns. A subject pronoun replaces the name or title of a person or thing and acts as the subject of a verb.

Carlos es estudiante. → Él es estudiante.

Subject pronouns

	Singular forms		Plural forms	
FIRST PERSON	yo	I	nosotros	we (masculine)
			nosotras	we (feminine)
SECOND PERSON	tú	you (familiar)	~~vosotros~~	you (masc., fam.)
	usted (Ud.)	you (formal)	~~vosotras~~	you (fem., fam.)
			ustedes (Uds.)	you (form.)
THIRD PERSON	él	he	ellos	they (masc.)
	ella	she	ellas	they (fem.)

▸ Notice that Spanish has two subject pronouns that mean *you* (singular). Use **tú** when talking to friends, family members, and children. Use **usted** when talking to someone with whom you have a more formal relationship, such as an employer, a professor, or someone who is older than you.

The present tense of ser

ser (to be)

Singular forms		Plural forms	
yo	soy (I am)	nosotros/as	somos (we are)
tú	eres (you are)	vosotros/as	sois (you are)
Ud./él/ella	es (you are; he/she is)	Uds./ellos/ellas	son (you/they are)

> ¡ojo!
>
> **De** does not form contractions with **la, los,** or **las.**
> Es la mochila **del** pasajero.
> Es la mochila **de la** pasajera.
> Es la mochila **de los** pasajeros.

▸ Use **ser** to identify people and things.

▸ There is no Spanish equivalent of the English subject pronoun *it.*

| ¿Quién **es** ella? | **Es** Marissa. | ¿Qué **es**? | **Es** una computadora. |
| Who is she? | She's Marissa. | What is it? | It's a computer. |

▸ Use **ser** to express possession, with the preposition **de. De** combines with **el** to form the contraction **del.** Note that Spanish does not use [*apostrophe*]+ *s* to indicate possession.

| ¿De quién **es** la mochila? | **Es** la mochila **de** María | ¿De quién **son** los lápices? | **Son** los lápices **del** chico. |
| Whose backpack is this? | It's María's backpack. | Whose pencils are these? | They are the boy's pencils. |

14 *catorce*

Hola, ¿qué tal?

▸ Express origin using **ser de**.

¿De dónde **es** Marissa? **Es de** los Estados Unidos.
Where is Marissa from? *She's from the U.S.*

▸ Use **ser** to talk about someone's occupation.

Jimena **es** estudiante. Isabel **es** profesora.
Jimena is a student. *Isabel is a teacher.*

¡ojo!
Spanish does not use **un** or **una** after **ser** when mentioning a person's occupation, unless the occupation is accompanied by an adjective.
Roberto **es** profesor.
Roberto **es un** profesor excelente.

Práctica y conversación

Practice more at vhlcentral.com.

1 ¿Qué es? Ask your partner what each object is and to whom it belongs.

MODELO
Estudiante 1: ¿Qué es?
Estudiante 2: Es un diccionario.

Estudiante 1: ¿De quién es?
Estudiante 2: Es del profesor.

1.
2.
3.
4.

2 En el dormitorio Using the items in the word bank, ask your partner questions about Susana's dorm room.

¿Cuántas?
¿Cuántos?
¿De dónde?
¿De quién?
¿Qué?
¿Quién?

3 ¿Quién es? With a partner, take turns asking who these people are and where they are from.

MODELO
Estudiante 1: ¿Quiénes son?
Estudiante 2: Son Jennifer López y Marc Anthony.

Estudiante 1: ¿De dónde son?
Estudiante 2: (Ellos) son de Nueva York.

Jennifer López y Marc Anthony
Nueva York

Gloria Estefan
Cuba

Penélope Cruz y Antonio Banderas
España

Shakira
Colombia

4 Personas famosas Pretend to be a person from either **Cuba**, **México**, **España** (Spain), **Canadá** or **los Estados Unidos** (U.S.) who is famous in one of these professions. Your classmates will try to guess who you are.

| actor | *actor* | cantante | *singer* | escritor(a) | *writer* |
| actriz | *actress* | deportista | *athlete* | músico/a | *musician* |

MODELO
Estudiante 3: ¿Eres de Cuba?
Estudiante 1: Sí.
Estudiante 2: ¿Eres mujer?
Estudiante 1: No. Soy hombre.
Estudiante 3: ¿Eres músico?
Estudiante 1: No. Soy actor.
Estudiante 2: ¿Eres Andy García?
Estudiante 1: ¡Sí! ¡Sí!

Andy García

quince 15

Lección 1

1.4 Telling time Tutorial

▶ Use numbers with the verb **ser** to tell time. To ask what time it is, use **¿Qué hora es?** To say what time it is, use **es la** with **una** and **son las** with other hours.

 Es la una.   Son las cuatro.

▶ Express time from the hour to the half hour by adding minutes.

 Son las dos y diez.   Son las ocho y veinte.

▶ Use **y cuarto** or **y quince** to say that it's fifteen minutes past the hour. Use **y media** or **y treinta** to say that it's thirty minutes past the hour.

 Son las cuatro y cuarto.
Son las cuatro y quince.

 Son las nueve y media.
Son las nueve y treinta.

▶ To express time from the half-hour to the hour in Spanish, use **menos** to subtract minutes or a portion of an hour from the next hour.

 Son las nueve menos diez.   Es la una menos cuarto.

Time-related expressions

▶ Here are some useful expressions related to telling time.

¿Qué hora es?
What time is it?

Son las nueve de la mañana.
It's 9 a.m. (in the morning).

Son las cuatro de la tarde.
It's 4 p.m. (in the afternoon).

Son las diez de la noche.
It's 10 p.m. (at night).

Son las once en punto.
It's 11 o'clock on the dot (sharp).

Es el mediodía.
It's noon.

Es la medianoche.
It's midnight.

¿A qué hora es la clase?
(At) what time is the class?

La clase es a la una.
The class is at one o'clock.

La clase es a las dos.
The class is at two o'clock.

¡ojo!
To ask at what time a particular event takes place, use the construction **¿A qué hora (...)?**. Use **A la(s)** + *time* to state when it occurs.

16   *dieciséis*

Práctica y conversación

1 Emparejar Match each watch with the correct statement.

1. Son las ocho menos veinticinco de la mañana.
2. Es la una menos diez de la mañana.
3. Son las tres y cinco de la mañana.
4. Son las dos menos cuarto de la tarde.
5. Son las seis y media de la mañana.
6. Son las once y veinte de la noche.

2 ¿Qué hora es? With a partner, take turns asking and answering the questions. Use the clocks as a guide.

MODELO
Estudiante 1: Son las siete de la noche en Los Ángeles. ¿Qué hora es en San Antonio?
Estudiante 2: Son las nueve de la noche.

Miami   San Antonio   Denver   Los Ángeles

1. Son las cinco en punto de la tarde en Los Ángeles. ¿Qué hora es en Miami?

2. Son las once menos cuarto en San Antonio. ¿Qué hora es en Los Ángeles?

3. Son las siete de la noche en Denver. ¿Qué hora es en Los Ángeles?

4. Son las dos y media de la tarde en Los Ángeles. ¿Qué hora es en Miami?

3 En la televisión With a partner, take turns asking and answering questions about these television listings.

MODELO
Estudiante 1: ¿A qué hora es el documental *Las computadoras*?
Estudiante 2: Es a las nueve y cuarto de la noche.

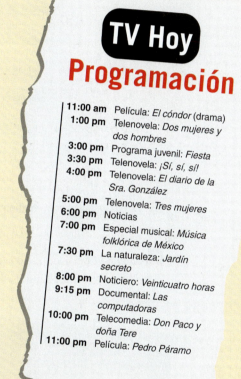

TV Hoy Programación

11:00 am	Película: *El cóndor* (drama)
1:00 pm	Telenovela: *Dos mujeres y dos hombres*
3:00 pm	Programa juvenil: *Fiesta*
3:30 pm	Telenovela: *¡Sí, sí, sí!*
4:00 pm	Telenovela: *El diario de la Sra. González*
5:00 pm	Telenovela: *Tres mujeres*
6:00 pm	Noticias
7:00 pm	Especial musical: *Música folklórica de México*
7:30 pm	La naturaleza: *Jardín secreto*
8:00 pm	Noticiero: *Veinticuatro horas*
9:15 pm	Documental: *Las computadoras*
10:00 pm	Telecomedia: *Don Paco y doña Tere*
11:00 pm	Película: *Pedro Páramo*

4 Entrevista Use the following questions to interview a classmate.

1. ¿Qué hora es?
2. ¿A qué hora es la clase de español?
3. ¿A qué hora es el programa *60 Minutes*?
4. ¿A qué hora es el programa *Today Show*?
5. ¿Hay una fiesta el sábado (*on Saturday*)? ¿A qué hora es?
6. ¿Hay un concierto (*concert*) el sábado? ¿A qué hora es?

Practice more at **vhlcentral.com**.

Lección 1

Ampliación

1 Escuchar 🎧

A Listen to the conversation between Srta. Martínez and a traveler. Then fill in the missing information on the form.

TIP **Listen for words you know.** You can get the gist of a conversation by listening for words and phrases you already know.

B When does this conversation take place, before or after the trip? How do you know?

2 Conversar

In small groups, act out an interview between school newspaper reporters and a visiting **profesor de literatura**. After introducing themselves, the reporters should find out the following information.

- The professor's name
- The start time of the class
- The number of students in class
- The number of dictionaries in the class
- Whether or not there are computers in class
- Whether or not there are maps in class

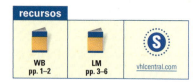

18   dieciocho

Hola, ¿qué tal?

3 Escribir Write an e-mail to Mrs. Suárez, the director of a language school in Madrid where you want to take a summer course. Introduce yourself and ask her questions about the program.

TIP Write in Spanish. Use grammar and vocabulary that you know. Also, look at your textbook for examples of style, format, and expressions in Spanish.

Organize — Make a list of the information that you can provide about yourself in Spanish (your name, your occupation, where you are from). In addition, make a list of questions that you want to ask Mrs. Suárez, such as what time class starts, the number of students in the class, and information about the other students (where they are from, number of males/females, etc).

Write — Using the material you have compiled, write the first draft of your e-mail.

Revise — Exchange papers with a classmate and comment on the organization, style, and grammatical accuracy of each other's work. Then revise your first draft, keeping your classmate's comments in mind.

Share — Read your e-mail aloud in small groups. What kind of greetings and expressions of courtesy were used in the e-mails?

4 Un paso más Prepare a presentation about how Hispanic cultures have influenced an American city. Include the following in your presentation:

- An introduction of yourself in Spanish
- A general description of the city
- Examples of how Hispanic cultures have influenced the city
- Photos, drawings, and charts to make your presentation more interesting

SAN ANTONIO

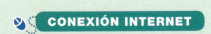
CONEXIÓN INTERNET

Investiga estos temas en **vhlcentral.com**.

- Emisoras de radio en Nueva York
- Dominó en Miami
- Calle Olvera en Los Ángeles

diecinueve **19**

1 LECTURA

Antes de leer  Audio: Reading / Additional Reading

Cognates are words that share similar meanings and spellings in two or more languages. The Spanish words **computadora**, **problema**, and **programa** are examples of cognates.

When you read in Spanish, look for cognates and use them to get the general meaning of what you're reading. But watch out for false cognates such as **librería**, which means *bookstore*, not *library*.

Laura, a university student, made a list of important names and numbers she needed to remember. Look for cognates while you read her list.

Phone numbers are usually read as pairs of numbers. However, for phone numbers with an odd number of digits, the first number is read separately. For example, Mrs. Ruiz's phone number would be read as 4-24-17-11. For e-mail addresses in Spanish, the "at" symbol (@) is called **arroba** and the period is called **punto**.

Teléfonos importantes

Sra. Ruiz (asistente de matemáticas) 424-1711
Oficina de ayuda financiera 427-1407
Administración universitaria
(número principal) 427-1300
Dormitorio Los Pinos 427-3023
Policía del campus 427-0710
Dra. Chen 313-2012
Estadio de béisbol 222-1514
Pizzería Roma 218-0723
Cooperativa Orgánica El Sol 310-1604

Llamar a la
Sra. Ruiz

10 a.m.

recursos
vhlcentral.com

20 veinte

Hola, ¿qué tal?

Después de leer

¿Comprendiste?

Mark each statement as **cierto** (*true*) or **falso** (*false*).

Cierto   Falso

_____ _____ **1.** Profesora González works in the math department.

_____ _____ **2.** If Laura wanted to get a student loan, she would call 427-3023.

_____ _____ **3.** Laura never eats pizza.

_____ _____ **4.** If Laura needed to report a crime, she would dial 427-0710.

_____ _____ **5.** To find out the price of organic apples, Laura would dial 310-1604.

_____ _____ **6.** Laura would call 427-1300 to get a baseball ticket.

Coméntalo

Think about the names, phone numbers, and e-mail addresses that Laura keeps in her address book. If you were preparing a similar address book, what names, telephone numbers, and e-mail addresses would you include?

Direcciones electrónicas

Oficina de matemáticas

ofna@matematicas.unimetro.edu.pe

Profesora González

a.gonzalez@matematicas.unimetro.edu.pe

Farmacia

rx@farmaciagomez.com.pe

Gimnasio

informacion@gimnasio.unimetro.edu.pe

veintiuno **21**

1 VOCABULARIO

Saludos

Hola.	Hello; Hi.
Buenos días.	Good morning.
Buenas tardes.	Good afternoon.
Buenas noches.	Good evening; Good night.

Despedidas

Adiós.	Goodbye.
Nos vemos.	See you.
Hasta luego.	See you later.
Hasta la vista.	See you later.
Hasta pronto.	See you soon.
Hasta mañana.	See you tomorrow.
Saludos a…	Greetings to…
Chau.	Bye.

¿Cómo está?

¿Cómo está usted?	How are you? (form.)
¿Cómo estás?	How are you? (fam.)
¿Qué hay de nuevo?	What's new?
¿Qué pasa?	What's happening?; What's going on?
¿Qué tal?	How are you?; How is it going?
(Muy) bien, gracias.	(Very) well, thanks.
Nada.	Nothing.
No muy bien.	Not very well.
Regular.	So-so; OK.

Expresiones de cortesía

De nada.	You're welcome.
Lo siento.	I'm sorry.
(Muchas) gracias.	Thank you (very much); Thanks (a lot).
No hay de qué.	You're welcome.
Por favor.	Please.

Presentaciones

¿Cómo se llama usted?	What's your name? (form.)
¿Cómo te llamas (tú)?	What's your name? (fam.)
Me llamo…	My name is…
¿Y tú?	And you? (fam.)
¿Y usted?	And you? (form.)
Mucho gusto.	Pleased to meet you.
El gusto es mío.	The pleasure is mine.
Encantado/a.	Delighted; Pleased to meet you.
Igualmente.	Likewise.
Éste/Ésta es…	This is…
Le presento a…	I would like to introduce you to (name). (form.)
Te presento a…	I would like to introduce you to (name). (fam.)

Verbos

ser	to be

¿De dónde es?

¿De dónde es usted?	Where are you from? (form.)
¿De dónde eres?	Where are you from? (fam.)
Soy de…	I'm from…

Expresiones adicionales

¿Cuántos/as?	How many?
¿De quién…?	Whose…? (sing.)
¿De quiénes…?	Whose…? (plural)
(No) Hay	There is (not); there are (not)
¿Qué es?	What is it?
¿Quién es?	Who is it?

Sustantivos

el autobús	bus
la capital	capital city
la chica	girl
el chico	boy
la computadora	computer
la comunidad	community
el/la conductor(a)	driver; chauffeur
la conversación	conversation
la cosa	thing
el cuaderno	notebook
el día	day
el diario	diary
el diccionario	dictionary
la escuela	school
el/la estudiante	student
la foto(grafía)	photograph
el hombre	man
el/la joven	youth; young person
el lápiz	pencil
la lección	lesson
la maleta	suitcase
la mano	hand
el mapa	map
la mochila	backpack
la mujer	woman
la nacionalidad	nationality
el número	number
el país	country
la palabra	word
el/la pasajero/a	passenger
el problema	problem
el/la profesor(a)	teacher
el programa	program
el/la turista	tourist
el video	video

Títulos	See page 4.
Numbers 0–30	See page 12.
Subject Pronouns	See page 14.
Time-related expressions	See page 16.

Audio: Vocabulary Flashcards

22 veintidós

2 Las clases

Communicative Goals

You will learn how to:
- talk about people, classes and college life
- express likes and dislikes
- ask questions
- describe the location of people and things

PREPARACIÓN
pages 24–27
- Words related to people, places, and classes at the university
- Days of the week
- Pronouncing Spanish vowels

ESCENAS
pages 28–29
- Felipe takes Marissa around Mexico City. Along the way, they meet some friends and discuss the upcoming semester.

EXPLORACIÓN
pages 30–31
- Bajo la lupa: *La elección de una carrera universitaria*
- Flash cultura: *Los estudios*

GRAMÁTICA
pages 32–41
- Present tense of **–ar** verbs
- Forming questions
- Present tense of **estar**
- Numbers 31–100

LECTURA
pages 42–43
- Brochure: *UAE: La mejor universidad de Europa*

Para empezar
- ¿Cuántas personas hay en la foto?
- ¿Son profesores o estudiantes?
- ¿Dónde están?, ¿en un laboratorio o en una universidad?

2 PREPARACIÓN

Las clases

el laboratorio laboratory

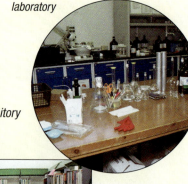

LOS LUGARES

la cafetería cafeteria
la librería bookstore
la residencia estudiantil dormitory
la universidad university

el estadio stadium

la biblioteca library

la química chemistry

LOS CURSOS

la administración business administration
de empresas
el arte art
la biología biology
la clase class
la contabilidad accounting
los cursos courses
el español Spanish
la física physics
la historia history

el inglés English
las lenguas extranjeras foreign languages
las matemáticas mathematics
el periodismo journalism
la psicología psychology
la sociología sociology

la computación computer science

la geografía geography

recursos

WB
pp. 9–10

LM
p. 7

vhlcentral.com

24 veinticuatro

Las clases

EN LA CLASE

el borrador eraser
el examen test; exam
el horario schedule
la mesa table
el papel paper
la pizarra blackboard
la pluma pen
la prueba test; quiz
la puerta door
el semestre semester
la silla chair
la tarea homework
la tiza chalk
el trimestre trimester; quarter
la ventana window

el reloj
clock; watch

el mapa
map

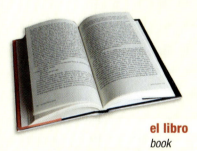
el libro
book

el escritorio
desk

el profesor
teacher; professor

LAS PERSONAS

el/la compañero/a de clase classmate
el/la compañero/a de cuarto roommate
el/la estudiante student

LOS DÍAS DE LA SEMANA

lunes Monday
martes Tuesday
miércoles Wednesday
jueves Thursday
viernes Friday
sábado Saturday
domingo Sunday

la semana week

Hoy es… Today is…

veinticinco **25**

Lección 2

Práctica y conversación

1 Mis clases Listen and fill in the calendar with María's class schedule. Then complete the sentences below.

Estudiante: María			Semestre Nº 1		
	lunes	martes	miércoles	jueves	viernes
AM					
PM					

1. Éste (*This*) es el primer (*first*) _____ de María en la universidad.
2. Este semestre María toma cuatro _____.
3. La clase de _____ es el lunes a las diez y media de la mañana.
4. La clase de _____ es el martes a las dos y quince de la tarde.
5. La clase de periodismo es el _____ a las once de la mañana.
6. La clase de _____ es el jueves a las tres y media de la tarde.
7. María estudia (*studies*) en la _____ los viernes.

2 Analogías Use these words to complete the analogies. Two words will not be used.

1. dos ↔ cuatro ⊜ martes ↔ _____
2. hoy ↔ mañana ⊜ viernes ↔ _____
3. EE.UU. ↔ mapa ⊜ hora ↔ _____
4. inglés ↔ lengua ⊜ miércoles ↔ _____
5. maleta ↔ turista ⊜ mochila ↔ _____
6. pluma ↔ papel ⊜ tiza ↔ _____

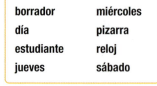

borrador	miércoles
día	pizarra
estudiante	reloj
jueves	sábado

3 Cursos What is the subject matter of each class?

MODELO
la cultura de España, los verbos
Es la clase de español.

1. los microbios, los animales
   _____

2. George Washington, Martin Luther King, Jr.
   _____

3. la geometría, la trigonometría
   _____

Frida Kahlo

El río Amazonas

4. Frida Kahlo, Leonardo da Vinci
   _____

5. África, el río Amazonas
   _____

Las clases

4 Entrevistas Use these questions to interview two classmates.

1. ¿Cómo te llamas?
2. ¿Cómo estás hoy?
3. ¿De dónde eres?
4. ¿Cuántas clases tomas?
5. ¿Cuándo tomas…?
6. ¿A qué hora es la clase de…?
7. ¿Quién es el/la profesor(a)?
8. ¿Cuál (*Which*) es tu clase favorita?

Practice more at vhlcentral.com.

Pronunciación Spanish vowels

Audio: Concepts, Activities

a   e   i   o   u

Spanish vowels are never silent; they are always pronounced in a short, crisp way without the glide sounds used in English.

Álex   cl**a**se   n**a**d**a**   enc**a**nt**a**d**a**

The letter **a** is pronounced like the *a* in *father*, but shorter.

el   **e**n**e**   m**e**sa   **e**l**e**fant**e**

The letter **e** is pronounced like the *e* in *they*, but shorter.

Inés   ch**i**ca   t**i**za   señor**i**ta

The letter **i** sounds like the *ee* in *beet*, but shorter.

h**o**la   c**o**n   libr**o**   d**o**n Francisc**o**

The letter **o** is pronounced like the *o* in *tone*, but shorter.

uno   reg**u**lar   sal**u**dos   g**u**sto

The letter **u** sounds like the *oo* in *room*, but shorter.

Refranes Practice the vowels by reading these sayings aloud.

Del dicho al hecho hay un gran trecho.[1]

Cada loco con su tema.[2]

1 Easier said than done.
2 To each their own.

recursos

LM p. 8

vhlcentral.com

Practice more at vhlcentral.com.

veintisiete 27

2 ESCENAS

¿Qué estudias? Video: *Fotonovela*

Felipe, Marissa, Juan Carlos y Miguel visitan Chapultepec y hablan de las clases.

Expresiones útiles

Talking about classes

¿Cuántas clases tomas?
How many classes are you taking?
Tomo cuatro clases.
I'm taking four classes.
Mi especialización es en arqueología.
My major is archeology.
Este año, espero sacar buenas notas y, por supuesto, viajar por el país.
This year, I hope / I'm hoping to get good grades. And, of course, travel through the country.

Talking about likes/dislikes

Me gusta mucho la cultura mexicana.
I like Mexican culture a lot.
Me gustan las ciencias ambientales.
I like environmental science.
Me gusta dibujar. *I like to draw.*
¿Te gusta este lugar? *Do you like this place?*

Paying for tickets

Dos boletos, por favor.
Two tickets, please.
Dos boletos son sesenta y cuatro pesos.
Two tickets are sixty-four pesos.
Aquí están cien pesos.
Here's a hundred pesos.
Son treinta y seis pesos de cambio.
That's thirty-six pesos change.

Talking about location and direction

¿Dónde está tu diccionario?
Where is your dictionary?
Está en casa de los Díaz.
It's at the Díaz's house.
Y ahora, ¿adónde? ¿A la biblioteca?
And now, where to? To the library?
Sí, pero primero a la librería.
Está al lado.
Yes, but first to the bookstore. It's next door.

recursos

VM
pp. 3–4

vhlcentral.com

FELIPE Dos boletos, por favor.

EMPLEADO Dos boletos son 64 pesos.
FELIPE Aquí están 100 pesos.
EMPLEADO 100 menos 64 son 36 pesos de cambio.

FELIPE Ésta es la Ciudad de México.

FELIPE Oye, Marissa, ¿cuántas clases tomas?
MARISSA Tomo cuatro clases: español, historia, literatura y también geografía. Me gusta mucho la cultura mexicana.

MIGUEL Marissa, hablas muy bien el español... ¿Y dónde está tu diccionario?
MARISSA En casa de los Díaz. Felipe necesita practicar inglés.
MIGUEL ¡Ay, Maru! Chicos, nos vemos más tarde.

28 veintiocho

Las clases

 MARISSA   **FELIPE**   **JUAN CARLOS**   **MIGUEL**   **EMPLEADO** **MARU**

FELIPE Juan Carlos, ¿quién enseña la clase de química este semestre?
JUAN CARLOS El profesor Morales. Ah, ¿por qué tomo química y computación?
FELIPE Porque te gusta la tarea.

FELIPE Los lunes y los miércoles, economía a las 2:30. Tú tomas computación los martes en la tarde, y química, a ver... Los lunes, los miércoles y los viernes ¿a las 10? ¡Uf!

FELIPE Y Miguel, ¿cuándo regresa?
JUAN CARLOS Hoy estudia con Maru.
MARISSA ¿Quién es Maru?

MIGUEL ¿Hablas con tu mamá?
MARU Mamá habla. Yo escucho. Es la 1:30.
MIGUEL Ay, lo siento. Juan Carlos y Felipe...
MARU Ay, Felipe.

MARU Y ahora, ¿adónde? ¿A la biblioteca?
MIGUEL Sí, pero primero a la librería. Necesito comprar unos libros.

Actividades

1 Identificar Indicate which person would say the following.

1. ¿Maru es compañera de ustedes? _____
2. Mi mamá habla (*talks*) mucho. _____
3. Mi diccionario está en casa de Felipe y Jimena. _____
4. Hoy yo estudio (*am studying*) con Maru en la biblioteca. _____
5. Yo tomo (*am taking*) computación los martes por la tarde. _____

2 Completar Complete each sentence with the correct words.

1. Marissa habla (*speaks*) muy bien el _____.
2. El profesor Morales enseña (*teaches*) _____.
3. Marissa toma cuatro _____.
4. Hay clase de economía los lunes y _____.
5. Maru necesita ir (*needs to go*) a la biblioteca y Miguel necesita ir a la _____.

3 Preguntas personales
Interview a classmate about his/her college life.

1. ¿Qué clases tomas en la universidad?
2. ¿Qué clases tomas los viernes?
3. ¿En qué clase hay más chicos?
4. ¿En qué clase hay más chicas?
5. ¿Te gusta la clase de español?

veintinueve 29

2 EXPLORACIÓN

BAJO LA LUPA

Additional Reading
Video: *Flash cultura*

La elección de una carrera universitaria

Since the Spanish-speaking world covers so many nations, there is a lot of variety in the educational systems within those countries. However, most countries share some important differences from the US educational system. In the Spanish-speaking world, higher education is heavily state-subsidized, so tuition is almost free; as a result, public universities see large enrollments. Spanish and Latin American students generally choose their **carrera universitaria** (major) when they're eighteen—which is the year they enter the university or the year before. In order to enroll, all students must complete a high school degree, known as the **bachillerato**. In countries like Bolivia and Mexico, the last year of high school (**colegio**) tends to be specialized in an area of study, such as the arts or natural sciences. (**Colegio** is a false cognate. In most countries, it means *high school,* but in some regions it refers to an elementary school.)

Students then choose their major according to their specialization. Similarly, university-bound students in Argentina focus their studies on specific fields, such as the humanities and social sciences,

Universidad Central de Venezuela en Caracas

natural sciences, communication, art and design, and economics and business, during their five years of high school. Finally, in Spain, students choose their major according to the score they receive on the **prueba de aptitud** (skills test or entrance exam).

University graduates receive a **licenciatura**, or bachelor's degree. In Peru and Venezuela, a bachelor's degree is a five-year process. Spanish and Colombian **licenciaturas** take four to five years, although some fields, such as medicine, require six or more. In Argentina or Chile, a **licenciatura** takes four to six years to complete, and may be considered equivalent to a master's degree.

Imagine, getting the equivalent of a bachelor's or even a master's degree with little or no cost to the student! How does that compare to your own college costs?

Estudiantes hispanos en los EE.UU.

In the 2010–11 academic year, almost 15,000 Mexican students (2.4% of all international students) studied at U.S. universities. Colombians were the second largest Spanish-speaking group, with over 6,000 students.

SOURCE: National Center for Education Statistics

Practice more at vhlcentral.com.

recursos
VM pp. 35–36
vhlcentral.com

Las clases

ACTIVIDADES

1 **¿Cierto o falso?** Indicate whether each statement is **cierto** or **falso**. Correct the false statements.

1. Students in Spanish-speaking countries must pay large amounts of money toward their college tuition.
2. **Carrera** refers to any undergraduate and/or graduate program students enroll in order to obtain a professional degree.
3. After studying at a **colegio**, students receive their **bachillerato**.
4. Undergraduates study at a **colegio** or an **universidad**.
5. In Latin America and Spain, students usually choose their majors in their second year at the university.
6. In Argentina, students focus their studies during their five years of high school.
7. Venezuelans complete a **licenciatura** in five years.
8. According to statistics, Colombians make the third largest Latin American group studying at the US universities.

2 **Universidades** In pairs, research a Spanish or Latin American university online and find five statistics about that institution. Using this information, create a dialogue between a prospective student and a university representative.

CONEXIÓN INTERNET

What **facultad** does your major belong to in Spain or Latin America? For more information about **Exploración**, go to **vhlcentral.com**.

Los estudios

1 **Preparación** What is the name of your school or university? What degree program are you in? What classes are you taking this semester?

2 **El video** Watch this **Flash cultura** episode.

Vocabulario

¿Qué estudias? *What do you study?*
¿Cuál es tu materia favorita? *What is your favorite subject?*
carrera (de medicina) *(medical) degree program, major*
derecho *law*

Estudio derecho en la UNAM.

¿Conoces algún° profesor famoso que dé clases... en la UNAM?

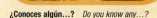

¿Conoces algún...? *Do you know any...?*

3 **Emparejar** Match the phrases in column A to each sentence in column B.

1. En la UNAM no hay
2. México, D.F. es
3. La UNAM es
4. La UNAM ofrece

a. una universidad muy grande.
b. 74 carreras de estudio.
c. residencias estudiantiles.
d. la ciudad más grande (*largest*) de Latinoamérica.

treinta y uno 31

2 GRAMÁTICA

2.1 The present tense of regular –ar verbs  Tutorial

▶ To create the forms of regular verbs, drop the infinitive endings (–ar, –er, –ir). Then add the endings that correspond to the different subject pronouns. The chart below demonstrates how to conjugate regular –ar verbs.

estudiar (to study)

yo	estudio	I study
tú	estudias	you (fam.) study
Ud./él/ella	estudia	you (form.) study; he/she studies
nosotros/as	estudiamos	we study
vosotros/as	estudiáis	you (pl.) study
Uds./ellos/ellas	estudian	you (pl.) study; they study

Common –ar verbs

bailar	to dance	descansar	to rest	explicar	to explain	preguntar	to ask (a question)
buscar	to look for	desear	to want; to wish	hablar	to talk; to speak	preparar	to prepare
caminar	to walk	dibujar	to draw	llegar	to arrive	regresar	to return
cantar	to sing	enseñar	to teach	llevar	to carry	terminar	to end; to finish
comprar	to buy	escuchar	to listen	mirar	to look (at); to watch	tomar	to take; to drink
contestar	to answer	esperar	to wait (for); to hope	necesitar	to need	trabajar	to work
conversar	to talk	estudiar	to study	practicar	to practice	viajar	to travel

Juan Carlos estudia ciencias ambientales.

▶ The Spanish present tense has several meanings in English. Note the following examples.

Ana **trabaja** en la cafetería.
Ana works in the cafeteria.
Ana is working in the cafeteria.
Ana does work in the cafeteria.

Paco **viaja** a Madrid mañana.
Paco travels to Madrid tomorrow.
Paco is traveling to Madrid tomorrow.
Paco does travel to Madrid tomorrow.

Using verbs in Spanish

Y tú, ¿qué estudias, Miguel?

▶ When two verbs are used together with no change of subject, the second verb is generally in the infinitive.

Deseo hablar con Maite.
I want to speak with Maite.

Necesito comprar lápices.
I need to buy pencils.

▶ To make a sentence negative, use **no** before the conjugated verb.

Yo **no** miro la televisión.
I don't watch TV.

Ella **no** desea bailar.
She doesn't want to dance.

▶ Subject pronouns are often omitted; the verb endings indicate who the subject is.

¿Habl**as** español?
Do you speak Spanish?

No, no habl**o** español.
No, I don't speak Spanish.

Las clases

▶ Subject pronouns may be used for clarification or for emphasis.

¿Qué enseñan **ellos**?
What do they teach?

Él enseña arte y **ella** enseña química.
He teaches art and she teaches chemistry.

¿Quién desea trabajar hoy?
Who wants to work today?

Yo no deseo trabajar.
I don't want to work.

Práctica y conversación

1 Completar Complete the conversation with the appropriate forms of the verbs.

JUAN ¡Hola, Linda! ¿Qué tal las clases?

LINDA Bien. (1) _____ [tomar] tres clases: química, biología y computación. Y tú, ¿cuántas clases (2) _____ [tomar]?

JUAN (3) _____ [tomar] cuatro: sociología, biología, arte y literatura. Yo (4) _____ [tomar] biología a las cuatro. ¿Y tú?

LINDA Lily, Alberto y yo (5) _____ [tomar] biología a las diez.

JUAN (6) ¿_____ [estudiar] ustedes mucho?

LINDA Sí, Alberto y yo (7) _____ [estudiar] dos horas todos los días (*every day*).

JUAN ¿Lily no (8) _____ [estudiar] con ustedes?

LINDA No, ella (9) _____ [estudiar] con Arturo.

2 ¿Te gusta…? Get together with a classmate and take turns asking each other if you like these activities. See the **Expresiones útiles** on p. 28 to see how to express likes and dislikes.

| ¿Te gusta…? (*Do you like…?*) | ▶ | Sí, me gusta…/No, no me gusta… (*Yes, I like…/No, I don't like…*) |

MODELO

Estudiante 1: ¿Te gusta tomar el autobús?
Estudiante 2: Sí, me gusta tomar el autobús. / No, no me gusta tomar el autobús.

	Sí	No		Sí	No
bailar	___	___	estudiar	___	___
cantar	___	___	mirar la televisión	___	___
dibujar	___	___	trabajar	___	___

3 Describir With a partner, describe what the people in the photos are doing.

MODELO
Ana María baila.

Ana María

Héctor

Ernesto

1. _____   3. _____

Gabriela

Mario y Laura

2. _____   4. _____

4 Entrevista Use these questions to interview a classmate.

1. ¿Qué clases tomas?
2. ¿Caminas a tus clases?
3. ¿A qué hora termina la clase de español?
4. ¿Cuántas lenguas hablas?
5. ¿Dónde estudias?
6. ¿Necesitas estudiar hoy para un examen?
7. ¿Miras mucho la televisión? ¿Qué programas te gustan?
8. ¿Te gusta viajar? ¿Deseas viajar a Suramérica?

Practice more at **vhlcentral.com.**

treinta y tres **33**

Lección 2

2.2 Forming questions in Spanish  Tutorial

¿Hablas con tu mamá?

▶ You can form a question by raising the pitch of your voice at the end of a sentence. In writing, be sure to use an upside-down question mark (¿) at the beginning of a question and a regular question mark (?) at the end.

Statement	Question
Miguel busca un mapa.	¿Miguel busca un mapa?
Miguel is looking for a map.	*Is Miguel looking for a map?*

Te gusta mucho la tarea, ¿no?

▶ You can also form a question by putting the subject after the verb. The subject may even be placed at the end of the sentence.

Statement	Question
SUBJECT VERB	VERB SUBJECT
Ustedes trabajan los sábados.	¿**Trabajan ustedes** los sábados?
You work on Saturdays.	*Do you work on Saturdays?*
SUBJECT VERB	VERB SUBJECT
Carlota regresa a las seis.	¿**Regresa** a las seis **Carlota**?
Carlota returns at six.	*Does Carlota return at six?*

¡ojo!
You may only add ¿**verdad**? to form a question with negative statements.
No trabajas mañana, ¿verdad?

▶ Questions can also be formed by adding ¿**no**? or ¿**verdad**? at the end of a statement.

Statement	Question
Ella regresa a las seis.	Ella regresa a las seis, ¿verdad?
She returns at six.	*She returns at six, right?*

▶ These interrogative words are used to form questions in Spanish.

Interrogative words

¿Cómo?	How?	¿Qué?	What?; Which?	¿De dónde?	From where?	¿Cuántos/as?	How many?
¿Cuál?	Which?			¿Por qué?	Why?	¿Quién?	Who?
¿Cuáles?	Which one(s)?	¿Dónde?	Where?	¿Cuánto/a?	How much?	¿Quiénes?	Who (plural)?
¿Cuándo?	When?	¿Adónde?	Where (to)?				

¡ojo!
Interrogative words always carry a written accent mark.
• • •
The answer to the question ¿**por qué**? is **porque**, which is written as one word without an accent.
¿**por qué**? *why?*
porque *because*

▶ Use interrogative words in questions that require more than a *yes* or *no* answer.

¿**Cuándo** descansan ustedes? ¿**Adónde** caminamos? ¿**Qué** clases tomas?
When do you rest? *Where are we walking to?* *What classes are you taking?*

▶ In questions that contain interrogative words, the pitch of your voice falls at the end of the sentence.

¿**Cómo** llegas a la escuela? ¿**Por qué** necesitas estudiar?
How do you get to school? *Why do you need to study?*

Las clases

Práctica y conversación

1 Una conversación Irene and Manolo are chatting (quietly!) in the library. Complete their conversation with the appropriate questions.

IRENE (1) _____
MANOLO Bien, gracias. (2) _____
IRENE Muy bien. (3) _____
MANOLO Son las nueve.
IRENE (4) _____
MANOLO Estudio historia.
IRENE (5) _____
MANOLO Porque hay un examen mañana.
IRENE (6) _____
MANOLO Sí, me gusta mucho la clase.
IRENE (7) _____
MANOLO El profesor Padilla enseña la clase.
IRENE (8) _____
MANOLO No, no tomo psicología este semestre.

2 Preguntas Change these statements into questions by inverting the word order.

MODELO
Ernesto / estudiar con Sara
¿Estudia Ernesto con Sara? /
¿Estudia con Sara Ernesto?

1. Sandra / hablar con su compañera de cuarto
   _____
2. La profesora Soto / buscar unos libros
   _____
3. Tú / preparar la tarea
   _____
4. Ustedes / trabajar en la cafetería
   _____
5. Los chicos / escuchar música en la radio
   _____

3 Encuesta Change the phrases in the first column into questions and use them to survey two or three classmates. Then report the results to the class.

Actividades	Nombres
1. Estudiar contabilidad	_____
2. Tomar una clase de sociología	_____
3. Dibujar bien	_____
4. Cantar rap	_____
5. Bailar bien	_____
6. Escuchar música en un iPod	_____
7. Necesitar comprar un reloj	_____
8. Tomar el autobús a la escuela	_____
9. Llevar una mochila a clase	_____
10. Desear viajar a España	_____

4 Entrevista Imagine that you are a reporter for the school newspaper. Use these questions and write three of your own to interview a classmate about student life.

1. ¿Dónde estudias? ¿Cuándo?
2. ¿Quién es tu profesor(a) favorito/a?
3. ¿Cuántas clases tomas?
4. ¿Necesitas estudiar más (*more*)?
5. ¿A qué hora llegas a la universidad?
6. ¿Trabajas? ¿Dónde?
7. ¿Cuál es tu día favorito de la semana? ¿Por qué?
8. ¿_____?
9. ¿_____?
10. ¿_____?

Practice more at vhlcentral.com.

treinta y cinco 35

Lección 2

2.3 The present tense of estar  Tutorial

Marissa está en México para estudiar este año.

▶ In Lesson 1, you learned how to conjugate and use the verb **ser** (*to be*). Spanish has another verb that also means *to be*: the verb **estar**.

▶ Although **estar** ends in **–ar**, it does not follow the pattern of regular **–ar** verbs. The **yo** form (**estoy**) is irregular. Also, all forms but the **yo** and **nosotros/as** forms have an accented **á**. As you will see, **ser** and **estar** are used in different ways. You will learn about these differences in depth in **Lección 5**.

Hola mamá. ¿Cómo estás?

estar (to be)

yo	est**oy**	*I am*
tú	est**ás**	*you (fam.) are*
Ud./él/ella	est**á**	*you (form.) are; he/she is*
nosotros/as	est**amos**	*we are*
vosotros/as	est**áis**	*you (pl.) are*
Uds./ellos/ellas	est**án**	*you (pl)/they are*

Uses of ser and estar

Uses of estar

LOCATION
Estoy en la biblioteca.
I am at the library.

Marissa **está** al lado de Felipe.
Marissa is next to Felipe.

HEALTH
Javier **está** enfermo hoy.
Javier is sick today.

WELL-BEING
¿Cómo **estás**, Juan Carlos?
How are you, Juan Carlos?

Estoy muy bien, gracias.
I'm very well, thank you.

Uses of ser

IDENTITY
Hola, **soy** Maru.
Hello, I'm Maru.

OCCUPATION
Soy estudiante.
I'm a student.

ORIGIN
¿**Eres** de España?
Are you from Spain?

Sí, **soy** de España.
Yes, I'm from Spain.

TELLING TIME
Son las cuatro.
It's four o'clock.

Marissa, Miguel y yo estamos muy lejos de casa.

Estar with prepositions of location

Prepositions of location

al lado de	next to; beside		delante de	in front of
a la derecha de	to the right of		detrás de	behind
a la izquierda de	to the left of		encima de	on top of
en	in; on; at		entre	between; among
cerca de	near		lejos de	far from
debajo de	below; under		sobre	on; over

La biblioteca está al lado de la librería.

36 treinta y seis

Las clases

▶ **Estar** is often used with certain prepositions to describe the location of a person or an object.

La cafetería está **al lado de** la biblioteca.
The cafeteria is beside the library.

Los libros están **encima del** escritorio.
The books are on top of the desk.

El estadio no está **lejos de** la librería.
The stadium isn't far from the bookstore.

Estamos **entre** la puerta y la ventana.
We are between the door and the window.

Práctica y conversación

1 Completar Complete this phone conversation between Daniela and her mother with the correct forms of **ser** or **estar**.

MAMÁ   Hola, Daniela. ¿Cómo (1) _____?
DANIELA Hola, mamá. (2) _____ bien. ¿Dónde (3) _____ papá? ¡Ya (*already*) (4) _____ las ocho de la noche!
MAMÁ   No (5) _____ aquí. (6) _____ en la oficina.
DANIELA Y Andrés y Margarita, ¿dónde (7) _____ ellos?
MAMÁ   (8) _____ en el restaurante García con Martín.
DANIELA ¿Quién (9) _____ Martín?
MAMÁ   (10) _____ un compañero de clase. (11) _____ de México.
DANIELA Y el restaurante García, ¿dónde (12) _____?
MAMÁ   (13) _____ cerca de la Plaza Mayor, en San Modesto.
DANIELA Gracias, mamá. Voy (*I'm going*) al restaurante. ¡Hasta pronto!

2 En la librería Imagine that you are in the school bookstore and can't find various items. Ask the clerk (your partner) where the items in the drawing are located.

MODELO
Estudiante 1: ¿Dónde están las mochilas?
Estudiante 2: Las mochilas están debajo de las computadoras.

3 ¿Dónde estás…? Find out where your partner is at these times.

1. ¿Dónde estás los viernes al mediodía?
2. ¿Dónde estás los miércoles a las nueve y cuarto de la mañana?
3. ¿Dónde estás los lunes a las once y diez de la mañana?
4. ¿Dónde estás los jueves a las doce y media de la tarde?

4 La ciudad universitaria You and your partner are at the **Facultad de Bellas Artes** (*School of Fine Arts*). Take turns asking each other where other buildings on the campus map are located.

1. ¿Está lejos la biblioteca de la Facultad (*school*) de Bellas Artes?
2. ¿Dónde está la Facultad de Medicina?
3. ¿Está la Facultad de Administración de Empresas a la derecha de la biblioteca?
4. ¿Dónde está el Colegio Mayor Cervantes?
5. ¿Está la Facultad de Administración de Empresas detrás del Colegio Mayor Cervantes?
6. ¿Dónde está la Facultad de Química?

Practice more at **vhlcentral.com**.

treinta y siete

Lección 2

2.4 Numbers 31–100 Tutorial

Numbers 31–100

31 treinta y uno	36 treinta y seis	41 cuarenta y uno	80 ochenta
32 treinta y dos	37 treinta y siete	42 cuarenta y dos	90 noventa
33 treinta y tres	38 treinta y ocho	50 cincuenta	100 cien, ciento
34 treinta y cuatro	39 treinta y nueve	60 sesenta	
35 treinta y cinco	40 cuarenta	70 setenta	

Hay cuarenta y siete estudiantes en la clase de geografía.

▶ The word **y** is used in most numbers from **31** through **99**.

Hay **ochenta y cinco** exámenes.   Hay **cuarenta y dos** estudiantes.
There are eighty-five exams.   *There are forty-two students.*

▶ With numbers that end in **uno** (31, 41, etc.), **uno** becomes **un** before a masculine noun and **una** before a feminine noun.

Hay **treinta y un** chicos.   Hay **treinta y una** chicas.
There are thirty-one guys.   *There are thirty-one girls.*

Cien menos sesenta y cuatro son treinta y seis pesos de cambio.

▶ **Cien** is used before nouns and in counting. The words **un**, **una**, and **uno** are never used before **cien** in Spanish.

¿Cuántos libros hay?   Hay **cien** libros.
How many books are there?   *There are one hundred books.*

¿Cuántas sillas hay?   Hay **cien** sillas.
How many chairs are there?   *There are one hundred chairs.*

▶ Note that most Spanish-speaking countries use a comma with numbers where English would use a decimal, and vice-versa.

$33,50   treinta y tres dólares y cincuenta centavos

ESPAÑOL EN VIVO

CONTENIDO

37 Correo
42 Mi álbum de fotos
56 Salud
57 Dinero
59 Amor
61 Familia
62 Educación
69 Mi cocina
74 Música
82 Horóscopo

59 Cuestionario
¿Dónde buscas amor?

62 Encuesta
Entrevistamos a 100 estudiantes de la universidad para preguntarles cuáles son los cursos más importantes para su futuro profesional.

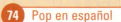

74 Pop en español
Conversamos con el cantante colombiano Juanes sobre su nuevo álbum.

Las clases

Práctica y conversación

1 Baloncesto Provide these basketball scores in Spanish.

1. _____

4. _____

2. _____

5. _____

3. _____

6. _____

2 Números de teléfono Imagine that you are a telephone operator in Spain. Take turns giving the appropriate phone numbers when callers ask for them.

122	MORALES – NAYA	
Morales Ballesteros, José	Venerable Centenares, 22	(91) 944-6662
Morales Benito, Francisco	Plaza Ahorro, 16	(91) 773-1216
Morales Borrego, Flora	Mayor, 51	(91) 634-3211
Morales Calvo, Emilio	Villafuerte, 49	(91) 472-2350
Morales Campos, María Josefa	Toledo, 35	(91) 419-7660
Morales Cid, Pedro	Rosal, 98	(91) 773-1382
Morales Conde, Ángel	Alameda, 67	(91) 944-3915
Morales de la Iglesia, Juliana	Buenavista, 80	(91) 834-5238
Morales Fraile, María Rosa	Plaza March, 74	(91) 834-3571

MODELO
Estudiante 1: ¿Cuál es el número de teléfono de José Morales Ballesteros, por favor?
Estudiante 2: Es el noventa y uno, noventa y cuatro, cuatro, sesenta y seis, sesenta y dos.

3 Precios (prices) With a partner, take turns asking how much the items in the ad cost.

MODELO
Estudiante 1: Deseo comprar papel. ¿Cuánto cuesta (does it cost)?
Estudiante 2: Un paquete cuesta cuatro dólares y cuarenta y un centavos.

4 Entrevista Find out the telephone numbers and e-mail addresses of four classmates.

MODELO
Estudiante 1: ¿Cuál es tu (your) número de teléfono?
Estudiante 2: Es el (416) 635-1951.
Estudiante 1: ¿Y tu dirección de correo electrónico (e-mail address)?
Estudiante 2: Es jota-Smith-arroba (@)-pe-ele-punto-e-de-u. (jsmith@pl.edu).

Practice more at
vhlcentral.com.

treinta y nueve 39

Lección 2

Ampliación

Audio: Activity
Video: TV Clip

1 Escuchar 🎧

A Listen to Armando and Julia's conversation. Then list the classes each person is taking.

TIP Listen for cognates. Cognates are words that have similar spellings and meanings in two or more languages. Listening for cognates will help you increase your comprehension.

Julia
1. _____
2. _____
3. _____
4. _____

Armando
1. _____
2. _____
3. _____
4. _____
5. _____

B ¿Cuántas clases toman Armando y Julia? ¿Cuántas clases tomas tú? ¿Qué clases te gustan y qué clases no te gustan?

2 Conversar

Greet a classmate, find out how he or she is, and get to know your classmate better by asking these questions.

- ¿Cómo te llamas?
- ¿De dónde eres?
- ¿Qué clases tomas?
- ¿Qué clases te gustan?
- ¿Cuántos estudiantes hay en tu (your) clase de...?
- ¿Cuántas horas estudias por (per) día?
- ¿Dónde estudias normalmente?

recursos

WB
pp. 11–18

LM
pp. 9–12

vhlcentral.com

Las clases

3 Escribir Write a description of yourself to post on a website in order to meet Spanish-speaking people.

TIP Brainstorm. Spend ten to fifteen minutes jotting down ideas about the topic you are going to write about. The more ideas you write down, the more you'll have to choose from later when you start to organize your thoughts.

Organízalo — Make a list of things you would like people to know about you, including your name, your major, where you go to school, what you're studying, where you work, and your likes and dislikes.

Escríbelo — Using the material you have compiled, write the first draft of your description.

Corrígelo — Exchange papers with a classmate and comment on the organization, style, and grammatical accuracy of each other's work. Then revise your first draft, keeping your classmate's comments in mind.

Compártelo — Read your descriptions aloud in small groups. Point out the three best features of each description.

4 Un paso más Create a poster that will encourage students to study at a university in a Spanish-speaking country. The poster might include these elements:

- A title
- Photos of the university's campus
- A campus map
- A short summary of the university's programs
- Photos of the town where the university is located

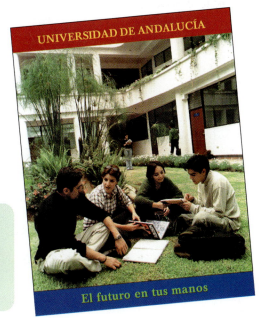

 **CONEXIÓN INTERNET**

Investiga estos temas en vhlcentral.com.

- Las universidades en España
- Las universidades en América Latina

cuarenta y uno 41

2 LECTURA

Antes de leer

 **Audio: Reading** **Additional Reading**

Examina el texto
Recognizing the format of a document can help you to predict its content. For instance, invitations and classified ads follow an easily identifiable format, which usually gives you a general idea of the information they contain. Glance at the document on this page and identify it based on its format.

Cognados
With a classmate, make a list of cognates in the text and guess their English meanings. What do the cognates reveal about the content of the document?

Piénsalo
If you guessed that this text is a brochure from a university, you are correct. You can now infer that the document contains information on departments, courses, and the university campus.

UAE
LA MEJOR° UNIVERSIDAD DE EUROPA
Universidad Autónoma de España

En el campus de la UAE hay ocho facultades:

- Ciencias
- Derecho°
- Medicina
- Psicología
- Filosofía y Letras
- Ciencias Económicas y Empresariales
- Escuela Técnica Superior de Computación
- Facultad° de Educación

Toma cursos de:

- Antropología Aplicada°
- Microbiología
- Contabilidad
- Derecho Privado
- Ecología
- Economía general
- Filosofía Antigua°
- Física General
- Geografía
- Historia Contemporánea
- Computación
- Literatura
- Matemáticas
- Psicología Social
- Química
- Sociología

recursos

vhlcentral.com

42 cuarenta y dos

Las clases

Después de leer

¿Comprendiste?
Indicate whether each statement is **cierto** (*true*) or **falso** (*false*).

Cierto	Falso	
_____	_____	1. La Universidad Autónoma de España está en Europa.
_____	_____	2. En la UAE hay diez facultades.
_____	_____	3. Filosofía y Letras es un curso.
_____	_____	4. Hay cursos de literatura china en la UAE.
_____	_____	5. Hay una facultad de psicología en la UAE.
_____	_____	6. La UAE está en Málaga, España.

Preguntas
Answer these questions using complete sentences.

1. ¿Hay clases de contabilidad en la UAE?
   _____
2. ¿Es posible estudiar medicina en la UAE?
   _____
3. ¿En qué facultad hay clases de economía general?
   _____
4. ¿En qué facultad hay clases de microbiología?
   _____
5. ¿En qué facultad hay clases de literatura?
   _____

Coméntalo
Look at the brochure and answer the following questions. Does your university offer the same courses? Are you taking any of those courses? Would you be interested in studying at the UAE? Why?

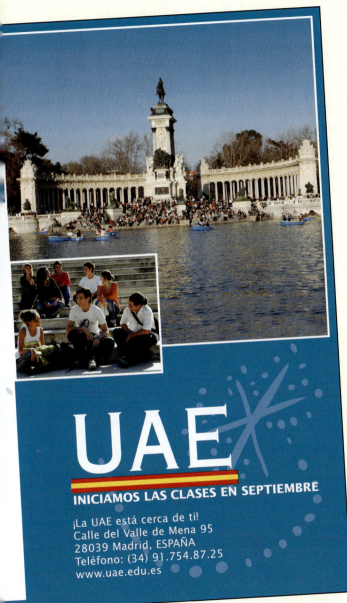

UAE
INICIAMOS LAS CLASES EN SEPTIEMBRE

¡La UAE está cerca de ti!
Calle del Valle de Mena 95
28039 Madrid, ESPAÑA
Teléfono: (34) 91.754.87.25
www.uae.edu.es

mejor *best*   derecho *law*   facultad *school*
aplicada *applied*   antigua *ancient*

cuarenta y tres 43

2 VOCABULARIO

La clase y la universidad

el borrador	eraser
la clase	class
el/la compañero/a de clase	classmate
el/la compañero/a de cuarto	roommate
el escritorio	desk
el/la estudiante	student
el libro	book
el mapa	map
la mesa	table
el papel	paper
la pizarra	blackboard
la pluma	pen
el/la profesor(a)	teacher; professor
la puerta	door
el reloj	clock; watch
la silla	chair
la tiza	chalk
la ventana	window
la biblioteca	library
la cafetería	cafeteria
el estadio	stadium
el laboratorio	laboratory
la librería	bookstore
la residencia estudiantil	dormitory
la universidad	university
el curso	course
el examen	test; exam
el horario	schedule
la prueba	test; quiz
el semestre	semester
la tarea	homework
el trimestre	trimester; quarter

Verbos

bailar	to dance
buscar	to look for
caminar	to walk
cantar	to sing
comprar	to buy
contestar	to answer
conversar	to talk; to chat
descansar	to rest
desear	to want; to wish
dibujar	to draw
enseñar	to teach
escuchar	to listen
esperar	to wait (for); to hope
estar	to be
estudiar	to study
explicar	to explain
gustar	to be pleasing to; to like
hablar	to talk; to speak
llegar	to arrive
llevar	to carry
mirar	to look (at); to watch
necesitar	to need
practicar	to practice
preguntar	to ask (a question)
preparar	to prepare
regresar	to return
terminar	to end; to finish
tomar	to take; to drink
trabajar	to work
viajar	to travel

Los cursos

la administración de empresas	business administration
el arte	art
la biología	biology
la computación	computer science
la contabilidad	accounting
el español	Spanish
la física	physics
la geografía	geography
la historia	history
el inglés	English
las lenguas extranjeras	foreign languages
las matemáticas	mathematics
el periodismo	journalism
la psicología	psychology
la química	chemistry
la sociología	sociology

Los días de la semana

lunes	Monday
martes	Tuesday
miércoles	Wednesday
jueves	Thursday
viernes	Friday
sábado	Saturday
domingo	Sunday
la semana	week
Hoy es...	Today is...

Interrogative words	See page 34.
Prepositions of location	See page 36.
Numbers 31–100	See page 38.

44 cuarenta y cuatro

¡VIVAN LOS PAÍSES HISPANOS!

Todos los años (*Every year*), en el mes de junio, Nueva York organiza un gran desfile (*parade*) en honor a los puertorriqueños.

Estados Unidos y Canadá

Estados Unidos
Población de EE.UU.: 308.745.538
Población de origen hispano: 50.477.594
País de origen de hispanos en los EE.UU.:
- 10,8% otros
- 9,2% Puerto Rico
- 3,5% Cuba
- 13,4% Centroamérica y Suramérica
- 63,1% México

Estados con mayor población hispana:
California, Texas, Florida y Nueva York

SOURCE: U.S. Census Bureau

Canadá
Población de Canadá: 33.000.000
Población de origen hispano: 300.000
País de origen de hispanos en Canadá:
- 12,4% México
- 11,6% Chile
- 67% otros
- 9% El Salvador

Ciudades con mayor población hispana:
Montreal, Toronto y Vancouver

SOURCE: Statistics Canada

¡Vivan los países hispanos!

Interactive map
Video: *Países hispanos*

Lugares

La Pequeña Habana

La Pequeña Habana (*Little Havana*) es un barrio (*neighborhood*) de Miami, Florida, donde viven (*live*) muchos cubanoamericanos. Es un lugar donde se encuentran (*are found*) las costumbres (*customs*) de la cultura cubana, los aromas y sabores (*flavors*) de su comida (*food*) y la música salsa. La Pequeña Habana es una parte de Cuba en los Estados Unidos.

Personalidades

Latinos famosos

Los estadounidenses de origen hispanoamericano contribuyen (*contribute*) en todos los niveles (*at all levels*) a la cultura y a la economía de los Estados Unidos.

Junot Díaz, escritor, de origen dominicano

John Quiñones, periodista, de origen mexicano

Nestor Carbonell, actor, de origen cubano

Ellen Ochoa, astronauta, de origen mexicano

Sonia Sotomayor, jueza de la Suprema Corte de Justicia de los EE.UU., de origen puertorriqueño

46 cuarenta y seis

Estados Unidos y Canadá

Comida

La comida mexicana

La comida (*food*) mexicana es muy popular en los Estados Unidos. Los tacos, las enchiladas y las quesadillas son platos (*dishes*) mexicanos que frecuentemente forman parte de las comidas (*meals*) de muchos norteamericanos. También (*Also*) son populares las variaciones de la comida mexicana en los Estados Unidos... el tex-mex y el cali-mex.

Comunidad

Hispanos en Canadá

La población hispana en Canadá crece (*grows*) cada año (*year*). Más (*More*) del 50% de los hispanos está en Toronto y en Montreal. La mayoría de ellos tiene (*have*) estudios universitarios y habla una de las lenguas oficiales: inglés o francés (*French*). Esto les permite (*This allows them*) participar activamente en la vida cotidiana (*daily life*) y profesional.

Familia colombiana en Mississauga, Ontario

cuarenta y siete 47

¡Vivan los países hispanos!

¿Qué aprendiste?

1 **¿Cierto o falso?** Indicate whether these statements are **cierto** or **falso**, based on what you have learned about Hispanics in the United States and Canada.

Cierto Falso

_____ _____ 1. Los mexicanos son el grupo hispano más grande (*biggest*) de los EE.UU.
_____ _____ 2. En Florida no hay muchas personas de origen hispano.
_____ _____ 3. En Texas hay muchos latinos.
_____ _____ 4. La Pequeña Habana está en la isla de Cuba.
_____ _____ 5. John Quiñones es de origen mexicano.
_____ _____ 6. Nestor Carbonell es de origen hispano.
_____ _____ 7. Los tacos y las quesadillas son los platos más populares en los restaurantes hispanos de los Estados Unidos.
_____ _____ 8. A los estadounidenses no les gustan los tacos.
_____ _____ 9. Los chilenos son el grupo hispano más grande de Canadá.
_____ _____ 10. Muchos hispanos en Canadá tienen estudios universitarios.

2 **Preguntas** Answer these questions in complete sentences.

1. ¿Qué ciudades en los Estados Unidos tienen una visible influencia hispana?
2. ¿Hay barrios hispanos en tu ciudad/pueblo? Si es así (*If so*), ¿los barrios son de algún (*any*) país hispano en particular?
3. ¿Estudias o trabajas con hispanos? ¿De dónde son?
4. ¿Qué otros estadounidenses de origen hispano conoces (*do you know*)?
5. ¿Qué platos de comida hispana te gustan?
6. ¿Qué música latina conoces? ¿Te gusta bailar música latina?

Investiga estos temas en el sitio vhlcentral.com.

- Estadounidenses famosos de origen hispano
- Lugares en Estados Unidos con nombres en español

48 cuarenta y ocho

3 La familia

Communicative Goals

You will learn how to:
- talk about your family and friends
- describe people and things
- express ownership

PREPARACIÓN
pages 50–53
- Words related to family and professions
- Diphthongs and linking

ESCENAS
pages 54–55
- The Díaz family spends Sunday afternoon in Xochimilco. Marissa meets the extended family and answers questions about her own family. The group has a picnic and takes a boat ride through the canals.

EXPLORACIÓN
pages 56–57
- Bajo la lupa: *¿Cómo te llamas?*
- Flash cultura: *La familia*

GRAMÁTICA
pages 58–67
- Descriptive adjectives
- Possessive adjectives
- Present tense of regular **-er** and **-ir** verbs
- Present tense of **tener** and **venir**

LECTURA
pages 68–69
- Magazine article: *Las familias*

Para empezar
- ¿Cuántas personas hay en la fotografía?
- ¿Son compañeros de clase o son una familia?
- ¿Cuántos años tiene la mamá: doce, treinta y cuatro o cincuenta y uno?
- ¿Ellos conversan, descansan o bailan?

3 PREPARACIÓN

La familia  Talking Picture Tutorial Games

LA FAMILIA

el/la esposo/a husband/wife
el/la hermanastro/a stepbrother/stepsister
el/la hermano/a brother/sister
el/la hijastro/a stepson/stepdaughter
la madrastra stepmother
el/la medio/a hermano/a half-brother/half-sister
el padrastro stepfather
los padres parents

el abuelo grandfather

la abuela grandmother

el padre father

la madre mother

LA FAMILIA EXTENDIDA

el/la cuñado/a brother-in-law/sister-in-law
el/la nieto/a grandson/granddaughter
la nuera daughter-in-law
los parientes relatives
el/la primo/a cousin
el/la sobrino/a nephew/niece
el/la suegro/a father-in-law/mother-in-law
el/la tío/a uncle/aunt
el yerno son-in-law

los hijos sons; children

la hija daughter

recursos

WB
pp. 21–22

LM
p. 13

vhlcentral.com

50 cincuenta

La familia

el artista
artist

LAS PROFESIONES

el/la ingeniero/a engineer
el/la médico/a doctor
el/la periodista journalist
el/la programador(a) computer programmer

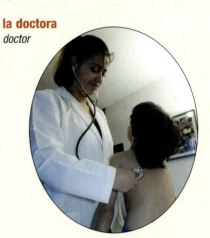

la doctora
doctor

OTRAS PALABRAS

el/la amigo/a friend
el/la gato/a cat
la gente people
el/la muchacho/a boy/girl
la persona person
el/la perro/a dog

mi my (sing.)
mis my (pl.)

el niño
boy; child

la niña
girl

la novia
girlfriend

el novio
boyfriend

cincuenta y uno 51

Lección 3

Práctica y conversación

1 Escuchar Find Luisa Moya Sánchez on the family tree. Then listen to her statements and indicate whether they are **cierto** (*true*) or **falso** (*false*), based on her family tree.

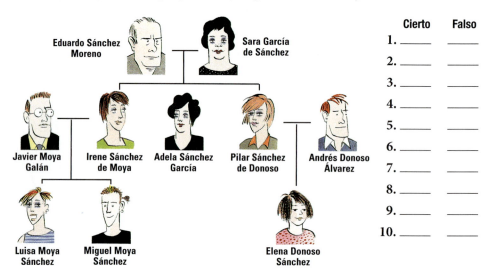

	Cierto	Falso
1.	_____	_____
2.	_____	_____
3.	_____	_____
4.	_____	_____
5.	_____	_____
6.	_____	_____
7.	_____	_____
8.	_____	_____
9.	_____	_____
10.	_____	_____

2 Completar Complete these sentences with the correct words.

1. Mi madre y mi padre son mis _____.
2. El padre de mi madre es mi _____.
3. El segundo (*second*) esposo de mi madre es mi _____.
4. La esposa de mi hijo es mi _____.
5. Yo soy el _____ de los padres de mi esposa.
6. La hija de mi hermana es mi _____.
7. Yo soy el _____ del hijo de mi hermana.
8. La hija de mi padre y de mi madrasta es mi _____.

3 Profesiones Complete the description of each photo.

1. Rosa María Ortiz es _____.

2. Héctor Ibarra es _____.

3. Luis Meléndez _____.

4. Elena Vargas es _____.

5. Daniela López es _____.

6. Irene González es _____.

recursos

vhlcentral.com

52 cincuenta y dos

La familia

4 **¿Y tú?** With a classmate, take turns asking each other these questions.

1. ¿Cuántas personas hay en tu familia?
2. ¿Cómo se llaman tus padres? ¿De dónde son?
3. ¿Cuántos hermanos tienes? ¿Cómo se llaman?
4. ¿Cuántos primos tienes? ¿Cuántos son niños y cuántos son adultos?
5. ¿Eres tío/a? ¿Cómo se llaman tus sobrinos/as?
6. ¿Tienes novio/a? ¿Tienes esposo/a? ¿Cómo se llama?

tengo *I have*	**tu** *your (sing.)*
tienes *you have*	**tus** *your (pl.)*

Practice more at vhlcentral.com.

Pronunciación — Diphthongs and linking

Audio: Concepts, Activities

hermano   **niña**   **cuñado**

In Spanish, **a**, **e**, and **o** are considered strong vowels. The weak vowels are **i** and **u**.

ruido   **parientes**   **periodista**

A diphthong is a combination of two weak vowels or of a strong vowel and a weak vowel. Diphthongs are pronounced as a single syllable.

la abuela   **mi hijo**   **una clase excelente**

Two identical vowel sounds that appear together are pronounced like one long vowel.

con Natalia   **sus sobrinos**   **las sillas**

Two identical consonants together sound like a single consonant.

es ingeniera   **mis abuelos**   **sus hijos**

A consonant at the end of a word is linked with the vowel at the beginning of the next word.

mi hermano   **su esposa**   **nuestro amigo**

A vowel at the end of a word is linked with the vowel at the beginning of the next word.

recursos

LM p. 14

vhlcentral.com

Refranes Read these sayings aloud to practice diphthongs and linking sounds.

Cuando una puerta se cierra, otra se abre.[1]

Hablando del rey de Roma, por la puerta se asoma.[2]

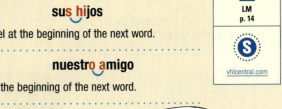

[1] When one door closes, another opens. [2] Speak of the devil and he will appear.

Practice more at vhlcentral.com.

cincuenta y tres 53

3 ESCENAS

Un domingo en familia

Marissa pasa el día en Xochimilco con la familia Díaz.

Expresiones útiles

Talking about your family

¿Tienes una familia grande?
Do you have a large family?
Tengo dos hermanos mayores y un hermano menor.
I have two older siblings and a younger brother.
La verdad, mi familia es pequeña.
The truth is, my family is small.
¿Pequeña? Yo soy hija única.
Small? I'm an only child.

Describing people

¡Qué bonitas son tus hijas! Y ¡qué simpáticas!
Your daughters are so pretty! And so nice!
Soy guapo y delgado.
I'm handsome and slim.
¡Por favor! Eres gordo, antipático y muy feo.
Please! You're fat, unpleasant, and very ugly.

Talking about plans

¿Compartimos una trajinera?
Shall we share a trajinera?
¡Claro que sí! ¡Qué bonitas son!
Of course! They're so pretty!
¿Vienes, Jimena?
Are you coming, Jimena?
No, gracias. Tengo que leer.
No, thanks. I have to read.

Saying how old people are

¿Cuántos años tienen tus hijas?
How old are your daughters?
Marta tiene ocho años y Valentina doce.
Marta is eight and Valentina twelve.

JIMENA Hola, tía Nayeli.
TÍA NAYELI ¡Hola, Jimena! ¿Cómo estás?
JIMENA Bien, gracias. Y, ¿dónde están mis primas?
TÍA NAYELI No sé. ¿Dónde están mis hijas? ¡Ah!

MARISSA ¡Qué bonitas son tus hijas! Y ¡qué simpáticas!

FELIPE Soy guapo y delgado.
JIMENA Ay, ¡por favor! Eres gordo, antipático y muy feo.

TÍO RAMÓN ¿Tienes una familia grande, Marissa?
MARISSA Tengo dos hermanos mayores, Zack y Jennifer, y un hermano menor, Adam.

MARISSA La verdad, mi familia es pequeña.
SRA. DÍAZ ¿Pequeña? Yo soy hija única. Bueno, y ¿qué más? ¿Tienes novio?
MARISSA No. Tengo mala suerte con los novios.

recursos

VM
pp. 5–6

vhlcentral.com

La familia

 FELIPE TÍA NAYELI JIMENA MARTA VALENTINA SRA. DÍAZ TÍO RAMÓN SR. DÍAZ MARISSA

MARISSA Tía Nayeli, ¿cuántos años tienen tus hijas?
TÍA NAYELI Marta tiene ocho años y Valentina doce.

SRA. DÍAZ Chicas, ¿compartimos una trajinera?
MARISSA ¡Claro que sí! ¡Qué bonitas son!
SRA. DÍAZ ¿Vienes, Jimena?
JIMENA No, gracias. Tengo que leer.

MARISSA Me gusta mucho este sitio. Tengo ganas de visitar otros lugares en México.
SRA. DÍAZ ¡Debes viajar a Mérida!
TÍA NAYELI ¡Sí, con tus amigos! Debes visitar a Ana María, la hermana de Roberto y de Ramón.

(La Sra. Díaz habla por teléfono con la tía Ana María.)
SRA. DÍAZ ¡Qué bien! Excelente. Sí, la próxima semana. Muchísimas gracias.

MARISSA ¡Gracias, Sra. Díaz!
SRA. DÍAZ Tía Ana María.
MARISSA Tía Ana María.
SRA. DÍAZ ¡Un beso, chau!
MARISSA Bye!

Practice more at vhlcentral.com.

Actividades

1 ¿Cierto o falso? Indicate whether each sentence is **cierto** or **falso**. Correct the false statements.

1. La señora Díaz tiene dos hermanos.
2. Marissa no tiene novio.
3. Valentina tiene veinte años.
4. Marissa comparte una trajinera con la señora Díaz y la tía Nayeli.
5. A Marissa le gusta mucho Xochimilco.

2 Identificar Indicate which person would make each statement.

1. Felipe es antipático y feo.
2. Mis hermanos se llaman Jennifer, Adam y Zach.
3. ¡Soy un joven muy guapo!
4. Mis hijas tienen doce y ocho años.
5. Tus hijas son bonitas y simpáticas.
6. Ana María es la hermana de Ramón y Roberto.

3 Conversar With a partner, use these questions to talk about your families.

1. ¿Tienes una familia grande o pequeña?
2. ¿Hay artistas en tu familia?
3. ¿Tienes hermanos menores? ¿Y hermanos mayores?
4. ¿Cuántos años tiene tu abuelo (tu hermana, tu primo...)?
5. ¿De dónde son tus padres?

cincuenta y cinco 55

3 EXPLORACIÓN

BAJO LA LUPA

¿Cómo te llamas?

In the Spanish-speaking world, it is common to have two last names: one paternal and one maternal. In some cases, the words **de** or **y** are used to connect the two. For example, in the name **Juan Martínez de Velasco**, *Martínez* is the paternal surname (**el apellido paterno**), and *Velasco* is the maternal surname (**el apellido materno**); **de** simply links the two. This convention of using two last names (**doble apellido**) is a European tradition that Spaniards brought to the Americas. It continues to be practiced in many countries, including Chile, Colombia, Mexico, Peru, and Venezuela. There are exceptions, however; in Argentina, the prevailing custom is for children to inherit only the father's last name.

Gabriel García Márquez

Mercedes Barcha Pardo

Rodrigo García Barcha

When a woman marries in a country where two last names are used, legally she retains her two maiden surnames. However, socially she may take her husband's paternal surname in place of her inherited maternal surname. For example, **Mercedes Barcha Pardo**, wife of Colombian writer **Gabriel García Márquez**, might use the names **Mercedes Barcha García** or **Mercedes Barcha de García** in social situations (although officially her name remains **Mercedes Barcha Pardo**). Adopting a husband's last name for social purposes, though widespread, is only legally recognized in Ecuador and Peru.

Most parents do not break tradition upon naming their children; regardless of the surnames the mother uses, they use the father's first surname followed by the mother's first surname, as in the name **Rodrigo García Barcha**. However, one should note that both surnames come from the grandfathers, and therefore all **apellidos** are effectively paternal.

Hijos en la casa

In Spanish-speaking countries, family and society place very little pressure on young adults to live on their own (**independizarse**). Consequently, children often live with their parents well into their thirties. For example, about 70% of Spaniards between the ages of 18 and 29 live at home with their parents. This delay in moving out is both cultural and economic—lack of job security or low wages coupled with a high cost of living may make it impractical for young adults to live independently before they marry.

56 cincuenta y seis

La familia

ACTIVIDADES

1 ¿Cierto o falso? Indicate whether these statements are **cierto** or **falso.** Correct the false statements.

1. Most Spanish speakers have three last names.
2. Hispanic last names generally consist of the paternal last name followed by the maternal last name.
3. It is common to see **de** or **y** used in Hispanic last names.
4. Someone from Argentina would most likely have two last names.
5. Generally, married women legally retain two maiden surnames.
6. In social situations, a married woman often uses her husband's last name in place of her inherited paternal surname.
7. Adopting a husband's surname is only legally recognized in Peru and Ecuador.
8. Hispanic last names are effectively a combination of the maternal surnames from the previous generation.

2 Una familia famosa Create a genealogical tree of a famous family, using photos or drawings labeled with their names and origins. Present the family tree to a classmate and explain who the people are and their relationships to each other.

CONEXIÓN INTERNET

What role do **padrinos** and **madrinas** have in today's Hispanic family? For more information about **Exploración**, go to **vhlcentral.com**.

Flash CULTURA

La familia

1 Preparación What is a "typical family" like where you live? Is there such a thing? What members of a family usually live together?

2 El video Watch this **Flash cultura** episode.

Vocabulario

familia grande y feliz	a big, happy family
familia numerosa	a large family
hacer (algo) juntos	to do (something) together
reuniones familiares	family gatherings, reunions

¡Qué familia tan° grande tiene!

Te presento a la familia Bolaños.

tan *so*

3 Completar Complete this paragraph with the appropriate words.

Los Valdivieso y los Bolaños son dos ejemplos de familias en Ecuador. Los Valdivieso son una familia (1) _____ (difícil/numerosa). Viven *(They live)* en una casa (2) _____ (grande/buena). En el patio, hacen *(they do)* muchas reuniones (3) _____ (familiares/con amigos). Los Bolaños son una familia pequeña *(small)*. Ellos comen *(eat)* (4) _____ (separados/juntos) y preparan canelazo, una bebida *(drink)* típica ecuatoriana.

cincuenta y siete 57

3 GRAMÁTICA

3.1 Descriptive adjectives

▶ Descriptive adjectives describe nouns. In Spanish, adjectives agree in gender and number with the nouns or pronouns they describe.

▶ Adjectives that end in **–o** and **–or** have four forms. The feminine singular is formed by changing the **–o** to **–a**. The plural is formed by adding **–s** to the singular forms.

Masculine	Feminine	Masculine	Feminine
el chico alt**o**	la chica alt**a**	el hombre trabajad**or**	la mujer trabajad**ora**
los chicos alt**os**	las chicas alt**as**	los hombres trabajad**ores**	las mujeres trabajad**oras**

▶ Adjectives that end in **–e** or a consonant have the same masculine and feminine forms. The plural for adjectives that end in a consonant is formed by adding **–es**.

Masculine	Feminine	Masculine	Feminine
el chico inteligent**e**	la chica inteligent**e**	el profesor difícil	la profesora difícil
los chicos inteligent**es**	las chicas inteligent**es**	los profesores difícil**es**	las profesoras difícil**es**

¡ojo!

Adjectives that refer to nouns of different genders use the masculine plural form.

¿Cómo son Paco y Ana?
Paco es alt**o**. Ana es alt**a**.
→ Paco y Ana son alt**os**.

• • •

Note that **joven** takes an accent in the plural: **jóvenes**. Also note that **mayor** is the polite way to refer to a person's age (not **viejo/a**).

Common descriptive adjectives

alto/a	tall	fácil	easy	inteligente	intelligent	rubio/a	blond(e)
antipático/a	unpleasant	feo/a	ugly	interesante	interesting	simpático/a	nice; likeable
bajo/a	short (in height)	gordo/a	fat	joven	young	tonto/a	silly; foolish
bonito/a	pretty	grande	big, large; great	malo/a	bad	trabajador(a)	hard-working
bueno/a	good	guapo/a	handsome; good looking	moreno/a	dark-haired	viejo/a	old
delgado/a	thin; slender			pelirrojo/a	red-haired		
difícil	hard, difficult	importante	important	pequeño/a	small		

▶ Adjectives of nationality that end in a consonant add **–a** to form the feminine.

Masculine	Feminine	Masculine	Feminine
Toño es mexican**o**.	Gloria es mexican**a**.	Héctor es español.	Sara es español**a**.
Ellos son mexican**os**.	Ellas son mexican**as**.	Ellos son español**es**.	Ellas son español**as**.

Adjectives of nationality

alemán, alemana	German	estadounidense	from the United States	japonés, japonesa	Japanese
canadiense	Canadian			mexicano/a	Mexican
ecuatoriano/a	Ecuadorian	francés, francesa	French	norteamericano/a	(North) American
español(a)	Spanish	inglés, inglesa	English	puertorriqueño/a	Puerto Rican

▶ Adjectives generally follow the nouns they modify.

La muchacha **rubia** es de España.   ¿Cómo se llama la mujer **ecuatoriana**?
The blond woman is from Spain.   *What is the Ecuadorian woman's name?*

▶ Adjectives of quantity such as **mucho/a** (*much; many; a lot*) come before the noun.

Hay **muchos** estudiantes.   **Mucha** gente viaja en el verano.
There are many students.   *A lot of people travel in the summer.*

La familia

▶ **Bueno/a** and **malo/a** can be placed before or after a noun. Before a masculine singular noun, the forms are shortened: **bueno → buen**; **malo → mal**.

José es un **buen** amigo. Hoy es un **mal** día.
José es un amigo **bueno**. Hoy es un día **malo**.
José is a good friend. *Today is a bad day.*

▶ When **grande** appears before a singular noun, it is shortened to **gran**. **Grande** also changes its definition depending on its position: **gran** = *great*, but **grande** = *big, large*.

Manuel es un **gran** hombre. La familia de Inés es **grande**.
Manuel is a great man. *Inés' family is large.*

Práctica y conversación

1 Emparejar Read the descriptions and match them with the photos.

1. __ Mateo es moreno.   4. __ Rayo es delgado.
2. __ Hideki es japonés. 5. __ César es muy pequeño.
3. __ Luisa es rubia.   6. __ Raquel es pelirroja.

A   B   C

D   E   F

2 Completar Look at the portrait of Amanda's family and imagine their personalities. Complete the sentences with appropriate adjectives.

1. Mi familia es _____.
2. Mis abuelos son _____.
3. Mi padre se llama Julio. Él es _____.
4. Mi madre es _____.
5. Mi hermana Rosa es _____.
6. Y mi hermano es muy _____.

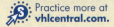
Practice more at vhlcentral.com.

3 Describir With a partner, take turns describing each photo. Tell your partner whether you agree (**Estoy de acuerdo**) or disagree (**No estoy de acuerdo**) with the descriptions.

MODELO
Estudiante 1: Los Ángeles es muy bonita.
Estudiante 2: Estoy de acuerdo. ¡Es muy interesante!/ No estoy de acuerdo. Es muy fea.

Los Ángeles

 1. Príncipe y Princesa de España

 2. La Torre (*Tower*) Sears

 3. Christina Aguilera

 4. Enrique Iglesias

 5. Taxco, México

 6. Bill Gates

4 Anuncio personal Write a personal ad that describes yourself and your ideal boyfriend, girlfriend, or mate. Compare your ad with a classmate's.

SOY ALTA, morena y bonita. Estudio arte en la universidad. Soy estadounidense, de Texas. Busco un chico similar a mí (*to me*). Mi novio ideal es alto, moreno, inteligente y muy simpático.

Lección 3

3.2 Possessive adjectives  Tutorial

¿Dónde están mis primas?

▶ Possessive adjectives express ownership or possession.

Forms of possessive adjectives

Singular forms	Plural forms	
mi	mis	my
tu	tus	your (fam.)
su	sus	his, her, its, your (form.)
nuestro/a	nuestros/as	our
vuestro/a	vuestros/as	your (fam.)
su	sus	their, its, your (form.)

Nuestra cuñada es muy simpática.

▶ Spanish possessive adjectives agree in number with the nouns they modify. **Nuestro** and **vuestro** agree in gender and number.

mi primo	mis primos		mi tía	mis tías
nuestro tío	nuestros tíos		nuestra tía	nuestras tías

▶ Possessive adjectives are placed before the nouns they modify.

▶ **Su** and **sus** have multiple meanings (*your, his, her, their, its*). To avoid confusion, use this construction instead: [*article*] + [*noun*] + **de** + [*subject pronoun*].

		los parientes de él/ella	his/her relatives
sus parientes		los parientes de usted/ustedes	your relatives
		los parientes de ellos/ellas	their relatives

ESPAÑOL EN VIVO

Vida Láctea
Su crecimiento° es vital

¡La leche es nuestra bebida favorita!

A mi hijo le gusta Vida Láctea por su excelente sabor°. Su vaso° de leche diario tiene vitaminas y minerales esenciales para su crecimiento. Sus huesos° están cada vez más grandes y fuertes.

crecimiento *growth* **sabor** *flavor* **vaso** *glass* **huesos** *bones*

60 sesenta

La familia

Práctica y conversación

1 Completar Marta just took a photo of her family. Complete her description of the photo.

Ésta es una foto de (1) _____ familia. Aquí están (2) _____ abuelos. Son los padres de (3) _____ papá. (4) _____ casa (*home*) está en Valparaíso, Chile. ¡Es muy bonita! ¡A mí me gusta mucho visitarlos (*visit them*)!

Este (*This*) hombre es (5) _____ papá. Se llama David y es médico. (6) _____ mamá se llama Rebeca; es periodista. (7) _____ hermana, (8) _____ tía Silvia, es una gran artista. Y aquí está (9) _____ hermano Ramón. (10) _____ esposa se llama Sonia. (11) _____ hijos Javier y Laura son (12) _____ sobrinos. Son muy simpáticos.

2 ¿Dónde está? Imagine that you can't remember where you put some of your belongings (pictured below). Your partner will help you by reminding you where things are. Take turns playing each role.

MODELO
Estudiante 1: ¿Dónde está mi pluma?
Estudiante 2: Tu pluma está al lado de la computadora.

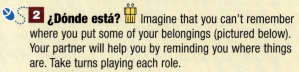

1.
2.
3.
4.
5.
6.

3 Describir With a partner, take turns describing these people and places.

MODELO
La biblioteca de su universidad
La biblioteca de nuestra universidad es muy grande. Hay muchos libros en la biblioteca. Mis amigos y yo estudiamos allí (there).

1. Tus padres
2. Tus abuelos
3. Tu mejor (*best*) amigo/a
4. Tu novio/a ideal
5. Su universidad
6. La librería de su universidad
7. Tu profesor
8. Su clase de español

4 Tres fotos Choose one of the three family photos and describe the family as if it were your own. Your partner will guess which photo you are describing. Then switch roles.

Familia 1

Familia 2

Familia 3

Practice more at **vhlcentral.com**.

sesenta y uno **61**

Lección 3

3.3 Present tense of regular –er and –ir verbs  Tutorial

Felipe y su tío **comen**.

Jimena **lee**.

▶ In Lesson 2, you learned how to form the present tense of regular **–ar** verbs. The chart below contains the forms of the regular **–ar** verb **trabajar**, which is conjugated just like the other **–ar** verbs you have learned. There are other regular verbs in Spanish: regular **–er** and **–ir** verbs. The chart also shows the forms of an **–er** verb and an **–ir** verb.

▶ **–Ar, –er,** and **–ir** verbs have very similar endings. Study this chart to detect the patterns that make it easier for you to use them to communicate in Spanish.

Present tense of –ar, –er, and –ir verbs

	trabajar to work	comer to eat	escribir to write
yo	trabajo	como	escribo
tú	trabajas	comes	escribes
Ud./él/ella	trabaja	come	escribe
nosotros/as	trabajamos	comemos	escribimos
vosotros/as	trabajáis	coméis	escribís
Uds./ellos/ellas	trabajan	comen	escriben

▶ Like **–ar** verbs, the **yo** forms of **–er** and **–ir** verbs end in **–o.**

trabajo   como   escribo

▶ The endings for **–ar** verbs begin with **–a**, except for the **yo** form.

hablo   habla   habláis
hablas   hablamos hablan

▶ The endings for **–er** verbs begin with **–e**, except for the **yo** form.

como   come   coméis
comes   comemos comen

▶ **–Er** and **–ir** verbs have the exact same endings, except in the **nosotros/as** and **vosotros/as** forms.

nosotros ◀ comemos / escribimos   vosotros ◀ coméis / escribís

Eugenia y Laura **corren** en el parque.

Ramón **escribe** una carta.

62   sesenta y dos

La familia

Common –er and –ir verbs

–er verbs
aprender	to learn
beber	to drink
comer	to eat
comprender	to understand
correr	to run
creer (en)	to believe (in)
deber (+ inf.)	should, ought to; must
leer	to read

–ir verbs
abrir	to open
asistir (a)	to attend
compartir	to share
decidir	to decide
describir	to describe
escribir	to write
recibir	to receive
vivir	to live

Práctica y conversación

Practice more at vhlcentral.com.

1 Emparejar Susana is describing her family. Complete each sentence with the correct verb form.

1. Mi familia y yo _____ [vivir] en Montevideo, Uruguay.
2. Mi hermano Alfredo es muy inteligente. Él _____ [asistir] a clases de lunes a viernes.
3. Los martes Alfredo y yo _____ [correr] en el parque.
4. Mis padres _____ [comer] mucho; ellos son un poco gordos.
5. Yo _____ [creer] que (*that*) mis padres _____ [deber] comer menos (*less*).

2 Completar Juan is talking about what he and his friends do after school. Complete his sentences.

MODELO
Yo _leo_ en la biblioteca.

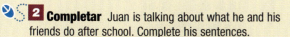

1. Nosotros _____ en el restaurante.

3. Elena _____ en su diario.

2. Sofía y Diego _____ café.

4. Ana y Lía _____ el almuerzo (*lunch*).

3 Entrevista Use these questions to interview a classmate. Then report the results of your interview to the class.

1. ¿Dónde vives?
2. ¿Con quién vives? ¿Compartes tu cuarto?
3. ¿Dónde comes al mediodía?
4. ¿Bebes leche (*milk*) todos los días?
5. ¿Qué días asistes a tus clases?
6. ¿Qué cursos debes tomar el próximo (*next*) semestre?
7. ¿Lees el periódico (*newspaper*)? ¿Cuál?
8. ¿Recibes muchos mensajes de texto (*text messages*)?
9. ¿Escribes poemas o cuentos (*stories*)?
10. ¿Crees en extraterrestres (*aliens*)?

4 Encuesta Walk around the class and ask your classmates if they do (or should do) the things mentioned on the survey. Try to find at least two people for each item.

Actividad	Nombres
1. Asistir siempre (*always*) a la clase de español	_____
2. Correr todos los días (*every day*)	_____
3. Aprender japonés	_____
4. Vivir en una residencia estudiantil	_____
5. Leer mucho para (*for*) un examen	_____
6. Escribir en un blog	_____
7. Beber un litro de agua al día	_____
8. Aprender contabilidad	_____

sesenta y tres 63

Lección 3

3.4 Present tense of **tener** and **venir**  Tutorial

¿Tienes una familia grande, Marissa?

▶ The verbs **tener** (*to have*) and **venir** (*to come*) are frequently used. Since most of their forms are irregular, you will have to learn each one individually.

Present tense of *tener* and *venir*

tener — to have				**venir** — to come			
yo	tengo	nosotros/as	tenemos	yo	vengo	nosotros/as	venimos
tú	tienes	vosotros/as	tenéis	tú	vienes	vosotros/as	venís
Ud./él/ella	tiene	Uds./ellos/ellas	tienen	Ud./él/ella	viene	Uds./ellos/ellas	vienen

¡ojo!

To express an obligation, use **tener que** (*to have to*) + [*infinitive*].

—¿**Tienes que** estudiar hoy?
Do you have to study today?

—Sí, **tengo que** estudiar física.
Yes, I have to study physics.

• • •

To ask people if they feel like doing something, use **tener ganas de** (*to feel like*) + [*infinitive*].

—¿**Tienes ganas de** comer?
Do you feel like eating?

—No, **tengo ganas de** dormir.
No, I feel like sleeping.

▶ Note that the **yo** forms are irregular:

tengo   vengo

▶ The **nosotros** and **vosotros** forms are regular:

tenemos   venimos
tenéis   venís

▶ In the second person singular and the third person singular and plural forms, there is also an **e:ie** stem change.

INFINITIVE	VERB STEM	VERB FORM	
tener	ten-	tú	tienes
		Ud./él/ella	tiene
		Uds./ellos/ellas	tienen
venir	ven-	tú	vienes
		Ud./él/ella	viene
		Uds./ellos/ellas	vienen

▶ In certain expressions, Spanish uses the construction **tener** + [*noun*] instead of **ser** or **estar** to express the English equivalent *to be* + [*adjective*].

Expressions with *tener*

tener... años	to be ... years old	tener (mucha) hambre	to be (very) hungry	tener razón	to be right
tener (mucho) calor	to be (very) hot	tener (mucho) miedo	to be (very) afraid/scared	no tener razón	to be wrong
tener (mucho) cuidado	to be (very) careful	tener (mucha) prisa	to be in a (big) hurry	tener (mucha) sed	to be (very) thirsty
tener (mucho) frío	to be (very) cold			tener (mucho) sueño	to be (very) sleepy
				tener (mucha) suerte	to be (very) lucky

64   sesenta y cuatro

La familia

Práctica y conversación

1 Completar Complete each sentence with the appropriate form of **tener** or **venir**.

1. Hoy nosotros _____ una reunión familiar.
2. Todos (*all*) mis parientes _____, excepto mi tío Ricardo y mi tía Luisa.
3. Él no _____ porque vive en Guayaquil.
4. Mi prima Inés y su novio no _____ hasta (*until*) las ocho porque ella _____ que trabajar.
5. En las fiestas, mis sobrinos siempre (*always*) _____ ganas de cantar y bailar.
6. Mi madre cree que mis sobrinos son muy simpáticos. Creo que ella _____ razón.

2 Describir Describe these people using **tener** expressions.

1. _____

4. _____

2. _____

5. _____

3. _____

6. _____

3 ¿Sí o no? Decide if these statements apply to you. Then interview a classmate by transforming each statement into a question. Report your results to the class.

MODELO
Estudiante 1: ¿Tiene tu madre cincuenta años?
Estudiante 2: No, tiene cuarenta y dos años.

	Yo	Mi amigo/a
1. Mi madre tiene cincuenta años.	Sí	No
2. Mi padre siempre (*always*) tiene razón.	___	___
3. Mis padres vienen a la universidad con frecuencia (*frequently*).	___	___
4. Vengo a clase los jueves.	___	___
5. Tengo dos pruebas hoy.	___	___
6. Mis amigos vienen a mi apartamento los días de semana.	___	___
7. Hoy tengo ganas de comer en un restaurante.	___	___
8. Tengo sed.	___	___
9. Tengo miedo de comer sushi.	___	___
10. Tengo que estudiar los domingos.	___	___
11. Tengo una familia grande.	___	___

4 Entrevista Use these questions to interview a classmate.

1. ¿Cuántos años tienes? ¿Y tus hermanos/as?
2. ¿Cuándo vienes a la universidad?
3. ¿Tienes que estudiar hoy? ¿Por qué?
4. Normalmente, ¿tienes hambre a la medianoche?
5. ¿Tienes sueño ahora (*now*)?
6. ¿Qué tienes ganas de hacer (*doing*) el sábado?
7. ¿De qué tienes miedo? ¿Por qué?
8. ¿Qué periódico (*newspaper*) lees?

sesenta y cinco **65**

Lección 3

Ampliación

1 Escuchar

A Listen to Cristina and Laura's conversation. Then indicate who would make each statement.

TIP Ask for repetition. During a conversation, you can ask someone to repeat by saying **¿Cómo?** (*What?*) or **¿Perdón?** (*Pardon me?*). In class, you can ask your teacher to repeat by saying **Repítalo, por favor** (*Repeat it, please*). If you don't understand a recorded activity, you can simply replay it.

	Cristina	Laura
1. Mi novio habla sólo (*only*) del fútbol y del béisbol.	☐	☐
2. Tengo un novio muy interesante y simpático.	☐	☐
3. Mi novio es alto y moreno.	☐	☐
4. Mi novio trabaja mucho.	☐	☐
5. Mi amiga no tiene buena suerte con los muchachos.	☐	☐
6. Mi novio es un poco gordo, pero guapo.	☐	☐

B ¿Cómo son Laura y Cristina? ¿Cómo son sus novios? ¿Tienes novio/a? ¿Cómo es?

2 Conversar

You are taking a friend to your family reunion. So that there will not be any surprises for your friend, you have a conversation with him or her to talk about your relatives. During the conversation, your friend should find out about the following:

- Which family members are coming, including their names and their relationship to you
- What each family member is like
- How old each person is
- Where each person is from
- Where each person lives

recursos

WB pp. 23–30

LM pp. 15–18

vhlcentral.com

La familia

3 Escribir One of your online friends wants to know about your family. Write an e-mail describing your family or an imaginary family.

TIP Use idea maps. Idea maps help you group your information.

Organízalo Use an idea map to help you list and organize information about your family. See the example.

Escríbelo Using the material you have compiled, write the first draft of your e-mail. Use an appropriate greeting, such as **Querido/a** (*Dear*), and an appropriate closing, such as **Un abrazo** (*A hug*).

Corrígelo Exchange papers with a classmate and comment on the organization, style, and grammatical accuracy of each other's work. Then revise your first draft, keeping your classmate's comments in mind.

Compártelo Read your e-mail aloud to a small group of classmates. Discuss how your families are similar (**semejantes**) and how they are different (**distintas**).

4 Un paso más Create an illustrated family tree for your family and share it with the class. Your family tree might include these elements:

- A simple title
- A format that clearly shows the relationships between family members
- Photos of family members and their names, following Hispanic naming conventions
- A few adjectives that describe each family member

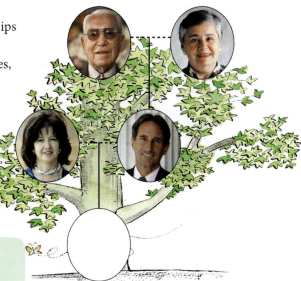

CONEXIÓN INTERNET

Investiga estos temas en vhlcentral.com.
- Tradiciones relacionadas con los nombres en el mundo hispano
- Origen y significado (*meaning*) de los nombres en español

Practice more at vhlcentral.com.

sesenta y siete 67

3 LECTURA

Antes de leer 🅢 Audio: Reading / Additional Reading

You do not need to understand every word you read in Spanish. When you come across words you have not learned, try to guess what they mean by looking at the context—the surrounding words and sentences. Look at this article about families and find a few words or phrases you do not know. Then guess what they mean, using the context as your guide.

Me llamo Armando y tengo setenta años, pero no me considero viejo. Tengo seis nietas y un nieto. Vivo con mi hija y tengo la oportunidad de pasar mucho tiempo con ella y con mi nieto. Por las tardes salgo a pasear por el parque con él y por la noche le leo cuentos°.

Armando. Tiene seis nietas y un nieto.

Mi prima Victoria y yo nos llevamos muy bien. Estudiamos juntas° en la universidad y compartimos un apartamento. Ella es muy inteligente y me ayuda° con los estudios. Además, es muy simpática y generosa. Si necesito cualquier cosa, ¡ella me la compra!

Diana. Vive con su prima.

Me llamo Ramona y soy paraguaya, aunque ahora vivo en los Estados Unidos. Tengo tres hijos, uno de nueve años, uno de doce y el mayor de quince. Es difícil a veces, pero mi esposo y yo tratamos° de ayudarlos y comprenderlos siempre.

Ramona. Sus hijos son muy importantes para ella.

Tengo mucha suerte. Aunque mis padres están divorciados, tengo una familia muy unida. Tengo dos hermanos y dos hermanas. Me gusta hablar y salir a fiestas con ellos. Ahora tengo novio en la universidad y él no conoce a mis hermanos. ¡Espero que se lleven bien!

68 *sesenta y ocho*

La familia

Después de leer

¿Comprendiste?
Look at the magazine article and see how the words and phrases in the first column are used in context. Then find their translations in the second column.

1. nos llevamos muy bien _____	a. the oldest
2. me la compra _____	b. movies
3. el mayor _____	c. better than
4. no conoce _____	d. buys it for me
5. películas _____	e. borrows it from me
6. mejor que _____	f. we see each other
	g. doesn't know
	h. we get along very well

Preguntas
Answer these questions using complete sentences.

1. ¿Cuántas personas hay en la familia de Ramona?
   _____
2. ¿Con quién vive Diana?
   _____
3. ¿Cómo se llama el sobrino de Santiago?
   _____
4. ¿Quién no tiene hermanos ni (*nor*) primos?
   _____
5. ¿Quién tiene novio?
   _____
6. ¿Cuántos nietos tiene Armando?
   _____

Coméntalo
¿Es similar tu familia a las familias del artículo? En tu opinión, ¿son ideales las familias del artículo? ¿Cómo es la familia ideal?

Ana María. Su familia es muy unida.

Antes quería° tener hermanos, pero ya no es tan importante. Ser hijo único tiene muchas ventajas°: no tengo que compartir mis cosas con hermanos, no hay discusiones° y, como soy nieto único también, ¡mis abuelos piensan° que soy perfecto!

Fernando. Es hijo único.

Como soy joven todavía, no tengo ni esposa ni hijos. Pero tengo un sobrino, el hijo de mi hermano, que es muy especial para mí. Se llama Benjamín y tiene diez años. Es un muchacho muy simpático. Siempre tiene hambre y por lo tanto vamos° frecuentemente a comer hamburguesas. Nos gusta también ir al cine° a ver películas de acción. Hablamos de todo. ¡Creo que ser tío es mejor que ser padre!

Santiago. Cree que ser tío es divertido.

---

cuentos *stories*   juntas *together*   me ayuda *she helps me*
tratamos *we try*   quería *I wanted*   ventajas *advantages*
discusiones *arguments*   piensan *think*   vamos *we go*
ir al cine *to go to the movies*

sesenta y nueve   **69**

3 VOCABULARIO

La familia

el/la abuelo/a	grandfather/grandmother
el/la cuñado/a	brother-in-law/sister-in-law
el/la esposo/a	husband/wife; spouse
la familia	family
el/la hermanastro/a	stepbrother/stepsister
el/la hermano/a	brother/sister
el/la hijastro/a	stepson/stepdaughter
el/la hijo/a	son/daughter
los/las hijos/as	children; sons, daughters
la madrastra	stepmother
la madre	mother
el/la medio/a hermano/a	half-brother/half-sister
el/la nieto/a	grandson/granddaughter
la nuera	daughter-in-law
el padrastro	stepfather
el padre	father
los padres	parents
los parientes	relatives
el/la primo/a	cousin
el/la sobrino/a	nephew/niece
el/la suegro/a	father-in-law/mother-in-law
el/la tío/a	uncle/aunt
el yerno	son-in-law

Otras palabras

el/la amigo/a	friend
el/la gato/a	cat
la gente	people
el/la muchacho/a	boy/girl
el/la niño/a	child; boy/girl
el/la novio/a	boyfriend/girlfriend
la persona	person
el/la perro/a	dog

Adjetivos

alto/a	tall
antipático/a	unpleasant
bajo/a	short (in height)
bonito/a	pretty
buen, bueno/a	good
delgado/a	thin; slender
difícil	difficult, hard
fácil	easy
feo/a	ugly
gordo/a	fat
gran; grande	big, large; great
guapo/a	handsome; good-looking
importante	important
inteligente	intelligent
interesante	interesting
joven	young
mal, malo/a	bad
moreno/a	dark-haired
mucho/a	much; many; a lot of
pelirrojo/a	red-haired
pequeño/a	small
rubio/a	blond(e)
simpático/a	nice; likeable
tonto/a	silly; foolish
trabajador(a)	hard-working
viejo/a	old

Las profesiones

el/la artista	artist
el/la doctor(a)	doctor; physician
el/la ingeniero/a	engineer
el/la médico/a	doctor; physician
el/la periodista	journalist
el/la programador(a)	computer programmer

Nationalities	See page 58.
Possessive adjectives	See page 60.

Verbos

abrir	to open
aprender	to learn
asistir (a)	to attend
beber	to drink
comer	to eat
compartir	to share
comprender	to understand
correr	to run
creer (en)	to believe (in)
deber (+ inf.)	to have to; should
decidir	to decide
describir	to describe
escribir	to write
leer	to read
recibir	to receive
tener	to have
venir	to come
vivir	to live

Expresiones con *tener*

tener… años	to be… years old
tener (mucho) calor	to be (very) hot
tener (mucho) cuidado	to be (very) careful
tener (mucho) frío	to be (very) cold
tener ganas de (+ inf.)	to feel like (doing something)
tener (mucha) hambre	to be (very) hungry
tener (mucho) miedo	to be (very) afraid/scared
tener (mucha) prisa	to be in a (big) hurry
tener que (+ inf.)	to have to (do something)
tener razón	to be right
no tener razón	to be wrong
tener (mucha) sed	to be (very) thirsty
tener (mucho) sueño	to be (very) sleepy
tener (mucha) suerte	to be (very) lucky

Audio: Vocabulary Flashcards

4 El fin de semana

Communicative Goals

You will learn how to:
- talk about pastimes, weekend activities, and sports
- make plans and invitations
- say what you are going to do

PREPARACIÓN
pages 72-75
- Words related to pastimes and sports
- Places in the city
- Word stress and accent marks

ESCENAS
pages 76-77
- The friends spend the day exploring Mérida and the surrounding area. Maru, Jimena, and Miguel take Marissa to a cenote. Felipe and Juan Carlos join Felipe's cousins for soccer and lunch.

EXPLORACIÓN
pages 78-79
- Bajo la lupa: *Real Madrid y Barça: rivalidad total*
- Flash cultura: *¡Fútbol en España!*

GRAMÁTICA
pages 80-89
- Present tense of **ir**
- Present tense of stem-changing verbs
- Verbs with irregular **yo** forms

LECTURA
pages 90-91
- Newspaper article: *Guía para el fin de semana*

Para empezar
- ¿Cómo son estas personas? ¿Gordas o delgadas?
- ¿Son jóvenes o viejas?
- ¿En qué tienen interés: en el fútbol o en el ciclismo?
- ¿Tienen calor o frío?

4 PREPARACIÓN

El fin de semana

 Talking Picture Tutorial Games

ACTIVIDADES Y DISTRACCIONES

escalar montañas to climb mountains
escribir una carta to write a letter
un mensaje electrónico to write an e-mail
esquiar to ski
ir de excursión (a las montañas) to go on a hike (in the mountains)
leer el periódico to read the newspaper
el correo electrónico to read e-mail
una revista to read a magazine
nadar en la piscina to swim in the pool
pasear por la ciudad/el pueblo to walk around the city/town
practicar deportes (m. pl.) to practice sports
ver películas to watch movies
visitar un monumento to visit a monument

pasear en bicicleta to ride a bicycle

patinar (en línea) to skate (in-line)

tomar el sol to sunbathe

bucear to scuba dive

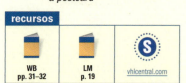
una (tarjeta) postal a postcard

recursos
WB pp. 31–32
LM p. 19
vhlcentral.com

72 setenta y dos

El fin de semana

LOS DEPORTES

el baloncesto basketball
el ciclismo cycling
el esquí (acuático) (water) skiing
el fútbol americano football
el golf golf
el hockey hockey
la natación swimming
el tenis tennis
el vóleibol volleyball

el equipo team
el/la jugador(a) player
el partido game
la pelota ball
ganar to win
ser aficionado/a (a) to be a fan (of)
deportivo/a sports-related

el/la excursionista
hiker

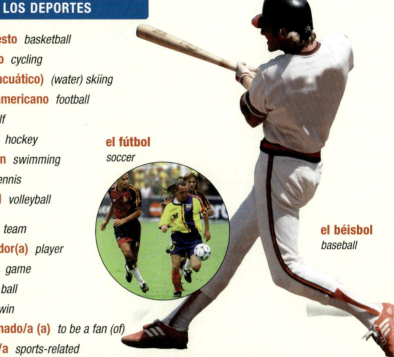
el fútbol soccer
el béisbol baseball

LUGARES

la casa house
el centro downtown
el cine movie theater
el gimnasio gym; gymnasium
el museo museum
el parque park
el restaurante restaurant

la iglesia
church

la piscina
pool

el café
café

OTRAS PALABRAS

la diversión entertainment; fun activity
el fin de semana weekend
el lugar place
el pasatiempo pastime; hobby
los ratos libres spare time
el tiempo libre free time
favorito/a favorite
pasar el tiempo to spend time

setenta y tres 73

Lección 4

Práctica y conversación  Audio: Activities

1 Una estudiante muy activa 🎧 Number the drawings in the order Laura mentions them.

a. _____

b. _____

c. _____

d. _____

e. _____

2 ¿Cierto o falso? Indicate whether each statement is **cierto** or **falso**.

Gustavo y Simón

los chicos

José   don Fernando

1. _____ Gustavo y Simón pasean en bicicleta.
2. _____ Los chicos juegan al fútbol.
3. _____ José hace una excursión a las montañas.
4. _____ Don Fernando lee en el parque.
5. _____ Maribel patina en línea.
6. _____ Doña Leonor pasea por la ciudad.

Maribel

doña Leonor

3 Dos amigos Complete the conversation with the words given.

LUISA ¿Cómo te gusta _____ los ratos libres, Manuel?
MANUEL Bueno, Luisa, no tengo mucho _____ libre, pero los fines de _____ me gusta ver películas. Y tú, Luisa, ¿cuáles son tus _____ favoritos?
LUISA Ir al _____, nadar en la _____ y jugar al _____.

centro	piscina
gimnasio	semana
pasar	tiempo
pasatiempos	vóleibol

recursos
vhlcentral.com

74 setenta y cuatro

El fin de semana

4 ¿Y tú? Interview a partner using these questions.

1. ¿Te gustan los deportes? ¿Qué deportes practicas?
2. ¿Eres aficionado/a a los deportes profesionales?
3. ¿Te gusta ir al cine? ¿Cuáles son tus películas favoritas?
4. ¿Hay lugares para esquiar o ir de excursión cerca de tu ciudad/pueblo? ¿Cuáles?
5. ¿Cuántos mensajes electrónicos escribes durante el día?

Practice more at vhlcentral.com.

Pronunciación Word stress

Audio: Concepts, Activities

| pe-**lí**-cu-la | e-di-**fi**-cio | **ver** | **yo** |

Every Spanish syllable contains at least one vowel. When two vowels (two weak vowels or one strong and one weak) are joined in the same syllable, they form a **diphthong**. A **monosyllable** is a word formed by a single syllable.

| bi-blio-**te**-ca | vi-si-**tar** | **par**-que | **fút**-bol |

The syllable of a Spanish word that is pronounced most emphatically is the "stressed" syllable.

| pe-**lo**-ta | pis-**ci**-na | **ra**-tos | **ha**-blan |

Words that end in **n**, **s**, or a **vowel** are usually stressed on the next-to-last syllable.

| na-ta-**ción** | pa-**pá** | in-**glés** | Jo-**sé** |

If words that end in **n**, **s**, or a **vowel** are stressed on the last syllable, they must carry an accent mark on the stressed syllable.

| bai-**lar** | es-pa-**ñol** | u-ni-ver-si-**dad** | tra-ba-ja-**dor** |

Words that do **not** end in **n**, **s**, or a **vowel** are usually stressed on the last syllable.

| **béis**-bol | **lá**-piz | **ár**-bol | **Gó**-mez |

If words that do **not** end in **n**, **s**, or a **vowel** are stressed on the next-to-last syllable, they must carry an accent mark on the stressed syllable.

Refranes Read these sayings aloud to practice word stress.

Practice more at vhlcentral.com.

En la unión está la fuerza.[2]

Quien ríe de último, ríe mejor.[1]

1 He who laughs last laughs loudest. 2 In unity, there is strength.

recursos

LM pp. 20

vhlcentral.com

setenta y cinco 75

4 ESCENAS

Fútbol, cenotes y mole Video: *Fotonovela*

Maru, Miguel, Jimena y Marissa visitan un cenote, mientras Felipe y Juan Carlos van a un partido de fútbol.

Expresiones útiles

Making invitations

¿Por qué no vamos al parque?
Why don't we go to the park?
¡Buena idea!
Good idea!
¿Por qué no jugamos al fútbol?
Why don't we play soccer?
Mmm… no quiero.
Hmm… I don't want to.
Lo siento, pero no puedo.
I'm sorry, but I can't.
¿Quieres pasear por la ciudad conmigo?
Do you want to walk around the city with me?
Sí, vamos.
Yes, let's go.

Making plans

¿Qué vas a hacer esta noche?
What are you going to do tonight?
No tengo planes.
I don't have any plans.

Talking about pastimes

¿Eres aficionado/a a los deportes?
Are you a sports fan?
Sí, me gustan todos los deportes.
Yes, I like all sports.
Sí, me gusta mucho el fútbol.
Yes, I like soccer a lot.

Apologizing

Mil perdones./Lo siento muchísimo.
I'm so sorry.

MIGUEL Buenos días a todos.
ANA MARÍA Hola, Miguel… Maru, ¿qué van a hacer hoy?
MARU Miguel y yo vamos a llevar a Marissa a un cenote.

MARISSA ¿No vamos a nadar? ¿Qué es un cenote?
MIGUEL Sí, sí, vamos a nadar. Un cenote… difícil de explicar… es una piscina natural en un hueco profundo….
MARU ¡Ya vas a ver! Seguro que te va a gustar.

ANA MARÍA Marissa, ¿qué te gusta hacer? ¿Escalar montañas? ¿Ir de excursión?
MARISSA Sí, me gusta ir de excursión y practicar el esquí acuático. Y usted, ¿qué prefiere hacer en sus ratos libres?

PABLO Uy, pues, mi mamá tiene muchos pasatiempos y actividades.
EDUARDO Sí. Ella nada y juega al tenis y al golf…
PABLO … va al cine y a los museos.
ANA MARÍA Sí, salgo mucho los fines de semana.

(*unos minutos después*)
EDUARDO Hay un partido de fútbol en el parque. ¿Quieren ir conmigo?
PABLO Y conmigo. Si no consigo más jugadores, nuestro equipo va a perder.

---

recursos

VM pp. 7–8

vhlcentral.com

76   setenta y seis

El fin de semana

 MIGUEL PABLO ANA MARÍA MARU MARISSA EDUARDO FELIPE JUAN CARLOS JIMENA DON GUILLERMO

FELIPE ¿Recuerdas el restaurante del mole?
EDUARDO ¿Qué restaurante?
JIMENA El mole de mi tía Ana María es mi favorito.
MARU Chicos, ya es hora, vamos.

(*más tarde, en el parque*)
PABLO ¡No puede ser! ¡Cinco a uno!
FELIPE Vamos a jugar. Si perdemos, compramos el almuerzo. Y si ganamos...
EDUARDO ¡Empezamos!

(*mientras tanto, en el cenote*)
MARISSA ¿Hay muchos cenotes en México?
MIGUEL Sólo en la península de Yucatán.
MARISSA ¡Vamos a nadar!

(*Los chicos visitan a don Guillermo, un vendedor de paletas heladas.*)
JUAN CARLOS Don Guillermo, ¿dónde podemos conseguir un buen mole?
FELIPE Eduardo y Pablo van a pagar el almuerzo. Y yo voy a pedir un montón de comida.

FELIPE Sí, éste es el restaurante. Recuerdo la comida.
EDUARDO Oye, Pablo... No tengo...
PABLO No te preocupes, hermanito.
FELIPE ¿Qué buscas? (*muestra la cartera de Pablo*) ¿Esto?

Practice more at **vhlcentral.com**.

Actividades

1 Identificar Identify the person who would make each statement.

____ a. Me gusta nadar, pero no sé (*I don't know*) qué es un cenote.
____ b. Me gustan las películas.
____ c. Voy a pedir mucha comida.
____ d. Nuestro equipo de fútbol juega en el parque.
____ e. Me gusta salir los fines de semana.

2 Preguntas Answer the questions using the information from **Escenas**.

1. ¿Qué van a hacer Miguel y Maru?
2. ¿Adónde va Ana María en sus ratos libres?
3. ¿Quiénes van al parque?
4. ¿Quiénes ganan el partido?
5. ¿Qué va a comer Felipe en el restaurante?

3 Conversación In pairs, talk about pastimes and plan an activity together. Use these expressions and the **Expresiones útiles** on page 76.

- ¿Eres aficionado/a a...?
- ¿Te gusta...?
- ¿Qué prefieres hacer en tus ratos libres?
- ¿Por qué no...?
- ¿Quieres... conmigo?
- Nos vemos a las siete.

setenta y siete 77

4 EXPLORACIÓN

BAJO LA LUPA

Additional Reading
Video: *Flash cultura*

Real Madrid y Barça: rivalidad total

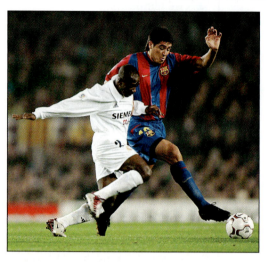

Soccer in Spain is a force to be reckoned with, and no two teams draw more attention than **Real Madrid** and the **Fútbol Club Barcelona.** Whether the venue is Madrid's **Santiago Bernabéu** or Barcelona's **Camp Nou,** the two cities shut down for the showdown, paralyzed by **fútbol** fever. A ticket to the actual game is always the hottest ticket in town.

The rivalry between **Real Madrid** and **Barça*** is about more than soccer. As the two biggest, most powerful cities in Spain, Barcelona and Madrid are constantly compared to one another and have a natural rivalry. There is also a political component to the dynamic. Barcelona, with its distinct language and culture, has long struggled for increased autonomy from Madrid's centralized government. Under Francisco Franco's rule (1939–1975), when repression of the Catalan identity was at its height, a game between **Real Madrid** and **FC Barcelona** was wrapped up with all the symbolism of the regime versus the resistance, even though both teams suffered casualties in Spain's civil war and the subsequent Franco dictatorship.

Although the dictatorship ended more than three decades ago, the momentum of all those decades of competition still transforms both cities into a frenzied, tense panic leading up to the game. Once the final score is announced, one of those cities is transformed again, this time into the best party in the country.

* Note that **ç** is pronounced like *s.*

Rivalidades del fútbol

Argentina: Boca Juniors vs. River Plate
México: Águilas del América vs. Chivas del Guadalajara
Chile: Colo Colo vs. Universidad de Chile
Guatemala: Comunicaciones vs. Municipal
Uruguay: Peñarol vs. Nacional
Colombia: Millonarios vs. Independiente Santa Fe

Practice more at **vhlcentral.com.**

El fin de semana

ACTIVIDADES

1 ¿Cierto o falso? Indicate whether each statement is **cierto** or **falso**. Correct the false statements.

1. Soccer is not a popular sport in Spain.
2. Madrid and Barcelona are the most important cities in Spain.
3. Santiago Bernabéu is a stadium in Barcelona.
4. The rivalry between Real Madrid and FC Barcelona is restricted to athletic competition.
5. Barcelona has resisted Madrid's centralized government.
6. Only the FC Barcelona team was affected by the civil war.
7. During Franco's regime, the Catalan culture thrived.
8. There are many famous rivalries between soccer teams in the Spanish-speaking world.
9. River Plate is a popular team from Argentina.
10. Comunicaciones and Peñarol are famous rivalries in Guatemala.

2 Comparación Compare soccer in Spain with a popular sport where you live. What are some famous rivalries? What is the source of their rivalries? How would you describe the different sets of fans?

CONEXIÓN INTERNET

¿Qué otras actividades y deportes son populares en los países hispanos? For more information about **Exploración**, go to **vhlcentral.com**.

¡Fútbol en España!

1 Preparación What is the most popular sport at your school? What teams are your rivals? How do students celebrate a win?

2 El video Watch this **Flash cultura** episode.

Vocabulario			
afición	fans	pierde	loses
celebran	they celebrate	rivalidad	rivalry

Hay mucha afición al fútbol en España.

—¿Y cuál es vuestro jugador favorito?

3 Escoger Select the correct answer.

1. Un partido entre el Barça y el Real Madrid es _____ (un deporte/un evento) importante en toda España.
2. Ronaldinho fue (*was*) el futbolista estrella (*soccer star*) del _____ (Barça/Real Madrid).
3. Los aficionados _____ (miran/celebran) las victorias de sus equipos en las calles (*streets*).
4. La rivalidad entre el Real Madrid y el Barça está relacionada con la _____ (religión/política).

setenta y nueve 79

4 GRAMÁTICA

4.1 The present tense of ir  Tutorial

ir (to go)

Singular forms		Plural forms	
yo	voy	nosotros/as	vamos
tú	vas	vosotros/as	vais
Ud./él/ella	va	Uds./ellos/ellas	van

¡Voy a ir con ellos!

▶ The verb **ir** (*to go*) is irregular in the present tense.

▶ **Ir** is often used with the preposition **a** (*to*). When **a** is followed by the article **el**, they form the contraction **al**. There is no contraction when **a** is followed by **la**, **las**, and **los**.

a + el = al

Voy al cine con María.
I'm going to the movies with María.

Ellos **van a** las montañas.
They are going to the mountains.

Vamos a jugar fútbol en el parque.

▶ The construction **ir a** + [*infinitive*] expresses actions that are going to happen in the future. It is equivalent to the English *to be going to* + [*infinitive*].

▶ **Vamos a** + [*infinitive*] can also express the idea of *let's (do something)*.

Vamos a pasear.
Let's take a stroll.

¡Vamos a ver!
Let's see!

¡ojo!
Use **adónde** instead of **dónde** when asking a question with **ir**.

¿Adónde vas?
Where are you going?

¿Dónde estás?
Where are you?

ESPAÑOL EN VIVO

Esta familia siempre va a estar unida,
porque el Banco Nacional siempre va a estar con ellos.

Luis va a trabajar lejos de su familia, pero ellos van a estar tranquilos. Luis va a depositar su sueldo en el Banco Nacional y, así, él va a ayudar a su familia.

Banco Nacional
Estamos siempre con usted

80 ochenta

Práctica y conversación

1 Adivina Roberto has gone to see Doña Imelda, a fortune teller. Using **ir a** + [*infinitive*], say what Doña Imelda predicts.

MODELO
Tu hermano Gabriel ___va a___ ir a Europa.

1. Tú _____ correr en el Maratón de Boston.
2. Tú y tu familia _____ escalar el monte Everest.
3. Tu hermano Pablo _____ jugar en la Liga Nacional de Fútbol.
4. Tu hermana Tina _____ recibir una carta misteriosa.
5. Tu hermana Rosario _____ patinar en los Juegos Olímpicos.
6. Tus padres _____ tomar el sol en Acapulco.
7. Tú _____ ver las pinturas (*paintings*) de tu amiga en el Museo Nacional de Arte.
8. ¡Y yo _____ ser muy, muy rica!

2 ¿Adónde vas? You are visiting Madrid with some friends. Work with a partner and ask each other which sites you will visit today. Use the clues provided in the map.

MODELO
Estudiante 1: ¿Adónde vamos nosotros?
Estudiante 2: Nosotros vamos a La Plaza de Santo Domingo.

3 Situaciones With a partner, say where you and your friends go in these situations.

1. Cuando (*When*) deseo descansar…
2. Cuando mi novio/a tiene que estudiar…
3. Si (*If*) mis amigos necesitan practicar el español…
4. Si deseo hablar con unos amigos…
5. Cuando tengo dinero (*money*)…
6. Cuando mis amigos y yo tenemos hambre…
7. Si tengo tiempo libre…
8. Cuando mis amigos desean esquiar…
9. Si estoy de vacaciones (*on vacation*)…
10. Si quiero leer…

4 Encuesta Walk around the class and ask your classmates if they are going to do these activities today. Try to find at least two people for each item and write their names on the worksheet. Report your findings to the class.

Actividades	Nombres
1. Comer en un restaurante	_____
2. Mirar la televisión	_____
3. Leer una revista	_____
4. Escribir un mensaje electrónico	_____
5. Correr	_____
6. Ver una película	_____
7. Pasear en bicicleta	_____
8. Estudiar en la biblioteca	_____

5 Entrevista Interview two classmates to find out what they are going to do this weekend.

MODELO
Estudiante 1: ¿Adónde vas este (*this*) fin de semana?
Estudiante 2: Voy a Guadalajara con mis amigos.
Estudiante 3: ¿Y qué van a hacer (*to do*) ustedes en Guadalajara?
Estudiante 2: Vamos a visitar unos monumentos y unos museos de arte. ¿Y tú?

Practice more at vhlcentral.com.

Lección 4

4.2 Stem-changing verbs: e → ie, o → ue  Tutorial

Los chicos empiezan a hablar de su visita al cenote.

▶ In stem-changing verbs, the stressed vowel of the stem changes when the verb is conjugated.

INFINITIVE	VERB STEM	STEM CHANGE	CONJUGATED FORM
empezar	empez–	empiez–	empiezo
volver	volv–	vuelv–	vuelvo

▶ In many verbs, such as **empezar** (*to begin*), the stem vowel changes from **e** to **ie**. Note that the **nosotros/as** and **vosotros/as** forms don't have a stem change.

empezar (e:ie)

Singular forms		Plural forms	
yo	empiezo	nosotros/as	empezamos
tú	empiezas	vosotros/as	empezáis
Ud./él/ella	empieza	Uds./ellos/ellas	empiezan

Ellos vuelven a comer en el restaurante.

▶ In many other verbs, such as **volver** (*to return*), the stem vowel changes from **o** to **ue**. The **nosotros/as** and **vosotros/as** forms have no stem change.

volver (e:ue)

Singular forms		Plural forms	
yo	vuelvo	nosotros/as	volvemos
tú	vuelves	vosotros/as	volvéis
Ud./él/ella	vuelve	Uds./ellos/ellas	vuelven

¡ojo!
To help you identify stem-changing verbs, they will appear as follows throughout the text:

empezar (e:ie)
volver (o:ue)

Common stem-changing verbs

e:ie				o:ue			
cerrar	to close	pensar	to think	dormir	to sleep	poder	to be able to; can
comenzar	to begin	perder	to lose; to miss	encontrar	to find	recordar	to remember
empezar	to begin	preferir	to prefer	mostrar	to show	volver	to return
entender	to understand	querer	to want; to love				

Los chicos juegan al fútbol.

▶ **Jugar** (*to play* a sport or a game) is the only Spanish verb that has a **u:ue** stem change. **Jugar** is followed by **a** + [*definite article*] when the name of a sport or game is mentioned.

▶ **Comenzar** and **empezar** require the preposition **a** when they are followed by an infinitive.

Comienzan a jugar a las siete.
They begin playing at seven.

Ana **empieza a** trabajar hoy.
Ana starts to working today.

82   ochenta y dos

El fin de semana

▶ **Pensar** + [*infinitive*] means *to plan* or *to intend to do something*. **Pensar en** means *to think about someone or something*.

¿**Piensan** ir al gimnasio?
Are you planning to go to the gym?

¿**En** qué **piensas**?
What are you thinking about?

Práctica y conversación

Practice more at vhlcentral.com.

1 El día del partido Complete this game-day conversation between two friends with the appropriate verb forms.

PABLO Óscar, voy al centro ahora. (1) ¿_____ [querer] venir?
ÓSCAR No, yo (2) _____ [preferir] descansar un poco y ver la televisión.
PABLO ¡Qué perezoso (*how lazy*) eres!
ÓSCAR No, hombre. Es que estoy muy cansado. Oye, ¿a qué hora (3) _____ [pensar] regresar? El partido de fútbol (4) _____ [empezar] a las dos.
PABLO A la una. (5) _____ [querer] ver el partido también.
ÓSCAR (6) ¿_____ [pensar] que (*that*) nuestro equipo (7) _____ [poder] ganar?
PABLO No, (8) _____ [pensar] que vamos a (9) _____ [perder]. Los jugadores del Guadalajara (10) _____ [jugar] muy bien.

2 Preferencias With a partner, take turns asking and answering questions about what these people want to do.

MODELO
Guillermo: estudiar / pasear en bicicleta
Estudiante 1: ¿Quiere estudiar Guillermo?
Estudiante 2: No, prefiere pasear en bicicleta.

1. **tú:** trabajar / dormir
   _____

2. **ustedes:** mirar la televisión / ir al cine
   _____

3. **tus amigos:** ir de excursión / descansar
   _____

4. **tú:** comer en la cafetería / ir a un restaurante
   _____

5. **Elisa:** ver una película / leer una revista
   _____

6. **María y su prima:** tomar el sol / esquiar
   _____

3 En la televisión In pairs, read this weekend's TV listing of sporting events. Discuss what sports you want to watch on TV and try to agree on one game you will watch together each day.

sábado
13:30 NATACIÓN
  1 Copa Mundial (*World Cup*) de Natación
15:00 TENIS
  8 Abierto (*Open*) Mexicano de Tenis: Cecilia Montero (México) vs. Sandra de la Paz (España) Semifinales
16:00 FÚTBOL NACIONAL
  3 Chivas vs. Monterrey
16:30 FÚTBOL AMERICANO PROFESIONAL
  21 Vaqueros de Dallas vs. Leones de Detroit
20:00 BALONCESTO PROFESIONAL
  16 Knicks de Nueva York vs. Toros de Chicago

domingo
13:00 GOLF
  40 Audi Senior Classic: Lorena Ochoa, Natalie Gulbis, Paula Creamer
14:30 VÓLEIBOL
  1 Campeonato (*Championship*) Nacional de México
16:00 BALONCESTO
  3 Campeonato de Cimeba: Correcaminos de Tampico vs. Santos de San Luis Final
17:00 ESQUÍ ALPINO
  19 Eslálom
18:30 FÚTBOL INTERNACIONAL
  30 Copa América: México vs. Argentina. Ronda final
20:00 PATINAJE ARTÍSTICO
  16 Exhibición mundial

4 Turistas You are taking two friends on a trip to your hometown. Talk about the things you want to do, then fill in the day-planner with the things you plan to do each day.

ochenta y tres 83

4 GRAMÁTICA

4.3 Stem-changing verbs: e → i

▶ In some verbs, such as **pedir** (*to ask for; to request*), the stressed vowel in the stem changes from **e** to **i**, as shown in the diagram.

INFINITIVE	VERB STEM	STEM CHANGE	CONJUGATED FORM
pedir	ped–	pid–	pido

▶ As with other stem-changing verbs you have learned, there is no stem change in the **nosotros/as** or **vosotros/as** forms in the present tense.

pedir (e:i)

Singular forms		Plural forms	
yo	pido	nosotros/as	pedimos
tú	pides	vosotros/as	pedís
Ud./él/ella	pide	Uds./ellos/ellas	piden

▶ The following are the most common **e:i** stem-changing verbs:

conseguir	repetir	seguir
to get; to obtain	to repeat	to follow; to continue; to keep (doing something)

Consiguen ver buenas películas.   **Repito** la pregunta.   **Sigue** esperando.
They get to see good movies.   *I repeat the question.*   *He keeps waiting.*

> **¡ojo!**
> To help you identify verbs with the **e:i** stem change, they will appear as follows throughout the text:
> **pedir (e:i)**

▶ The **yo** forms of **seguir** and **conseguir** have a spelling change as well as a stem change.

Sigo su plan.   **Consigo** novelas en la librería.
I'm following their plan.   *I get novels at the bookstore.*

conseguir (e:i)

Singular forms		Plural forms	
yo	consigo	nosotros/as	conseguimos
tú	consigues	vosotros/as	conseguís
Ud./él/ella	consigue	Uds./ellos/ellas	consiguen

seguir (e:i)

Singular forms		Plural forms	
yo	sigo	nosotros/as	seguimos
tú	sigues	vosotros/as	seguís
Ud./él/ella	sigue	Uds./ellos/ellas	siguen

repetir (e:i)

Singular forms		Plural forms	
yo	repito	nosotros/as	repetimos
tú	repites	vosotros/as	repetís
Ud./él/ella	repite	Uds./ellos/ellas	repiten

El fin de semana

Práctica y conversación

1 En la clase You're teaching Spanish at an elementary school. Fill in the blanks to describe a typical day in your class.

1. Yo entro en la clase y _____ [cerrar] la puerta.
2. La clase _____ [comenzar] a las nueve en punto.
3. Yo _____ [pedir] la tarea del día anterior (*previous*).
4. Los estudiantes _____ [repetir] las palabras del vocabulario.
5. Pablo no _____ [seguir] mis instrucciones.
6. Pedro _____ [perder] su lápiz.
7. Algunos estudiantes _____ [dormir] en sus escritorios.
8. La clase termina y yo _____ [volver] a casa muy cansado/a.

2 Combinar Combine words from the columns to create sentences about yourself and people you know.

Yo	pedir muchos favores
Mi compañero/a de cuarto	nunca (*never*) repetir los cursos
Mi mejor (*best*) amigo/a	nunca pedir perdón
Mi familia	nunca seguir las instrucciones del profesor
Mis amigos/as	siempre seguir las instrucciones del profesor
Mis amigos/as y yo	conseguir libros en Internet
Mis padres	conseguir viajar a lugares exóticos
Mi hermano/a	repetir el vocabulario
Mi profesor(a) de español	siempre perder sus libros

3 Las películas Use these questions to interview a classmate.

1. ¿Dónde consigues información sobre (*about*) cine y televisión?
2. ¿Prefieres las películas románticas, las películas de acción o las películas de terror? ¿Por qué?
3. ¿Dónde consigues las entradas (*tickets*) para ver una película?
4. Para decidir qué películas vas a ver, ¿sigues las recomendaciones de los críticos de cine?
5. ¿Qué cines en tu comunidad muestran las mejores (*best*) películas?
6. ¿Vas a ver una película esta semana? ¿A qué hora empieza la película?

4 El fin de semana Ask a classmate if he or she does these things on a weekend. Report the results to the class.

Actividad	Sí	No
1. Dormir hasta la una de la tarde	___	___
2. Pedir una pizza por teléfono	___	___
3. Jugar al tenis	___	___
4. Ir a un partido de fútbol/baloncesto/béisbol	___	___
5. Pasear	___	___
6. Ir a un museo	___	___
7. Escribir mensajes electrónicos	___	___
8. Patinar	___	___
9. Ir al gimnasio	___	___

Practice more at vhlcentral.com.

4 GRAMÁTICA

4.4 Verbs with irregular yo forms Tutorial

▶ In Spanish, several verbs have irregular **yo** forms in the present tense. The verbs **hacer** (*to do, to make*), **poner** (*to put, to place*), **salir** (*to leave*), **suponer** (*to suppose*), and **traer** (*to bring*) have **yo** forms that end in **–go**. The other forms are regular.

Salgo mucho los fines de semana.

Verbs with irregular yo forms

	hacer	poner	salir	suponer	traer
yo	hago	pongo	salgo	supongo	traigo
tú	haces	pones	sales	supones	traes
Ud./él/ella	hace	pone	sale	supone	trae
nosotros/as	hacemos	ponemos	salimos	suponemos	traemos
vosotros/as	hacéis	ponéis	salís	suponéis	traéis
Uds./ellos/ellas	hacen	ponen	salen	suponen	traen

▶ **Salir de** is used to indicate that someone is leaving a particular place.

Hoy **salgo del** hospital.
Today I leave the hospital.

Sale de la clase a las cuatro.
He leaves class at four.

▶ **Salir para** is used to indicate someone's destination.

Mañana **salgo para** México.
Tomorrow I leave for Mexico.

Hoy **salen para** España.
Today they leave for Spain.

▶ **Salir con** means *to leave with someone or something*, or *to date someone*.

Alberto **sale con** su amigo.
Alberto is leaving with his friend.

Margarita **sale con** Guillermo.
Margarita is going out with Guillermo.

▶ The verb **ver** (*to see*) has an irregular **yo** form. The other forms of **ver** are regular.

▶ The verb **oír** (*to hear*) has an irregular **yo** form and a spelling change in the **tú**, **usted**, **él**, **ella**, **ustedes**, **ellos**, and **ellas** forms. The **nosotros/as** and **vosotros/as** forms have an accent mark.

ver (to see)

Singular forms		Plural forms	
yo	veo	nosotros/as	vemos
tú	ves	vosotros/as	veis
Ud./él/ella	ve	Uds./ellos/ellas	ven

oír (to hear)

Singular forms		Plural forms	
yo	oigo	nosotros/as	oímos
tú	oyes	vosotros/as	oís
Ud./él/ella	oye	Uds./ellos/ellas	oyen

Oigo a unas personas en la otra sala.
I hear some people in the other room.

¿**Oyes** la música?
Do you hear the music?

El fin de semana

Práctica y conversación

1 Completar Complete this conversation with the appropriate verb forms.

ERNESTO David, ¿qué (1) _____ [hacer] hoy?
DAVID Ahora estudio biología, pero esta noche (2) _____ [salir] con Luisa. Vamos al cine. Queremos (3) _____ [ver] la nueva (*new*) película de Almodóvar.
ERNESTO ¿Y Diana? ¿Qué (4) _____ [hacer] ella?
DAVID (5) _____ [salir] a comer con sus padres.
ERNESTO ¿Qué (6) _____ [hacer] Andrés y Javier?
DAVID Tienen que (7) _____ [hacer] las maletas. (8) _____ [salir] para Monterrey mañana.
ERNESTO Pues, ¿qué (9) _____ [hacer] yo?
DAVID (10) _____ [suponer] que puedes estudiar.
ERNESTO No quiero estudiar. Mejor (11) _____ [hacer] la tarea.

2 Oraciones Form sentences using the cues given.

MODELO
Tú / ? / los libros / debajo de / escritorio
Tú *pones los libros debajo del escritorio.*

1. Nosotros / ? / mucha / tarea
2. ¿Tú / ? / la radio?
3. Yo / no / ? / el problema
4. Marta / ? / una grabadora / clase
5. Los señores Marín / ? / su casa / siete
6. Yo / ? / que (*that*) / tú / ir / cine / ¿no?

3 Describir In pairs, form complete sentences with the cues provided.

1. Fernán/poner

2. Yo/traer

3. Nosotras/ver

4. El estudiante/hacer

4 Preguntas Get together with a classmate and ask each other these questions.

1. ¿A qué hora sales de tu residencia o de tu casa por la mañana? ¿A qué hora llegas a la universidad?
2. ¿Traes un diccionario a la clase de español? ¿Por qué? ¿Qué más traes?
3. ¿A qué hora salimos de la clase de español?
4. Cuando vuelves a casa, ¿dónde pones tus libros? ¿Siempre (*always*) pones tus cosas en su lugar?
5. ¿Oyes la radio o prefieres ver la televisión?
6. ¿Oyes la radio cuando estudias?
7. ¿Qué haces los fines de semana? ¿Sales con amigos? ¿Adónde van?

5 Charadas In groups, play a game of charades. Each person should think of a phrase using **hacer**, **poner**, **salir**, **oír**, **traer**, or **ver** and act out the phrase. The first person to guess correctly acts out the next charade.

6 Típico fin de semana Interview a classmate about what he or she does on a typical weekend.

- What time does he/she leave the house on the weekend?
- What does he/she do in the afternoon?
- What TV shows does he/she watch?
- Does he/she go out with friends?...

Practice more at vhlcentral.com.

ochenta y siete 87

Lección 4

Ampliación

Audio: Activity
Video: TV Clip

1 Escuchar

A First you will hear José talking, then Anabela. Which person does each statement best describe?

TIP **Listen for gist.** When you listen for the gist, try to capture the general meaning of what you hear without focusing on individual words. You will be surprised at how much you can understand!

Descripción	José	Anabela
1. Es muy aficionado/a a los deportes.	☐	☐
2. Pasa el tiempo con sus amigos.	☐	☐
3. Va mucho al cine.	☐	☐
4. Es una persona muy activa.	☐	☐
5. Le gusta descansar por la tarde.	☐	☐
6. Es una persona estudiosa.	☐	☐
7. Su deporte favorito es el ciclismo.	☐	☐
8. A veces va a ver partidos de béisbol.	☐	☐

B ¿Tienes más en común (*more in common*) con José o con Anabela? Explica tu respuesta.

2 Conversar

You and a friend haven't seen each other in a long time and plan to get together in a new city. Role-play a phone conversation to discuss your plans. Include this information:

- When you are planning to arrive and return
- What places you want to visit
- A few activities you can do together

recursos

WB
pp. 33–40

LM
pp. 21–24

vhlcentral.com

88 *ochenta y ocho*

El fin de semana

3 Escribir Create a short article for your school's student website. Describe at least six leisure activities that students enjoy on campus.

TIP **Use bilingual dictionaries carefully.** Use a Spanish-English dictionary to look up words you don't know. Consider whether the first option given is really what you are trying to say.

Organízalo	List the activities you could include in the article. Use an idea map to organize them.
Escríbelo	Using your idea map, write the first draft of your article.
Corrígelo	Exchange drafts with a classmate and comment on the organization, style, and grammatical accuracy of each other's work. Then revise your first draft, keeping your classmate's comments in mind.
Compártelo	Exchange drafts with a different partner. Note any words that are new to you, so you can look them up later. Then turn your final draft in to your instructor.

4 Un paso más Prepare a radio broadcast of weekend sports events for a major city in the Spanish-speaking world. Include this information in your broadcast:

- An introduction of yourself and your program
- A list of local sports events
- The location and time of each event
- A brief sign-off

CONEXIÓN INTERNET

Investiga estos temas en **vhlcentral.com**.

- Los deportes más (*most*) populares del mundo hispano
- Los pasatiempos más populares del mundo hispano

ochenta y nueve 89

4 LECTURA

Antes de leer

**Audio: Reading
Additional Reading**

This article appeared in one of Mexico City's newspapers. Scan the article's headlines and visual elements. Based on what you see, what do you think it is about?

Can you guess the meaning of these cognates from the article?

baladas	_____
concierto	_____
contemporáneo/a	_____
creativo/a	_____
festival	_____
fotógrafo/a	_____
origen	_____
pasión	_____
recomendar	_____
romántico/a	_____

GUÍA para el fi

CINE

Festival de cine latinoamericano

Para los aficionados al cine, este fin d semana comienza el Festival de Cir Latinoamericano en el cine Plaza. S muestran las últimas° producciones de Juan Pablo Reátegui, Lore Suárez, Álvaro del Carpio y Die Bianchi. Recomendamos especialmen *Un día sin° fútbol* del director Ju Pablo Reátegui. *Un día sin fút* cuenta la historia° de un grupo aficionados al fútbol y su enor pasión por este deporte.

Fechas: 10–14 de marzo
Hora: 8:00 p.m.
Lugar: Cine Plaza
Dirección: Calle Principal #152

CONCIERTO
Canta Maribel Puértolas

Si quiere escuchar buena música, la cantante° Maribel Puértolas va a ofrecer° un concierto en el café Los Amigos. De origen puertorriqueño, esta joven cantante ha conquistado° a los románticos con *Cuando tú no estás,* su último CD de baladas. "Va a ser un concierto para recordar", dice Puértolas.

Fecha: 11 de marzo
Hora: 7:00 p.m.
Lugar: Café La Gloria
Dirección: Avenida Bolívar #345

recursos

vhlcentral.com

90 noventa

El fin de semana

de semana

EXPOSICIÓN
Lucía Velasco: Cuarenta años de fotografía

Este fin de semana se va a inaugurar la exposición° de la fotógrafa uruguaya Lucía Velasco en el Museo de Arte Contemporáneo. Las cien fotografías que forman parte de la exposición muestran el desarrollo° creativo de Velasco durante sus 40 años de carrera.

Fechas: 10 de marzo – 8 de abril
Lugar: Museo de Arte Contemporáneo
Dirección: Avenida Juárez #248

últimas *latest*   **sin** *without*   **cuenta la historia** *tells the story*
cantante *singer*   **ofrecer** *offer*   **ha conquistado** *has won over*
inaugurar la exposición *to open the exhibit*   **desarrollo** *development*

Después de leer

¿Comprendiste?
Based on the reading, indicate whether each statement is **cierto** or **falso**?

Cierto	Falso	
_____	_____	1. La guía presenta noticias sobre eventos deportivos.
_____	_____	2. *Un día sin fútbol* cuenta la historia de un equipo de fútbol.
_____	_____	3. Maribel Puértolas es una cantante de baladas.
_____	_____	4. Las fotografías de Juan Pablo Reátegui se exhiben en el cine Plaza.
_____	_____	5. Lucía Velasco es una fotógrafa uruguaya.
_____	_____	6. En el café La Gloria hay una exposición de arte.

Preguntas
Answer these questions with a complete sentence.

1. ¿De dónde es Maribel Puértolas?
   _____

2. ¿Qué clase de canciones (*songs*) canta ella?
   _____

3. ¿Cuántas fotografías de Lucía Velasco hay en la exposición?
   _____

4. ¿Dónde está la exposición de Lucía Velasco?
   _____

5. ¿Qué película recomienda la guía?
   _____

6. ¿Dónde es el festival de cine?
   _____

Coméntalo
In small groups, discuss which of the activities in the article you would each prefer to do on a weekend and why.

noventa y uno   **91**

4 VOCABULARIO

Audio: Vocabulary Flashcards

Las actividades

bucear	to scuba dive
escalar montañas (*f. pl.*)	to climb mountains
escribir una carta/ un mensaje electrónico/ una (tarjeta) postal	to write a letter/ an e-mail message/ a postcard
esquiar	to ski
ganar	to win
ir de excursión (a las montañas)	to go for a hike (in the mountains)
leer el correo electrónico/ el periódico/ una revista	to read e-mail/ a newspaper/ a magazine
nadar	to swim
pasar el tiempo	to spend time
pasear en bicicleta	to ride a bicycle
pasear por la ciudad/el pueblo	to walk around the city/town
patinar (en línea)	to skate (in-line)
practicar deportes (*m. pl.*)	to play sports
ser aficionado/a (a)	to be a fan (of)
tomar el sol	to sunbathe
ver películas (*f. pl.*)	to watch movies
visitar un monumento	to visit a monument
la diversión	entertainment; fun activity
el/la excursionista	hiker
el fin de semana	weekend
el pasatiempo	pastime; hobby
los ratos libres	spare time
el tiempo libre	free time

Verbos

cerrar (e:ie)	to close
comenzar (e:ie)	to begin
conseguir (e:i)	to get; to obtain
dormir (o:ue)	to sleep
empezar (e:ie)	to begin
encontrar (o:ue)	to find
entender (e:ie)	to understand
hacer	to do; to make
ir	to go
ir a (+ inf.)	to be going to do something
jugar (u:ue)	to play
mostrar (o:ue)	to show
oír	to hear
pedir (e:i)	to ask for; to request
pensar (e:ie)	to think
pensar (+ inf.)	to intend; to plan
pensar en	to think about
perder (e:ie)	to lose; to miss
poder (o:ue)	to be able to; can
poner	to put; to place
preferir (e:ie)	to prefer
querer (e:ie)	to want; to love
recordar (o:ue)	to remember
repetir (e:i)	to repeat
salir	to leave
seguir (e:i)	to follow; to continue; to keep (doing something)
suponer	to suppose
traer	to bring
ver	to see
volver (o:ue)	to return

Los deportes

el baloncesto	basketball
el béisbol	baseball
el ciclismo	cycling
el equipo	team
el esquí (acuático)	(water) skiing
el fútbol	soccer
el fútbol americano	football
el golf	golf
el hockey	hockey
el/la jugador(a)	player
la natación	swimming
el partido	game
la pelota	ball
el tenis	tennis
el vóleibol	volleyball

Los lugares

el café	café
la casa	house
el centro	downtown
el cine	movie theater
el gimnasio	gym; gymnasium
la iglesia	church
el lugar	place
el museo	museum
el parque	park
la piscina	swimming pool
el restaurante	restaurant

Adjetivos

deportivo/a	sports-related
favorito/a	favorite

92 *noventa y dos*

¡VIVAN LOS PAÍSES HISPANOS!

En Acapulco, un hombre salta desde un acantilado (*cliff*) frente al océano Pacífico. El lugar se llama La Quebrada y miles de turistas lo visitan cada (*each*) día. ¿Te gustaría (*Would you like*) visitarlo algún (*some*) día?

México

México

Área: 1.972.550 km^2 (761.603 millas^2)
Población: 110.645.000
Capital: México, D.F. 19.460.000
Ciudades importantes: Guadalajara, Monterrey, Ciudad Juárez, Puebla, Cancún, Acapulco
Moneda: peso mexicano

SOURCE: Population Division, UN Secretariat

¡Vivan los países hispanos!

Interactive map
Video: *Países hispanos*

Celebraciones

La independencia de México

El 16 de septiembre los mexicanos celebran la independencia de su país. En todas las ciudades se ponen decoraciones con los colores de la bandera (*flag*) mexicana y se hacen fiestas con mariachis, comida típica y bailes (*dances*) tradicionales. A estas celebraciones se les llaman las fiestas patrias.

Historia

Los mayas

La civilización maya construyó (*built*) impresionantes ciudades con templos religiosos en forma de pirámide, que hoy en día visitan millones de turistas. Los descendientes de esta civilización siguen tradiciones de su pasado y muchos aún (*still*) viven en esa misma área: el sur (*south*) de México y partes de Centroamérica.

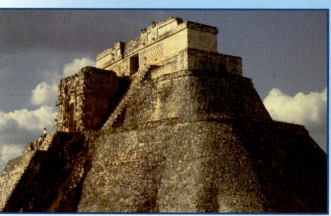
Pirámide de Uxmal

México

Arte

Diego Rivera y Frida Kahlo

Frida Kahlo y Diego Rivera son los pintores mexicanos más famosos. Se casaron (*They got married*) en 1929. Los dos se interesaron (*became interested*) en las condiciones sociales de la gente indígena y de los campesinos (*farmers*) de su país. Puedes ver algunas de sus obras (*works*) en el Museo de Arte Moderno de la Ciudad de México.

Detalle de un mural de Diego Rivera

Economía

La plata

México es el mayor (*largest*) productor de plata (*silver*) del mundo (*world*). Estados como Zacatecas y Durango tienen ciudades fundadas cerca de los más grandes yacimientos (*deposits*) de plata del país. Estas ciudades fueron (*were*) en la época colonial unas de las más ricas e importantes. Hoy en día, aún conservan mucho de su encanto (*charm*) y esplendor.

noventa y cinco 95

¡Vivan los países hispanos!

¿Qué aprendiste?

1 ¿Cierto o falso? Indicate if these statements are **cierto** or **falso**.

Cierto	Falso	
_____	_____	1. La Quebrada está en México, D.F.
_____	_____	2. Frida Kahlo es una pintora.
_____	_____	3. El 16 de septiembre en México organizan una celebración religiosa.
_____	_____	4. México es el mayor productor de pinturas (*paintings*) del mundo (*world*).
_____	_____	5. Los mexicanos celebran la independencia con las fiestas patrias.
_____	_____	6. En México no hay ciudades fundadas cerca de los yacimientos (*deposits*) de plata.
_____	_____	7. Diego Rivera fue (*was*) el esposo de Frida Kahlo.
_____	_____	8. Puebla es la capital de México.
_____	_____	9. Pocos turistas visitan los templos mayas.
_____	_____	10. La moneda mexicana es el dólar mexicano.

2 Preguntas Answer the questions in complete sentences.

1. ¿Qué elementos en común hay en las celebraciones de la independencia de tu país y las celebraciones en México? ¿Qué diferencias hay?
2. ¿Qué piensas del estilo artístico de Diego Rivera? ¿Prefieres el arte realista o el abstracto?
3. ¿Sigues alguna (*any*) tradición de tus antepasados? ¿Cuál(es)?
4. ¿Hay yacimientos de minerales cerca de donde vives?
5. ¿Cuál es la actividad económica más (*more*) importante de tu ciudad o estado: la agricultura, la minería, la industria, el turismo, los servicios o el comercio (*trade*)?

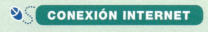

Investiga estos temas en el sitio vhlcentral.com.
- Lugares para visitar en México
- Pintores famosos de México

5 Las vacaciones

Communicative Goals

You will learn how to:
- talk about vacations
- describe a hotel
- talk about seasons and the weather
- talk about how you feel

PREPARACIÓN
pages 98–101
- Words related to vacationing, travel, weather, seasons, months, and ordinal numbers
- Pronouncing **b** and **v**

ESCENAS
pages 102–103
- Felipe plays a practical joke on Miguel, then the friends take a trip to the coast. They check in to their hotel and go to the beach, where Miguel gets his revenge.

EXPLORACIÓN
pages 104–105
- Bajo la lupa: *El Camino Inca*
- Flash cultura: *¡Vacaciones en Perú!*

GRAMÁTICA
pages 106–115
- **Estar** with conditions and emotions
- The present progressive
- Comparing **ser** and **estar**
- Direct object nouns and pronouns

LECTURA
pages 116–117
- Brochure: *Turismo ecológico en Puerto Rico*

Para empezar
- ¿Es vieja o joven la persona de la foto?
- ¿Es rubio o moreno?
- ¿Está en su casa o de vacaciones?
- ¿Dónde está él, en la playa o en la montaña?
- ¿Qué hace: nada, bucea o toma el sol?

5 PREPARACIÓN

Las vacaciones Talking Picture Tutorial Games

la estación del tren
train station

LAS VACACIONES Y LOS VIAJES

el aeropuerto airport
la agencia de viajes travel agency
el/la agente de viajes travel agent
la estación de autobuses bus station
del metro subway station
el/la inspector(a) de aduanas customs officer
el pasaje (de ida y vuelta) (round-trip) ticket
la tienda de campaña tent
el/la viajero/a traveler

el pasaporte
passport

¿QUÉ TIEMPO HACE?

¿Qué tiempo hace? How's the weather?; What's the weather like?
Está despejado. It's clear.
    (muy) nublado. It's (very) cloudy.
Hace buen/mal tiempo. The weather is nice/bad.
    (mucho) calor. It's (very) hot.
    fresco. It's cool.
    (mucho) frío. It's (very) cold.
    (mucho) sol. It's (very) sunny.
    (mucho) viento. It's (very) windy.
Hay (mucha) niebla. It's (very) foggy.

llover (o:ue) to rain
Llueve. It's raining.
nevar (e:ie) to snow
Nieva. It's snowing.

el botones
bellhop

EN EL HOTEL

el alojamiento lodging
la cama bed
el/la empleado/a employee
la habitación room
    individual single room
    doble double room
el hotel hotel
el/la huésped guest
la pensión boarding house
el piso floor (of a building)
la planta baja ground floor

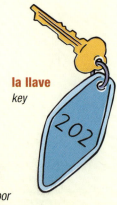

la llave
key

recursos

WB pp. 45–46 | LM p. 25 | vhlcentral.com

98 noventa y ocho

Las vacaciones

ir en motocicleta (f.) to go by motorcycle

LAS ACTIVIDADES

acampar to camp
confirmar una reservación to confirm a reservation
estar de vacaciones to be on vacation
hacer las maletas to pack (one's suitcases)
hacer turismo (m.) to go sightseeing
  un viaje to take a trip
  una excursión to go on a hike, to go on a tour
ir a la playa to go to the beach
ir de pesca to go fishing
  de vacaciones to go on vacation
ir en autobús (m.) to go by bus
  en auto(móvil) (m.) to go by car
  en avión (m.) to go by plane
  en barco (m.) to go by boat
  en taxi (m.) to go by taxi
pasar por la aduana to go through customs
pescar to fish

sacar fotos (f. pl.) to take pictures

montar a caballo to ride a horse

LOS NÚMEROS ORDINALES

primer, primero/a first
segundo/a second
tercer, tercero/a third
cuarto/a fourth
quinto/a fifth
sexto/a sixth
séptimo/a seventh
octavo/a eighth
noveno/a ninth
décimo/a tenth

LAS ESTACIONES Y LOS MESES

el invierno winter
la primavera spring
el verano summer
el otoño fall, autumn

el año year
la estación season
el mes month

OTRAS PALABRAS Y EXPRESIONES

el ascensor elevator
la cabaña cabin
el campo countryside
el equipaje luggage
la llegada arrival
el mar ocean, sea
la salida departure; exit

¿Cuál es la fecha de hoy? What is today's date?
Hoy es el primero (dos, tres,...) de marzo.
  Today is March first (second, third,...).

enero	January
febrero	February
marzo	March
abril	April
mayo	May
junio	June
julio	July
agosto	August
septiembre	September
octubre	October
noviembre	November
diciembre	December

noventa y nueve **99**

Lección 5

Práctica y conversación

1 Escuchar Indicate who would probably make each statement you hear. Each answer is used twice.

El agente de viajes

La inspectora de aduanas

El empleado del hotel

1. ____   4. ____
2. ____   5. ____
3. ____   6. ____

1. ____   4. ____
2. ____   5. ____
3. ____   6. ____

1. ____   4. ____
2. ____   5. ____
3. ____   6. ____

2 ¿Cierto o falso? Listen to each sentence and indicate whether it is **cierto** or **falso**. Correct the false statements.

Cierto	Falso	
____	____	1. _____
____	____	2. _____
____	____	3. _____
____	____	4. _____
____	____	5. _____
____	____	6. _____
____	____	7. _____
____	____	8. _____

3 Describir With a partner, take turns describing what these people are doing.

1. Enrique y Gustavo

2. Yo
3. Tú

4. Don Luis
5. Marcela

6. Juan y yo

recursos
vhlcentral.com

100 *cien*

4 Contestar With a classmate, take turns asking each other these questions.

1. ¿Cuál es la fecha de hoy?
2. ¿Qué estación es? ¿Te gusta esta (*this*) estación?
3. ¿Cuál es el segundo mes del verano?
4. ¿Cuál es el primer mes del invierno?
5. ¿Cuál es la cuarta estación del año?
6. ¿Prefieres el otoño o la primavera? ¿Por qué?
7. ¿Prefieres el mar o las montañas? ¿Por qué?
8. ¿Te gusta más el campo o la ciudad? ¿Por qué?
9. Cuando vas de vacaciones, ¿qué haces?

Practice more at vhlcentral.com.

Pronunciación Spanish b and v

Audio: Concepts, Activities

| **b**ueno | **v**óleibol | **b**iblioteca | vi**v**ir |

There is no difference in pronunciation between the Spanish letters **b** and **v**. However, each letter can be pronounced two different ways, depending on which letters appear next to them.

| **b**onito | **v**iajar | tam**b**ién | in**v**estigar |

B and **v** are pronounced like the English hard **b** when they appear either as the first letter of a word, at the beginning of a phrase, or after **m** or **n**.

| de**b**er | no**v**io | a**b**ril | cer**v**eza |

In all other positions, **b** and **v** have a softer pronunciation, which has no equivalent in English. Unlike the hard **b**, which is produced by tightly closing the lips and stopping the flow of air, the soft **b** is produced by keeping the lips slightly open.

| **b**ola | **v**ela | Cari**b**e | decli**v**e |

In both pronunciations, there is no difference between **b** and **v**. The English *v* sound, produced by friction between the upper teeth and lower lip, does not exist in Spanish. Instead, the soft **b** comes from friction between the two lips.

Verónica y su esposo canta**n b**oleros.

When **b** or **v** begins a word, its pronunciation depends on the previous word. At the beginning of a phrase or after a word that ends in **m** or **n**, it is pronounced as a hard **b**.

Benito es de **B**oquerón pero **v**ive en **V**ictoria.

Words that begin with **b** or **v** are pronounced with a soft **b** if they appear immediately after a word that ends in a vowel or any consonant other than **m** or **n**.

Refranes Read these sayings aloud to practice the **b** and the **v**.

No hay mal que por bien no venga.[1]

Hombre prevenido vale por dos.[2]

1 *Every cloud has a silver lining.*
2 *Forewarned is forearmed.*

Practice more at vhlcentral.com.

recursos

LM p. 26

vhlcentral.com

5 ESCENAS

¡Vamos a la playa! Video: *Fotonovela*

Los seis amigos hacen un viaje a la playa.

Expresiones útiles

Talking to hotel personnel

¿En qué puedo servirles?
How can I help you?
Tenemos una reservación.
We have a reservation.
¿A nombre de quién?
In whose name?
¿Quizás López? ¿Tal vez Díaz?
Maybe López? Maybe Díaz?
Ahora lo veo, aquí está. Díaz.
Now I see it. Here it is. Díaz.
Dos habitaciones en el primer piso para seis huéspedes.
Two rooms on the first floor for six guests.
Aquí tienen las llaves.
Here are your keys.

Describing a hotel

No está nada mal el hotel.
The hotel isn't bad at all.
Todo está tan limpio y cómodo.
Everything is so clean and comfortable.
Es excelente/estupendo/fabuloso/
fenomenal/increíble/magnífico/
maravilloso/perfecto.
*It's excellent/stupendous/fabulous/
phenomenal/incredible/magnificent/
marvelous/perfect.*

Talking about how you feel

Yo estoy un poco cansado/a.
I am a little tired.
Estoy confundido/a. *I'm confused.*
Todavía estoy/Sigo enojado/a contigo.
I'm still angry with you.

TÍA ANA MARÍA ¿Están listos para su viaje a la playa?
TODOS Sí.
TÍA ANA MARÍA Excelente... ¡A la estación de autobuses!
MARU ¿Dónde está Miguel?
FELIPE Yo lo traigo.

(*se escucha un grito de Miguel*)
FELIPE Ya está listo. Y tal vez enojado. Ahorita vamos.

EMPLEADO Bienvenidas. ¿En qué puedo servirles?
MARU Hola. Tenemos una reservación para seis personas para esta noche.
EMPLEADO ¿A nombre de quién?
JIMENA ¿Díaz? ¿López? No estoy segura.

EMPLEADO No encuentro su nombre. Ah, no, ahora sí lo veo, aquí está. Díaz. Dos habitaciones en el primer piso para seis huéspedes.

FELIPE No está nada mal el hotel, ¿verdad? Limpio, cómodo... ¡Oye, Miguel! ¿Todavía estás enojado conmigo? (*a Juan Carlos*) Miguel está de mal humor. No me habla.
JUAN CARLOS ¿Todavía?

recursos

VM pp. 9–10

vhlcentral.com

102 ciento dos

Las vacaciones

FELIPE

JUAN CARLOS

MARISSA

JIMENA

MARU

MIGUEL

MAITE FUENTES

ANA MARÍA

EMPLEADO

EMPLEADO Aquí están las llaves de sus habitaciones.
MARU Gracias. Una cosa más. Mi novio y yo queremos hacer windsurf, pero no tenemos tablas.
EMPLEADO El botones las puede conseguir para ustedes.

JUAN CARLOS ¿Qué hace este libro aquí? ¿Estás estudiando en la playa?
JIMENA Sí, es que tengo un examen la próxima semana.

JUAN CARLOS Ay, Jimena. ¡No! ¿Vamos a nadar?
JIMENA Bueno, como estudiar es tan aburrido y el tiempo está tan bonito...

MARISSA Yo estoy un poco cansada. ¿Y tú? ¿Por qué no estás nadando?
FELIPE Es por causa de Miguel.

MARISSA Hmm, estoy confundida.
FELIPE Esta mañana. ¡Sigue enojado conmigo!
MARISSA No puede seguir enojado tanto tiempo.

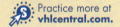
Practice more at vhlcentral.com.

Actividades

1 Identificar Identify the person who would say the following.

1. No lo encuentro, ¿a nombre de quién está su reservación?
2. ¿Por qué estás estudiando en la playa? ¡Mejor vamos a nadar!
3. Nuestra reservación es para seis personas en dos habitaciones.
4. Miguel está enojado conmigo.
5. No tengo ganas de nadar. Estoy cansada.

2 Ordenar Place these events in the correct order.

____ a. El empleado busca la reservación.
____ b. Marissa dice que (*says that*) está confundida.
____ c. Felipe, Juan Carlos, Marissa y Jimena están listos para ir a la playa.
____ d. El empleado da (*gives*) las llaves de las habitaciones a las chicas.
____ e. Miguel da un grito.

3 Conversar With a partner, use these cues to create a conversation between a hotel employee and a guest in Mexico.

1. Greet the employee and ask for your reservation.
2. Tell the employee that the reservation is in your name.
3. Tell the employee that the hotel is very clean and comfortable.
4. Ask the employee to call the bellhop because you have a lot of luggage.

ciento tres 103

5 EXPLORACIÓN

BAJO LA LUPA

El Camino Inca

Early in the morning, Larry rises, packs up his campsite, fills his water bottle in a stream, eats a quick breakfast, and begins his day. By tonight, the seven miles he and his group hiked yesterday to a height of 9,700 feet will seem easy; today the hikers will cover seven miles to a height of almost 14,000 feet, all the while carrying fifty-pound backpacks.

While not everyone is cut out for such a rigorous trip, Larry is on the journey of a lifetime: **el Camino Inca**. Between 1438 and 1533, when the vast and powerful **Imperio Incaico** (*Incan Empire*) was at its height, the Incas built an elaborate network of **caminos** (*trails*) that traversed the Andes Mountains and converged on the empire's capital, Cuzco. Today, hundreds of thousands of tourists come to Peru annually to walk the surviving **caminos** and enjoy the spectacular landscapes. The most popular trail, **el Camino Inca**, leads from Cuzco to the ancient mountain city of Machu Picchu. Many trekkers opt for a guided four-day itinerary, starting at a suspension bridge over the Urubamba River, and ending at **Intipunku** (*Sun Gate*), the entrance to Machu Picchu. Guides organize campsites and meals for travelers, as well as one night in a hostel en route.

Wiñay Wayna

To preserve **el Camino Inca**, the National Cultural Institute of Peru limits the number of hikers to five hundred per day. Those that make the trip must book in advance and should be in good physical condition in order to endure the high altitude and difficult terrain.

Sitios en el Camino Inca

Highlights of a four-day hike along the Inca Trail:

Warmiwañusqua (*Dead Woman's Pass*), at 13,800 feet, hiker's first taste of the Andes' extreme sun and wind

Sayacmarca (*Inaccessible Town*), fortress ruins set on a sheer cliff

Phuyupatamarca (*Town in the Clouds*), an ancient town with stone baths, probably used for water worship

Wiñay Wayna (*Forever Young*), a town named for the pink orchid native to the area, famous for its innovative agricultural terraces which transformed the mountainside into arable land

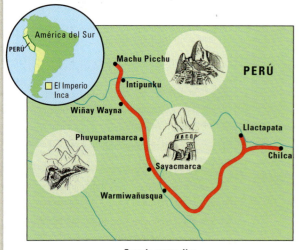

Ruta de cuatro días

Las vacaciones

ACTIVIDADES

1 ¿Cierto o falso? Indicate whether these statements are **cierto** or **falso**. Correct the false statements.

1. **El Imperio Incaico** reached its height between 1438 and 1533.
2. Lima was the capital of the Incan Empire.
3. Hikers on **el Camino Inca** must camp out every night.
4. The Incas invented a series of terraces to make the rough mountain landscape suitable for farming.
5. Along **el Camino Inca**, one can see village ruins, native orchids, and agricultural terraces.
6. High altitude is one of the challenges faced by hikers on **el Camino Inca**.
7. At Sayacmarca, hikers can see Incan pyramids set on a sheer cliff.
8. Travelers can complete **el Camino Inca** on their own at any time.

2 De vacaciones Spring break is coming up, and you want to hike **el Camino Inca** with some friends. In groups, decide how you will get there, where you prefer to stay and for how long, and what each of you will do during free time. Present your trip to the class.

CONEXIÓN INTERNET

¿Qué otro lugar turístico es muy visitado en Cuzco? For more information about **Exploración** go to **vhlcentral.com**.

¡Vacaciones en Perú!

1 Preparación Have you ever visited an archeological or historic site? Where? Why did you go there?

2 El video Watch this **Flash cultura** episode.

Vocabulario

ciudadela	citadel
el/la guía	guide
quechua	Quechua (*indigenous Peruvian*)
sector (urbano)	(*urban*) sector

Machu Picchu se salvó° de la invasión española [...] se encuentra aislada°...

Me encantan° las civilizaciones antiguas°.

se salvó *was saved* se encuentra aislada *it is isolated* Me encantan *I love*
antiguas *ancient*

3 Completar Complete these sentences. Make the necessary changes.

1. Las ruinas de Machu Picchu son una antigua _____ inca.
2. La ciudadela estaba (*was*) dividida en tres sectores: _____, religioso y de cultivo (*farming*).
3. Cada año los _____ reciben a cientos (*hundreds*) de turistas de diferentes países.
4. Hoy en día, la cultura _____ está presente en las comunidades andinas (*Andean*) del Perú.

ciento cinco **105**

5 GRAMÁTICA

5.1 Estar with conditions and emotions

▸ In Spanish, the verb **estar** is used to talk about how people feel and to say where people, places, and things are located.

Estoy bien, gracias.   *I'm fine, thanks.*   Juan **está** en la biblioteca.   *Juan is at the library.*

▸ **Estar** is used with adjectives to describe the physical condition of nouns.

La puerta **está** cerrada.   *The door is closed.*   Todo **está** muy limpio.   *Everything is very clean.*

▸ Use **estar** with adjectives to describe how people feel.

Yo estoy cansada.

¿Están listos para su viaje?

Adjectives that describe emotions and conditions

abierto/a	open	contento/a	happy, content	nervioso/a	nervous
aburrido/a	bored; boring	desordenado/a	disorderly; messy	ocupado/a	busy
alegre	happy; joyful	enamorado/a (de)	in love (with)	ordenado/a	orderly
amable	friendly	enojado/a	mad, angry	preocupado/a (por)	worried (about)
avergonzado/a	embarrassed	equivocado/a	wrong; mistaken	seguro/a	sure; confident; safe
cansado/a	tired	feliz	happy	sucio/a	dirty
cerrado/a	closed	limpio/a	clean	triste	sad
cómodo/a	comfortable				

▸ Note that the plural of **feliz** is **felices**. Also, note that **seguro** means *safe* when referring to an object and *confident* when referring to people.

ESPAÑOL EN VIVO

TÚ: en la ciudad. Estás muy ocupado, cansado y nervioso. Si crees que el invierno es así para todos, estás equivocado.

CURAÇAO
Donde siempre es verano

El paquete incluye:
- Pasaje de ida y vuelta
- Cómoda estancia de 5 días en habitación doble
- Excursiones en barco a los maravillosos lugares de la isla

OFERTA
$797
ESPECIAL

Consulte su agencia de viajes.   **ELLOS:** de vacaciones en Curaçao. Están felices y relajados. ¿Estás listo para hacer tus maletas?

106 *ciento seis*

Las vacaciones

Práctica y conversación

1 Un viaje Claudia is going on a trip. Say how she, her family, and her friends are feeling. In the first blank, fill in the correct form of **estar**. In the second blank, fill in the adjective that best fits the context. Make the necessary changes.

contento	ocupado
enojado	preocupado
nervioso	triste

Claudia

1. ¡Qué bueno! Hoy yo _____ muy _____ porque mañana voy a hacer un viaje a Chicago.
2. ¡Qué nervios! También _____ un poco _____ porque voy en avión y no me gusta mucho volar (*to fly*).
3. Mis padres _____ _____ porque viajo sola (*alone*).
4. Mi amiga Patricia y yo _____ muy _____ porque ella no puede ir. Ella tiene que estudiar para un examen.
5. Es que Patricia _____ muy _____ porque este semestre toma muchas clases.
6. Mi novio César _____ muy _____ porque él piensa que yo voy a ir a bailar todas las noches.

2 ¿Cómo están? Describe these places and people.

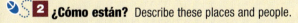

La habitación de Teresa

La habitación de César

1. _____
2. _____

Yo

El profesor Olmos

3. _____
4. _____

3 Situaciones With a partner, use **estar** to talk about how you feel in these situations.

1. Cuando estoy de vacaciones…
2. Cuando tomo un examen…
3. Cuando estoy con mi familia…
4. Cuando estoy en la clase de español…
5. Cuando llueve…
6. Cuando asisto a un funeral…
7. Cuando mi novio/a sale con otro/a chico/a…
8. Cuando llega el invierno…

4 Describir With a partner, say how these people are feeling and explain why. Use your imagination.

María Laura

Juan y Luisa

Sebastián

Olivia y Marco

5 Preguntas Use these questions to interview your partner.

1. ¿Estás ocupado/a este fin de semana? ¿Qué vas a hacer?
2. ¿Estás enamorado/a? ¿De quién?
3. ¿Qué haces cuando estás preocupado/a por algo (*something*)?
4. ¿Qué haces cuando estás aburrido/a?
5. ¿Cómo estás ahora? ¿Por qué?

Practice more at **vhlcentral.com**.

ciento siete 107

Lección 5

5.2 The present progressive  Tutorial

Las chicas están hablando con el empleado del hotel.

▶ Both Spanish and English use the present progressive, which consists of the present tense of the verb *to be* and the present participle (the *–ing* form in English).

Los chicos **están jugando.**	**Estoy haciendo** las maletas.	**Estás mirando** la televisión.
The kids are playing.	*I am packing.*	*You are watching TV.*

▶ Form the present progressive with the present tense of **estar** and a present participle.

Están cantando.	**Estamos** esperando.	**Estoy** comiendo.	Ella **está** trabajando.
They are singing.	*We are waiting.*	*I am eating.*	*She is working.*

▶ The present participle of regular verbs is formed as follows:

▶ When the stem of an **–er** or **–ir** verb ends in a vowel, the present participle ends in **–yendo**.

▶ The verbs **ir**, **poder**, and **venir** have irregular present participles (**yendo**, **pudiendo**, **viniendo**). Several other verbs have irregular present participles.

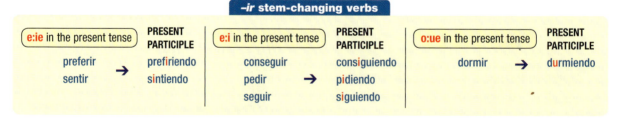

▶ The present progressive is used less in Spanish than in English. In Spanish, the present progressive emphasizes that an action is *in progress*.

Ella todavía **está escuchando** música.	Javier **está estudiando** ahora mismo.
She is still listening to music.	*Javier is studying right now.*

108 ciento ocho

Las vacaciones

▶ In English, the present progressive is used with actions that occur over time or in the future. In Spanish, the simple present tense is used.

Practican fútbol este verano.
They're playing soccer this summer.

Salgo hoy a las tres.
I'm leaving today at three.

Práctica y conversación

1 De vacaciones Mauricio and his family are vacationing. Complete his description of what everyone is doing right now.

1. Yo _____
4. Mi mamá _____

2. Mi hermana Elena _____
5. Mis hermanos _____

3. Mi papá _____
6. Mi abuela _____

2 Un amigo preguntón You are on summer vacation. A nosy friend calls you at all hours to see what you are doing. Look at the clocks and tell him.

MODELO
Estoy descansando.

 1. _____
 3. _____
2. _____
 4. _____

3 Describir With a partner, use the present progressive to describe what is going on in this beach scene.

4 Conversar You and a classmate are each babysitting a group of children. In pairs, prepare a telephone conversation using these cues. Be creative!

ESTUDIANTE 1	Say hello and ask what the kids are doing.
ESTUDIANTE 2	Say hello and tell your partner that two of your kids are doing their homework. Then ask what the kids at his/her house are doing.
ESTUDIANTE 1	Tell your partner that two of your kids are running and dancing in the house.
ESTUDIANTE 2	Tell your partner that one kid is reading.
ESTUDIANTE 1	Tell your partner that you are tired and that two kids are watching TV and eating pizza.
ESTUDIANTE 2	Tell your partner that one kid is sleeping.
ESTUDIANTE 1	Tell your partner you have to go; the kids are playing soccer in the house.
ESTUDIANTE 2	Say goodbye and good luck (**¡Buena suerte!**).

Practice more at vhlcentral.com.

ciento nueve 109

Lección 5

5.3 Comparing ser and estar  Tutorial

▶ **Ser** and **estar** both mean *to be*, but are used for different purposes.

Jimena, Juan Carlos y Marissa son muy amables conmigo.

Uses of ser

Nationality and place of origin	Los Gómez **son** peruanos. Luisa **es** de Cuzco.	**Possession**	Las maletas **son** de Silvia.
Profession or occupation	Liliana **es** ingeniera. Ana y yo **somos** médicos.	**What something is made of**	Las llaves **son** de metal.
Characteristics of people and things	Sus padres **son** amables. El hotel **es** muy grande.	**Time and date**	¿Qué hora **es**? **Son** las tres. ¿Qué día **es** hoy? Hoy **es** lunes. Hoy **es** el dos de abril.
Generalizations	**Es** necesario trabajar.	**Where or when an event occurs**	La fiesta **es** en mi casa. El concierto **es** a las ocho.

Miguel está enojado.

Uses of estar

Location or spatial relationships	El hotel no **está** lejos. Álex **está** en el cine.	**Emotional states**	Ignacio **está** aburrido. **Estoy** contenta con el viaje.
Health	¿Cómo **estás**? **Estoy** enfermo.	**Certain weather expressions**	**Está** despejado. **Está** nublado.
Physical states and conditions	El conductor **está** cansado. Las puertas **están** cerradas.	**Ongoing actions (progressive tenses)**	**Estamos** buscando el museo. María **está** durmiendo.

Ser and estar with adjectives

▶ With many adjectives, both **ser** and **estar** can be used, but the meaning changes. Statements with **ser** describe inherent qualities, while statements with **estar** describe temporary and changeable conditions.

Juan **es** nervioso.
Juan is a nervous person.

Juan **está** nervioso hoy.
Juan is nervous today.

Ana **es** elegante.
Ana is an elegant person.

Ana **está** elegante hoy.
Ana looks elegant today.

▶ Some adjectives change in meaning depending on whether they are used with **ser** or **estar**.

ser vs. **estar**

El chico **es** listo.
The boy is smart.

El chico **está** listo.
The boy is ready.

La niña **es** mala.
The girl is bad.

La niña **está** mala.
The girl is sick.

Él **es** aburrido.
He is boring.

Él **está** aburrido.
He is bored.

ser vs. **estar**

Las peras **son** verdes.
The pears are green.

Las peras **están** verdes.
The pears are not ripe.

El gato **es** muy vivo.
The cat is very clever.

El gato **está** vivo.
The cat is alive.

Él **es** seguro.
He's confident.

Él no **está** seguro.
He's not sure.

Las vacaciones

Práctica y conversación

1 Completar Complete this dialogue with **ser** and **estar**.

- **TINA** ¡Hola, Ricardo! ¿Cómo (1) _____?
- **RICARDO** Bien, gracias. Oye... ¡Qué guapa (2) _____ hoy!
- **TINA** Gracias. (3) _____ muy amable. Oye, ¿qué (4) _____ haciendo? (5) ¿_____ ocupado?
- **RICARDO** No, sólo (6) _____ escribiendo un mensaje electrónico a mi amigo Sancho.
- **TINA** ¿De dónde (7) _____ él?
- **RICARDO** Sancho (8) _____ de Ponce, pero ahora él y su familia (9) _____ de vacaciones en Miami.
- **TINA** Y... ¿cómo (10) _____ Sancho?
- **RICARDO** (11) _____ moreno y un poco bajo. También (12) _____ muy listo. ¿Lo quieres conocer?

2 En el aeropuerto Use **ser** and **estar** to describe this scene at an airport in Spain. Tell what these people look like, how they are feeling, and what they are doing.

MODELO
Anita es una niña pequeña, delgada y morena. Ella está triste y ahora está llorando (*crying*).

3 Describir With a partner, take turns describing the people in the drawing without saying their names. Use these questions to guide your descriptions. Your partner has to guess who the person is.

- ¿Dónde está(n)?
- ¿Cómo es? / ¿Cómo son?
- ¿Cómo está(n)?
- ¿Qué está(n) haciendo?
- ¿Qué estación es?
- ¿Qué tiempo hace?
- ¿Qué hora es?

4 Advinar Using these questions as a guide, describe one classmate and one celebrity to your partner. Don't mention their names. Your partner will guess whom you are describing.

- ¿Cómo es?
- ¿Cómo está?
- ¿De dónde es?
- ¿Dónde está?
- ¿Qué está haciendo?

Practice more at **vhlcentral.com**.

ciento once 111

Lección 5

5.4 Direct object nouns and pronouns Tutorial

¿Dónde está Miguel?
Yo lo traigo.

▶ A direct object receives the action of the verb directly and generally follows the verb. In this example, the direct object answers the question *what is Jimena reading?*

SUBJECT	VERB	DIRECT OBJECT NOUN
Jimena	está leyendo	un libro.
Jimena	is reading	a book.

▶ When a direct object noun is a person or a pet, it is preceded by the word **a**. This is called the "personal **a**" and it has no English equivalent. When the direct object is not a person or pet, but a place, for example, the personal **a** is not needed.

Marta busca **a** su perro Lucas.
Marta is looking for her dog, Lucas.

Escucho **al** profesor.
I am listening to the professor.

Ustedes visitan el museo.
You are visiting the museum.

▶ Direct object pronouns replace direct object nouns. Like English, Spanish sometimes uses a direct object pronoun to avoid repetition.

No tenemos tablas de windsurf.
El botones las puede conseguir para ustedes.

DIRECT OBJECT	DIRECT OBJECT PRONOUN	DIRECT OBJECT	DIRECT OBJECT PRONOUN
Ella hace las maletas.	Ella las hace.	Él tiene el carro.	Él lo tiene.

Direct object pronouns

Singular forms			Plural forms		
me	me	lo	you (m., form.); him; it (m.)	nos	us	los	you (m., form.); them (m.)
te	you (fam.)	la	you (f., form.); her; it (f.)	os	you (fam.)	las	you (f., form.); them (f.)

¡ojo!
It is common to use the direct object pronoun when the direct object noun has been mentioned before.
¿Quieres a tu mamá?
Do you love your mom?
Sí, la quiero mucho.
Yes, I love her very much.

▶ In affirmative sentences, direct object pronouns generally appear before the conjugated verb. In negative sentences, the pronoun is placed between the word **no** and the verb.

Katia tiene las llaves. → Katia las tiene.   Él no practica el tenis. → Él no lo practica.

▶ In the present progressive and in infinitive constructions, the direct object pronoun can be placed before the conjugated form, or attached to the present participle or infinitive.

Vamos a hacer las maletas. → Las vamos a hacer. / Vamos a hacerlas.
Quiero ver el estadio. → Lo quiero ver. / Quiero verlo.

▶ When a pronoun is attached to the present participle, an accent mark is added to maintain the proper stress.

Están buscando la llave. → La están buscando. / Están buscándola.

112   *ciento doce*

Las vacaciones

Práctica y conversación

1 Sustitución Professor Vega's class is planning a trip to Costa Rica. Describe their preparations by changing the direct object nouns to direct object pronouns.

MODELO
La profesora Vega tiene su pasaporte.
La profesora Vega lo tiene.

1. Gustavo y Héctor confirman las reservaciones.
2. Nosotros leemos los folletos (*brochures*).
3. Ana María estudia el mapa.
4. Yo aprendo los nombres de los monumentos de San José.
5. Alicia escucha a la profesora.
6. Miguel escribe las instrucciones para llegar al hotel.

2 Vacaciones Ramón is going to San Juan, Puerto Rico, with his friends, Javier and Marcos. Express his thoughts more succinctly using direct object pronouns.

MODELO
Quiero hacer una excursión.
Quiero hacerla./La quiero hacer.

1. Voy a hacer mi maleta.
2. Necesitamos llevar los pasaportes.
3. Marcos está pidiendo el folleto turístico.
4. Javier debe llamar a sus padres.
5. Ellos esperan visitar el Viejo San Juan.
6. Puedo llamar a Javier por la mañana.

3 ¿Qué estás haciendo? A classmate has called to find out what you are doing to prepare for your trip to Cancún. Answer your partner's questions. Follow the model.

MODELO
preparar el itinerario de viaje
Estudiante 1: ¿Estás preparando el itinerario de viaje?
Estudiante 2: No, no lo estoy preparando.
Estudiante 1: ¿Cuándo lo vas a preparar?
Estudiante 2: Voy a prepararlo mañana (el lunes, a los dos, etc.).

1. preparar los documentos de viaje
2. buscar información de hoteles en Internet
3. practicar español
4. pensar en actividades para hacer

4 En un café Get together with a partner and take turns asking each other questions about the drawing.

MODELO
Estudiante 1: ¿Quién está leyendo el mapa?
Estudiante 2: El Sr. Torres está leyéndolo.

5 Entrevista Use these questions to interview a classmate. Your partner should respond using direct object pronouns.

1. ¿Quién prepara la comida (*food*) en tu casa?
2. ¿Visitas parientes con frecuencia (*frequently*)?
3. ¿Cuándo ves a tus amigos?
4. ¿Estudias español todos los días?
5. ¿Traes tu libro a clase? ¿Y tu cuaderno?
6. ¿Cuándo vas a hacer la tarea de la clase de español?
7. ¿Ves mucho la televisión? ¿Cuándo vas a ver tu programa favorito?
8. ¿Quieres visitar otro país? ¿Por qué?

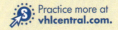
Practice more at vhlcentral.com.

Lección 5

Ampliación

1 Escuchar 🎧

A Listen to the weather report by Hernán Jiménez and indicate which of these phrases are correct.

TIP **Listen for key words.** Listening for key words and phrases will help you identify the subject and main ideas of what you hear, as well as some of the details.

Santo Domingo

___ 1. hace sol
___ 2. va a hacer frío
___ 3. una mañana de mal tiempo
___ 4. va a estar nublado
___ 5. buena tarde para tomar el sol
___ 6. buena mañana para ir a la playa

San Francisco de Macorís

___ 1. hace frío
___ 2. hace sol
___ 3. va a nevar
___ 4. va a llover
___ 5. hay niebla
___ 6. buen día para excursiones

B ¿Qué tiempo hace hoy en tu ciudad?

2 Conversar

While you're on summer vacation, you run into a classmate from last year. With a partner, role-play a conversation that includes these topics.

- Las clases
- La familia
- Los amigos
- Los pasatiempos
- Las vacaciones
- Los deportes
- El tiempo
- Los compañeros de clase

114 *ciento catorce*

Las vacaciones

3 Escribir Write a tourist brochure for a hotel or resort.

TIP Make an outline. Identify topics and subtopics in order to provide a framework for the information you want to present.

Descripción del sitio (con foto)		
A. Playa Grande		
1. Playas seguras y limpias		
2. Ideal para tomar el sol y descansar		
B. El hotel		
1. Abierto los 365 días del año		
2. Piscina grande		

Organízalo — Jot down the most attractive aspects of your hotel or resort. Then, organize your ideas into an outline.

Escríbelo — Using your outline as a reference, write the first draft of your brochure.

Corrígelo — Exchange papers with a classmate and comment on the brochure's completeness, organization, grammatical accuracy, and level of interest. Then revise your first draft, keeping your classmate's comments in mind.

Compártelo — Swap brochures with a classmate. After you have read the brochure, name the three aspects of the hotel or resort that appeal to you the most or least.

4 Un paso más Create a real or simulated website to promote a travel package to a resort in a Spanish-speaking country. Include images whenever possible. Your website should include these pages:

- A home page (**página principal**) with a general description of the tour and links to the other pages
- A page describing the means of transportation
- A page describing hotels and accommodations
- A page about the nearby sites to visit
- A page detailing activities available to travelers

CONEXIÓN INTERNET

Investiga estos temas en **vhlcentral.com**.

- Balnearios (*resorts*) de España
- Balnearios de Latinoamérica

ciento quince **115**

5 LECTURA

Antes de leer

By scanning for specific information, you can learn a great deal about a text without reading it word for word. For example, you can scan a document to identify its format, to find cognates, or to find specific facts.

Examinar el texto
Scan the reading selection for cognates and write a few of them down.

1. _____
2. _____
3. _____
4. _____
5. _____

Based on the cognates you found, what do you think this document is about?
_____
_____

Preguntas
Read these questions. Then scan the document again to look for answers to the questions.

1. What is the format of the reading?
_____

2. What place is the document about?
_____

3. What are some of the visual cues this document provides? What do they tell you about the content of the document?
_____
_____

4. Who produced the document, and what do you think it is for?
_____
_____

116 ciento dieciséis

Turismo ecológico en Puerto Rico

Hotel Vistahermosa ~ Lajas, Puerto Rico

- 40 habitaciones individuales
- 15 habitaciones dobles
- Teléfono/TV por cable/Internet
- Aire acondicionado
- Restaurante (Bar)
- Piscina
- Área de juegos
- Cajero automático°

El hotel está situado en Playa Grande, un pequeño pueblo de pescadores del mar Caribe. Es el lugar perfecto para el viajero que viene de vacaciones. Las playas son seguras y limpias, ideales para tomar el sol, descansar, tomar fotografías y nadar. Está abierto los 365 días del año. Hay una rebaja° especial para estudiantes universitarios.

DIRECCIÓN: Playa Grande 406, Lajas, PR 00667, cerca del Parque Nacional Foresta.

Las vacaciones

Atracciones cercanas

Playa Grande ¿Busca la playa perfecta? Playa Grande es la playa que está buscando. Usted puede pescar, sacar fotos, nadar y pasear en bicicleta. Playa Grande es un paraíso para el turista que quiere practicar deportes acuáticos. El lugar es bonito e interesante y usted va a tener muchas oportunidades para descansar y disfrutar en familia.

Valle Niebla Ir de excursión, tomar café, montar a caballo, caminar, hacer picnics. Más de cien lugares para acampar.

Bahía Fosforescente Sacar fotos, salidas de noche, excursión en barco. Una maravillosa experiencia llena de luz°.

Arrecifes de Coral Sacar fotos, bucear, explorar. Es un lugar único en el Caribe.

Playa Vieja Tomar el sol, pasear en bicicleta, jugar a las cartas, escuchar música. Ideal para la familia.

Parque Nacional Foresta Sacar fotos, visitar el Museo de Arte Nativo. Reserva Mundial de la Biosfera.

Santuario de las Aves Sacar fotos, observar aves°, seguir rutas de excursión.

Después de leer

¿Comprendiste?

Indicate whether each statement is **cierto** or **falso**.

Cierto	Falso	
_____	_____	1. El hotel Vistahermosa tiene 55 habitaciones
_____	_____	2. Playa Grande es un lugar ideal para montar a caballo.
_____	_____	3. Hay muchos lugares para acampar en Valle Niebla.
_____	_____	4. El hotel Vistahermosa está cerrado en invierno.
_____	_____	5. Es posible sacar fotos de las aves en el Santuario de las aves.
_____	_____	6. No hay museos cerca del hotel.

Preguntas

Answer these questions.

1. ¿Dónde está el hotel Vistahermosa?

_____

2. ¿Cómo son las playas cerca del hotel?

_____

3. ¿Dónde podemos hacer picnics?

_____

4. ¿Qué lugar es único en el Caribe?

_____

5. ¿Dónde podemos ir de pesca?

_____

Coméntalo

Imagina que vas de vacaciones a Lajas. ¿En qué mes del año deseas ir? ¿Por qué? ¿Cómo prefieres viajar, en avión o en barco? ¿Quieres visitar los lugares mencionados aquí? ¿Por qué?

Cajero automático *ATM*   rebaja *discount*   llena de luz *full of light*   aves *birds*

ciento diecisiete **117**

5 VOCABULARIO

Las vacaciones y los viajes

el aeropuerto	airport
la agencia de viajes	travel agency
el/la agente de viajes	travel agent
la estación de autobuses	bus station
del metro	subway station
del tren	train station
el/la inspector(a) de aduanas	customs inspector
el pasaje (de ida y vuelta)	(round-trip) ticket
el pasaporte	passport
la tienda de campaña	tent
el/la viajero/a	traveler
acampar	to camp
confirmar una reservación	to confirm a reservation
estar de vacaciones	to be on vacation
hacer las maletas	to pack (one's suitcases)
hacer turismo (m.)	to go sightseeing
hacer un viaje	to take a trip
una excursión	to go on a hike, to go on a tour
ir a la playa	to go to the beach
ir de pesca	to go fishing
ir de vacaciones	to go on vacation
ir en autobús (m.), en auto(móvil) (m.),	to go by bus to go by car
en avión (m.),	to go by plane
en barco (m.),	to go by boat
en motocicleta (f.),	to go by motorcycle
en taxi (m.)	to go by taxi
montar a caballo	to ride a horse
pasar por la aduana	to go through customs
pescar	to fish
sacar fotos (f. pl.)	to take pictures

En el hotel

el alojamiento	lodging
el/la botones	bellhop
la cama	bed
el/la empleado/a	employee
la habitación individual, doble	single, double room
el hotel	hotel
el/la huésped	guest
la llave	key
la pensión	boarding house
el piso	floor (of a building)
la planta baja	ground floor

Adjetivos

abierto/a	open
aburrido/a	bored; boring
alegre	happy, joyful
amable	nice; friendly
avergonzado/a	embarrassed
cansado/a	tired
cerrado/a	closed
cómodo/a	comfortable
contento/a	happy, content
desordenado/a	disorderly; messy
enamorado/a (de)	in love (with)
enojado/a	mad, angry
equivocado/a	wrong; mistaken
feliz	happy
limpio/a	clean
listo/a	ready; smart
malo/a	bad; sick
nervioso/a	nervous
ocupado/a	busy
ordenado/a	orderly
preocupado/a (por)	worried (about)
seguro/a	sure; confident; safe
sucio/a	dirty
triste	sad
verde	green; ripe
vivo/a	clever; alive

¿Qué tiempo hace?

¿Qué tiempo hace?	How's the weather?; What's the weather like?
Está despejado.	It's clear.
Está (muy) nublado.	It's (very) cloudy.
Hace buen/mal tiempo.	It's nice/bad weather.
(mucho) calor.	It's (very) hot.
fresco.	It's cool.
(mucho) frío.	It's (very) cold.
(mucho) sol.	It's (very) sunny.
(mucho) viento.	It's (very) windy.
Hay (mucha) niebla.	It's (very) foggy.
llover (o:ue)	to rain
Llueve.	It's raining.
nevar (e:ie)	to snow
Nieva.	It's snowing.

Palabras y expresiones adicionales

el ascensor	elevator
la cabaña	cabin
el campo	countryside
el equipaje	luggage
la llegada	arrival
el mar	ocean, sea
la salida	departure; exit
ahora mismo	right now
todavía	yet; still
¿Cuál es la fecha de hoy?	What is today's date?
Hoy es el primero (dos, tres,...) de marzo.	Today is March first (second, third,...).

Las estaciones y los meses	See page 99.
Los números ordinales	See page 99.
Direct object pronouns	See page 112.

118 ciento dieciocho

6 ¡De compras!

Communicative Goals
You will learn how to:
- talk about clothing
- negotiate and pay for items
- express preferences while shopping

PREPARACIÓN
pages 120–123
- Words related to clothing and shopping
- Colors and other adjectives
- Pronouncing **d** and **t**

ESCENAS
pages 124–125
- The friends are back in Mérida where they go to the market to do some shopping. Who will get the best deal?

EXPLORACIÓN
pages 126–127
- Bajo la lupa: *Los mercados al aire libre*
- Flash cultura: *Comprar en los mercados*

GRAMÁTICA
pages 128–137
- Numbers 101 and higher
- Preterite tense of regular verbs
- Indirect object pronouns
- Demonstrative adjectives and pronouns

LECTURA
pages 138–139
- Newspaper advertisement: *Corona*

Para empezar
- ¿Quiénes son las tres personas de la foto?
- ¿Cómo son ellas?
- ¿Dónde están, en un restaurante o en una tienda?
- ¿Qué están haciendo, comprando o trabajando?

6 PREPARACIÓN

¡De compras! Talking Picture Tutorial Games

DE COMPRAS

el almacén department store
la caja cash register
el centro comercial shopping mall
el/la cliente/a client
el/la dependiente/a clerk
el mercado (al aire libre) (open-air) market
la rebaja sale
la tienda shop, store
el/la vendedor(a) salesperson

costar (o:ue) to cost
gastar to spend (money)
hacer juego (con) to match
ir de compras to go shopping
llevar to wear; to take
pagar (con) to pay (with)
regatear to bargain
usar to wear; to use
vender to sell

el precio (fijo) (fixed, set) price

el dinero money

la tarjeta de crédito credit card

recursos

 WB pp. 53–54
 LM p. 31
vhlcentral.com

120 ciento veinte

¡De compras!

LA ROPA Y LOS ACCESORIOS

la corbata tie

- **el abrigo** coat
- **los bluejeans** jeans
- **la blusa** blouse
- **la bolsa** bag; purse
- **las botas** boots
- **los calcetines** socks
- **la camisa** shirt
- **la camiseta** t-shirt
- **la cartera** wallet
- **la chaqueta** jacket
- **el cinturón** belt
- **la falda** skirt
- **los guantes** gloves
- **el impermeable** raincoat
- **las medias** pantyhose, stockings
- **los pantalones** pants
- **cortos** shorts
- **la ropa** clothing, clothes
- **interior** underwear
- **las sandalias** sandals
- **el sombrero** hat
- **el suéter** sweater
- **el traje** suit
- **de baño** bathing suit
- **el vestido** dress
- **los zapatos de tenis** sneakers

las gafas (de sol) sunglasses

el par de zapatos pair of shoes

LOS COLORES

- **amarillo/a** yellow
- **anaranjado/a** orange
- **blanco/a** white
- **rojo/a** red
- **gris** gray
- **rosado/a** pink
- **negro/a** black
- **morado/a** purple
- **café** brown
- **verde** green
- **azul** blue

ADJETIVOS

- **barato/a** cheap
- **bueno/a** good
- **cada** each
- **caro/a** expensive
- **corto/a** short (in length)
- **elegante** elegant
- **hermoso/a** beautiful
- **largo/a** long
- **loco/a** crazy
- **nuevo/a** new
- **otro/a** other; another
- **pobre** poor
- **rico/a** rich

ciento veintiuno **121**

Lección 6

Práctica y conversación

1 Escuchar Listen to Juanita and Vicente talk about what they're packing for their vacations. Indicate who is packing each item. If neither is packing an item, write an **X**.

Juanita

Vicente

	Juanita	Vicente		Juanita	Vicente
1. abrigo	_____	_____	7. gafas de sol	_____	_____
2. zapatos de tenis	_____	_____	8. camisetas	_____	_____
3. impermeable	_____	_____	9. traje de baño	_____	_____
4. chaqueta	_____	_____	10. botas	_____	_____
5. sandalias	_____	_____	11. pantalones cortos	_____	_____
6. bluejeans	_____	_____	12. suéter	_____	_____

2 Anita la contraria Your friend Liliana always contradicts you. Indicate how she would respond to each sentence.

MODELO El suéter nuevo de Liliana es muy grande.
No, su suéter es muy pequeño.

1. El cinturón de Liliana es caro. _____
2. El impermeable de don José es muy feo. _____
3. La corbata del Sr. Ramos es larga. _____
4. Los zapatos de tenis de Noelia son viejos. _____
5. Los trajes de Mauricio son baratos. _____
6. Las botas de Marta están sucias. _____

3 Preguntas Answer these questions with a classmate.

1. ¿De qué color es el suéter?
2. ¿De qué color es la corbata?
3. ¿De qué color es la planta?
4. ¿De qué color es la rosa de Texas?
5. ¿De qué color es la casa donde vive el presidente de EE.UU.?
6. ¿De qué color es una cebra?

122 *ciento veintidós*

¡De compras!

4 Entrevista  Use these questions to interview a classmate. Then report your findings to the class.

1. ¿Cuál es tu marca (*brand*) de ropa preferida? ¿Es cara o barata?
2. ¿Cuál es tu artículo de ropa preferido? ¿Cuándo lo usas?
3. ¿Adónde vas para (*in order to*) comprar ropa? ¿Por qué?
4. ¿Cuánto dinero gastas en ropa cada mes? ¿Cada año?
5. Cuando vas de compras, ¿buscas rebajas? ¿Regateas?
6. En tu opinión, ¿es importante comprar frecuentemente ropa nueva?

Practice more at vhlcentral.com.

Pronunciación The consonants d and t

Audio: Concepts, Activities

| ¿Dónde? | vender | nadar | verdad |

Like **b** and **v**, the Spanish **d** can also have a hard sound or a soft sound, depending on which letters appear next to it.

| Don | dinero | tienda | falda |

At the beginning of a phrase and after **n** or **l**, the letter **d** is pronounced with a hard sound. This sound is similar to the English *d* in *dog*, but a little softer and duller. The tongue should touch the back of the upper teeth, not the roof of the mouth.

| medias | verde | vestido | huésped |

In all other positions, **d** has a soft sound. It is similar to the English *th* in *there*, but a little softer.

Don Diego no tiene el diccionario.

When **d** begins a word, its pronunciation depends on the previous word. At the beginning of a phrase or after a word that ends in **n** or **l**, it is pronounced as a hard **d**.

Doña Dolores es de la capital.

Words that begin with **d** are pronounced with a soft **d** if they appear immediately after a word that ends in a vowel or any consonant other than **n** or **l**.

| traje | pantalones | tarjeta | tienda |

When pronouncing the Spanish **t**, the tongue should touch the back of the upper teeth, not the roof of the mouth. Unlike the English *t*, no air is expelled from the mouth.

Refranes Read these sayings aloud to practice the **d** and the **t**.

En la variedad está el gusto.[1]

Aunque la mona se vista de seda, mona se queda.[2]

1 Variety is the spice of life. 2 You can't make a silk purse out of a sow's ear.

Practice more at vhlcentral.com.

recursos

LM p. 32

vhlcentral.com

6 ESCENAS

En el mercado Video: *Fotonovela*

Los chicos van de compras al mercado. ¿Quién hizo la mejor compra?

Expresiones útiles

Talking about clothing

¡Qué ropa más bonita!
What nice clothes!
Esta falda azul es muy elegante.
This blue skirt is very elegant.
Está de moda.
It's in style.
Éste rojo es de algodón/lana.
This red one is cotton/wool.
Ésta de rayas/lunares/cuadros es de seda.
This striped/polka-dotted/plaid one is silk.
Es de muy buena calidad.
It's very good quality.
¿Qué talla usas/llevas?
What size do you wear?
Uso/Llevo talla 4.
I wear a size 4.
¿Qué número calza?
What size shoe do you wear?
Yo calzo siete.
I wear a size seven.

Negotiating a price

¿Cuánto cuesta?
How much does it cost?
Demasiado caro/a.
Too expensive.
Es una ganga.
It's a bargain.

Saying what you bought

¿Qué compraste?/¿Qué compró usted?
What did you buy?
Sólo compré esto.
I only bought this.
¡Qué bonitos aretes!
What beautiful earrings!
Y ustedes, ¿qué compraron?
And you guys, what did you buy?

Additional vocabulary

híjole   *wow*

MARISSA Oigan, vamos al mercado.
JUAN CARLOS ¡Sí! Los chicos en un equipo y las chicas en otro.
FELIPE Tenemos dos horas para ir de compras.
MARU Y don Guillermo decide quién gana.

JIMENA Esta falda azul es muy elegante.
MARISSA ¡Sí! Además, este color está de moda.
MARU Éste rojo es de algodón.

MARISSA ¿Me das aquella blusa rosada? Me parece que hace juego con esta falda, ¿no? ¿No tienen otras tallas?
JIMENA Sí, aquí. ¿Qué talla usas?
MARISSA Uso talla 4.
JIMENA La encontré. ¡Qué ropa más bonita!

(*En otra parte del mercado*)
FELIPE Juan Carlos compró una camisa de muy buena calidad.
MIGUEL (*a la vendedora*) ¿Puedo ver ésos, por favor?
VENDEDORA Sí, señor. Le doy un muy buen precio.

(*Las chicas encuentran unas bolsas.*)
VENDEDOR Ésta de rayas cuesta 190 pesos, ésta 120 pesos y ésta 220 pesos.

---

recursos

VM
pp. 11–12

vhlcentral.com

124   ciento veinticuatro

¡De compras!

FELIPE   **JUAN CARLOS**   **MARISSA**   **JIMENA**   **MARU**   **MIGUEL**   **DON GUILLERMO**   **VENDEDORA**   **VENDEDOR**

VENDEDOR Son 530 por las tres bolsas. Pero como ustedes son tan bonitas, son 500 pesos.
MARU Señor, no somos turistas ricas. Somos estudiantes pobres.
VENDEDOR Bueno, son 480 pesos.

JUAN CARLOS Miren, mi nueva camisa. Elegante, ¿verdad?
FELIPE A ver, Juan Carlos... te queda bien.

MARU ¿Qué compraste?
MIGUEL Sólo esto.
MARU ¡Qué bonitos aretes! Gracias, mi amor.

JUAN CARLOS Y ustedes, ¿qué compraron?
JIMENA Bolsas.
MARU Acabamos de comprar tres bolsas por sólo 480 pesos. ¡Una ganga!

FELIPE Don Guillermo, usted tiene que decidir quién gana. ¿Los chicos o las chicas?
DON GUILLERMO El ganador es... Miguel. ¡Porque no compró nada para él, sino para su novia!

Actividades

1 **¿Cierto o falso?** Indicate whether each sentence is **cierto** or **falso**. Correct the false statements.

1. Jimena dice que la falda azul no es elegante.
2. Juan Carlos compra una camisa.
3. Marissa dice que el azul es un color que está de moda.
4. Miguel compra unas sandalias para Maru.
5. Miguel es el ganador.

2 **Identificar** Provide the name of the person who would make each statement.

1. ¿Te gusta cómo se me ven mis nuevos aretes?
2. Juan Carlos compró una camisa de muy buena calidad.
3. No podemos pagar 500, señor, eso es muy caro.
4. Aquí tienen ropa de muchas tallas.
5. Esta falda me gusta mucho, el color azul es muy elegante.
6. Hay que darnos prisa, sólo tenemos dos horas para ir de compras.

3 Conversar With a classmate, role-play a conversation in which the salesperson greets a customer in an open-air market and offers assistance. The customer is looking for a particular item of clothing. The salesperson and the customer discuss colors and sizes, and negotiate a price.

Practice more at **vhlcentral.com**.

ciento veinticinco **125**

6 EXPLORACIÓN

BAJO LA LUPA

Additional Reading
Video: *Flash cultura*

Los mercados al aire libre

El Rastro

Mercados al aire libre are an integral part of commerce and culture in the Spanish-speaking world. Whether they take place daily or weekly, these markets are an important forum where tourists, locals, and vendors interact. People come to the marketplace to shop, socialize, taste local foods, and watch street performers. Wandering from one **puesto** (*stand*) to the next, one can browse for fresh fruits and vegetables, clothing, CDs and DVDs, and **artesanías** (*crafts*). Some markets offer a mix of products, while others specialize in food, fashion, or used merchandise, such as antiques and books.

When shoppers see an item they like, they can bargain with the vendor. Friendly bargaining is an expected ritual and may result in a significantly lower price. When selling food, vendors may give the customer a little extra of what they purchase; this free addition is known as **la ñapa**.

Many open-air markets are also tourist attractions. The market in Otavalo, Ecuador, is world-famous and has taken place every Saturday since pre-Incan times. This market is well-known for the colorful textiles woven by the **otavaleños**, the indigenous people of the area. One can also find leather goods and wood carvings from nearby towns. Another popular market is **El Rastro**, held every Sunday in Madrid, Spain. Sellers set up **puestos** along the streets to display their wares, which range from local artwork and antiques to inexpensive clothing and electronics.

Otros mercados famosos

Mercado	Lugar	Productos
Feria Artesanal de Recoleta	Buenos Aires, Argentina	artesanías
Mercado Central	Santiago, Chile	mariscos°, pescado°, frutas, verduras°
Tianguis Cultural del Chopo	Ciudad de México, México	ropa, música, revistas, libros, arte, artesanías
El mercado de Chichicastenango	Chichicastenango, Guatemala	frutas, verduras, flores°, cerámica, textiles

Mercado de Otavalo

mariscos *seafood*   pescado *fish*   verduras *vegetables*   flores *flowers*

Practice more at vhlcentral.com.

recursos

VM pp. 43–44

vhlcentral.com

¡De compras!

ACTIVIDADES

1 ¿Cierto o falso? Indicate whether these statements are **cierto** or **falso**. Correct the false statements.

1. In the Hispanic world, markets are vital centers of commerce and culture.
2. Generally, open-air markets specialize in one type of goods.
3. Bargaining is commonplace at outdoor markets.
4. Only new goods can be found at open-air markets.
5. A **ñapa** is a tax on open-air market goods.
6. The **otavaleños** weave colorful textiles to sell on Saturdays.
7. The market in Otavalo opened recently.
8. A Spaniard in search of antiques could search at **El Rastro**.
9. Santiago's **Mercado Central** is known for books and music.
10. If you are in Guatemala and want to buy ceramics, you can go to Chichicastenango.

2 Comparación Compare a market in the Hispanic world with a market where you live. How popular are markets? What items can you typically find there? How do customers negotiate prices?

CONEXIÓN INTERNET

¿Qué marcas de ropa son populares en el mundo hispano? For more information about **Exploración**, go to **vhlcentral.com**.

Comprar en los mercados

1 Preparación Have you ever been to an open-air market? What did you buy? Have you ever negotiated a price? What did you say?

2 El video Watch this **Flash cultura** episode.

Vocabulario	
colones (pl.)	currency from Costa Rica
descuento	discount
¿Cuánto vale?	¿Cuánto cuesta?
el regateo	bargaining

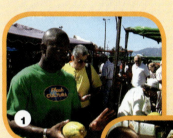

…pero me hace un buen descuento.

¿Qué compran en el Mercado Central?

3 Completar Select the option that best summarizes this episode.

A. Randy Cruz va al mercado al aire libre para comprar papayas. Luego va al Mercado Central. Él les pregunta a clientes qué compran, prueba (*tastes*) platos típicos y busca la heladería.

B. Randy Cruz va al mercado al aire libre para comprar papayas y pedir un descuento. Luego va al Mercado Central para preguntarles a los clientes qué compran en los mercados.

ciento veintisiete 127

6 GRAMÁTICA

6.1 Numbers 101 and higher

Costaron sólo doscientos pesos.

Son cuatrocientos ochenta por las tres bolsas en efectivo.

▸ Spanish uses a period, rather than a comma, to indicate thousands and millions.

Numbers 101 and higher

101	ciento uno	700	setecientos/as	5.000	cinco mil
200	doscientos/as	800	ochocientos/as	100.000	cien mil
300	trescientos/as	900	novecientos/as	200.000	doscientos mil
400	cuatrocientos/as	1.000	mil	550.000	quinientos cincuenta mil
500	quinientos/as	1.100	mil cien	1.000.000	un millón (de)
600	seiscientos/as	2.000	dos mil	8.000.000	ocho millones (de)

▸ The numbers **200** through **999** agree in gender with the nouns they modify.

324 tiendas
trescient**as** veinticuatro tiendas

605 clientes
seiscient**os** cinco clientes

873 habitaciones
ochocient**as** setenta y tres habitaciones

990 euros
novecient**os** noventa euros

500 mujeres
quinient**as** mujeres

257 estudiantes
doscient**os** cincuenta y siete estudiantes

¡ojo!

Notice this difference between Spanish and English:

mil millones
a billion
(1.000.000.000)

un billón
a trillion
(1.000.000.000.000)

Hay **mil millones** de personas en China.
There are a billion people in China.

Hay un **billón** de planetas en el universo.
There are a trillion planets in the universe.

▸ **Mil** can mean *a thousand* or *one thousand*. The plural form of **un millón** (*a million* or *one million*) is **millones**, which has no accent.

1.000 dólares
mil dólares

2.000.000 de pesos
dos millones de pesos

1.000 aviones
mil aviones

1.000.000 de personas
un millón de personas

5.000 bicicletas
cinco mil bicicletas

1.000.000 de aficionados
un millón de aficionados

▸ In Spanish, years are never expressed as pairs of 2-digit numbers as they sometimes are in English (*1979, nineteen seventy-nine*):

1945
mil novecientos cuarenta y cinco

2015
dos mil quince

1898
mil ochocientos noventa y ocho

1220
mil doscientos veinte

▸ When **millón** or **millones** is used before a noun, place **de** between the two.

1.000.000 **de** hombres = un **millón de** hombres
12.000.000 **de** aviones = doce **millones de** aviones
15.000.000 **de** personas = quince **millones de** personas

128   *ciento veintiocho*

¡De compras!

Práctica y conversación

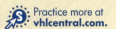

1 Completar Complete these sequences in Spanish. Write out the words, not the digits.

1. 100, 120, 140, … 200
   _____
   _____

2. 5.000, 10.000, 15.000, … 30.000
   _____
   _____

3. 50.000, 100.000, 150.000, … 300.000
   _____
   _____

4. 100.000.000, 200.000.000, 300.000.000, … 900.000.000
   _____
   _____

2 Resolver In pairs, read these math problems aloud and solve them.

MODELO
```
  300
+ 400
-----
  700
```
Trescientos más cuatrocientos son setecientos.

+ mas – menos = es (*singular*)/son (*plural*)

1. 150
   + 150
   _____

2.   43.000
   – 10.000
   _____

3. 20.000
   +   555
   _____

4. 32.000
   – 30.000
   _____

5. 3.000
   + 753
   _____

6. 200.000
   + 350.000
   _____

7. 1.000.000
   –   75.000
   _____

8. 800.000
   + 175.000
   _____

3 ¿Cuánto cuesta? Ask your partner how much each item costs.

MODELO
Estudiante 1: ¿Cuánto cuestan las gafas de sol?
Estudiante 2: Cuarenta mil pesos.

1. 210.000 pesos

4. 61.500 pesos

2. 160.150 pesos

5. 84.450 pesos

3. 48.200 pesos

6. 22.790 pesos

4 ¿En qué año? Take turns with a classmate asking and answering these questions. Follow the model.

MODELO
Estudiante 1: ¿En qué año terminaste (*did you finish*) la escuela secundaria?
Estudiante 2: En el año 2009.

1. ¿En qué año llegó (*arrived*) tu familia a los Estados Unidos?
2. ¿Cuál es el año de tu nacimiento (*birth*)?
3. ¿En qué año empezaste (*started*) a estudiar en la universidad?
4. ¿En qué año te vas a graduar?
5. ¿Cuándo te quieres jubilar (*retire*)?
6. ¿Cuál es hasta ahora (*so far*) el año en que has sido (*you have been*) más feliz?

ciento veintinueve 129

Lección 6

6.2 The preterite tense of regular verbs  Tutorial

¿Qué compraste?

Compré estos aretes.

▸ The preterite is used to talk about actions or states completed in the past.

Preterite of –ar, –er, and –ir verbs

	comprar	vender	escribir
yo	compré / *I bought*	vendí / *I sold*	escribí / *I wrote*
tú	compraste	vendiste	escribiste
usted/él/ella	compró	vendió	escribió
nosotros/as	compramos	vendimos	escribimos
vosotros/as	comprasteis	vendisteis	escribisteis
ustedes/ellos/ellas	compraron	vendieron	escribieron

▸ The preterite endings for regular **–er** and **–ir** vebs are identical. Also, note that the **yo** and **usted/él/ella** forms of all three conjugations have written accents on the last syllable.

▸ Note that the **nosotros/as** forms of regular **–ar** and **–ir** verbs in the preterite are identical to the present-tense forms. Context will help you determine which tense is being used.

En invierno **compramos** suéteres.
In the winter we buy sweaters.

Anoche **compramos** unas sandalias.
Last night we bought some sandals.

Escribimos poemas en clase.
We write poems in class.

Ya **escribimos** dos veces al presidente.
We already wrote to the president twice.

▸ **–Ar** and **–er** verbs that have a stem change in the present tense do *not* have a stem change in the preterite.

INFINITIVE	PRESENT	PRETERITE
cerrar (e:ie)	Ana cierra la puerta.	Ana cerró la puerta.
volver (o:ue)	Juan vuelve a las dos.	Juan volvió a las dos.
jugar (u:ue)	Él juega al fútbol.	Él jugó al fútbol.
pensar (e:ie)	Pienso mucho.	Pensé mucho.

¡ojo!

Use **acabar de** + [*infinitive*] to say that something *has just occurred*. Note that **acabar** is in the present tense in this construction:

Acabo de comprar un suéter.
I just bought a sweater.

Acabas de ir de compras.
You just went shopping.

▸ Verbs that end in **–car**, **–gar**, and **–zar** have a spelling change in the **yo** form of the preterite. All the other forms are regular.

bus**car** → bus**qué**   lle**gar** → lle**gué**   empe**zar** → empe**cé**

▸ **Creer, leer,** and **oír** have spelling changes in the preterite.

creer   creí, creíste, creyó, creímos, creísteis, creyeron
leer   leí, leíste, leyó, leímos, leísteis, leyeron
oír   oí, oíste, oyó, oímos, oísteis, oyeron

▸ **Ver** is regular in the preterite, but none of its forms has an accent.

ver → vi, viste, vio, vimos, visteis, vieron

¡De compras!

Words commonly used with the preterite

anoche	last night	ayer	yesterday	la semana pasada	last week
anteayer	the day before yesterday	de repente	suddenly	una vez	once; one time
		desde... hasta...	from... until...	dos veces	twice; two times
el año pasado	last year	pasado/a	(adj.) last; past	ya	already

Useful phrases

¿Qué hiciste?	What did you (fam., sing.) do?	¿Qué hizo él/ella?	What did he/she do?
¿Qué hizo usted?	What did you (form., sing.) do?	¿Qué hicieron ellos/ellas?	What did they do?
¿Qué hicieron ustedes?	What did you (form., pl.) do?		

Práctica y conversación

1 **Un día fantástico** Complete what Isabel says about her day with the appropriate verb forms.

Ayer (1) _____ [pasar] un día fantástico. Por la mañana (2) _____ [estudiar] y luego (3) _____ [salir] de compras con mis amigas al nuevo centro comercial. (4) _____ [Comprar] un vestido y un suéter muy baratos porque el vendedor me hizo un buen descuento. ¡(5) _____ [Gastar] sólo 40 dólares! Más tarde, nosotras (6) _____ [comer] en un restaurante mexicano. Mi amiga Estela (7) _____ [gastar] mucho dinero porque pidió platos (*dishes*) muy caros. Por la noche, nosotras (8) _____ [salir] a bailar a una discoteca y (9) _____ [regresar] muy tarde. Hoy me levanté (*I got up*) muy temprano porque tengo que estudiar para la clase de español. ¡Uy! ¡Qué cansada (*tired*) estoy!

2 **¿Qué hicieron?** Combine words from each list to talk about things you and others did.

MODELO Yo leí un buen libro la semana pasada.

¿Quién?	¿Qué?	¿Cuándo?
yo	ver la televisión	anoche
mi compañero/a de cuarto	hablar con un(a) chico/a guapo/a	anteayer
mis amigos/as y yo	estudiar español	ayer
mis padres	comprar ropa	la semana pasada
mi abuelo/a	leer un buen libro	el año pasado
el/la profesor(a)	bailar en una discoteca latina	una vez
el/la presidente/a		dos veces

3 **Nuestras vacaciones** Imagine that you took these photos on a vacation with friends. Use the pictures to tell your partner about the trip.

1.

2.

3.

4.

4 **¿Qué hiciste?** Get together with a partner and take turns asking each other what you did yesterday, the day before yesterday, and last week.

MODELO
Estudiante 1: ¿Qué hiciste ayer?
Estudiante 2: Ayer estudié toda la mañana y en la tarde mis amigos y yo vimos una película.

Practice more at vhlcentral.com.

ciento treinta y uno 131

Lección 6

6.3 Indirect object pronouns  Tutorial

Bueno, le doy un descuento.

Acabo de mostrarles que sí sabemos regatear.

▶ An indirect object is the noun or pronoun that answers the question *to whom or for whom* an action is done. In this example, the indirect object answers this question: **¿A quién le prestó Roberto cien pesos?** *To whom did Roberto loan 100 pesos?*

SUBJECT	INDIRECT OBJECT PRONOUN	VERB	DIRECT OBJECT	INDIRECT OBJECT
Roberto	le	prestó	cien pesos	a Luisa.
Roberto		loaned	100 pesos	to Luisa.

Indirect object pronouns

Singular forms
- me — (to, for) me
- te — (to, for) you (fam.)
- le — (to, for) you (form.); (to, for) him; (to, for) her

Plural forms
- nos — (to, for) us
- os — (to, for) you (fam.)
- les — (to, for) you (form.); (to, for) them

▶ Spanish speakers often use the indirect object pronoun and the noun to which it refers in the same sentence to emphasize or clarify *to whom* the pronoun refers. The indirect object pronoun is often used without the noun when the person for whom the action is being done is known.

Iván **le** prestó un lápiz **a Juan**.
Iván loaned a pencil to Juan.

También **le** prestó papel.
He also loaned him paper.

▶ Since **le** and **les** have multiple meanings, **a** + [*noun*] or **a** + [*pronoun*] are often used to clarify to whom the pronouns refer.

Unclear: Ella **les** vendió ropa.
She sold clothing (to them or to you all).

Clear: Ella **les** vendió ropa **a ellos**.
She sold clothing to them.

▶ Indirect object pronouns usually precede the conjugated verb. In negative sentences, place the pronoun between **no** and the conjugated verb.

Te compré un abrigo.
I bought you a coat.

No te compré nada.
I didn't buy you anything.

▶ When an infinitive or present participle is used, there are two options for indirect object pronoun placement: before the conjugated verb, or attached to the infinitive or present participle. When a pronoun is attached to a present participle, an accent mark is added to maintain the proper stress.

¿Vas a comprar**le** un regalo a Carla?
¿**Le** vas a comprar un regalo a Carla?
Are you going to buy a gift for Carla?

Estoy mostrándo**les** las fotos a ellos.
Les estoy mostrando las fotos a ellos.
I'm showing them the photos.

132 ciento treinta y dos

¡De compras!

▶ The irregular verbs **dar** (*to give*) and **decir** (*to say; to tell*) are often used with indirect object pronouns.

Dar and decir

dar

yo	doy	vosotros/as	dais
tú	das	Uds./ellos/ellas	dan
Ud./él/ella	da	Present Participle	dando
nosotros/as	damos		

decir

yo	digo	vosotros/as	decís
tú	dices	Uds./ellos/ellas	dicen
Ud./él/ella	dice	Present Participle	diciendo
nosotros/as	decimos		

Ella **me da** regalos.
She gives me gifts.

Voy a **darle** un beso.
I'm going to give her a kiss.

Te digo la verdad.
I'm telling you the truth.

No **les estoy diciendo** mentiras a mis padres.
I am not telling lies to my parents.

Práctica y conversación

1 Completar Fill in the correct indirect object pronouns to complete Emilio's description of his family's holiday shopping.

1. Yo _____ compré una cartera a mi padre.
2. Mi prima _____ compró una corbata muy fea (a mí).
3. Mis tíos _____ compraron guantes a mis padres.
4. Yo _____ compré un suéter azul a mi mamá.
5. Mis abuelos _____ compraron regalos a nosotros.
6. Y yo _____ compré una camiseta bonita a mi novia.

2 Combinar Use an item from each column and an indirect object pronoun to create logical sentences.

MODELO
Mis padres les dan regalos a mis primos.

A	B	C	D
yo	dar	beso	mí
mis padres	decir	mentiras	ustedes
tú		regalos	novio/a
¿?		¿?	¿?

3 Entrevista Take turns with a classmate asking and answering questions using the cues provided.

MODELO
escribir mensajes electrónicos
Estudiante 1: ¿A quién le escribes mensajes electrónicos?
Estudiante 2: Le escribo mensajes electrónicos a mi hermano.

> 1. Cantar canciones de amor (*love songs*)
> 2. Dar besos
> 3. Decir mentiras
> 4. Escribir mensajes electrónicos
> 5. Hablar por teléfono
> 6. Mostrar fotos de un viaje

4 ¡Somos ricos! You and your classmates won the lottery! Now you want to spend money on your loved ones. In groups of three, discuss what each person is buying for their family and friends.

MODELO
Estudiante 1: Quiero comprarle un vestido a mi mamá.
Estudiante 2: Y yo voy a darles un auto nuevo a mis padres y una blusa a mi amiga.
Estudiante 3: Voy a comprarles una casa a mis padres, pero a mis amigos no les voy a dar nada.

Practice more at **vhlcentral.com**.

Lección 6

6.4 Demonstrative adjectives and pronouns Tutorial

▶ Demonstrative adjectives demonstrate or point out nouns. They precede the nouns they modify and agree with them in gender and number.

este vestido	**esos** zapatos	**aquella** tienda	**aquellas** bolsas
this dress	those shoes	that store (over there)	those bags (over there)

Me gusta **este** vestido.

Demonstrative adjectives

Singular forms		Plural forms		
MASCULINE	FEMININE	MASCULINE	FEMININE	
este	esta	estos	estas	this; these
ese	esa	esos	esas	that; those
aquel	aquella	aquellos	aquellas	that; those (over there)

¡Pero **esos** zapatos son feos!

▶ The demonstrative adjectives **este**, **esta**, **estos**, and **estas** are used to point out nouns that are close to the speaker and the listener.

▶ The demonstrative adjectives **ese**, **esa**, **esos**, and **esas** are used to point out nouns that are not close in space and time to the speaker. They may, however, be close to the listener.

▶ The demonstrative adjectives **aquel**, **aquella**, **aquellos**, and **aquellas** are used to point out nouns that are far away from the speaker and the listener.

▶ Demonstrative pronouns are identical to demonstrative adjectives, except that they traditionally carry an accent mark on the stressed vowel. They agree in number and gender with the corresponding noun.

No me gusta **este** suéter. Prefiero **ése**.
I don't like this sweater. I prefer that one.

Ella quiere comprar **esa** bolsa, no **aquélla**.
She wants to buy that purse, not that one over there.

¿Qué pantalón te gusta?

Me gusta **éste**.

Demonstrative pronouns

Singular forms		Plural forms		
MASCULINE	FEMININE	MASCULINE	FEMININE	
éste	ésta	éstos	éstas	this one; these
ése	ésa	ésos	ésas	that one; those
aquél	aquélla	aquéllos	aquéllas	that one; those (over there)

¿Cuáles tiendas son tus favoritas?

Mis favoritas son **aquéllas**.

▶ There are three neuter forms: **esto**, **eso**, and **aquello**. These forms refer to unidentified or unspecified nouns, situations, and ideas. They do not change in gender or number and never carry an accent mark.

¿Qué es **esto**?
What's this?

Eso es interesante.
That's interesting.

Aquello es bonito.
That's pretty.

134 ciento treinta y cuatro

¡De compras!

Práctica y conversación

1 En un almacén Emilio and María are shopping. Complete their conversation with the appropriate demonstrative adjectives and pronouns.

MARÍA No me gustan (1) _____ (*those*) pantalones. Voy a comprar (2) _____ (*these*).

GABRIEL Yo prefiero (3) _____ (*those over there*).

MARÍA Sí, a mí también me gustan. ¿Qué piensas de (4) _____ (*these*) cinturones?

GABRIEL (5) _____ (*These*) cuestan demasiado.

MARÍA También busco un vestido elegante. ¿Te gusta (6) _____ (*this one*)?

GABRIEL No, es muy feo. ¿Necesitas una falda nueva? (7) _____ (*This one*) es bonita.

MARÍA No, no necesito una falda. Vamos, Gabriel. Me gusta (8) _____ (*this*) almacén, pero (9) _____ (*that one over there*) es mejor (*better*).

2 Oraciones Form sentences using the words provided and the appropriate forms of the preterite. Make all the necessary changes.

MODELO
Este / clientes / gastar / mucho dinero
Estos clientes gastaron mucho dinero.

1. aquel / mujer / comprar / chaqueta
2. cliente / pagar / muy caro / ese / abrigos
3. tú / salir / de compras / ese / centro comercial
4. yo / buscar / aquel / sombreros / por mucho tiempo
5. empleados / vender / este / corbatas / en rebaja

3 ¿De qué color es? In pairs, use demonstrative adjectives and pronouns to discuss the colors of items in your classroom.

MODELO
Estudiante 1: ¿Esos zapatos son azules?
Estudiante 2: No, ésos son verdes. Aquéllos son azules.
Estudiante 1: Y esa mochila, ¿es roja?
Estudiante 2: No, ésa es blanca. Aquélla es roja.

4 En una tienda Imagine that you and a classmate are in a small clothing store. Look at the illustration, then talk about what you see around you.

MODELO
Estudiante 1: ¿Te gusta esa chaqueta de mujer que está debajo de las camisas?
Estudiante 2: No, prefiero aquélla que está al lado de los pantalones. ¿Dónde están los zapatos?
Estudiante 1: Están en el centro de la tienda.

Practice more at vhlcentral.com.

ciento treinta y cinco 135

Lección 6

Ampliación

1 Escuchar

A Listen to Marisol and Alicia's conversation. Make a list of the clothing items that each person mentions, then note if she actually purchased it.

TIP **Listen for linguistic cues.** By listening for the endings of conjugated verbs, you can identify whether an event already took place, is taking place now, or will take place in the future. Verb endings also give clues about who is participating in the action.

B ¿Crees que la moda es importante para Alicia? ¿Y para Marisol? ¿Por qué? En tu opinión, ¿es importante estar a la moda?

2 Conversar

With a classmate, take turns playing the roles of a shopper and a clerk in a clothing store. Use these guidelines.

- The shopper talks about the clothing he/she is looking for as a gift, mentions for whom the clothes are intended, and says what he/she bought for the same person last year.
- The clerk recommends items.
- The shopper asks how much the items cost.

recursos

WB
pp. 55–62

LM
pp. 33–36

vhlcentral.com

136 ciento treinta y seis

¡De compras!

3 Escribir Write a report for the school newspaper about an interview you conducted with a student concerning his or her opinion on the latest fashion trends at your school.

TIP Reporting an interview. You may transcribe the interview verbatim, or simply summarize it with occasional quotes from the speaker. Your report should begin with an interesting title and brief introduction, include some examples or a quote, and end with a conclusion.

Organízalo	Use an idea map to organize the interview questions and develop an outline for your report. Then brainstorm a title for the report.
Escríbelo	Using your outline as a guide, write the first draft of your report.
Corrígelo	Exchange papers with a classmate and comment on the report's title, introduction, organization, level of interest, grammatical accuracy, and conclusion. Then revise your first draft with your classmate's comments in mind.
Compártelo	Exchange reports in groups of four. Give a superlative title to each report on the basis of its strongest points, for example, "best use of Spanish" or "most interesting questions."

4 Un paso más Develop a business plan to open a clothing store in a Spanish-speaking country.

- Choose a location for your store.
- Decide which products you are going to sell and select an appealing name for your store.
- Include a visual presentation of your products.
- Itemize your prices and expected profits.
- Explain why you think your store will be successful (**va a tener éxito**).

CONEXIÓN INTERNET

Investiga estos temas en vhlcentral.com.

- Tiendas y almacenes hispanos
- Las monedas de los países hispanos

ciento treinta y siete 137

6 LECTURA

Antes de leer

Audio: Reading
Additional Reading

Skimming involves quickly reading through a document to absorb its general meaning. This strategy allows you to understand the main ideas without having to read word for word.

Examinar el texto

Look at the format of the reading selection. How is it organized? What does the organization of the document tell you about its content?

Buscar cognados

Scan the reading selection to locate at least five cognates. Based on the cognates, what do you think the reading selection is about?

1. _____
2. _____
3. _____
4. _____
5. _____
6. The reading selection is about _____.

Impresiones generales

Now skim the reading selection to understand its general meaning. Jot down your impressions. What new information did you learn about the document by skimming it? Based on all the information you now have, answer these questions in Spanish.

1. Who created this document?
2. What is its purpose?
3. Who is its intended audience?

Corona

¡Corona tiene las ofertas más locas del verano!

La tienda más elegante de la ciudad con precios increíbles

Carteras
ELEGANCIA
Colores anaranjado, blanco, rosado y amarillo
Ahora: 15.000 pesos
50% de rebaja

Sandalias de playa
GINO
Números del 35 al 38
A sólo 12.000 pesos
50% de descuento

Faldas largas
ROPA BONITA
Algodón. De distintos colores
Talla mediana
Precio especial: 8.000 pesos

Blusas de seda
BAMBÚ
De cuadros y de lunares
Ahora: 21.000 pesos
40% de rebaja

Vestido de algodón
PANAMÁ
Colores blanco, azul y verde
Ahora: 18.000 pesos
30% de rebaja

Accesorios
BELLEZA
Cinturones, gafas de sol, sombreros, medias
Diversos estilos
Todos con un 40% de rebaja

Lunes a sábado de 9 a 21 horas.
Domingo de 10 a 14 horas.

138 ciento treinta y ocho

¡De compras!

¡Grandes rebajas!
Real° Liquidación°
¡La rebaja está de moda en Corona!
con la tarjeta de crédito más conveniente del mercado.

Chaquetas
CASINO
Microfibra. Colores negro, café y gris
Tallas: P, M, G, XG
Ahora: 22.500 pesos

Zapatos
COLOR
Italianos y franceses
Números del 40 al 45
A sólo 20.000 pesos

Pantalones
OCÉANO
Colores negro, gris y café
Ahora: 11.500 pesos
30% de rebaja

Ropa interior
ATLÁNTICO
Tallas: P, M, G
Colores blanco, negro y gris
40% de rebaja

Traje inglés
GALES
Modelos originales
Ahora: 105.000 pesos
30% de rebaja

Accesorios
GUAPO
Gafas de sol, corbatas, cinturones, calcetines
Diversos estilos
Todos con un 40% de rebaja

Real *Royal*   Liquidación *Clearance sale*

Por la compra de 40.000 pesos, puede llevar un regalo gratis.
- Un hermoso cinturón de señora
- Un par de calcetines
- Una corbata de seda
- Una bolsa para la playa
- Una mochila
- Unas medias

Después de leer

¿Comprendiste?
Indicate whether each statement is **cierto** or **falso**. Correct the false statements.

Cierto	Falso	
_____	_____	1. Hay sandalias de playa.
_____	_____	2. El almacén Corona tiene un departamento de zapatos.
_____	_____	3. Corona abre a las nueve de la mañana los domingos.
_____	_____	4. Una elegante chaqueta café cuesta 22.500 pesos.
_____	_____	5. Las corbatas para hombre tienen una rebaja del 25%.
_____	_____	6. Normalmente las sandalias cuestan 22.000 pesos.
_____	_____	7. El almacén Corona acepta tarjetas de crédito.
_____	_____	8. Cuando gastas 30.000 pesos en la tienda, llevas un regalo gratis.

Preguntas
1. ¿Cuánto cuestan los zapatos de hombre?
   _____
2. ¿Hay rebaja de blusas de algodón (*cotton*)?
   _____
3. ¿Hay rebaja de ropa para niños en Corona?
   _____
4. ¿Hay rebaja de minifaldas?
   _____

Coméntalo
Imagina que vas a ir a Corona. ¿Qué ropa vas a comprar? ¿Hay tiendas similares a Corona en tu comunidad? ¿Cómo se llaman? ¿Tienen muchas rebajas?

recursos
vhlcentral.com

ciento treinta y nueve 139

6 VOCABULARIO

La ropa y los accesorios

el abrigo	coat
los bluejeans	jeans
la blusa	blouse
la bolsa	bag; purse
las botas	boots
los calcetines	socks
la camisa	shirt
la camiseta	t-shirt
la cartera	wallet
la chaqueta	jacket
el cinturón	belt
la corbata	tie
la falda	skirt
las gafas (de sol)	(sun)glasses
los guantes	gloves
el impermeable	raincoat
las medias	pantyhose, stockings
los pantalones	pants
los pantalones cortos	shorts
el par de zapatos	pair of shoes
la ropa	clothing, clothes
la ropa interior	underwear
las sandalias	sandals
el sombrero	hat
el suéter	sweater
el traje	suit
el traje de baño	bathing suit
el vestido	dress
los zapatos de tenis	sneakers

Adjetivos

barato/a	cheap
bueno/a	good
cada	each
caro/a	expensive
corto/a	short (in length)
elegante	elegant
hermoso/a	beautiful
largo/a	long
loco/a	crazy
nuevo/a	new
otro/a	other; another
pobre	poor
rico/a	rich

De compras

el almacén	department store
la caja	cash register
el centro comercial	shopping mall
el/la cliente/a	client
el/la dependiente/a	clerk
el dinero	money
el mercado (al aire libre)	(open-air) market
el precio (fijo)	(fixed, set) price
la rebaja	sale
la tarjeta de crédito	credit card
la tienda	shop, store
el/la vendedor(a)	salesperson
costar (o:ue)	to cost
gastar	to spend (money)
hacer juego (con)	to match
ir de compras	to go shopping
llevar	to wear; to take
pagar (con)	to pay (with)
regatear	to bargain
usar	to wear; to use
vender	to sell

Palabras y expresiones

anoche	last night
anteayer	the day before yesterday
el año pasado	last year
ayer	yesterday
de repente	suddenly
desde	from
hasta	until
pasado/a	(adj.) last; past
la semana pasada	last week
una vez	once; one time
dos veces	twice; two times
ya	already
el beso	kiss
la mentira	lie
el regalo	gift
la verdad	truth
¿Qué hiciste?	What did you (fam., sing.) do?
¿Qué hizo usted?	What did you (form., sing.) do?
¿Qué hizo él/ella?	What did he/she do?
¿Qué hicieron ustedes?	What did you (form., pl.) do?
¿Qué hicieron ellos/ellas?	What did they do?
acabar de (+ inf.)	to have just done something
dar	to give
decir	to say; to tell
prestar	to loan

Los colores	See page 121.
Numbers 101 and higher	See page 128.
Indirect object pronouns	See page 132.
Demonstrative adjectives and pronouns	See page 134.

¡VIVAN LOS PAÍSES HISPANOS!

Cada año miles de personas de todo el mundo (*world*) llegan al Caribe para disfrutar (*to enjoy*) de sus encantos. De aguas cálidas (*warm*) y transparentes, el mar caribeño rodea (*surrounds*) las costas (*coasts*) de Cuba, Puerto Rico y la República Dominicana. Además de sus increíbles playas, el Caribe goza de (*enjoys*) un clima tropical todo el año y posee una enorme variedad de plantas y animales exóticos. ¿Te gustaría (*Would you like*) ir al Caribe algún (*some*) día?

El Caribe

Puerto Rico

Área: 8.959 km^2 (3.459 millas^2)
Población: 3.999.000
Capital: San Juan – 2.758.000
Ciudades principales: Caguas, Mayagüez, Ponce
Moneda: dólar estadounidense

SOURCE: Population Division, UN Secretariat & CIA World Factbook

Cuba

Área: 110.860 km^2 (42.083 millas^2)
Población: 11.075.000
Capital: La Habana – 2.159.000
Ciudades principales: Santiago de Cuba, Camagüey, Holguín, Guantánamo
Moneda: peso cubano

SOURCE: Population Division, UN Secretariat & CIA World Factbook

República Dominicana

Área: 48.730 km^2 (18.815 millas^2)
Población: 10.089.000
Capital: Santo Domingo – 2.240.000
Ciudades principales: Santiago de los Caballeros, La Vega
Moneda: peso dominicano

SOURCE: Population Division, UN Secretariat & CIA World Factbook

¡Vivan los países hispanos!

Interactive map
Video: *Países hispanos*

Lugares

La Habana Vieja

La Habana Vieja es uno de los lugares más maravillosos de Cuba. Este distrito fue declarado (*was declared*) Patrimonio (*Heritage*) Cultural de la Humanidad por la UNESCO en 1982. En la Plaza de Armas, se puede visitar el majestuoso Palacio de Capitanes Generales, que ahora es un museo. En la calle (*street*) Obispo, frecuentada por el escritor Ernest Hemingway, hay hermosos cafés, clubes nocturnos y tiendas elegantes.

Plaza de la Catedral en La Habana

Deportes

El béisbol

Para algunos latinoamericanos, el béisbol es más que un deporte. Los primeros países hispanos en tener una liga fueron Cuba y México, donde se empezó a jugar al béisbol en el siglo (*century*) XIX. Hoy día este deporte es una afición nacional en la República Dominicana. Pedro Martínez y David Ortiz son sólo dos de los muchísimos beisbolistas dominicanos que han alcanzado (*have reached*) gran éxito e inmensa popularidad entre los aficionados.

142 ciento cuarenta y dos

El Caribe

Océano Atlántico

Música
La salsa y el merengue
Hoy día Puerto Rico es el centro internacional de la salsa. El Gran Combo de Puerto Rico, por ejemplo, es una de las orquestas de salsa más famosas del mundo. Sin embargo (*Nevertheless*), este género musical, que comúnmente (*commonly*) se asocia con el Caribe, nació (*was born*) en barrios latinos de Nueva York como resultado de una mezcla (*mix*) de influencias puertorriqueñas y cubanas.

El merengue, el ritmo más conocido de la República Dominicana, tiene sus raíces (*roots*) en el campo. Tradicionalmente las canciones hablaban de los problemas sociales de los campesinos (*farmers*). Entre 1930 y 1960, el merengue se popularizó en las ciudades y adoptó un tono más urbano. Uno de los cantantes y compositores de merengue más famosos es Juan Luis Guerra.

Monumentos
El Morro
El Morro, el gran tesoro (*treasure*) de Puerto Rico, es un fuerte (*fort*) que está en la bahía (*bay*) de San Juan. Lo construyeron (*built*) los españoles en el siglo (*century*) XVI para defenderse de los piratas. Desde mil novecientos sesenta y uno, El Morro es un museo que atrae (*attracts*) a miles de turistas. También es el sitio más fotografiado de Puerto Rico. La arquitectura del fuerte es impresionante: tiene túneles misteriosos, mazmorras (*dungeons*) y vistas (*views*) fabulosas de la bahía.

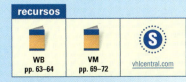

ciento cuarenta y tres 143

¡Vivan los países hispanos!

¿Qué aprendiste?

1 ¿Cierto o falso? Indica si estas oraciones son **ciertas** o **falsas**.

Cierto	Falso	
_____	_____	1. El mar Caribe está al oeste de América Central.
_____	_____	2. El área de Cuba es mayor que el área de Puerto Rico.
_____	_____	3. San Juan es la capital de Puerto Rico.
_____	_____	4. La Habana Vieja es Patrimonio Cultural de la Humanidad.
_____	_____	5. La Habana Vieja es la parte nueva de la capital de Cuba.
_____	_____	6. Los primeros países hispanos en tener una liga de béisbol fueron Cuba y Puerto Rico.
_____	_____	7. El béisbol es el deporte nacional de la República Dominicana.
_____	_____	8. La salsa nació en Nueva York.
_____	_____	9. El merengue tiene sus raíces en la ciudad.
_____	_____	10. Juan Luis Guerra es un cantante de merengue.
_____	_____	11. El Morro fue construido (*was built*) por piratas en el siglo XVI.
_____	_____	12. El Morro es actualmente un museo.

2 Preguntas Answer the questions in complete sentences.

1. ¿Cuál de los países del Caribe te parece interesante visitar? ¿Por qué?
2. ¿Por qué crees que la Habana Vieja fue declarada Patrimonio Cultural de la Humanidad?
3. ¿Practicas béisbol? ¿Qué equipos de béisbol conoces? ¿Cuál es tu equipo favorito?
4. ¿Te gustan la salsa y el merengue? ¿Conoces (*Do you know*) bandas o artistas famosos de estos géneros musicales?
5. ¿Qué país del Caribe quieres visitar en tus próximas vacaciones? ¿Por qué?

CONEXIÓN INTERNET

Investiga estos temas en el sitio **vhlcentral.com**.

- Cubanos y puertorriqueños célebres
- Ecoturismo y lugares para visitar en el Caribe

Practice more at **vhlcentral.com**.

7 La vida diaria

Communicative Goals
You will learn how to:
- talk about daily routines and personal hygiene
- reassure someone
- tell where you went

PREPARACIÓN
pages 146–149
- Words related to personal hygiene and daily routines
- Sequencing expressions
- Pronouncing **r** and **rr**

ESCENAS
pages 150–151
- Marissa, Felipe, and Jimena all compete for space in front of the mirror as they get ready to go out on Friday night.

EXPLORACIÓN
pages 152–153
- Bajo la lupa: *La siesta*
- Flash cultura: *Tapas para todos los días*

GRAMÁTICA
pages 154–163
- Reflexive verbs
- Indefinite and negative words
- Preterite of **ser** and **ir**
- **Gustar** and verbs like **gustar**

LECTURA
pages 164–165
- Magazine article: *¡Una mañana desastrosa!*

Para empezar
- ¿Dónde están ellas: en el patio o en el baño?
- ¿Crees que es de día o de noche? ¿Por qué?
- ¿Van a salir o acaban de llegar?
- ¿Crees que a ellas les gusta estar a la moda? ¿Por qué?

7 PREPARACIÓN

La vida diaria

LA HIGIENE PERSONAL

cepillarse el pelo to brush one's hair
ducharse to shower
lavarse la cara to wash one's face
las manos to wash one's hands
maquillarse to put on makeup
peinarse to comb one's hair

el baño bathroom
el champú shampoo
la crema de afeitar shaving cream
el maquillaje makeup
la toalla towel

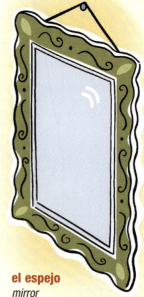

el espejo
mirror

el despertador
alarm clock

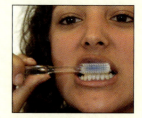

cepillarse los dientes
to brush one's teeth

el jabón
soap

afeitarse
to shave

bañarse
to bathe; to take a bath

recursos

WB pp. 65–66
LM p. 37
vhlcentral.com

146 ciento cuarenta y seis

La vida diaria

POR LA MAÑANA Y POR LA NOCHE

la rutina diaria daily routine

acostarse (o:ue) to lie down; to go to bed
despertarse (e:ie) to wake up
vestirse (e:i) to get dressed

dormirse (o:ue)
to go to sleep; to fall asleep

levantarse
to get up

OTRAS PALABRAS Y EXPRESIONES

Se acuesta. He/she goes to bed; you (form.) go to bed.
Se afeita. He/she shaves; you shave.
Se cepilla los dientes. He/she brushes his/her teeth; you brush your teeth.
Se despierta. He/she wakes up; you wake up.
Se peina. He/she combs his/her hair; you comb your hair.
Se viste. He/she gets dressed; you get dressed.

ADVERBIOS Y PREPOSICIONES DE TIEMPO

antes (de) before
después afterward; then
después de after
durante during
entonces then
luego afterward; then
más tarde later (on)
por la mañana in the morning
por la noche at night
por la tarde in the afternoon; in the (early) evening
por último finally

Se lava las manos.
She washes her hands.

Se ducha.
He takes a shower.

ciento cuarenta y siete **147**

Lección 7

Práctica y conversación

Audio: Activities

1 ¿Cierto o falso? Escucha las oraciones, mira las fotos e indica si cada frase es **cierta** o **falsa**.

	Cierto	Falso
1.		
2.		
3.		
4.		
5.		
6.		
7.		
8.		

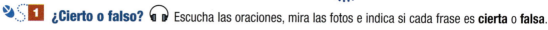

1. 2. 3. 4.

5. 6. 7. 8.

2 Escuchar Escucha las oraciones e indica si cada oración es **lógica** o **ilógica**.

	1.	2.	3.	4.	5.	6.
Lógico						
Ilógico						

3 Identificar Con un(a) compañero/a, indica qué necesitan estas personas para realizar (*to perform*) estas acciones.

MODELO
Manuel / vestirse
Estudiante 1: ¿Qué necesita Manuel para (*in order to*) vestirse?
Estudiante 2: Necesita una camiseta y unos pantalones.

1. Daniel / acostarse   **2.** Raúl / despertarse   **3.** Mercedes / lavarse la cara

4. Leonardo / afeitarse   **5.** Sofía / lavarse el pelo   **6.** Yolanda / maquillarse

recursos
vhlcentral.com

148 ciento cuarenta y ocho

La vida diaria

4 Describir Trabajen en parejas (*pairs*) para describir la rutina diaria de dos o tres de estas personas. Usen las palabras de la lista.

antes	después	durante el día	luego	por último
antes de	después de	entonces	por fin	primero

1. mi mejor (*best*) amigo/a
2. nuestro/a profesor(a) de español
3. mi padre/madre
4. mi compañero/a de cuarto
5. Gabriel García Márquez
6. Jennifer López
7. Juanes
8. el presidente de los Estados Unidos

Practice more at vhlcentral.com.

Pronunciación   The consonant r

Audio: Concepts, Activities

ropa   **rutina**   **rico**   **Ramón**

In Spanish, **r** has a strong trilled sound at the beginning of a word. No English words have a trill, but English speakers often produce a trill when they imitate the sound of a motor.

gustar   **durante**   **primero**   **crema**

In any other position, **r** has a weak sound similar to the English *tt* in *better* or the English *dd* in *ladder*. In contrast to English, the tongue touches the roof of the mouth behind the teeth.

pizarra   **corro**   **marrón**   **aburrido**

The letter combination **rr**, which only appears between vowels, always has a strong trilled sound.

caro   **carro**   **pero**   **perro**

Between vowels, the difference between the strong trilled **rr** and the weak **r** is very important, as a mispronunciation could lead to confusion between two different words.

Refranes Lee en voz alta los refranes, prestando atención a la **r** y a la **rr**.

Perro que ladra no muerde.[1]

No se ganó Zamora en una hora.[2]

1 The dog's bark is worse than its bite.
2 Rome wasn't built in a day.

recursos

LM p. 38

vhlcentral.com

Practice more at vhlcentral.com.

ciento cuarenta y nueve   149

7 ESCENAS

¡Necesito arreglarme!  Video: *Fotonovela*

Es viernes por la tarde y Marissa, Jimena y Felipe se preparan para salir.

Expresiones útiles

Talking about getting ready

Necesito arreglarme.
I need to get ready.
Me estoy lavando la cara.
I'm washing my face.
¿Te importa si me maquillo primero?
Is it OK with you if I put on my makeup first?
Tú te arreglas el pelo y después yo me maquillo.
You fix your hair and then I'll put on my makeup.
Todavía me falta cambiarme la camisa.
I still have to change my shirt.

Reassuring someone

Tranquilo/a.
Relax.
No te preocupes.
Don't worry.

Talking about past actions

¿Cuándo fue la última vez que viste a Juan Carlos?
When was the last time you saw Juan Carlos?
Cuando fuimos a Mérida.
When we went to Mérida.

Talking about likes and dislikes

Me fascinan las películas de Almodóvar.
I love Almodóvar's movies.
Me encanta la música en vivo.
I love live music.
Me molesta compartir el baño.
It bothers me to share the bathroom.

Additional vocabulary

encontrarse con *to meet up with*
molestar *to bother*
nadie *no one*

recursos

VM pp. 13–14

vhlcentral.com

MARISSA ¿Hola? ¿Está ocupado?
JIMENA Sí. Me estoy lavando la cara.
MARISSA Necesito usar el baño.

MARISSA Tengo que terminar de arreglarme. Voy al cine esta noche.
JIMENA Yo también tengo que salir. ¿Te importa si me maquillo primero? Me voy a encontrar con mi amiga Elena en una hora.

JIMENA ¡Felipe! ¿Qué estás haciendo?
FELIPE Me estoy afeitando. ¿Hay algún problema?
JIMENA ¡Siempre haces lo mismo!
FELIPE Pues, yo no vi a nadie aquí.

JIMENA ¿Por qué no te afeitaste por la mañana?
FELIPE Porque cada vez que quiero usar el baño, una de ustedes está aquí. O bañándose o maquillándose.

JIMENA No te preocupes, Marissa. Llegaste primero. Entonces, te arreglas el pelo y después me maquillo.
FELIPE ¿Y yo? Tengo crema de afeitar en la cara. No me voy a ir. Estoy aquí y aquí me quedo.

150 ciento cincuenta

La vida diaria

MARISSA

JIMENA

FELIPE

MARISSA Tú ganas. ¿Adónde vas a ir esta noche, Felipe?

FELIPE Juan Carlos y yo vamos a ir a un café en el centro. Siempre hay música en vivo. Me siento guapísimo. Todavía me falta cambiarme la camisa.

MARISSA ¿Adónde vas esta noche?

JIMENA A la biblioteca.

MARISSA ¡Es viernes! ¡Nadie debe estudiar los viernes! Voy a ver una película de Pedro Almodóvar con unas amigas.

MARISSA ¿Por qué no vienen tú y Elena al cine con nosotras? Después, podemos ir a ese café y molestar a Felipe.

JIMENA No sé.

MARISSA ¿Cuándo fue la última vez que viste a Juan Carlos?

JIMENA Cuando fuimos a Mérida.

MARISSA A ti te gusta ese chico.

JIMENA No tengo idea de qué estás hablando. Si no te importa, nos vemos en el cine.

Practice more at vhlcentral.com.

Actividades

1 ¿Cierto o falso? Indica si lo que dicen estas oraciones es **cierto** o **falso**. Corrige las oraciones falsas.

1. Marissa va a ver una película de Pedro Almodóvar con unas amigas.
2. Jimena se va a encontrar con Elena en dos horas.
3. Felipe se siente muy feo después de afeitarse.
4. Jimena quiere maquillarse.
5. Marissa quiere ir al café para molestar a Juan Carlos.

2 Ordenar Ordena correctamente los planes que tiene Marissa.

____ a. Voy al café.
____ b. Me arreglo el pelo.
____ c. Molesto a Felipe.
____ d. Me encuentro con unas amigas.
____ e. Entro al baño.
____ f. Voy al cine.

3 En el baño Trabajen en parejas para representar el conflicto entre dos compañeros/as de cuarto que deben usar el baño al mismo tiempo.

Estudiante 1
1. Di (*Say*) que quieres arreglarte porque vas a ir al cine.
2. Pregunta si puedes secarte el pelo.
3. Di que puede lavarse la cara, pero que después necesitas secarte el pelo.

Estudiante 2
1. Di (*Say*) que tienes que arreglarte porque te vas a encontrar con tus amigos/as.
2. Responde que no porque necesitas lavarte la cara.
3. Di que después necesitas peinarte.

ciento cincuenta y uno 151

7 EXPLORACIÓN

BAJO LA LUPA

La siesta

Additional Reading
Video: Flash cultura

¿Sientes cansancio° después de comer? ¿Te cuesta° volver al trabajo° o a clase después del almuerzo? Estas sensaciones son normales. A muchas personas les gusta relajarse° después de almorzar. Este momento de descanso es la siesta. La siesta es popular en los países hispanos y viene de una antigua costumbre° del área del Mediterráneo. La palabra *siesta* viene del latín, es una forma corta de decir "sexta hora". La sexta hora del día es después del mediodía, el momento de más calor. Debido al° calor y al cansancio, los habitantes de España, Italia, Grecia e incluso Portugal tienen la costumbre de dormir la siesta desde hace° más de° dos mil años. Los españoles y los portugueses llevaron la costumbre a los países americanos.

Aunque° hoy día esta costumbre está desapareciendo° en las grandes ciudades, la siesta todavía es importante en la cultura hispana. En pueblos pequeños, por ejemplo, muchas oficinas° y tiendas tienen la costumbre de cerrar por dos o tres horas después del mediodía. Los empleados van a su casa, almuerzan con sus familias, duermen la siesta o hacen actividades, como ir al gimnasio, y luego regresan al trabajo entre las 2:30 y las 4:30 de la tarde.

Los estudios científicos explican que una siesta corta después de almorzar ayuda° a trabajar más y mejor° durante la tarde. Pero ¡cuidado! Esta siesta debe durar° sólo entre veinte y cuarenta minutos. Si dormimos más, entramos en la fase de sueño profundo y es difícil despertarse.

Hoy, algunas empresas° de los EE.UU., Canadá, Japón, Inglaterra y Alemania tienen salas° especiales donde los empleados pueden dormir la siesta.

Sientes cansancio *Do you feel tired* **Te cuesta** *Is it hard for you* **trabajo** *work* **relajarse** *to relax* **antigua costumbre** *old custom* **Debido al** *Because (of the)* **desde hace** *for* **más de** *more than* **Aunque** *Although* **está desapareciendo** *is disappearing* **oficinas** *offices* **ayuda** *helps* **mejor** *better* **durar** *last* **algunas empresas** *some businesses* **salas** *rooms*

¿Dónde duermen la siesta?

Costumbre antigua
Costumbre nueva

En los lugares donde la siesta es una costumbre antigua, las personas la duermen en su casa. En los países donde la siesta es una costumbre nueva, la gente duerme en sus lugares de trabajo o en centros de siesta.

recursos

VM
pp. 45–46

vhlcentral.com

152 ciento cincuenta y dos

La vida diaria

ACTIVIDADES

1 ¿Cierto o falso? Indica si lo que dicen las oraciones es **cierto** o **falso**. Corrige la información falsa.

1. La costumbre de la siesta empezó en Asia.
2. La palabra *siesta* está relacionada con la sexta hora del día.
3. Los españoles y los portugueses llevaron la costumbre de la siesta a Latinoamérica.
4. La siesta ayuda a trabajar más y mejor durante la tarde.
5. Los horarios de trabajo de las grandes ciudades hispanas son los mismos que en los pueblos pequeños.
6. Una siesta larga siempre es mejor que una siesta corta.
7. En los Estados Unidos, los empleados de algunas empresas pueden dormir la siesta en el trabajo.
8. Es fácil despertar de un sueño profundo.

2 Una nueva costumbre En parejas, imaginen que las tiendas y comercios en donde viven deciden adoptar la costumbre de la hora de la siesta. ¿Es una buena idea? ¿Cómo va a afectar esta nueva costumbre a su vida diaria? ¿Qué deben hacer ustedes para adaptarse?

CONEXIÓN INTERNET

¿Qué costumbres son populares en los países hispanos? For more information about **Exploración**, go to **vhlcentral.com**.

Tapas para todos los días

1 Preparación En el área donde vives, ¿qué hacen las personas normalmente después del trabajo (*work*)? ¿Van a sus casas? ¿Salen con amigos? ¿Comen?

2 El video Mira el episodio de **Flash cultura**.

Vocabulario
económicas *inexpensive*
montaditos *bread slices with assorted toppings*
pagar propinas *to tip*
tapar el hambre *to take the edge off (lit. putting the lid on one's hunger)*

—¿Cuándo suelesº venir a tomar tapas?
—Generalmente después del trabajo.

Estos son los montaditos, o también llamados pinchos. ¿Te gustan?

º**sueles** *do you tend*

3 Ordenar Ordena estos eventos de manera lógica.

_____ a. El empleado cuenta los palillos (*counts the toothpicks*) de los montaditos que Mari Carmen comió.
_____ b. Mari Carmen va al barrio de la Ribera.
_____ c. Un hombre dice cuándo toma tapas.
_____ d. Un hombre explica la tradición de los montaditos o pinchos.
_____ e. Mari Carmen le pregunta a la chica si los montaditos son buenos para la salud.

ciento cincuenta y tres 153

7 GRAMÁTICA

7.1 Reflexive verbs Tutorial

▶ A reflexive verb is used to indicate that the subject does something to or for himself or herself. Reflexive verbs always use reflexive pronouns.

SUBJECT   REFLEXIVE VERB
Carlos   **se afeita** todos los días.

¿Te importa si me maquillo primero?

The verb **lavarse** (*to wash oneself*)

yo	me lavo	I wash (myself)	nosotros/as	nos lavamos	we wash (ourselves)
tú	te lavas	you wash (yourself)	vosotros/as	os laváis	you wash (yourself)
usted	se lava	you wash (yourself)	ustedes	se lavan	you wash (yourself)
él/ella	se lava	he/she washes (himself/herself)	ellos/ellas	se lavan	they wash (themselves)

A las chicas les encanta maquillarse durante horas y horas.

¡OJO!
Unlike English, Spanish uses the definite article, not a possessive adjective, when referring to clothing or parts of the body.
Se quitó **los** zapatos.
He took off his shoes.
Me cepillé **los** dientes.
I brushed my teeth.

▶ When a reflexive verb is conjugated, the reflexive pronoun agrees with the subject:
Me peino.

▶ Reflexive pronouns follow the same rules for placement as object pronouns. They are placed before the conjugated verb, or attached to the infinitive or present participle. When a pronoun is attached to the participle, an accent mark is added.

José **se** levanta temprano.
José gets up early.

José **se** va a levantar temprano.
José va a levantar**se** temprano.
José is going to get up early.

Carlos **se** afeita.
Carlos shaves.

Carlos **se** está afeitando.
Carlos está afeitándo**se**.
Carlos is shaving.

Common reflexive verbs

acordarse (de) (o:ue)	to remember	irse	to go away; to leave	preocuparse (por)	to worry (about)
acostarse (o:ue)	to go to bed				
afeitarse	to shave	lavarse	to wash oneself	probarse (o:ue)	to try on
bañarse	to bathe; to take a bath	levantarse	to get up	quedarse	to stay, to remain
		llamarse	to be called; to be named	quitarse	to take off
cepillarse	to brush			sentarse (e:ie)	to sit down
despertarse (e:ie)	to wake up	maquillarse	to put on makeup	sentirse (e:ie)	to feel
dormirse (o:ue)	to go to sleep	peinarse	to comb one's hair	vestirse (e:i)	to get dressed
ducharse	to shower	ponerse	to put on		
enojarse (con)	to get angry (with)	ponerse + (adj.)	to become + (adj.)		

La vida diaria

▸ Many Spanish verbs can be reflexive. If the verb acts upon the subject, use the reflexive form. If the verb acts upon something else, use the non-reflexive form.

Lola **lava** los platos.   Lola **se lava** la cara.
Lola washes dishes.   *Lola washes her face.*

▸ Reflexive verbs and their non-reflexive counterparts sometimes have different meanings.

acordar	acordarse	levantar	levantarse
to agree	*to remember*	*to lift*	*to get up*

Práctica y conversación

 Practice more at **vhlcentral.com**.

1 Emparejar Empareja cada foto con la oración correspondiente. Luego, indica qué oraciones tienen verbos reflexivos.

1.   2.

3.   4.

¿Reflexivo?

_____ a. Julia se enoja.   _____
_____ b. Manuela baña a su hija.   _____
_____ c. Estela se pone los calcetines.   _____
_____ d. Ramón se cepilla los dientes.   _____

2 Nuestra rutina La familia de Blanca sigue la misma rutina todos los días. Según Blanca, ¿qué hacen ellos?

MODELO
mamá / despertarse a las 5:00
Mamá se despierta a las cinco.

1. Roberto y yo / levantarse a las 7:00
2. papá / ducharse primero y / luego afeitarse
3. yo / lavarse la cara y / vestirse antes de tomar café
4. mamá / peinarse y / luego maquillarse
5. todos (nosotros) / sentarse a la mesa para comer
6. Roberto / cepillarse los dientes después de comer

3 Conversaciones Completa las conversaciones.

MARIO Tú (1) _____ [lavar / lavarse] los platos ayer, ¿no?
TOMÁS Sí, los (2) _____ [lavar / lavarse] en la noche.

• • •

BEATRIZ ¿Normalmente (tú) (3) _____ [duchar / ducharse] antes de ir a clase?
DAVID Sí, (4) _____ [duchar / ducharse] por la mañana.

• • •

MAMÁ Niños, ¿a qué hora (5) _____ [acostar / acostarse] ustedes anoche?
PABLO Daniela (6) _____ [acostar / acostarse] a las nueve, pero nosotros (7) _____ [acostar / acostarse] a las ocho.

• • •

ANA Yo (8) _____ [sentir / sentirse] nerviosa hoy.
PATRICIA Bueno… tú siempre (9) _____ [sentir / sentirse] nerviosa antes de un examen.

4 Charadas En grupos, jueguen a las charadas. Cada persona debe pensar en dos oraciones con verbos reflexivos. La primera persona que adivina la charada dramatiza la siguiente (*next one*).

5 Entrevista Primero, prepara una lista con las actividades que hiciste (*you did*) anoche. Luego, compara con un(a) compañero/a las actividades y toma apuntes (*notes*) de lo que hizo él/ella (*what he/she did*). Sigue el modelo para el primer paso (*step*).

6:00 p.m.	En el Centro Comercial. Me probé un vestido bien bonito.
7:30 p.m.	Cine con Javier. Muy aburrido. Casi me dormí.
9:00 p.m.	Cena en el restaurante "El cangrejo". Me enojé con Ana.
11:00 p.m.	Fiesta de Antonio. Me acosté tarde.

ciento cincuenta y cinco 155

Lección 7

7.2 Indefinite and negative words  Tutorial

¿Hay algún problema?

▶ Indefinite words, such as *someone* or *something*, refer to people and things that are not specific. Negative words, like *no one* or *nothing*, deny the existence of people and things or contradict statements.

Indefinite and negative words

Indefinite words		Negative words	
algo	something; anything	nada	nothing; not anything
alguien	someone; somebody; anyone	nadie	no one; nobody; not anyone
alguno/a(s), algún	some; any	ninguno/a, ningún	no; none; not any
o... o	either... or	ni... ni	neither... nor
siempre	always	nunca, jamás	never, not ever
también	also; too	tampoco	neither; not either

Yo tampoco me voy a ir.

▶ There are two ways to form negative sentences in Spanish. You can place the negative word before the verb, or you can place **no** before the verb and the negative word after the verb.

Nadie piensa en mí.
No piensa **nadie** en mí.
Nobody thinks of me.

Ellos **nunca** se enojan.
Ellos **no** se enojan **nunca**.
They never get angry.

Ninguno me gusta.
No me gusta **ninguno**.
I don't like any.

Nada me despierta.
No me despierta **nada**.
Nothing wakes me up.

▶ In Spanish, sentences frequently contain two or more negative words. Once a sentence is negative, all indefinite ideas must be expressed in the negative.

Ella **no** tiene **ninguna** idea.
She doesn't have any idea.

Jamás me preocupo por **nada**.
I never worry about anything.

Nunca te pido **nada**.
I never ask you for anything.

Tampoco me despido de **nadie**.
I don't say goodbye to anyone either.

¡ojo!

Before a masculine, singular noun, **alguno** and **ninguno** are shortened to **algún** and **ningún**.

—¿Tienen ustedes **algún** amigo peruano?
Do you have a Peruvian friend?

—No, no tenemos **ningún** amigo peruano.
No, we don't have any Peruvian friends.

▶ **Alguien** and **nadie** are often used with the personal **a**. The personal **a** is also used before **alguno/a, algunos/as**, and **ninguno/a** when these words refer to people and they are the direct object of a verb.

Carlos, ¿ves **a alguien** allí?
Carlos, do you see someone there?

No, no veo **a nadie**.
No, I don't see anyone.

¿Oyes **a alguno** de los chicos?
Do you hear any of the boys?

No, no oigo **a ninguno**.
No, I don't hear any of them.

▶ Although **pero** and **sino** both mean *but*, they are not interchangeable. **Sino** is used when the first part of a sentence is negative and the second part contradicts it. In this context, **sino** means *but rather* or *on the contrary*. In all other cases, **pero** is used to mean *but*.

No se acuesta temprano, **sino** tarde.
*He doesn't get up early, **but rather** late.*

No queremos irnos, **sino** quedarnos.
*We don't want to leave, **but rather** stay.*

Canto, **pero** nunca en público.
*I sing, **but** never in public.*

Me desperté a las once, **pero** estoy cansada.
*I woke up at eleven, **but** I'm tired.*

156 ciento cincuenta y seis

Práctica y conversación

1 La familia de Margarita González Arjona Completa las oraciones con **pero** o **sino**.

MODELO
Mi abuela es aburrida, ___pero___ amable.

1. No me ducho por la mañana, _____ por la noche.
2. A mí no me gusta nadar, _____ correr.
3. Mi hermana María Luisa es alta, _____ delgada.
4. Mi hermano Emilio no es moreno, _____ rubio.
5. Mis padres y mis tíos no se acuestan temprano, _____ tarde.
6. Mi primo Manuel es inteligente, _____ no es interesante.
7. Mi madre y yo siempre nos despertamos temprano, _____ nunca estamos cansadas.
8. Mi amiga Mariana es pequeña, _____ fuerte.

2 Completar Completa esta conversación con oraciones que tengan (*have*) palabras negativas.

MODELO
ALFONSO Ana María, ¿encontraste algún regalo para Elena?
ANA MARÍA No, no encontré ningún regalo/nada para Elena.

ALFONSO ¿Viste a alguna amiga en el centro comercial?
ANA MARÍA (1) _____

ALFONSO ¿Quieres ir al teatro o al cine esta noche?
ANA MARÍA (2) _____

ALFONSO ¿Quieres salir a comer?
ANA MARÍA (3) _____

ALFONSO ¿Hay algo interesante en la televisión esta noche?
ANA MARÍA (4) _____

ALFONSO ¿Tienes algún problema?
ANA MARÍA (5) _____

ALFONSO ¿Eres siempre antipática?
ANA MARÍA (6) _____

3 Quejas Con un(a) compañero/a, prepara una lista de cinco quejas (*complaints*) comunes que tienen los estudiantes universitarios. Usen expresiones negativas.

MODELO
Nadie me entiende.
¡Jamás puedo levantarme tarde!

Ahora preparen una lista de cinco quejas que los padres tienen de sus hijos.

MODELO
Nunca limpian sus habitaciones.
¡No se lavan las manos tampoco!

4 Anuncios En parejas, lean el anuncio (*ad*) y preparen otro anuncio similar, sobre algún producto de higiene personal, usando expresiones afirmativas y negativas.

¿Buscas algún producto especial?

¡No vas a poder resistirte jamás a las ofertas de las tiendas García!

Practice more at vhlcentral.com.

La vida diaria

ciento cincuenta y siete 157

7.3 Preterite of ser and ir  Tutorial

▶ The preterite forms of **ser** (*to be*) and **ir** (*to go*) are irregular, so you will need to memorize them. None of these forms has an accent mark.

¿Cuándo fue la última vez que viste a Juan Carlos?

Cuando fuimos a Mérida.

Preterite of *ser* and *ir*

	ser (to be)	ir (to go)
yo	fui	fui
tú	fuiste	fuiste
usted/él/ella	fue	fue
nosotros/as	fuimos	fuimos
vosotros/as	fuisteis	fuisteis
ustedes/ellos/ellas	fueron	fueron

▶ Since the preterite forms of **ser** and **ir** are identical, the context clarifies which verb is being used.

Lina **fue** a ver una película.
Lina went to see a film.

Fui a Barcelona el año pasado.
I went to Barcelona last year.

La película **fue** muy interesante.
The film was very interesting.

Fue un viaje maravilloso.
It was a wonderful trip.

olvidé *I forgot*
despedirme de *to say goodbye to*
descubrir *to discover*
agua *water* **cansancio** *fatigue*

La vida diaria

Práctica y conversación

1 Conversación Completa esta conversación con la forma correcta del pretérito de **ser** o **ir**.

ANDRÉS Cristina y Vicente (1) _____ novios, ¿no?
LAURA Sí, pero ahora Cristina sale con Luis. Anoche ella (2) _____ a comer con él y la semana pasada ellos (3) _____ al partido de fútbol.
ANDRÉS ¿Ah, sí? Mercedes y yo (4) _____ al partido y no los vimos.
LAURA ¿(5) _____ tú con Mercedes? Y, ¿cómo (6) _____ el partido?
ANDRÉS (7) _____ muy divertido. ¡Lo pasamos genial! Pero... ¡qué extraño! Nosotros (8) _____ al café Paraíso y vimos a Vicente con la hermana de Cristina.
LAURA ¿Él (9) _____ al café Paraíso con su hermana? ¡Qué horror!

2 Oraciones Forma oraciones con los siguientes elementos. Usa el pretérito.

Sujetos	Verbos	Actividades
yo		a un restaurante
tú		en autobús a Nueva York
mis amigos/as		estudiante(s)
nosotros/as	(no) ir	a una discoteca en Buenos Aires
ustedes	(no) ser	muy amable
Antonio Banderas		a casa muy tarde
Gloria Estefan		a la playa con su novio/a
		dependiente/a en una tienda

3 Preguntas En parejas, túrnense para hacerse las siguientes preguntas.

1. ¿Adónde fuiste de vacaciones el año pasado?
2. ¿Con quién fuiste?
3. ¿Cómo fueron tus vacaciones?
4. ¿Fuiste de compras esta semana? ¿Qué compraste?
5. ¿Cómo se llama la última película que viste?
6. ¿Cuándo fuiste a ver la película?
7. ¿Cómo fue?
8. ¿Adónde fuiste durante el fin de semana? ¿Por qué?

4 El fin de semana pasado En parejas, hablen de lo que hicieron ustedes el fin de semana pasado por la mañana, por la tarde y por la noche. Luego compartan la información con la clase.

	Yo	Mi compañero/a
Por la mañana	_____	_____
	_____	_____
	_____	_____
Por la tarde	_____	_____
	_____	_____
	_____	_____
Por la noche	_____	_____
	_____	_____
	_____	_____

5 20 preguntas En grupos pequeños, jueguen a las veinte preguntas. Una persona elige un personaje famoso. El resto del grupo hace preguntas hasta adivinar quién es. Los estudiantes deben hacer preguntas afirmativas o negativas con los verbos en el pretérito que conocen. Pueden usar a estas personas famosas o a otras que ustedes conocen.

- Barack Obama
- Oprah Winfrey
- Donald Trump
- Jennifer Aniston
- Alex Rodriguez

ciento cincuenta y nueve 159

7.4 Gustar and verbs like gustar

▶ **Me gusta(n)** and **te gusta(n)** express the concepts of *I like* and *you* (fam.) *like*. The literal meaning of **gustar** is *to be pleasing to (someone)*.

Me gusta ese champú.
That shampoo is pleasing to me.
I like that shampoo.

¿Te gustan los deportes?
Are sports pleasing to you?
Do you like sports?

▶ **Me gusta(n)** and similar constructions require an indirect object pronoun. In Spanish, the object or thing being liked (**el champú**) is the subject of the sentence. The person who likes the object is an indirect object that answers the question *to whom is the shampoo pleasing?*

I. O. PRONOUN	VERB	SUBJECT	SUBJECT	VERB	DIRECT OBJECT
Me	gusta	ese champú.	I	like	that shampoo.

¿Te gusta Juan Carlos?

Me gustan los cafés que tienen música en vivo.

▶ **Gustar** and similar verbs are usually used in the third-person singular and plural. When the object or person liked is singular, the form **gusta** is used. When two or more objects or persons are liked, **gustan** is used.

| SINGULAR | me, te, le | gusta / gustó | la película / el concierto |
| PLURAL | nos, os, les | gustan / gustaron | las computadoras / los libros |

▶ To express what someone likes or does not like to do, the singular form **gusta** is used, followed by one or more infinitives.

Me gusta levantarme tarde.
I like to get up late.

Me gusta comer y **dormir**.
I like to eat and sleep.

▶ The construction **a** + [*personal pronoun*] (**a mí, a ti, a usted, a él, a ella, a nosotros/as, a vosotros/as, a ustedes, a ellos, a ellas**) clarifies or emphasizes the people who are pleased. **A** + [*noun*] can also be used.

A mí me gusta levantarme temprano. ¿Y **a ti**?
I like to get up early. How about you?

Al profesor le gustó el libro.
The teacher liked the book.

▶ Here is a list of common verbs used in the same way as **gustar**.

Verbs like *gustar*

aburrir	to bore	fascinar	to fascinate; to like very much	interesar	to be interesting to; to interest
encantar	to like very much; to love (objects)	importar	to be important to; to matter	molestar	to bother; to annoy
faltar	to lack; to need			quedar	to be left over; to fit (clothing)

¡ojo!

To express the English equivalent of *would like* (*something* or *to do something*), use the construction [*i.o. pronoun*] + **gustaría(n)**.

¿**Te gustaría** ver esa película?
Would you like to see that movie?

Me gustarían unos días sin clases.
I would like a few days without class.

160 ciento sesenta

La vida diaria

▶ **Faltar** expresses what is lacking or missing. **Quedar** expresses how much of something is left and is also used to talk about how clothing fits or looks on someone.

Le falta dinero.	**Me faltan** dos pesos.	**Nos quedan** cinco libros.	La falda **te queda** bien.
He/she is short of money.	*I need two pesos.*	*We have five books left.*	*The skirt looks good on you.*

Práctica y conversación

1 Completar Completa estas oraciones con los elementos necesarios.

1. _____ Ana _____ [encantar] las canciones (*songs*) de Enrique Iglesias.
2. A _____ me _____ [gustar] más la música de Marc Anthony.
3. A mis amigos _____ [molestar] la música de Gloria Estefan.
4. _____ nosotros _____ [fascinar] los grupos de pop latino.
5. Creo que a Elena _____ [interesar] más la salsa.
6. ¿A _____ te _____ [faltar] dinero para el concierto de Jennifer López?
7. Sí. Sólo _____ [faltar] cinco dólares.
8. ¿Cuánto dinero te _____ [quedar] a _____ ?

2 Describir Describe los dibujos con uno de los siguientes verbos: **aburrir, encantar, faltar, interesar, molestar, quedar.**

1. A Mauricio / libros

3. A Lorena / despertador

2. A nosotros / bailar

4. A ti / camisa

3 Preguntas En parejas, túrnense para hacer y contestar estas preguntas.

1. ¿Te gusta levantarte temprano o tarde? ¿Por qué?
2. ¿Te molesta cuando tu compañero/a de cuarto se levanta muy temprano?
3. ¿Te gustaría poder dormir la siesta todos los días? ¿Por qué?
4. ¿Te gusta ducharte por la mañana o por la noche?
5. ¿Te gustaría ir de tapas todos los días después de las clases?
6. ¿Te aburren los fines de semana que no sales con amigos?
7. ¿Qué te gusta de esta universidad? ¿Qué te molesta? ¿Hay algo que le falta a esta universidad?
8. ¿Te interesan más las ciencias o las humanidades?

4 Conversar En parejas, representen una conversación entre un(a) cliente/a y un(a) dependiente/a en una tienda de ropa. Sigan las instrucciones.

Dependiente/a	Cliente/a
1. Saluda al/a la cliente/a y pregúntale en qué le puedes servir.	2. Saluda al/a la dependiente/a y dile (*tell him/her*) qué quieres comprar.
3. Pregúntale qué estilos le interesan y empieza a mostrarle la ropa.	4. Explícale que te interesan los estilos modernos. Escoge las cosas que te interesan.
5. Habla de las preferencias de la temporada (*trends*).	6. Habla de la ropa (me queda(n) bien/mal, me encanta(n)…).
7. Da opiniones favorables al/a la cliente/a (las botas le quedan fantásticas…).	8. Decide qué cosas te gustan y qué vas a comprar.

Practice more at vhlcentral.com.

Lección 7

Ampliación

1 Escuchar

A Escucha la entrevista entre Carolina y Julián, teniendo en cuenta (*taking into account*) lo que ya sabes sobre este tipo de situación. Elige la opción que completa correctamente cada oración.

TIP **Use background information.** Use what you already know about a topic to help you guess the meaning of unknown words or linguistic structures.

1. Julián es…
   a. político.   b. deportista profesional.
   c. artista de cine.

2. El público (*audience*) de Julián quiere saber de…
   a. sus películas.   b. su vida (*life*).   c. su novia.

3. Julián habla de…
   a. sus viajes y sus rutinas.   b. sus parientes y amigos.
   c. sus comidas (*foods*) favoritas.

4. Julián…
   a. se levanta y se acuesta a horas diferentes todos los días.
   b. tiene una rutina diaria.   c. no quiere hablar de su vida.

B ¿Crees que Julián siempre fue rico? ¿Por qué? ¿Qué piensas de Julián como persona?

2 Conversar
En parejas, conversen sobre lo que hicieron ayer, siguiendo estas preguntas.

- ¿A qué hora te levantaste ayer? ¿Usaste un despertador?
- ¿Cuántas veces te cepillaste los dientes ayer?
- ¿Adónde fuiste ayer después de las clases?
- ¿Te gusta mirar la televisión antes de acostarte?
- ¿A qué hora te acostaste anoche?

162   *ciento sesenta y dos*

La familia

3 Escribir Escribe una composición en la que describes tu rutina diaria en algún lugar interesante (una isla desierta, el Polo Norte, el desierto, etc.). Considera cómo pueden cambiar los elementos básicos de tu rutina: ¿Dónde te acuestas? ¿Cómo te bañas?

TIP Use adverbs to sequence events. You can use adverbs and adverbial phrases as transitions between the introduction, the body, and the conclusion of a narrative.

Organízalo Utiliza estos adverbios para organizar la secuencia de tu composición: **primero, después, luego, más tarde** y **al final**. Anota ideas que respondan a estas preguntas: ¿qué?, ¿quién?, ¿cuándo?, ¿dónde?, ¿cómo? y ¿por qué?

Escríbelo Utiliza tus notas para escribir el primer borrador *(draft)* de la composición.

Corrígelo Intercambia tu composición con un(a) compañero/a. Comenta sobre la introducción, la secuencia de eventos, el nivel *(level)* de interés y los errores de gramática o de ortografía. Revisa el primer borrador según las indicaciones de tu compañero/a.

Compártelo Intercambia tu composición con otro/a compañero/a. Lee su trabajo y comparte con la clase tres ideas que te gustaron *(you liked)* de su composición.

4 Un paso más Planea un viaje a un lugar famoso del mundo hispano. Haz un folleto *(brochure)* con elementos visuales y esta información:

- Presenta el itinerario de cada día del viaje e indica la hora para cada actividad.
- Describe el país, una breve *(brief)* historia del lugar y también las actividades programadas para el viaje.
- Comenta sobre los restaurantes, el transporte y los hoteles.
- Describe la rutina diaria de un viajero típico.

CONEXIÓN INTERNET

Investiga estos temas en **vhlcentral.com**.
- Lugares de interés en España
- Lugares de interés en Latinoamérica

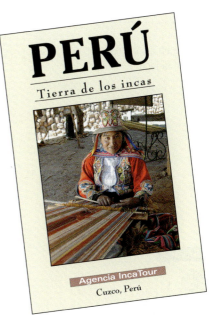

ciento sesenta y tres **163**

7 LECTURA

Antes de leer

Predicting content from the title will help you increase your reading comprehension in Spanish. We can usually predict the content of a newspaper article in English from its headline, for example.

Examinar el texto

Lee el título de la lectura y haz tres predicciones sobre el contenido. Escribe tus predicciones en una hoja de papel.

Compartir

Comparte tus ideas con un(a) compañero/a.

Cognados

Escribe una lista de cuatro cognados que encuentres en la lectura.

1. _____
2. _____
3. _____
4. _____

¿Qué te dicen los cognados sobre el tema de la lectura?

15 de octubre
¡Una mañana desastrosa!

—Me levanté de la cama a las seis y media.

Esta mañana me levanté de la cama a las seis y media y corrí a despertar a mis dos hijas. —Yolanda, Dolores, van a perder el autobús de la escuela, —les grité°. Pero ellas no se despertaron. Jamás se despiertan temprano. Siempre se sientan a ver la televisión por la noche y se acuestan muy tarde.

—Corrimos para llegar a la parada del autobús.

Yolanda y Dolores salieron de la casa sin° cepillarse los dientes, pero eso no importa. Por lo menos se acordaron de ponerse las botas y el abrigo antes de irse. Corrimos para llegar a la parada° del autobús de la escuela, que pasa a las siete de la mañana.

—Nunca llegó el autobús.

Esperamos media hora, pero nu[nca] llegó el autobús. Regresamos a casa. Llamamos por teléfono° a [la] escuela, pero nadie contestó. Tomamos el automóvil y salim[os] de casa.

La vida diaria

—¡Por fin se despertaron mis hijas!

¡Por fin se despertaron! Medio dormidas y medio enojadas°, entraron al baño para lavarse la cara y peinarse. Luego fueron a su habitación para vestirse. Yo fui a la cocina a prepararles el desayuno°. A mis hijas les encanta comer un buen desayuno, pero hoy les di° cereales y les preparé dos sándwiches para el almuerzo°.

—¡Hoy es sábado!

Llegamos a la escuela antes de las ocho y entonces me di cuenta de que° hoy es sábado. ¡Y los sábados no hay clases!

grité / *shouted*   Medio dormidas y medio enojadas *Half asleep and half mad*
desayuno *breakfast*   di / *gave*   almuerzo *lunch*   sin *without*
parada *stop*   Llamamos por teléfono *We called on the phone*
me di cuenta de que / *realized that*

Después de leer

¿Comprendiste?
Selecciona la respuesta correcta.
1. ¿Quién es el/la narrador(a)?
   a. el padre de las chicas   b. Yolanda
   c. Dolores
2. ¿A qué hora se despertó el papá?
   a. a las seis de la mañana   b. a las seis y media
   c. a las siete y media
3. ¿Qué comieron las chicas antes de salir de la casa?
   a. un sándwich   b. cereales
   c. dos sándwiches
4. ¿Cómo fueron las chicas a la escuela?
   a. Corrieron.   b. Fueron en autobús.
   c. Fueron en automóvil.

Preguntas
Responde a estas preguntas con oraciones completas.
1. ¿Por qué nunca se despiertan temprano las chicas?
   _____
2. ¿Se bañaron las chicas esta mañana?
   _____
3. ¿A qué hora llega generalmente el autobús?
   _____
4. ¿A qué hora llegó el autobús hoy?
   _____
5. ¿Por qué no contestó nadie cuando llamaron a la escuela?
   _____

Coméntalo
¿Qué crees que le dicen Yolanda y Dolores a su papá después de volver de la escuela? Imagina que eres el papá, ¿cómo responderías (*would you respond*) a lo que te dicen las chicas?

ciento sesenta y cinco **165**

7 VOCABULARIO

Los verbos reflexivos

acordarse (de) (o:ue)	to remember
acostarse (o:ue)	to lie down; to go to bed
afeitarse	to shave
bañarse	to bathe; to take a bath
cepillarse el pelo	to brush one's hair
cepillarse los dientes	to brush one's teeth
despertarse (e:ie)	to wake up
dormirse (o:ue)	to go to sleep; to fall asleep
ducharse	to shower, to take a shower
enojarse (con)	to get angry (with)
irse	to go away; to leave
lavarse la cara	to wash one's face
lavarse las manos	to wash one's hands
levantarse	to get up
llamarse	to be called; to be named
maquillarse	to put on makeup
peinarse	to comb one's hair
ponerse	to put on
ponerse + [adj.]	to become + [adj.]
preocuparse (por)	to worry (about)
probarse (o:ue)	to try on
quedarse	to stay; to remain
quitarse	to take off
sentarse (e:ie)	to sit down
sentirse (e:ie)	to feel
vestirse (e:i)	to get dressed

En el baño

el baño	bathroom
el champú	shampoo
la crema de afeitar	shaving cream
el espejo	mirror
el jabón	soap
el maquillaje	makeup
la toalla	towel

Adverbios y preposiciones de tiempo

antes (de)	before
después	afterward; then
después de	after
durante	during
entonces	then
luego	afterward; then
más tarde	later (on)
por último	finally

Verbos como *gustar*

aburrir	to bore
encantar	to like very much; to love (inanimate objects)
faltar	to lack; to need
fascinar	to fascinate; to like very much
gustar	to be pleasing to; to like
importar	to be important to; to matter
interesar	to be interesting to; to interest
me gustaría(n)…	I would like…
molestar	to bother; to annoy
quedar	to be left over; to fit (clothing)

Otras palabras y expresiones

el despertador	alarm clock
la rutina diaria	daily routine
por la mañana	in the morning
por la noche	at night
por la tarde	in the afternoon; in the (early) evening

Indefinite and negative words	See page 156.

8 ¡A comer!

Communicative Goals

You will learn how to:
- talk about food
- order at a restaurant
- discuss familiar people and places

PREPARACIÓN
pages 168–171
- Words related to restaurants and meals
- Adjectives that describe food
- The letters **ll**, **ñ**, **c**, and **z**

ESCENAS
pages 172–173
- Miguel and Maru are at one of Mexico City's best restaurants enjoying a romantic dinner... until Felipe and Juan Carlos show up.

EXPLORACIÓN
pages 174–175
- Bajo la lupa: *Frutas y verduras de América*
- Flash cultura: *La comida latina*

GRAMÁTICA
pages 176–185
- Preterite of stem-changing verbs
- Double object pronouns
- **Saber** and **conocer**
- Comparisons and superlatives

LECTURA
pages 186–187
- Newspaper restaurant review: *Cinco estrellas para El Palmito*

Para empezar
- ¿Quiénes son los muchachos?
- ¿Dónde están?
- ¿Qué están haciendo?
- ¿Crees que están contentos?

8 PREPARACIÓN

¡A comer!

el camarero waiter

EN UN RESTAURANTE

el/la dueño/a owner
el plato (principal) (main) dish
la sección de (no) fumadores (non) smoking section
el almuerzo lunch
la cena dinner
la comida food; meal
el desayuno breakfast
almorzar (o:ue) to have lunch
cenar to have dinner
desayunar to have breakfast
pedir (e:i) to order (food)
probar (o:ue) to taste; to try
recomendar (e:ie) to recommend
servir (e:i) to serve

el menú menu

LAS CARNES, LOS PESCADOS Y LOS MARISCOS

el atún tuna
los camarones shrimp
la carne meat
la carne de res beef
la chuleta de cerdo pork chop
la hamburguesa hamburger
el jamón ham
la langosta lobster
el pavo turkey
el pescado fish
la salchicha sausage
el salmón salmon
los mariscos seafood

el bistec steak

los entremeses hors d'oeuvres

LOS SABORES

agrio/a sour
delicioso/a delicious
dulce sweet
picante hot, spicy
rico/a tasty; delicious
sabroso/a tasty; delicious
salado/a salty

el pollo (asado) (roast) chicken

recursos

WB pp. 75–76 | LM p. 43 | vhlcentral.com

168 ciento sesenta y ocho

¡A comer!

LAS FRUTAS

la banana banana
el limón lemon
la manzana apple
la naranja orange
las uvas grapes

las frutas
fruit

LOS GRANOS Y LAS VERDURAS

el ajo garlic
el arroz rice
las arvejas peas
la cebolla onion
los cereales cereal; grain
los frijoles beans
la lechuga lettuce
el maíz corn
la papa/patata potato
el tomate tomato
las verduras vegetables
la zanahoria carrot

los champiñones
mushrooms

la ensalada
salad

LOS CONDIMENTOS Y OTRAS COMIDAS

el aceite oil
el azúcar sugar
el huevo egg
la mantequilla butter
la margarina margarine
la mayonesa mayonnaise
el pan (tostado) (toasted) bread
las papas/patatas fritas French fries
el queso cheese
la sal salt
la sopa soup
el vinagre vinegar

la pimienta
pepper

LAS BEBIDAS

la bebida drink
la cerveza beer
el jugo (de fruta) (fruit) juice
la leche milk
el refresco soft drink
el té (helado) (iced) tea
el vino (blanco/tinto) (white/red) wine

el café
coffee

el agua (f.) (mineral)
(mineral) water

el sándwich
sandwich

ciento sesenta y nueve **169**

Lección 8

Práctica y conversación  Audio: Activities

1 **¿Lógico o ilógico?** Escucha las oraciones e indica si son **lógicas** o **ilógicas**.

	1.	2.	3.	4.	5.	6.	7.	8.
Lógico								
Ilógico								

2 **¿Qué pide Nora?** Escucha la conversación entre Nora y el camarero en un restaurante. Luego indica las comidas y las bebidas que Nora pide.

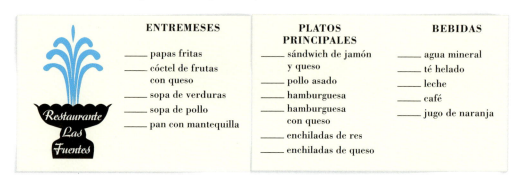

ENTREMESES
____ papas fritas
____ cóctel de frutas con queso
____ sopa de verduras
____ sopa de pollo
____ pan con mantequilla

PLATOS PRINCIPALES
____ sándwich de jamón y queso
____ pollo asado
____ hamburguesa
____ hamburguesa con queso
____ enchiladas de res
____ enchiladas de queso

BEBIDAS
____ agua mineral
____ té helado
____ leche
____ café
____ jugo de naranja

3 **Completar** Completa las oraciones con las palabras correctas.

1. La persona que sirve la comida en un restaurante es el _____.
2. Camarero, ¿puedo ver el _____, por favor?
3. El bistec y el jamón son dos tipos de _____.
4. El té helado, el café y los refrescos son _____.
5. Algo de color blanco que pongo en el café es el _____.
6. Las tres comidas principales del día son el _____, el almuerzo y la cena.

4 **¿Qué es?** Describe cada uno de estos alimentos con alguna característica. Puedes decir de qué color es, qué sabor tiene o cuándo lo comes o lo tomas.

MODELO
El limón es una fruta de color amarillo./Es una fruta agria./Le pongo limón a la ensalada.

1. _____ 2. _____ 3. _____

4. _____ 5. _____ 6. _____ 7. _____ 8. _____

recursos
vhlcentral.com

5 Conversación En parejas, contesten las preguntas.

1. ¿Desayunas? ¿Qué comes y bebes por la mañana?
2. ¿Qué comes generalmente a la hora del almuerzo?
3. ¿Qué comidas prefieres para la cena?
4. ¿Qué tipos de comidas te gustan más: las dulces o las saladas?
5. ¿Te gustan las comidas picantes? ¿Cuáles?
6. ¿Te importa pagar más dinero por comer alimentos orgánicos?

Practice more at vhlcentral.com

Pronunciación ll, ñ, c, and z

Audio: Concepts, Activities

pollo **llave** **ella** **cebolla**

Most Spanish speakers pronounce the letter **ll** like the *y* in *yes*.

mañana **señor** **baño** **niña**

The letter **ñ** is pronounced much like the *ny* in *canyon*.

café **colombiano** **cuando** **rico**

Before **a**, **o**, or **u**, the Spanish **c** is pronounced like the *c* in *car*.

cereales **delicioso** **conducir** **conocer**

Before **e** or **i**, the Spanish **c** is pronounced like the *s* in *sit*. (In parts of Spain, **c** before **e** or **i** is pronounced like the *th* in *think*.)

zeta **zanahoria** **almuerzo** **cerveza**

The Spanish **z** is pronounced like the *s* in *sit*. (In parts of Spain, **z** is pronounced like the *th* in *think*.)

Refranes Lee los refranes en voz alta.

Las apariencias engañan.[1]

Panza llena, corazón contento.[2]

1. Looks can be deceiving.
2. The way to a man's heart is through his stomach.

recursos

LM p. 44

vhlcentral.com

Practice more at vhlcentral.com

¡A comer!

ciento setenta y uno 171

8 ESCENAS

Una cena... romántica **S** Video: *Fotonovela*

Maru y Miguel quieren tener una cena romántica, pero les espera una sorpresa.

Expresiones útiles

Ordering food

¿Qué me recomiendas?
What do you recommend?
Las chuletas de cerdo se ven muy buenas.
The pork chops look good.
¿Les gustaría saber nuestras especialidades del día?
Would you like to hear our specials?
Para el entremés, tenemos ceviche de camarón.
For an appetizer, we have shrimp ceviche.
De plato principal ofrecemos bistec con verduras a la plancha.
For a main course, we have beef with grilled vegetables.
Voy a probar el jamón.
I am going to try the ham.

Describing people and things

¡Qué bonitos! ¿Quién te los dio?
How pretty! Who gave them to you?
Me los compró un chico muy guapo e inteligente.
A really handsome, intelligent guy bought them for me.
¿Es tan guapo como yo?
Is he as handsome as I am?
Sí, como tú, guapísimo.
Yes, like you, gorgeous.
Soy el peor camarero del mundo.
I am the worst waiter in the world.
Él es más responsable que yo.
He is more responsible than I am.

Additional vocabulary
el/la gerente manager
caballero gentleman, sir

MARU No sé qué pedir. ¿Qué me recomiendas?
MIGUEL No estoy seguro. Las chuletas de cerdo se ven muy buenas.
MARU ¿Vas a pedirlas?
MIGUEL No sé.

MIGUEL ¡Qué bonitos! ¿Quién te los dio?
MARU Me los compró un chico muy guapo e inteligente.
MIGUEL ¿Es tan guapo como yo?
MARU Sí, como tú, guapísimo.

(*El camarero llega a la mesa.*)
CAMARERO ¿Les gustaría saber nuestras especialidades del día?
MARU Sí, por favor.
CAMARERO Para el entremés, tenemos ceviche de camarón. De plato principal ofrecemos bistec con verduras a la plancha.

MARU Voy a probar el jamón.
CAMARERO Perfecto. ¿Y para usted, caballero?
MIGUEL Pollo asado con champiñones y papas, por favor.
CAMARERO Excelente.

MIGUEL Por nosotros.
MARU Dos años.

recursos

VM pp. 15–16

vhlcentral.com

172 ciento setenta y dos

¡A comer!

MARU **MIGUEL** **CAMARERO** **JUAN CARLOS** **FELIPE** **GERENTE**

(*en otra parte del restaurante*)
JUAN CARLOS Disculpe. ¿Qué me puede contar del pollo? ¿Dónde lo consiguió el chef?
CAMARERO ¡Oiga! ¿Qué está haciendo?

FELIPE Los espárragos están sabrosísimos esta noche. Usted pidió el pollo, señor. Estos champiñones saben a mantequilla.

GERENTE ¿Qué pasa aquí, Esteban?
CAMARERO Lo siento señor. Me quitaron la comida.
GERENTE (*a Felipe*) Señor, ¿quién es usted? ¿Qué cree que está haciendo?

JUAN CARLOS Felipe y yo les servimos la comida a nuestros amigos. Pero desafortunadamente, salió todo mal.
FELIPE Soy el peor camarero del mundo. ¡Lo siento! Nosotros vamos a pagar la comida.
JUAN CARLOS ¿Nosotros?

FELIPE Todo esto fue idea tuya, Juan Carlos.
JUAN CARLOS ¿Mi idea? ¡Felipe! (*al gerente*) Señor, él es más responsable que yo.
GERENTE Tú y tú, vamos.

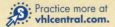

Actividades

1 Escoger Escoge la respuesta que completa mejor cada oración.

1. Miguel lleva a Maru a un restaurante para (almorzar / cenar).
2. El camarero les ofrece como plato principal (ceviche de camarón / bistec con verduras a la plancha).
3. Miguel va a pedir (langosta al horno / pollo asado con champiñones y papas).
4. Felipe les lleva la comida a sus amigos y prueba (el atún y la lechuga / los espárragos y los champiñones).

2 Identificar Indica quién puede decir estas oraciones.

1. Qué desastre. Soy un camarero muy malo.
2. Les recomiendo el bistec con verduras a la plancha.
3. Tal vez escoja las chuletas de cerdo, creo que son muy sabrosas.
4. ¿Qué pasa aquí?
5. Dígame las especialidades del día, por favor.
6. No fue mi idea. Felipe es más responsable que yo.

3 Situaciones En parejas, preparen este diálogo.

- El/La camarero/a le pregunta a un(a) cliente/a qué le puede servir.
- El/La cliente/a pregunta cuál es la especialidad del restaurante.
- El/La camarero/a dice la especialidad y recomienda algunos platos del menú.
- El/La cliente/a pide entremeses, un plato principal y una bebida.
- El/La camarero/a le sirve la comida.

ciento setenta y tres **173**

8 EXPLORACIÓN

BAJO LA LUPA

Frutas y verduras de América

Additional Reading
Video: *Flash cultura*

Imagínate una pizza sin salsa° de tomate o una hamburguesa sin papas fritas. Ahora piensa que quieres ver una película, pero las palomitas de maíz° y el chocolate no existen. ¡Qué mundo° tan insípido°! Muchas de las comidas más populares del mundo tienen ingredientes esenciales que son originarios del continente llamado Nuevo Mundo. Estas frutas y verduras no fueron introducidas en Europa sino hasta° el siglo° XVI.

El tomate, por ejemplo, era° usado como planta ornamental cuando llegó por primera vez a Europa porque pensaron que era venenoso°. El maíz, por su parte, era ya la base de la comida de muchos países latinoamericanos muchos siglos antes de la llegada de los españoles.

La papa fue un alimento° básico para los incas. Incluso consiguieron deshidratarla para almacenarla° por largos períodos de tiempo. El cacao (planta con la que se hace el chocolate) fue muy importante para los aztecas y los mayas. Ellos usaban sus semillas° como moneda° y como ingrediente de diversas salsas. También las molían° para preparar una bebida, mezclándolas° con agua ¡y con chile!

El aguacate°, la guayaba°, la papaya, la piña y el maracuyá (o fruta de la pasión) son otros ejemplos de frutas originarias de América que son hoy día conocidas en todo el mundo.

¿En qué alimentos encontramos estas frutas y verduras?

Tomate: pizza, ketchup, salsa de tomate, sopa de tomate
Maíz: palomitas de maíz, tamales, tortillas, arepas (Colombia y Venezuela), pan
Papa: papas fritas, frituras de papa°, puré de papas°, sopa de papas, tortilla de patatas (España)
Cacao: mole (México), chocolatinas°, cereales, helados°, tartas°
Aguacate: guacamole (México), cóctel de camarones, sopa de aguacate, nachos, enchiladas hondureñas

Mole

recursos

VM pp. 47–48

vhlcentral.com

Practice more at vhlcentral.com.

salsa *sauce*   palomitas de maíz *popcorn*   mundo *world*   insípido *flavorless*
hasta *until*   siglo *century*   era *was*   venenoso *poisonous*   alimento *food*
almacenarla *to store it*   semillas *seeds*   moneda *currency*   las molían *they used to grind them*   mezclándolas *mixing them*   aguacate *avocado*
guayaba *guava*   frituras de papa *chips*   puré de papas *mashed potatoes*
chocolatinas *chocolate bars*   helados *ice cream*   tartas *cakes*

174 ciento setenta y cuatro

¡A comer!

ACTIVIDADES

1 **¿Cierto o falso?** Indica si lo que dicen las oraciones es **cierto** o **falso**.

1. El tomate se introdujo en Europa como planta ornamental.
2. Los incas sólo consiguieron almacenar las papas por poco tiempo.
3. Los aztecas y los mayas usaron las papas como moneda.
4. El maíz era una comida poco popular en Latinoamérica.
5. El aguacate era el alimento básico de los incas.
6. El mole se hace con chocolate.
7. El aguacate, la guayaba, la papaya, la piña y el maracuyá son originarios de América.
8. Las arepas se hacen con cacao.
9. El aguacate es un ingrediente del cóctel de camarones.
10. En España hacen una tortilla con papas.

2 **¿Qué te gusta?** Describe tres de tus comidas favoritas que tengan como ingredientes alguna fruta o verdura de América. ¿Qué ingredientes tienen? ¿Cuándo las comes? ¿Cómo se sirven?

La comida latina

1 **Preparación** ¿Probaste alguna vez comida latina? ¿Qué plato? ¿La compraste en un supermercado o fuiste a un restaurante? ¿Te gustó?

2 **El video** Mira el episodio de **Flash cultura**.

Vocabulario

cocinar to cook	**el plato** dish (in a meal)
¿Está lista para ordenar? Are you ready to order?	**pruébala** try it, taste it

Marta nos mostrará° algunos de los platos de la comida mexicana.

… hay más lugares donde podemos comprar productos hispanos.

°**mostrará** will show

3 **¿Cierto o falso?** Indica si las oraciones son **ciertas** o **falsas**.

1. En Los Ángeles hay comida de países latinoamericanos y de España.
2. Leticia explica que la tortilla del taco americano es blanda *(soft)* y la del taco mexicano es dura *(hard)*.
3. Las ventas *(sales)* de salsa son bajas en los Estados Unidos.
4. Leticia fue a un restaurante ecuatoriano.
5. Leticia probó Inca Kola en un supermercado.

CONEXIÓN INTERNET

¿Qué otro plato típico puedes encontrar en los países hispanos? For more information about **Exploración**, go to **vhlcentral.com**.

ciento setenta y cinco 175

8 GRAMÁTICA

8.1 Preterite of stem-changing verbs  Tutorial

¿Quién pidió el jamón?

Yo lo pedí.

▶ As you know, **–ar** and **–er** stem-changing verbs have no stem change in the preterite. **–Ir** stem-changing verbs, however, do have a stem change.

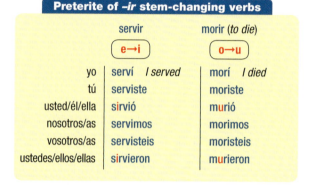

Preterite of –ir stem-changing verbs

	servir (e→i)	morir (to die) (o→u)
yo	serví / I served	morí / I died
tú	serviste	moriste
usted/él/ella	s**i**rvió	m**u**rió
nosotros/as	servimos	morimos
vosotros/as	servisteis	moristeis
ustedes/ellos/ellas	s**i**rvieron	m**u**rieron

▶ In the preterite, stem-changing **–ir** verbs have an **e** to **i** or **o** to **u** stem change in the **Ud./él/ella** and **Uds./ellos/ellas** forms.

INFINITIVE	VERB STEM	STEM CHANGE	PRETERITE
pedir	ped–	pid–	pidió, pidieron
dormir	dor–	dur–	durmió, durmieron

¡ojo!
Conseguir, divertirse *(to have fun)*, **preferir, repetir, seguir, sentir, sugerir** *(to suggest)*, and **vestirse** are other **-ir** verbs that change their stem vowel in the preterite.

ESPAÑOL EN VIVO

Tu_cocina.com

Tu_cocina.com te prepara los mejores platos para eventos sociales y personalizados. ¡Pruébalos ya°!

¿Viste° los comentarios de nuestros clientes? ¿Qué esperas?

Carmen Moreno ¡Prefiero este servicio a cualquier otro!

Ana Tejada Pedí cuarenta arepas° y me las prepararon en menos de dos horas.

Manuel Sánchez Serví cachapas° en la cena y todos mis invitados repitieron.

ya *now* **arepas** *cornmeal pancakes* **cachapas** *grilled pancakes made from fresh corn dough* **Viste** *Did you see*

176 ciento setenta y seis

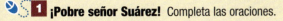

Práctica y conversación

1 ¡Pobre señor Suárez! Completa las oraciones.

1. Los señores Suárez llegaron al restaurante a las ocho y _____ [seguir] al camarero a una mesa.
2. El señor Suárez _____ [pedir] una chuleta de cerdo. La señora Suárez decidió probar los camarones.
3. El camarero _____ [repetir] el pedido (*the order*).
4. La comida tardó mucho (*took a long time*) en llegar y los señores Suárez casi (*almost*) _____ [dormirse] esperándola.
5. A las nueve el camarero les _____ [servir] la comida.
6. Después de comer la chuleta de cerdo, el señor Suárez _____ [sentirse] muy mal.
7. ¡Pobre señor Suárez! ¿Por qué no _____ [pedir] los camarones?

2 El camarero distraído Indica lo que los clientes pidieron y lo que un camarero distraído (*distracted*) les sirvió.

MODELO
Claudia / hamburguesa
Claudia pidió una hamburguesa, pero el camarero le sirvió zanahorias.

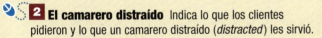

1. Juan y Rafael / té helado   3. Laura / arroz
   _____   _____

2. Nosotros / papas fritas   4. Tú / salmón
   _____   _____

3 Preguntas Averigua (*Find out*) si tu compañero/a hizo estas actividades la semana pasada. Comparte los resultados con la clase.

¿Pediste una pizza con champiñones?
No, pedí una pizza con carne.

Actividades	Respuestas
1. pedir una pizza con salame	_____
2. dormir más de diez horas	_____
3. quedarse dormido en clase	_____
4. pedir un plato muy caro en un restaurante elegante	_____
5. preferir quedarse en casa en lugar de (*instead of*) salir con amigos	_____
6. ir a una fiesta y vestirse con ropa muy formal	_____

4 Una cena romántica En grupos, imaginen que sus amigos, Eduardo y Rosa, salieron a cenar en su primera cita (*date*). Usen las preguntas como guía (*as a guide*).

- ¿Adónde salieron a cenar?
- ¿Qué pidieron?
- ¿Les sirvieron la comida rápidamente (*quickly*)?
- ¿Les gustó la comida?
- ¿Cuánto costó? ¿Quién pagó?
- ¿Van a volver otra vez a ese restaurante en el futuro?
- ¿Van a salir juntos otra vez? ¿Por qué?

Practice more at vhlcentral.com.

ciento setenta y siete 177

Lección 8

8.2 Double object pronouns  Tutorial

▸ You have already learned that direct and indirect object pronouns replace nouns. You'll now learn how to use these pronouns together.

INDIRECT OBJECT PRONOUNS			DIRECT OBJECT PRONOUNS	
me	nos		lo	los
te	os	+		
le (se)	les (se)		la	las

▸ When object pronouns are used together, the indirect object pronoun precedes the direct object pronoun.

¿Quién te los dio?

Me los compró un chico muy guapo.

▸ The indirect object pronouns **le** and **les** always change to **se** when they precede **lo**, **los**, **la**, and **las**.

El camarero está sirviéndoselas.

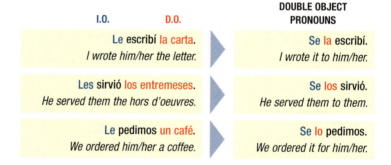

Lo siento, señor, ¡no me dejaron traérsela!

▸ Because **se** has multiple meanings, you can clarify to whom the pronoun refers by adding **a usted**, **a él**, **a ella**, **a ustedes**, **a ellos**, or **a ellas**.

¿El sombrero? Carlos **se** lo vendió **a ella**.
The hat? Carlos sold it to her.

¿Las llaves? Ya **se** las di **a ella**.
The keys? I already gave them to her.

▸ Double object pronouns are placed before a conjugated verb. With infinitives and present participles, double object pronouns may be placed before the conjugated verb or attached to the end of the infinitive or present participle.

178   ciento setenta y ocho

¡A comer!

▶ When double object pronouns are attached to an infinitive or a present participle, an accent mark is added to maintain the original stress.

Me lo estoy poniendo.
Estoy poniéndo**melo**.
I am putting it on.

Se la van a traer.
Van a traér**sela**.
They are going to bring it to you.

Práctica y conversación

1 ¿Quién? Cambia los sustantivos subrayados (*underlined nouns*) por pronombres de objeto directo.

MODELO
¿Quién va a traerme la carne del supermercado? [Mi esposo]
Mi esposo va a traérmela./Mi esposo me la va a traer.

1. ¿Quién les mandó las invitaciones a los invitados (*guests*)? [Mi hija] _____
2. ¿Quién me puede comprar el pan? [Mi hijo] _____
3. ¿Quién puede prestarme los platos que necesito? [Mi mamá] _____
4. ¡Los postres (*desserts*)! ¿Quién está preparándonos los postres? [Silvia y Renata] _____
5. Nos falta mantequilla. ¿Quién nos trae la mantequilla? [Mi cuñada] _____

2 En un restaurante En parejas, representen las conversaciones entre un(a) camarero/a y unos clientes.

MODELO
Sra. Guzmán: Una hamburguesa, por favor.
Camarero/a: Enseguida (*right away*) se la traigo.

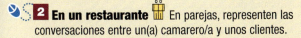

Sra. Guzmán

1. Tus compañeros/as de cuarto
2. Tu profesor(a) de español
3. Tú

4. Tus padres
5. Srta. Salas
6. Dr. Cifuentes

3 Contestar En parejas, háganse preguntas usando las palabras interrogativas **¿Quién?** o **¿Cuándo?**

MODELO
nos enseña español
Estudiante 1: ¿Quién nos enseña español?
Estudiante 2: La profesora Castro nos lo enseña.

1. te escribe mensajes electrónicos
2. me vas a prestar tu computadora
3. les vende los libros de texto a los estudiantes
4. le enseñó español al/a la profesor(a)
5. te compró esa camiseta
6. me vas a mostrar tu casa o apartamento

4 Preguntas En parejas, háganse estas preguntas. Usen pronombres de objeto directo e indirecto en cada respuesta.

MODELO
Estudiante 1: ¿Quién te va a preparar el desayuno esta mañana?
Estudiante 2: Yo me lo voy a preparar.

1. ¿Me prestas tu coche (*car*)?
2. ¿Me puedes comprar un coche nuevo?
3. ¿Quién te presta dinero cuando lo necesitas?
4. ¿Les prestas tu casa a tus amigos? ¿Por qué?
5. ¿Nos compras el almuerzo a mí y a los otros compañeros de clase?
6. ¿Me describes tu casa?
7. ¿Quién te va a preparar la cena esta noche?
8. ¿Vas a leerles el cuento (*story*) de "Blancanieves" (*Snow White*) a tus nietos? ¿Qué otros cuentos les vas a leer?

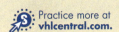

Lección 8

8.3 Saber and conocer  Tutorial

▶ Spanish has two verbs that mean *to know*, **saber** and **conocer**, but they are used differently. Note that only the **yo** forms of **saber** and **conocer** are irregular in the present tense.

Saber and conocer

	saber	conocer
yo	sé	conozco
tú	sabes	conoces
usted/él/ella	sabe	conoce
nosotros/as	sabemos	conocemos
vosotros/as	sabéis	conocéis
ustedes/ellos/ellas	saben	conocen

▶ **Saber** means *to know a fact or piece(s) of information* or *to know how to do something.*

No **sé** tu número de teléfono.
I don't know your telephone number.

Mi hermana **sabe** hablar francés.
My sister knows how to speak French.

▶ **Conocer** means *to know or be familiar/acquainted with a person, place, or thing.*

¿**Conoces** la ciudad de Nueva York?
Do you know New York City?

No **conozco** a tu amigo Esteban.
I don't know your friend Esteban.

▶ As you learned in **Lección 5**, when the direct object of **conocer** is a person or pet, the personal **a** is used.

¿**Conoces a** Rigoberta Menchú?
Do you know Rigoberta Menchú?

¿**Conoces** ese restaurante?
Do you know that restaurant?

▶ These verbs are conjugated like **conocer** in the **yo** form in the present. You will learn how to use **saber**, **conocer**, and related verbs in the preterite in Lesson 9.

conducir (*to drive*)	conduzco, conduces, conduce, etc.
ofrecer (*to offer*)	ofrezco, ofreces, ofrece, etc.
parecer (*to seem*)	parezco, pareces, parece, etc.
traducir (*to translate*)	traduzco, traduces, traduce, etc.

cumpleaños *birthday* **divertirse** *to have fun* **un poco de todo** *a little bit of everything*

180 ciento ochenta

¡A comer!

Práctica y conversación

1 Completar Completa las oraciones con la forma apropiada de **saber** o **conocer**.

1. —Nosotros no _____ Guatemala.
   —Ah, ¿no? Pues yo _____ bien las ciudades de Escuintla, Quetzaltenango y Antigua.
2. —¿_____ ustedes dónde vive Pilar?
   —No, nosotras no _____.
3. Mi amiga Carla _____ conducir, pero yo no _____.
4. —¿_____ a Mateo, mi hermano mayor?
   —No, no lo _____.
5. —Todavía no _____ a tu novio.
   —Sí, ya lo _____.
6. Tú _____ esquiar, pero Tino y Luis son pequeños y no _____.
7. Roberto _____ bien el *Popol Vuh*, el libro sagrado de los mayas; también _____ leer los jeroglíficos de los templos mayas.

2 Oraciones Combina las palabras de las tres columnas para formar oraciones.

MODELO
No conozco a Cameron Díaz. Yo conozco a Angelina Jolie.

Sujetos	Verbos	Objetos directos
Jessica Sánchez	(no) conocer	Cameron Díaz
Lady Gaga	(no) saber	Angelina Jolie
Ozzy Osbourne		cantar
Brad Pitt		la ciudad de Montreal en Canadá
Enrique Iglesias		hablar dos lenguas extranjeras
Miguel Cabrera		hacer reír (*laugh*) a la gente
yo		actuar (*perform*) bien
tú		escribir novelas de terror
tu compañero/a		programar computadoras
tu profesor(a)		muchas personas importantes

3 Deportes Pregúntale a un(a) compañero/a qué deportes practica y por qué. Usen los verbos **saber** y **conocer**.

MODELO
Estudiante 1: ¿Sabes esquiar?
Estudiante 2: Sí, sé esquiar./No, no sé esquiar.
Estudiante 1: ¿Por qué?
Estudiante 2: Porque mi papá me enseñó./Porque no me gusta el invierno.

1.   2.   3.

4.   5.   6.

4 Preguntas Con un(a) compañero/a, contesten las siguientes preguntas.

1. ¿Qué restaurantes buenos conoces? ¿Cenas en esos restaurantes frecuentemente (*frequently*)?
2. En tu familia, ¿quién sabe cocinar mejor (*best*)?
3. ¿Conoces algún mercado cerca que tenga (*has*) productos orgánicos? ¿Vas allí con frecuencia?
4. ¿Sabes recetas de comidas latinas? ¿Cuáles?
5. ¿Conoces a algún/alguna chef famoso/a? ¿Qué tipo de comida prepara?
6. ¿Sabes preparar algún plato especial? ¿Cuál es?
7. ¿Sabes que el ajo es bueno para la salud (*health*)? ¿Qué otras comidas o condimentos saludables conoces?
8. ¿Conoces a alguna persona que come solamente hamburguesas y papas fritas?

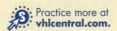
Practice more at **vhlcentral.com**.

ciento ochenta y uno 181

Lección 8

8.4 Comparisons and superlatives  Tutorial

▶ Comparisons of inequality are formed by placing **más** (*more*) or **menos** (*less*) before adjectives, adverbs, and nouns and **que** (*than*) after them. When the comparison involves a numerical expression, use **de** before the number.

La ensalada es menos cara que la sopa.

El té es **más caro que** el jugo.
Tea is more expensive than juice.

Susana es **menos generosa que** su prima.
Susana is less generous than her cousin.

Luis se despierta **más temprano que** yo.
Luis gets up earlier than I (do).

Tomo **más clases que** Enrique.
I take more classes than Enrique (does).

▶ With verbs, use this construction to make comparisons of inequality:
[*verb*] + **más/menos que**.

¿El pollo es más rico que el jamón?

Mis hermanos **comen más que** yo.
My brothers eat more than I (do).

Arturo **duerme menos que** su padre.
Arturo sleeps less than his father (does).

▶ The constructions **tan** + [*adverb, adjective*] + **como** and **tanto/a(s)** + [*singular noun, plural noun*] + **como** are used to make comparisons of equality.

Este plato es **tan delicioso como** aquél.
This dish is as delicious as that one.

Yo comí **tanta comida como** tú.
I ate as much food as you (did).

Tu amigo es **tan simpático como** tú.
Your friend is as nice as you (are).

Ustedes probaron **tantos platos como** ellos.
You tried as many dishes as they (did).

▶ Comparisons of equality with verbs are formed by placing **tanto como** after the verb. Note that **tanto** does not change in number or gender.

No **duermo tanto como** mi tía.
I don't sleep as much as my aunt (does).

Estudiamos tanto como ustedes.
We study as much as you (do).

▶ Form the superlative with this construction: **el/la/los/las** + [*noun*] + **más/menos** + [*adjective*] + **de** Note that the noun is preceded by a definite article. **De** is equivalent to the English *in* or *of*.

Es **el café más rico del** país.
It's the most delicious coffee in the country.

Son **las tiendas menos caras de** la ciudad.
They are the least expensive stores in the city.

¡ojo!

The absolute superlative, which ends in **–ísimo/a(s)**, is equivalent to the English *extremely/very* + [*adjective/adverb*]. For example: **muchísimo/a(s)** (*very much*), **malísimo/a(s)** (*very bad*), **facilísimo/a(s)** (*extremely easy*).

▶ The noun in a superlative construction can be omitted if it is clear to whom or what the superlative refers.

¿El restaurante El Cráter? Es **el más elegante de** la ciudad.
The El Cráter restaurant? It's the most elegant (one) in the city.

¡ojo!

Note that **joven** takes an accent in its plural form. **Los jóvenes estudian mucho.**

Irregular comparative and superlative forms

Adjectives		Comparative form		Superlative form	
bueno/a	good	mejor	better	el/la mejor	(the) best
malo/a	bad	peor	worse	el/la peor	(the) worst
grande	big; old	mayor	bigger	el/la mayor	(the) biggest
pequeño/a	small; young	menor	smaller	el/la menor	(the) smallest
joven	young	menor	younger	el/la menor	(the) youngest
viejo/a	old	mayor	older	el/la mayor	(the) oldest

¡A comer!

▶ When **grande** and **pequeño/a** refer to age, use the irregular comparative and superlative forms, **mayor/menor**. However, when **grande** and **pequeño/a** refer to size, use the regular forms, **más grande/más pequeño/a**.

Isabel es **la mayor**.
Isabel is the oldest.

Tu ensalada es **más grande que** ésa.
Your salad is bigger than that one.

▶ **Bien** and **mal** have the same comparative forms as **bueno/a** and **malo/a**.

Julio nada **mejor que** los otros chicos.
Julio swims better than the other boys.

Ellas cantan **peor que** las otras chicas.
They sing worse than the other girls.

Práctica y conversación

Practice more at vhlcentral.com.

1 Dos parejas de hermanos Escoge (*choose*) la palabra correcta para comparar a las hermanas Lucila y Teresa y a los hermanos Mario y Luis.

Lucila y Teresa

Mario y Luis

1. Lucila es más alta y más atractiva _____ [de, más, menos, que] Teresa.
2. Teresa es más delgada porque practica _____ [de, más, menos, que] deportes que Lucila.
3. Mario es _____ [tan, tanto, tantos, tantas] interesante como Luis.
4. Mario viaja _____ [tan, tanto, tantos, tantas] como Luis.
5. A Teresa le gusta quedarse en casa. Va a _____ [de, más, menos, que] fiestas que su hermana.
6. Lucila es _____ [más, menos de, más que] simpática que Teresa porque es alegre.
7. Luis habla _____ [tan, tanto, tantos, tantas] lenguas extranjeras como Mario.
8. ¡Qué casualidad (*coincidence*)! Mario y Luis también son hermanos, pero no hay _____ [tan, tanto, tanta, tantos, tantas] diferencia entre ellos como entre Lucila y Teresa.

2 La familia García  En grupos, túrnense (*take turns*) para hacer comparaciones entre Rafael, Eva, Esteban y Lourdes.

MODELO
Estudiante 1: Esteban es el más activo de la familia.
Estudiante 2: Pues yo creo que Rafael es tan activo como Esteban.
Estudiante 1: Mmm, pero Esteban es mucho más delgado.

3 Comparaciones En parejas, conversen sobre estos temas: cafés y restaurantes, comidas favoritas, los cursos que toman, libros favoritos, periódicos, personas famosas, los profesores, música de moda. Luego, compartan tres datos interesantes con la clase.

MODELO artistas de moda
Estudiante 1: Creo que Adele es la mejor artista de estos tiempos.
Estudiante 2: ¡Pero qué dices! Esa artista es malísima. Rihanna y Snoop son los mejores. Además, Adele no se viste tan bien como Rihanna.
Estudiante 1: Estás loco. Adele siempre está a la moda. Además, te repito que es la mejor. Por ejemplo, ya tiene más de veinte millones de copias vendidas (*copies sold*).

ciento ochenta y tres **183**

Lección 8

Ampliación

1 Escuchar

A Rosa y Roberto están en un restaurante. Escucha la conversación entre ellos y la camarera y toma nota de cuáles son los especiales del día.

> **TIP** **Jot down notes as you listen.** Jotting down notes while you listen can help you keep track of the important points or details. Focus actively on comprehension rather than on remembering what you have heard.

Los especiales del día

_____ _____ _____

B Usa tus notas para completar las oraciones con la opción correcta.

1. La camarera les dio información sobre _____ (dos / tres / cuatro) especiales del día.
2. Rosa pidió _____ (el arroz con pollo / bistec a la criolla / cerdo con salsa de champiñones y papas).
3. Roberto pidió _____ (los entremeses / bistec a la criolla / cerdo con salsa de champiñones y papas).
4. Roberto va a comer _____ (más platos que / menos platos que / tantos platos como) Rosa.

2 Conversar

En parejas, conversen sobre la última vez (*the last time*) que fueron a un restaurante. Utilicen las preguntas como guía.

- ¿Cuándo fue la última vez que fuiste a un restaurante?
- ¿Con quién comiste?
- ¿A qué restaurante fueron?
- ¿Qué pidieron? ¿Les gustó la comida?
- ¿Se la sirvieron rápidamente (*quickly*)?
- ¿Fue mejor o peor que la comida que comes en casa?
- ¿Van a volver a ese restaurante en el futuro?

¡A comer!

3 **Escribir** Escribe una crítica sobre un restaurante local.

TIP **Expressing and supporting opinions.** Use details, facts, examples, and other forms of evidence to convince your readers to take your opinions seriously.

Organízalo — Usa un mapa de ideas para organizar comentarios sobre la comida, el servicio, el ambiente (*atmosphere*) y otros datos sobre el restaurante.

Escríbelo — Utiliza tus notas para escribir el primer borrador de la crítica.

Corrígelo — Intercambia (*exchange*) tu composición con la de un(a) compañero/a. Comenta sobre el título, la organización, los detalles específicos y los errores de gramática o de ortografía.

Compártelo — Revisa el primer borrador teniendo en cuenta los comentarios de tu compañero/a. Incorpora nuevas ideas o más información para reforzar (*support*) tu opinión. Luego entrégale (*hand it in*) la crítica a tu profesor(a).

4 **Un paso más** Diseña el menú de un nuevo restaurante en la capital de un país hispano.

- Decide en qué país y ciudad vas a abrir el restaurante.
- Investiga cuáles son las comidas típicas y los platos más populares del país.
- Elige el nombre del restaurante.
- Diseña el menú, incluyendo entremeses, platos principales, ensaladas, postres y bebidas.
- Indica los precios de los platos en la moneda del país.
- Intercambia tu menú con los de tres o cuatro compañeros/as y comparen los platos que escogieron.

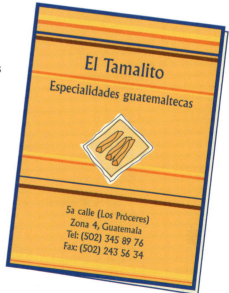

Investiga estos temas en vhlcentral.com.

- Capitales de los países hispanos
- Comidas del mundo hispano

ciento ochenta y cinco **185**

8 LECTURA

Antes de leer

Reading for the main idea is a useful strategy. Locate the topic sentences of each paragraph to determine the author's purpose for writing. In particular, the first sentence in each paragraph usually provides clues about its content, as well as impressions of how the entire reading selection is organized.

Examinar el texto
Aquí se presentan dos textos distintos. ¿Qué estrategias puedes usar para leer la crítica? ¿Cuáles son las estrategias apropiadas para familiarizarte con el menú? Utiliza las más eficaces para cada texto. Luego, identifica las estrategias similares que se aplican en los dos textos.

Identificar la idea principal
Lee la primera oración de cada párrafo de la crítica del restaurante **El Palmito**. Apunta el tema principal de cada párrafo. Luego lee el primer párrafo. ¿Crees que el restaurante le gustó a la autora? ¿Por qué? Ahora lee la crítica entera. En tu opinión, ¿cuál es la idea principal de la crítica? ¿Por qué la escribió la autora? Compara tus opiniones con las de un(a) compañero/a.

El Tiempo de Guatemala   37E

Restaurantes
Domingo 9 de mayo, Antigua, Guatemala

Cinco estrellas para El Palmito

Margarita Galán, crítica de restaurantes

El viernes pasado me sorprendí° cuando encontré un restaurante fantástico en el barrio donde vivo. Cené en el restaurante **El Palmito**, donde se mezclan° de una manera extraordinaria la comida tradicional de Centroamérica y la belleza arquitectónica de nuestra ciudad. Su propietario, Héctor Suárez, es uno de los chefs más respetados de Guatemala.

El exterior del restaurante refleja el estilo colonial de la ciudad. Por dentro°, la decoración rústica crea un ambiente cálido°. Hay que mencionar también el hermoso patio, lleno° de plantas y flores, donde muchas personas se reúnen para tomar un café en un ambiente relajado° y cordial.

Uno no se puede quejar° del servicio de **El Palmito**. El personal del restaurante es muy amable y atento, desde los cocineros que preparan la comida hasta los camareros que la sirven.

La comida del restaurante es exquisita. Las tortillas, que se sirven con ajiaceite, son deliciosas. La sopa de pollo y huevo es excelente, y los frijoles enchilados, ricos. También recomiendo el tomaticán, cocinado con una gran variedad de verduras muy ricas. De postre°, don Héctor me preparó su especialidad, un rico pastel de yogur.

Les recomiendo que visiten **El Palmito** cuando tengan ocasión°.

El Palmito
*de lunes a sábado 10:00a.m.-11:00p.m.
domingo 11:00a.m.-10:00p.m.*

Comida ★★★★★
Servicio ★★★★★
Ambiente ★★★★★
Precio ★★★★

---

recursos

vhlcentral.com

186   ciento ochenta y seis

¡A comer!

Después de leer

¿Comprendiste?
Completa cada oración con la opción correcta.

1. La arquitectura del restaurante es _____ [moderna, colonial, fea].
2. A muchos clientes les gusta tomar el café en _____ [las mesas, el bar, el patio].
3. El dueño del restaurante es uno de los _____ [peores, menores, mejores] chefs de Guatemala.
4. La comida en este restaurante, según la autora, es _____ [muy buena, mala, regular].
5. La crítica _____ [no da información, habla bien, se queja] del restaurante.

Preguntas
Responde a estas preguntas con oraciones completas.

1. ¿Cómo se llama el dueño del restaurante?
   _____
2. ¿Qué tipo de comida se sirve en El Palmito?
   _____
3. ¿Cómo es el ambiente del restaurante?
   _____
4. ¿Quién escribió este artículo?
   _____
5. ¿Cuál es la profesión de la autora del artículo?
   _____
6. ¿Cuántos platos probó la autora del artículo?
   _____

Coméntalo
¿Te interesan las comidas y bebidas que sirven en El Palmito? ¿Cuáles te parecen más interesantes? ¿Por qué? ¿Se sirven platos y bebidas similares a éstos en donde vives?

MENÚ

Entremeses
Pan tostado con
• Queso frito   • Huevos revueltos°

Tortillas con
• Ajicomino (chile, comino°)   • Ajiaceite (chile, aceite)

Sopas
• Cebolla   • Verduras   • Pollo y huevo   • Mariscos

Platos Principales
Chilaquil
(tortilla de maíz, queso y chile)

Tomaticán
(tomate, papas, maíz, chile, arvejas y zanahorias)

Tamales
(maíz, azúcar, ajo, cebolla)

Frijoles enchilados
(frijoles negros, carne de cerdo o de res, arroz, chile)

Postres
• Helado° de limón   • Plátanos° caribeños
• Uvate (uvas, azúcar y ron°)   • Pastel de yogur

Bebidas
• Té helado   • Vino tinto
• Vino blanco   • Agua mineral   • Jugos
• Chilate (maíz, chile y cacao)

---

sorprendí *was surprised*   mezclan *mix*   Por dentro *Inside*   ambiente cálido *warm atmosphere*   Hay que *One must*   lleno *full*   ambiente *atmosphere*
relajado *relaxed*   Uno no se puede quejar *One can't complain*   postre *dessert*
cuando tengan ocasión *when you have the opportunity*   Huevos revueltos
Scrambled eggs   comino *cumin*   Helado *Ice cream*   Plátanos *Plantains*   ron *rum*

ciento ochenta y siete **187**

VOCABULARIO

Las comidas

el/la camarero/a	waiter/waitress
el/la dueño/a	owner
el menú	menu
la sección de (no) fumadores	(non) smoking section
el almuerzo	lunch
la cena	dinner
la comida	food; meal
el desayuno	breakfast
los entremeses	hors d'oeuvres
el plato (principal)	(main) dish
agrio/a	sour
delicioso/a	delicious
dulce	sweet
picante	hot, spicy
rico/a	tasty; delicious
sabroso/a	tasty; delicious
salado/a	salty
almorzar (o:ue)	to have lunch
cenar	to have dinner
desayunar	to have breakfast
pedir (e:i)	to order (food)
probar (o:ue)	to taste; to try
recomendar (e:ie)	to recommend
servir (e:i)	to serve

Las bebidas

el agua (f.) (mineral)	(mineral) water
la bebida	drink
el café	coffee
la cerveza	beer
el jugo (de fruta)	(fruit) juice
la leche	milk
el refresco	soft drink
el té (helado)	(iced) tea
el vino (blanco/tinto)	(white/red) wine

Los granos y las verduras

el ajo	garlic
el arroz	rice
las arvejas	peas
la cebolla	onion
los cereales	cereal; grains
el champiñón	mushroom
la ensalada	salad
los frijoles	beans
la lechuga	lettuce
el maíz	corn
las papas/patatas	potatoes
el tomate	tomato
las verduras	vegetables
la zanahoria	carrot

Las carnes, los pescados y los mariscos

el atún	tuna
el bistec	steak
los camarones	shrimp
la carne	meat
la carne de res	beef
la chuleta de cerdo	pork chop
la hamburguesa	hamburger
el jamón	ham
la langosta	lobster
los mariscos	seafood
el pavo	turkey
el pescado	fish
el pollo (asado)	(roast) chicken
la salchicha	sausage
el salmón	salmon

Las frutas

la banana	banana
las frutas	fruit
el limón	lemon
la manzana	apple
la naranja	orange
las uvas	grapes

Los condimentos y otras comidas

el aceite	oil
el azúcar	sugar
el huevo	egg
la mantequilla	butter
la margarina	margarine
la mayonesa	mayonnaise
el pan (tostado)	(toasted) bread
las papas/patatas fritas	French fries
la pimienta	pepper
el queso	cheese
la sal	salt
el sándwich	sandwich
la sopa	soup
el vinagre	vinegar

Verbos

conocer	to know; to be acquainted with
conducir	to drive
morir (o:ue)	to die
ofrecer	to offer
parecer	to seem; to appear
saber	to know; to know how
traducir	to translate

Comparisons and superlatives	See pages 182–183.

¡VIVAN LOS PAÍSES HISPANOS!

El Amazonas es el río más caudaloso (*the most vast*) del mundo. Por ser muy profundo (*deep*) y ancho (*wide*), tiene otro nombre: "río océano". Desde barcos muy grandes hasta barcos pequeños, como la canoa que vemos en la foto, navegan en él. Alrededor (*around*) del río Amazonas hay una gran selva (*jungle*) y muy poca gente vive allí.

Suramérica I

Venezuela

Área: 912.050 km^2 (352.144 millas^2)
Población: 28.048.000
Capital: Caracas–3.051.000
Ciudades principales: Maracaibo, Valencia, Maracay, Barquisimeto
Moneda: bolívar

SOURCE: Population Division, UN Secretariat & CIA World Factbook

Colombia

Área: 1.138.910 km^2 (439.734 millas^2)
Población: 45.239.000
Capital: Bogotá–8.262.000
Ciudades principales: Cali, Medellín, Barranquilla, Cartagena
Moneda: peso colombiano

SOURCE: Population Division, UN Secretariat & CIA World Factbook

Ecuador

Área: 283.560 km^2 (109.483 millas^2)
Población: 15.224.000
Capital: Quito–1.801.000
Ciudades principales: Guayaquil, Cuenca, Machala, Portoviejo
Moneda: dólar estadounidense

SOURCE: Population Division, UN Secretariat & CIA World Factbook

Perú

Área: 1.285.220 km^2 (496.224 millas^2)
Población: 29.550.000
Capital: Lima–8.769.000
Ciudades principales: Arequipa, Trujillo, Chiclayo, Iquitos
Moneda: nuevo sol

SOURCE: Population Division, UN Secretariat & CIA World Factbook

¡Vivan los países hispanos!

S Interactive map
Video: *Países hispanos*

Gente

Indígenas de Ecuador

Ecuador tiene una gran población indígena *(native)*. La lengua oficial de Ecuador es el español, pero hoy día también se hablan *(are spoken)* otras lenguas. Aproximadamente unos cuatro millones de ecuatorianos hablan lenguas indígenas; la mayoría de ellos habla quechua. Las comunidades indígenas de Ecuador son excelentes tejedores *(weavers)*; sus tejidos son famosos en todo el mundo por sus colores vivos y sus hermosos diseños *(designs)*. En el mercado de Otavalo se venden mantas *(blankets)*, ropas tradicionales y tapices *(tapestries)* hechos por estas comunidades.

Lugares

El Salto Ángel

El Salto Ángel, en el sureste de Venezuela, es la catarata *(waterfall)* más alta del mundo. Tiene 979 metros (3.212 pies) de altura *(height)*. Es diecisiete veces más alta que las cataratas del Niágara. James C. Angel "descubrió" esta catarata en 1937 y por eso lleva su nombre. Está en el Parque Nacional Canaima y los indígenas la llaman *Kerepakupai Merú*, que significa "catarata".

190 *ciento noventa*

Suramérica I

Literatura

Gabriel García Márquez

Gabriel García Márquez es uno de los escritores contemporáneos más importantes del mundo. Publicó su primer cuento (*short story*) en 1947, cuando era estudiante universitario. Su libro más conocido, *Cien años de soledad*, está escrito en el estilo (*style*) literario llamado "realismo mágico", un estilo que mezcla (*mixes*) la realidad con lo irreal y lo mítico (*mythical*). García Márquez recibió el Premio Nobel de Literatura en 1982.

Economía

Las alpacas del Perú

La alpaca es un animal suramericano de la familia de la llama y la vicuña. Vive en rebaños (*herds*) en los Andes del Perú. Es un animal muy importante para la economía del país, ya que da una lana muy buena que los peruanos utilizan para hacer ropa, mantas (*blankets*) y bolsas de alta calidad (*quality*). Pero cuidado: ¡las alpacas escupen (*spit*) para defenderse!

Familia peruana esquilando (*shearing*) una alpaca.

recursos

WB pp. 85–86

VM pp. 73–76

vhlcentral.com

ciento noventa y uno 191

¡Vivan los países hispanos!

¿Qué aprendiste?

1 ¿Cierto o falso? Indica si las oraciones son **ciertas** o **falsas**.

Cierto	Falso	
____	____	1. El río Amazonas es el más caudaloso del mundo.
____	____	2. Alrededor del río Amazonas hay una gran playa.
____	____	3. La moneda de Ecuador es el dólar estadounidense.
____	____	4. Arequipa es una de las ciudades principales de Venezuela.
____	____	5. La lengua oficial de Ecuador es el quechua.
____	____	6. Los tejidos de Ecuador son famosos en todo el mundo.
____	____	7. Las cataratas del Niágara son más altas que el Salto Ángel.
____	____	8. Los indígenas llaman *Kerepakupai Merú* al Salto Ángel.
____	____	9. García Márquez ganó el Premio Nobel en 1982.
____	____	10. García Márquez publicó su primer cuento en 1999.
____	____	11. La alpaca es de la familia de la llama y la vicuña.
____	____	12. La alpaca escupe para defenderse.

2 Preguntas Contesta las siguientes preguntas.

1. ¿Te gustaría navegar en el río Amazonas? ¿Por qué?
2. ¿Qué te gustaría comprar en el mercado de Otavalo?
3. ¿Conoces alguna catarata similar a la de Salto Ángel? ¿Dónde está? ¿Cómo es comparada con la de Salto Ángel?
4. ¿Leíste alguna obra de Márquez? ¿Cuál? Si no, ¿crees que te gustaría leer algo de él?
5. ¿Tienes ropa, mantas o bolsas de alpaca? ¿Te gusta la calidad de la alpaca?

CONEXIÓN INTERNET

Investiga estos temas en el sitio el sitio **vhlcentral.com**.

- La cultura inca y personajes importantes de Perú, Venezuela y Colombia.
- Ecoturismo en el Orinoco y lugares para visitar en Colombia y Ecuador

9 Las celebraciones

Communicative Goals

You will learn how to:
- talk about celebrations and personal relationships
- express congratulations
- ask for the bill in a restaurant
- express gratitude

PREPARACIÓN
pages 194–197
- Words related to celebrations and desserts
- Personal relationships and stages of life
- The letters **h**, **j**, and **g**

ESCENAS
pages 198–199
- The Díaz family gets ready for their annual **Día de Muertos** celebration. The whole family participates in the preparations, and even friends are invited to the main event.

EXPLORACIÓN
pages 200–201
- Bajo la lupa: *Semana Santa: vacaciones y tradición*
- Flash cultura: *Las fiestas*

GRAMÁTICA
pages 202–211
- Irregular preterites
- Verbs that change meaning in the preterite
- Relative pronouns
- **¿Qué?** and **¿cuál?**

LECTURA
pages 212–213
- Newspaper article: *Vida Social: Matrimonio, Bautismo, Fiesta de quince años, Expresión de gracias*

Para empezar
- ¿Cómo se sienten estas personas, alegres o tristes?
- ¿Qué hay en la mesa?
- ¿Qué crees que está celebrando la familia?

9 PREPARACIÓN

Las celebraciones

Talking Picture
Tutorial
Games

la boda
wedding

LAS FIESTAS

el aniversario (de bodas) (wedding) anniversary
el día de fiesta holiday
la fiesta party
el/la invitado/a guest
la Navidad Christmas
la quinceañera young woman celebrating her fifteenth birthday
la sorpresa surprise

el cumpleaños
birthday

celebrar to celebrate
cumplir años to have a birthday
dejar una propina to leave a tip
divertirse (e:ie) to have fun
invitar to invite; to treat
pagar la cuenta to pay the bill

brindar
to toast

graduarse (de)
to graduate (from)

pasarlo bien/mal to have a good/bad time
regalar to give (a gift)
reírse (e:i) to laugh
relajarse to relax
sonreír (e:i) to smile
sorprender to surprise

LOS POSTRES Y OTRAS COMIDAS

la botella de vino bottle of wine
los dulces sweets; candy
el helado ice cream
el pastel cake
   de cumpleaños birthday cake
los postres desserts

las galletas
cookies

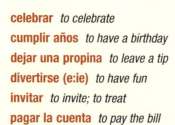

el flan
baked custard

el champán
champagne

recursos

WB
pp. 89–90

LM
p. 49

vhlcentral.com

194 ciento noventa y cuatro

Las celebraciones

LAS ETAPAS DE LA VIDA

la etapa stage
la juventud youth
el nacimiento birth
la vida life

jubilarse to retire (from work)
nacer to be born

la niñez
childhood

la adolescencia
adolescence

LAS RELACIONES PERSONALES

la alegría happiness
la amistad friendship
el amor love
el divorcio divorce
el estado civil marital status
el matrimonio marriage; married couple
la pareja couple; partner
el/la recién casado/a newlywed

casado/a married
divorciado/a divorced
juntos/as together
separado/a separated
soltero/a single
viudo/a widowed

la madurez
maturity; middle age

la vejez
old age

cambiar (de) to change
casarse (con) to get married (to)
comprometerse (con) to get engaged (to)
divorciarse (de) to get divorced (from)
enamorarse (de) to fall in love (with)
llevarse bien/mal (con) to get along well/badly (with)
odiar to hate
romper (con) to break up (with)
salir (con) to go out (with); to date
separarse (de) to separate (from)
tener una cita to have a date; to have an appointment

OTRAS PALABRAS

el apellido last name
el consejo advice
la respuesta answer

la muerte
death

ciento noventa y cinco **195**

Lección 9

Práctica y conversación

1 ¿Lógico o ilógico? Escucha las oraciones e indica si son **lógicas** o **ilógicas**.

	1.	2.	3.	4.	5.	6.
Lógico						
Ilógico						

2 ¡Feliz cumpleaños! Los amigos de Silvia están preparándole una fiesta de cumpleaños. Escucha la conversación y contesta las preguntas.

1. ¿Sabe Silvia que sus amigos le van a organizar una fiesta? _____
2. ¿Qué van a comer los amigos en la fiesta? _____
3. ¿A Silvia le gusta el chocolate? _____
4. ¿Dónde compraron el helado? _____
5. ¿Por qué no quieren comer el helado de la cafetería? _____
6. ¿Cuántos años cumple Silvia? _____
7. ¿Con qué brindan los amigos? _____
8. ¿Silvia es mayor o menor que sus amigos? _____

3 Completar Completa las oraciones.

dejó una propina	se jubiló
lo pasaron mal	se llevan bien
nació	sonrió
nos divertimos	tenemos una cita
se casaron	pagó la cuenta

1. Nelson y Mónica _____ en septiembre. La boda fue maravillosa.
2. Mi tía le _____ muy grande al camarero.
3. Mi padrastro _____ hace un año.
4. A Alejandra le gustan las galletas. Ella se puso contenta y _____ después de comérselas todas.
5. Luis y yo _____ en la fiesta. Bailamos y comimos mucho.
6. ¡Tengo una nueva sobrina! Ella _____ ayer por la mañana y se llama Sofía.
7. Irene y su esposo _____. Ellos casi nunca se pelean y disfrutan haciendo actividades juntos.
8. Rocío y Eddie _____ en el cine. La película fue muy mala y Rocío estaba (*was*) tan aburrida que se quedó dormida a los cinco minutos de empezar la película.
9. Isabel y yo _____ esta noche. Vamos a ir a un restaurante muy elegante.

196 ciento noventa y seis

Las celebraciones

4 Planes para una fiesta Trabaja con dos compañeros/as para planear una fiesta. Describan la fiesta a la clase. Recuerden incluir la siguiente información.

1. ¿Qué tipo de fiesta es?
2. ¿Dónde va a ser? ¿Cuándo va a ser?
3. ¿A quiénes van a invitar?
4. ¿Qué van a comer? ¿Quiénes van a llevar la comida?
5. ¿Qué van a beber? ¿Quiénes van a llevar las bebidas?
6. ¿Cómo planean entretener a los invitados? ¿Van a bailar o jugar algún juego?

5 Una fiesta inolvidable Cuéntale a un(a) compañero/a cómo fue la fiesta más divertida que tuviste *(had)*. Usa estas preguntas como guía. ¿Qué? ¿Por qué? ¿Cuándo? ¿Dónde? ¿Cómo? ¿Quién(es)?

Practice more at vhlcentral.com.

Pronunciación The letters h, j, and g

Audio: Concepts, Activities

| helado | hombre | hola | hermosa |

The Spanish **h** is always silent.

| José | jubilarse | dejar | pareja |

The letter **j** is pronounced much like the English *h* in *his*.

| a**g**encia | **g**eneral | **G**il | **G**isela |

The letter **g** can be pronounced three different ways. Before **e** or **i**, the letter **g** is pronounced much like the English *h*.

Gustavo, **g**racias por llamar el domi**ng**o.

At the beginning of a phrase or after the letter **n**, the Spanish **g** is pronounced like the English *g* in *girl*.

Me **g**radué en a**g**osto.

In any other position, the Spanish **g** has a somewhat softer sound.

| **Gue**rra | conse**gui**r | **gua**ntes | a**gua** |

In the combinations **gue** and **gui**, the **g** has a hard sound and the **u** is silent. In the combination **gua**, the **g** has a hard sound and the **u** is pronounced like the English *w*.

Refranes Lee los refranes en voz alta, prestando atención a la **h**, la **j** y la **g**.

A la larga, lo más dulce amarga.[1]

Practice more at vhlcentral.com.

El hábito no hace al monje.[2]

[1] Too much of a good thing.
[2] The clothes don't make the man.

recursos

LM p. 50

vhlcentral.com

ciento noventa y siete 197

9 ESCENAS

El Día de Muertos
Video: *Fotonovela*

La familia Díaz conmemora el Día de Muertos.

MARISSA · JIMENA · FELIPE

Expresiones útiles

Discussing family history
El mole siempre fue el plato favorito de mi papá.
Mole was always my dad's favorite dish.
Mi hijo Eduardo nació el día de su cumpleaños.
My son Eduardo was born on his birthday.
Por eso le pusimos su nombre.
That's why we named him after him (after my father).
¿Cómo se conocieron sus padres?
How did your parents meet?
En la fiesta de un amigo. Fue amor a primera vista.
At a friend's party. It was love at first sight.

Talking about a party/celebration
Ésta es una fiesta única que todos deben ver por lo menos una vez.
This is a unique celebration that everyone should see at least once.
Gracias por invitarme.
Thanks for inviting me.
Brindamos por ustedes.
A toast to you.

Additional vocabulary
alma *soul*
altar *altar*
ángel *angel*
calavera de azúcar *skull made out of sugar*
cementerio *cemetery*
cocina *kitchen*
disfraz *costume*

MAITE FUENTES El Día de Muertos se celebra en México el primero y el segundo de noviembre. Como pueden ver, hay calaveras de azúcar, flores, música y comida por todas partes. Ésta es una fiesta única que todos deben ver por lo menos una vez en la vida.

MARISSA Holy moley! ¡Está delicioso!
TÍA ANA MARÍA Mi mamá me enseñó a prepararlo. El mole siempre fue el plato favorito de mi papá. Mi hijo Eduardo nació el día de su cumpleaños. Por eso le pusimos su nombre.

TÍO RAMÓN ¿Dónde están mis hermanos?
JIMENA Mi papá y Felipe están en el otro cuarto. Esos dos antipáticos no quieren decirnos qué están haciendo. Y la tía Ana María...
TÍO RAMÓN ... está en la cocina.

TÍA ANA MARÍA Marissa, ¿le puedes llevar esa foto que está ahí a Carolina? La necesita para el altar.
MARISSA Sí. ¿Son sus padres?
TÍA ANA MARÍA Sí, el día de su boda.

MARISSA ¿Cómo se conocieron?
TÍA ANA MARÍA En la fiesta de un amigo. Fue amor a primera vista.
MARISSA (*Señala la foto.*) La voy a llevar al altar.

Practice more at vhlcentral.com

recursos

VM pp. 17–18

vhlcentral.com

Las celebraciones

JUAN CARLOS | SRA. DÍAZ | SR. DÍAZ | TÍA ANA MARÍA | TÍO RAMÓN | TÍA NAYELI | DON DIEGO | MARTA | VALENTINA | MAITE FUENTES

TÍA ANA MARÍA Ramón, ¿cómo estás?
TÍO RAMÓN Bien, gracias. ¿Y Mateo? ¿No vino contigo?
TÍA ANA MARÍA No. Ya sabes que me casé con un doctor y, pues, trabaja muchísimo.

SR. DÍAZ Familia Díaz, deben prepararse...
FELIPE ... ¡para la sorpresa de sus vidas!

JUAN CARLOS Gracias por invitarme.
SR. DÍAZ Juan Carlos, como eres nuestro amigo, ya eres parte de la familia.

(*En el cementerio*)
JIMENA Yo hice las galletas y el pastel. ¿Dónde los puse?
MARTA Postres... ¿Cuál prefiero? ¿Galletas? ¿Pastel? ¡Dulces!
VALENTINA Me gustan las galletas.

SR. DÍAZ Brindamos por ustedes, mamá y papá.
TÍO RAMÓN Todas las otras noches estamos separados. Pero esta noche estamos juntos.
TÍA ANA MARÍA Con gratitud y amor.

Actividades

1 Identificar Identifica quién puede decir estas oraciones. Vas a usar un nombre dos veces.

1. Mis padres se conocieron en la fiesta de un amigo.
2. El Día de Muertos se celebra con flores, calaveras de azúcar, música y comida.
3. Gracias por invitarme a celebrar este Día de Muertos.
4. Los de la foto son mis padres el día de su boda.
5. A mí me gustan mucho las galletas.

2 Completar Completa las oraciones con la información correcta.

1. El Día de Muertos es una _____ única que todos deben ver.
2. La tía Ana María preparó _____ para celebrar.
3. Marissa lleva la _____ al altar.
4. Jimena hizo las _____ y el _____.
5. Marta no sabe qué _____ prefiere.

3 Una cena Trabajen en grupos para representar una conversación en una cena de Año Nuevo. Usen la guía para representar la situación.

- Una persona brinda por el año que está por comenzar y por estar con su familia y amigos.
- Cada persona del grupo habla de cuál es su comida favorita en Año Nuevo.
- Después de la cena, una persona del grupo dice que es hora de (*it's time to*) comer las uvas.
- Cada persona del grupo dice qué desea para el año que empieza.

ciento noventa y nueve **199**

9 EXPLORACIÓN

BAJO LA LUPA

Additional Reading
Video: *Flash cultura*

Semana Santa: vacaciones y tradición

¿Te imaginas pasar veinticuatro horas tocando un tambor° entre miles de personas? Así es como mucha gente celebra el Viernes Santo° en el pequeño pueblo de **Calanda**, España. De todas las celebraciones hispanas, la **Semana Santa°** es una de las más espectaculares y únicas.

Semana Santa es la semana antes de Pascua°, una celebración religiosa que conmemora la Pasión de Jesucristo. Generalmente, la gente tiene unos días de vacaciones en esta semana. Algunas personas aprovechan° estos días para viajar, pero otras prefieren participar en las tradicionales celebraciones religiosas en las calles°. En **Antigua**, Guatemala, hacen alfombras° de flores° y altares; también organizan Vía Crucis° y danzas.

Alfombra de flores en Antigua, Guatemala

En las famosas procesiones y desfiles° religiosos de **Sevilla**, España, los fieles° sacan a las calles imágenes religiosas. Las imágenes van encima de plataformas ricamente decoradas con abundantes flores y velas°. En la procesión, los penitentes llevan túnicas y unos sombreros cónicos que les cubren° la cara°. En sus manos llevan faroles° o velas encendidas.

Si visitas algún país hispano durante la Semana Santa, debes asistir a un desfile. Las playas y las discotecas pueden esperar hasta la semana siguiente.

Procesión en Sevilla, España

Otras celebraciones famosas

Ayacucho, Perú: Además de alfombras de flores y procesiones, aquí hay una antigua tradición llamada "quema de la chamiza"°.

Iztapalapa, Ciudad de México: Es famoso el Vía Crucis del cerro° de la Estrella. Es una representación del recorrido° de Jesucristo con la cruz°.

Popayán, Colombia: En las procesiones "chiquitas" los niños llevan imágenes que son copias pequeñas de las que llevan los mayores.

tocando un tambor playing a drum *Viernes Santo* Good Friday *Semana Santa* Holy Week *Pascua* Easter Sunday *aprovechan* take advantage of *calle* streets *alfombras* carpets *flores* flowers *Vía Crucis* Stations of the Cross *desfiles* parades *fieles* faithful *velas* candles *cubren* cover *cara* face *faroles* lamps *quema de la chamiza* burning of brushwood *cerro* hill *recorrido* route *cruz* cross

Practice more at vhlcentral.com.

recursos

VM pp. 49–50

vhlcentral.com

200 *doscientos*

Las celebraciones

ACTIVIDADES

1 ¿Cierto o falso? Indica si lo que dicen las oraciones sobre la Semana Santa en los países hispanos es **cierto** o **falso**.

1. La Semana Santa se celebra después de Pascua.
2. Las personas tienen días libres durante la Semana Santa.
3. Todos asisten a las celebraciones religiosas.
4. En los países hispanos, las celebraciones se hacen en las calles.
5. En Antigua y en Ayacucho es típico hacer alfombras de flores.
6. En Sevilla, sacan imágenes religiosas a las calles.
7. En Sevilla, las túnicas cubren la cara.
8. En la procesión en Sevilla algunas personas llevan flores en sus manos.
9. El Vía Crucis de Iztapalapa es en el interior de una iglesia.
10. Las procesiones "chiquitas" son famosas en Sevilla, España.

2 Comparación Compara una celebración del mundo hispano con una celebración importante de tu país. ¿Cómo celebra la gente? ¿Cuáles son actividades típicas? ¿En qué se parecen? ¿En qué se diferencian? Comparte tus ideas con la clase.

CONEXIÓN INTERNET

¿Qué celebraciones hispanas hay en los Estados Unidos? For more information about **Exploración**, go to **vhlcentral.com**.

Las fiestas

1 Preparación ¿Se celebra la Navidad en tu país? ¿Qué otras fiestas importantes se celebran? En cada caso, ¿cuánto tiempo dura? ¿Cuáles son las tradiciones y actividades típicas?

2 El video Mira el episodio de **Flash cultura**.

Vocabulario
los cabezudos *carnival figures with large heads*
los carteles *posters*
fiesta de pueblo *local celebration*
santos de palo *wooden sculptures of saints*

Los cabezudos son una tradición […] de España.

Es una fiesta de pueblo… una tradición. Vengo todos los años.

3 Elegir Indica cuál de las dos opciones resume mejor este episodio.

a. Las Navidades puertorriqueñas son las más largas y terminan después de las fiestas de la calle San Sebastián. Esta fiesta de pueblo se celebra con baile, música y distintas expresiones artísticas típicas.

b. En la celebración de las Navidades puertorriqueñas, los cabezudos son una tradición de España y son el elemento más importante de la fiesta. A la gente le gusta bailar y hacer procesiones por la noche.

9 GRAMÁTICA

9.1 Irregular preterites

Marissa le dio la foto a la Sra. Díaz.

▶ You already know that **ir** and **ser** are irregular in the preterite. Here are some other verbs that are irregular in the preterite.

Preterite of tener, venir, and decir

	tener (u-stem)	venir (i-stem)	decir (j-stem)
yo	tuve	vine	dije
tú	tuviste	viniste	dijiste
Ud./él/ella	tuvo	vino	dijo
nosotros/as	tuvimos	vinimos	dijimos
vosotros/as	tuvisteis	vinisteis	dijisteis
Uds./ellos/ellas	tuvieron	vinieron	dijeron

Hubo una celebración en casa de los Díaz.

▶ Observe the stem changes in the chart: the **e** in **tener** changes to **u**, and the **e** in **venir** and **decir** changes to **i**. Note also that the **c** in **decir** changes to **j**. None of these verbs have written accents in the **yo** or **usted/él/ella** forms.

▶ These verbs have similar stem changes to **tener**, **venir**, and **decir**.

INFINITIVE	U-STEM	PRETERITE FORMS
poder	pud–	pude, pudiste, pudo, pudimos, pudisteis, pudieron
poner	pus–	puse, pusiste, puso, pusimos, pusisteis, pusieron
saber	sup–	supe, supiste, supo, supimos, supisteis, supieron
estar	estuv–	estuve, estuviste, estuvo, estuvimos, estuvisteis, estuvieron

INFINITIVE	I-STEM	PRETERITE FORMS
querer	quis–	quise, quisiste, quiso, quisimos, quisisteis, quisieron
hacer	hic–	hice, hiciste, hizo, hicimos, hicisteis, hicieron

INFINITIVE	J-STEM	PRETERITE FORMS
traer	traj–	traje, trajiste, trajo, trajimos, trajisteis, trajeron
conducir	conduj–	conduje, condujiste, condujo, condujimos, condujisteis, condujeron
traducir	traduj–	traduje, tradujiste, tradujo, tradujimos, tradujisteis, tradujeron

¡ojo!

Verbs with **j**-stems omit the letter **i** in the **Uds./ellos/ellas** endings.

For example:

tener → tuvieron, but **decir → dijeron**.

Most verbs that end in **–cir** are j-stem verbs in the preterite.

For example:

producir → produje, produjiste, produjo, produjimos, produjisteis, produjeron.

202 doscientos dos

Las celebraciones

The preterite of dar

| yo | di | Ud./él/ella | dio | vosotros/as | disteis |
| tú | diste | nosotros/as | dimos | Uds./ellos/ellas | dieron |

▸ The endings for **dar** are the same as the regular preterite endings for **–er** and **–ir** verbs, but there are no written accent marks.

La camarera me **dio** el menú.
The waitress gave me the menu.

Le **di** a Juan algunos consejos.
I gave Juan some advice.

▸ The preterite of **hay** (*inf.* **haber**) is **hubo** (*there was/were*).

Hubo una fiesta el sábado pasado.
There was a party last Saturday.

Hubo muchos invitados.
There were a lot of guests.

Práctica y conversación

 Practice more at vhlcentral.com.

1 Una fiesta sorpresa Completa estas oraciones con el pretérito de los verbos indicados.

1. El sábado _____ [haber] una fiesta para Elsa.
2. Sofía _____ [hacer] un pastel para la fiesta y Miguel _____ [traer] un flan.
3. Los amigos de Elsa _____ [traer] regalos.
4. El hermano de Elsa no _____ [venir] porque _____ [tener] que trabajar.
5. Su tía María Dolores tampoco _____ [poder] venir.
6. ¡La fiesta le _____ [dar] a Elsa tanta alegría!

2 ¿Qué hicieron? Usa los siguientes verbos para describir lo que hicieron estas personas: **dar, estar, poner, tener, traer.**

1. El señor López/dinero
_____

3. Nosotros/fiesta
_____

2. Norma/pavo
_____

4. Roberto y Elena/regalo
_____

3 Preguntas En parejas, túrnense para contestar estas preguntas.

1. ¿Qué hiciste anoche? ¿Y el domingo pasado?
2. ¿Quiénes no estuvieron en clase la semana pasada?
3. ¿Qué trajiste a clase hoy?
4. ¿Hubo una fiesta en tu casa o residencia el sábado?
5. ¿Cuándo fue la última (*last*) vez que tus parientes vinieron a visitarte? ¿Te trajeron algo? ¿Qué te trajeron?
6. ¿Les diste a tus padres un regalo para su aniversario de bodas? ¿Qué les regalaste?

4 Encuesta Averigua (*Find out*) quién de tus compañeros/as hizo cada una de estas actividades. Luego, comparte los resultados con la clase.

Descripciones	Nombres
1. Tuvo un examen ayer.	_____
2. Trajo dulces a clase.	_____
3. Condujo su auto a clase.	_____
4. Estuvo en la biblioteca ayer.	_____
5. Le dio consejos a alguien ayer.	_____
6. No pudo levantarse esta mañana.	_____
7. Tuvo una cita anoche.	_____
8. Hizo un viaje por más de dos semanas el verano pasado.	_____

Lección 9

9.2 Verbs that change meaning in the preterite

▶ **Conocer**, **saber**, **poder**, and **querer** change meanings in the preterite.

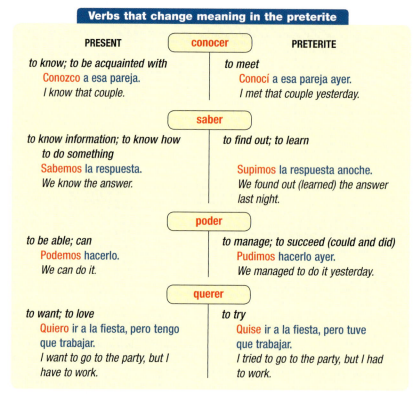

Verbs that change meaning in the preterite

PRESENT	conocer	PRETERITE
to know; to be acquainted with		to meet
Conozco a esa pareja.		Conocí a esa pareja ayer.
I know that couple.		I met that couple yesterday.

	saber	
to know information; to know how to do something		to find out; to learn
Sabemos la respuesta.		Supimos la respuesta anoche.
We know the answer.		We found out (learned) the answer last night.

	poder	
to be able; can		to manage; to succeed (could and did)
Podemos hacerlo.		Pudimos hacerlo ayer.
We can do it.		We managed to do it yesterday.

	querer	
to want; to love		to try
Quiero ir a la fiesta, pero tengo que trabajar.		Quise ir a la fiesta, pero tuve que trabajar.
I want to go to the party, but I have to work.		I tried to go to the party, but I had to work.

▶ In the preterite, **poder** and **querer** have different meanings, depending on whether they are used in affirmative or negative sentences.

Affirmative		Negative	
pude	I was able (to)/succeeded	no pude	I failed (to)
quise	I tried (to)	no quise	I refused (to)

ESPAÑOL EN VIVO

Hubo un día en el que la humanidad quiso ir más allá de sus límites.
Pudo conocer un mundo° increíble.
Supo asegurar° su futuro.

Ahora todos lo pueden hacer.

BANCO COLÓN
El banco de Puerto Rico

mundo world
asegurar to ensure

Las celebraciones

Práctica y conversación

1 Oraciones Forma oraciones con estos elementos. Usa el pretérito.

MODELO
Mis padres / no querer / venir / fiesta
Mis padres no quisieron venir a la fiesta.

1. Anoche / nosotros / saber / que / Carlos y Eva / divorciarse _____
2. Tú / conocer / Nora / clase / historia / ¿no? _____
3. ¿Poder / ustedes / visitar / la Isla de Pascua? _____
4. Ayer / yo / saber / que / Paco / querer / romper / Olivia _____
5. El señor Navarro / querer / jubilarse / pero / no poder _____
6. Gustavo y Elena / conocer / mi esposo / fiesta de Ana _____
7. Yolanda / no poder / dormir / anoche _____
8. Irma / saber / que / nosotros / traer / galletas _____
9. Ayer / yo / no poder / llamar / tú _____
10. Nosotros / querer / pagar la cuenta _____

2 Completar Completa estas frases de una manera lógica.

1. La semana pasada yo supe…
2. Ayer mi compañero/a de cuarto supo…
3. Esta mañana no pude…
4. El fin de semana pasado mis amigos y yo no pudimos…
5. Conocí a mi mejor amigo/a en…
6. Mis padres no quisieron…
7. Mi mejor amigo/a no pudo…
8. Mi novio/a y yo nos conocimos en…
9. El mes pasado en clase no pudimos…
10. Ayer mis amigos quisieron…
11. Mis abuelos pudieron…

3 El fin de semana Prepara dos listas: una con las actividades que hiciste el fin de semana pasado y la otra lista con las actividades que quisiste hacer, pero no pudiste hacer. Luego, compara tu lista con la de un(a) compañero/a, y expliquen por qué no pudieron hacer esas cosas.

Cosas que hice	Cosas que quise hacer
1. _____	1. _____
2. _____	2. _____
3. _____	3. _____
4. _____	4. _____
5. _____	5. _____
6. _____	6. _____
7. _____	7. _____
8. _____	8. _____
9. _____	9. _____
10. _____	10. _____

4 Telenovela En grupos de tres, escriban el guión (*script*) de una escena amorosa entre los tres personajes de la telenovela (*soap opera*) llamada **La mujer doble**. Usen el pretérito de **conocer**, **poder**, **querer** y **saber**. ¡Sean creativos!

Daniel

Mirta

Raúl

Practice more at vhlcentral.com.

doscientos cinco 205

Lección 9

9.3 Relative pronouns

La comida que prepararon fue muy rica.

La Sra. Díaz, quien tiene las flores, preparó la comida.

> **¡ojo!**
> Note that relative pronouns never carry an accent, unlike interrogative words (**qué, quién,** etc.).

▶ Relative pronouns are used to combine two sentences or clauses that share a common element, such as a noun or pronoun. Study these diagrams.

Éste es **el flan**.
This is the flan.

Manuela preparó **el flan**.
Manuela made the flan.

Éste es **el flan que** Manuela preparó.
This is the flan that Manuela made.

Lourdes es muy inteligente.
Lourdes is very intelligent.

Lourdes estudia español.
Lourdes studies Spanish.

Lourdes, quien estudia español, es muy inteligente.
Lourdes, who studies Spanish, is very intelligent.

▶ Spanish has three commonly used relative pronouns.

Common relative pronouns

que | *that; which; who* **quien(es)** | *who; whom; that* **lo que** | *that which; what*

▶ **Que**, the most frequently used relative pronoun, can refer to things or to people. Unlike the English *that*, **que** is never omitted.

¿Dónde está el pastel **que** pedí?
Where is the cake (that) I ordered?

El hombre **que** sirve la comida se llama Diego.
The man who serves the food is named Diego.

▶ **Que** is used like the English *that* after verbs like **creer, decir, pensar,** and **suponer.**

Creo que la fiesta es mañana.
I think (that) the party is tomorrow.

Pienso que hiciste bien.
I think (that) you did well.

Ana **dice que** no puede venir.
Ana says (that) she can't come.

Supongo que va a llover.
I suppose (that) it's going to rain.

▶ **Quien** (singular) and **quienes** (plural) refer only to people and are often used after a preposition or the personal **a**.

Eva, **a quien** vi anoche, cumple veinticinco años hoy.
Eva, whom I saw last night, turns twenty-five today.

¿Son ésas las chicas **de quienes** me hablaste la semana pasada?
Are those the girls you told me about last week?

▶ **Quien(es)** is occasionally used instead of **que** in clauses set off by commas.

Lola, **quien** es cubana, es médica.
Lola, who is Cuban, is a doctor.

Mi hermana, **quien** vive en Madrid, me llamó por teléfono.
My sister, who lives in Madrid, called me on the phone.

Las celebraciones

▶ **Lo que** refers to an idea, a situation, or a past event and means *what* or *the thing that*.

Juana tiene todo **lo que** necesitamos.
Juana has everything we need.

Lo que quiero es verte.
What I want is to see you.

Lo que me molesta es el calor.
What bothers me is the heat.

Lo que más te gusta es divertirte.
What you like most is to have fun.

Práctica y conversación

1 Una fiesta de aniversario Amparo está hablando de la fiesta de aniversario de sus abuelos. Completa las oraciones con las expresiones de la lista.

a quien conozco muy bien	**que se graduó**
de quienes te hablé	**quien es la novia**
que saqué	**quien se jubiló**

1. El sábado fui a la fiesta de aniversario de mis abuelos, _____ la semana pasada.
2. Éstas son las fotos _____ durante la fiesta.
3. Éste es Ramón, mi primo. Es el chico _____ de la universidad en junio.
4. Éste es mi abuelo, _____ el año pasado.
5. Esta mujer, _____ , se llama Ana.
6. Y ésta es Lucía, _____ de Ramón.

2 Una fiesta de cumpleaños Describe la fiesta sorpresa que van a dar Jaime y Tina, usando los pronombres relativos **que, quien, quienes** y **lo que**.

1. Manuela, _____ cumple veintiún años mañana, no sabe que sus amigos están planeando una fiesta.
2. Jaime y Laura son los amigos _____ planean la fiesta.
3. Éstas son las personas _____ van a invitar.
4. Juan y Luz, _____ son los hermanos de Manuela, van a venir.
5. Marco, _____ es el novio de Manuela, va a venir también.
6. _____ Jaime y Laura van a servir de postre es un pastel de chocolate.
7. Todos van a bailar salsa y rock hasta la una de la mañana, _____ va a ser muy divertido.

3 Definiciones En parejas, túrnense para definir estas palabras, usando **que, quien(es)** y **lo que.** Luego compartan sus definiciones con la clase.

MODELO
un pastel de cumpleaños
Estudiante 1: *¿Qué es un pastel de cumpleaños?*
Estudiante 2: *Es un postre que comes en tu cumpleaños./ Es lo que comes en tu cumpleaños.*

1. el helado
2. el champán
3. una propina
4. una boda
5. un invitado
6. la Navidad
7. una recién casada
8. el divorcio
9. la juventud
10. la vejez
11. una viuda
12. una fiesta de quince años

4 Entrevista En parejas, túrnense para hacerse las siguientes preguntas.

1. ¿Qué es lo que más te gusta de las fiestas familiares? ¿Por qué?
2. ¿Qué es lo que menos te gusta de las fiestas familiares? ¿Por qué?
3. ¿Quiénes son las personas con quienes celebras tu cumpleaños?
4. ¿Quién es el/la pariente o amigo/a a quien más le gustan los cumpleaños? ¿Por qué le gustan tanto?
5. ¿Dónde compras los regalos que le das a tu mejor amigo/a?
6. ¿Tienes hermanos/as o amigos/as que están casados/as? ¿Dónde viven?
7. ¿Quién es la persona que más te importa?
8. ¿Quiénes son las personas con quienes te diviertes más? ¿Por qué lo pasas bien con ellos/ellas?

Practice more at
vhlcentral.com.

doscientos siete **207**

Lección 9

9.4 ¿Qué? and ¿cuál?  Tutorial

▶ As you know, **¿qué?** and **¿cuál?** or **¿cuáles?** mean *what?* or *which?* However, they are not interchangeable.

▶ **¿Qué?** is used to ask for a definition or explanation.

¿Qué es un flan?
What is flan?

¿Qué estudias?
What do you study?

▶ **¿Cuál(es)?** is used when there is a choice between two or more possibilities.

¿Cuáles quieres, éstos o ésos?
Which (ones) do you want, these ones or those ones?

¿Cuál es tu apellido, Martínez o Vásquez?
What is your last name, Martínez or Vásquez?

▶ **¿Cuál(es)?** cannot be used before a noun; **¿qué?** is used instead.

¿Cuál es tu color favorito?
What is your favorite color?

¿Qué colores te gustan?
What colors do you like?

▶ **¿Qué?** used before a noun has the same meaning as **¿cuál?**.

Qué + [noun]
¿**Qué regalo** te gusta?
¿**Qué dulces** quieren ustedes?

Cuál + [verb]
¿**Cuál** te gusta?
¿**Cuáles** quieren ustedes?

Review of interrogative words and phrases

¿a qué hora?	at what time?	¿cuándo?	when?	¿dónde?	where?
¿adónde?	(to) where?	¿cuánto/a?	how much?	¿por qué?	why?
¿cómo?	how?	¿cuántos/as?	how many?	¿qué?	what?; which?
¿cuál(es)?	what?; which?	¿de dónde?	from where?	¿quién(es)?	who?

prioridades *priorities*
eliges *choose*

208 doscientos ocho

Las celebraciones

Práctica y conversación

1 Minidiálogos Completa los minidiálogos con las palabras interrogativas correctas.

- **SILVIA** ¿(1) _____ es la fiesta de aniversario de tus padres?
- **ERNESTO** El sábado por la noche.

• • •

- **MICAELA** ¿(2) _____ va a ser la fiesta de cumpleaños?
- **DIEGO** En casa de mi primo.

• • •

- **CAMILA** ¿(3) _____ es tu clase favorita?
- **CARLOS** La clase de arte es mi favorita.

• • •

- **TOMÁS** ¿(4) _____ dinero te van a dar tus abuelos para tu graduación de la universidad?
- **MERCEDES** Dicen que van a darme dos mil dólares.

• • •

- **LIDIA** ¿(5) _____ compraste para tu sobrino?
- **MARTA** Una raqueta de tenis.

• • •

- **PEDRO** ¿(6) _____ vas después de la boda?
- **JUAN** Mi novia y yo vamos al cine. ¿Quieres venir?

2 Completar Completa estas preguntas con una palabra interrogativa. En algunos casos se puede usar más de una palabra interrogativa.

1. ¿En _____ país nacieron tus padres?
2. ¿_____ es la fecha de tu cumpleaños?
3. ¿_____ naciste?
4. ¿_____ es tu estado civil?
5. ¿_____ te relajas?
6. ¿_____ son tus programas de televisión favoritos?
7. ¿_____ es tu mejor amigo?
8. ¿_____ van tus amigos para divertirse?
9. ¿_____ postres te gustan? ¿_____ te gusta más?
10. ¿_____ problemas tuviste el primer día de clase?
11. ¿_____ primos tienes?

Practice more at vhlcentral.com.

3 Una invitación En parejas, lean esta invitación. Luego, cada estudiante debe pensar en tres preguntas que su compañero/a debe responder sobre el texto.

MODELO
Estudiante 1: ¿Quiénes se casan?
Estudiante 2: María Luisa y José Antonio

> Fernando Sandoval Valera   Lorenzo Vásquez Amaral
> Isabel Arzipe de Sandoval   Elena Soto de Vásquez
>
> tienen el agrado de invitarlos
> a la boda de sus hijos
>
> María Luisa y José Antonio
>
> La ceremonia religiosa tendrá lugar
> el sábado 10 de junio a las dos de la tarde
> en el Templo de Santo Domingo
> (Calle Santo Domingo, 961).
>
> Después de la ceremonia, sírvanse pasar a la recepción en el salón de baile del Hotel Metrópoli (Sotero del Río, 465).

4 Fotos En parejas, túrnense para hacerse preguntas sobre estas personas.

MODELO
Estudiante 1: ¿Quién es esta mujer?
Estudiante 2: Es una estudiante.
Estudiante 1: ¿Dónde está?
Estudiante 2: Está en la biblioteca.
Estudiante 1: ¿Qué está haciendo?
Estudiante 2: Está estudiando para un examen.

1.
2.
3.
4.

doscientos nueve 209

Lección 9

Ampliación

Audio: Activity
Video: TV Clip

1 Escuchar

A Escucha la conversación entre Josefina y Rosa. Cuando oigas una de las palabras de la **columna A**, usa el contexto para identificar un sinónimo en la **columna B**.

TIP **Guess the meaning of the words through context.** Listen to the words and phrases around an unfamiliar word to guess its meaning.

A	B
_____ 1. festejar	a. conmemoración religiosa de una muerte
_____ 2. te divertiste	b. tolera
_____ 3. dicha	c. suerte
_____ 4. bien parecido	d. celebrar
_____ 5. finge (fingir)	e. lo pasaste bien
_____ 6. soporta (soportar)	f. horror
	g. pretende ser algo que no es
	h. guapo

B ¿Son solteras Rosa y Josefina? ¿Cómo lo sabes?

Margarita Robles de García
y Roberto García Olmos

Piden su presencia en la celebración del segundo aniversario de bodas el día 13 de marzo con una misa en la Iglesia Virgen del Coromoto a las 6:30 p.m.

Seguida por cena y baile en el restaurante El Campanero, Calle Principal, Las Mercedes a las 8:30 p.m.

2 Conversar

En parejas, conversen sobre cómo celebraron ustedes el Día de Acción de Gracias (*Thanksgiving*) el año pasado. Incluyan esta información.

- ¿Dónde celebraron el día de fiesta? ¿A qué hora fue?
- ¿Cuántos invitados hubo? ¿Quiénes fueron los invitados? ¿Conocieron a alguien?
- ¿Cuál fue el menú? ¿Quién hizo la comida?
- ¿Lo pasaron bien? ¿Qué fue lo que más (*more*) les gustó de la celebración?

recursos
WB pp. 91–97
LM pp. 51–54
vhlcentral.com

210 *doscientos diez*

Las celebraciones

3 Escribir En una composición, compara dos celebraciones a las que tú asististe recientemente.

TIP Use Venn diagrams. Use Venn diagrams to organize your ideas visually before comparing and contrasting people, places, objects, events, or issues. Differences are listed in the outer rings of the two circles; similarities appear where the circles overlap.

Boda de Silvia Reyes y Carlos Espinoza
Diferencias:
1. Primero hay una celebración religiosa.
2. Se celebra el matrimonio de dos personas.

Similitudes:
1. Las dos fiestas se celebran por la noche.
2. Hay música y baile.

Fiesta de quince años de Ana Ester Larenas Vera
Diferencias:
1. Se celebra en un club.
2. Vienen invitados especiales.

Organízalo Utiliza un diagrama de Venn para anotar las similitudes y las diferencias entre las dos celebraciones.

Escríbelo Utiliza tus notas para escribir el primer borrador de la composición.

Corrígelo Intercambia tu composición con la de un(a) compañero/a. Dale sugerencias para mejorar su borrador y si ves errores gramaticales u ortográficos, coméntaselos.

Compártelo Revisa el primer borrador según las indicaciones de tu compañero/a. Incorpora nuevas ideas o más información para ampliar la comparación. Luego comparte tu composición con otro/a compañero/a.

4 Un paso más Imagina que eres periodista en un país hispano. Escribe un artículo sobre un día de fiesta o una celebración que viste.

- Investiga las fiestas, las celebraciones y los festivales de ese país. Elige la celebración que más te interese.
- Explica el nombre de la celebración, cuándo fue y cómo la celebraron.
- Incluye información sobre la ropa especial que llevaron, la comida, la música y el baile.
- Indica qué hiciste tú durante la celebración.
- Presenta el artículo a la clase. Es importante explicar los detalles y mostrar fotos.

CONEXIÓN INTERNET

Investiga estos temas en **vhlcentral.com**.

- Festivales nacionales del mundo hispano
- Fiestas religiosas del mundo hispano

doscientos once **211**

9 LECTURA

Antes de leer

Audio: Reading
Additional Reading

Recognizing root words and word families can help you guess the meaning of words in context, ensuring better comprehension of a reading selection. Using this strategy will enrich your Spanish vocabulary as well.

Examinar el texto
Familiarízate con el texto usando las estrategias de lectura más efectivas para ti. ¿Qué tipo de documento es? ¿De qué tratan las cuatro secciones del documento? Explica tus respuestas.

Raíces
Completa el siguiente cuadro para ampliar tu vocabulario. Usa palabras de la lectura de esta lección y vocabulario de las lecciones anteriores. ¿Qué significan las palabras que escribiste en el cuadro?

Verbs	Nouns	Other forms
1. agradecer *to thank, to be grateful for*	agradecimiento/ gracias *gratitude/thanks*	agradecido *grateful, thankful*
2. estudiar	_____	_____
3. _____	_____	celebrando
4. _____	baile	_____
5. bautizar	_____	_____

Vida social

Matrimonio
Espinoza Álvarez-Reyes Salazar

El día sábado 17 de junio a las 19 horas, se celebró el matrimonio de Silvia Reyes y Carlos Espinoza en la catedral de Santiago. La ceremonia fue oficiada por el pastor Federico Salas y participaron los padres de los novios, el señor Jorge Espinoza y señora y el señor José Alfredo Reyes y señora. Después de la ceremonia, los padres de los recién casados ofrecieron una fiesta bailable en el restaurante La Misión.

Bautismo
José María recibió el bautismo el 26 de junio.

Sus padres, don Roberto Lagos Moreno y doña María Angélica Sánchez, compartieron la alegría de la fiesta con todos sus parientes y amigos. La ceremonia religiosa tuvo lugar° en la catedral de Aguas Blancas. Después de la ceremonia, padres, parientes y amigos celebraron una fiesta en la residencia de la familia Lagos.

recursos

vhlcentral.com

Las celebraciones

Fiesta de quince años

El doctor don Amador Larenas Fernández y la señora Felisa Vera de Larenas celebraron los quince años de su hija Ana Ester junto a sus parientes y amigos. La quinceañera reside en la ciudad de Valparaíso y es estudiante del Colegio Francés. La fiesta de presentación en sociedad de la señorita Ana Ester fue el día viernes 2 de mayo a las 19 horas en el Club Español. Entre los invitados especiales asistieron el alcalde° de la ciudad, don Pedro Castedo, y su esposa. La música estuvo a cargo de la Orquesta Americana. ¡Feliz cumpleaños, le deseamos a la señorita Ana Ester en su fiesta bailable!

Expresión de gracias
Carmen Godoy Tapia

Agradecemos° sinceramente a todas las personas que nos acompañaron en el último adiós a nuestra apreciada esposa, madre, abuela y tía, la señora Carmen Godoy Tapia. El funeral tuvo lugar el día 28 de junio en la ciudad de Viña del Mar. La vida de Carmen Godoy fue un ejemplo de trabajo, amistad, alegría y amor para todos nosotros. Su esposo, hijos y familia agradecen de todo corazón° su asistencia° al funeral a todos los parientes y amigos.

tuvo lugar *took place*   alcalde *mayor*   Agradecemos *We thank*
de todo corazón *sincerely*   asistencia *attendance*

Después de leer

¿Comprendiste?
Indica si lo que se dice en cada oración es **cierto** o **falso**. Corrige las oraciones falsas.

Cierto   Falso

_____   _____   1. El alcalde y su esposa asistieron a la boda de Silvia y Carlos.

_____   _____   2. Todos los anuncios (*announcements*) describen eventos felices.

_____   _____   3. Ana Ester Larenas cumple quince años.

_____   _____   4. Roberto Lagos y María Angélica Sánchez son hermanos.

_____   _____   5. La familia de Carmen Godoy Tapia les dio las gracias a las personas que asistieron al funeral.

Preguntas
Responde a estas preguntas con oraciones completas.

1. ¿Quién murió el 28 de junio?
   _____

2. ¿Dónde tuvo lugar el funeral?
   _____

3. ¿Dónde fue la fiesta de bautismo de José María?
   _____

4. ¿Qué hicieron los recién casados y sus invitados después de la ceremonia?
   _____

5. ¿Quién estuvo a cargo de la música en la fiesta de quince años de Ana Ester?
   _____

Coméntalo
¿Hay una sección de notas sociales en el periódico de tu universidad, comunidad o región? ¿Qué tipo de información encuentras en la sección de notas sociales? ¿La lees normalmente? ¿Por qué?

doscientos trece 213

9 VOCABULARIO

Las celebraciones

el aniversario (de bodas)	(wedding) anniversary
la boda	wedding
el cumpleaños	birthday
el día de fiesta	holiday
la fiesta	party
el/la invitado/a	guest
la Navidad	Christmas
la quinceañera	young woman celebrating her fifteenth birthday
la sorpresa	surprise
brindar	to toast (drink)
celebrar	to celebrate
cumplir años	to have a birthday
dejar una propina	to leave a tip
divertirse (e:ie)	to have fun
graduarse (de)	to graduate (from)
invitar	to invite; to treat
pagar la cuenta	to pay the bill
pasarlo bien/mal	to have a good/bad time
regalar	to give (a gift)
reírse (e:i)	to laugh
relajarse	to relax
sonreír (e:i)	to smile
sorprender	to surprise

Los postres y otras comidas

la botella de vino	bottle of wine
el champán	champagne
los dulces	sweets; candy
el flan	baked custard
las galletas	cookies
el helado	ice cream
el pastel	cake
el pastel de cumpleaños	birthday cake
los postres	desserts

Las relaciones personales

la alegría	happiness
la amistad	friendship
el amor	love
el divorcio	divorce
el estado civil	marital status
el matrimonio	marriage; married couple
la pareja	couple; partner
el/la recién casado/a	newlywed
casado/a	married
divorciado/a	divorced
juntos/as	together
separado/a	separated
soltero/a	single
viudo/a	widowed
cambiar (de)	to change
casarse (con)	to get married (to)
comprometerse (con)	to get engaged (to)
divorciarse (de)	to get divorced (from)
enamorarse (de)	to fall in love (with)
llevarse bien/mal (con)	to get along well/badly (with)
odiar	to hate
romper (con)	to break up (with)
salir (con)	to go out (with); to date
separarse (de)	to separate (from)
tener una cita	to have a date; to have an appointment

Palabras adicionales

el apellido	last name
el consejo	advice
la respuesta	answer

Las etapas de la vida

la adolescencia	adolescence
la etapa	stage
la juventud	youth
la madurez	maturity; middle age
la muerte	death
el nacimiento	birth
la niñez	childhood
la vejez	old age
la vida	life
jubilarse	to retire (from work)
nacer	to be born

Relative pronouns	See page 206.
Interrogative words and phrases	See page 208.

214 doscientos catorce

10 En el consultorio

Communicative Goals
You will learn how to:
- discuss medical conditions
- talk about parts of the body
- talk about health and medical visits

PREPARACIÓN
pages 216–219
- Words related to sickness, symptoms, medicine, and the doctor's office
- Parts of the body
- Written accent marks and word stress

ESCENAS
pages 220–221
- While out with a friend, Jimena comes down with a bug. Despite medical remedies from friends and family, she still needs to see a doctor.

EXPLORACIÓN
pages 222–223
- Bajo la lupa: *Servicios de salud*
- Flash cultura: *La salud*

GRAMÁTICA
pages 224–231
- The imperfect tense
- Constructions with **se**
- Adverbs

LECTURA
pages 232–233
- Newspaper column: *El consultorio: Dra. Fernanda Jiménez Ocaña*

Para empezar
- ¿Están en una farmacia o en un hospital?
- ¿El hombre es médico o dentista?
- ¿Qué hace él, una operación o un examen médico?
- ¿Cómo se siente la paciente?

10 PREPARACIÓN

En el consultorio

Talking Picture Tutorial Games

EL CUERPO

el corazón heart
el cuerpo body
el estómago stomach
el hueso bone
la rodilla knee
el tobillo ankle

el ojo eye
la nariz nose
la boca mouth
la oreja (outer) ear
el pie foot
la pierna leg
la cabeza head
el cuello neck
la garganta throat
el brazo arm
el dedo finger

LA SALUD

el accidente accident
la clínica clinic
el consultorio doctor's office
el/la doctor(a) doctor
el/la enfermero/a nurse
el examen médico physical exam
el hospital hospital
el/la paciente patient
la operación operation
la radiografía X-ray
la sala de emergencia(s) emergency room
la salud health

la farmacia pharmacy

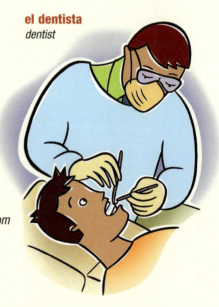
el dentista dentist

recursos

WB pp. 99–100
LM p. 55
vhlcentral.com

216 doscientos dieciséis

En el consultorio

tomar(le) la temperatura (a alguien)
to take (someone's) temperature

estornudar
to sneeze

VERBOS

caerse to fall (down)
doler (o:ue) to hurt
enfermarse to get sick
estar enfermo/a to be sick
lastimarse (el pie) to injure (one's foot)
poner una inyección to give an injection
recetar to prescribe
romperse (la pierna) to break (one's leg)
sacar(se) una muela to have a tooth pulled
ser alérgico/a (a) to be allergic (to)
tener fiebre (f.) to have a fever
torcerse (el tobillo) to sprain (one's ankle)
toser to cough

LAS ENFERMEDADES Y LOS SÍNTOMAS

el dolor (de cabeza) (head)ache; pain
la enfermedad illness; sickness
la gripe flu
la infección infection
el resfriado cold
el síntoma symptom
la tos cough

congestionado/a congested; stuffed-up
mareado/a dizzy; nauseated

LOS MEDICAMENTOS

el antibiótico antibiotic
el medicamento medication
la medicina medicine
las pastillas pills; tablets
la receta prescription

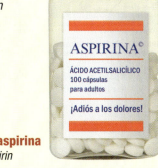

la aspirina
aspirin

ADJETIVOS

embarazada pregnant
grave grave; serious
médico/a medical
saludable healthy
sano/a healthy

doscientos diecisiete 217

Lección 10

Práctica y conversación

1 Escuchar 🎧 Escucha las preguntas y selecciona la respuesta más adecuada.

1. _____   a. Tengo dolor de cabeza y fiebre.
2. _____   b. No fui a la clase porque estaba (*I was*) enfermo.
3. _____   c. Me caí ayer jugando al tenis.
4. _____   d. Debes ir a la farmacia.
5. _____   e. Porque tengo gripe.
6. _____   f. Sí, tengo mucha tos por las noches.
7. _____   g. Lo llevaron directamente a la sala de emergencia.
8. _____   h. No sé. Todavía tienen que tomarme la temperatura.

2 Actividades En parejas, identifiquen las partes del cuerpo que asocian con estas actividades.

MODELO
nadar
Estudiante 1: Usamos los brazos para nadar.
Estudiante 2: También usamos las piernas.

1. conducir
2. caminar
3. toser
4. comer arroz con pollo
5. comprar un perfume
6. ver una película
7. hablar por teléfono
8. correr en el parque
9. tocar el piano

3 Cuestionario Selecciona las respuestas que reflejen mejor tu estado de salud. Suma (*add*) los puntos de cada respuesta y anota el resultado. Después, compara los resultados con el resto de la clase.

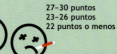

¿Tienes buena salud?

27–30 puntos Salud y hábitos excelentes
23–26 puntos Salud y hábitos buenos
22 puntos o menos Salud y hábitos problemáticos

1. ¿Con qué frecuencia te enfermas (resfriados, gripe, etc.)?
   - Cuatro veces por año o más. (1 punto)
   - Dos o tres veces por año. (2 puntos)
   - Casi nunca. (3 puntos)
2. ¿Con qué frecuencia tienes dolor de estómago o problemas digestivos?
   - Con mucha frecuencia. (1 punto)
   - A veces. (2 puntos)
   - Casi nunca. (3 puntos)
3. ¿Con qué frecuencia tienes dolor de cabeza?
   - Frecuentemente. (1 punto)
   - A veces. (2 puntos)
   - Casi nunca. (3 puntos)
4. ¿Comes verduras y frutas?
   - No, casi nunca. (1 punto)
   - Sí, a veces. (2 puntos)
   - Sí, todos los días. (3 puntos)
5. ¿Eres alérgico/a a algo?
   - Sí, a muchas cosas. (1 punto)
   - Sí, a algunas cosas. (2 puntos)
   - No. (3 puntos)
6. ¿Haces ejercicios aeróbicos?
   - No, casi nunca hago ejercicios aeróbicos. (1 punto)
   - Sí, a veces. (2 puntos)
   - Sí, con frecuencia. (3 puntos)
7. ¿Con qué frecuencia te haces un examen médico?
   - Nunca o casi nunca. (1 punto)
   - Cada dos años. (2 puntos)
   - Cada año o antes de practicar un deporte. (3 puntos)
8. ¿Con qué frecuencia vas al dentista?
   - Nunca voy al dentista. (1 punto)
   - Sólo cuando me duele una muela. (2 puntos)
   - Por lo menos una vez por año. (3 puntos)
9. ¿Qué desayunas normalmente por la mañana?
   - No como nada. (1 punto)
   - Tomo una bebida dietética. (2 puntos)
   - Como cereales y fruta. (3 puntos)
10. ¿Con qué frecuencia te sientes mareado/a?
    - Frecuentemente. (1 punto)
    - A veces. (2 puntos)
    - Casi nunca. (3 puntos)

En el consultorio

4 ¿Cuáles son sus síntomas? En parejas, túrnense para representar los papeles (*roles*) de un(a) médico/a y su paciente.

5 Un accidente En parejas, conversen sobre un accidente que ustedes, un(a) amigo/a o un miembro de la familia tuvo. Usen estas preguntas de guía: ¿Qué ocurrió? ¿Dónde y cuándo ocurrió? ¿Cómo ocurrió? ¿Quién te ayudó y cómo?

Practice more at vhlcentral.com.

Ortografía El acento y las sílabas fuertes

In Spanish, written accent marks are used on many words. Here is a review of some of the principles governing word stress and the use of written accents.

as-pi-ri-na   **gri-pe**   **to-man**   **an-tes**

In Spanish, when a word ends in a vowel, **–n**, or **–s**, the spoken stress usually falls on the next-to-last syllable. Words of this type are very common and do not need a written accent.

a-sí   **in-glés**   **in-fec-ción**   **hé-ro-e**

When a word ends in a vowel, **–n**, or **–s**, and the spoken stress does *not* fall on the next-to-last syllable, then a written accent is needed.

hos-pi-tal   **na-riz**   **re-ce-tar**   **to-ser**

When a word ends in any consonant *other* than **–n** or **–s**, the spoken stress usually falls on the last syllable. Words of this type are very common and do not need a written accent.

lá-piz   **fút-bol**   **hués-ped**   **sué-ter**

When a word ends in any consonant *other* than **–n** or **–s**, and the spoken stress does *not* fall on the last syllable, then a written accent is needed.

far-ma-cia   **bio-lo-gí-a**   **su-cio**   **frí-o**

Diphthongs (two weak vowels or a strong and weak vowel together) are normally pronounced as a single syllable. A written accent is needed when a diphthong is broken into two syllables.

sol   **pan**   **mar**   **tos**

Spanish words of only one syllable do not usually carry a written accent.

El ahorcado Juega al ahorcado (*hangman*) para adivinar las palabras.

1. __ l __ __ __ __ __ a   Vas allí cuando estás enfermo/a.
2. __ __ __ e __ c __ __ n   Se usa para poner una vacuna (*vaccination*).
3. __ __ d __ o __ __ __ __ __ a   Se usa para ver los huesos.

10 ESCENAS

¡Qué dolor! Video: *Fotonovela*

Jimena no se siente bien y tiene que ir al doctor.

Expresiones útiles

Discussing medical conditions

¿Cómo te sientes?
How do you feel?
Me duele un poco la garganta.
My throat hurts a little.
No me duele el estómago.
My stomach doesn't hurt.
De niño/a apenas me enfermaba.
As a child, I rarely got sick.
¡Soy alérgico/a al chile!
I'm allergic to chili powder!

Discussing remedies

Se dice que el té de jengibre es bueno para el dolor de estómago.
They say ginger tea is good for stomach aches.
Aquí están las pastillas para el resfriado.
Here are the pills for your cold.
Se debe tomar una cada seis horas.
You should take one every six hours.

Expressions with hacer

Hace + [*period of time*] **que** + [*present/ preterite*]
¿Cuánto tiempo hace que tienes estos síntomas?
How long have you had these symptoms?
Hace dos días que me duele la garganta.
My throat has been hurting for two days.
¿Cuánto tiempo hace que lo llamaste?
How long has it been since you called him?
Hace media hora.
It's been a half hour (since I called).

Additional vocabulary

canela *cinnamon*
miel *honey*
terco/a *stubborn*

recursos

VM
pp. 19–20

vhlcentral.com

ELENA ¿Cómo te sientes?
JIMENA Me duele un poco la garganta. Pero no tengo fiebre.
ELENA Creo que tienes un resfriado. Te voy a llevar a casa.

ELENA ¿Don Diego ya fue a la farmacia? ¿Cuánto tiempo hace que lo llamaste?
JIMENA Hace media hora. Ay, qué cosas, de niña apenas me enfermaba. No perdí ni un solo día de clases.
ELENA Yo tampoco.

ELENA Nunca tenía resfriados, pero me rompí el brazo dos veces. Mi hermana y yo estábamos paseando en bicicleta y casi me di con un señor que caminaba por la calle. Me caí y me rompí el brazo.

JIMENA ¿Qué es esto?
ELENA Es té de jengibre. Cuando me dolía el estómago, mi mamá siempre me hacía tomarlo. Se dice que es bueno para el dolor de estómago.
JIMENA Pero no me duele el estómago.

JIMENA Hola, don Diego. Gracias por venir.
DON DIEGO Fui a la farmacia. Aquí están las pastillas para el resfriado. Se debe tomar una cada seis horas con las comidas. Y no se deben tomar más de seis pastillas al día.

En el consultorio

 ELENA   JIMENA   DON DIEGO   SRA. DÍAZ   DR. MELÉNDEZ

(*La Sra. Díaz llama a Jimena*)
JIMENA Hola, mamá. Don Diego me trajo los medicamentos... ¿Al doctor? ¿Estás segura? Allá nos vemos. (*A Elena*) Mi mamá ya hizo una cita para mí con el Dr. Meléndez.

SRA. DÍAZ ¿Te pusiste un suéter anoche?
JIMENEZ No, mamá. Se me olvidó.
SRA. DÍAZ Doctor, esta jovencita salió anoche, se le olvidó ponerse un suéter y parece que le dio un resfriado.

DR. MELÉNDEZ Jimena, ¿cuáles son tus síntomas?
JIMENA Toso con frecuencia y me duele la garganta.
DR. MELÉNDEZ ¿Cuánto tiempo hace que tienes estos síntomas?
JIMENA Hace dos días que me duele la garganta.

DR. MELÉNDEZ Muy bien. Aquí no tienes infección. No tienes fiebre. Te voy a mandar algo para la garganta. Puedes ir por los medicamentos inmediatamente a la farmacia.

SRA. DÍAZ Doctor, ¿cómo está? ¿Es grave?
DR. MELÉNDEZ No, no es nada grave. Jimena, la próxima vez, escucha a tu mamá. ¡Tienes que usar suéter!

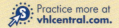
Practice more at vhlcentral.com.

Actividades

1 ¿Cierto o falso? Decide si lo que dicen estas oraciones sobre Jimena es **cierto** o **falso**. Corrige las oraciones falsas.

1. Dice que de niña apenas se enfermaba.
2. Tiene dolor de garganta y fiebre.
3. Olvidó ponerse un suéter anoche.
4. Hace tres días que le duele la garganta.
5. El doctor le dice que tiene una infección.

2 Ordenar Pon estos eventos en el orden correcto.

a. Jimena va a ver al doctor. ___
b. El doctor le dice a la Sra. Díaz que no es nada serio. ___
c. Elena le habla a Jimena de cuando se rompió el brazo. ___
d. El doctor le receta medicamentos. ___
e. Jimena le dice a Elena que le duele la garganta. ___
f. Don Diego le trae a Jimena las pastillas para el resfriado. ___

3 En el consultorio En parejas, preparen una conversación entre un(a) médico/a y su paciente. Sigan la guía.

- El médico le pregunta al/a la paciente qué le pasó.
- El/La paciente se cayó en su casa y piensa que se rompió un dedo.
- El/La médico/a le pregunta al/a la paciente si le duele y cuánto tiempo hace que se cayó.
- El/La paciente describe el dolor.
- El/la médico/a le recomienda un tratamiento (*treatment*).

10 EXPLORACIÓN

BAJO LA LUPA

Servicios de salud

¿Sabías que en los países hispanos no necesitas pagar por los servicios de salud? Ésta es una de las diferencias que hay entre países como los Estados Unidos y los países hispanos.

En la mayor parte de estos países, el gobierno ofrece servicios médicos muy baratos o gratuitos° a sus ciudadanos°. Los turistas y extranjeros también pueden tener acceso a los servicios médicos a bajo° costo. La Seguridad Social y organizaciones similares son las responsables de gestionar° estos servicios.

Naturalmente, esto no funciona igual° en todos los países. En Ecuador, México y Perú, la

Cruz verde de farmacia en Madrid, España

situación varía según las regiones. Los habitantes de las ciudades y pueblos grandes tienen acceso a más servicios médicos, mientras que quienes viven en pueblos remotos sólo cuentan con° pequeñas clínicas.

Por su parte, Costa Rica, Colombia, Cuba y España tienen sistemas de salud muy desarrollados°. En España, por ejemplo, la mayoría de las personas tienen acceso a ellos y en muchos casos son completamente gratuitos. Según un informe de la Organización Mundial de la Salud, el sistema de salud español ocupa uno de los primeros diez lugares del mundo. Esto se debe no sólo al buen funcionamiento° del sistema, sino también al nivel de salud general de la población. Impresionante, ¿no?

Consulta médica en la República Dominicana

Las farmacias

Farmacia de guardia: Las farmacias generalmente tienen un horario comercial. Sin embargo°, en cada barrio° hay una farmacia de guardia que abre las veinticuatro horas del día.

Productos farmacéuticos: Todavía hay muchas farmacias tradicionales que están más especializadas en medicinas y productos farmacéuticos. No venden productos de otro tipo.

Recetas: Muchos medicamentos se venden sin receta. Los farmacéuticos aconsejan° a las personas sobre problemas de salud y les dan las medicinas.

Cruz° verde: En muchos países, las farmacias tienen el signo de una cruz verde. Cuando la cruz verde está encendida°, la farmacia está abierta.

gratuitos *free (of charge)*   ciudadanos *citizens*   bajo *low*
gestionar *to manage*   igual *in the same way*   cuentan con *have*
desarrollados *developed*   funcionamiento *operation*
Sin embargo *However*   barrio *neighborhood*   aconsejan *advise*
Cruz *Cross*   encendida *lit (up)*

222   doscientos veintidós

En el consultorio

ACTIVIDADES

1 ¿Cierto o falso? Indica si lo que dicen las oraciones es **cierto** o **falso**.

1. En los países hispanos los gobiernos ofrecen servicios de salud accesibles a sus ciudadanos.
2. En los países hispanos los extranjeros tienen que pagar mucho dinero por los servicios médicos.
3. El sistema de salud español es uno de los mejores del mundo.
4. Las farmacias de guardia abren sólo los sábados y domingos.
5. En los países hispanos las farmacias venden una gran variedad de productos.
6. Los farmacéuticos de los países hispanos aconsejan a los enfermos y venden algunas medicinas sin necesidad de receta.
7. En México y otros países, los pueblos remotos cuentan con grandes centros médicos.
8. Muchas farmacias usan una cruz verde como símbolo.

2 Comparación En parejas, comparen el sistema de salud de los países hispanos con el de su país. ¿En qué se parecen? ¿En qué se diferencian? ¿Cuál prefieren ustedes? ¿Por qué?

CONEXIÓN INTERNET

¿Qué otra forma de servicio de atención médica se ofrece en los países hispanos?

For more information about **Exploración**, go to **vhlcentral.com**.

La salud

1 Preparación ¿Qué haces si tienes un pequeño accidente o quieres hacer una consulta? ¿Visitas a tu médico general o vas al hospital? ¿Debes pedir un turno (*appointment*)?

2 El video Mira el episodio de **Flash cultura**.

Vocabulario
la cita previa *previous appointment*
la guardia *emergency room*
Me di un golpe. *I got bumped.*
la práctica *rotation (hands-on medical experience)*

¿Le podría° pedir que me explique qué es la guardia?

Nuestro hospital público es gratuito para todas las personas.

podría *could*

3 ¿Cierto o falso? Indica si las oraciones son **ciertas** o **falsas**.

1. Silvina tuvo un accidente en su automóvil.
2. Silvina fue a la guardia del hospital.
3. La guardia del hospital está abierta sólo durante el día y es necesario tener cita previa.
4. Los entrevistados (*interviewees*) tienen enfermedades graves.
5. En Argentina, los médicos reciben la certificación cuando terminan la práctica.

doscientos veintitrés 223

10 GRAMÁTICA

10.1 The imperfect tense  Tutorial

▶ In Lessons 6–9, you learned the preterite tense. Now you will learn the imperfect tense, which describes past activities in a different way.

De niña apenas me enfermaba.

The imperfect of regular verbs

	cantar	beber	escribir
yo	cantaba	bebía	escribía
tú	cantabas	bebías	escribías
Ud./él/ella	cantaba	bebía	escribía
nosotros/as	cantábamos	bebíamos	escribíamos
vosotros/as	cantabais	bebíais	escribíais
Uds./ellos/ellas	cantaban	bebían	escribían

Cuando me dolía el estómago, mi mamá me daba té de jengibre.

▶ There are no stem changes in the imperfect tense.

Me **duelen** los pies.	Me **dolían** los pies.
My feet hurt.	*My feet were hurting.*

▶ The imperfect form of **hay** (*inf.* **haber**) is **había** (*there was/were/used to be*).

Había sólo un médico.	**Había** dos pacientes allí.
There was only one doctor.	*There were two patients there.*

¡ojo!

The imperfect endings of **–er** and **–ir** verbs are the same. The **nosotros** form of **–ar** verbs has an accent on the first **a** of the ending. **–Er** and **–ir** verb forms carry an accent on the first **i** of the ending.

• • •

Ir, ser, and **ver** are the only irregular verbs in the imperfect.

Irregular verbs in the imperfect

	ir	ser	ver
yo	iba	era *soy*	veía
tú	ibas	eras *eres*	veías
Ud./él/ella	iba	era *es*	veía
nosotros/as	íbamos	éramos *somos*	veíamos
vosotros/as	ibais	erais	veíais
Uds./ellos/ellas	iban	eran *son*	veían

▶ The imperfect is used to describe past events in a different way than the preterite. Generally, the imperfect describes actions which are seen by the speaker as incomplete or continuing, while the preterite describes actions that have been completed. The imperfect expresses what was happening at a certain time or how things used to be.

¿Qué te **pasó**?	Me **torcí** el tobillo.	¿Dónde **vivías** de niño?	**Vivía** en San José.
What happened to you?	*I sprained my ankle.*	*Where did you live as a child?*	*I lived in San José.*

▶ Use these expressions with the imperfect to express habitual or repeated actions:
de niño/a (*as a child*), **todos los días** (*every day*), **mientras** (*while*).

En el consultorio

Uses of the imperfect

Habitual or repeated actions	Íbamos al parque los domingos. *We used to go to the park on Sundays.*	**Age**	Los niños tenían seis años. *The children were 6 years old.*
Events or actions that were in progress	Yo leía mientras él estudiaba. *I was reading while he was studying.*	**Physical characteristics**	Era alto y guapo. *He was tall and handsome.*
Telling time	Eran las tres y media. *It was 3:30.*	**Mental or emotional states**	Quería mucho a su familia. *He loved his family very much.*

Práctica y conversación

1 La salud Completa las oraciones con el imperfecto. Algunos verbos se repiten. Hay dos verbos que no vas a usar.

caerse	esperar	mirar	sentirse
doler	estar	poder	tener
enfermarse	estornudar	querer	toser

1. Después de correr, a Dora le _____ los pies.
2. Ana _____ el termómetro; con tanta fiebre no _____ leerlo.
3. El paciente _____ mientras el doctor _____ ocupado atendiendo a otros pacientes.
4. Lorenzo _____ dolor de muelas, pero no _____ ir al dentista porque tenía miedo.
5. Paco y Luis _____ dolor de estómago y _____ unas pastillas para el dolor.
6. Le _____ la cabeza y _____ mareado.
7. Luisa _____ siempre porque era alérgica al polen.
8. Juan Carlos siempre _____ de la bicicleta.

2 ¡Pobre Miguelito! Completa las oraciones con el imperfecto. Luego, ordénalas lógicamente del 1 al 7.

___ a. Finalmente, Miguelito no _____ [ir] a jugar más. Ahora quería ir a casa a descansar.
___ b. El doctor dijo que no _____ [ser] nada grave.
___ c. El niño le dijo a la enfermera que _____ [dolerle] la nariz.
___ d. _____ [ser] las dos de la tarde y los niños _____ [jugar] en el patio.
___ e. Su mamá _____ [estar] dibujando cuando Miguelito entró llorando.
___ f. Miguelito _____ [tener] mucho dolor.
___ g. El doctor _____ [querer] examinar su nariz.

3 Entrevista En parejas, un(a) estudiante debe entrevistar a su compañero/a. Luego compartan los resultados de la entrevista con la clase.

1. ¿Cuántos años tenías en 1998? ¿Y en 2007?
2. ¿Veías mucha televisión cuando eras niño/a?
3. Cuando eras niño/a, ¿qué hacías durante las vacaciones?
4. Cuando eras estudiante de primaria, ¿te gustaban tus maestros?
5. Cuando tenías diez años, ¿cuál era tu programa de televisión favorito?
6. Cuando tenías quince años, ¿cuál era tu grupo musical favorito?
7. Cuando eras estudiante de secundaria, ¿qué hacías con tus amigos/as después de la escuela?
8. Antes de tomar esta clase, ¿sabías hablar español?

4 Describir En parejas, túrnense para describir lo que hacían de niños. Elijan una de estas preguntas y compartan la anécdota con su compañero/a.

MODELO
De niña, mi familia y yo siempre íbamos a Tortuguero. Tomábamos un barco desde Limón, y por las noches mirábamos las tortugas (*turtles*) en la playa. Algunas veces teníamos suerte porque las tortugas venían a poner (*lay*) huevos. Otras veces, volvíamos al hotel sin ver ninguna tortuga.

- ¿Qué hacías durante las vacaciones cuando eras niño/a?
- ¿Qué hacías en ocasiones especiales?
- ¿Cómo eran las celebraciones con tus amigos/as o familia?
- ¿Cómo era tu escuela? ¿Te gustaban tus maestros/as y compañeros/as?
- ¿Cómo eran tus amigos/as? ¿A qué jugabas con ellos/as?

doscientos veinticinco 225

Lección 10

10.2 Constructions with se  Tutorial

▶ As you know, **se** can be used as a reflexive pronoun (**Él se despierta.**).

▶ Non-reflexive verbs can also be used with **se** to form impersonal constructions. In impersonal constructions, the person performing the action is not defined. In English, the passive voice or indefinite subjects (*you, they, one*) are used.

> **¡ojo!**
> The third person singular verb form is used with singular nouns and the third person plural form is used with plural nouns:
> **Se vende ropa.**
> **Se venden camisas.**

Se habla español en Costa Rica.
Spanish is spoken in Costa Rica.

Se puede leer en la sala de espera.
You can read in the waiting room.

▶ You often see the impersonal **se** in signs and advertisements.

SE PROHÍBE NADAR

Se necesitan programadores
GRUPO TECNO
Tel. 778-34-34

ENTRADA
Se entra por la izquierda

▶ **Se** can also be used to de-emphasize the person who performs an action, implying that the accident or event is not his/her direct responsibility. Use this construction:

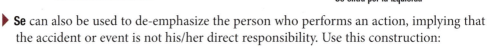

se	+	INDIRECT OBJECT PRONOUN	+	VERB	+	SUBJECT
Se		me		cayó		la pluma.

I dropped the pen.

¿Se te perdió el suéter anoche?

▶ In this construction, what would normally be the direct object of the sentence becomes the subject and agrees with the verb.

No, mamá. Se me olvidó.

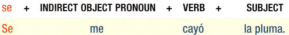

I.O. PRONOUN	+	VERB	+	SUBJECT
me		perdieron		las llaves.
te		cayó		la taza.
Se le		dañó		el radio.
nos		rompieron		las botellas.
os		olvidaron		las pastillas.
les				

▶ These verbs are often used with **se** to describe unplanned events.

> **¡ojo!**
> **Dejar caer** (*to let fall*) is often used to mean *to drop*.
> Elena **dejó caer** el libro.
> *Elena dropped the book.*
> El médico **dejó caer** la aspirina.
> *The doctor dropped the aspirin.*

| caer | to fall; to drop | olvidar | to forget | quedar | to be left behind |
| dañar | to damage; to break down | perder (e:ie) | to lose | romper | to break |

▶ **A** + [*noun*] or **a** + [*prepositional pronoun*] is frequently used to clarify or emphasize who is involved in the action.

Al estudiante se le perdió la tarea.
The student lost his homework.

A mí se me olvidó ir a clase ayer.
I forgot to go to class yesterday.

226 doscientos veintiséis

Práctica y conversación

1 ¿Cierto o falso? Lee estas oraciones sobre la vida en 1901. Indica si lo que dice cada oración es **cierto** o **falso**. Luego corrige las oraciones falsas.

Cierto   Falso
_____   _____   1. Se veía mucha televisión.
_____   _____   2. Se escribían muchos libros.
_____   _____   3. Se viajaba mucho en tren.
_____   _____   4. Se montaba a caballo.
_____   _____   5. Se mandaban correos electrónicos.
_____   _____   6. Se llevaban minifaldas.

2 Anuncios Traduce estos anuncios (*ads*) al español con el **se** impersonal.

ENGINEERS NEEDED
1. _____

EATING AND DRINKING PROHIBITED
2. _____

PROGRAMMERS SOUGHT
3. _____

WE SPEAK ENGLISH
4. _____

WE SELL COMPUTERS
5. _____

NO TALKING
6. _____

TEACHER NEEDED
7. _____

WE SELL BOOKS
8. _____

DO NOT ENTER
9. _____

SPANISH SPOKEN
10. _____

3 Preguntas Trabajen en parejas y usen estas preguntas para entrevistarse.

1. ¿Qué comidas se sirven en tu restaurante favorito?
2. ¿Se te olvidó invitar a alguien a tu última fiesta o cena? ¿A quién?
3. ¿A qué hora se abre la cafetería de tu universidad?
4. ¿Alguna vez se te quedó algo importante en casa?
5. ¿Alguna vez se te perdió algo importante durante un viaje? ¿Qué?
6. ¿Qué se vende en la librería de la universidad?
7. ¿Sabes si en la librería se aceptan cheques?
8. ¿Alguna vez se te rompió un plato o un vaso (*glass*)? ¿Dónde?

4 Minidiálogos En parejas, preparen estos minidiálogos. Luego preséntenlos a la clase.

1. Un(a) profesor(a) de español le pide a un(a) estudiante su cuaderno de práctica (*workbook*). El/La estudiante le explica por qué él/ella no lo tiene.
2. Un(a) turista le pregunta al botones (*bellhop*) dónde se sirve la mejor comida en la ciudad. El botones hace varias sugerencias.
3. Un(a) paciente le dice al/a la doctor(a) que él/ella no puede caminar. El/La doctor(a) examina al/a la paciente y le explica el problema.
4. Un padre le pregunta a su hijo/a qué le pasó al plato que está roto (*broken*) en el piso. El/La hijo/a se disculpa y le explica lo que sucedió.

5 Anuncios En grupos, preparen dos anuncios (*ads*) de televisión para presentar a la clase. Deben usar el imperfecto y dos construcciones con **se**.

MODELO
Se me cayeron unos libros sobre el pie. Me dolía mucho. Pero ahora no, gracias a Superaspirina 500. ¡Tomé dos pastillas y se me fue el dolor! Se puede comprar Superaspirina 500 en todas las farmacias Recetamax.

doscientos veintisiete 227

Lección 10

10.3 Adverbs Tutorial

▶ Adverbs describe how, when, and where actions take place. They modify verbs, adjectives, and even other adverbs. The list below contains some adverbs you have already learned.

bien	muy	hoy	temprano	aquí
mal	nunca	siempre	ayer	allí

▶ Most adverbs end in **–mente**. These are equivalent to the English adverbs which end in *–ly*.

lentamente	slowly	generalmente	generally
verdaderamente	truly, really	simplemente	simply

¡ojo!
When a sentence contains two or more adverbs in sequence, the suffix **-mente** is dropped from all but the last adverb.
Ex: **El médico nos habló simple y abiertamente.** *The doctor spoke to us simply and openly.*

▶ To form adverbs which end in **–mente**, add **–mente** to the feminine form of the adjective. If the adjective does not have a feminine form, just add **–mente** to the standard form.

ADJECTIVE	FEMININE FORM	SUFFIX	ADVERB
lento	lenta	–mente	lentamente
fabuloso	fabulosa	–mente	fabulosamente
enorme		–mente	enormemente
feliz		–mente	felizmente

▶ Adverbs that end in **–mente** generally follow the verb, while adverbs that modify an adjective or another adverb precede the word they modify.

Javier dibuja **maravillosamente.**
Javier draws wonderfully.

Inés está **casi siempre** ocupada.
Inés is almost always busy.

Common adverbs and adverbial expressions

a menudo	often	así	like this; so	menos	less
a tiempo	on time	bastante	enough; quite	muchas veces	a lot; many times
a veces	sometimes	casi	almost		
además (de)	furthermore; besides	con frecuencia	frequently	poco	little
		de vez en cuando	from time to time	por lo menos	at least
apenas	hardly; scarcely			pronto	soon

ESPAÑOL EN VIVO

No hay tiempo para el dolor de cabeza.

Si tienes prisa o si simplemente quieres que tu dolor de cabeza se vaya muy pronto, piensa en Capalivia. Se asimila mejor y actúa rápidamente. Ya no se puede perder tiempo por un dolor de cabeza.

228 doscientos veintiocho

En el consultorio

Práctica y conversación

1 En la clínica
Completa las oraciones con los adverbios adecuados.

1. La cita era a las nueve, pero llegamos _____ [aquí, nunca, tarde].
2. El problema fue que _____ [aquí, ayer, así] se nos rompió el despertador.
3. La recepcionista no se enojó porque sabía que normalmente llegamos _____ [a veces, a tiempo, poco].
4. _____ [Por lo menos, Muchas veces, Poco] el doctor estaba listo.
5. _____ [Lentamente, Además, Apenas] tuvimos que esperar cinco minutos.
6. El doctor dijo que nuestra hija Irene necesitaba una operación _____ [casi, a veces, inmediatamente].
7. Cuando Irene salió de la operación, le preguntamos _____ [con frecuencia, nerviosamente, muchas veces] al doctor cómo estaba nuestra hija.
8. _____ [Bastante, Afortunadamente, A menudo], el médico nos contestó que Irene estaba bien.

2 Oraciones
Combina palabras de las tres columnas para formar oraciones completas.

MODELO
Mi mejor amigo se enferma frecuentemente.
Jennifer López conduce rápidamente.

Sujetos	Verbos	Adverbios
mi mejor amigo/a	caerse	bien
mi(s) padre(s)	casarse	fabulosamente
el/la profesor(a) de español	conducir	felizmente
yo	divertirse	frecuentemente
los jóvenes	enfermarse	mal
Charlie Sheen	estornudar	muchas veces
Jennifer López	ir	poco
las celebridades	levantarse	pronto
todos nosotros	llevarse	rápidamente
	vestirse	tarde
		temprano
		tranquilamente

3 Preguntas
Usa estas preguntas para entrevistar a un(a) compañero/a.

1. ¿Qué sabes hacer muy bien?
2. ¿Qué estudias además de español?
3. ¿Hay compañeros/as de clase a quienes apenas conoces?
4. ¿Qué gustos (*treats*) te das de vez en cuando?
5. ¿Cenas bastante en restaurantes?
6. ¿Te enfermas a menudo?
7. ¿Con qué frecuencia vas al doctor?
8. ¿Qué haces si te sientes congestionado/a y estornudas muchas veces?

4 ¿Con qué frecuencia?
Averigua (*Find out*) con qué frecuencia tus compañeros/as hacen estas actividades. Comparte los resultados con la clase.

MODELO
pasear en bicicleta
Estudiante 1: ¿Paseas en bicicleta con mucha frecuencia?
Estudiante 2: Sí, paseo en bicicleta con mucha frecuencia./No, casi nunca paseo en bicicleta.

Actividades	con mucha frecuencia	de vez en cuando	casi nunca	nunca
1. Nadar	___	___	___	___
2. Jugar al tenis	___	___	___	___
3. Hacer la tarea	___	___	___	___
4. Salir a bailar	___	___	___	___
5. Mirar la televisión	___	___	___	___
6. Dormir en clase	___	___	___	___
7. Perder las gafas	___	___	___	___
8. Tomar medicina	___	___	___	___
9. Ir al dentista	___	___	___	___

doscientos veintinueve 229

Lección 10

Ampliación

1 Escuchar

A Escucha la conversación de la señorita Méndez y Carlos Peña. Marca las oraciones donde se mencionan los síntomas de Carlos.

TIP **Listen for specific information.** Identify the subject of a conversation and use your background knowledge to predict what kind of information you might hear. For example, what would you expect to hear in a conversation between a sick person and a doctor's receptionist?

_____ 1. Tiene infección en los ojos. _____ 8. No puede dormir.
_____ 2. Se lastimó el dedo. _____ 9. Es alérgico a la aspirina.
_____ 3. Tiene tos. _____ 10. Le duele la garganta.
_____ 4. Está congestionado. _____ 11. Tiene frío.
_____ 5. Está mareado. _____ 12. Se rompió la pierna.
_____ 6. Le duele la cabeza. _____ 13. Le duele la rodilla.
_____ 7. Le duele el estómago. _____ 14. Siente dolor en los huesos.

B En tu opinión, ¿qué tiene Carlos? ¿Gripe? ¿Un resfriado? ¿Alergia? Explica tu opinión.

2 Conversar
En parejas, preparen una conversación entre un(a) estudiante hipocondríaco/a y un(a) enfermero/a. Presenten la conversación a la clase.

- Decidan qué síntomas tiene el/la estudiante y con qué frecuencia los tiene.
- Decidan qué preguntas le va a hacer el/la enfermero/a. Por ejemplo: ¿Cuánto tiempo hace que comenzaron los síntomas? ¿Tenía el mismo problema cuando era niño/a? ¿Lo tenía la semana pasada?
- Decidan qué consejos le va a dar el/la enfermero/a.

En el consultorio

3 Escribir Imagina que eres enfermero/a en la sala de emergencia de un hospital. Tienes que escribir cada día un parte (*report*) médico para tu supervisor(a).

TIP Avoid redundancies. To avoid repetition of verbs and nouns, consult a Spanish-language thesaurus. You can also use direct object pronouns, possessive adjectives, demonstrative adjectives and pronouns, and prepositional pronouns to streamline your writing.

Susana se lastimó la rodilla ayer. ~~Susana~~ Ella estaba corriendo por el parque cuando se cayó y se ~~la~~ lastimó la rodilla.

Organízalo Utiliza un mapa de ideas para organizar tu parte médico. Incluye información sobre los pacientes, sus síntomas y el resultado de los tratamientos.

Escríbelo Utiliza tus apuntes para escribir el primer borrador del parte médico.

Corrígelo Intercambia tu composición con un(a) compañero/a. Lee su borrador y anota los aspectos mejor escritos (*written*). Ofrécele sugerencias para evitar (*avoid*) redundancias, y si ves algunos errores gramaticales u ortográficos, coméntaselos.

Compártelo Revisa el primer borrador según las indicaciones de tu compañero/a. Incorpora nuevas ideas o más información si es necesario antes de escribir la versión final del parte médico.

4 Un paso más Prepara una presentación sobre el sistema de servicios médicos de un país hispano. Tu presentación debe contestar estas preguntas.

- ¿Qué servicios médicos públicos hay en el país?
- ¿Cuál es el papel (*role*) de las clínicas y los hospitales privados?
- ¿Cómo son los servicios médicos en las ciudades y en las áreas rurales?
- ¿Son populares los tratamientos alternativos?
- ¿Hay personas reconocidas por sus contribuciones a la medicina?

CONEXIÓN INTERNET

Investiga estos temas en vhlcentral.com.

- Hospitales y clínicas en el mundo hispano
- Facultades de medicina en el mundo hispano
- Médicos famosos del mundo hispano

10 LECTURA

Antes de leer

Using what you already know about a particular subject will often help you better understand a reading selection. For example, if you read an article about a recent medical discovery, you might think about what you already know about health in order to understand unfamiliar words or concepts.

1. A primera vista, ¿cuál es el tema de esta lectura?
   _____
   _____

2. ¿Qué tipo de documento es? ¿Cómo lo sabes?
   _____
   _____

3. Basándote en documentos similares que conoces, ¿qué tipo de información esperas encontrar en esta lectura?
   _____
   _____

El consultorio
Dra. Fernanda Jiménez Ocaña

P: Soy una madre española y le escribo para hacerle una consulta sobre mi hijo. Tiene ocho años y hace una semana que ni come ni duerme bien. Además, desde hace cuatro días° tose constantemente. Al no consumir la cantidad de alimentos° necesarios ni dormir lo suficiente, mi hijo no tiene energía para realizar sus actividades diarias. Estoy un poco preocupada porque es la primera vez que el niño presenta este tipo de síntomas. Todavía no hemos ido° al médico porque me interesa conocer primero su punto de vista°. Muchísimas gracias por su ayuda.

R: Querida° madre española: Gracias por escribir en mi columna. Cuando un niño de la edad de su hijo presenta este tipo de síntomas, puede ser señal° de que tiene una pequeña infección en las vías° respiratorias, producida por una bacteria o por un virus. Creo que debe llevar pronto a su hijo al consultorio de su médico para evitar° la aparición de una enfermedad crónica como la bronquitis. Si tiene más preguntas o si desea contarme cómo evoluciona su hijo, ya sabe que puede escribirme otra vez.

232 doscientos treinta y dos

En el consultorio

P: Hola, doctora. Soy un ciclista profesional de Colombia. Hace dos semanas tuve un accidente con mi bicicleta y me lastimé la rodilla. Fui a la sala de emergencias y el médico me hizo una radiografía para ver si tenía un hueso roto. Afortunadamente, los resultados de la radiografía fueron muy buenos y sólo me recetaron unas pastillas y mucho reposo. Le escribo porque, después de este tiempo, sigo sintiendo dolor en la zona de la rodilla. ¿Qué puedo hacer?

R: Querido amigo ciclista: Creo que, en su caso, necesita tener más paciencia. Hay que° comprender que algunas veces el cuerpo requiere más tiempo para recuperarse. Creo que tiene que esperar dos semanas más para ver si el dolor va desapareciendo o no. Si sigue las indicaciones de su médico y no nota ningún cambio, debe volver al hospital. En mi opinión, no debe hacer ningún movimiento con la pierna y debe seguir tomándose las pastillas que le recetaron.

P: Le escribo desde Puerto Rico para pedirle su opinión. Durante este mes y el anterior°, tengo los síntomas de un resfriado que no desaparece nunca. Toso, estoy congestionado y tengo la garganta y los ojos irritados. Mi novia opina que soy alérgico a algo. ¿Cree que eso es posible?

R: Estimado° amigo puertorriqueño: Debe empezar por observar dónde y cuándo aparecen sus síntomas. El otoño y la primavera son las épocas del año en que suele haber° más reacciones alérgicas del tipo que usted presenta. Creo que debe ir al médico y esperar los resultados de las pruebas°. Si le diagnostican un tipo de alergia, no debe preocuparse. En la actualidad, existen tratamientos excelentes, incluyendo antihistamínicos e inyecciones, que calman los efectos de las reacciones alérgicas y lo ayudan a llevar una vida normal.

¡Salud!

Dra. Fernanda Jiménez Ocaña

desde hace cuatro días *for four days*   alimentos *foods*   no hemos ido *we haven't been*
punto de vista *point of view*   Querido/a *Dear*   señal *sign*   vías *passages*   evitar
to avoid   Hay que *It is necessary to*   el anterior *the previous one*   Estimado/a *Dear*
suele haber *there are customarily*   pruebas *tests*

Después de leer

¿Comprendiste?

Indica si cada oración es **cierta** o **falsa**. Corrige las oraciones falsas.

Cierto   Falso

_____   _____   1. La madre española no come bien.

_____   _____   2. La doctora piensa que el hijo de la española puede tener una infección.

_____   _____   3. La doctora piensa que el ciclista debe practicar más el ciclismo.

_____   _____   4. La radiografía indica que el ciclista colombiano tiene algunos huesos rotos.

_____   _____   5. La doctora cree que el chico puertorriqueño puede tener alergias.

_____   _____   6. Hace dos meses que el puertorriqueño tiene los síntomas de un resfriado.

Preguntas

Responde a estas preguntas con oraciones completas.

1. ¿Con qué frecuencia tose el hijo de la madre española?

2. ¿Cuánto tiempo hace que el colombiano se lastimó la rodilla?

3. ¿Qué hizo el médico cuando el ciclista fue a la sala de emergencias?

4. ¿Por qué debe ser paciente el ciclista?

5. ¿Qué debe hacer la madre española?

6. Según (*According to*) la doctora, ¿cuándo ocurren más frecuentemente las reacciones alérgicas?

Coméntalo

¿Hay una columna de consejos médicos en el periódico de tu ciudad? ¿La lees frecuentemente? ¿Por qué sí o por qué no? Imagina que tú escribes las respuestas de esta columna, ¿qué deben hacer las tres personas que pidieron consejos?

doscientos treinta y tres **233**

10 VOCABULARIO

El cuerpo

la boca	mouth
el brazo	arm
la cabeza	head
el corazón	heart
el cuello	neck
el cuerpo	body
el dedo	finger
el estómago	stomach
la garganta	throat
el hueso	bone
la nariz	nose
el ojo	eye
la oreja	(outer) ear
el pie	foot
la pierna	leg
la rodilla	knee
el tobillo	ankle

Adjetivos

congestionado/a	congested; stuffed-up
embarazada	pregnant
grave	grave; serious
mareado/a	dizzy; nauseated
médico/a	medical
saludable	healthy
sano/a	healthy

La salud

el accidente	accident
el antibiótico	antibiotic
la aspirina	aspirin
la clínica	clinic
el consultorio	doctor's office
el/la dentista	dentist
el/la doctor(a)	doctor
el dolor (de cabeza)	(head)ache; pain
la enfermedad	illness; sickness
el/la enfermero/a	nurse
el examen médico	physical exam
la farmacia	pharmacy
la gripe	flu
el hospital	hospital
la infección	infection
el medicamento	medication
la medicina	medicine
la operación	operation
el/la paciente	patient
las pastillas	pills; tablets
la radiografía	X-ray
la receta	prescription
el resfriado	cold
la sala de emergencia(s)	emergency room
la salud	health
el síntoma	symptom
la tos	cough

Verbos

caer	to fall; to drop
caerse	to fall (down)
dañar	to damage; to break down
doler (o:ue)	to hurt
enfermarse	to get sick
estar enfermo/a	to be sick
estornudar	to sneeze
lastimarse (el pie)	to injure (one's foot)
olvidar	to forget
poner una inyección	to give an injection
prohibir	to prohibit
quedar	to be left behind
recetar	to prescribe
romper	to break
romperse (la pierna)	to break (one's leg)
sacar(se) una muela	to have a tooth pulled
ser alérgico/a (a)	to be allergic (to)
tener fiebre (f.)	to have a fever
tomar(le) la temperatura (a alguien)	to take (someone's) temperature
torcerse (el tobillo)	to sprain (one's ankle)
toser	to cough

Otras palabras y expresiones

de niño/a	as a child
mientras	while
todos los días	every day

Adverbs	See page 228.

234 doscientos treinta y cuatro

¡VIVAN LOS PAÍSES HISPANOS!

Un *snowboarder* salta (*jumps*) en el centro de esquí Portillo, uno de los más famosos y antiguos (*old*) de Chile. El esquí y el *snowboard* se pueden practicar en las montañas nevadas (*snow-capped*) de la cordillera de los Andes, que se extiende por todo el país. Gente de todo el mundo va a Chile a practicar los deportes de invierno. ¿Te gustaría esquiar en Chile?

Suramérica II

Argentina

Área: 2.780.400 km² (.074.000 millas²)

Población: 42.193.000

Capital: Buenos Aires–2.990.000

Ciudades principales: órdoba, Rosario, Mendoza

Moneda: peso argentino

SOURCE: Population Division, Secretariat & CIA World Factbook

Chile

Área: 756.100 km² (292.000 millas²)

Población: 17.067.000

Capital: Santiago de Chile–5.883.000

Ciudades principales: Concepción, Viña del Mar, Valparaíso, Temuco

Moneda: peso chileno

SOURCE: Population Division, UN Secretariat & CIA World Factbook

Uruguay

Área: 176.220 km² (68.039 millas²)

Población: 3.316.000

Capital: Montevideo–1.633.000

Ciudades principales: Salto, Paysandú, Las Piedras, Rivera

Moneda: peso uruguayo

SOURCE: Population Division, UN Secretariat & CIA World Factbook

Paraguay

Área: 406.750 km² (157.046 millas²)

Población: 6.542.000

Capital: Asunción–1.977.000

Ciudades principales: Ciudad del Este, San Lorenzo, Lambaré, Fernando de la Mora

Moneda: guaraní

SOURCE: Population Division, UN Secretariat & CIA World Factbook

Bolivia

Área: 1.098.580 km² (412.162 millas²)

Población: 10.290.000

Capital: La Paz, sede del gobierno (*seat of government*), capital administrativa–1.642.000; **Sucre,** capital constitucional y judicial

Ciudades principales: Santa Cruz de la Sierra, Cochabamba, Oruro, Potosí

Moneda: peso boliviano

SOURCE: Population Division, UN Secretariat & CIA World Factbook

¡Vivan los países hispanos!

Interactive map
Video: *Países hispanos*

Artes

El tango argentino

El tango es un símbolo cultural muy importante de Argentina. Este género (*genre*) musical es una mezcla de ritmos de origen africano, italiano y español, y surgió a finales del siglo XIX entre los porteños (*people of Buenos Aires*). Poco después se hizo popular entre el resto de los argentinos y su fama llegó hasta París. Como baile, el tango en un principio (*at first*) era provocativo y violento, pero se hizo más romántico durante los años 30. Hoy día, este estilo musical es popular en muchas partes del mundo (*world*).

Lugares

El lago Titicaca

Situado en los Andes de Bolivia y Perú, éste es el lago navegable más alto del mundo, a una altitud de 3.815 metros (12.500 pies). Con un área de más de 8.000 kilómetros^2 (3.000 millas^2), también es el segundo lago más grande de Suramérica, después del lago de Maracaibo, en Venezuela. La mitología inca cuenta que los hijos del dios (*god*) Sol emergieron de las profundas aguas del lago Titicaca para fundar su imperio (*empire*).

Suramérica II

Costumbres
La carne y el mate
En Chile, Uruguay y Argentina, la carne de res es un elemento esencial de la dieta diaria. Los platos más representativos de estas naciones son el asado (*barbecue*), la parrillada (*grilled meat*) y el chivito (*goat*). El mate, una infusión similar al té, también es típico de la región. Esta bebida de origen indígena se bebe a diario y reemplaza al café. Tradicionalmente se toma en una calabaza (*gourd*) con una bombilla (*straw*) de metal.

Naturaleza
Los ríos Paraguay y Paraná
Los ríos Paraguay y Paraná sirven de frontera (*border*) natural entre Argentina y Paraguay, y son las principales rutas de transporte de este último (*last*) país. El río Paraguay divide el Gran Chaco de la meseta (*plateau*) Paraná, donde vive la mayoría de los paraguayos. El Paraná tiene unos 3.200 kilómetros navegables; por esta ruta pasan barcos de más de 5.000 toneladas, los cuales viajan desde el estuario (*estuary*) del Río de la Plata hasta la ciudad de Asunción. El río Paraná confluye (*meets*) con el río Iguazú en la frontera entre Brasil, Argentina y Paraguay. Allí forman las cataratas (*waterfalls*) del Iguazú, uno de los sitios turísticos más visitados en Suramérica. Estas extensas cataratas miden unos 70 metros (230 pies) de altura (*height*).

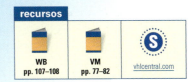

recursos
WB pp. 107–108
VM pp. 77–82
vhlcentral.com

doscientos treinta y siete 237

¡Vivan los países hispanos!

¿Qué aprendiste?

1 ¿Cierto o falso? Decide si lo que dicen las siguientes oraciones es **cierto** o **falso**.

Cierto	Falso	
_____	_____	1. Portillo es un centro de esquí en Argentina.
_____	_____	2. Viña del Mar y Concepción son dos de las ciudades principales de Chile.
_____	_____	3. Asunción es la capital de Uruguay.
_____	_____	4. En un principio, el tango era un baile tranquilo.
_____	_____	5. El tango es uno de los símbolos culturales más importantes de Argentina.
_____	_____	6. El lago Titicaca es el más bajo del mundo.
_____	_____	7. El lago Titicaca es el lago más grande de Suramérica después del lago de Maracaibo.
_____	_____	8. La carne de res forma parte de la dieta diaria de Argentina y Uruguay.
_____	_____	9. El mate es una bebida similar al té.
_____	_____	10. El río Paraguay pasa entre Argentina y Chile.
_____	_____	11. En la meseta Paraná vive muy poca gente.
_____	_____	12. Las cataratas del Iguazú están en la frontera entre Brasil, Paraguay y Argentina.

2 Preguntas Contesta las siguientes preguntas.

1. ¿En qué lugares de los Estados Unidos se puede practicar esquí y *snowboard*? ¿Te gustaría practicarlos en las montañas nevadas de la cordillera de Los Andes?
2. ¿Sabes bailar tango? ¿Te gusta ese tipo de baile? ¿Por qué?
3. ¿Qué otros lagos navegables conoces? ¿Cuál te gustaría visitar?
4. ¿Probaste alguna vez el mate? ¿Te gustaría probarlo? ¿Qué otras comidas típicas de estos países conoces?
5. ¿Qué otras cataratas conoces? ¿Qué río(s) afecta(n)?

CONEXIÓN INTERNET

Investiga estos temas en el sitio **vhlcentral.com**.

- El tango en Argentina
- Deportes de invierno en Chile
- Preferencias gastronómicas en Uruguay
- La historia de Paraguay
- El sitio arqueológico Tiahuanaco en Bolivia

11 El carro y la tecnología

Communicative Goals
You will learn how to:
- talk about using technology and electronics
- talk about car trouble
- use common expressions on the telephone
- say how far away things are

PREPARACIÓN
pages 240–243
- Cars and driving
- Home electronics and the Internet
- Written accents with homophones

ESCENAS
pages 244–245
- Miguel's car has broken down again, and he has to take it to the mechanic. In the meantime, Maru has a similar streak of bad luck with her computer. Can their problems with technology be resolved?

EXPLORACIÓN
pages 246–247
- Bajo la lupa: *El teléfono celular*
- Flash cultura: *Maravillas de la tecnología*

GRAMÁTICA
pages 248–255
- The preterite and the imperfect
- **Por** and **para**
- Stressed possessive adjectives and pronouns

LECTURA
pages 256–257
- Comic strip: *El celular*

Para empezar
- ¿Quiénes son las personas de la foto?
- ¿Dónde están: en un consultorio o en un taller mecánico?
- ¿Qué están haciendo?
- ¿Cómo crees que se sienten estas personas? ¿Por qué?

11 PREPARACIÓN

El carro y la tecnología

Talking Picture Tutorial Games

EN LA CALLE

la calle street
el camino route
el garaje garage; (mechanic's) repair shop
la gasolina gasoline
la gasolinera gas station
el kilómetro kilometer
el/la mecánico/a mechanic
la milla mile
la multa fine; ticket
el policía/la mujer policía police officer
la policía police (force)
el taller (mecánico) (mechanic's) repair shop
el tráfico traffic
la velocidad máxima speed limit

arrancar to start
arreglar to fix; to arrange
bajar to go down
bajar(se) de to get off of/out of (a vehicle)
chocar (con) to run into; to crash
conducir to drive
estacionar to park
manejar to drive
parar to stop
revisar (el aceite) to check (the oil)
subir to go up
subir(se) a to get on/into (a vehicle)

LAS PARTES DEL CARRO

el carro car
el coche car
los frenos brakes

el semáforo
traffic light

el capó
(car) hood

el parabrisas
windshield

el volante
steering wheel

el baúl
trunk

el motor
motor

la llanta
tire

la licencia de conducir
driver's license

llenar (el tanque)
to fill up (the tank)

recursos

WB
pp. 109–110

LM
p. 61

vhlcentral.com

240 doscientos cuarenta

El carro y la tecnología

LA TECNOLOGÍA

el buzón de voz voicemail
la cámara digital digital camera
el control remoto remote control
el disco compacto CD (compact disc)
el estéreo stereo
el fax fax (machine)
el mensaje de texto text message
el navegador GPS GPS
el radio radio (set)
el reproductor de CD CD player
                  de DVD DVD player
                  de MP3 MP3 player
el teléfono celular cell phone
la televisión por cable cable television

apagar to turn off
funcionar to work
llamar to call
poner to turn on
prender to turn on
sonar (o:ue) to ring

el televisor
television set

la cámara (de video)
(video) camera

la calculadora
calculator

ADJETIVOS

descompuesto/a not working; out of order
lento/a slow
lleno/a full

INTERNET Y LA COMPUTADORA

el archivo file
la computadora portátil laptop
la conexión inalámbrica wireless (connection)
el disco disk
Internet Internet
la página principal home page
la pantalla screen
el programa de computación software
la red network; Web
el sitio web website

guardar to save
imprimir to print
navegar en Internet to surf the Internet

la computadora computer
el monitor monitor
el ratón mouse
la impresora printer
el teclado keyboard

doscientos cuarenta y uno 241

Lección 11

Práctica y conversación  Audio: Activities

1 **¿Qué necesitas?** Identifica oralmente los dibujos. Luego escucha las oraciones e indica el objeto que necesitas para cada actividad.

1. _____ _____   4. _____ _____

2. _____ _____   5. _____ _____

3. _____ _____

2 **Problemas con la computadora** Completa la conversación con las palabras de la lista.

arreglar	funciona	llamar	prendiste
descompuesto	la impresora	navegar	el ratón
el disco	imprimir	la pantalla	el teléfono celular

JUAN CARLOS Mariana, la computadora no (1) _____. No veo nada en (2) _____.

MARIANA Pues, ¿la (3) _____?

JUAN CARLOS Tienes razón, no estaba prendida. Ahora no puedo conectarme a Internet. Parece que el sistema de conexión inalámbrica está (4) _____. ¿Cómo lo puedo (5) _____?

MARIANA ¡Ay, mi amor! Si (*If*) quieres, puedo (6) _____ a la compañía de Internet para ver qué pasa. Mientras tanto, creo que es mejor que uses (7) _____ para conectarte.

JUAN CARLOS Sí, gracias… Bueno, ahora sí estoy conectado. Voy a (8) _____ en Internet un rato y después voy a (9) _____ el trabajo para mi clase de historia. Pero… ¿dónde está (10) _____?

MARIANA Lo siento, ésa sí que está descompuesta.

JUAN CARLOS No te preocupes. Puedo llevar (11) _____ a la universidad e imprimirlo allá.

MARIANA ¡Qué buena idea!

recursos
vhlcentral.com

3 **Preguntas** Trabajen en grupos para contestar las siguientes preguntas. Después compartan sus respuestas con la clase.

¿Qué utilizas más: el teléfono celular, el correo electrónico o el *chat*? ¿Cuáles son las ventajas (*advantages*) y desventajas de los diferentes modos de comunicación? ¿Cómo usas la tecnología para divertirte? ¿Y para comunicarte? ¿Y para trabajar?

242 *doscientos cuarenta y dos*

El carro y la tecnología

4 En el taller En parejas, preparen una conversación entre un(a) mecánico/a y un(a) cliente/a cuyo (*whose*) coche se dañó en un accidente. El/La cliente/a le dice al/a la mecánico/a qué ocurrió en el accidente y los dos hablan de las partes dañadas.

5 Situación En parejas, preparen una conversación entre el/la director(a) de ventas (*sales*) de una tienda de computadoras y un(a) cliente/a. El cliente puede ser el padre de un niño de seis años, una mujer que va a crear una nueva empresa (*business*) en su casa, un hombre que viaja mucho o un estudiante que no sabe nada de computadoras. El/La director(a) de ventas pregunta lo que el/la cliente/a desea hacer con la computadora y le muestra la computadora que éste/a necesita.

Ortografía La acentuación de palabras similares

Although accent marks usually indicate which syllable in a word is stressed, they are also used to distinguish between words that have the same or similar spellings.

Él maneja **el** coche.   **Sí**, voy **si** quieres.

Although one-syllable words do not usually carry written accents, some *do* have accent marks to distinguish them from words that have the same spelling but different meanings.

Sé cocinar.   **Se** baña.   ¿Tomas **té**?   **Te** duermes.

Sé (*I know*) and **té** (*tea*) have accent marks to distinguish them from the pronouns **se** and **te**.

para **mí**   **mi** cámara   **Tú** lees.   **tu** estéreo

Mí (*me*) and **tú** (*you*) have accent marks to distinguish them from the possessive adjectives **mi** and **tu**.

¿**Por qué** vas?   Voy **porque** quiero.

Several words of many syllables have accent marks to distinguish them from words that have similar spellings.

Éste es rápido.   **Este** módem es rápido.

Demonstrative pronouns have accent marks to distinguish them from demonstrative adjectives.

¿**Cuándo** fuiste?   Fui **cuando** me llamó.

Adverbs have accent marks when they are used to convey a question.

Crucigrama Utiliza las siguientes pistas (*clues*) para completar el crucigrama. ¡Ojo con los acentos!

Horizontales
1. Él _____ levanta.
4. No voy _____ no puedo.
7. Tú _____ acuestas.
9. ¿_____ es el examen?
10. Quiero este video y _____.

Verticales
2. ¿Cómo _____ usted?
3. Eres _____ mi hermano.
5. ¿_____ tal?
6. Me gusta _____ suéter.
8. Navego _____ la red.

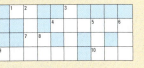

doscientos cuarenta y tres 243

11 ESCENAS

En el taller
Video: *Fotonovela*

El coche de Miguel está descompuesto y Maru tiene problemas con su computadora.

Expresiones útiles

Giving instructions to a friend

¿Me pasas la llave?
Can you pass me the wrench?
No lo manejes en carretera.
Don't drive it on the highway.
Revisa el aceite cada 1.500 kilómetros.
Check the oil every 1,500 kilometers.
Asegúrate de llenar el tanque.
Make sure to fill up the tank.
No manejes con el cofre abierto.
Don't drive with the hood open.
Recomiéndame con tus amigos.
Recommend me to your friends.

Taking a phone call

Aló./Bueno./Diga.
Hello.
¿Quién habla? / ¿De parte de quién?
Who is speaking/calling?
Con él/ella habla.
Speaking.
¿Puedo dejar un recado?
May I leave a message?

Reassuring someone

Tranquilo/a, cariño.
Relax, sweetie.
Nos ayudamos los unos a los otros.
We help each other out.
No te preocupes.
Don't worry.

Additional vocabulary

entregar *to hand in*
el intento *attempt*
la noticia *news*
el proyecto *project*
recuperar *to recover*

MIGUEL ¿Cómo lo ves?
JORGE Creo que puedo arreglarlo. ¿Me pasas la llave?

JORGE ¿Y dónde está Maru?
MIGUEL Acaba de enviarme un mensaje de texto: "Última noticia sobre la computadora portátil: todavía está descompuesta. Moni intenta arreglarla. Voy para allá".

JORGE ¿Está descompuesta tu computadora?
MIGUEL No, la mía no, la suya. Una amiga la está ayudando.
JORGE Un mal día para la tecnología, ¿no?

MIGUEL Ella está preparando un proyecto para ver si puede hacer sus prácticas profesionales en el Museo de Antropología.
JORGE ¿Y todo está en la computadora?
MIGUEL Y claro.

MARU Buenos días, Jorge.
JORGE ¡Qué gusto verte, Maru! ¿Cómo está la computadora?
MARU Mi amiga Mónica recuperó muchos archivos, pero muchos otros se borraron.

recursos

VM pp. 21–22

vhlcentral.com

244 doscientos cuarenta y cuatro

El carro y la tecnología

MIGUEL

JORGE

MARU

MARU Estamos en una triste situación. Yo necesito una computadora nueva, y Miguel necesita otro coche.

JORGE Y un televisor nuevo para mí, por favor.

MARU ¿Qué vamos a hacer, Miguel?

MIGUEL Tranquila, cariño. Por eso tenemos amigos como Jorge y Mónica. Nos ayudamos los unos a los otros.

JORGE ¿No te sientes afortunada, Maru? No te preocupes. Sube.

MIGUEL ¡Por fin!

MARU Gracias, Jorge. Eres el mejor mecánico de la ciudad.

MIGUEL ¿Cuánto te debo por el trabajo?

JORGE Hombre, no es nada. Guárdalo para el coche nuevo. Eso sí, recomiéndame con tus amigos.

MIGUEL Gracias, Jorge.

JORGE No manejes en carretera. Revisa el aceite cada 1.500 kilómetros y asegúrate de llenarle el tanque... No manejes con el cofre abierto. Nos vemos.

Practice more at vhlcentral.com.

Actividades

1 Seleccionar Selecciona las respuestas que completan correctamente estas oraciones.

1. Jorge intenta arreglar _____.
   a. la computadora de Maru b. el coche de Miguel c. el teléfono celular de Felipe
2. Maru dice que se borraron muchos _____ de su computadora.
   a. archivos b. sitios web c. mensajes de texto
3. Jorge dice que necesita un _____.
   a. navegador GPS b. reproductor de DVD c. televisor

2 Identificar Identifica quién puede decir estas oraciones.

1. Debes comprarte un coche nuevo y recomendarme con tus amigos. _____
2. El mensaje de texto de Maru dice que su computadora todavía está descompuesta. _____
3. Mi amiga Mónica me ayudó a recuperar muchos archivos, pero necesito una computadora nueva. _____
4. No debes conducir con el cofre abierto y debes recordar que el tanque tiene que estar lleno. _____

3 Situación En parejas, representen una conversación entre un(a) mecánico/a y un(a) cliente/a. Sigan la guía.

- El/La cliente/a llama al taller y explica el problema del carro.
- El/La mecánico/a le pregunta dónde está.
- El/La cliente/a le pregunta cuánto dinero cuesta el servicio mecánico y si acepta tarjeta de crédito.
- El/La mecánico/a dice que va enseguida.

doscientos cuarenta y cinco **245**

EXPLORACIÓN

BAJO LA LUPA

Los cibercafés

¿Estás pensando pasar un semestre en Latinoamérica y no quieres llevar tu computadora portátil? ¡No te preocupes! En casi cualquier ciudad latinoamericana, grande o pequeña, te puedes encontrar con **el cibercafé**. Pagando una tarifa° muy barata (¡a veces menos de un dólar por hora!), uno puede disfrutar de° un refresco o un café mientras navega en Internet, escribe correo electrónico o chatea° en múltiples foros virtuales.

De hecho°, el negocio° del cibercafé está mucho más desarrollado° en Latinoamérica que en los Estados Unidos. En las grandes ciudades hispanas, es común ver varios cibercafés en una misma cuadra°. Muchos extranjeros piensan que no puede haber suficientes clientes para todos, pero los cibercafés ofrecen servicios especializados que permiten su coexistencia. Por ejemplo, algunos cibercafés informales atraen° a adolescentes y jóvenes con videojuegos en línea° o servicio de *chat* con cámara. Otros centros de Internet, como los centros telefónicos, atraen a estudiantes o profesionales, ya que generalmente son más tranquilos para hacer las tareas de la escuela o del trabajo.

Sin embargo, para los fanáticos que no se pueden despegar° de las computadoras portátiles, también hay bares, restaurantes y librerías que ofrecen el servicio inalámbrico° de Internet como lo hace Starbucks en los Estados Unidos y en Canadá. Como ves, Internet está en cada esquina°. ¿Qué esperas para hacer tus maletas y salir para Latinoamérica?

tarifa *fee* **disfrutar de** *enjoy* **chatea** *chat (from the English verb "to chat")* **De hecho** *In fact* **negocio** *business* **desarrollado** *developed* **cuadra** *(city) block* **atraen** *attract* **en línea** *online* **despegar** *detach* **inalámbrico/a** *wireless* **esquina** *corner*

Mensajes de texto en español

Al igual que en otros idiomas, el chateo está cambiando la forma en que la gente escribe el español. Ésta es una lista de expresiones comunes en el *chat*.

¿K TL?	¿Qué tal?	CONT, XFA	Contesta, por favor.
Toy cansada	Estoy cansada.	TB	también
TQ MXO.	Te quiero mucho.	1 BSO	Un beso.
A2	Adiós.	¿Q T PARECE?	¿Qué te parece?
¿XQ?	¿Por qué?	T MANDO 1 MSG DSPS	Te mando un mensaje después.
GNL	genial		

Practice more at vhlcentral.com.

VM pp. 53–54

vhlcentral.com

El carro y la tecnología

ACTIVIDADES

1 ¿Cierto o falso? Indica si estas oraciones son **ciertas** o **falsas**.

1. Los cibercafés son más populares en las ciudades grandes que en las pequeñas.
2. El servicio de Internet es caro en los cibercafés.
3. Hay más cibercafés en Latinoamérica que en los Estados Unidos.
4. Todos los cibercafés ofrecen servicios similares.
5. Muchos turistas se quejan de que no hay suficientes cibercafés en las ciudades de Latinoamérica.
6. Hay cibercafés con videojuegos en línea.
7. Si eres estudiante, puedes hacer tus tareas en los centros de Internet.
8. En los países hispanos, no hay servicio inalámbrico de Internet.
9. La primera palabra de la expresión **Toy cansada** viene del verbo **ser**.
10. TB significa "también".

2 ¿Cómo te comunicas? Escribe un párrafo breve para explicar qué utilizas para comunicarte con tus amigos/as (correo electrónico, teléfono, *chat*, etc.) y de qué hablan cuando se comunican.

Maravillas de la tecnología

1 Preparación ¿Con qué frecuencia navegas en Internet? ¿Dónde lo haces, en tu casa o en un lugar público?

2 El video Mira el episodio de **Flash cultura**.

Vocabulario

chateando *chatting*	romper con la barrera
comunidad indígena	de la distancia
indigenous community	*to break the distance barrier*
	usuarios *users*

… los cibercafés se conocen como "cabinas de Internet" y están localizados° por todo el país.

… el primer *hotspot* de Cuzco, que permite a los usuarios navegar de manera inalámbrica…

localizados *located*

3 Elegir Indica cuál de las dos opciones resume mejor este episodio.
- En Cuzco, Internet es un elemento importante para los indígenas peruanos que quieren vender sus productos en otros países. Con Internet inalámbrico, ellos chatean con clientes en otros países.
- En Cuzco, la comunidad y los turistas usan la tecnología de los celulares e Internet para comunicarse con sus familias o vender productos. Para navegar en Internet, se pueden visitar las cabinas de Internet o ir a la Plaza de Armas con una computadora portátil.

CONEXIÓN INTERNET

¿Qué sitios web son populares entre los jóvenes hispanos?

For more information about **Exploración**, go to **vhlcentral.com**.

11 GRAMÁTICA

11.1 The preterite and the imperfect Tutorial

▶ The preterite and the imperfect are not interchangeable. The choice between these two tenses depends on the context and on the point of view of the speaker.

¡ojo!
These words and expressions, as well as similar ones, commonly occur with the preterite: **ayer, anteayer, una vez, dos veces, tres veces, el año pasado, de repente**. They usually imply that an action has happened at a specific point in time.

¡ojo!
These words and expressions, as well as similar ones, commonly occur with the imperfect: **de niño/a, todos los días, mientras, siempre, con frecuencia, todas las semanas**. They usually express habitual or repeated actions in the past.

Uses of the preterite

To express actions that are viewed by the speaker as completed
Don Alejandro **estacionó** el autobús.
Don Alejandro parked the bus.
Fueron a Valparaíso ayer.
They went to Valparaíso yesterday.

To express the beginning or end of a past action
La película **empezó** a las nueve.
The movie began at nine o'clock.
Ayer **terminé** el proyecto.
I finished the project yesterday.

To narrate a series of past actions or events
Don Alejandro **paró** el autobús, **abrió** la ventanilla y **saludó** a doña Rosa.
Don Alejandro stopped the bus, opened the window, and greeted Doña Rosa.

Uses of the imperfect

To describe an ongoing past action with no reference to its beginning or end
Mónica **conducía** muy rápido en Madrid.
Mónica was driving very fast in Madrid.
Jorge **esperaba** en el garaje.
Jorge was waiting in the garage.

To express habitual past actions and events
Cuando **era** joven, **jugaba** al tenis.
When I was young, I used to play tennis.
Raúl siempre **revisaba** su correo electrónico a las tres.
Raúl always checked his e-mail at three o'clock.

To describe physical and emotional states or characteristics
La chica **quería** descansar. **Se sentía** mal y **tenía** dolor de cabeza.
The girl wanted to rest. She felt ill and had a headache.
Ellos **eran** altos y **tenían** ojos verdes.
They were tall and had green eyes.
Estábamos felices de ver a la familia.
We were happy to see the family.

¿Y revisaste el aceite?

▶ When the preterite and the imperfect appear in the same sentence, the imperfect describes what was happening while the preterite describes the action that "interrupted" the ongoing activity.

Navegaba en la red cuando **sonó** el teléfono.
I was surfing the Web when the phone rang.

Jimena **leía** un libro cuando **llegó** Juan Carlos.
Jimena was reading a book when Juan Carlos arrived.

▶ You will see the preterite and the imperfect together in narratives such as fiction, news, and the retelling of events. The imperfect provides background information, such as time, weather, and location. The preterite indicates the specific events that occurred.

Pensé que podía arreglar el coche, pero no puedo.

Eran las dos de la mañana y el detective ya no **podía** mantenerse despierto. **Se bajó** lentamente del coche, **estiró** las piernas y **levantó** los brazos.
It was two in the morning, and the detective could no longer stay awake. He slowly stepped out of the car, stretched his legs, and raised his arms.

La luna **estaba** llena y no **había** en el cielo ni una sola nube. De repente, el detective **escuchó** un grito espeluznante.
The moon was full and there wasn't a single cloud in the sky. Suddenly, the detective heard a piercing scream.

El carro y la tecnología

Práctica y conversación

1 Un accidente Completa este artículo de periódico con las formas correctas del pretérito o del imperfecto.

Un trágico accidente

Ayer temprano por la mañana (1) _____ [haber] un trágico accidente en el centro de Lima, cuando un autobús (2) _____ [chocar] con un carro. La mujer que (3) _____ [manejar] el carro (4) _____ [morir] al instante. Los paramédicos llevaron al conductor del autobús al hospital porque (5) _____ [tener] varias fracturas. Su estado de salud es todavía muy grave. El conductor del autobús (6) _____ [decir] que no (7) _____ [ver] el carro hasta el último momento porque (8) _____ [haber] mucha niebla y (9) _____ [llover]. Él (10) _____ [intentar] (*to attempt*) dar un viraje brusco (*to swerve*), pero (11) _____ [perder] el control del autobús y no (12) _____ [poder] evitar (*to avoid*) el accidente. Según nos informaron, no (13) _____ [lastimarse] ningún pasajero que (14) _____ [viajar] en el autobús.

2 Combinar Combina elementos de las tres columnas para hablar de lo que hicieron y lo que hacían las personas de la primera columna.

Sujetos	Verbos	Adverbios
el mecánico	arreglar	ayer
Adrián González	caerse	bien
la mujer policía	chocar	con frecuencia
Maria Sharapova	conducir	de vez en cuando
mis padres	decir	fácilmente
mis amigos y yo	enamorarse	lentamente
John Mayer	lastimarse	por aquí
yo	llamar	por fin
	navegar (en)	todos los días
	olvidar	la semana pasada

3 Oraciones En parejas, completen las oraciones usando el pretérito o el imperfecto. Luego comparen sus respuestas.

MODELO
De niño/a, yo…
Estudiante 1: De niña, yo vivía con mis abuelos en un apartamento cerca de la escuela.
Estudiante 2: Pues, mi mamá, mis hermanos y yo vivíamos en una casita con un jardín.
Estudiante 1: De niña, me lastimé una vez la rodilla. Mientras corría, me caí.
Estudiante 2: En cambio, yo nunca me lastimé la rodilla, pero me torcía constantemente el tobillo.

1. El verano pasado…
2. Yo manejaba el coche mientras…
3. Anoche mi novio/a…
4. Ayer el/la profesor(a)…
5. La semana pasada un(a) amigo/a…
6. A menudo mi madre…
7. Esta mañana en la cafetería…
8. Navegábamos en la red cuando…

4 Tu primer(a) novio/a Entrevista a un(a) compañero/a acerca de su primer(a) novio/a. Si quieres, puedes añadir (*add*) otras preguntas.

1. ¿Quién fue tu primer(a) novio/a?
2. ¿Cuántos años tenías cuando lo/la conociste?
3. ¿Cómo era él/ella?
4. ¿Qué le gustaba hacer? ¿Tenían ustedes los mismos pasatiempos?
5. ¿Por cuánto tiempo salieron ustedes?
6. ¿Adónde iban ustedes cuando salían?
7. ¿Pensaban casarse?
8. ¿Cuándo y por qué rompieron ustedes?

5 Un robo misterioso Anoche alguien robó (*stole*) el examen de la Lección 11 de la oficina de tu profesor(a) y tú tienes que averiguar (*to find out*) quién lo hizo. Pregúntales a varios compañeros dónde estaban, con quién estaban y qué hicieron entre las ocho y las doce de la noche. Luego decide quién robó el examen.

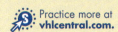
Practice more at vhlcentral.com.

11.2 Por and para Tutorial

▶ Both **por** and **para** mean *for*, but they are not interchangeable. Study their uses in the charts.

Uses of *por*

Motion or a general location (around, through, along, by)	La excursión nos llevó **por** el centro. *The tour took us through downtown.* Pasamos **por** el parque y **por** el río. *We passed by the park and along the river.*	**Means by which something is done** (by, by way of, by means of)	Ellos viajan **por** la autopista. *They travel by (way of) highway.* ¿Hablaste con la policía **por** teléfono? *Did you talk to the police by (on the) phone?*
Duration of an action (for, during, in)	Estuve en Montevideo **por** un mes. *I was in Montevideo for a month.* Miguel estudió **por** la noche. *Miguel studied during the night.*	**Exchange or substitution** (for, in exchange for)	Le di dinero **por** el estéreo. *I gave him money for the stereo.* Cambiamos este carro **por** uno nuevo. *We exchanged this car for a new one.*
Object of a search (for, in search of)	Vengo **por** ti a las ocho. *I am coming for you at eight.* Paola fue **por** su cámara. *Paola went in search of her camera.*	**Unit of measure** (per, by)	Manejé a 120 kilómetros **por** hora. *I drove 120 kilometers per hour.* Me pagan **por** hora. *I get paid by the hour.*

Uses of *para*

Destination (toward, in the direction of)	Salimos **para** Mérida hoy. *We are leaving for Mérida today.* Voy **para** el banco. *I'm going to the bank.*	**Purpose or goal +** [infinitive] (in order to)	Juan estudia **para** (ser) mecánico. *Juan is studying to be a mechanic.*
Deadline or a specific time in the future (by, for)	Él va a arreglarlo **para** el viernes. *He will fix it by Friday.*	**The recipient of something** (for)	Compré una calculadora **para** mi hijo. *I bought a calculator for my son.*
Purpose + [noun/verb] (for, used for)	Es una llanta **para** el carro. *It's a tire for the car.* Uso mi celular **para** navegar en Internet. *I use my cell phone to surf the Internet.*	**Comparisons or opinions** (for, considering)	**Para** ser joven, es demasiado serio. *For a young person, he is too serious.* **Para** mí, esta lección no es difícil. *For me, this lesson isn't difficult.*
		Employment (for)	Sara trabaja **para** Telecom. *Sara works for Telecom.*

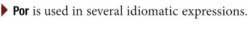

Maru habla por teléfono.

▶ **Por** is used in several idiomatic expressions.

| por aquí | around here | por eso | that's why; therefore |
| por ejemplo | for example | por fin | finally |

▶ When giving an exact time, **de** is used instead of **por** before **la mañana, la tarde,** and **la noche.**

La clase es a las nueve **de** la mañana.
The class is at nine a.m.

La clase es **por** la mañana.
The class is in the morning.

Llegué a las diez **de** la noche.
I arrived at ten p.m.

Me gusta estudiar **por** la noche.
I like to study at night.

¡Y un televisor nuevo para mí, por favor!

El carro y la tecnología

▶ Often, either **por** or **para** can be used in a sentence, although the meaning may change.

Caminé **por** el parque.
I walked through the park.

Caminé **para** el parque.
I walked to (toward) the park.

Trabajó **por** su padre.
He worked for (in place of) his father.

Trabajó **para** su padre.
He worked for his father('s business).

Se exhibió **por** el pueblo.
It was shown throughout (around) the town.

Se exhibió **para** todo el pueblo.
It was shown for the whole town.

Práctica y conversación

Practice more at vhlcentral.com.

1 Un viaje a Buenos Aires Completa este párrafo con las preposiciones **por** o **para**.

El mes pasado, mi esposo y yo hicimos un viaje a Buenos Aires y sólo pagamos dos mil dólares (1) _____ los pasajes. Estuvimos en Buenos Aires (2) _____ una semana y exploramos toda la ciudad. Durante el día caminamos (3) _____ la plaza San Martín, el microcentro y el barrio de La Boca, donde viven muchos artistas. (4) _____ la noche fuimos a una tanguería, que es un tipo de teatro, (5) _____ ver a la gente bailar tango. Dos días después decidimos hacer una excursión (6) _____ las Pampas (7) _____ ver el paisaje y un rodeo con gauchos. (8) _____ eso, alquilamos (*we rented*) un carro y pasamos unos días muy agradables. El último día fuimos a Galerías Pacífico (9) _____ comprar recuerdos (*souvenirs*) (10) _____ nuestros hijos y nietos. Compramos tantos regalos que, al regresar, tuvimos que pagar impuestos (*duties*) cuando pasamos (11) _____ la aduana.

2 Completar Habla con un(a) compañero/a para completar estas oraciones sobre él/ella. Usa **por** y **para** en las respuestas.

1. El año pasado compró un regalo…
2. Ayer fue al taller…
3. Necesita hacer la tarea…
4. En casa, habla con sus amigos/as…
5. Los miércoles tiene clases…
6. A veces va a la biblioteca…
7. Necesita… dólares…
8. Esta noche tiene que estudiar…
9. Su padre/madre trabaja…
10. Su mejor amigo/a estudia…

3 ¿Qué pasa aquí?  Usa **por** o **para** y el tiempo presente para describir estos dibujos. Luego, compara tus respuestas con las de un(a) compañero/a.

1. _____   4. _____

2. _____   5. _____

3. _____   6. _____

4 Una subasta En grupos, dramaticen una subasta (*auction*). Cada estudiante debe traer a la clase un objeto o una foto del objeto para vender. Luego, un(a) estudiante es el/la vendedor(a) y los otros son los postores (*bidders*).

MODELO
Vendedor(a): Aquí tengo una cámara de video. ¿Quién ofrece $400,00 por ella?
Postor(a) 1: Te doy $175,00.

doscientos cincuenta y uno 251

Lección 11

11.3 Stressed possessive adjectives and pronouns Tutorial

¿También está descompuesta tu computadora?

No, la mía no, la suya.

▶ Spanish has two types of possessive adjectives: the unstressed (short) forms you learned in Lesson 3 and the stressed (long) forms. The stressed possessive adjectives are used for emphasis or to express *(of) mine, (of) yours, (of) his,* and so on.

Stressed possessive adjectives

Singular forms		Plural forms		
MASCULINE	FEMININE	MASCULINE	FEMININE	
mío	mía	míos	mías	my; (of) mine
tuyo	tuya	tuyos	tuyas	your; (of) yours (fam.)
suyo	suya	suyos	suyas	your; (of) yours (form.); his; (of) his; her; (of) hers; its
nuestro	nuestra	nuestros	nuestras	our; (of) ours
vuestro	vuestra	vuestros	vuestras	your; (of) yours (fam.)
suyo	suya	suyos	suyas	your; (of) yours (form.); their; (of) theirs

▶ Stressed possessive adjectives agree in gender and number with the nouns they modify.

mi impresora	▶	la impresora mía		nuestros televisores	▶	los televisores nuestros
my printer		*my printer*		*our television sets*		*our television sets*

▶ Stressed possessive adjectives are placed after the nouns they modify. Unstressed possessive adjectives are placed before the noun.

Son **mis** llaves.   Son las llaves **mías**.
They are my keys.   *They are my keys.*

▶ A definite article, an indefinite article, or a demonstrative adjective usually precedes a noun modified by a stressed possessive adjective.

	unos discos **tuyos**.	*Alberto had some disks of yours.*
Alberto tenía	**los** discos **tuyos**.	*Alberto had your disks.*
	estos discos **tuyos**.	*Alberto had these disks of yours.*

▶ Since **suyo, suya, suyos,** and **suyas** have more than one meaning, you can avoid confusion by using the construction: [*article*] + [*noun*] + **de** + [*subject pronoun or noun*].

	el teclado **de él/ella**	*his/her keyboard*
el teclado **suyo**	el teclado **de usted(es)**	*your keyboard*
	el teclado **de ellos/ellas**	*their keyboard*
	el teclado **de Ramón**	*Ramón's keyboard*

▶ **El** and **la** are usually omitted when a stressed possessive adjective follows the verb **ser**.

¿**Es suya** esta cámara?   No, no **es mía**.

252 *doscientos cincuenta y dos*

El carro y la tecnología

▶ Possessive pronouns are used to replace [*noun*] + [*possessive adjective*]. In Spanish, the possessive pronouns have the same forms as the stressed possessive adjectives, and they are preceded by a definite article.

la calculadora nuestra ▶ la nuestra   el fax tuyo ▶ el tuyo   los archivos suyos ▶ los suyos

▶ Possessive pronouns agree in number and gender with the nouns they replace.

Aquí está **mi coche**. ¿Dónde está **el tuyo**?
Here's my car. Where is yours?

¿Tienes **los archivos** de Carlos?
Do you have Carlos' files?

El mío está en el taller de mi hermano Armando.
Mine is at my brother Armando's garage.

No, pero tengo **los nuestros**.
No, but I have ours.

Práctica y conversación

Practice more at vhlcentral.com.

1 Oraciones Forma oraciones con estos elementos. Usa el presente y haz todos los cambios necesarios.

1. yo / necesitar / usar / impresora / de Miguel / porque / mío / no / funcionar
2. pero / él / no poder / ayudarme / porque / suyo / tampoco / funcionar
3. me gustaría / pedirle / a Juana / su ratón, / pero / suyo / estar / descompuesto
4. yo / no poder / usar / teclado / de Valeria / porque / suyo / también / estar descompuesto
5. si / yo / pedirte / computadora, / estar / seguro de que / ir a / decirme / que / no poder / usar / tuyo

2 Anuncios Lee este anuncio (*ad*) con un(a) compañero/a. Luego, preparen su propio (*own*) anuncio usando los adjetivos o los pronombres posesivos. Después, conviértanlo en un anuncio de televisión (*commercial*) y preséntenlo a la clase.

3 ¿Es suyo? Un policía ha capturado (*has captured*) al hombre que robó (*robbed*) en tu casa. Ahora quiere saber qué cosas son tuyas. Túrnate con un(a) compañero/a para hacer el papel del policía y usa las pistas (*clues*) para contestar las preguntas.

MODELO
No / pequeño
Policía: Esta computadora, ¿es suya?
Estudiante: No, no es mía. La mía es más pequeña.

1. Sí   4. No / viejo

2. Sí   5. Sí

3. No / nuevo   6. No / caro

doscientos cincuenta y tres 253

Lección 11

Ampliación

1 Escuchar

A Escucha a Ricardo Moreno y luego contesta las preguntas.

TIP **Recognize the genre of spoken discourse.** Identifying the genre (for example: political speech, radio interview, news broadcast) of what you hear can help you figure out what kinds of things you are likely to hear. It will also help you identify the speaker's motives and intentions.

1. ¿Qué tipo de discurso es?
   a. noticias (*news*) por radio o televisión   b. un anuncio comercial
   c. una reseña (*review*) de una película

2. ¿De qué habla?
   a. de su vida   b. de un producto o servicio   c. de algo que oyó o vio

3. ¿Cuál es el propósito?
   a. relacionarse con alguien   b. informar   c. vender

B ¿Qué pistas (*clues*) te ayudaron a identificar el género de la grabación (*recording*)?

2 Conversar
Con un(a) compañero/a, prepara una conversación sobre la primera vez que manejaste un carro o el día en que fuiste al Departamento de Tráfico para conseguir tu licencia de conducir. Incluye la siguiente información:

- ¿Cuántos años tenías?
- ¿A qué hora fue? ¿Te levantaste temprano para practicar?
- ¿Cómo estaba el tiempo?
- ¿Fuiste solo/a? ¿Quién fue contigo (*with you*)?
- ¿Cómo te sentías antes de hacerlo? ¿Y cómo te sentiste después?
- ¿Fue una experiencia linda? ¿Te gustaría repetirla? ¿Por qué?

254 *doscientos cincuenta y cuatro*

El carro y la tecnología

3 Escribir Escribe una historia acerca de una experiencia tuya con una máquina electrónica o con el carro.

TIP **Master the simple past tenses.** To be able to write about events that occurred in the past, you will need to know when to use the preterite and the imperfect. The box on this page contains a summary of their uses.

Preterite
- Past actions viewed as completed
- Beginning or end of past actions
- Series of past actions

Imperfect
- Ongoing past actions
- Habitual past actions
- Physical and emotional states in the past

Organízalo Prepara una lista de todos los detalles que quieres narrar (*narrate*). Identifica qué acciones fueron completadas (pretérito) y cuáles están incompletas o cuáles describen (imperfecto).

Escríbelo Utiliza tu lista para escribir el primer borrador de tu historia.

Corrígelo Intercambia tu historia con un(a) compañero/a. Lee su borrador y reflexiona sobre las partes mejor escritas. Da sugerencias sobre los detalles, la lógica de la secuencia de eventos y el uso del pretérito y del imperfecto.

Compártelo Revisa el primer borrador según las indicaciones de tu compañero/a. Incorpora las nuevas ideas y prepara la versión final. Luego, comparte la historia con la clase.

4 Un paso más Busca información sobre los cibercafés en los países hispanos e inventa un cibercafé nuevo. Crea un anuncio de revista para promocionarlo. El anuncio debe incluir estos elementos:

- Nombre del cibercafé
- Una descripción del lugar donde está ubicado (*located*)
- Una descripción de la tecnología y de los servicios que se ofrecen a los clientes
- Fotos o dibujos
- Por qué este cibercafé es mejor que otros
- Los precios

CONEXIÓN INTERNET

Investiga estos temas en **vhlcentral.com**.
- Cibercafés en el mundo hispano
- Internet en el mundo hispano
- La tecnología en el mundo hispano

doscientos cincuenta y cinco 255

11 LECTURA

Antes de leer

One way languages grow is by borrowing words from each other. English words that relate to technology are often borrowed by Spanish and other languages throughout the world. Sometimes the words are modified slightly to fit the sounds of the languages that borrow them. When reading in Spanish, you can often increase your understanding by looking for words borrowed from English or other languages you know.

Examinar el texto

Observa la tira cómica (*comic strip*). ¿De qué trata (*is it about*)? ¿Cómo lo sabes?

Buscar

Esta lectura contiene una palabra tomada (*taken*) del inglés. Trabaja con un(a) compañero/a para encontrarla.

_____

Repasa (*Review*) las nuevas palabras relacionadas con la tecnología que aprendiste en **Preparación** y expande la lista de palabras tomadas del inglés.

_____   _____
_____   _____
_____   _____

Juan Matías Loiseau (1974) Más conocido como *Tute*, este artista nació en el año 1974 en Buenos Aires, Argentina. Estudió diseño gráfico, humorismo y cine. Sus tiras cómicas se publican en Estados Unidos, Francia y toda Latinoamérica.

El carro y la tecnología

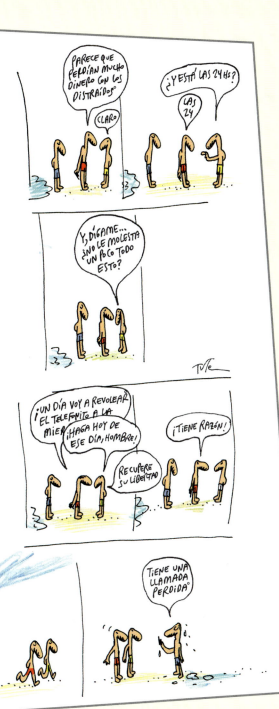

Después de leer

¿Comprendiste?

Indica si las oraciones son **ciertas** o **falsas**. Corrige las falsas.

Cierto   Falso

____   ____   1. Hay tres personajes en la tira cómica: un usuario de teléfono, un amigo y un empleado de la empresa (*company*) telefónica.

____   ____   2. El nuevo servicio de teléfono incluye las llamadas telefónicas únicamente.

____   ____   3. El empleado duerme en su propia casa.

____   ____   4. El contrato de teléfono dura (*lasts*) un año.

____   ____   5. El usuario y el amigo están trabajando (*working*).

Preguntas

Responde a estas preguntas con oraciones completas. Usa el pretérito y el imperfecto.

1. ¿Al usuario le gustaba usar el teléfono celular todo el tiempo? _____
2. ¿Por qué el usuario decidió tirar el teléfono al mar? _____
3. Según el amigo, ¿para qué tenía el usuario que tirar el teléfono celular al mar? _____
4. ¿Qué ocurrió cuando el usuario tiró el teléfono? _____
5. ¿Qué le dijo el empleado al usuario cuando salió del mar? _____

Coméntalo

¿Cuáles son los aspectos positivos y los negativos de tener teléfono celular? ¿Te sientes identificado/a con el usuario del teléfono? ¿Por qué?

te viene *comes with*   **tipo** *guy, dude*   **te avisa** *alerts you*   **escuchás** *listen (Arg.)*   **distraídos** *careless*   **piso** *floor*   **bolsa de dormir** *sleeping bag*
darle de baja *to suspend*   **harto** *fed up*   **revolear** *throw away forcefully (S. America)*   **bien hecho** *well done*   **llamada perdida** *missed call*

VOCABULARIO

El carro

el baúl	trunk
la calle	street
el camino	route
el capó	(car) hood
el carro	car
el coche	car
los frenos	brakes
el garaje	garage; (mechanic's) repair shop
la gasolina	gasoline
la gasolinera	gas station
el kilómetro	kilometer
la licencia de conducir	driver's license
la llanta	tire
el/la mecánico/a	mechanic
la milla	mile
el motor	motor
la multa	fine; ticket
el parabrisas	windshield
el policía/la mujer policía	police officer
la policía	police (force)
el semáforo	traffic light
el taller (mecánico)	(mechanic's) repair shop
el tráfico	traffic
la velocidad máxima	speed limit
el volante	steering wheel
arrancar	to start
arreglar	to fix; to arrange
bajar	to go down
bajar(se) de	to get off of/out of (a vehicle)
chocar (con)	to run into; to crash
conducir	to drive
estacionar	to park
llenar (el tanque)	to fill up (the tank)
manejar	to drive
parar	to stop
revisar (el aceite)	to check (the oil)
subir	to go up
subir(se) a	to get on/into (a vehicle)

La tecnología

la calculadora	calculator
la cámara (de video)	(video) camera
digital	digital camera
el buzón de voz	voicemail
el control remoto	remote control
el disco compacto	CD (compact disc)
el estéreo	stereo
el fax	fax (machine)
el mensaje de texto	text message
el navegador GPS	GPS
el radio	radio (set)
el reproductor de CD	CD player
de DVD	DVD player
de MP3	MP3 player
el teléfono (celular)	(cell) phone
la televisión por cable	cable television
el televisor	television set
apagar	to turn off
funcionar	to work
llamar	to call
poner	to turn on
prender	to turn on
sonar (o:ue)	to ring
descompuesto/a	not working; out of order
lento/a	slow
lleno/a	full

Stressed possessive adjectives and pronouns	See pages 252–253.

Internet y la computadora

el archivo	file
la computadora	computer
la computadora portátil	laptop
la conexión inalámbrica	wireless (connection)
el disco	disk
la impresora	printer
Internet	Internet
el monitor	monitor
la página principal	home page
la pantalla	screen
el programa de computación	software
el ratón	mouse
la red	network, Web
el sitio web	website
el teclado	keyboard
guardar	to save
imprimir	to print
navegar en Internet	to surf the Internet

Otras palabras y expresiones

para	for; in order to; toward; in the direction of; by; used for; considering
por	for; by; by means of; through; along; during; in; in exchange for; around; in search of; by way of; per
por aquí	around here
por ejemplo	for example
por eso	that's why; therefore
por fin	finally

258 doscientos cincuenta y ocho

12 Hogar, dulce hogar

Communicative Goals
You will learn how to:
- welcome people
- show people around the house
- give instructions

PREPARACIÓN
pages 260–263
- Words related to the home
- Household chores
- Capital and lowercase letters

ESCENAS
pages 264–265
- Felipe and Jimena have promised to clean the apartment in exchange for permission to take a trip to the Yucatán Peninsula. Can Marissa and Juan Carlos help them finish on time?

EXPLORACIÓN
pages 266–267
- Bajo la lupa: *El patio central*
- Flash cultura: *La casa de Frida*

GRAMÁTICA
pages 268–277
- **Usted** and **ustedes** commands
- The present subjunctive
- Subjunctive with verbs of will and influence

LECTURA
pages 278–279
- Brochure: *¡Bienvenidos a la Casa Colorada!*

Para empezar
- ¿En dónde están: en una oficina o en una casa?
- ¿Qué están haciendo?
- ¿Cómo es la decoración de la casa: moderna o tradicional?

12 PREPARACIÓN

Hogar, dulce hogar

Talking Picture Tutorial Games

LA CASA Y SUS CUARTOS

la alcoba bedroom
el altillo attic
el balcón balcony
la cocina kitchen
el comedor dining room
la entrada entrance
el garaje garage
la oficina office
el pasillo hallway
el patio patio; yard
la sala living room
el sótano basement; cellar
la escalera stairs; stairway

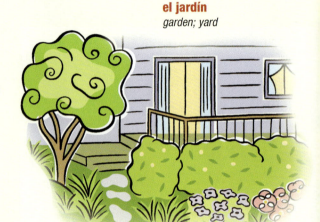

el jardín garden; yard

LA MESA

la copa wineglass; goblet
la cuchara spoon
el cuchillo knife
el plato plate
la servilleta napkin
la taza cup; mug
el tenedor fork
el vaso glass

LOS ELECTRODOMÉSTICOS

la estufa stove
el horno (de microondas) (microwave) oven
la lavadora washing machine
el lavaplatos dishwasher
el refrigerador refrigerator
la secadora clothes dryer

los electrodomésticos
electrical appliances

recursos
WB pp. 119–120
LM p. 67
vhlcentral.com

260 doscientos sesenta

Hogar, dulce hogar

barrer el suelo
to sweep the floor

LOS QUEHACERES DOMÉSTICOS

arreglar to neaten; to straighten up
cocinar to cook
hacer los quehaceres domésticos
 to do household chores
lavar (el suelo, los platos) to wash (the floor, the dishes)
limpiar la casa to clean the house
pasar la aspiradora to vacuum
poner la mesa to set the table
quitar la mesa to clear the table
sacar la basura to take out the trash
sacudir los muebles to dust the furniture

hacer la cama
to make the bed

planchar la ropa
to iron clothes

LOS MUEBLES Y OTRAS COSAS

la alfombra carpet; rug
la almohada pillow
el armario closet
la cómoda chest with drawers
las cortinas curtains
el cuadro picture
el estante bookcase; bookshelves
la lámpara lamp
la luz light; electricity
la manta blanket
la mesita end table
la mesita de noche nightstand
la pared wall
la pintura painting; picture
el sillón armchair
el sofá couch; sofa

los muebles
furniture

OTRAS PALABRAS

las afueras suburbs; outskirts
la agencia de bienes raíces real estate agency
el alquiler rent (payment)
el ama (f.) de casa homemaker
el barrio neighborhood
el edificio de apartamentos apartment building
el hogar home
el/la vecino/a neighbor
la vivienda housing

alquilar to rent
ensuciar to get (something) dirty
mudarse to move (residences)

doscientos sesenta y uno **261**

Lección 12

Práctica y conversación Audio: Activities

1 Escoger Escucha las preguntas e indica la respuesta correcta.

1. ____ Al pasillo.
   ____ Al balcón.
2. ____ En el lavaplatos.
   ____ En la mesita de noche.
3. ____ Al edificio.
   ____ A las afueras.
4. ____ En la secadora.
   ____ En la basura.
5. ____ El balcón.
   ____ Las escaleras.
6. ____ En las paredes.
   ____ En el horno.
7. ____ La estufa.
   ____ La aspiradora.
8. ____ En la alfombra.
   ____ En la alcoba.

2 Escuchar Escucha la conversación y completa las oraciones.

1. Paula va a comenzar por _____.
2. Pedro va a limpiar _____ primero.
3. Pedro también va a limpiar _____.
4. Pedro le dice a Paula que debe _____ en la alcoba de huéspedes.
5. Pedro va a _____ en el sótano.
6. Ellos están limpiando la casa porque _____ va a visitarlos.

3 Emparejar Empareja cada dibujo con su descripción. Luego, nombra los dibujos.

____ 1. Lo usas para tomar agua.
____ 2. Lo necesitas para comer un bistec.
____ 3. Necesitas este objeto para la sopa.
____ 4. La necesitas para tomar café.
____ 5. La necesitas para tomar vino.
____ 6. Necesitas este objeto para limpiarte la boca después de comer.

a. _____   b. _____   c. _____
d. _____   e. _____   f. _____

4 Los quehaceres domésticos Trabajen en grupos para indicar quién hace los siguientes quehaceres domésticos en sus casas. Luego contesten las preguntas.

barrer el suelo	lavar la ropa	planchar la ropa
cocinar	lavar los platos	sacar la basura
hacer las camas	pasar la aspiradora	sacudir los muebles

- ¿Quién es la persona de tu grupo que hace más quehaceres?
- ¿Cúales son los quehaceres que más te molestan y los que más te gustan? ¿Por qué?
- ¿Piensas que debes hacer más quehaceres? ¿Por qué?

recursos
vhlcentral.com

262 doscientos sesenta y dos

5 **¿Una casa o un apartamento?** En parejas, comparen las ventajas y desventajas de vivir en una casa o en un apartamento. Consideren el espacio, la comodidad, el precio del alquiler (*rent*), las reglas para las visitas, la organización de fiestas, etc.

Ortografía Las mayúsculas y las minúsculas

Here are the Spanish rules for capitals (**mayúsculas**) and lowercase letters (**minúsculas**).

Los estudiantes llegaron al aeropuerto a las dos. Luego fueron al hotel.

In both Spanish and English, the first letter of every sentence is capitalized.

Rubén Blades   **Panamá**   **Colón**   **los Andes**

The first letter of all proper nouns (names of people, countries, cities, etc.) is capitalized.

Cien años de soledad   Don Quijote de la Mancha   El País   Muy Interesante

The first letter of the first word in titles of books, films, and works of art is generally capitalized, as well as the first letter of any proper names. In newspaper and magazine titles, as well as other short titles, the initial letter of each word is often capitalized.

la señora Ramos   **don Francisco**   **el presidente**   **Sra. Vives**

Titles associated with people are *not* capitalized unless they appear as the first word in a sentence. Note, however, that the first letter of an abbreviated title is capitalized.

Último   **Álex**   **MENÚ**   **PERDÓN**

Accent marks should be retained on capital letters. In practice, however, this rule is often ignored.

lunes   **viernes**   **marzo**   **primavera**

The first letter of days, months, and seasons is *not* capitalized.

español   **estadounidense**   **japonés**   **panameños**

The first letter of nationalities and languages is *not* capitalized.

Oraciones Lee el diálogo de las serpientes. Ordena las letras para saber de qué palabras se trata. Después escribe las letras indicadas para descubrir por qué llora Pepito.

m n a a P á   ◯ ▢ ▢ ▢ ▢ ▢   y a U r u g u   ▢ ▢ ▢ ▢ ◯ ▢ ▢
s t e m r a   ◯ ▢ ▢ ▢ ▢ ▢   r o ñ e s a   ▢ ▢ ▢ ▢ ▢ ◯
i g s l é n   ▢ ▢ ▢ ▢ ◯ ▢

¡ ▢ orque ▢ e acabo de morder° la ▢ en ▢ u ▢ !

venenosas *venomous*
morder *to bite*

Respuestas: Panamá, martes, inglés, Uruguay, señora
¡Porque me acabo de morder la lengua!

Profesor Herrera, ¿es cierto que somos venenosas°?

Sí, Pepito. ¿Por qué lloras?

recursos

LM
p. 68

vhlcentral.com

12 ESCENAS

Los quehaceres Video: *Fotonovela*

Jimena y Felipe deben limpiar el apartamento para poder ir de viaje con Marissa.

Expresiones útiles

Making recommendations

Le(s) sugiero que arregle(n) este apartamento.
I suggest you tidy up this apartment.
Le(s) aconsejo que prepare(n) la cena para las ocho y media.
I recommend that you have dinner ready for eight thirty.

Organizing work

Recomiendo que se organicen en equipos para limpiar.
I recommend that you divide yourselves into teams to clean.
Yo lleno el lavaplatos... después de vaciarlo.
I'll fill the dishwasher… after I empty it.
¿Por qué no terminas de pasar la aspiradora?
Why don't you finish vacuuming?
¡Ya casi acaban!
You're almost finished!
Felipe, tú quita el polvo.
Felipe, you dust.

Making polite requests

Don Diego, quédese a cenar con nosotros.
Don Diego, stay and have dinner with us.
Venga.
Come on.
Don Diego, pase.
Don Diego, come in.

Additional vocabulary
el plumero duster

SR. DÍAZ Quieren ir a Yucatán con Marissa, ¿verdad?
SRA. DÍAZ Entonces, les sugiero que arreglen este apartamento. Regresamos más tarde.
SR. DÍAZ Les aconsejo que preparen la cena para las 8:30.

MARISSA ¿Qué pasa?
JIMENA Nuestros papás quieren que Felipe y yo arreglemos toda la casa.
FELIPE Y que, además, preparemos la cena.
MARISSA ¡Pues, yo les ayudo!

MARISSA Mis padres siempre quieren que mis hermanos y yo ayudemos con los quehaceres. No me molesta ayudar. Pero odio limpiar el baño.
JIMENA Lo que más odio yo es sacar la basura.

JUAN CARLOS Hola, Jimena. ¿Está Felipe? (*a Felipe*) Te olvidaste del partido de fútbol.
FELIPE Juan Carlos, ¿verdad que mi papá te considera como de la familia?
JUAN CARLOS Sí.

(*Don Diego llega a ayudar a los chicos.*)
FELIPE Tenemos que limpiar la casa hoy.
JIMENA ¿Nos ayuda, don Diego?
DON DIEGO Claro. Recomiendo que se organicen en equipos para limpiar.

Hogar, dulce hogar

JIMENA **FELIPE** **SRA. DÍAZ** **SR. DÍAZ** **MARISSA** **JUAN CARLOS** **DON DIEGO**

MARISSA Yo lleno el lavaplatos... después de vaciarlo.
DON DIEGO Juan Carlos, ¿por qué no terminas de pasar la aspiradora? Y Felipe, tú limpia el polvo. ¡Ya casi acaban!

(*Los chicos preparan la cena y ponen la mesa.*)
JUAN CARLOS ¿Dónde están los tenedores?
JIMENA Allá.
JUAN CARLOS ¿Y las servilletas?
MARISSA Aquí están.

FELIPE La sala está tan limpia. Le pasamos la aspiradora al sillón y a las cortinas. ¡Y también a las almohadas!
JIMENA Yucatán, ¡ya casi llegamos!

(*Papá y mamá regresan a casa.*)
SRA. DÍAZ ¡Qué bonita está la casa!
SR. DÍAZ Buen trabajo, muchachos. ¿Qué hay para cenar?
JIMENA Quesadillas. Vengan.

SRA. DÍAZ Don Diego, quédese a cenar con nosotros. Venga.
SR. DÍAZ Sí, don Diego. Pase.
DON DIEGO Gracias.

Practice more at **vhlcentral.com**.

Actividades

1 ¿Cierto o falso? Indica si lo que dicen estas oraciones es **cierto** o **falso**. Corrige las oraciones falsas.

1. Felipe y Jimena tienen que preparar el desayuno.
2. Don Diego ayuda a los chicos organizando los quehaceres domésticos.
3. Jimena le dice a Juan Carlos dónde están los tenedores.
4. A Marissa no le molesta limpiar el baño.
5. Juan Carlos termina de lavar los platos.

2 Completar Los chicos y don Diego están haciendo los quehaceres. Adivina en qué cuarto está cada uno de ellos.

1. Jimena limpia el congelador. Jimena está en _____.
2. Don Diego limpia el escritorio. Don Diego está en _____.
3. Felipe pasa la aspiradora debajo de la mesa y las sillas. Felipe está en _____.
4. Juan Carlos sacude el sillón. Juan Carlos está en _____.
5. Marissa hace la cama. Marissa está en _____.

3 La casa Describe la casa de una celebridad o de una persona que conoces bien. Luego, comparte la descripción con la clase.

MODELO

La mansión de 50 Cent es espectacular. Tiene una sala muy grande con muebles muy originales. En la cocina hay un estéreo donde él escucha su música. Su mansión tiene 19 alcobas y 35 baños.

doscientos sesenta y cinco   265

12 EXPLORACIÓN

BAJO LA LUPA

El patio central

En las tardes cálidas° de Oaxaca, México; Córdoba, España, o Popayán, Colombia, es un placer sentarse en **el patio central** de una casa y tomar un refresco disfrutando de° una buena conversación. De influencia árabe, esta característica arquitectónica° fue traída° a las Américas por los españoles. En la época° colonial, se construyeron casas, palacios, monasterios, hospitales y escuelas con patio central. Éste es un espacio privado e íntimo en donde se puede disfrutar del sol y de la brisa° y se puede estar, al mismo tiempo, aislado° de la calle.

El centro del patio es un espacio abierto. Alrededor de° él, separado por columnas, hay un pasillo cubierto°. Así, en el patio hay zonas de sol y de sombra°. El patio es una parte importante de la vivienda familiar y su decoración se cuida° mucho. En el centro del patio muchas veces hay una fuente°, plantas e incluso árboles°. El agua es un elemento muy importante en la ideología islámica porque simboliza la purificación del cuerpo y del alma°. Por esta razón y para disminuir° la temperatura, el agua en estas construcciones es muy importante. El agua y la vegetación ayudan a mantener la temperatura fresca y el patio proporciona° luz y ventilación a todas las habitaciones.

cálidas *hot*   disfrutando de *enjoying*   arquitectónica *architectural*
traída *brought*   época *era*   brisa *breeze*   aislado *isolated*
Alrededor de *Surrounding*   cubierto *covered*   sombra *shade*
se cuida *is looked after*   fuente *fountain*   árboles *trees*   alma *soul*
disminuir *lower*   proporciona *provides*   adineradas *wealthy*

La distribución

Las casas con patio central eran usualmente las viviendas de familias adineradas°. Son casas de dos o tres pisos. Los cuartos de la planta baja son las áreas comunes: cocina, comedor, sala, etc., y tienen puertas al patio. En los pisos superiores están las habitaciones privadas de la familia.

Hogar, dulce hogar

ACTIVIDADES

1 ¿Cierto o falso? Indica si lo que dicen las oraciones es **cierto** o **falso**.

1. Los patios centrales de Latinoamérica tienen su origen en la tradición indígena.
2. Los españoles llevaron a América el concepto del patio.
3. En la época colonial las casas eran las únicas construcciones con patio central.
4. El patio es una parte importante en estas construcciones, y es por ello que se le presta atención a su decoración.
5. El patio central es un lugar de descanso que da luz y ventilación a las habitaciones.
6. Las fuentes en los patios tienen importancia por razones ideológicas y porque bajan la temperatura.
7. En la ideología española el agua simboliza salud y bienestar del cuerpo y del alma.
8. Las casas con patio central eran de personas con dinero.
9. Los cuartos de la planta baja son privados.
10. Las alcobas están en los pisos superiores.

2 Viviendas tradicionales Escribe cuatro oraciones sobre una vivienda tradicional que conoces. Explica su origen, en qué lugar se encuentra, qué materiales tiene y cómo es.

CONEXIÓN INTERNET

¿Cuáles son las características de la arquitectura moderna de los países hispanos? For more information about **Exploración**, go to **vhlcentral.com**.

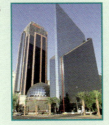

La casa de Frida

1 Preparación Imagina que eres un(a) artista, ¿cómo sería (*would be*) tu casa? ¿Sería muy diferente de la casa en donde vives ahora?

2 El video Mira el episodio de **Flash cultura**.

Vocabulario

jardinero *gardener* **la silla de ruedas** *wheelchair*
muros *walls* **las valiosas obras** *valuable works*

El hogar [de] Frida Kahlo… se caracteriza por su arquitectura típicamente mexicana…

Uno de los espacios más atractivos de esta casa es este estudio que Diego instaló…

3 ¿Cierto o falso? Indica si lo que dicen estas oraciones es **cierto** o **falso**.

1. La casa de Frida Kahlo está en el centro de México, D.F.
2. La casa de Frida se transformó en un museo en los años 50.
3. Frida Kahlo vivió sola en su casa.
4. Entre las obras que se exhiben está el cuadro (*painting*) de *Las dos Fridas*.
5. El jardinero actual (*current*) jamás conoció ni a Frida ni a Diego.
6. En el museo se exhiben la silla de ruedas y los aparatos ortopédicos de Frida.

doscientos sesenta y siete **267**

12 GRAMÁTICA

12.1 Usted and ustedes commands  Tutorial

Don Diego, quédese a cenar con nosotros.

▶ Command forms are used to give orders or advice. **Usted** and **ustedes** can be used to refer to a group of people or in formal situations.

Hable con ellos, don Francisco.
Talk to them, Don Francisco.

Coma frutas y verduras.
Eat fruits and vegetables.

Laven los platos ahora mismo.
Wash the dishes right now.

▶ Form **usted** and **ustedes** commands (**mandatos**) by dropping the final **–o** of the **yo** form of the present tense. For **–ar** verbs, add **–e** or **–en**. For **–er** and **–ir** verbs, add **–a** or **–an**.

Formal commands (Ud. and Uds.)

Infinitive	Present tense *yo* form	Ud. command	Uds. command
barrer	barro	barra	barran
decir (e:i)	digo	diga	digan
limpiar	limpio	limpie	limpien
sacudir	sacudo	sacuda	sacudan
salir	salgo	salga	salgan
servir (e:i)	sirvo	sirva	sirvan
venir	vengo	venga	vengan
volver (o:ue)	vuelvo	vuelva	vuelvan

No se preocupen, yo los ayudo.

▶ Verbs with irregular **yo** forms have the same irregularity in their formal commands. These verbs include **conducir, conocer, decir, hacer, ofrecer, oír, poner, salir, tener, traducir, traer, venir,** and **ver.**

Oiga, don Alejandro…
Listen, Don Alejandro…

¡**Salga** inmediatamente!
Leave immediately!

Ponga la mesa, por favor.
Set the table, please.

▶ Stem-changing verbs maintain their stem changes in **usted** and **ustedes** commands.

e:ie
No **pierda** la llave.
Cierren la puerta.

o:ue
Vuelva temprano, joven.
Duerman bien, chicos.

e:i
Sirva la sopa, por favor.
Repitan las oraciones.

¡ojo!

These spelling changes are necessary to ensure that the words are pronounced correctly. It may help you to study the following five series of syllables. Note that, within each series, the consonant sound doesn't change.

ca que qui co cu
za ce ci zo zu
ga gue gui go gu
ja ge gi jo ju

▶ Verbs ending in **–car, –gar,** and **–zar** have a spelling change in the command forms.

sacar	c	qu	saque, saquen
jugar	g	gu	juegue, jueguen
almorzar	z	c	almuerce, almuercen

▶ These verbs have irregular formal commands:

INFINITIVE	UD. COMMAND	UDS. COMMAND	INFINITIVE	UD. COMMAND	UDS. COMMAND
dar	dé	den	saber	sepa	sepan
estar	esté	estén	ser	sea	sean
ir	vaya	vayan			

268 doscientos sesenta y ocho

Hogar, dulce hogar

▶ In affirmative commands, reflexive and object pronouns are attached to the end of the verb. Note that when a pronoun is attached to a verb that has two or more syllables, an accent mark is added.

Siéntense, por favor.   Dígamelo.   Acuéstense ahora.   Pónganlas en el suelo, por favor.

▶ To make a command negative, place **no** before the verb. Note that the pronouns precede the verb.

No ponga las maletas en la cama.   **No ensucien** los sillones.   No **se** preocupe.   No **me lo** dé.
Don't put the suitcases on the bed.   *Don't dirty the armchairs.*   *Don't worry.*   *Don't give it to me.*

▶ **Usted** and **ustedes** can be used after command forms for a more formal, polite tone.

Muéstrele usted la foto a su amigo.   **Tomen ustedes** esta alcoba.
Show the photo to your friend.   *Take this bedroom.*

Práctica y conversación

Practice more at **vhlcentral.com**.

1 ¡A mudarse! La señora González quiere mudarse. Ayúdala a organizarse, indicando el mandato formal de cada verbo.

1. _____ [leer] los anuncios (*ads*) del periódico y _____ [guardarlos].
2. Decida qué casa quiere y _____ [llamar] al agente. _____ [pedirle] un contrato de alquiler.
3. _____ [decirles] a todos que tienen que ayudar. No _____ [hacerles] las maletas a los niños.
4. El día de la mudanza no _____ [estar] nerviosa.
5. No _____ [preocuparse]. _____ [saber] que todo va a salir bien.

2 ¿Qué dicen? En parejas, miren los dibujos y escriban un mandato lógico para cada uno.

MODELO

Arreglen estas cosas, por favor.

1.

2.

3.

4.

3 Problemas  En parejas, túrnense para representar a un(a) estudiante y un(a) profesor(a). El/La estudiante cuenta sus problemas y el/la profesor(a) le da órdenes. Sigan el modelo.

MODELO
Me torcí el tobillo jugando al tenis. Es la tercera vez.
Estudiante 1: Me torcí el tobillo jugando al tenis. Es la tercera vez.
Estudiante 2: No juegue más al tenis. / Vaya a ver a un médico.

1. Me enfermé después de volver de las vacaciones.
2. Nuestro cuarto es demasiado ruidoso para estudiar.
3. Me duele la cabeza y no puedo hacer la presentación para la clase hoy.
4. ¡Se me olvidó estudiar para el examen!

4 Un programa de consejos En parejas, túrnense para representar los papeles de una persona que da consejos en la radio y los radioyentes (*radio listeners*) que la llaman con estos problemas.

- problemas sentimentales
- problemas académicos
- problemas con los amigos
- problemas financieros
- problemas médicos
- problemas con el coche

5 Un anuncio de televisión En grupos, presenten un anuncio de televisión a la clase. Debe tratar de (*be about*) un detergente, un electrodoméstico o una agencia de bienes raíces. Usen mandatos, los pronombres relativos (**que, quien(es)** o **lo que**) y el **se** impersonal.

MODELO
Compre el lavaplatos Cristal. Tiene todo lo que usted desea. Es el lavaplatos que mejor funciona. Venga a verlo ahora mismo... No pierda ni un minuto más.

Lección 12

12.2 The present subjunctive

▶ The subjunctive mood expresses the speaker's attitude toward events, actions, or states that the speaker views as uncertain or hypothetical.

Es bueno que estudies más.
It is good that you study more.

Es necesario que no lleguemos tarde.
It is necessary that we don't arrive late.

▶ The subjunctive is mainly used to express: 1) will and influence; 2) emotion; 3) doubt, disbelief, and denial; and 4) indefiniteness and nonexistence.

▶ Some expressions are always followed by clauses in the subjunctive. These include:

Es bueno que... *It's good that...*	**Es mejor que...** *It's better that...*	**Es malo que...** *It's bad that...*
Es importante que... *It's important that...*	**Es necesario que...** *It's necessary that...*	**Es urgente que...** *It's urgent that...*

Es bueno que coma verduras.
It is good that I eat vegetables.

Es mejor que vayas con él.
It is better that you go with him.

Es malo que el niño no hable mucho.
It is bad that the boy does not speak much.

Es importante que traigamos la tarea.
It is important that we bring our homework.

Es necesario que los estudiantes traduzcan la lectura.
It is necessary that the students translate the reading.

Es urgente que Luisa sepa la verdad.
It is urgent that Luisa know the truth.

▶ To form the present subjunctive of regular verbs, drop the **–o** ending from the **yo** form of the present indicative, and replace it with the subjunctive endings.

INFINITIVE	PRESENT INDICATIVE	PRESENT SUBJUNCTIVE
hablar	hablo	hable
comer	como	coma
escribir	escribo	escriba

▶ Note the following endings for the subjunctive:

Present subjunctive of regular verbs

	hablar	comer	escribir
yo	hable	coma	escriba
tú	hables	comas	escribas
Ud./él/ella	hable	coma	escriba
nosotros/as	hablemos	comamos	escribamos
vosotros/as	habléis	comáis	escribáis
Uds./ellos/ellas	hablen	coman	escriban

¡ojo!
You may think that English doesn't have the subjunctive, but it does! While once common, it now mostly survives in set expressions, such as *If I were you...* and *Be that as it may...*

Hogar, dulce hogar

▸ Verbs ending in **–car, –gar,** and **–zar** have a spelling change in all forms.

sacar	saque, saques, saque, saquemos, saquéis, saquen
jugar	juegue, juegues, juegue, juguemos, juguéis, jueguen
almorzar	almuerce, almuerces, almuerce, almorcemos, almorcéis, almuercen

Present subjuntive of stem-changing verbs

▸ **–Ar** and **–er** stem-changing verbs have the same stem changes in the subjunctive as they do in the present indicative.

pensar (e:ie)	piense, pienses, piense, pensemos, penséis, piensen
mostrar (o:ue)	muestre, muestres, muestre, mostremos, mostréis, muestren
entender (e:ie)	entienda, entiendas, entienda, entendamos, entendáis, entiendan
volver (o:ue)	vuelva, vuelvas, vuelva, volvamos, volváis, vuelvan

▸ **–Ir** stem-changing verbs have the same stem changes in the subjunctive as in the present indicative. In addition, the **nosotros/as** and **vosotros/as** forms also undergo a stem change. The unstressed **e** changes to **i** and the unstressed **o** changes to **u**.

pedir (e:i)	pida, pidas, pida, pidamos, pidáis, pidan
sentir (e:ie)	sienta, sientas, sienta, sintamos, sintáis, sientan
dormir (o:ue)	duerma, duermas, duerma, durmamos, durmáis, duerman

▸ Verbs with irregular **yo** forms in the present indicative tense have the same irregularity in the present subjunctive.

INFINITIVE	PRESENT INDICATIVE	PRESENT SUBJUNCTIVE
conducir	conduzco	conduzca
conocer	conozco	conozca
decir	digo	diga
hacer	hago	haga
ofrecer	ofrezco	ofrezca
oír	oigo	oiga
parecer	parezco	parezca
poner	pongo	ponga
tener	tengo	tenga
traducir	traduzco	traduzca
traer	traigo	traiga
venir	vengo	venga
ver	veo	vea

doscientos setenta y uno **271**

Irregular verbs in the present subjuntive

▶ These five verbs are irregular in the present subjunctive:

Irregular verbs in the present subjunctive

	dar	estar	ir	saber	ser
yo	dé	esté	vaya	sepa	sea
tú	des	estés	vayas	sepas	seas
Ud./él/ella	dé	esté	vaya	sepa	sea
nosotros/as	demos	estemos	vayamos	sepamos	seamos
vosotros/as	deis	estéis	vayáis	sepáis	seáis
Uds./ellos/ellas	den	estén	vayan	sepan	sean

▶ The subjunctive form of **hay** (*there is, there are*) is also irregular: **haya**.

▶ The subjunctive is usually used in complex sentences that consist of a main clause and a subordinate clause. The main clause contains a verb or expression that triggers the use of the subjunctive. The word **que** connects the subordinate clause to the main clause.

Es necesario que pidas permiso antes de entrar a mi oficina.
It's necessary that you ask permission before you enter my office.

Es bueno que haya clases de español en mi universidad.
It's good that there are Spanish classes at my university.

ESPAÑOL EN VIVO

Para que tenga dientes más sanos...

- Es bueno que vaya al dentista con frecuencia.
- Es necesario que use blanqueador.
- ¡Y lo más importante es que se limpie los dientes con *Dentabrit*!

272   doscientos setenta y dos

Hogar, dulce hogar

Práctica y conversación

1 Emparejar Completa las oraciones con el subjuntivo de los verbos. Luego, empareja las oraciones del grupo **A** con las del grupo **B**.

A
1. Es mejor que _____ [nosotros, cenar] en casa. ___
2. Es importante que _____ [yo, tomar] algo para el dolor de cabeza. ___
3. Señora, es urgente que le _____ [yo, sacar] la muela. Parece que tiene una infección. ___
4. Es malo que Ana les _____ [dar] tantos dulces a los niños. ___
5. Es necesario que _____ [ustedes, llegar] a la una de la tarde. ___
6. Es importante que _____ [nosotros, acostarse] temprano esta noche. ___

B
a. Es importante que _____ [ellos, comer] más verduras y frutas.
b. No, es mejor que _____ [nosotros, salir] a comer.
c. Y yo creo que es urgente que _____ [tú, llamar] al médico inmediatamente.
d. En mi opinión, no es necesario que _____ [nosotros, dormir] tanto.
e. ¿Ah, sí? ¿Es necesario que me _____ [yo, tomar] un antibiótico también?
f. Para llegar a tiempo, es necesario que _____ [nosotros, almorzar] temprano.

2 Oraciones Combina los elementos de las tres columnas para formar oraciones. Usa el subjuntivo.

Expresiones	Sujetos	Actividades
Es bueno que	yo	hacer la cama
Es mejor que	mi hermano	levantarse
Es malo que	los padres	sacar la basura
Es importante que	Sofía Vergara	mudarse
Es necesario que	mis amigos	lavar los platos
Es urgente que	Kevin Durant	cocinar
	el/la profesor(a)	barrer el suelo
		despertarse
		ensuciar la casa
		comer

3 Minidiálogos En parejas, completen los minidiálogos de una manera lógica usando el subjuntivo.

MODELO
Miguelito: Mamá, no quiero arreglar mi cuarto.
Sra. Casas: Es necesario que lo arregles. Y es importante que sacudas los muebles también.

MIGUELITO Mamá, no quiero estudiar. Quiero salir a jugar con mis amigos.
SRA. CASAS (1) _____.

• • •

MIGUELITO Mamá, es que no me gustan las verduras. Prefiero comer pasteles.
SRA. CASAS (2) _____.

• • •

MIGUELITO ¿Tengo que poner la mesa, mamá?
SRA. CASAS (3) _____.

• • •

MIGUELITO No me siento bien, mamá. Me duele todo el cuerpo y tengo fiebre.
SRA. CASAS (4) _____.

4 Entrevista En parejas, usen estas preguntas para entrevistarse. Expliquen sus respuestas.

1. ¿Es importante que los niños ayuden con los quehaceres domésticos?
2. ¿Es urgente que los norteamericanos aprendan otras lenguas?
3. Si un(a) norteamericano/a quiere aprender francés, ¿es mejor que lo aprenda en Francia?
4. En tu universidad, ¿es necesario que los estudiantes vivan en residencias estudiantiles?
5. ¿Es bueno que todos los estudiantes practiquen algún deporte?
6. ¿Es importante que los estudiantes asistan a las clases?

doscientos setenta y tres **273**

Lección 12

12.3 Subjunctive with verbs of will and influence

▶ The subjunctive is used with verbs and expressions of will and influence. Verbs of will and influence are often used when someone wants to affect the actions of other people.

Enrique **quiere** que **salgamos** a cenar.
Enrique wants us to go out for dinner.

Mi madre nos **ruega** que **vayamos** a verla.
My mother is begging us to come see her.

▶ Here are some verbs of will and influence:

Verbs of will and influence

aconsejar	to advise	mandar	to order	recomendar (e:ie)	to recommend
desear	to wish; to desire	necesitar	to need	rogar (o:ue)	to beg; to plead
importar	to be important; to matter	pedir (e:i)	to ask (for)	sugerir (e:ie)	to suggest
insistir (en)	to insist (on)	prohibir	to prohibit		
		querer (e:ie)	to want		

¡ojo!
In English, constructions using the infinitive, such as *I want you to go*, are often used with verbs of will and influence. This is not the case with Spanish, where the subjunctive would be used in the subordinate clause.
Quiero que vayas.

▶ Some impersonal expressions convey will or influence, such as **es necesario que, es importante que, es mejor que,** and **es urgente que.**

Es importante que duermas bien.
It's important that you sleep well.

Es urgente que él lo **haga** hoy.
It's urgent that he do it today.

▶ When the main clause contains an expression of will or influence and the subordinate clause has a different subject, the subjunctive is required.

Les sugiero que arreglen este apartamento.

▶ Indirect object pronouns are often used with the verbs **aconsejar, mandar, pedir, recomendar, rogar,** and **sugerir.**

Te aconsejo que estudies.
I advise you to study.

Le ruego que no venga.
I beg you not to come.

Le sugiero que vaya a casa.
I suggest that you go home.

Recomiendo que se organicen en equipos.

▶ All the forms of **prohibir** in the present tense carry a written accent, except for the **nosotros** form: **prohíbo, prohíbes, prohíbe, prohibimos, prohibís, prohíben.**

Ella les **prohíbe** que miren la televisión.
She prohibits them from watching TV.

Nos **prohíben** que nademos en la piscina.
They prohibit us from swimming in the pool.

▶ The infinitive is used if there is no change of subject.

No quiero **sacudir** los muebles.
I don't want to dust the furniture.

Es importante **sacar** la basura.
It's important to take out the trash.

Paco prefiere **descansar**.
Paco prefers to rest.

No es necesario **quitar** la mesa.
It's not necessary to clear the table.

Hogar, dulce hogar

Práctica y conversación

1 Entre amigas
Completa el diálogo con palabras de la lista.

cocina	haga	ponga	quiere	sé	ser
diga	mires	prohíbe	saber	sea	vaya

IRENE Tengo problemas con Vilma. ¿Qué me recomiendas que le (1) _____?

JULIA Necesito (2) _____ más para aconsejarte.

IRENE Me (3) _____ que mire televisión cuando llego de la escuela.

JULIA Tiene razón. Es mejor que tú no (4) _____ tanta televisión.

IRENE Quiero que (5) _____ más flexible, pero insiste en que yo (6) _____ todo en la casa.

JULIA No es verdad. Yo (7) _____ que Vilma (8) _____ y hace los quehaceres todos los días.

IRENE Sí, pero siempre me pide que (9) _____ los cubiertos en la mesa y que (10) _____ al sótano por las servilletas.

JULIA ¡Vilma sólo (11) _____ que ayudes en la casa!

2 Unos consejos
Lee lo que dice cada persona. Luego da consejos lógicos usando verbos como **aconsejar**, **recomendar** y **prohibir**. Sigue el modelo.

MODELO
El presidente: Quiero comprar la Casa Blanca.
Le aconsejo que compre otra casa.

1. **Tu mamá:** Pienso poner la secadora en la entrada de la casa.
2. **Martha Stewart:** Voy a ir a la gasolinera para comprar unas elegantes copas de cristal.
3. **Tu profesor(a):** No voy a corregir los exámenes.
4. **Enrique Iglesias:** Pienso llevar todos mis muebles nuevos al altillo.
5. **Katy Perry:** Hay una fiesta en mi casa esta noche, pero no quiero arreglar la casa.
6. **Tu papá:** Hoy no tengo ganas de hacer las camas.

3 Preguntas
En parejas, túrnense para contestar las preguntas. Usen el subjuntivo.

1. ¿Te dan consejos tus amigos/as? ¿Qué te aconsejan? ¿Aceptas sus consejos? ¿Por qué?
2. ¿Qué te sugieren tus profesores/as que hagas antes de terminar los cursos que tomas?
3. ¿Insisten tus amigos/as en que salgas mucho con ellos/as?
4. ¿Qué quieres que te regalen tu familia y tus amigos/as para tu cumpleaños?
5. ¿Qué le recomiendas tú a un(a) amigo/a que no quiere salir los sábados con su novio/a?
6. ¿Qué les aconsejas a los/las nuevos/as estudiantes de tu universidad?

4 Recomendaciones
En parejas, preparen una lista de seis personas famosas. Un(a) estudiante da el nombre de una persona famosa y el/la otro/a le da un consejo.

MODELO
Estudiante 1: Judge Judy.
Estudiante 2: Le recomiendo que sea más simpática con la gente.
Estudiante 1: Will Ferrell.
Estudiante 2: Le aconsejo que haga más películas.

5 El apartamento de Luisa
En parejas, miren la ilustración. Denle consejos a Luisa sobre cómo arreglar su apartamento. Usen expresiones impersonales y verbos como **aconsejar**, **sugerir** y **recomendar**.

MODELO
Es mejor que arregles el apartamento más a menudo. Te aconsejo que guardes (*put away*) la tabla de planchar (*ironing board*).

doscientos setenta y cinco 275

Lección 12

Ampliación

Audio: Activity
Video: TV Clip

1 Escuchar

A Mira los anuncios en esta página y escucha la conversación entre el señor Núñez, Adriana y Felipe. Luego indica si cada descripción se refiere a la casa del anuncio o al apartamento del anuncio.

TIP Use visual cues. Visual cues, like illustrations and headings, provide useful clues about what you will hear.

18G

Bienes raíces

Se vende.
4 alcobas, 3 baños, cocina moderna, jardín con árboles frutales. B/. 225.000

Se alquila.
2 alcobas, 1 baño. Balcón. Urbanización Las Brisas. 525

Descripciones	La casa del anuncio	El apartamento del anuncio
1. Es barato.	☐	☐
2. Tiene cuatro alcobas.	☐	☐
3. Tiene oficina.	☐	☐
4. Tiene balcón.	☐	☐
5. Tiene una cocina moderna.	☐	☐
6. Tiene un jardín muy grande.	☐	☐
7. Tiene patio.	☐	☐

B Vuelve a escuchar la conversación e indica cómo es la casa ideal de Adriana y Felipe.

2 Conversar
Con un(a) compañero/a, preparen una conversación entre un(a) psicólogo/a y un(a) paciente que le consulta sobre un problema personal (la familia, el/la novio/a, etc.). Luego presenten la conversación a la clase. Incluyan la siguiente información:

- ¿Cuál es el problema que tiene el/la paciente?
- ¿Por qué tiene este problema?
- ¿Qué soluciones le da el/la psicólogo/a?

276 doscientos setenta y seis

Hogar, dulce hogar

3 Escribir Eres el/la administrador(a) de un edificio de apartamentos. Prepara un contrato de arrendamiento (*lease*) para los nuevos inquilinos (*tenants*).

TIP **Use linking words.** To make your writing more cohesive, use linking words to connect simple sentences or ideas. Some common linking words are: **cuando, mientras, o, pero, porque, pues, que, quien(es), sino,** and **y.**

Here are some technical terms that might help you in writing your contract:
el/la arrendatario/a (*tenant*)
el/la arrendador(a) (*landlord*)
el/la propietario/a (*owner*)
las estipulaciones (*stipulations*)
la parte (*party*)
por adelantado/anticipado / con antelación (*in advance*)

Organízalo — Utiliza un mapa de ideas para organizar la información sobre las fechas del contrato, el precio del alquiler y otros aspectos importantes.

Escríbelo — Escribe el primer borrador de tu contrato de arrendamiento.

Corrígelo — Intercambia el contrato con un(a) compañero/a. Anota los mejores aspectos, especialmente el uso de las palabras de enlace (*linking words*). Dale sugerencias y, si ves algunos errores, coméntaselos.

Compártelo — Revisa el primer borrador según las indicaciones de tu compañero/a. Incorpora nuevas ideas y/o más información, si es necesario, antes de escribir la versión final.

4 Un paso más Imagina que quieres construir (*to build*) una casa de vacaciones en un país hispano. Prepara una presentación sobre la casa. Considera estas preguntas.

- ¿Dónde quieres construir la casa? ¿Prefieres que esté en la selva (*jungle*), en una isla, en una montaña o en un lugar con vistas al mar?
- ¿Cómo va a ser la casa? ¿Quieres que sea grande? ¿Cuántos pisos y cuántos cuartos va a tener?
- ¿Qué muebles quieres poner en cada cuarto?
- ¿Qué efectos visuales puedes usar para hacer más interesante la presentación? ¿Tienes mapas, fotos o planos (*blueprints*) de la casa?

 CONEXIÓN INTERNET

Investiga estos temas en vhlcentral.com.

- Lugares turísticos del mundo hispano
- Agencias de bienes raíces en el mundo hispano
- Mueblerías (*furniture stores*) en el mundo hispano

doscientos setenta y siete

12 LECTURA

Antes de leer

**Audio: Reading
Additional Reading**

Did you know that a text written in Spanish is often longer than the same text written in English? Since the Spanish language frequently uses more words to express ideas, you will often encounter long sentences when reading in Spanish. Of course, sentence length varies with genre and with authors' individual styles. To help you understand long sentences, identify the main parts of the sentence before trying to read it in its entirety. First, locate the main verb of the sentence, along with its subject, ignoring any words or phrases set off by commas. Then re-read the sentence, adding details like direct and indirect objects, transitional words, and prepositional phrases. Practice this strategy on a few sentences from this reading selection.

For example, locate the main subject and verb in the first sentence of this reading: _____

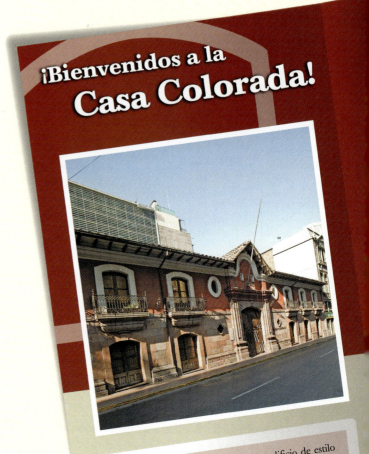

¡Bienvenidos a la Casa Colorada!

La Casa Colorada es un atractivo edificio de estilo colonial, construido° en 1769. Está situado en el centro de Santiago de Chile, en la calle Merced. En sus orígenes fue la vivienda de Mateo de Toro y Zambrano, un aristócrata chileno conocido por sus actividades en el ejército°, los negocios° y la administración de la ciudad. En la actualidad°, la Casa Colorada no está habitada por nadie.

recursos

vhlcentral.com

Hogar, dulce hogar

El edificio se convirtió en un espacio público en el siglo° XX y en su interior están el Museo de Santiago, la Oficina de Turismo y la Fundación de Vicente Huidobro, donde se encuentra abundante información sobre la vida y la obra° de este escritor chileno. El Museo de Santiago ofrece una exhibición permanente sobre la historia de la ciudad, desde la época precolombina hasta nuestros días.

La Casa Colorada es una obra del arquitecto portugués Joseph de la Vega. Los materiales fundamentales que se utilizaron en su construcción fueron el adobe, la madera° y la cal°. Desde el primer momento, esta casa se convirtió en el centro de atención de la sociedad santiaguina° por la elegancia de su diseño°. Además, una característica que la diferenciaba de otras viviendas del mismo estilo arquitectónico es que su fachada° estaba recubierta de piedra° hasta el primer piso. El edificio empezó a llamarse Casa Colorada en 1888, año en que pintaron su fachada de color rojo.

La composición exterior del edificio es simétrica. En el centro de la fachada hay una gran puerta que sirve de acceso principal a la vivienda; a los lados se ven unos arcos que forman puertas adicionales en el primer piso y ventanas con balcones de hierro forjado° en el segundo. Otra característica interesante del exterior de la casa es la elevación triangular del tejado° sobre la puerta principal.

construido *built* ejército *army* negocios *business* En la actualidad *At the present time* siglo *century* obra *work* madera *wood* cal *lime* santiaguina *of Santiago* diseño *design* fachada *façade* recubierta de piedra *covered with stone* hierro forjado *wrought iron* tejado *roof*

Después de leer

¿Comprendiste?

Completa las oraciones con las palabras adecuadas.

1. Mateo de Toro y Zambrano, un aristócrata de _____, vivió en la Casa Colorada.

2. Ahora _____ vive en la Casa Colorada.

3. El exterior de la casa es de color _____.

4. La _____ principal está en el centro de la fachada.

5. Los materiales que se utilizaron en su construcción fueron _____, la madera y la cal.

6. En el Museo de Santiago hay una exhibición sobre la _____ de la ciudad.

Preguntas

Responde a estas preguntas con oraciones completas.

1. ¿Cuándo se construyó la Casa Colorada?

_____

2. ¿Cuándo se convirtió en lugar público?

_____

3. ¿Dónde están el Museo de Santiago, la Oficina de Turismo y la Fundación de Vicente Huidobro?

_____

4. ¿Cómo se llamaba el arquitecto de la Casa Colorada?

_____

5. ¿Por qué la Casa Colorada se diferenciaba de otras viviendas del mismo estilo arquitectónico?

_____

6. ¿Por qué este edificio se llama la Casa Colorada?

_____

Coméntalo

¿Te gustaría visitar la Casa Colorada? ¿Te gustaría vivir en una casa similar a ésta? ¿Hay edificios históricos en tu ciudad o comunidad? Explica tus respuestas.

doscientos setenta y nueve **279**

12 VOCABULARIO

La casa y sus cuartos

la alcoba	bedroom
el altillo	attic
el balcón	balcony
la cocina	kitchen
el comedor	dining room
la entrada	entrance
la escalera	stairs; stairway
el garaje	garage
el jardín	garden; yard
la oficina	office
el pasillo	hallway
el patio	patio; yard
la sala	living room
el sótano	basement; cellar

Los muebles y otras cosas

la alfombra	carpet; rug
la almohada	pillow
el armario	closet
la cómoda	chest of drawers
las cortinas	curtains
el cuadro	picture
el estante	bookcase; bookshelf
la lámpara	lamp
la luz	light; electricity
la manta	blanket
la mesita	end table
la mesita de noche	nightstand
los muebles	furniture
la pared	wall
la pintura	painting; picture
el sillón	armchair
el sofá	sofa; couch

Los quehaceres domésticos

arreglar	to neaten; to straighten up
barrer el suelo	to sweep the floor
cocinar	to cook
hacer la cama	to make the bed
hacer los quehaceres domésticos	to do household chores
lavar (el suelo, los platos)	to wash (the floor, the dishes)
limpiar la casa	to clean the house
pasar la aspiradora	to vacuum
planchar la ropa	to iron clothes
poner la mesa	to set the table
quitar la mesa	to clear the table
sacar la basura	to take out the trash
sacudir los muebles	to dust the furniture

Los electrodomésticos

la estufa	stove
los electrodomésticos	electric appliances
el horno (de microondas)	(microwave) oven
la lavadora	washing machine
el lavaplatos	dishwasher
el refrigerador	refrigerator
la secadora	clothes dryer

La mesa

la copa	wineglass; goblet
la cuchara	spoon
el cuchillo	knife
el plato	plate
la servilleta	napkin
la taza	cup; mug
el tenedor	fork
el vaso	glass

Otras palabras

las afueras	suburbs; outskirts
la agencia de bienes raíces	real estate agency
el alquiler	rent (payment)
el ama (f.) de casa	homemaker
el barrio	neighborhood
el edificio de apartamentos	apartment building
el hogar	home
el/la vecino/a	neighbor
la vivienda	housing
alquilar	to rent
ensuciar	to get (something dirty)
mudarse	to move (residences)

Verbs and expressions of will and influence	See page 274.

280 doscientos ochenta

¡VIVAN LOS PAÍSES HISPANOS!

La ropa tradicional de los guatemaltecos se llama *huipil* y en ella se puede observar el amor de la cultura maya por la naturaleza (*nature*). El diseño (*design*) y los colores de cada *huipil* indican el pueblo de origen y a veces también el sexo y la edad (*age*) de la persona que lo lleva.

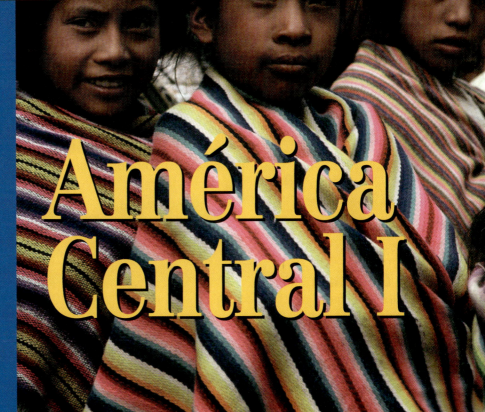

América Central I

Guatemala
Área: 108.890 km² (42.042 millas²)
Población: 14.099.032
Capital: Ciudad de Guatemala–1.075.000
Ciudades principales: Quetzaltenango, Escuintla, Mazatenango, Puerto Barrios
Moneda: quetzal

SOURCE: Population Division, UN Secretariat & CIA World Factbook

Honduras
Área: 112.492 km² (43.870 millas²)
Población: 8.296.693
Capital: Tegucigalpa–1.000.000
Ciudades principales: San Pedro Sula, El Progreso
Moneda: lempira

SOURCE: Population Division, UN Secretariat & CIA World Factbook

El Salvador
Área: 21.040 km² (8.124 millas²)
Población: 6.090.646
Capital: San Salvador–1.534.000
Ciudades principales: Soyapango, Santa Ana, San Miguel
Moneda: dolar estadounidense

SOURCE: Population Division, UN Secretariat & CIA World Factbook

¡Vivan los países hispanos!

S Interactive map
Video: *Países hispanos*

Deportes

El surfing

El Salvador es uno de los destinos favoritos en Latinoamérica para la práctica del surfing. Cuenta con 300 kilómetros de costa a lo largo del océano Pacífico y sus olas (*waves*) altas son ideales para quienes practican este deporte. De sus playas, La Libertad es la más visitada por surfistas de todo el mundo, gracias a que está muy cerca de la capital salvadoreña.

Ciudades

Antigua Guatemala

Antigua Guatemala fue fundada en 1543. Fue una capital de gran importancia hasta 1773, cuando un terremoto (*earthquake*) la destruyó. Hoy día, conserva el carácter original de su arquitectura y es un gran centro turístico. Su celebración de la Semana Santa es, para muchas personas, la más importante del hemisferio.

282 *doscientos ochenta y dos*

América Central I

Lugares
Copán

Copán es una zona arqueológica muy importante de Honduras. Fue construida por los mayas. Se calcula que en el año 400 d.C. era una ciudad con más de 150 edificios y una gran cantidad de plazas y canchas (*courts*) para el juego de pelota (*ceremonial ball game*). Las ruinas más famosas del lugar son los edificios adornados con esculturas pintadas a mano, los cetros (*scepters*) ceremoniales de piedra y el templo Rosalila. Una de las actividades más importantes de Copán era la astronomía. ¡Hasta se hacían congresos (*conventions*) de astrónomos!

Naturaleza
El Parque Nacional Montecristo

El Parque Nacional Montecristo se encuentra en la región norte de El Salvador. Se le conoce también como El Trifinio porque se ubica (*it is located*) en el punto donde se unen las fronteras de Guatemala, Honduras y El Salvador. Este bosque reúne muchas especies vegetales y animales, como orquídeas, monos araña (*spider monkeys*), pumas, quetzales y tucanes. En este hermoso bosque, las copas de sus enormes árboles forman una bóveda que impide (*blocks*) que entre la luz del sol.

doscientos ochenta y tres 283

¡Vivan los países hispanos!

¿Qué aprendiste?

1 ¿Cierto o falso? Indica si lo que dicen estas oraciones es **cierto** o **falso**.

Cierto	Falso	
_____	_____	1. La ropa tradicional de los guatemaltecos se llama Quetzaltenango.
_____	_____	2. Los diseños del *huipil* indican el origen de la persona que lo lleva.
_____	_____	3. Tegucigalpa es la capital de Honduras.
_____	_____	4. La lempira es la moneda de Guatemala.
_____	_____	5. En Copán se hacían congresos de geografía.
_____	_____	6. Los mayas eran muy buenos astrónomos.
_____	_____	7. Antigua Guatemala es la capital de Guatemala.
_____	_____	8. Antigua Guatemala es muy famosa por su celebración de la Semana Santa.
_____	_____	9. El Parque Nacional Montecristo está en El Salvador, en el límite con Honduras y Guatemala.
_____	_____	10. Las plantas pequeñas en el bosque del Parque Nacional Montecristo reciben mucho sol.

2 Preguntas Contesta estas preguntas.

1. ¿Conoces la ropa tradicional de algún lugar en el mundo? ¿De dónde?
2. ¿En qué lugares de los Estados Unidos se puede practicar el surfing? ¿Te gustaría practicarlo en las playas de América Central?
3. ¿Conoces algún país donde se celebra la Semana Santa? ¿Cómo se celebra?
4. ¿Qué otros países en el mundo son famosos por sus ruinas arqueológicas?
5. ¿Cuáles son algunos de los parques naturales más famosos en los Estados Unidos?

CONEXIÓN INTERNET

Investiga estos temas en el sitio **vhlcentral.com**.

- Rigoberta Menchú
- Lugares para visitar en América Central
- Base de la economía hondureña

13 La naturaleza

Communicative Goals

You will learn how to:
- talk about nature
- discuss environmental conditions
- express wishes, desires, and doubts

PREPARACIÓN
pages 286–289
- Words related to nature and the environment
- Animals
- Spanish punctuation

ESCENAS
pages 290–291
- Jimena, Felipe, Juan Carlos, and Marissa take a trip to the Yucatán Peninsula. While Marissa and Jimena visit a turtle sanctuary and the Mayan ruins of Tulum, the boys take a trip to the jungle.

EXPLORACIÓN
pages 292–293
- Bajo la lupa: ¡Los Andes se mueven!
- Flash cultura: Naturaleza en Costa Rica

GRAMÁTICA
pages 294–301
- The subjunctive with verbs of emotion
- The subjunctive with doubt, disbelief, and denial
- The subjunctive with conjunctions

LECTURA
pages 302–303
- Fables: El perro y el cocodrilo and El pato y la serpiente

Para empezar
- ¿Dónde están estas personas?
- ¿Qué hacen?
- ¿Qué ropa y objetos llevan? ¿Por qué?
- ¿Crees que a ellos les importa la naturaleza?

13 PREPARACIÓN

La naturaleza

el volcán volcano

EL MEDIO AMBIENTE

la caza hunting
el calentamiento global global warming
la conservación conservation
la contaminación (del aire; del agua) (air; water) pollution
la ecología ecology
el ecoturismo ecotourism
la energía (solar) (solar) energy
la extinción extinction
la fábrica factory
el gobierno government
la ley law
el medio ambiente environment
el peligro danger
la población population
el reciclaje recycling
el recurso natural natural resource
la solución solution

ecologista ecological; ecologist
renovable renewable

LA NATURALEZA

el árbol tree
el bosque (tropical) (tropical; rain) forest
el césped grass
el cielo sky
el cráter crater
el desierto desert
la estrella star
la hierba grass
el lago lake
la luna moon
el mundo world
la naturaleza nature
la nube cloud
el océano ocean
el paisaje landscape
la piedra rock; stone
la planta plant
la región region; area
el río river
la selva jungle
el sendero trail
el sol sun
la tierra land; soil
el valle valley

la flor *flower*

la energía nuclear nuclear energy

recursos
WB pp. 131–132
LM p. 73
vhlcentral.com

la deforestación deforestation

286 doscientos ochenta y seis

La naturaleza

la tortuga marina
sea turtle

LOS ANIMALES

el animal animal
la ballena whale
el pez fish

el pájaro
bird

el mono
monkey

VERBOS

conservar to conserve
contaminar to pollute
controlar to control
cuidar to take care of
dejar de (+ *inf.*) to stop (doing something)
desarrollar to develop
descubrir to discover
destruir to destroy
estar afectado/a (por) to be affected (by)
evitar to avoid
mejorar to improve
proteger to protect
reciclar to recycle
recoger to pick up
reducir to reduce
resolver (o:ue) to resolve; to solve
respirar to breathe

la botella de vidrio
glass bottle

OTRAS PALABRAS Y EXPRESIONES

el envase de plástico plastic container
puro/a pure

estar contaminado/a
to be polluted

la lata de aluminio
aluminum can

doscientos ochenta y siete **287**

Lección 13

Práctica y conversación

1 Escuchar Escucha estas oraciones y anota los sustantivos (*nouns*) que se refieren a **las plantas**, **los animales**, **la tierra** y **el cielo**.

Plantas	Animales	Tierra	Cielo
_____	_____	_____	_____
_____	_____	_____	_____
_____	_____	_____	_____

2 Seleccionar Escucha las descripciones y escribe el número de la descripción que corresponda a cada foto.

a. _____   b. _____   c. _____   d. _____

3 Completar Completa las oraciones.

contaminar	destruyen	reciclamos
controlan	están afectadas	recoger
cuidan	mejoramos	resolver
descubrir	proteger	se desarrollaron

1. Si vemos basura en las calles, la debemos _____.
2. Los científicos trabajan para _____ nuevas soluciones.
3. Es necesario que todos trabajemos juntos para _____ los problemas del medio ambiente.
4. Debemos _____ el medio ambiente porque está en peligro.
5. Muchas leyes nuevas _____ el número de árboles que se pueden cortar (*cut down*).
6. Las primeras civilizaciones _____ cerca de los ríos, los lagos y los océanos.
7. Todas las personas del mundo _____ por la contaminación.
8. Los turistas deben tener cuidado y no _____ las regiones que visitan.
9. Podemos conservar los recursos si _____ el aluminio, el vidrio y el plástico.
10. La lluvia ácida, la contaminación y la deforestación _____ el medio ambiente.

4 Definir En parejas, definan cada palabra.

1. la población
2. una ballena
3. la lluvia
4. la naturaleza
5. un desierto
6. la caza
7. la ecología
8. un mono
9. el sendero

¿Qué es el calentamiento global?

El calentamiento global significa que la temperatura de la Tierra sube.

288 *doscientos ochenta y ocho*

5 **Situaciones** En grupos pequeños, representen estas situaciones.

- Un(a) ecologista habla con un grupo de familias sobre qué se puede hacer en la casa para proteger el medio ambiente.
- Un(a) representante de una universidad habla con un grupo de estudiantes nuevos sobre la campaña (*campaign*) ambiental de la universidad.

Ortografía Los signos de puntuación

In Spanish, as in English, punctuation marks are important because they help you express your ideas in a clear, organized way.

No podía ver las llaves. Las buscó por los estantes, las mesas, las sillas, el suelo; minutos después, decidió mirar por la ventana. Allí estaban...

The **punto y coma (;)**, the **puntos suspensivos (...)**, and the **punto (.)** are used in very similar ways in Spanish and English.

Argentina, Brasil, Paraguay y Uruguay son miembros del Mercosur.

In Spanish, the **coma (,)** is not used in a series before **y** or **o**.

| 13,5% | 29,2° | 3.000.000 | $2.999,99 |

In numbers, Spanish uses a **coma** where English uses a decimal point and a **punto** where English uses a comma.

¿Cómo te llamas?   ¿Dónde está?   ¡Ven aquí!   ¡Hola!

Questions in Spanish are preceded and followed by **signos de interrogación (¿ ?)**, and exclamations are preceded and followed by **signos de exclamación (¡ !)**.

¿Palabras de amor? El siguiente diálogo tiene diferentes significados (*meanings*), dependiendo de los signos de puntuación que utilizas y el lugar donde los pones. Intenta encontrar los diferentes significados.

JULIÁN   me quieres
MARISOL no puedo vivir sin ti
JULIÁN   me quieres dejar
MARISOL no me parece mala idea
JULIÁN   no eres feliz conmigo
MARISOL no soy feliz

13 ESCENAS

Aventuras en la naturaleza Video: *Fotonovela*

Las chicas visitan un santuario de tortugas, mientras los chicos pasean por la selva.

Expresiones útiles

Talking about the environment

Aprendimos sobre las normas que existen para proteger a las tortugas marinas.
We learned about the regulations that exist to protect sea turtles.

Afortunadamente, ahora la población está aumentando.
Fortunately, the population is now growing.

No cabe duda de que necesitamos aprobar más leyes para protegerlas.
There is no doubt that we need to pass more laws to protect them.

Es maravilloso que México tenga tantos programas estupendos para proteger a las tortugas.
It's marvelous that Mexico has so many wonderful programs to protect the turtles.

A menos que protejamos a los animales de la contaminación y la deforestación, muchos van a estar en peligro de extinción.
Unless we protect animals from pollution and deforestation, many of them will become endangered.

Additional vocabulary

aumentar *to grow; to get bigger*
meterse en problemas *to get into trouble*
perdido/a *lost*
el recorrido *tour*
sobre todo *above all*

MARISSA Querida tía Ana María, lo estoy pasando muy bien. Es maravilloso que México tenga tantos programas estupendos para proteger a las tortugas. Hoy estamos en Tulum, y ¡el paisaje es espectacular! Con cariño, Marissa.

MARISSA Estoy tan feliz de que estés aquí conmigo.
JIMENA Es mucho más divertido cuando se viaja con amigos.
(*Llegan Felipe y Juan Carlos*)
JIMENA ¿Qué pasó?
JUAN CARLOS No lo van a creer.

GUÍA A menos que protejamos a los animales de la contaminación y la deforestación, muchos van a estar en peligro de extinción. Por favor, síganme y eviten pisar las plantas.

FELIPE Nos retrasamos sólo cinco minutos... Qué extraño. Estaban aquí hace unos minutos.
JUAN CARLOS ¿Adónde se fueron?
FELIPE No creo que puedan ir muy lejos.
(*Se separan para buscar al grupo.*)

FELIPE Juan Carlos encontró al grupo. ¡Yo esperaba encontrarlos también! ¡Pero nunca vinieron por mí! Yo estaba asustado. Regresé al lugar de donde salimos y esperé. Me perdí todo el recorrido.

recursos

VM
pp. 25–26

vhlcentral.com

La naturaleza

MARISSA **JIMENA** **JUAN CARLOS** **FELIPE** **GUÍA**

FELIPE Decidí seguir un río y...

MARISSA No es posible que un guía continúe el recorrido cuando hay dos personas perdidas.

JIMENA Vamos a ver, chicos, ¿qué pasó? Dígannos la verdad.

JUAN CARLOS Felipe se cayó. Él no quería contarles.

JIMENA ¡Lo sabía!

FELIPE Y ustedes, ¿qué hicieron hoy?

JIMENA Marissa y yo fuimos al santuario de las tortugas

MARISSA Aprendimos sobre las normas que existen para proteger a las tortugas marinas.

JIMENA Pero no cabe duda de que necesitamos aprobar más leyes para protegerlas.

MARISSA Fue muy divertido verlas tan cerca.

JUAN CARLOS Entonces se divirtieron. ¡Qué bien!

JIMENA Gracias, y tú, pobrecito, pasaste todo el día con mi hermano. Siempre te mete en problemas.

Actividades

1 Identificar Identifica quién puede decir estas oraciones. Puedes usar algunos nombres más de una vez.

1. Fue divertido ver a las tortugas y aprender las normas para protegerlas. _____
2. Tenemos que evitar la contaminación y la deforestación. _____
3. Estoy feliz de estar aquí, Tulum es maravilloso. _____
4. Es una lástima que me pierda el recorrido. _____
5. No es posible que esa historia que nos dices sea verdad. _____

2 Preguntas Contesta las siguientes preguntas.

1. ¿Qué lugar visitan Marissa y Jimena?
2. ¿Adónde fueron Juan Carlos y Felipe?
3. Según la guía, ¿por qué muchos animales están en peligro de extinción?
4. ¿Por qué Jimena y Marissa no creen la historia de Felipe?
5. ¿Qué esperaba Felipe cuando se perdió?

3 Situación En grupos de tres o cuatro, imaginen que un(a) estudiante es un(a) guía y el resto son turistas que van a hacer una excursión a las montañas. Los/Las turistas preguntan al/a la guía lo que van a ver y lo que deben o no hacer durante la excursión. Usen las **Expresiones útiles.**

doscientos noventa y uno 291

13 EXPLORACIÓN

BAJO LA LUPA

¡Los Andes se mueven!

Additional Reading
Video: *Flash cultura*

Los Andes, la cadena° de montañas más extensa de América, son conocidos como "la espina dorsal° de Suramérica". Sus 7.240 kilómetros (4.500 millas) van desde el norte° de la región entre Venezuela y Colombia, hasta el extremo sur°, entre Argentina y Chile, y pasan por casi todos los países suramericanos. La cordillera° de los Andes, formada hace 27 millones de años, es la segunda más alta del mundo, después de la del Himalaya (aunque° esta última es mucho más "joven", ya que se formó hace apenas cinco millones de años).

Para poder atravesar° de un lado a otro de los Andes, existen varios pasos o puertos° de montaña. Situados a grandes alturas°, son generalmente estrechos° y peligrosos. En algunos de ellos hay, también, vías ferroviarias°.

De acuerdo con° varias instituciones científicas, la cordillera de los Andes se eleva° y se hace más angosta° cada año. La capital de Chile se acerca° a la capital de Argentina a un ritmo° de 19,4 milímetros por año. Si ese ritmo se mantiene°, Santiago y Buenos Aires podrían unirse° en unos... 63 millones de años, ¡casi el mismo tiempo que ha transcurrido° desde la extinción de los dinosaurios!

cadena *range*   **espina dorsal** *spine*   **norte** *north*   **sur** *south*   **cordillera** *mountain range*   **aunque** *although*   **atravesar** *to cross*   **puertos** *passes*   **alturas** *heights*   **estrechos** *narrow*   **vías ferroviarias** *railroad tracks*   **De acuerdo con** *According to*   **se eleva** *rises*   **angosta** *narrow*   **se acerca** *gets closer*   **ritmo** *rate*   **se mantiene** *keeps going*   **podrían unirse** *could join together*   **ha transcurrido** *has gone by*   **a.C.** *Before Christ (B.C.)*   **desarrollo** *development*   **pico** *peak*

Los Andes en números

3 Cordilleras que forman los Andes: Las cordilleras Central, Occidental y Oriental
900 (a.C.°) Año aproximado en que empezó el desarrollo° de la cultura chavín, en los Andes peruanos
600 Número aproximado de volcanes que hay en los Andes
6.962 Metros (**22.841** pies) de altura del Aconcagua (Argentina), el pico° más alto de los Andes

Volcán Misti, Arequipa, Perú

recursos

VM pp. 57–58   vhlcentral.com

Practice more at **vhlcentral.com.**

292   doscientos noventa y dos

La naturaleza

ACTIVIDADES

1 Escoger Escoge la opción que completa mejor cada oración.

1. Los Andes es la cadena montañosa más extensa del…
   a. mundo.
   b. continente americano.
   c. hemisferio norte.
2. "La espina dorsal de Suramérica" es…
   a. los Andes.
   b. el Himalaya.
   c. el Aconcagua.
3. La cordillera de los Andes se extiende…
   a. de este a oeste.
   b. de sur a oeste.
   c. de norte a sur.
4. El Himalaya y los Andes tienen…
   a. diferente altura.
   b. la misma altura.
   c. el mismo color.
5. Es posible atravesar los Andes por medio de…
   a. montañas
   b. puertos
   c. aviones
6. El Aconcagua es…
   a. una montaña.
   b. un grupo indígena.
   c. un volcán.

2 Maravillas de la naturaleza Escribe un párrafo breve donde describas alguna maravilla de la naturaleza que has (*you have*) visitado y que te impresionó. Puede ser cualquier (*any*) sitio natural: un río, una montaña, una selva, etc.

CONEXIÓN INTERNET

¿En qué otros lugares de Latinoamérica se puede hacer ecoturismo? For more information about **Exploración**, go to **vhlcentral.com**.

Naturaleza en Costa Rica

1 Preparación ¿Qué sabes de los volcanes de Costa Rica? ¿Y de sus aguas termales? Si no sabes nada, escribe tres predicciones sobre cada tema.

2 El video Mira el episodio de **Flash cultura**.

Vocabulario
aguas termales hot springs
hace erupción erupts
los poderes curativos healing powers
rocas incandescentes incandescent rocks

Aquí existen más de cien volcanes. Hoy visitaremos el Parque Nacional Volcán Arenal.

En los alrededores del volcán […] nacen aguas termales de origen volcánico…

3 ¿Cierto o falso? Indica si estas oraciones son **ciertas** o **falsas**.

1. Centroamérica es una zona de pocos volcanes.
2. El volcán Arenal está en un parque nacional.
3. El volcán Arenal hace erupción pocas veces.
4. Las aguas termales cerca del volcán vienen del mar.
5. Cuando Alberto sale del agua, tiene calor.
6. Se pueden ver las rocas incandescentes desde algunos hoteles.

doscientos noventa y tres   293

13 GRAMÁTICA

13.1 The subjunctive with verbs of emotion

Es una lástima que ellos no estén aquí con nosotros.

Me alegra que te diviertas.

Main clause	Connector	Subordinate clause
Marta espera	que	yo vaya al lago este fin de semana.

▶ When the main clause of a sentence expresses an emotion or feeling, use the subjunctive in the subordinate clause.

Nos alegramos de que te **gusten** las flores.
We are happy that you like the flowers.

Siento que tú no **vengas** mañana.
I'm sorry that you're not coming tomorrow.

Temo que Ana no **pueda** ir mañana con nosotros.
I'm concerned that Ana won't be able to go with us tomorrow.

Le **sorprende** que Juan **sea** tan joven.
It surprises him that Juan is so young.

Common verbs and expressions of emotion

alegrarse (de)	to be happy	esperar	to hope; to wish	sentir (e:ie)	to be sorry; to regret
es extraño	it's strange	gustar	to be pleasing; to like	sorprender	to surprise
es ridículo	it's ridiculous				
es terrible	it's terrible	molestar	to bother	temer	to be worried, concerned
es triste	it's sad	ojalá (que)	I hope (that); I wish (that)		
es una lástima	it's a shame			tener miedo (de)	to be afraid (of)

Me molesta que la gente no **recicle** el plástico.
It bothers me that people don't recycle plastic.

Me preocupa que no **respiremos** aire puro.
I worry that we don't breathe clean air.

Es una lástima que no **controlemos** la deforestación.
It's a shame we don't control deforestation.

Espera que el gobierno **proteja** el medio ambiente.
He hopes that the government protects the environment.

Using the subjunctive

▶ Use the infinitive after an expression of emotion when there is no change of subject.

Temo **llegar** tarde.
I'm concerned I'll arrive late.

Me molesta **ver** el bosque tropical en peligro.
It bothers me to see the rainforest in danger.

Temo que mi novio **llegue** tarde.
I'm worried my boyfriend will arrive late.

Me alegro de que algunas fábricas **se preocupen** por el medio ambiente.
I'm happy that some factories worry about the environment.

▶ The expression **ojalá (que)** is always followed by the subjunctive. The use of **que** is optional.

Ojalá (que) se conserven nuestros recursos naturales.
I hope (that) our natural resources will be conserved.

Ojalá (que) recojan la basura muy pronto.
I hope (that) they collect the garbage soon.

294 *doscientos noventa y cuatro*

La naturaleza

Práctica y conversación

1 Olga y Sara Completa esta conversación.

alegro	molesta	temer
conozcan	ojalá	tengo miedo de
estén	puedan	vayan
lleguen	sorprender	visitar

OLGA Me alegro de que Adriana y Raquel (1) _____ a Colombia.

SARA Sí… Es una lástima que (2) _____ cuando ya comenzaron las clases. Ojalá que la universidad las ayude a buscar casa. (3) _____ que no consigan dónde vivir.

OLGA Me (4) _____ que seas tan pesimista. Yo espero que (5) _____ gente simpática.

SARA ¿Sabías que ellas van a estudiar la deforestación en las costas? Es triste que en tantos países los recursos naturales (6) _____ en peligro.

OLGA Me (7) _____ de que no se queden en la capital por la contaminación, pero (8) _____ tengan tiempo de viajar por el país.

SARA Sí, espero que (9) _____ ir al Museo del Oro. Sé que también esperan (10) _____ la Catedral de Sal de Zipaquirá.

2 Diálogo Usa los siguientes elementos para crear una conversación entre Juan y la madre de su novia. Añade palabras si es necesario. Luego, con un(a) compañero/a, preséntala a la clase.

1. Juan, / esperar / (tú) llamar / Raquel. / Ser / tu / novia. / Ojalá / no / sentirse / sola
2. Molestarme / (usted) decirme / lo que / tener / hacer. / Ahora / mismo / estar / llamándola
3. Alegrarme / oírte / decir / eso. / Ser / terrible / estar / lejos / cuando / nadie / recordarte
4. Señora, / ¡yo / tener / miedo / (ella) no recordarme / mí! / Ser / triste / estar / sin / novia
5. Ser / ridículo / (tú) sentirte / así. / Mi hija / esperar / (tú) casarte / con ella
6. Ridículo / o / no, / sorprenderme / todos preocuparse / ella / y / (nadie) acordarse / mí

3 Oraciones Combina elementos de las tres columnas para formar oraciones.

MODELO Es triste que tú no cuides la naturaleza.

Expresiones	Sujetos	Actividades
Me alegro de que	yo	desarrollar programas de reciclaje
Espero que	tú	proteger las ballenas
Es extraño que	el gobierno	destruir los bosques
Me gusta que	el/la profesor(a)	poner en peligro las tortugas marinas
Tengo miedo de que	la universidad	cuidar la naturaleza
Es triste que	las fábricas	
Ojalá que	algunas personas	
	los centros comerciales	

4 Comentar En parejas, compartan sus opiniones sobre las clases que más les gustan y las que menos les gustan. Usen expresiones como **me alegro de que**, **temo que** y **es extraño que**.

MODELO
Estudiante 1: Mi clase favorita es español. Me alegra que mi profesor nos ayude con la tarea.
Estudiante 2: Yo, en cambio, odio las matemáticas. Temo que mi profesor piense darnos más tarea.

5 Problemas Prepara una lista de tres o cuatro problemas ambientales en tu escuela. Luego, en grupos escriban una oración, con el subjuntivo, para cada problema expresando su reacción. Compartan la información con la clase.

MODELO la basura de la cafetería
Tememos que la basura de la cafetería no se pueda reducir.

6 ¡Es terrible! En parejas, miren el dibujo y digan qué piensan sobre el comportamiento (*behavior*) de esta familia. Usen el subjuntivo y expresiones como **es una lástima que**, **es ridículo que** y **es terrible que**.

Practice more at vhlcentral.com.

doscientos noventa y cinco   295

Lección 13

13.2 The subjunctive with doubt, disbelief, and denial

▶ The subjunctive is used with expressions of doubt, disbelief, and denial. Tutorial

Main clause	Connector	Subordinate clause
Dudan	que	su hijo les **diga** la verdad.

No creo que puedan ir muy lejos.

▶ The subjunctive is used in a subordinate clause when there is a change of subject and the main clause implies negation or uncertainty.

Expressions of doubt, disbelief, or denial

dudar	to doubt	no es cierto	it's not true; it's not certain	es improbable	it's improbable
negar (e:ie)	to deny			(no) es posible	it's (not) possible
no creer	not to believe	no es seguro	it's not certain	(no) es probable	it's (not) probable
no estar seguro/a (de)	not to be sure (of)	no es verdad	it's not true		
		es imposible	it's impossible		

No es posible que el guía continúe el recorrido sin ustedes.

El gobierno **niega** que el agua **esté** contaminada.
The government denies that the water is polluted.

Dudo que el gobierno **resuelva** el problema.
I doubt that the government will solve the problem.

▶ In English, the expression *it is probable/possible* indicates a fairly high degree of certainty. In Spanish, however, **es probable/posible** implies inherent uncertainty and therefore triggers the subjunctive in the subordinate clause.

Es posible que **haya** menos bosques y selvas en el futuro.
It's possible that there will be fewer forests and jungles in the future.

Es muy **probable** que **contaminemos** el medio ambiente.
It's very probable that we're polluting the environment.

¡ojo!

Use the infinitive after an expression of uncertainty, doubt, disbelief, or denial when there is no change of subject.

Dudo llegar temprano.
I doubt I will arrive early.

Mauricio duda llegar temprano.
Mauricio doubts he will arrive early.

▶ The expressions **quizás** and **tal vez** imply an uncertain possibility and are usually followed by the subjunctive.

Quizás haga sol mañana.
Perhaps it will be sunny tomorrow.

Tal vez veamos la luna esta noche.
Perhaps we will see the moon tonight.

▶ Use the indicative in a subordinate clause when the main clause expresses certainty.

Expressions of certainty

es cierto	it's true; it's certain	es verdad	it's true	no dudar	not to doubt
es obvio	it's obvious	estar seguro/a (de)	to be sure (of)	no hay duda de	there is no doubt
es seguro	it's certain	no cabe duda de	there is no doubt	no negar (e:ie)	not to deny

296 *doscientos noventa y seis*

No negamos que **hay** demasiados carros en las carreteras.
We don't deny that there are too many cars on the highways.

Es cierto que los tigres **están** en peligro de extinción.
It's certain that tigers are in danger of extinction.

▶ The verb **creer** expresses belief or certainty, so it is followed by the indicative. **No creer** implies doubt and is followed by the subjunctive.

Creo que **debemos** usar la energía solar.
I believe we should use solar energy.

No creo que **haya** vida en Marte.
I don't believe that there is life on Mars.

Práctica y conversación

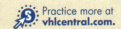

1 Conversación
Completa el diálogo con las palabras adecuadas.

RAÚL Ustedes dudan que yo (1) _____ [estudio/estudie]. No niego que a veces me (2) _____ [divierto/divierta], pero no cabe duda de que (3) _____ [tomo/tome] mis estudios en serio. Creo que no (4) _____ [tienen/tengan] razón.

PAPÁ Es posible que tu mamá y yo no (5) _____ [tenemos/tengamos] razón. Pero no hay duda de que te (6) _____ [pasas/pases] toda la noche en Internet y escuchando música. No es seguro que (7) _____ [estás/estés] estudiando.

RAÚL Es verdad que (8) _____ [uso/use] mucho Internet, pero ¿no es posible que (9) _____ [es/sea] para buscar información para mis clases?

PAPÁ Dudo que esta conversación nos (10) _____ [va/vaya] a ayudar. Pero tal vez (11) _____ [puedes/puedas] estudiar sin música.

2 Dudas
Carolina siempre miente. Expresa tus dudas sobre lo que ella dice.

MODELO
El próximo año mi familia y yo vamos a ir de vacaciones por diez meses. [dudar]
¡Ja! Dudo que vayan a ir de vacaciones por diez meses.

1. Mi tía es la directora del Sierra Club. [no ser verdad]
2. Dos profesores míos juegan para los Osos (*Bears*) de Chicago. [ser imposible]
3. Mi mejor amiga conoce al chef Emeril. [no ser cierto]
4. Mi padre es dueño del Rockefeller Center. [no ser posible]

3 Hablando con un(a) burócrata
En parejas, preparen una conversación entre un(a) activista ambiental y un(a) funcionario/a público/a (*government official*). Usen el subjuntivo. Luego presenten la conversación a la clase.

MODELO
Activista: Queremos reducir la contaminación del aire, pero dudo que el gobierno nos ayude.
Funcionario: No es cierto. ¡Lea las noticias del periódico! Es obvio que el gobierno está haciendo muchas cosas para reducir la contaminación del aire.

4 Adivinar
Escribe cinco oraciones sobre tu vida presente y futura. Cuatro deben ser falsas y sólo una debe ser cierta. Preséntalas al grupo. El grupo adivina (*guesses*) cuál es la oración cierta y expresa sus dudas sobre las falsas.

MODELO
Estudiante 1: Quiero irme un año a trabajar en la selva.
Estudiante 2: Dudo que te guste vivir en la selva.
Estudiante 3: En cinco años voy a ser presidente de los Estados Unidos.
Estudiante 2: No creo que vayas a ser presidente de los Estados Unidos en cinco años. ¡Tal vez en treinta!

5 Debate
En parejas, conversen sobre sus dudas y miedos para cuando se gradúen de la universidad.

MODELO
Estudiante 1: Es improbable que me case inmediatamente.
Estudiante 2: Dudo que nosotros podamos comprarnos una casa después de terminar la universidad.

Lección 13

13.3 The subjunctive with conjunctions  Tutorial

▶ Conjunctions are words or phrases that connect clauses in sentences. Certain conjunctions introduce adverbial clauses, which describe *how, why, when,* and *where* an action takes place. These conjunctions always require the subjunctive.

Conjunctions that require the subjunctive

a menos que	unless	con tal (de) que	provided that	para que	so that
antes (de) que	before	en caso (de) que	in case (that)	sin que	without

Muchos animales van a estar en peligro de extinción, a menos que los protejamos.

Voy a dejar un recado **en caso de que** Gustavo me **llame**.
I'm going to leave a message in case Gustavo calls me.

Voy al supermercado **para que tengas** algo de comer.
I'm going to the supermarket so that you'll have something to eat.

▶ Use the infinitive after the prepositions **antes de, para,** and **sin** when there is no change of subject. Compare these sentences.

Marissa habla con Jimena antes de que lleguen los chicos.

Te llamamos el viernes **antes de salir** de la casa.
We will call you on Friday before leaving the house.

Te llamamos mañana **antes de que salgas.**
We will call you tomorrow before you leave.

Conjunctions used with subjunctive or indicative

cuando	when	en cuanto	as soon as	tan pronto como	as soon as
después (de) que	after	hasta que	until		

Cuando veo basura, la recojo.

▶ With the conjunctions above, use the subjunctive in the subordinate clause if the main clause expresses a future action or command.

Vamos a resolver el problema **cuando desarrollemos** nuevas tecnologías.
We are going to solve the problem when we develop new technology.

Después de que ustedes **tomen** sus refrescos, reciclen las botellas.
After you drink your soft drinks, recycle the bottles.

Voy a formar un club de ecología tan pronto como vuelva al DF.

▶ Use the indicative if the verb in the main clause expresses an action that habitually happens or that happened in the past.

Contaminan los ríos **cuando construyen** nuevos edificios.
They pollute the rivers when they build new buildings.

Contaminaron el río **cuando construyeron** ese edificio.
They polluted the river when they built that building.

Siempre vamos de excursión **tan pronto como llega** Rafael.
We always go hiking as soon as Rafael arrives.

Salimos **tan pronto como llegó** Rafael.
We left as soon as Rafael arrived.

La naturaleza

Práctica y conversación

1 Una excursión Completa las oraciones.

1. Voy a llevar a mis hijos al parque para que _____ [hacer] actividades al aire libre.
2. Vamos a pasar todo el día allí con tal de que ellos no _____ [aburrirse] en casa.
3. Vamos a alquilar bicicletas en cuanto _____ [llegar] al parque.
4. En bicicleta, podemos explorar el parque sin _____ [caminar] demasiado.
5. Siempre llevamos al perro cuando _____ [ir] al parque.
6. En caso de que _____ [llover], vamos a regresar temprano a la casa.
7. Queremos almorzar a la orilla (*shore*) del río cuando _____ [tener] hambre.
8. Mis hijos van a ver muchas cosas interesantes antes de _____ [salir] del parque.

2 Oraciones Completa las siguientes oraciones.

1. No podemos controlar la contaminación del aire a menos que…
2. Voy a reciclar los productos de papel en cuanto…
3. Protegemos los animales en peligro de extinción para que…
4. Mis amigos y yo vamos a recoger la basura de la universidad después de que…
5. Todos podemos conservar energía cuando…
6. No podemos desarrollar nuevas fuentes (*sources*) de energía sin…
7. Debemos comprar coches eléctricos tan pronto como…
8. Hay que eliminar la contaminación del agua para…
9. No podemos proteger la naturaleza sin que…
10. Los gobiernos deben alertar a la población de que las tortugas marinas están en peligro de extinción, antes de que…

3 ¿Yo, ambientalista? En parejas, túrnense para hacerse preguntas sobre sus conductas (*behavior*) ambientales. Usen el subjuntivo para las acciones que todavía no han hecho y el indicativo para las acciones que hacen habitualmente.

MODELO reciclar la basura
Estudiante 1: ¿Reciclas la basura?
Estudiante 2: Sí, siempre reciclo la basura cada semana./ No, no voy a reciclar la basura a menos que tenga recipientes para reciclar.

1. Venir en bicicleta a la universidad
2. Comer alimentos orgánicos
3. Usar excesiva calefacción en invierno
4. Comprar productos ecológicos
5. Interesarse por los animales en peligro de extinción
6. Pensar en las consecuencias del calentamiento global

4 El fin de semana Antes de salir de viaje, Javier le deja una lista de instrucciones a su compañero de cuarto. En parejas, túrnense para escribir las instrucciones con el subjuntivo y las conjunciones de la lista.

MODELO
No dejes las luces prendidas cuando salgas de la casa.

a menos que
cuando
en caso de que
en cuanto
tan pronto como

Instrucciones
- *Darles de comer a los peces*
- *Comprar productos ecológicos*
- *Reciclar la basura orgánica*
- *Usar sólo papel reciclado*
- *Llamarme por cualquier problema*

5 Tres en línea Formen dos equipos. En la pizarra, una persona comienza a escribir una frase y otra persona de su equipo la termina, usando palabras de la gráfica. El primer equipo que forme tres oraciones seguidas (*in a row*) gana.

MODELO
Estudiante 1: Dudo que podamos eliminar la deforestación…
Estudiante 2: … sin que nos ayude el gobierno.

cuando	con tal de que	para que
antes de que	para	sin que
hasta que	en caso de que	antes de

Practice more at **vhlcentral.com**.

doscientos noventa y nueve **299**

Lección 13

Ampliación  Audio: Activity / Video: TV Clip

1 Escuchar 🎧

A Soledad Morales es una activista preocupada por el medio ambiente. Observa el dibujo y escribe tres predicciones sobre lo que piensas que va a decir.

TIP Use your background knowledge. / Guess meaning from context. Your background knowledge helps you anticipate the content. If you hear words or expressions you do not understand, you can often guess their meanings based on the surrounding words.

B Escucha lo que Soledad dice e indica si estas oraciones son **ciertas** o **falsas**.

	Cierto	Falso
1. Soledad conversa con unos compañeros de trabajo.	_____	_____
2. Soledad teme que el futuro del medio ambiente no sea bueno.	_____	_____
3. Soledad cree que las distintas formas de vida— la naturaleza, los animales y los humanos— están relacionadas.	_____	_____
4. Soledad dice que la caza ilegal de animales es un problema grave.	_____	_____
5. La contaminación del río afecta la ecología de las playas de Barranquilla.	_____	_____
6. Soledad dice que la comunidad debe dejar de cazar animales en peligro de extinción.	_____	_____

C Compara tus predicciones con las respuestas correctas. ¿Fueron tus predicciones correctas? ¿Qué elementos te ayudaron a anticipar el discurso de Soledad?

2 Conversar
Conversa con un(a) compañero/a sobre los animales en peligro de extinción. Usa las siguientes preguntas como guía:

- ¿Cuáles son las causas de la extinción de los animales?
- ¿Cuáles son sus consecuencias?
- ¿Que medidas (measures) debería (should) tomar el gobierno?
- ¿Qué medidas debería tomar cada persona?

En América, el puma del Este o de montaña está en peligro de extinción debido a la caza excesiva y la falta de hábitat.

recursos

 WB pp. 133–138

 LM pp. 75–77

 vhlcentral.com

La naturaleza

3 Escribir Escribe una carta a un periódico sobre una situación importante que afecta el medio ambiente en tu comunidad.

TIP Consider your audience and purpose. Once you have defined both your audience and your purpose, you will be able to decide which tone, vocabulary, and grammatical structures will best serve your needs.

- Are you going to comment on one topic or several?
- Are you intending to register a complaint or to inform others?
- Are you hoping to persuade others to adopt your point of view or to take specific action?

Organízalo — Decide cuál es el propósito de tu carta y planéala.

Escríbelo — Utiliza tus apuntes para escribir el primer borrador de tu carta.

Corrígelo — Intercambia tu carta con un(a) compañero/a. Lee su carta y anota los mejores aspectos. Dale sugerencias para mejorarla. Si ves algunos errores, coméntaselos.

Compártelo — Revisa el primer borrador teniendo en cuenta las indicaciones de tu compañero/a. Si es necesario, incorpora nuevas ideas y/o más información.

4 Un paso más Escribe una carta al/a la presidente/a de un país hispano para hablarle de tus dudas, deseos y preocupaciones sobre el futuro de una de las atracciones naturales del país.

Las tortugas marinas están en grave peligro de extinción.

- Investiga algunas de las atracciones naturales del mundo hispano.
- Escoge una y piensa en lo que se puede hacer para protegerla.
- Explica lo que temes de los problemas ambientales, lo que esperas y tus dudas sobre el futuro.
- Presenta recomendaciones para proteger este lugar en el futuro.

CONEXIÓN INTERNET

Investiga estos temas en vhlcentral.com.
- Atracciones naturales de España
- Atracciones naturales de Latinoamérica

trescientos uno 301

13 LECTURA

Antes de leer

 **Audio: Reading Additional Reading**

Identifying the purpose of a text will help you anticipate the content of a reading selection. For example, if you are reading an advice column in a newspaper, you know to expect questions about people's problems and suggestions from the columnist. The reading selection for this lesson consists of two fables: "El perro y el cocodrilo" by Félix María Samaniego and "El pato y la serpiente" by Tomás de Iriarte. What's a fable? What do the writers of fables attempt to accomplish? What kinds of characters do you expect to read about in fables? How do fables typically end?

_____
_____
_____

Sobre los autores

Félix María Samaniego (1745–1801), nacido en España, escribió las *Fábulas morales*, que ilustran de manera humorística el carácter humano. Los protagonistas de muchas de sus fábulas son animales que hablan.

Tomás de Iriarte (1750–1791), nacido en las Islas Canarias, tuvo gran éxito (*success*) con su libro *Fábulas literarias*. Su tendencia a representar la lógica a través de símbolos de la naturaleza fue de gran influencia para muchos autores de su época.

El perro y el cocodrilo

Bebiendo un perro en el Nilo°,
al mismo tiempo corría.
"Bebe quieto°", le decía
un taimado° cocodrilo.

Díjole° el perro prudente:
"Dañoso° es beber y andar°;
pero ¿es sano el aguardar
a que me claves el diente?°"

¡Oh qué docto° perro viejo!
Yo venero° su sentir°
en esto de no seguir
del enemigo el consejo.

Nilo *Nile*   **quieto** *in peace*   **taimado** *sly*   **Díjole** *Said to him*
Dañoso *Harmful*   **andar** *to walk*   **¿es sano... diente?** *is it good for me to wait for you to sink your teeth into me?*
docto *learned; wise*   **venero** *revere*   **sentir** *wisdom*

302 trescientos dos

La naturaleza

Después de leer

¿Comprendiste?

Escoge la mejor opción para completar cada oración.

1. El cocodrilo _____ perro.

   a. está preocupado por el   b. quiere comerse al
   c. tiene miedo del

2. El perro _____ cocodrilo.

   a. le tiene miedo al   b. es amigo del
   c. quiere quedarse con el

3. El pato cree que es un animal

   a. muy famoso.   b. muy hermoso.
   c. de muchos talentos.

4. La serpiente cree que el pato es

   a. muy inteligente.   b. muy tonto.
   c. muy feo.

Preguntas

Responde a estas preguntas con oraciones completas.

1. ¿Qué representa el cocodrilo?
   _____

2. ¿Qué representa el pato?
   _____

3. ¿Cuál es la moraleja (*moral*) de "El perro y el cocodrilo"?
   _____

4. ¿Cuál es la moraleja de "El pato y la serpiente"?
   _____

Coméntalo

¿Estás de acuerdo (*Do you agree*) con las moralejas (*moral lessons*) de estas fábulas? ¿Por qué? ¿Cuál de estas fábulas te gusta más? ¿Por qué? ¿Conoces otras fábulas? Cuál es su propósito (*purpose*)?

El pato° y la serpiente

A orillas° de un estanque°,
diciendo estaba un pato:
"¿A qué animal dio el cielo°
los dones que me ha dado?°

"Soy de agua, tierra y aire:
cuando de andar me canso°,
si se me antoja, vuelo°;
si se me antoja, nado".

Una serpiente astuta
que le estaba escuchando,
le llamó con un silbo°,
y le dijo "¡Seo° guapo!

"No hay que echar tantas plantas°;
pues ni anda como el gamo°,
ni vuela como el sacre°,
ni nada como el barbo°;

"y así tenga sabido
que lo importante y raro°
no es entender de todo,
sino ser diestro° en algo".

---

pato *duck* orillas *bank* estanque *pond* cielo *heaven*
los dones… dado *the gifts that it has given me*
me canso *I get tired* si se me antoja, vuelo *If I feel like it,*
I fly silbo *hiss*

Seo *Señor* No hay que… plantas *There's no reason to boast*
gamo *deer* sacre *falcon* barbo *barbel (a type of fish)*
lo… raro *the important and rare thing* diestro *skillful*

trescientos tres **303**

13 VOCABULARIO

La naturaleza

el árbol	tree
el bosque (tropical)	(tropical; rain) forest
el césped	grass
el cielo	sky
el cráter	crater
el desierto	desert
la estrella	star
la flor	flower
la hierba	grass
el lago	lake
la luna	moon
el mundo	world
la naturaleza	nature
la nube	cloud
el océano	ocean
el paisaje	landscape
la piedra	rock; stone
la planta	plant
la región	region; area
el río	river
la selva	jungle
el sendero	trail
el sol	sun
la tierra	land; soil
el valle	valley
el volcán	volcano

Conjunciones

a menos que	unless
antes (de) que	before
con tal (de) que	provided that
después (de) que	after
en caso (de) que	in case (that)
en cuanto	as soon as
hasta que	until
para que	so that
sin que	without
tan pronto como	as soon as

El medio ambiente

la caza	hunting
el calentamiento global	global warming
la conservación	conservation
la contaminación (del aire; del agua)	(air; water) pollution
la deforestación	deforestation
la ecología	ecology
el ecoturismo	ecotourism
la energía (nuclear; solar)	(nuclear; solar) energy
la extinción	extinction
la fábrica	factory
el gobierno	government
la ley	law
el medio ambiente	environment
el peligro	danger
la población	population
el reciclaje	recycling
el recurso natural	natural resource
la solución	solution
conservar	to conserve
contaminar	to pollute
controlar	to control
cuidar	to take care of
dejar de (+ *inf.*)	to stop (doing something)
desarrollar	to develop
descubrir	to discover
destruir	to destroy
estar afectado/a (por)	to be affected (by)
estar contaminado/a	to be polluted
evitar	to avoid
mejorar	to improve
proteger	to protect
reciclar	to recycle
recoger	to pick up
reducir	to reduce
resolver (o:ue)	to resolve; to solve
respirar	to breathe
la botella de vidrio	glass bottle
el envase de plástico	plastic container
la lata de aluminio	aluminum can
ecologista	ecological; ecologist
puro/a	pure
renovable	renewable

Las emociones

alegrarse (de)	to be happy
esperar	to hope; to wish
sentir (e:ie)	to be sorry; to regret
temer	to be afraid/concerned; to fear
es extraño	it's strange
es una lástima	it's a shame
es ridículo	it's ridiculous
es terrible	it's terrible
es triste	it's sad
ojalá (que)	I hope (that); I wish (that)

Las dudas y las certezas

(no) creer	(not) to believe
(no) dudar	(not) to doubt
(no) estar seguro/a (de)	(not) to be sure (of)
(no) negar (e:ie)	(not) to deny
es imposible	it's impossible
es improbable	it's improbable
es obvio	it's obvious
no cabe duda de	there is no doubt
no hay duda de	there is no doubt
(no) es posible	it's (not) possible
(no) es probable	it's (not) probable
(no) es cierto	it's (not) true; it's (not) certain
(no) es verdad	it's (not) true
(no) es seguro	it's (not) certain

Los animales

el animal	animal
la ballena	whale
el mono	monkey
el pájaro	bird
el pez	fish
la tortuga marina	sea turtle

304 *trescientos cuatro*

14 En la ciudad

Communicative Goals

You will learn how to:
- talk about errands
- ask for and give directions
- give advice

PREPARACIÓN

pages 306–309
- City life
- At the bank and post office
- Abbreviations

ESCENAS

pages 310–311
- Maru is racing against the clock to turn in her application for an internship at the **Museo de Antropología**. Between a car that won't start and long lines all over town, she'll need some help if she wants to meet her deadline.

EXPLORACIÓN

pages 312–313
- Bajo la lupa: *Paseando en metro*
- Flash cultura: *El metro del D.F.*

GRAMÁTICA

pages 314–321
- The subjunctive in adjective clauses
- Familiar (**tú**) commands
- **Nosotros/as** commands

LECTURA

pages 322–323
- Short story: *Esquina peligrosa*

Para empezar

- ¿Dónde están ellos, en una ciudad o en un pueblo?
- ¿Qué están haciendo?
- ¿Cómo crees que es la vida en esta ciudad?

14 PREPARACIÓN

En la ciudad

EN LA CIUDAD

el banco bank
la carnicería butcher shop
el correo post office; mail
la heladería ice cream shop
la joyería jewelry store
la lavandería laundromat
la panadería bakery
la pastelería pastry shop
la peluquería hairdressing salon
el salón de belleza beauty salon
el supermercado supermarket
la zapatería shoe store

hacer cola to stand in line
hacer diligencias to run errands

EN EL CORREO

el correo mail
el paquete package
los sellos stamps
el sobre envelope

echar (una carta) al buzón to put (a letter) in the mailbox; to mail (a letter)
enviar to send
mandar to send

la pescadería
fish market

la ciudad
city

la frutería
fruit store

las estampillas
stamps

el cartero
mail carrier

recursos

WB
pp. 139–140

LM
p. 79

vhlcentral.com

306 trescientos seis

En la ciudad

EN EL BANCO

el cheque de viajero traveler's check
la cuenta corriente checking account
la cuenta de ahorros savings account

ahorrar to save (money)
cobrar to cash (a check); to charge (for a product or service)
depositar to deposit
llenar (un formulario) to fill out (a form)
pagar al contado to pay in cash
pagar a plazos to pay in installments
pedir prestado to borrow
pedir un préstamo to apply for a loan
ser gratis to be free of charge

el cheque check

firmar to sign

el cajero automático automatic teller machine, ATM

CÓMO LLEGAR

la cuadra (city) block
la dirección address
la esquina corner

cruzar to cross
doblar to turn
estar perdido/a to be lost
quedar to be located

(al) este (to the) east
(al) oeste (to the) west
(al) norte (to the) north
(al) sur (to the) south

derecho straight (ahead)
enfrente de opposite; facing
hacia toward

el letrero sign

indicar cómo llegar to give directions

Lección 14

Práctica y conversación

1 ¿Lógico o ilógico? Escucha las oraciones e indica si cada oración es **lógica** o **ilógica**.

	1.	2.	3.	4.	5.	6.	7.	8.
Lógico								
Ilógico								

2 ¿Adónde fue? Óscar está hablándote de las diligencias que hizo ayer. Indica adónde fue.

1. _____

2. _____

3. _____

4. _____

5. _____

6. _____

3 Emparejar Indica la actividad que se puede hacer en cada lugar.

Lugares
1. carnicería _____
2. pastelería _____
3. frutería _____
4. joyería _____
5. lavandería _____
6. pescadería _____
7. salón de belleza _____
8. zapatería _____

Actividades
a. comprar galletas
b. conseguir manzanas
c. comprar un collar (*necklace*)
d. cortarse (*to cut*) el pelo
e. lavar la ropa
f. comprar pescado
g. comprar pollo
h. probarse unas sandalias

4 Completar Completa las oraciones con las palabras de la lista.

1. El banco me regaló un reloj. Lo conseguí _____.
2. Me gusta _____ dinero, pero no me molesta gastarlo.
3. Tengo que _____ el cheque en el dorso (*on the back*) para cobrarlo.
4. Mi madre va a un _____ para obtener dinero.
5. Julio lleva su cheque al banco y lo _____ para tener dinero en efectivo.
6. Anoche en el restaurante, Marcos _____ en vez de usar una tarjeta de crédito.

ahorrar	firmar
cajero automático	gratis
cobra	pagó al contado

recursos
vhlcentral.com

308 trescientos ocho

En la ciudad

5 Situaciones En parejas, representen una conversación entre un(a) empleado/a de banco y uno/a de estos/as clientes/as.

- un(a) estudiante universitario/a que quiere abrir una cuenta corriente
- una persona que quiere pedir un préstamo para comprar una casa
- una persona que quiere información de los servicios que ofrece el banco

6 ¿Dónde está? En grupos, escriban un minidrama en el que unos/as turistas piden ayuda para llegar a tres diferentes sitios de la comunidad en la que viven ustedes. Luego preséntenlo a la clase.

Practice more at vhlcentral.com

Ortografía Las abreviaturas   Concepts

In Spanish, as in English, abbreviations are often used in order to save space and time while writing. Here are some of the most commonly used abbreviations in Spanish.

usted → **Ud.**   **ustedes** → **Uds.**

As you have already learned, the subject pronouns **usted** and **ustedes** are often abbreviated.

don → **D.**   **doña** → **Dña.**   **doctor(a)** → **Dr(a).**
señor → **Sr.**   **señora** → **Sra.**   **señorita** → **Srta.**

These titles are frequently abbreviated.

centímetro → **cm**   **metro** → **m**   **kilómetro** → **km**
litro → **l**   **gramo** → **g; gr** **kilogramo** → **kg**

The abbreviations for these units of measurement are often used, but without periods.

por ejemplo → **p. ej.**   **página(s)** → **pág(s).**

These abbreviations are often seen in books.

derecha → **dcha.**   **izquierda** → **izq. (izqda.)**
código postal → **C.P.**   **número** → **n.º**

These abbreviations are often used in mailing addresses.

Practice more at vhlcentral.com

Banco → **Bco.**   **Compañía** → **Cía.**
cuenta corriente → **c/c.**   **Sociedad Anónima (Inc.)** → **S.A.**

These abbreviations are frequently used in the business world.

recursos

LM p. 80

vhlcentral.com

Emparejar En la tabla hay nueve abreviaturas. Empareja los cuadros necesarios para formarlas.

S.	c.	C.	c	co.	U
B	c/	Sr	A.	D	dc
ta.	P.	ña.	ha.	m	d.

trescientos nueve 309

14 ESCENAS

Corriendo por la ciudad   Video: *Fotonovela*

Maru necesita entregar unos documentos en el Museo de Antropología.

Expresiones útiles

Getting/giving directions

Estoy en la esquina de Zaragoza y Francisco Sosa.
I'm at the corner of Zaragoza and Francisco Sosa.
Dobla en la avenida Hidalgo.
Turn on Hidalgo Avenue.
Luego cruza la calle Independencia y dobla a la derecha.
Then cross Independencia Street and turn right.
El coche está enfrente de la pastelería.
The car is in front of the bakery.
En el semáforo, a la izquierda y sigue derecho.
Left at the light, then straight ahead.

Talking about errands

Voy a pasar al banco porque necesito dinero.
I'm going to the bank because I need money.
No tengo tiempo.   *I don't have time.*
Estoy haciendo diligencias, y me gasté casi todo el efectivo.
I'm running errands, and I spent most of my cash.

Asking for a favor

¿Me puedes prestar algo de dinero?
Could you lend me some money?
¿Me podrías prestar tu coche?
Could I borrow your car?

Talking about deadlines

Tengo que entregar mi proyecto.
I have to turn in my project.
El plazo para mandarlo por correo se venció la semana pasada.
The deadline to mail it in passed last week.

Additional vocabulary

aguantar   to endure, to hold
pálido/a   pale
¿Qué onda?   *What's up?*

recursos

VM
pp. 27–28

vhlcentral.com

MARU Miguel, ¿estás seguro de que tu coche está estacionado en la calle Independencia? Estoy en la esquina de Zaragoza y Francisco Sosa. OK. Estoy enfrente del salón de belleza.

MIGUEL Dobla en la avenida Hidalgo. Luego cruza la calle Independencia y dobla a la derecha. El coche está enfrente de la pastelería.

MARU ¡Ahí está! Gracias, cariño. Hablamos luego.

MARU Vamos, arranca. Pensé que podías aguantar unos kilómetros más. Necesito un coche que funcione bien. (*en el teléfono*) Miguel, tu coche está descompuesto. Voy a pasar al banco porque necesito dinero, y luego me voy en taxi al museo.

MARU Hola, Moni. Lo siento, tengo que ir a entregar un paquete y todavía tengo que ir a un cajero.

MÓNICA ¡Uf! Y la cola está súper larga.

MARU ¿Me puedes prestar algo de dinero?

MÓNICA Déjame ver cuánto tengo. Estoy haciendo diligencias, y me gasté casi todo el efectivo en la carnicería y en la panadería y en la frutería.

310   trescientos diez

En la ciudad

MARU

MIGUEL

MÓNICA

MÓNICA ¿Estás bien? Te ves pálida. Sentémonos un minuto.
MARU ¡No tengo tiempo! Tengo que llegar al Museo de Antropología. Necesito entregar...
MÓNICA ¡Ah, sí, tu proyecto!

MÓNICA ¿Puedes mandarlo por correo? El correo está muy cerca de aquí.
MARU El plazo para mandarlo por correo se venció la semana pasada. Tengo que entregarlo personalmente.

MARU ¿Me podrías prestar tu coche?
MÓNICA Estás muy nerviosa para manejar con este tráfico. Te acompaño. ¡No!, mejor, yo te llevo. Mi coche está en el estacionamiento de la calle Constitución.

MARU En esta esquina dobla a la derecha. En el semáforo, a la izquierda y sigue derecho.
MÓNICA Hay demasiado tráfico. No sé si podemos...

MARU Hola, Miguel. No, no hubo más problemas. Lo entregué justo a tiempo. Nos vemos más tarde. (*a Mónica*) ¡Vamos a celebrar!

Actividades

1 ¿Cierto o falso? Decide si lo que dicen estas oraciones es **cierto** o **falso**. Corrige las oraciones falsas.

1. Miguel dice que su coche está estacionado enfrente de la carnicería.
2. Maru necesita pasar al banco porque necesita dinero.
3. Mónica gastó el efectivo en la joyería y el supermercado.
4. Maru puede mandar el paquete por correo.
5. Maru va al museo en taxi.

2 Ordenar Pon los sucesos de la Fotonovela en el orden correcto.

a. Maru le pide dinero prestado a Mónica. ___
b. Maru entregó el paquete justo a tiempo (*just in time*). ___
c. Mónica dice que hay una cola súper larga en el banco. ___
d. Mónica lleva a Maru en su coche. ___
e. Maru dice que se va a ir en taxi al museo. ___
f. Maru le dice a Mónica que doble a la derecha en la esquina. ___

3 Conversación Un(a) compañero/a y tú son vecinos/as. Uno/a de ustedes acaba de mudarse y necesita ayuda porque no conoce la ciudad. Preparen una conversación que incluya instrucciones para ir a estos lugares. Usen las **Expresiones útiles**.

- un banco
- una lavandería
- una panadería
- un supermercado
- una heladería

trescientos once 311

14 EXPLORACIÓN

BAJO LA LUPA

 Additional Reading
Video: *Flash cultura*

Paseando en metro

Hoy es el primer día de Teresa en la Ciudad de México. Debe tomar el metro para ir del centro de la ciudad a Coyoacán, en el sur. Llega a la estación Zócalo y compra un pasaje por el equivalente a veintitrés centavos° de dólar, ¡qué ganga! Con este pasaje puede ir a cualquier° parte de la ciudad o del área metropolitana.

No sólo en México, sino también en ciudades de Venezuela, Chile, Argentina y España, hay sistemas de transporte público eficientes y muy económicos. También suele haber° varios tipos de transporte: autobús, metro, tranvía°, microbús y tren. Generalmente se pueden comprar abonos° de uno o varios días para un determinado tipo de transporte. En algunas ciudades también existen

abonos de transporte combinados que permiten usar, por ejemplo, el metro y el autobús o el autobús y el tren. En estas ciudades, los metros, autobuses y trenes pasan con mucha frecuencia. Las paradas° y estaciones están bien señalizadas°.

Vaya°, Teresa ya está llegando a Coyoacán. Con lo que ahorró en el pasaje del metro, puede comprarse un helado de mango y unos esquites° en el jardín Centenario.

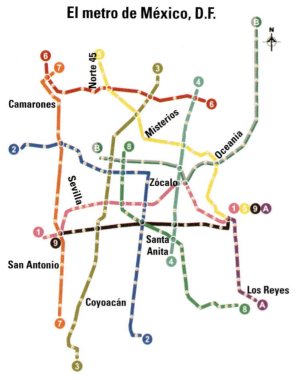

El metro de México, D.F.

El metro

El primer metro de Suramérica que se abrió al público fue el de Buenos Aires, Argentina (1° de diciembre de 1913); el último, el de Lima, Perú (11 de Julio de 2011).

Ciudad	Pasajeros/Día (aprox.)
México D.F., México	4.500.000
Madrid, España	2.500.000
Santiago, Chile	2.500.000
Buenos Aires, Argentina	1.700.000
Caracas, Venezuela	1.623.216
Medellín, Colombia	500.000
Guadalajara, México	161.910

centavos *cents* cualquier *any* suele haber *there usually are* tranvía *streetcar* abonos *passes* paradas *stops* señalizadas *labeled* Vaya *Well* esquites *toasted corn kernels*

 Practice more at vhlcentral.com.

 recursos
VM pp. 59–60

 vhlcentral.com

312 trescientos doce

En la ciudad

ACTIVIDADES

1 ¿Cierto o falso? Indica si lo que dice cada oración es **cierto** o **falso**.

1. En la Ciudad de México, el pasaje de metro cuesta veintitrés dólares.
2. En México, un pasaje se puede usar sólo para ir al centro de la ciudad.
3. En Chile hay varios tipos de transporte público.
4. Un abono es una multa que tienes que pagar si no compras el pasaje de metro de antemano (*in advance*).
5. Los abonos de transporte no sirven para más de un tipo de transporte.
6. En ciudades con varios tipos de transporte, los trenes, autobuses y metros pasan con mucha frecuencia.
7. Hay pocos letreros en las paradas y estaciones.
8. Los metros en los que viaja más gente cada día están en México, España y Chile.
9. La ciudad de Buenos Aires tiene el sistema de metro más viejo de Suramérica.
10. El metro que lleva menos tiempo en servicio es el de la ciudad de Medellín, Colombia.

2 Comparación Compara el servicio de metro en México con el servicio de un transporte público en el área donde vives. Da información de la frecuencia, el precio del pasaje, cuántas personas lo usan y cuál prefieres tú.

CONEXIÓN INTERNET

¿Qué edificios están ubicados alrededor de las plazas (*squares*) principales en los países hispanos? For more information about **Exploración**, go to **vhlcentral.com**.

Flash Cultura

El metro del D.F.

1 Preparación Imagina que estás en México, D.F., una de las ciudades más grandes del mundo. ¿Qué transporte usas para ir de un lugar a otro? ¿Por qué?

2 El video Mira el episodio de **Flash cultura**.

Vocabulario

concurrido *busy, crowded*   **transbordo** *transfer, change*
se esconde *is hidden*   **el rincón** *corner*

Viajando en el metro... puedes conocer más acerca de la cultura de este país.

Para la gente... mayor de 60 años, es el transporte totalmente gratuito.

3 Seleccionar Selecciona la respuesta correcta para completar cada oración.

1. El Parque de _____ (Chapultepec/Los Leones) es uno de los lugares más concurridos de la ciudad.
2. En las estaciones _____ (de transbordo/de una sola línea) los pasajeros pueden cambiar de trenes para llegar fácilmente a su destino.
3. Algunas líneas de metro son _____ (subterráneas/superficiales), es decir, circulan al nivel de la calle.
4. Dentro de algunas estaciones hay _____ (danzas indígenas/exposiciones de arte).

trescientos trece 313

14 GRAMÁTICA

14.1 The subjunctive in adjective clauses

¿Conoces una joyería que esté cerca?

No, no conozco ninguna joyería que esté cerca de aquí.

▶ Adjective clauses modify nouns or pronouns. The subjunctive can be used in adjective clauses to indicate that the existence of someone or something is uncertain or indefinite.

▶ The subjunctive is used in an adjective clause that refers to a person, place, thing, or idea that either does not exist or whose existence is uncertain or indefinite.

Busco **un profesor** que **enseñe** japonés.
I'm looking for a professor who teaches Japanese.

¿Conoces **un buen restaurante** que **esté** cerca de mi casa?
Do you know a good restaurant that is near my house?

▶ The indicative is used when the adjective clause refers to a person, place, thing, or idea that is clearly known, certain, or definite.

Quiero ir **al restaurante** que **está** en frente de la biblioteca.
I want to go to the restaurant that's in front of the library.

Conozco a **alguien** que **va** a esa peluquería.
I know someone who goes to that beauty salon.

Adjective clauses

Indicative	Subjunctive
Necesito **el libro** que **tiene** información sobre Venezuela. *I need the book that has information about Venezuela.*	Necesito **un libro** que **tenga** información sobre Venezuela. *I need a book that has information about Venezuela.*
Quiero vivir en **esta casa** que **tiene** jardín. *I want to live in this house that has a garden.*	Quiero vivir en **una casa** que **tenga** jardín. *I want to live in a house that has a garden.*
En mi barrio, hay **una heladería** que **vende** helado de mango. *In my neighborhood, there's an ice cream shop that sells mango ice cream.*	En mi barrio, no hay **ninguna heladería** que **venda** helado de mango. *In my neighborhood, there isn't an ice cream shop that sells mango ice cream.*

¡ojo!

These verbs are commonly followed by adjective clauses in the subjunctive:

buscar   conocer
encontrar   haber
necesitar   querer

▶ The personal **a** is not used with direct objects that are hypothetical people. However, **alguien** and **nadie** are always preceded by the personal **a** when they function as direct objects.

Necesitamos **un empleado** que **sepa** usar computadoras.
We need an employee who knows how to use computers.

Necesitamos **al empleado** que **sabe** usar computadoras.
We need the employee who knows how to use computers.

Busco **a alguien** que **pueda** cocinar hoy.
I'm looking for someone who can cook today.

No conozco **a nadie** que **pueda** cocinar hoy.
I don't know anyone who can cook today.

▶ The subjunctive is commonly used in questions when the speaker is unsure. However, if the person who responds to the question knows the information, the indicative is used.

—¿Hay un parque que **esté** cerca de nuestro hotel?
Is there a park that's close to our hotel?

—Sí, hay un parque que **está** muy cerca del hotel.
Yes, there's a park that's very close to the hotel.

En la ciudad

Práctica y conversación

1 Minidiálogos Completa los minidiálogos con la forma correcta de los verbos indicados.

MARCELA Buscamos un hotel que (1) _____ [tener] piscina.

MARTÍN Hay tres o cuatro hoteles por aquí que (2) _____ [tener] piscina.

•••

EDUARDO ¿Hay algún buzón por aquí donde yo (3) _____ [poder] echar una carta?

SUSANA Sí, hay uno en la esquina donde (4) _____ [poder] echar una carta.

•••

ANA Queremos encontrar un restaurante que (5) _____ [servir] comida venezolana.

ROBERTO Creo que el restaurante en esta cuadra (6) _____ [servir] comida venezolana.

•••

VICENTE Necesitas al empleado que (7) _____ [entender] este nuevo programa de computación.

MARISOL No hay nadie que (8) _____ [entender] este programa.

2 Completar Completa estas oraciones de manera lógica. Luego, compara tus respuestas con las de un(a) compañero/a.

1. Tengo un(a) amigo/a que…
2. Algún día espero tener un apartamento o una casa que…
3. Quiero visitar un país que…
4. No tengo ningún/ninguna profesor(a) que…
5. Es importante conocer a alguien que…
6. Mi compañero/a de cuarto busca una lavandería que…
7. Un(a) consejero/a (*advisor*) debe ser una persona que…
8. Mi novio/a quiere un perro que…
9. En esta clase no hay nadie que…
10. Mis padres buscan un carro que…

3 Encuesta Averigua (*Find out*) cuál de tus compañeros/as conoce a alguien que haga estas actividades. Si responde que sí, pregunta quién es y anota sus respuestas. Comparte los resultados con la clase.

Actividades	Nombres	Respuestas
1. Conocer bien su ciudad	_____	_____
2. Hablar japonés	_____	_____
3. Comprender el subjuntivo	_____	_____
4. Odiar ir de compras	_____	_____
5. Estudiar música	_____	_____
6. Trabajar en una zapatería	_____	_____
7. No tener tarjeta de crédito	_____	_____
8. Graduarse este año	_____	_____

4 Anuncios clasificados En parejas, lean estos anuncios y describan el tipo de persona u objeto que se busca. Usen el subjuntivo.

CLASIFICADOS

CLASES DE INGLÉS Profesor de Inglaterra con diez años de experiencia ofrece clases para grupos o instrucción privada para individuos. Llamar al 933-4110 de 16:30 a 18:30.

SE BUSCA CONDOMINIO Se busca condominio en Sabana Grande con 3 alcobas, 2 baños, sala, comedor, lavadora, secadora y aire acondicionado. Tel: 977-2018.

EJECUTIVO DE CUENTAS Se requiere joven profesional con al menos dos años de experiencia en el sector financiero. Se ofrecen beneficios excelentes. Enviar currículum vitae al Banco Mercantil, Avda. Urdaneta 263, Caracas.

VENDEDOR(A) Se necesita persona dinámica y responsable con buena presencia. Experiencia mínima de un año. Horario de trabajo flexible. Llamar a Joyería Aurora de 10 a 13h y de 16 a 18h. Tel: 263-7553.

PELUQUERÍA UNISEX Se busca persona con experiencia en peluquería y maquillaje para trabajar tiempo completo. Llamar de 9 a 13h. Tel: 261-3548.

COMPARTIR APARTAMENTO Se necesita compañera para compartir apartamento de 2 alcobas en el Chaco. Alquiler 3.000 bolívares por mes. No fumar. Llamar al 951-3642 entre 19 y 22h.

Practice more at vhlcentral.com.

trescientos quince 315

Lección 14

14.2 Familiar (tú) commands  Tutorial

▶ Use familiar (**tú**) commands when you want to give an order or advice to someone that you normally address with **tú**.

▶ Affirmative **tú** commands usually have the same form as the **usted/él/ella** form of the present indicative. The pronoun **tú** is only used for emphasis.

Paga al contado.
Pay in cash.

Pide un préstamo.
Ask for a loan.

Llámame cuando termine tu clase.

Dobla en la avenida Hidalgo y luego cruza la calle Independencia.

Affirmative *tú* commands

Infinitive	Present subjunctive	Affirmative *tú* command
cuidar	él/ella/Ud. cuida	cuida (tú)
tocar	él/ella/Ud. toca	toca (tú)
temer	él/ella/Ud. teme	teme (tú)
volver	él/ella/Ud. vuelve	vuelve (tú)
insistir	él/ella/Ud. insiste	insiste (tú)
pedir	él/ella/Ud. pide	pide (tú)

▶ There are eight irregular affirmative **tú** commands.

decir / hacer	→	di / haz
ir / poner	→	ve / pon
salir / ser	→	sal / sé
tener / venir	→	ten / ven

Haz los ejercicios.
Do the exercises.

¡**Sal** de aquí ahora mismo!
Leave here at once!

¡**Ten** cuidado con el perro!
Be careful with the dog!

¡ojo!
Verbs ending in **-car**, **-gar**, and **-zar** have a spelling change in the negative **tú** commands.

c → qu
sacar — no saques
g → gu
apagar — no apagues
z → c
almorzar — no almuerces

▶ Negative **tú** commands have the same form as the **tú** form of the present subjunctive.

Carlos, **no eches** eso al buzón.
Carlos, don't put that in the mailbox.

Julia, **no cruces** la calle.
Julia, don't cross the street.

Negative *tú* commands

Infinitive	Present subjunctive	Negative *tú* command
cuidar	tú cuides	no cuides (tú)
tocar	tú toques	no toques (tú)
temer	tú temas	no temas (tú)
volver	tú vuelvas	no vuelvas (tú)
insistir	tú insistas	no insistas (tú)
pedir	tú pidas	no pidas (tú)

¡ojo!
These verbs have irregular negative tú commands:

dar	no des
estar	no estés
ir	no vayas
saber	no sepas
ser	no seas

▶ The negative familiar commands keep the same stem changes as the indicative.

No p**ie**rdas el mapa.
Don't lose the map.

No v**ue**lvas a esa gasolinera.
Don't go back to that gas station.

316 *trescientos dieciséis*

En la ciudad

▶ **Ir** and **ver** have the same **tú** command. Context will determine the meaning.

Ve al supermercado con José. **Ve** ese programa… es muy interesante.
Go to the supermarket with José. *Watch that program… it's very interesting.*

▶ The placement of reflexive and object pronouns in **tú** commands follows the same rules as in formal commands. When a pronoun is attached to a command of more than two syllables, a written accent is used.

Informal		Formal	
¡Alégra**te**!	**Di**me.	¡Alégren**se**!	**Díga**me.
Be happy!	*Tell me.*	*Be happy!*	*Tell me.*
No **te** sientas triste.	No **me** lo digas.	No **se** sientan tristes.	No **me** lo diga.
Don't feel sad.	*Don't tell me (it).*	*Don't feel sad.*	*Don't tell me (it).*

Práctica y conversación

Practice more at vhlcentral.com.

1 Unas diligencias Completa los pedidos que la señora Ramos le hace a su esposo. Usa las formas correctas de los mandatos informales.

1. Enrique, _____ [ir] al banco, por favor.
2. Cuando llegues al banco, _____ [depositar] este cheque en nuestra cuenta corriente.
3. No _____ [depositarlo] en la cuenta de ahorros y, por favor, no _____ [pedir] un préstamo.
4. Luego _____ [pasar] por la zapatería y _____ [recoger] mis zapatos.
5. No _____ [pagar] al contado, sino con un cheque.

2 Quehaceres Pedro y Marina no se ponen de acuerdo (*agree*) cuando le dan órdenes a su hijo Miguel. Lee los quehaceres que Pedro le da a Miguel. Después, usa la información entre paréntesis para formar las órdenes que le da Marina. Sigue el modelo.

MODELO
Recoge los libros. (poner la mesa)
No los recojas, Miguel. Pon la mesa.

1. Barre el suelo. (pasar la aspiradora)
2. Plancha la ropa. (hacer las camas)
3. Saca la basura. (quitar la mesa)
4. Ve a la joyería. (ir a la frutería)
5. Dale los libros a Isabel. (dárselos a Juan)
6. Prepara la cena. (limpiar el carro)

3 Estoy perdido/a  Con un(a) compañero/a, preparen una conversación breve entre un(a) estudiante nuevo/a en la universidad y otro/a estudiante que le indica cómo llegar a varios lugares.

MODELO
Estudiante 1: Quiero ir al laboratorio de Ciencias, pero estoy perdido. ¿Me puedes ayudar?
Estudiante 2: Sí. Sigue derecho hasta llegar a la Facultad de Negocios. Dobla a la izquierda…

4 Órdenes En grupos, intercambien tres órdenes con cada uno. Luego, cada uno debe seguir las órdenes que el resto del grupo le da o reaccionar apropiadamente.

MODELO
Estudiante 1: Dame todo tu dinero.
Estudiante 2: No, no quiero dártelo. Muéstrame tu cuaderno.
Estudiante 1: Aquí está.
Estudiante 3: Ve a la pizarra y escribe tu nombre.
Estudiante 4: No quiero. Hazlo tú.

trescientos diecisiete **317**

Lección 14

14.3 Nosotros/as commands  Tutorial

▸ **Nosotros/as** commands, which correspond to the English *let's* + [*verb*], are used to give orders or suggestions that include yourself and other people.

    Crucemos la calle.   **No crucemos** la calle.
    Let's cross the street.   *Let's not cross the street.*

▸ Both affirmative and negative **nosotros/as** commands are generally formed by using the first person plural form of the present subjunctive.

▸ The affirmative *let's* + [*verb*] may also be expressed with **vamos a** + [*infinitive*]. Remember, however, that **vamos a** + [*infinitive*] can also mean *we are going to (do something)*. Context and tone will determine which meaning is being expressed.

    Vamos a caminar por la ciudad.   **Vamos a ir** a Chile este verano.
    Let's walk around the city.   *We're going to Chile this summer.*

Pensemos, ¿adónde fuiste hoy?

▸ To express *let's go*, the present indicative form of **ir** (**vamos**) is used, not the subjunctive. For the negative command, however, the subjunctive (**vayamos**) is used.

Affirmative	Negative
Vamos a la pescadería.	**No vayamos** a la pescadería.
Let's go to the fish market.	*Let's not go to the fish market.*

¡Eso es! ¡El carro de Miguel! ¡Vamos!

▸ Object pronouns are attached to affirmative **nosotros/as** commands. A written accent is added to maintain the original stress.

    Firmemos el cheque.   **Firmémoslo.**
    Let's sign the check.   *Let's sign it.*

    Escribamos a Ana y a Raúl.   **Escribámosles.**
    Let's write to Ana and Raúl.   *Let's write to them.*

▸ When **nos** or **se** is attached to an affirmative **nosotros/as** command, the final **–s** of the command verb is dropped.

    Démoselo a ella.   **Mandémoselo** a ellos.
    Let's give it to her.   *Let's send it to them.*

    Sentémonos allí.   **Levantémonos** temprano.
    Let's sit down there.   *Let's get up early.*

▸ Object pronouns are placed in front of negative **nosotros/as** commands.

    No **les paguemos** el préstamo.   No **se lo digamos** a ellos.
    Let's not pay them the loan.   *Let's not tell them (it).*

    No **lo compremos.**   No **se la presentemos.**
    Let's not buy it.   *Let's not introduce her.*

▸ The **nosotros/as** command form of **irse** (*to go away*) is **vámonos**. Its negative form is **no nos vayamos.**

    ¡Vámonos de vacaciones!   **No nos vayamos** de aquí.
    Let's go away on vacation!   *Let's not go away from here.*

En la ciudad

Práctica y conversación

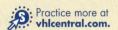
Practice more at **vhlcentral.com**.

1 Conversación Completa esta conversación con mandatos de **nosotros/as**.

MARÍA Sergio, ¿quieres hacer diligencias por la tarde?
SERGIO No (1) _____ [dejarlas] para más tarde.
(2) _____ [Hacerlas] ahora.
MARÍA Necesito comprar sellos.
SERGIO Yo también. (3) _____ [Ir] al correo.
MARÍA Pues, antes de ir al correo, necesito sacar dinero de mi cuenta corriente.
SERGIO Bueno, (4) _____ [buscar] un cajero automático.
MARÍA ¿Tienes hambre?
SERGIO Sí. (5) _____ [Cruzar] la calle y (6) _____ [comer] algo en ese café.
MARÍA Buena idea.
SERGIO ¿Nos sentamos aquí?
MARÍA No, no (7) _____ [sentarse] aquí; (8) _____ [sentarse] enfrente de la ventana.
SERGIO ¿Qué pedimos?
MARÍA (9) _____ [Pedir] café y pan dulce.

2 Hagámoslo Responde a cada oración; sigue el modelo.

MODELO
Vamos a vender el carro. (Sí)
Sí, vendámoslo.

1. Vamos a levantarnos a las seis. (Sí)
2. Vamos a enviar los paquetes. (No)
3. Vamos al supermercado. (No)
4. Vamos a mandar esta tarjeta postal a nuestros amigos. (No)
5. Vamos a limpiar la habitación. (Sí)
6. Vamos a mirar la televisión. (No)
7. Vamos a bailar. (Sí)
8. Vamos a arreglar la sala. (No)

3 Decisiones Imagina que estás con un(a) amigo/a. Túrnense para hacerse estas preguntas. Usen mandatos de **nosotros/as** en sus respuestas.

1. ¿Vamos al cine en taxi o en autobús?
2. ¿Volvemos al hotel después de la película o tomamos algo en un café?
3. ¿Pagamos la cuenta al contado o con tarjeta de crédito?

4 Preguntar Tú y un(a) compañero/a están de vacaciones y se hacen sugerencias para resolver las situaciones. Usen mandatos de **nosotros/as**.

MODELO
Se nos olvidaron las tarjetas de crédito.
Paguemos en efectivo./ No compremos más regalos.

1. El museo está a sólo una cuadra de aquí.
2. Tenemos hambre.
3. Hay una cola larga en el cine.
4. Tenemos muchos cheques de viajero.
5. Tenemos prisa para llegar al cine.
6. Estamos cansados y queremos dormir.

5 Turistas En grupos pequeños, imaginen que están en Caracas por dos días. Lean esta página de una guía turística sobre la ciudad y decidan qué van a hacer hoy por la mañana, por la tarde y por la noche. Usen mandatos de **nosotros/as**.

MODELO
Visitemos el Museo de Arte Contemporáneo Sofía Imber esta mañana. Quiero ver las esculturas (sculptures) de Jesús Rafael Soto.

Guía de Caracas

MUSEOS
- **Museo de Arte Colonial** Avenida Panteón
- **Museo de Arte Contemporáneo Sofía Imber** Parque Central. Esculturas de Jesús Rafael Soto y pinturas de Miró, Chagall y Picasso.
- **Galería de Arte Nacional** Parque Central. Colección de más de 4.000 obras de arte venezolano.

SITIOS DE INTERÉS
- **Plaza Bolívar**
- **Jardín Botánico** Avenida Interna UCV. De 8:00 a 5:00.
- **Parque del Este** Avenida Francisco de Miranda. Parque más grande de la ciudad con serpentarium.
- **Casa Natal de Simón Bolívar** Esquinas San Jacinto y Traposos. Casa colonial donde nació Simón Bolívar.

RESTAURANTES
- **El Barquero** Avenida Luis Roche
- **Restaurante El Coyuco** Avenida Urdaneta
- **Restaurante Sorrento** Avenida Francisco Solano
- **Café Tonino** Avenida Andrés Bello

trescientos diecinueve **319**

Lección 14

Ampliación

1 Escuchar

A Lee estas oraciones y luego escucha la conversación entre Alberto y Eduardo. Indica si cada verbo se refiere a algo en el pasado, en el presente o en el futuro.

TIP **Listen for specific information and linguistic cues.** You can often get the facts you need by listening for specific pieces of information. You should also be aware of the linguistic structures you hear. By listening for verb endings, you can figure out whether the verbs describe past, present, or future actions. Verb endings also indicate who is performing the action.

1. Demetrio / comprar en Macro _____
2. Alberto / comprar en Macro _____
3. Alberto / estudiar psicología _____
4. carro / tener frenos malos _____
5. Eduardo / comprar un anillo (*ring*) para Rebeca _____
6. Eduardo / estudiar _____

B ¿Crees que Alberto y Eduardo viven en una ciudad grande o en un pueblo? ¿Cómo lo sabes?

2 Conversar
Imagina que tú y tu compañero/a de cuarto tienen problemas económicos. Preparen una conversación en la que hablen de cuatro problemas y propongan soluciones para cada uno/a. Usen mandatos de **nosotros/as**.

MODELO

Estudiante 1: *No sé qué hacer. Casi no tengo el dinero para el alquiler.*
Estudiante 2: *Debes ahorrar más dinero… y yo también. No comamos en restaurantes. Preparemos comida en casa.*
Estudiante 1: *Tal vez necesitemos mudarnos. Necesitamos un apartamento que sea más barato.*
Estudiante 2: *¡Uy! No quiero mudarme. Pídele un préstamo a tu papá, mejor.*
Estudiante 1: *No lo puedo hacer cada mes. Pero tienes razón, podemos ahorrar dinero comiendo en casa.*
Estudiante 2: *Y no usemos más las tarjetas de crédito. Paguemos todo al contado para saber mejor adónde va el dinero.*

En la ciudad

3 Escribir Escribe una carta a un(a) amigo/a en la cual le explicas claramente cómo llegar a tu casa desde el aeropuerto. Incluye también un mapa detallado para que no se confunda.

TIP **List key words.** When you give directions, you use prepositions that describe location, such as **enfrente de, al lado de,** and **detrás de.** Making a list of these expressions will help you write your directions more efficiently.

Organízalo — Planea la mejor ruta para llegar a tu casa. Apunta las expresiones útiles para indicar cómo llegar, como los nombres de las calles y de los monumentos.

Escríbelo — Dibuja un mapa y utilízalo para escribir el primer borrador de tu carta.

Corrígelo — Intercambia tu carta con un(a) compañero/a. Anota los aspectos mejor escritos. Ofrécele sugerencias. ¿Hay suficientes detalles? ¿Está claro el mapa? Si ves algunos errores, coméntaselos.

Compártelo — Revisa el primer borrador de la carta y el mapa según las indicaciones de tu compañero/a. Incorpora nuevas ideas y prepara la versión final.

4 Un paso más Imagina que eres miembro de un grupo que está promocionando una comunidad modelo en un país hispano. Diseña un folleto (*brochure*) informativo para dar a conocer la comunidad.

- Escoge el lugar ideal para el proyecto. Considera el acceso a las ciudades grandes, los eventos culturales y los recursos naturales.
- Incluye un mapa del país elegido que indique dónde está localizada la comunidad modelo.
- Crea un mapa de la zona que muestre las atracciones principales del centro de la comunidad.
- Explica las características de la comunidad.

CONEXIÓN INTERNET

Investiga estos temas en vhlcentral.com.
- Ciudades de España
- Ciudades de Latinoamérica

14 LECTURA

Antes de leer

You can understand a narrative more completely if you identify the point of view of the narrator. You can do this by simply asking yourself from whose perspective is the story being told. Some stories are narrated in the first person. That is, the narrator is a character in the story, and everything you read is filtered through that person's thoughts, emotions, and opinions. Other stories have an omniscient narrator who is not one of the story's characters, but reports the thoughts and actions of all the characters. This reading selection is a short story by Marco Denevi. Is this short story narrated in the first person or by an omniscient narrator? How can you tell?

_____

_____

Sobre el autor

Marco Denevi (1922–1998) escritor y dramaturgo argentino. Estudió derecho y más tarde se convirtió en escritor. Algunas de sus obras, como *Rosaura a las diez*, han sido (*have been*) llevadas al cine. Denevi se caracteriza por su gran creatividad e ingenio, que jamás dejan de sorprender al lector (*reader*).

Esquina peligrosa

Marco Denevi

El señor Epidídimus, el magnate de las finanzas°, uno de los hombres más ricos del mundo, sintió un día el vehemente deseo de visitar el barrio donde había vivido cuando era niño y trabajaba como dependiente de almacén.

Le ordenó a su chofer que lo condujese hasta aquel barrio humilde° y remoto. Pero el barrio estaba tan cambiado que el señor Epidídimus no lo reconoció. En lugar de calles de tierra había bulevares asfaltados°, y las míseras casitas de antaño° habían sido reemplazadas por torres de departamentos°.

Al doblar una esquina vio el almacén, el mismo viejo y sombrío° almacén donde él había trabajado como dependiente cuando tenía doce años.

—Deténgase aquí— le dijo al chofer. Descendió del automóvil y entró en el almacén. Todo se conservaba igual que en la época de su infancia: las estanterías, la anticuada caja registradora°, la balanza de pesas° y, alrededor, el mudo asedio° de la mercadería.

El señor Epidídimus percibió el mismo olor de sesenta años atrás: un olor picante y agridulce a

322 trescientos veintidós

En la ciudad

abón amarillo, a aserrín° húmedo, a vinagre, a aceitunas, a acaroína°. El recuerdo de su niñez lo puso nostálgico. Se le humedecieron los ojos. Le pareció que retrocedía en el tiempo.

Desde la penumbra del fondo° le llegó la voz ruda del patrón:

—¿Estas son horas de venir? Te quedaste dormido, como siempre.

El señor Epidídimus tomó la canasta de mimbre, fue llenándola con paquetes de azúcar, de yerba y de fideos, y salió a hacer el reparto°.

La noche anterior había llovido y las calles de tierra estaban convertidas en un lodazal°.

(1974)

© Denevi, Marco, Cartas peligrosas y otros cuentos. *Obras Completas*, Tomo 5, Buenos Aires, Corregidor, 1999, págs. 192-193.

finanzas *finance*   **humilde** *humble, modest*   **asfaltados** *paved with asphalt*
antaño *yesteryear*   **torres de departamentos** *apartment buildings*   **sombrío** *somber*
anticuada caja registradora *old-fashioned cash register*   **balanza de pesas** *scale*
mudo asedio *silent siege*   **aserrín** *sawdust*   **acaroína** *disinfectant*
penumbra del fondo *half-light from the back*   **reparto** *delivery*   **lodazal** *bog*

Después de leer

¿Comprendiste?

Indica si las oraciones son **ciertas** o **falsas**. Corrige las falsas.

Cierto	Falso	
____	____	1. El señor Epidídimus tiene una tienda con la que gana poco dinero.
____	____	2. Epidídimus vivía en un barrio humilde cuando era pequeño.
____	____	3. Epidídimus le ordenó al chofer que lo llevara a un barrio de gente con poco dinero.
____	____	4. Cuando Epidídimus entró al almacén se acordó de experiencias pasadas.
____	____	5. Epidídimus les dio órdenes a los empleados del almacén.

Preguntas

Responde a estas preguntas con oraciones completas.

1. ¿Qué deseo tuvo Epidídimus?
   _____

2. ¿Por qué Epidídimus va al almacén?
   _____

3. ¿De quién es la voz "ruda" que Epidídimus escucha? ¿Qué orden crees que le dio a Epidídimus?
   _____

4. ¿Qué hace Epidídimus al final?
   _____

Coméntalo

¿Te sorprendió el final de este cuento? ¿Por qué? ¿Qué va a hacer Epidídimus el resto del día?

trescientos veintitrés **323**

14 VOCABULARIO

Audio: Vocabulary Flashcards

En la ciudad

el banco	bank
la carnicería	butcher's shop
el correo	post office
la frutería	fruit store
la heladería	ice cream shop
la joyería	jewelry store
la lavandería	laundromat
la panadería	bakery
la pastelería	pastry shop
la peluquería	hairdressing salon
la pescadería	fish market
el salón de belleza	beauty salon
el supermercado	supermarket
la zapatería	shoe store
hacer cola	to stand in line
hacer diligencias	to run errands

En el banco

el cajero automático	automatic teller machine, ATM
el cheque	check
el cheque de viajero	traveler's check
la cuenta corriente	checking account
la cuenta de ahorros	savings account
ahorrar	to save (money)
cobrar	to cash (a check); to charge (for a product or service)
depositar	to deposit
firmar	to sign
llenar (un formulario)	to fill out
pagar a plazos	to pay in installments
pagar al contado	to pay in cash
pedir prestado	to borrow
pedir un préstamo	to apply for a loan
ser gratis	to be free of charge

Las direcciones

la cuadra	(city) block
la dirección	address
la esquina	corner
el letrero	sign
cruzar	to cross
doblar	to turn
estar perdido/a	to be lost
indicar cómo llegar	to give directions
quedar	to be located
(al) este	(to the) east
(al) oeste	(to the) west
(al) norte	(to the) north
(al) sur	(to the) south
derecho	straight (ahead)
enfrente de	opposite; facing
hacia	toward

En el correo

el cartero	mail carrier
el correo	mail
las estampillas	stamps
el paquete	package
los sellos	stamps
el sobre	envelope
echar (una carta) al buzón	to put (a letter) in the mailbox; to mail (a letter)
enviar	to send
mandar	to send

recursos

vhlcentral.com

324   trescientos veinticuatro

¡VIVAN LOS PAÍSES HISPANOS!

El Canal de Panamá conecta el océano Pacífico con el océano Atlántico. La construcción de este cauce (*channel*) artificial empezó en 1903 y concluyó diez años después. Es la fuente (*source*) principal de ingresos (*income*) del país, gracias al dinero que aportan los más de 12.000 buques (*ships*) que transitan anualmente por esta ruta.

América Central II

Nicaragua

Área: 130.370 km² (50.336 millas²)
Población: 5.728.000
Capital: Managua–934.000
Ciudades principales: León, Masaya, Granada
Moneda: córdoba

SOURCE: Population Division, UN Secretariat & CIA World Factbook

Costa Rica

Área: 51.100 km² (19.730 millas²)
Población: 4.636.000
Capital: San José–1.416.000
Ciudades principales: Alajuela, Cartago, Puntarenas, Heredia
Moneda: colón costarricense

SOURCE: Population Division, UN Secretariat & CIA World Factbook

Panamá

Área: 75.420 km² (29.119 millas²)
Población: 3.510.000
Capital: Ciudad de Panamá–1.346.000
Ciudades principales: Colón, David
Moneda: balboa (es equivalente al dólar estadounidense)

SOURCE: Population Division, UN Secretariat & CIA World Factbook

¡Vivan los países hispanos!

Interactive map
Video: *Países hispanos*

Sociedad

Costa Rica: una nación progresista

Costa Rica es un país progresista. Tiene un nivel de alfabetización del 95%, uno de los más altos de Latinoamérica. Además, en 1870, Costa Rica abolió la pena de muerte (*death penalty*) y, en 1948, disolvió el ejército (*army*) e hizo obligatoria y gratis la educación para todos los costarricenses.

Museo Nacional de Costa Rica, antiguo cuartel (*barracks*) del ejército (*army*).

Indígenas

La mola

La mola es una forma de arte textil de los kunas, una tribu indígena que vive en las islas San Blas de Panamá. Las molas se hacen con fragmentos de tela (*material*) de colores vivos. Las molas tradicionales tienen diseños (*patterns*) geométricos. Antes se usaban como ropa, pero hoy día también sirven para decorar casas.

326 trescientos veintiséis

América Central II

Escritores

Ernesto Cardenal

El nicaragüense Ernesto Cardenal es poeta, escultor y sacerdote (*priest*) católico. Es uno de los escritores más famosos de América Latina. Ha escrito (*He has written*) más de treinta y cinco libros. Desde joven creyó en el poder (*power*) de la poesía para mejorar la sociedad, y trabajó por establecer la igualdad y la justicia en su país.

Política

Óscar Arias

Óscar Arias es el ex presidente de Costa Rica.[1] Fue elegido presidente dos veces. Su primer período presidencial fue de 1986 a 1990 y su segundo período fue de 2006 a 2010. Arias tiene una amplia formación académica: estudió en Costa Rica, Estados Unidos e Inglaterra y fue profesor de Ciencias Políticas en la Universidad de Costa Rica. Durante su primer período como presidente, trabajó incansablemente (*tirelessly*) para establecer la paz (*peace*) en Centroamérica. Finalmente, logró (*he achieved*) un acuerdo (*agreement*) de paz con los presidentes de El Salvador, Nicaragua, Honduras y Guatemala. Por sus esfuerzos (*efforts*), ganó el Premio Nobel de la Paz en 1987.

[1] A la fecha de publicación, la actual presidenta de Costa Rica es Laura Chinchilla Miranda, quien es la primera mujer costarricense que ocupa este puesto y la sexta presidenta de América Latina.

recursos
WB pp. 147–148
VM pp. 87–90
vhlcentral.com

¡Vivan los países hispanos!

¿Qué aprendiste?

1 ¿Cierto o falso? Indica si estas oraciones son **ciertas** o **falsas**.

Cierto   Falso

_____ _____ 1. El Canal de Panamá conecta los océanos Pacífico y Atlántico.
_____ _____ 2. Por el Canal de Panamá pasan más de 12.000 barcos por día.
_____ _____ 3. La población de Nicaragua es mayor que la de Panamá.
_____ _____ 4. San José es la capital de Panamá.
_____ _____ 5. En Costa Rica, la educación es gratis y obligatoria para todos los turistas.
_____ _____ 6. Costa Rica disolvió el ejército en 1948.
_____ _____ 7. La mola es una tribu indígena que vive en Panamá.
_____ _____ 8. Las molas se usan hoy para decorar casas.
_____ _____ 9. Ernesto Cardenal es uno de los escritores más famosos de América Latina.
_____ _____ 10. Ernesto Cardenal escribió menos de veinte libros.
_____ _____ 11. Óscar Arias fue presidente de Panamá.
_____ _____ 12. Óscar Arias ganó el Premio Nobel de la Paz en 1987.

2 Preguntas Contesta estas preguntas.

1. ¿Te gustaría visitar el Canal de Panamá? ¿Por qué crees que es importante para el comercio de los países del continente americano?
2. ¿Fuiste a Costa Rica o conoces a alguien que visitó alguna vez Costa Rica? ¿Qué sabes sobre ese país?
3. ¿Te gusta la artesanía de Latinoamérica? ¿Te gusta su variedad de colores?
4. ¿Conoces a artistas o escritores de Latinoamérica? ¿A quién conoces?
5. ¿Conoces a alguna persona importante en el área de la política en Latinoamérica? ¿Y en los Estados Unidos?

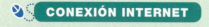

CONEXIÓN INTERNET

Investiga estos temas en el sitio **vhlcentral.com**.

- Personajes importantes de Nicaragua, Costa Rica y Panamá
- Economía y derechos humanos en Nicaragua
- El Canal de Panamá

Practice more at **vhlcentral.com**.

15 El bienestar

Communicative Goals

You will learn how to:
- discuss health, well-being, and nutrition
- describe an action or event in the immediate past
- describe an event that occurred before another past event

PREPARACIÓN
pages 330–333
- Words related to being healthy
- The gym and nutrition
- The letters *b* and *v*

ESCENAS
pages 334–335
- Marissa, Felipe, Jimena, and Juan Carlos visit the famous ruins of Chichén Itzá. After exploring the archeological site, they visit a spa to escape the sun and unwind.

EXPLORACIÓN
pages 336–337
- Bajo la lupa: *Spas naturales*
- Flash cultura: *¿Estrés? ¿Qué estrés?*

GRAMÁTICA
pages 338–345
- Past participles used as adjectives
- The present perfect
- The past perfect

LECTURA
pages 346–347
- Novel: excerpt from *El viaje* (de *Indicios pánicos*)

Para empezar
- ¿Qué están haciendo ellas?
- ¿Dónde están?
- ¿Tienen estrés?
- ¿Crees que tienen buena salud? ¿Por qué?

15 PREPARACIÓN

El bienestar

Talking Picture
Tutorial
Games

EL BIENESTAR

el bienestar *well-being*

aliviar el estrés/la tensión *to relieve stress/tension*

disfrutar (de) *to enjoy; to reap the benefits (of)*

llevar una vida sana *to lead a healthy lifestyle*

(no) fumar *(not) to smoke*

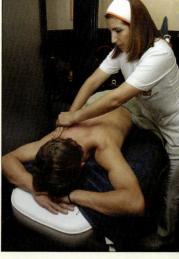
el masaje
massage

EN EL GIMNASIO

el músculo *muscle*

calentarse (e:ie) *to warm up*
entrenarse *to practice; to train*
estar en buena forma *to be in good shape*
hacer ejercicio *to exercise*
hacer ejercicios aeróbicos *to do aerobics*
hacer gimnasia *to work out*
mantenerse en forma *to stay in shape*
sudar *to sweat*

hacer ejercicios de estiramiento
to do stretching exercises

levantar pesas
to lift weights

la clase de ejercicios aeróbicos
aerobics class

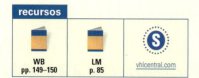
recursos
WB pp. 149–150
LM p. 85
vhlcentral.com

330 trescientos treinta

El bienestar

LA NUTRICIÓN

la caloría calorie
el colesterol cholesterol
la grasa fat
la merienda (afternoon) snack
los minerales minerals
la nutrición nutrition
la proteína protein

adelgazar to lose weight; to slim down
aumentar de peso to gain weight
consumir alcohol to consume alcohol
engordar to gain weight
estar a dieta to be on a diet
seguir una dieta equilibrada
   to eat a balanced diet

descafeinado/a decaffeinated

las vitaminas
vitamins

merendar (e:ie)
to have a(n) (afternoon) snack

la bebida alcohólica
alcoholic beverage

ADJETIVOS

activo/a active
débil weak
flexible flexible
sedentario/a sedentary
tranquilo/a calm; quiet

OTRAS PALABRAS Y EXPRESIONES

la droga drug
el/la drogadicto/a drug addict
el/la teleadicto/a couch potato

apurarse to hurry; to rush
darse prisa to hurry; to rush
sufrir muchas presiones to be under a
   lot of pressure
tratar de (+ *inf.*) to try (to do something)

en exceso in excess; too much
sin without

fuerte
strong

trescientos treinta y uno 331

Lección 15

Práctica y conversación

1 Seleccionar Escucha el anuncio del gimnasio Sucre. Marca los servicios que se ofrecen.

_____ 1. dietas para adelgazar
_____ 2. programa para aumentar de peso
_____ 3. clases de gimnasia
_____ 4. entrenador personal (*personal trainer*)
_____ 5. programas privados de pesas
_____ 6. clases de estiramiento
_____ 7. masajes
_____ 8. programa para dejar de fumar
_____ 9. programas para teleadictos
_____ 10. clases de ejercicios aeróbicos

2 Combinar Combina las oraciones de las dos columnas para formar ocho oraciones lógicas.

___ 1. David levanta pesas…	a. aumentó de peso.
___ 2. Estás en buena forma…	b. estiramiento.
___ 3. Felipe se lastimó…	c. presiones de sus pacientes.
___ 4. Mi hermano…	d. porque quieren adelgazar.
___ 5. Sara hace ejercicios de…	e. porque haces ejercicio.
___ 6. Mis primos están a dieta…	f. un músculo de la pierna.
___ 7. Para llevar una vida sana,…	g. no se debe fumar.
___ 8. Los médicos sufren muchas…	h. y corre mucho.

3 Describir Describe lo que ocurre en los dibujos.

1.   2.   3.   4.

4 Un anuncio En grupos pequeños, imaginen que son dueños/as de un gimnasio con equipo (*equipment*) moderno, entrenadores cualificados y un(a) nutricionista. Preparen un anuncio para la televisión que atraiga (*attracts*) a nuevos clientes. Incluyan esta información: **las ventajas de estar en buena forma, el equipo que tienen, las características únicas del gimnasio, los servicios y las clases que ofrecen, la dirección y el teléfono del gimnasio, el precio para los socios** (*members*).

5 Recomendaciones En parejas, imaginen que están preocupados/as por los malos hábitos de un(a) amigo/a suyo/a que no está bien últimamente (*lately*). Escriban y representen un diálogo en el cual hablan de lo que está pasando en la vida de su amigo/a y los cambios que necesita hacer para llevar una vida sana.

recursos

vhlcentral.com

332   *trescientos treinta y dos*

El bienestar

6 El teleadicto  Con un(a) compañero/a, representen una conversación entre un(a) nutricionista y un(a) teleadicto/a. La persona sedentaria habla de sus malos hábitos de salud. El/La nutricionista debe sugerir una dieta equilibrada y una rutina para mantenerse en forma.

Ortografía Las letras **b** y **v**

Since there is no difference in pronunciation between the Spanish letters *b* and *v*, spelling words that contain these letters can be tricky. Here are some tips.

nomb**re**   **bl**usa   **a**bs**oluto**   **descu**br**ir**

The letter *b* is always used before consonants.

bon**ita**   **bo**t**ella**   **bus**car   **bi**en**estar**

At the beginning of words, the letter **b** is usually used when it is followed by the letter combinations –**on**, –**or**, –**ot**, –**u**, –**ur**, –**us**, –**ien**, and –**ene**.

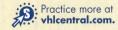

adelgazab**a**   **disfruta**ban   **i**b**as**   **í**b**amos**

The letter *b* is used in the verb endings of the imperfect tense for –**ar** verbs and **ir**.

voy   **v**amos   **estu**vo   **tu**vieron

The letter *v* is used in the present tense forms of **ir** and in the preterite forms of **estar** and **tener**.

octa**vo**   **hu**e**vo**   **act**i**va**   **gr**a**ve**

The letter *v* is used in these noun and adjective endings: –**avo/a**, –**evo/a**, –**ivo/a**, –**ave**, –**eve**.

El ahorcado Juega al ahorcado (*hangman*) para adivinar las palabras.

1. _ u _ _ s   Están en el cielo.
2. _ u _ _ n   Relacionado con el correo.
3. _ o _ e _ _ a   Está llena de líquido.
4. _ i _ _ e   Fenómeno meteorológico.
5. _ e _ _ _ s   Los "ojos" de la casa.

recursos

LM p. 86

15 ESCENAS

Chichén Itzá Video: *Fotonovela*

Los chicos exploran Chichén Itzá y se relajan en un spa.

Expresiones útiles

Wishing a friend were with you
Qué lástima que no hayan podido venir.
What a shame that they were not able to come.
Sobre todo Maru.
Especially Maru.
Él/Ella ha estado bajo mucha presión.
He/She has been under a lot of pressure.
Creo que ellos ya habían venido antes.
I think they had already come (here) before.

Talking about a trips
¿Ustedes ya habían venido antes?
Had you been (here) before?
Sí. He querido regresar desde que leí el *Chilam Balam*.
Yes. I have wanted to come back ever since I read the Chilam Balam.
¿Recuerdas cuando nos trajo papá?
Remember when Dad brought us?
Al llegar a la cima, comenzaste a llorar.
When we got to the top, you started to cry.

Talking about a well-being
Siempre había llevado una vida sana antes de entrar a la universidad.
I had always maintained a healthy lifestyle before starting college.
Ofrecemos varios servicios para aliviar el estrés.
We offer many services to relieve stress.
Me gustaría un masaje.
I would like a massage.

Additional vocabulary
la cima *top, peak*
el escalón *step*
el muro *wall*
tomar una decisión *to make a decision*

MARISSA ¡Chichén Itzá es impresionante! Qué lástima que Maru y Miguel no hayan podido venir. Sobre todo Maru.
FELIPE Ha estado bajo mucha presión.

MARISSA ¿Ustedes ya habían venido antes?
FELIPE Sí. Nuestros papás nos trajeron cuando éramos niños.

(*en otro lugar de las ruinas*)
JUAN CARLOS ¡Hace calor!
JIMENA ¡Sí! Hay que estar en buena forma para recorrer las ruinas.

JUAN CARLOS Siempre había llevado una vida sana antes de entrar a la universidad.
JIMENA Tienes razón. La universidad hace que seamos muy sedentarios.
JUAN CARLOS ¡Busquemos a Felipe y a Marissa!

FELIPE El otro día le gané a Juan Carlos en el parque.
JUAN CARLOS Estaba mirando hacia otro lado, cuando me di cuenta, Felipe ya había empezado a correr.

334 trescientos treinta y cuatro

El bienestar

MARISSA   FELIPE   JUAN CARLOS   JIMENA   EMPLEADA

FELIPE ¡Gané!
JIMENA Qué calor. Tengo una idea. Vamos.

EMPLEADA Ofrecemos varios servicios para aliviar el estrés: masajes, saunas...

FELIPE Me gustaría un masaje.
MARISSA Yo prefiero un baño mineral.

JUAN CARLOS ¿Crees que tienes un poco de tiempo libre la semana que viene? Me gustaría invitarte a salir.
JIMENA ¿Sin Felipe?
JUAN CARLOS Sin Felipe.

EMPLEADA ¿Ya tomaron una decisión?
JIMENA Sí.

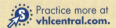

Actividades

1 Seleccionar Selecciona la respuesta que completa mejor cada oración.

1. Felipe y Marissa piensan que Maru _____.
   a. debe hacer ejercicios b. aumentó de peso c. ha estado bajo mucha presión
2. Felipe y Jimena visitaron Chichén Itzá _____.
   a. para aliviar el estrés b. cuando eran niños c. para llevar una vida sana
3. Jimena dice que la universidad hace a los estudiantes _____.
   a. comer una dieta equilibrada b. ser sedentarios c. levantar pesas
4. En el spa ofrecen servicios para _____.
   a. sudar b. aliviar el estrés c. ser flexibles

2 Identificar Identifica quién puede decir estas oraciones.

1. No me di cuenta (*I didn't realize*) de que empezaste a correr antes, por eso ganaste.
2. Miguel y Maru no visitaron Chichén Itzá, ¡qué lástima que no pudieron venir!
3. Se necesita estar en buena forma para visitar este tipo de lugares.
4. Los masajes, saunas y baños minerales que ofrecemos alivian la tensión.
5. Salgamos sin mi hermano Felipe.
6. Yo corro más rápido que Juan Carlos.

3 Minidrama En grupos pequeños, preparen un minidrama sobre este episodio. Incluyan un evento dramático e inesperado (*unexpected*) que cambie el final.

trescientos treinta y cinco   335

15 EXPLORACIÓN

BAJO LA LUPA

Spas naturales

¿Hay algo mejor que un buen baño° para descansar y aliviar la tensión? Y si el baño se toma en una terma°, el beneficio° es mayor. Los tratamientos con agua y lodo° para mejorar la salud y el bienestar son populares en Latinoamérica desde hace muchos siglos°. Las termas son manantiales° naturales de agua caliente. La temperatura facilita la absorción de minerales y otros elementos que el agua contiene y que son buenos para la salud. El agua de las termas se usa en piscinas, baños y duchas o en el sitio natural en el que surge° el agua: pozas°, estanques° o cuevas°.

En Baños de San Vicente, en Ecuador, son muy populares los tratamientos° con lodo volcánico.

Ecotermales en Arenal, Costa Rica

Volcán de lodo El Totumo, Colombia

El lodo caliente se extiende por el cuerpo y, de esta manera, la piel° absorbe los minerales beneficiosos para la salud. El lodo también se usa para dar masajes. La lodoterapia es útil para tratar varias enfermedades; además, hace que la piel se vea radiante.

En Costa Rica, la actividad volcánica también ha dado° origen a fuentes° y pozas termales. Si te gusta cuidarte y amas la naturaleza, recuerda estos nombres: Las Hornillas y Las Pailas. Son pozas naturales de aguas termales que están cerca del volcán Rincón de la Vieja. ¡Un baño termal en medio de un paisaje tan hermoso es una experiencia única!

Otros balnearios°

Todos ofrecen piscinas, baños, pozas y duchas de aguas termales y además...

Lugar	Servicios
El Edén y Yanasara, Curgos (Perú)	cascadas° de aguas termales
Montbrió del Camp, Tarragona (España)	baños de algas°
Termas de Puyuhuapi (Chile)	duchas de agua de mar; baños de algas
Termas de Río Hondo, Santiago del Estero (Argentina)	baños de lodo
Tepoztlán, Morelos (México)	temazcales° aztecas
Uyuni, Potosí (Bolivia)	baños de sal

Practice more at **vhlcentral.com**.

baño *bath* terma *hot spring* beneficio *benefit* lodo *mud* siglos *centuries* manantiales *springs* surge *springs forth* pozas *small pools* estanques *ponds* cuevas *caves* tratamientos *treatments* piel *skin* ha dado *has given* fuentes *springs* balnearios *spas* cascadas *waterfalls* algas *seaweed* temazcales *steam and medicinal herb baths*

336 trescientos treinta y seis

El bienestar

ACTIVIDADES

1 ¿Cierto o falso? Indica si lo que dicen las oraciones es **cierto** o **falso**.

1. Las aguas termales son beneficiosas para algunas enfermedades, incluido el estrés.
2. Los tratamientos con agua y lodo se conocen sólo desde hace pocos años.
3. Las termas son manantiales naturales de agua caliente.
4. La temperatura de las aguas termales no afecta la absorción de los minerales.
5. Mucha gente va a Baños de San Vicente, Ecuador, por sus playas.
6. Las Hornillas y Las Pailas son pozas de aguas termales en Costa Rica.
7. Es posible ver aguas termales en forma de cascadas.
8. Tepoztlán ofrece temazcales aztecas.

2 Para sentirte mejor Entrevista a un(a) compañero/a sobre sus hábitos de salud diarios y semanales y lo que le ayuda a sentirse mejor. Incluyan las actividades deportivas, la alimentación y lo que hacen en sus ratos libres.

CONEXIÓN INTERNET

¿Qué atletas hispanos conoces? For more information about **Exploración**, go to **vhlcentral.com**.

¿Estrés? ¿Qué estrés?

1 Preparación ¿Sufres de estrés? ¿Qué situaciones te producen estrés? ¿Qué haces para combatirlo?

2 El video Mira el episodio de **Flash cultura**.

Vocabulario

árabe *Moorish, Arab*
el bullicio *hustle and bustle*
combatir el estrés *to fight against stress*
el ruido *noise*

El tráfico, el ruido de las calles... Todos quieren llegar al trabajo a tiempo.

... la gente viene a "retirarse", a escapar del estrés y el bullicio de la ciudad.

3 ¿Cierto o falso? Indica si las oraciones son **ciertas** o **falsas**. Corrige las oraciones falsas.

1. Madrid es la segunda ciudad más grande de España, después de Barcelona.
2. Madrid es una ciudad muy poco congestionada (*congested*) gracias a los policías de tráfico.
3. Un turista estadounidense intenta saltearse la cola (*cut the line*) para entrar a un espectáculo.
4. En el Parque del Retiro, puedes descansar, hacer gimnasia, etc.
5. Los baños termales Medina Mayrit son de influencia cristiana.
6. En Medina Mayrit es posible bañarse en aguas termales, tomar el té y hasta comer.

trescientos treinta y siete **337**

15 GRAMÁTICA

15.1 Past participles used as adjectives Tutorial

Forming past participles

Sólo tomo café descafeinado.

▶ The past participles of English verbs often end in **–ed** (*to turn* ➔ *turned*), but many are irregular (*to buy* ➔ *bought*; *to drive* ➔ *driven*).

▶ In Spanish, regular **–ar** verbs form the past participle with **–ado**. Regular **–er** and **–ir** verbs form the past participle with **–ido**.

INFINITIVE	STEM	PAST PARTICIPLE
bailar	bail–	bailado
comer	com–	comido
vivir	viv–	vivido

Estoy cansada.

▶ You already know several past participles used as adjectives: **aburrido, cansado, cerrado, enamorado, interesado, nublado, perdido**, etc.

▶ All irregular past participles, except for those of **decir (dicho)** and **hacer (hecho)**, end in **–to**.

Irregular past participles

abrir	abierto	escribir	escrito	resolver	resuelto
decir	dicho	hacer	hecho	romper	roto
describir	descrito	morir	muerto	ver	visto
descubrir	descubierto	poner	puesto	volver	vuelto

▶ The past participles of **–er** and **–ir** verbs whose stems end in **–a**, **–e**, or **–o** carry a written accent mark on the **i** of the **–ido** ending.

caer	caído	oír	oído	sonreír	sonreído
creer	creído	reír	reído	traer	traído
leer	leído				

La ventana está rota.

Past participles used as adjectives

▶ In Spanish, as in English, past participles can be used as adjectives. They are often used with the verb **estar** to describe a condition or state that results from an action. Like other Spanish adjectives, past participles must agree in gender and number with the nouns they modify.

El gimnasio **está cerrado**.
The gym is closed.

El cheque ya **está firmado**.
The check is already signed.

En la entrada, hay algunos letreros **escritos** en español.
In the entrance, there are some signs written in Spanish.

Tenemos la mesa **puesta** y la cena **hecha**.
We have the table set and dinner made.

La puerta está abierta.

338 *trescientos treinta y ocho*

El bienestar

Práctica y conversación

1 Completar Completa estas oraciones con la forma adecuada del participio pasado.

1. El hombre _____ [describir] en ese panfleto es un entrenador personal (*personal trainer*) de gimnasia.
2. Lindsey Vonn es una atleta muy _____ [conocer].
3. ¿Está _____ [hacer] la cena?
4. Los libros _____ [usar] son más baratos que los nuevos.
5. Los documentos están _____ [firmar].
6. Creo que el gimnasio está _____ [abrir] veinticuatro horas al día.

2 Describir Completa las frases con las palabras de la lista. Haz los cambios necesarios.

estar cerrado	estar aburrido
estar muerto	estar descrito
estar roto	estar firmado
estar abierto	no estar hecho

1. Los estudiantes _____.

2. Los cheques _____.

3. La ventana _____.

4. La cama _____.

5. La puerta _____.

6. El señor Vargas _____.

3 Preguntas En parejas, túrnense para hacerse estas preguntas.

1. ¿Qué haces cuando no estás preparado/a para una clase?
2. ¿Qué haces cuando estás perdido/a en una ciudad?
3. ¿Está ordenado tu cuarto?
4. ¿Dejas la luz prendida en tu cuarto?
5. ¿Prefieres comprar libros usados o nuevos? ¿Por qué?
6. ¿Tienes mucho dinero ahorrado?
7. ¿Necesitas pedirles dinero prestado a tus padres?
8. ¿Quiénes están aburridos en la clase?
9. ¿Hay alguien que esté dormido en la clase?
10. ¿Cuándo está abierto el gimnasio de la universidad?

4 Encuesta Averigua quién de tus compañeros/as se identifica con estas descripciones. Anota sus respuestas y comparte los resultados con la clase.

Descripciones	Nombres	Respuestas
1. Tiene algo roto en casa. (¿Qué es?)	_____	_____
2. Lleva algo hecho en Europa o en un país hispano. (¿Qué es?)	_____	_____
3. Deja la puerta de su cuarto abierta por la noche. (¿Por qué?)	_____	_____
4. Toma café descafeinado. (¿Cuándo?)	_____	_____
5. Está interesado/a en trabajar en un banco. (¿Por qué?)	_____	_____
6. Le gusta comprar ropa usada. (¿Dónde y por qué?)	_____	_____
7. Tiene un pariente o un(a) amigo/a muy conocido/a. (¿Quién?)	_____	_____
8. Es teleadicto/a. (¿Cuáles son sus programas favoritos?)	_____	_____

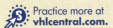
Practice more at vhlcentral.com.

Lección 15

15.2 The present perfect  Tutorial

▶ The present perfect indicative tense (**el pretérito perfecto de indicativo**) is used to talk about what someone *has done*. It is formed with the present tense of **haber** and a past participle.

Maru ha estado bajo mucha presión.

He querido regresar desde que leí el Chilam Balam.

Present indicative of *haber*

Singular forms		Plural forms	
yo	he	nosotros/as	hemos
tú	has	vosotros/as	habéis
Ud./él/ella	ha	Uds./ellos/ellas	han

Tú no **has cerrado** la puerta.
You haven't closed the door.

Yo ya **he leído** esos libros.
I've already read those books.

¿**Ha asistido** Juan a la clase?
Has Juan attended class?

Hemos presentado el proyecto.
We have presented the project.

¡ojo!

To say that someone has *just done something*, use **acabar de** + [*infinitive*].

Juan **acaba de llegar**.
Juan has just arrived.

Ellos **acaban de salir**.
They have just left.

Acabo de terminar.
I have just finished.

Acabamos de comer.
We have just eaten.

▶ The past participle agrees with the noun when it functions as an adjective, but not when it is part of the present perfect tense.

Clara **ha abierto** las ventanas.
Clara has opened the windows.

Las ventanas están **abiertas**.
The windows are open.

▶ The present perfect is generally used just as in English: to talk about what *has occurred*. It usually refers to the recent past.

He trabajado cuarenta horas.
I have worked forty hours.

¿Cuál es el último libro que **has leído**?
What is the last book that you have read?

▶ **Haber** and the past participle cannot be separated by any word.

Siempre **hemos vivido** en Bolivia.
We have always lived in Bolivia.

Usted nunca **ha venido** a mi oficina.
You have never come to my office.

▶ The word **no** and any object or reflexive pronouns are placed immediately before **haber**.

Yo **no he cobrado** el cheque.
I have not cashed the check.

Susana ya **lo ha hecho**.
Susana has already done it.

¿Por qué **no lo has cobrado**?
Why haven't you cashed it?

Ellos **no lo han arreglado**.
They haven't fixed it.

¿Y Juan Carlos todavía no te ha invitado a salir?

▶ In English, *to have* can be either a main verb or an auxiliary verb. As a main verb, it corresponds to **tener**, while as an auxiliary, it corresponds to **haber**.

Tengo un problema.
I have a problem.

He resuelto mi problema.
I have resolved my problem.

▶ The present perfect of **hay** is **ha habido**.

Ha habido muchos problemas.
There have been a lot of problems.

Ha habido un accidente.
There has been an accident.

Últimamente hemos sufrido muchas presiones en la universidad.

El bienestar

Práctica y conversación

1 Completar Completa estas oraciones sobre el estado de salud y bienestar de algunos estudiantes con el pretérito perfecto del indicativo de estos verbos.

| adelgazar | hacer | seguir |
| aumentar | llevar | sufrir |

1. Luisa _____ muchas presiones este año.
2. Juan y Raúl _____ de peso porque no hacen ejercicio.
3. Pero María _____ porque trabaja demasiado y siempre se olvida de comer.
4. Hasta ahora, yo _____ una vida muy sana.
5. Pero tú y yo no _____ gimnasia este semestre.
6. Tú tampoco _____ una dieta equilibrada recientemente.

2 Estilos de vida Indica si has hecho estas actividades. Sigue el modelo.

MODELO
Encontrar un buen gimnasio
*He encontrado un buen gimnasio. /
Yo no he encontrado un buen gimnasio.*

1. Tratar de estar en forma
2. Estar a dieta los últimos dos meses
3. Dejar de tomar refrescos
4. Hacerse una prueba de colesterol
5. Entrenarse cinco días a la semana
6. Cambiar de una vida sedentaria a una vida activa
7. Tomar vitaminas por las noches y por las mañanas
8. Practicar yoga para relajarse
9. Consumir mucha proteína
10. Quedarse despierto/a toda una noche
11. Levantar pesas tres días a la semana
12. Aliviar el estrés

3 ¿Qué han hecho? En parejas, describan lo que han hecho y lo que no han hecho estas personas. Usen su imaginación.

1. Jorge y Raúl

2. Natalia y Diego

3. Luisa

4. Ricardo

5. Jorge

6. Carmen

4 Describir En parejas, piensen en una persona que conozcan bien o en una celebridad que lleve una vida muy sana. Luego, describan en un párrafo lo que la persona ha hecho para mantener ese estilo de vida.

MODELO
Michael Phelps ha llevado una vida muy sana. Ha hecho todo lo posible para mantenerse en forma. Para ganar las competencias de natación, él ha...

Practice more at vhlcentral.com.

Lección 15

15.3 The past perfect Tutorial

Creo que ya habían venido antes.

▶ The past perfect indicative (**el pretérito pluscuamperfecto de indicativo**) is used to talk about what someone *had done* or what *had occurred* before another past action, event, or state. The past perfect uses the imperfect of **haber** plus the past participle.

Past perfect indicative

	cerrar	**perder**	**asistir**
yo	había cerrado	había perdido	había asistido
tú	habías cerrado	habías perdido	habías asistido
Ud./él/ella	había cerrado	había perdido	había asistido
nosotros/as	habíamos cerrado	habíamos perdido	habíamos asistido
vosotros/as	habíais cerrado	habíais perdido	habíais asistido
Uds./ellos/ellas	habían cerrado	habían perdido	habían asistido

Siempre había llevado una vida sana.

Pensé que ya se **habían ido**.
I thought you had already left.

Cuando llegamos, Luis ya **había salido**.
When we arrived, Luis had already left.

¡ojo!

The past perfect is often used in conjunction with **antes de** + [*noun*] or **antes de** + [*infinitive*] to describe when the action(s) occurred.

Antes de este año, nunca había estudiado español.
Before this year, I had never studied Spanish.

Luis me había llamado antes de venir.
Luis had called me before he came.

▶ The past perfect is often used with the word **ya** (*already*). Note that **ya** cannot be placed between **haber** and the past participle.

Ella **ya había empezado** cuando llamaron.
She had already begun when they called.

Cuando llegué a casa, Raúl **ya se había acostado**.
When I arrived home, Raúl had already gone to bed.

ESPAÑOL EN VIVO

Hasta el año pasado, siempre había mirado la tele sentado en el sofá durante mis ratos libres. ¡Era un sedentario y un teleadicto! Había aumentado mucho de peso porque jamás había practicado ningún deporte.

Este año, he empezado a seguir una dieta más sana y voy al gimnasio todos los días. He comenzado a ser una persona muy activa y he adelgazado. Disfruto de una vida sana y... ¡Me siento muy feliz!

Manténgase en forma.

¡Acabo de descubrir una nueva vida!

¡Venga al **Gimnasio Olímpico** hoy mismo!

Práctica y conversación

1 Completar Completa los minidiálogos con las formas correctas del pretérito pluscuamperfecto del indicativo.

SARA Antes de cumplir los 15 años, ¿ (1) _____ [estudiar] tú otra lengua?

JOSÉ Sí, (2) _____ [tomar] clases de inglés y de italiano.

• • •

DIANA Antes del 2009, ¿ (3) _____ [viajar] tú y tu familia a Europa?

TOMÁS Sí, (4) _____ [visitar] Europa tres veces.

• • •

ANTONIO Antes de este año, ¿ (5) _____ [correr] usted en un maratón?

SRA. VERA No, nunca lo (6) _____ [hacer].

• • •

SOFÍA Antes de su enfermedad, ¿ (7) _____ [sufrir] muchas presiones tu tío?

IRENE Sí… y él nunca antes (8) _____ [mantenerse] en forma.

2 Quehaceres Indica lo que ya había hecho cada miembro de la familia antes de la llegada de la madre, la señora Ferrer.

3 Tu vida En oraciones completas, indica si ya habías hecho estas cosas cuando cumpliste los dieciséis años.

1. Escalar una montaña
2. Escribir un poema
3. Leer una novela
4. Enamorarte
5. Montar a caballo
6. Ir de pesca
7. Manejar un carro
8. Navegar en Internet

4 Oraciones En parejas, túrnense para completar estas oraciones, usando el pretérito pluscuamperfecto del indicativo.

1. Cuando yo llamé a mi mejor amigo/a la semana pasada, él/ella ya…
2. Antes de este año, mis amigos/as y yo nunca…
3. Hasta el año pasado, yo siempre…
4. Antes de cumplir los dieciocho años, mi mejor amigo/a…
5. Antes de cumplir los treinta años, mis padres ya…
6. Hasta que cumplí los dieciocho años, yo nunca…
7. Antes de este semestre, el/la profesor(a) de español nunca…
8. Antes de tomar esta clase, yo nunca…

5 Lo dudo Escribe cinco oraciones, algunas ciertas y otras falsas, sobre cosas que habías hecho antes de venir a la universidad. Luego, en grupos, túrnense para leer sus oraciones. Cada miembro del grupo debe decir "es cierto" o "lo dudo" después de escuchar cada oración. Luego, el que leyó escribe la reacción de cada compañero/a para ver quién obtiene más respuestas ciertas.

MODELO

Estudiante 1: Cuando tenía diez años, ya había manejado el carro de mi papá.
Estudiante 2: Lo dudo.
Estudiante 3: Es cierto.

6 Entrevista En parejas, preparen una conversación en la que un(a) periodista de televisión está entrevistando (*interviewing*) a un(a) actor/actriz famoso/a que está haciendo un video de ejercicios aeróbicos. El/la periodista le hace preguntas para descubrir esta información:

- Si siempre se había mantenido en forma antes de hacer este video
- Si había seguido alguna dieta especial antes de hacer este video
- Qué le recomienda a la gente que quiere mantenerse en forma
- Qué le recomienda a las personas que quieren adelgazar
- Qué va a hacer cuando termine el video

trescientos cuarenta y tres **343**

Lección 15

Ampliación

1 Escuchar

A Escucha lo que dice Ofelia Cortez de Bauer. Anota algunos de los cognados que escuchas y también la idea general del discurso.

TIP **Listen for the gist and cognates.** By listening for the gist, you can get the general idea of what you're hearing. Listening for cognates will help you to fill in the details.

Cognados   **Idea general**
_____   _____
_____   _____
_____   _____

Ahora indica si estas oraciones son **ciertas** o **falsas**.

Cierto   Falso

_____ _____ 1. La señora Bauer habla de la importancia de estar en buena forma.
_____ _____ 2. Según la señora Bauer, es importante que todos sigan el mismo programa.
_____ _____ 3. La señora Bauer participa en actividades individuales y de grupo.
_____ _____ 4. Según la señora Bauer, el objetivo más importante de cada persona debe ser adelgazar.

B ¿Qué piensas de los consejos que ella da? ¿Hay otra información que ella debía haber incluido (*included*)?

2 Conversar
Con un(a) compañero/a, preparen una conversación entre el/la enfermero/a de la clínica de la universidad y un(a) estudiante que no se siente bien. Usen estas preguntas como guía.

- ¿Qué problema tiene y de dónde viene?
- ¿Tiene buenos hábitos el/la estudiante?
- ¿Qué ha hecho el/la estudiante en los últimos meses? ¿Cómo se ha sentido?
- ¿Qué recomendaciones tiene el/la enfermero/a para el/la estudiante?
- ¿Qué va a hacer el/la estudiante para llevar una vida más sana?

recursos

344 trescientos cuarenta y cuatro

El bienestar

3 Escribir Desarrolla un plan personal para mejorar tu bienestar físico y emocional. Considera la nutrición, el ejercicio y el estrés.

TIP Organize your information logically. To make your writing and message clearer to your readers, organize information chronologically, sequentially, or in order of importance.

Organízalo — Escribe tus objetivos. Anota lo que has hecho hasta ahora, lo que no has hecho y lo que todavía tienes que hacer para conseguir tus objetivos.

Escríbelo — Organiza tus apuntes y escribe el primer borrador de tu plan personal.

Corrígelo — Intercambia tu plan personal con un(a) compañero/a. Dale sugerencias para mejorar la organización. ¿Incluye toda la información pertinente? ¿Es lógica la organización? Si ves algunos errores, coméntaselos.

Compártelo — Prepara la versión final, tomando en cuenta los comentarios de tu compañero/a. Luego con otro/a compañero/a, comparen lo que han escrito. ¿Son similares sus planes? ¿Son diferentes?

4 Un paso más Imagina que estás a cargo de (*in charge of*) promocionar una excursión de aventuras con actividades deportivas en algún país hispano. Crea un folleto (*brochure*) atractivo para vender la idea de la excursión. Luego compara tu folleto con los de tus compañeros/as.

- Escoge el país y los lugares que van a visitar.
- Describe las actividades deportivas y de aventura que van a hacer en cada lugar.
- Explica los aspectos de la excursión que son importantes para la salud.
- Incluye el costo del viaje.

CONEXIÓN INTERNET

Investiga estos temas en vhlcentral.com.
- Actividades deportivas en el mundo hispano
- Turismo alternativo en el mundo hispano

15 LECTURA

Antes de leer

Audio: Reading
Additional Reading

For dramatic effect and to achieve a smoother writing style, authors often do not explicitly supply the reader with all the details of a story. Clues in the text can help you infer those things the writer chooses not to state in a direct manner. You simply "read between the lines" to fill in the missing information and draw conclusions about the story.

Sobre la autora

Cristina Peri Rossi (1941) Nació en Uruguay, pero ahora vive en España. En sus cuentos, novelas y poemas explora las pasiones, el aislamiento (*isolation*) y las incertidumbres (*uncertainties*) que sentimos como seres humanos (*human beings*).

El viaje

Cristina Peri Rossi

Ella me ha entregado la felicidad dentro de una caja° bien cerrada, y me la ha dado, diciéndome:

—Ten cuidado, no vayas a perderla, no seas distraída, me ha costado un gran esfuerzo° conseguirla: los mercados estaban cerrados, en las tiendas ya no había y los pocos vendedores ambulantes que existían se han jubilado, porque tenían los pies

recursos
vhlcentral.com

El bienestar

cansados. Ésta es la única que pude hallar° en la plaza, pero es de las legítimas. Tiene un poco menos brillo° que aquella que consumíamos mientras éramos jóvenes y está un poco arrugada°, pero si caminas bien, no notarás° la diferencia. Si la apoyas en alguna parte°, por favor, recógela antes de irte, y si decides tomar un ómnibus, apriétala° bien entre las manos: la ciudad está llena de ladrones° y fácilmente te la podrían arrebatar°.

Después de todas estas recomendaciones soltó° la caja y me la puso entre las manos. Mientras caminaba, noté que no pesaba° mucho pero que era un poco incómoda de usar: mientras la sostenía no podía tocar otra cosa, ni me animaba a dejarla depositada, para hacer las compras. De manera que no podía entretenerme, y menos aún, detenerme a explorar, como era mi costumbre. A la mitad de la tarde tuve frío. Quería abrirla, para saber si era de las legítimas, pero ella me dijo que se podía evaporar. Cuando desprendí° el papel, noté que en la etiqueta° venía una leyenda°:

"Consérvese sin usar."

Desde ese momento tengo la felicidad guardada en una caja. Los domingos de mañana la llevo a pasear, por la plaza, para que los demás me envidien° y lamenten su situación; de noche la guardo en el fondo del ropero°. Pero se aproxima el verano y tengo un temor: ¿cómo la defenderé° de las polillas°?

Después de leer

¿Comprendiste?

1. La persona que narra el cuento, ¿es hombre o es mujer?
2. El regalo, la felicidad, ¿fue fácil o difícil de conseguir?
3. ¿Dónde compró la persona la felicidad, en la calle o en una tienda?
4. Según la persona que la dio, ¿esta felicidad es de mejor o de peor calidad que la que tenía de joven?
5. Según ella, ¿hay mucho o poco riesgo (*risk*) de perder la felicidad?
6. ¿Por qué no puede abrir la caja la narradora?
7. Al final, ¿qué hace la narradora con la felicidad?

Preguntas

Responde a estas preguntas, sobre la narradora de la historia, con oraciones completas.

1. ¿Qué debe hacer para cuidar la felicidad?
2. ¿Qué límites le impone la felicidad a ella?
3. ¿Cómo quiere que su felicidad afecte a otras personas?
4. ¿Por qué les tiene miedo a las polillas?

Coméntalo

En parejas, conversen sobre estas preguntas: ¿Por qué a la persona le resulta (*results*) difícil conseguir la felicidad? ¿Por qué está encerrada en una caja? ¿Vale la pena (*Is it worth it*) tener la "felicidad" guardada en una caja sin usar? ¿Qué simboliza la felicidad en este cuento?

me… caja *handed me happiness in a box* esfuerzo *effort*
la única que pude hallar *the only one I could find* brillo *shine*
arrugada *wrinkled* no notarás *you won't notice* Si… parte *If you set it down
somewhere* apriétala *hold* ladrones *thieves* podrían arrebatar *could snatch*
soltó *let go of* no pesaba *it didn't weigh* desprendí *I took off* etiqueta *label*
leyenda *inscription* envidien *envy* en… ropero *in the back of the closet*
defenderé *will I defend* polillas *moths*

trescientos cuarenta y siete **347**

15 VOCABULARIO

El bienestar

el bienestar	well-being
la clase de ejercicios aeróbicos	aerobics class
la droga	drug
el/la drogadicto/a	drug addict
el masaje	massage
el músculo	muscle
el/la teleadicto/a	couch potato
adelgazar	to lose weight; to slim down
aliviar el estrés/ la tensión	to relieve stress/ tension
apurarse	to hurry; to rush
aumentar de peso	to gain weight
calentarse (e:ie)	to warm up
darse prisa	to hurry; to rush
disfrutar (de)	to enjoy; to reap the benefits (of)
engordar	to gain weight
entrenarse	to practice; to train
estar a dieta	to be on a diet
estar en buena forma	to be in good shape
(no) fumar	(not) to smoke
hacer ejercicio	to exercise
hacer ejercicios aeróbicos	to do aerobics
hacer ejercicios de estiramiento	to do stretching exercises
hacer gimnasia	to work out
levantar pesas	to lift weights
llevar una vida sana	to lead a healthy lifestyle
mantenerse en forma	to stay in shape
sudar	to sweat
sufrir muchas presiones	to be under a lot of pressure
tratar de (+ *inf.*)	to try (to do something)

El bienestar: adjetivos

activo/a	active
débil	weak
flexible	flexible
fuerte	strong
sedentario/a	sedentary
tranquilo/a	calm; quiet

La nutrición

la bebida alcohólica	alcoholic beverage
la caloría	calorie
el colesterol	cholesterol
la grasa	fat
la merienda	(afternoon) snack
los minerales	minerals
la nutrición	nutrition
la proteína	protein
las vitaminas	vitamins
consumir alcohol	to consume alcohol
merendar (e:ie)	to have a(n) (afternoon) snack
seguir una dieta equilibrada	to eat a balanced diet
descafeinado/a	decaffeinated

Palabras adicionales

en exceso	in excess; too much
sin	without

Irregular past participles	See page 338.

348 trescientos cuarenta y ocho

16 El mundo del trabajo

Communicative Goals
You will learn how to:
- discuss the world of work
- talk about future plans
- reminisce
- express hopes

PREPARACIÓN
pages 350-353
- Words related to working
- Occupations
- The letters **y**, **ll** and **h**

ESCENAS
pages 354-355
- As Marissa prepares to go back to the States, the friends reflect on their plans for the future. In the meantime, Sra. Díaz helps Miguel with a mock job interview, and Maru gets some good news.

EXPLORACIÓN
pages 356–357
- Bajo la lupa: *Beneficios en los empleos*
- Flash cultura: *El mundo del trabajo*

GRAMÁTICA
pages 358-365
- The future tense
- The conditional tense
- The past subjunctive

LECTURA
pages 366-367
- Short story: *Imaginación y destino*

Para empezar
- ¿Está estudiando o trabajando esta persona?
- ¿Lleva ella ropa profesional?
- ¿Cuál es su profesión?
- ¿Crees que ella sufre de mucho estrés?

16 PREPARACIÓN

El mundo del trabajo

Talking Picture Tutorial Games

el científico
scientist

LAS OCUPACIONES

el/la abogado/a lawyer
la actriz actress
el/la arqueólogo/a archaeologist
el/la arquitecto/a architect
el bailarín dancer
la bailarina dancer
el/la cantante singer
el/la carpintero/a carpenter
el/la consejero/a counselor; advisor
el/la contador(a) accountant
el/la corredor(a) de bolsa stockbroker
el/la diseñador(a) designer
el/la electricista electrician
el/la escritor(a) writer
el/la escultor(a) sculptor
el/la gerente manager
el hombre/la mujer de negocios businessperson
el/la jefe/a boss
el/la maestro/a elementary school teacher
el/la pintor(a) painter
el/la poeta poet
el/la político/a politician
el/la reportero/a reporter
el/la secretario/a secretary
el/la técnico/a technician

el cocinero
cook; chef

la peluquera
hairdresser

el actor
actor

el bombero
firefighter

el psicólogo
psychologist

recursos

WB pp. 157–158
LM p. 91
vhlcentral.com

350 trescientos cincuenta

El mundo del trabajo

Se busca diseñador gráfico.

Ofrecemos excelentes beneficios. Para mayor información, diríjase a nuestra oficina principal, Calle Castilla, no. 44.

el anuncio advertisement

LAS ENTREVISTAS

el/la aspirante candidate; applicant
los beneficios benefits
el/la entrevistador(a) interviewer
el puesto position; job
el salario salary
la solicitud (de trabajo) (job) application
el sueldo salary

contratar to hire
entrevistar to interview
ganar to earn
obtener to obtain; to get
solicitar to apply (for a job)

el currículum
résumé

DATOS PERSONALES

Nombre y apellidos: Carmela Roca
Fecha de nacimiento: 14 de diciembre de 1988
Lugar de nacimiento: Salamanca
D.N.I.: 7885270-R
Dirección: Calle Ferrara 17, 5
37500 Salamanca
Teléfono: 923 270 118
Correo electrónico: rocac@teleline.com

FORMACIÓN ACADÉMICA
- 2010-2013 Máster en Administración y Dirección de Empresas, Universidad Autónoma de Madrid
- 2006-2010 Licenciada en Administración y Dirección de Empresas por la Universidad de Salamanca

CURSOS Y SEMINARIOS
- 2007 "Gestión y Creación de Empresas", Universidad de Córdoba

EXPERIENCIA PROFESIONAL
- 2008-2010 Contrato de un año en la empresa RAMA, S.L., realizando tareas administrativas
- 2006-2008 Contrato de trabajo haciendo prácticas en Banco Sol

IDIOMAS
- INGLÉS Nivel alto. Título de la Escuela Oficial de Idiomas
- ITALIANO Nivel medio

INFORMÁTICA/COMPUTACIÓN
- Conocimientos de usuario de Mac / Windows
- MS Office

EL MUNDO DEL TRABAJO

el ascenso promotion
el aumento de sueldo raise
la carrera career
la compañía company; firm
el empleo job; employment
la empresa company; firm
la especialización field of study
los negocios business; commerce
la ocupación occupation
el oficio trade
la profesión profession
el teletrabajo telecommuting
el trabajo job; work
la videoconferencia videoconference

dejar to quit; to leave behind
despedir (e:i) to fire
invertir (e:ie) to invest
renunciar (a) to resign (from)
tener éxito to be successful

comercial commercial; business-related

la reunión
meeting

la entrevista
interview

trescientos cincuenta y uno 351

Lección 16

Práctica y conversación

1 ¿Lógico o ilógico? Escucha las oraciones e indica si son **lógicas** o **ilógicas**.

	1.	2.	3.	4.	5.	6.	7.	8.
Lógico								
Ilógico								

2 Completar Escoge la respuesta que completa cada oración.

1. Quiero conseguir un puesto con ____.
   a. oficios   b. beneficios   c. ocupación
2. Luisa tiene la oportunidad de ____ la empresa donde trabaja.
   a. despedir   b. entrevistar   c. invertir en
3. Mi vecino dejó su ____ porque no le gustaba su jefe.
   a. puesto   b. anuncio   c. sueldo
4. Raúl va a ____ su empleo antes de empezar su propia empresa.
   a. solicitar   b. tener éxito   c. renunciar a
5. Mi madre ____ su carrera como escultora.
   a. tuvo éxito en   b. contrató   c. entrevistó
6. ¿Cuándo obtuviste ____ más reciente?
   a. los negocios   b. la videoconferencia   c. el aumento de sueldo
7. Jorge llegó tarde a la ____ esta mañana.
   a. reunión   b. especialización   c. carrera

3 Asociaciones Escribe las profesiones que asocias con estas palabras.

1. pelo ____
2. novelas ____
3. emociones ____
4. teatro ____
5. periódico ____
6. pinturas ____
7. elecciones ____
8. baile ____
9. leyes ____
10. luz artificial ____

4 Conversación Contesta las preguntas con un(a) compañero/a.

1. ¿Te gusta tu especialización? ¿Cuál es tu carrera ideal? ¿Por qué?
2. ¿Cómo te preparas para una entrevista? ¿Obtienes siempre los puestos que quieres?
3. ¿Qué características tiene un(a) jefe/a bueno/a?
4. ¿Te gustaría más un teletrabajo o un trabajo en una oficina? ¿Por qué?

El mundo del trabajo

5 **Una feria de trabajo**  La clase va a organizar una feria (*fair*) de trabajo. Unos estudiantes son representantes de compañías y otros están buscando empleo.

Representantes
- Preparan carteles con el nombre de su compañía.
- Escriben los puestos de trabajo que ofrecen.
- Contestan las preguntas de los aspirantes y describen los puestos disponibles.
- Consiguen los nombres y referencias de los aspirantes.

Aspirantes
- Circulan por la feria de trabajo.
- Hablan con tres representantes y formulan preguntas sobre los puestos que tienen.
- Muestran sus referencias y currículums.
- Escogen el puesto que les gustó más.

Practice more at vhlcentral.com

Ortografía Las letras y, ll y h *Concepts*

The letters *ll* and *y* were not pronounced alike in Old Spanish. Nowadays, however, *ll* and *y* have the same or similar pronunciations in many parts of the Spanish-speaking world. This similarity results in frequent misspellings. The letter *h*, as you already know, is silent in Spanish, and it is often difficult to know whether words should be written with or without it. Here are some of the word groups that are spelled with each letter.

ta**lla**   se**llo**   bote**lla**   amari**llo**

The letter *ll* is used in these endings: **–allo/a, –ello/a, –illo/a**.

llave   **ll**ega   **ll**orar   **ll**uvia

The letter *ll* is used at the beginning of words in these combinations: **lla–, lle–, llo–, llu–**.

ca**y**endo   le**y**eron   o**y**e   inclu**y**e

The letter *y* is used in some forms of the verbs **caer**, **leer**, and **oír**, and of verbs ending in **–uir**.

hiperactivo   **h**ospital   **h**ipopótamo   **h**umor

The letter *h* is used at the beginning of words in these combinations: **hiper–, hosp–, hidr–, hipo–, hum–**.

hiato   **h**ierba   **h**ueso   **h**uir

The letter *h* is also used in words that begin with these combinations: **hia–, hie–, hue–, hui–**.

recursos — LM p. 92 — vhlcentral.com

Adivinanza Aquí tienes una adivinanza (*riddle*). Intenta descubrir de qué se trata.

Una cajita chiquita, blanca como la nieve: todos la saben abrir, nadie la sabe cerrar.[1]

Pista: Es una comida.

1 El huevo

16 ESCENAS

La entrevista de trabajo
Video: *Fotonovela*

Los chicos hablan de sus planes para el futuro. Y la Sra. Díaz prepara a Miguel para unas entrevistas de trabajo.

Expresiones útiles

Talking about future plans

En menos de dos meses, ya habré regresado a mi casa en Wisconsin.
In less than two months, I'll have gone back home to Wisconsin.

¿Qué piensas hacer después de graduarte?
What do you think you'll do after graduating?

Vamos a crear una compañía de asesores de negocios.
We're going to open a consulting firm.

Les enseñaremos a las empresas a disminuir la cantidad de contaminación que producen.
We'll teach businesses how to reduce the amount of pollution they produce.

No sé cómo vaya a ser mi vida a los treinta años.
I don't know what my life will be like when I am thirty.

Probablemente me habré ido de Wisconsin.
I'll probably have left Wisconsin.

Seré arqueóloga en un país exótico.
I'll be an archeologist in some exotic country.

Reactions

Estoy seguro/a de que tendrán mucho éxito.
I'm sure you'll be very successful.
¡Genial! *Great!*

Additional Vocabulary

ejercer to practice/exercise (a degree/profession)
enterarse to find out
establecer to establish
extrañar to miss
por el porvenir for/to the future
el título title

recursos

VM pp. 31–32

vhlcentral.com

MARISSA En menos de dos meses, ya habré regresado a mi casa en Wisconsin.
FELIPE No pensé que el año terminara tan pronto.
JIMENA ¡Todavía no se ha acabado! Tengo que escribir tres ensayos.

MARISSA ¿Qué piensas hacer después de graduarte, Felipe?
JUAN CARLOS Vamos a crear una compañía de asesores de negocios.
FELIPE Les enseñaremos a las empresas a disminuir la cantidad de contaminación que producen.

MARISSA Estoy segura de que tendrán mucho éxito.
FELIPE También me gustaría viajar. Me muero por ir a visitarte a los Estados Unidos.
JIMENA Pues date prisa. Pronto estará lejos trabajando como arqueóloga.

MARISSA No sé cómo vaya a ser mi vida a los 30 años. Probablemente me habré ido de Wisconsin y seré arqueóloga en un país exótico.
JUAN CARLOS (*a Jimena*) Para entonces ya serás doctora.

(*Mientras tanto, en la oficina de la Sra. Díaz*)
MIGUEL Gracias por recibirme hoy.
SRA. DÍAZ De nada, Miguel. Estoy muy feliz de poder ayudarte con las entrevistas de trabajo.

354 trescientos cincuenta y cuatro

El mundo del trabajo

MARISSA **FELIPE** **JIMENA** **JUAN CARLOS** **MIGUEL** **SRA. DÍAZ**

SRA. DÍAZ Durante la entrevista, tienes que convencer al entrevistador de que tú eres el mejor candidato. ¿Estás listo para comenzar?
MIGUEL Sí.

MIGUEL Mucho gusto. Soy Miguel Ángel Lagasca Martínez.
SRA. DÍAZ Encantada, Miguel. Veamos. Hábleme sobre su trabajo en el Museo Guggenheim de Bilbao.
MIGUEL Estuve allí seis meses en una práctica.

SRA. DÍAZ ¿Cuáles son sus planes para el futuro?
MIGUEL Seguir estudiando historia del arte, especialmente la española y la latinoamericana. Me encanta el arte moderno. En el futuro, quiero trabajar en un museo y ser un pintor famoso.

SRA. DÍAZ ¿Qué te hace especial, Miguel?
MIGUEL ¿Especial?
SRA. DÍAZ Bueno. Paremos un momento. Necesitas relajarte. Vamos a caminar.

MIGUEL Estamos esperando noticias del museo. (*al teléfono*) Hola. ¿Maru? ¡Genial! (*a la Sra. Díaz*) ¡La aceptaron!
SRA. DÍAZ Felicidades. Ahora quiero que tomes ese mismo entusiasmo y lo lleves a la entrevista.

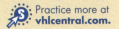

Actividades

1 ¿Cierto o falso? Indica si lo que dicen las oraciones es **cierto** o **falso**. Corrige las oraciones falsas.

1. Juan Carlos y Felipe quieren crear su propia empresa.
2. En el futuro, Marissa va a viajar porque va a ser psicóloga.
3. La Sra. Díaz ayuda a Miguel con su currículum.
4. Miguel quiere seguir estudiando historia del arte.

2 Identificar Identifica quién puede decir estas oraciones.

1. Nosotros vamos a ayudar a que se reduzca la contaminación.
2. Me gustan los hospitales, por eso quiero ser doctora.
3. No imagino cómo será mi vida en el futuro.
4. Quiero ser un pintor famoso, como Salvador Dalí.
5. Lleva ese entusiasmo a la entrevista y serás el mejor candidato.

3 Profesiones Los protagonistas de **Escenas** mencionan estas profesiones. En parejas, túrnense para identificar cada profesión.

1. arqueólogo/a
2. doctor(a)
3. artista
4. administrador(a) de empresas
5. abogado/a
6. pintor(a)
7. profesor(a)
8. hombre/mujer de negocios

trescientos cincuenta y cinco 355

16 EXPLORACIÓN

BAJO LA LUPA

Beneficios en los empleos

Additional Reading
Video: Flash cultura

¿Qué piensas si te ofrecen un trabajo que te da treinta días de vacaciones pagadas? Los beneficios laborales° en los Estados Unidos, España e Hispanoamérica son diferentes en varios sentidos°. En España, por ejemplo, los empleados tienen treinta días de vacaciones pagadas al año. Por otra parte, mientras que° en los Estados Unidos se otorga° una licencia por maternidad° de doce semanas, la ley° no especifica que sea pagada, esto depende de cada empresa. En muchos países hispanoamericanos las leyes dictan que esta licencia sea pagada. Países como Cuba y Venezuela ofrecen a las madres trabajadoras° dieciocho semanas de licencia pagada. Chile cuenta con la licencia por maternidad más larga de Suramérica: veinticuatro meses.

Otra diferencia está en los sistemas de jubilación° de los países hispanoamericanos. Hasta la década de 1990, la mayoría de los países de Centroamérica y Suramérica tenía un sistema de jubilación público. Es decir que las personas no tenían que pagar directamente por su jubilación, sino que el Estado la administraba. Sin embargo, en las últimas décadas las cosas han cambiado en Hispanoamérica: casi todos los países han incorporado el sistema privado° de jubilación y en muchos países podemos encontrar los dos sistemas (público y privado) funcionando al mismo tiempo, como en Colombia, Perú o Costa Rica.

El currículum vitae

- El currículum vitae contiene información personal y es fundamental que sea muy detallado°. En general, mientras más páginas tenga, mejor.
- Normalmente incluye la educación completa del aspirante, todos los trabajos que ha tenido e incluso sus gustos personales y pasatiempos.
- Puede también incluir detalles que no se suelen incluir en los Estados Unidos: una foto del aspirante, su estado civil e incluso si tiene auto y de qué tipo.

beneficios laborales *job benefits* **varios sentidos** *many ways* **mientras que** *while* **se otorga** *is given* **licencia por maternidad** *maternity leave* **ley** *law* **madres trabajadoras** *working mothers* **jubilación** *retirement* **privado** *private* **detallado** *detailed*

recursos

VM
pp. 63–64

vhlcentral.com

356 trescientos cincuenta y seis

El mundo del trabajo

ACTIVIDADES

1 ¿Cierto o falso? Indica si lo que dicen estas oraciones es **cierto** o **falso**.

1. Los trabajadores de los Estados Unidos y los de España tienen beneficios laborales diferentes.
2. La licencia por maternidad es igual en Hispanoamérica y los Estados Unidos.
3. En Venezuela, la licencia por maternidad es de cuatro meses y medio.
4. En España, los empleados tienen treinta días de vacaciones al año.
5. Hasta 1990, muchos países hispanoamericanos tenían un sistema de jubilación privado.
6. En Perú sólo tienen sistema de jubilación privado.
7. En general, el currículum vitae hispano y el estadounidense tienen contenido distinto.
8. En Hispanoamérica, es importante que el currículum vitae tenga pocas páginas.

2 Futuro laboral En parejas, hagan una lista con expectativas que tienen sobre su futuro como trabajadores/as y sobre el trabajo que quieren tener. Luego, respondan estas preguntas: ¿Conocen bien las reglas para conseguir un trabajo? ¿Les gustan? ¿Les disgustan? Presenten sus ideas ante la clase para un debate.

CONEXIÓN INTERNET

¿Qué tipo de trabajo voluntario se puede realizar en Latinoamérica?
For more information about **Exploración**, go to **vhlcentral.com**.

El mundo del trabajo

1 Preparación ¿Trabajas? ¿Cuáles son tus metas (*goals*) profesionales?

2 El video Mira el episodio de **Flash cultura**.

Vocabulario
el desarrollo development	**promover** to promote
el horario schedule	**las ventas** sales

Gabriela, ¿qué es lo más difícil de ser una mujer policía?

Nuestra principal estrategia de ventas es promover nuestra naturaleza…

3 Escoger Escoge la opción correcta de cada par de afirmaciones.

1. a. Todos los ecuatorianos que trabajan en Ecuador son muy felices en su trabajo.
   b. En Ecuador, como en todos los países del mundo, hay personas que aman su trabajo y hay otras que lo odian.
2. a. El objetivo principal de la agencia Klein Tours es mostrar al mundo las maravillas de Ecuador.
   b. La agencia de viajes Klein Tours quiere mostrar al mundo que tiene los empleados más fieles y profesionales de toda Latinoamérica.

16 GRAMÁTICA

16.1 The future tense

▶ You have already learned how to use **ir a** + [*infinitive*] to express the near future. You will now learn the future tense. Compare these different ways of expressing the future.

PRESENT INDICATIVE

Voy al cine mañana.
I'm going to the movies tomorrow.

PRESENT SUBJUNCTIVE

Ojalá **vaya al cine** mañana.
I hope I will go to the movies tomorrow.

IR A + INFINITIVE

Voy a ir al cine.
I'm going to go to the movies.

FUTURE

Iré al cine.
I will go to the movies.

Future tense of regular verbs

	estudiar	aprender	recibir
yo	estudiaré	aprenderé	recibiré
tú	estudiarás	aprenderás	recibirás
Ud./él/ella	estudiará	aprenderá	recibirá
nosotros/as	estudiaremos	aprenderemos	recibiremos
vosotros/as	estudiaréis	aprenderéis	recibiréis
Uds./ellos/ellas	estudiarán	aprenderán	recibirán

¡ojo!
All the forms of the future tense have written accents, except the **nosotros/as** form.

...

The future of **hay** (*inf.* **haber**) is **habrá** (*there will be*).

La próxima semana **habrá** dos reuniones.
Next week there will be two meetings.

Habrá muchos gerentes en la conferencia.
There will be many managers at the conference.

▶ In Spanish, the future tense consists of one word, whereas in English it is made up of the auxiliary verb *will* or *shall* and the main verb.

¿Cuándo **recibirás** el ascenso?
When will you receive the promotion?

Mañana **aprenderemos** más.
Tomorrow we will learn more.

▶ The future endings are the same for all verbs. For regular verbs, add the endings to the infinitive. For irregular verbs, add the endings to the irregular stem.

Irregular verbs in the future

INFINITIVE	STEM	FUTURE FORMS	INFINITIVE	STEM	FUTURE FORMS
decir	dir–	diré	querer	querr–	querré
haber	habr–	habré	saber	sabr–	sabré
hacer	har–	haré	salir	saldr–	saldré
poder	podr–	podré	tener	tendr–	tendré
poner	pondr–	pondré	venir	vendr–	vendré

▶ Although the English verb *will* can refer to future time, it also refers to someone's willingness to do something. In this case, Spanish uses **querer** + [*infinitive*].

¿**Quieres llamarme**, por favor?
Will you please call me?

¿**Quieren ustedes escucharnos**, por favor?
Will you please listen to us?

El mundo del trabajo

▶ English sentences involving expressions such as *I wonder, I bet, must be, may, might,* and *probably* are often conveyed in Spanish using the future of probability. This use of the future tense expresses conjecture about *present* conditions, events, or actions.

—¿Dónde **estarán** mis llaves?
I wonder where my keys are?

—**Estarán** en la cocina.
They're probably in the kitchen.

▶ The future may be used in the main clause of sentences in which the present subjunctive follows a conjunction of time such as **cuando, después (de) que, en cuanto, hasta que,** and **tan pronto como.**

Cuando llegues a la oficina, **hablaremos**.
When you arrive at the office, we will talk.

Saldremos tan pronto como termine su trabajo.
We will leave as soon as you finish your work.

Práctica y conversación

Practice more at vhlcentral.com.

1 Planes Celia está hablando de sus planes. Repite lo que dice usando el tiempo futuro.

MODELO
Voy a consultar un diccionario en la biblioteca.
Consultaré un diccionario en la biblioteca.

1. Julián me va a decir dónde puedo buscar trabajo.
2. Voy a buscar un puesto que ofrezca ascensos.
3. Álvaro y yo nos vamos a casar pronto.
4. Voy a obtener un puesto en mi especialización.
5. Mis amigos van a intentar (*try*) obtener un teletrabajo.

2 Preguntas En parejas, túrnense para hablar del puesto que prefieren y por qué, basándose en los anuncios. Usen las preguntas como guía y hagan también sus propias preguntas.

1. ¿Cuál será tu trabajo?
2. ¿Cuánto te pagarán?
3. ¿Te ofrecerán beneficios?
4. ¿Qué horario tendrás?
5. ¿Crees que te gustará?
6. ¿Cuándo comenzarás?

3 Conversar Tú y un(a) compañero/a viajarán a la República Dominicana por siete días. Indiquen lo que harán y no harán. Digan dónde, cómo, con quién o cuándo lo harán usando el anuncio como guía. Pueden usar sus propias ideas también.

MODELO
Estudiante 1: ¿Qué haremos el martes?
Estudiante 2: Visitaremos el Jardín Botánico.

¡Bienvenido a la República Dominicana!

Se divertirá desde el momento en que llegue al Aeropuerto Internacional de las Américas.
- Visite la ciudad colonial de Santo Domingo con su interesante arquitectura.
- Vaya al Jardín Botánico y disfrute de nuestra abundante naturaleza.
- En el Mercado Modelo, no va a poder resistir la tentación de comprar artesanías.
- No deje de escalar la montaña del Pico Duarte (se recomiendan 3 días).
- ¿Le gusta bucear? Cabarete tiene todo el equipo que Ud. necesita.
- ¿Desea nadar? Punta Cana le ofrece hermosas playas.

4 Una empresa privada En grupos pequeños, hagan planes para formar una empresa privada. Usen las preguntas como guía. Después presenten su plan a la clase.

1. ¿Cómo se llamará y qué tipo de empresa será?
2. ¿Cuántos empleados tendrá y cuáles serán sus oficios?
3. ¿Qué tipo de beneficios se ofrecerán?
4. ¿Quién será el/la gerente y quién será el/la jefe/a?
5. ¿Permitirá su empresa el teletrabajo? ¿Por qué?
6. ¿Dónde pondrán anuncios para buscar empleados?

5 Predicciones En grupos pequeños, especulen sobre lo que ocurrirá en estos años: 2020, 2050 y 2080. Usen su imaginación. Luego compartan sus predicciones con la clase.

trescientos cincuenta y nueve **359**

Lección 16

16.2 The conditional tense

▸ The conditional tense in Spanish expresses what you *would do* or what *would happen* under certain circumstances. In Lesson 7, you learned the polite expression **me gustaría...** (*I would like...*), which uses a conditional form of **gustar**.

The conditional tense

	visitar	comer	aplaudir
yo	visitaría	comería	aplaudiría
tú	visitarías	comerías	aplaudirías
Ud./él/ella	visitaría	comería	aplaudiría
nosotros/as	visitaríamos	comeríamos	aplaudiríamos
vosotros/as	visitaríais	comeríais	aplaudiríais
Uds./ellos/ellas	visitarían	comerían	aplaudirían

▸ The conditional endings are the same for all verbs, and all forms carry a written accent. For regular verbs, add the endings to the infinitive. For irregular verbs, add the conditional endings to the irregular stems.

Irregular verbs in the conditional

INFINITIVE	STEM	CONDITIONAL	INFINITIVE	STEM	CONDITIONAL
decir	dir–	diría	querer	querr–	querría
haber	habr–	habría	saber	sabr–	sabría
hacer	har–	haría	salir	saldr–	saldría
poder	podr–	podría	tener	tendr–	tendría
poner	pondr–	pondría	venir	vendr–	vendría

¡ojo!
The conditional form of **hay** (*inf.* **haber**) is **habría** (*there would be*).

¡ojo!
Keep in mind the two parallel combinations shown in the example sentences:
1) present tense in main clause → future tense in subordinate clause
2) past tense in main clause → conditional tense in subordinate clause

▸ While in English the conditional is made up of the auxiliary verb *would* and a main verb, in Spanish it consists of one word.

Este aspirante **sería** perfecto para el puesto.
This candidate would be perfect for the job.

¿**Vivirían** ustedes en otro país por un trabajo?
Would you live in another country for a job?

Querría un puesto con un buen salario.
I would like a job with a good salary.

Ganarían más en otra compañía.
They would earn more in another company.

▸ The conditional is commonly used to make polite requests.

¿**Podrías** llamar al gerente, por favor?
Would you call the manager, please?

¿**Sería** tan amable de venir ahora?
Would you be so kind as to come now?

▸ In both Spanish and English, the conditional expresses the future in relation to a past action or state of being. The future indicates what *will happen*, whereas the conditional indicates what *would happen*. The future tense is often used if the main verb is in the present tense. The conditional is often used if the main verb is in one of the past tenses.

Creo que mañana **hará** sol.
I think it will be sunny tomorrow.

Creía que hoy **haría** sol.
I thought it would be sunny today.

360 *trescientos sesenta*

El mundo del trabajo

▶ The English *would* can also mean *used to*, in the sense of past habitual action. To express past habitual actions, Spanish uses the imperfect instead of the conditional.

Íbamos al parque los sábados.
We would go to the park on Saturdays.

De adolescentes, **comíamos** mucho.
As teenagers, we used to eat a lot.

▶ English sentences involving expressions such as *I wondered if, probably*, and *must have been* are often conveyed in Spanish using the conditional of probability. This use of the conditional expresses conjecture or probability about *past* conditions, events, or actions.

Serían las nueve cuando el jefe me llamó.
It must have been (It was probably) 9 o'clock when my boss called me.

Sonó el teléfono. ¿**Llamaría** Tina para cancelar nuestra cita?
The phone rang. I wondered if it was Tina calling to cancel our date.

Práctica y conversación

Practice more at vhlcentral.com.

1 Un viaje A la empresa Día le gustaría tener una conferencia en Puerto Rico. Los empleados nos cuentan sus planes de viaje. Complétalos con el condicional.

1. Me _____ [gustar] venir unos días antes de la conferencia para viajar por el país.
2. Ana y Rubén _____ [salir] primero a la playa.
3. Yo _____ [decir] que fuéramos a San Juan.
4. Nosotras _____ [preferir] tener las reuniones por la mañana. Así, por la tarde _____ [poder] visitar la ciudad.
5. Y nosotros _____ [visitar] la zona comercial de la ciudad. Y tú, Luisa, ¿qué _____ [hacer]?
6. El jefe _____ [tener] interés en hacer una videoconferencia. Él _____ [visitar] los museos.

2 Preguntas Forma preguntas con estos elementos. Luego, en parejas, inventen las respuestas. Usen el condicional.

MODELO
hacer (ustedes) / videoconferencia / con / empresa de Chile
—¿Harían ustedes una videoconferencia con una empresa de Chile?
—Sí, haríamos una videoconferencia con una empresa de Chile.

1. contratar (tú) / primo / para / puesto nuevo
2. invertir (ellos) / dinero / en / compañía nueva
3. solicitar (ella) / trabajo / de abogado
4. renunciar (tú) / puesto / trabajo con más beneficios

3 En tu lugar… Lee las situaciones. Responde con lo que harías en esta situación usando la frase **Yo en tu lugar…** (*If I were you…*). Después, compara tus ideas con las de un(a) compañero/a.

MODELO
Me encanta mi puesto, pero mi jefe nunca me deja hablar.
Estudiante 1: Me encanta mi puesto, pero mi jefe nunca me deja hablar.
Estudiante 2: Pues, yo en tu lugar hablaría con mi jefe sobre este problema.

1. El año pasado escogí la contabilidad como mi especialización, pero ahora he descubierto que no me gusta trabajar con números todo el día.
2. Me ofrecen un puesto interesantísimo, pero tiene un horario horrible. No volveré a ver a mis amigos jamás.
3. Mi peluquero es maravilloso, pero se va de viaje por dos meses a San Juan. Los otros peluqueros que trabajan en su salón no me gustan. Y tengo que hacer varias presentaciones durante esos dos meses.

4 ¿Qué harías? Quieres saber qué harían tus compañeros/as por un millón de dólares. Escribe ocho preguntas usando el tiempo condicional. Circula por la clase y hazles las preguntas a tus compañeros/as. Anota las respuestas e informa a la clase de los resultados de la encuesta.

MODELO
Estudiante 1: ¿Trabajarías como cantante en Las Vegas?
Estudiante 2: Sí, lo haría. Sería un puesto muy interesante.

trescientos sesenta y uno 361

Lección 16

16.3 The past subjunctive  Tutorial

▸ The past subjunctive (**el pretérito imperfecto de subjuntivo**) is also called the imperfect subjunctive. Like the present subjunctive, it is mainly used in multiple-clause sentences that express will, influence, emotion, commands, indefiniteness, and non-existence.

¡ojo!
The past subjunctive endings are the same for all verbs. Also, note that the **nosotros/as** form always has a written accent.

The past subjunctive

	estudiar	aprender	recibir
yo	estudiara	aprendiera	recibiera
tú	estudiaras	aprendieras	recibieras
Ud./él/ella	estudiara	aprendiera	recibiera
nosotros/as	estudiáramos	aprendiéramos	recibiéramos
vosotros/as	estudiarais	aprendierais	recibierais
Uds./ellos/ellas	estudiaran	aprendieran	recibieran

Cuando llegaste, no creí que tuviéramos muchas cosas en común.

▸ For *all* verbs, the past subjunctive is formed with the **Uds./ellos/ellas** form of the preterite. By dropping the **–ron** ending, you establish the stem for all the past subjunctive forms. You then add the past subjunctive endings.

Me sorprendió que el año terminara tan pronto.

INFINITIVE	PRETERITE FORM	STEM	PAST SUBJUNCTIVE
hablar	ellos habla~~ron~~	habla–	hablara, hablaras, habláramos…
beber	ellos bebie~~ron~~	bebie–	bebiera, bebieras, bebiéramos…
escribir	ellos escribie~~ron~~	escribie–	escribiera, escribieras, escribiéramos…

▸ For verbs with irregular preterites, add the past subjunctive endings to the irregular stem.

¡ojo!
Quisiera is often used to make polite requests.
Quisiera hablar con Marco.
I would like to speak with Marco.
¿Quisiera usted algo más?
Would you like anything else?

dar	die~~ron~~	die–	diera, dieras, diéramos…
decir	dije~~ron~~	dije–	dijera, dijeras, dijéramos…
estar	estuvie~~ron~~	estuvie–	estuviera, estuvieras, estuviéramos…
hacer	hicie~~ron~~	hicie–	hiciera, hicieras, hiciéramos…
ir/ser	fue~~ron~~	fue–	fuera, fueras, fuéramos…
poder	pudie~~ron~~	pudie–	pudiera, pudieras, pudiéramos…
poner	pusie~~ron~~	pusie–	pusiera, pusieras, pusiéramos…
querer	quisie~~ron~~	quisie–	quisiera, quisieras, quisiéramos…
saber	supie~~ron~~	supie–	supiera, supieras, supiéramos…
tener	tuvie~~ron~~	tuvie–	tuviera, tuvieras, tuviéramos…
venir	vinie~~ron~~	vinie–	viniera, vinieras, viniéramos…

trescientos sesenta y dos

El mundo del trabajo

▶ **–Ir** stem-changing verbs and other verbs with spelling changes follow a similar process to form the past subjunctive.

INFINITIVE	PRETERITE FORM	STEM	PAST SUBJUNCTIVE
preferir	prefirie~~ron~~	prefirie–	prefiriera, prefirieras, prefiriéramos
repetir	repitie~~ron~~	repitie–	repitiera, repitieras, repitiéramos
dormir	durmie~~ron~~	durmie–	durmiera, durmieras, durmiéramos
conducir	conduje~~ron~~	conduje–	condujera, condujeras, condujéramos
creer	creye~~ron~~	creye–	creyera, creyeras, creyéramos
destruir	destruye~~ron~~	destruye–	destruyera, destruyeras, destruyéramos
oír	oye~~ron~~	oye–	oyera, oyeras, oyéramos

▶ The past subjunctive is used in the same contexts and situations as the present subjunctive, except that it describes actions, events or conditions that have already happened. The verb in the main clause is usually in the preterite or the imperfect.

Me pidieron que no **llegara** tarde.
They asked me not to arrive late.

Ellos querían que yo les **escribiera**.
They wanted me to write to them.

Práctica y conversación

Practice more at vhlcentral.com.

1 Conversaciones Completa los minidiálogos con el pretérito imperfecto de subjuntivo de los verbos.

PACO ¿Qué le dijo el consejero a Andrés?
JULIA Le aconsejó que (1) _____ [dejar] los estudios de arte y que (2) _____ [estudiar] una carrera que (3) _____ [pagar] mejor.
PACO ¿No se enojó él de que le (4) _____ [aconsejar] eso?
JULIA Sí, y le dijo que no creía que ninguna carrera le (5) _____ [ir] a gustar más.

• • •

EVA Qué lástima que ellos no te (6) _____ [ofrecer] el puesto de gerente.
LUIS Querían a alguien que (7) _____ [tener] experiencia.
EVA ¿No te molestó que te (8) _____ [decir] eso?
LUIS No, me pidieron que (9) _____ [volver] en un año y (10) _____ [solicitar] el puesto otra vez.

• • •

CARLA Cuánto me alegró que tus hijas (11) _____ [venir] ayer a visitarte. ¿Cuándo se van?
ANA Bueno, yo esperaba que (12) _____ [quedarse] dos semanas, pero no pueden. Ojalá (13) _____ [poder]. Hace muchísimo tiempo que no las veo.

2 Transformar Cambia las oraciones al pasado. Sigue el modelo.

MODELO
Temo que Juanita no consiga el trabajo.
Temía que Juanita no consiguiera el trabajo.

1. Esperamos que Miguel no renuncie.
2. No hay nadie que responda al anuncio.
3. Me sorprende que ellos no inviertan su dinero.
4. Te piden que no llegues tarde a la oficina.

3 Minidiálogos Trabajen en parejas. Uno/a ha comprado una casa; la otra persona es responsable de las reformas (*improvements*) de la casa. El/la cliente/a llama para quejarse (*to complain*). Usen estas palabras y el modelo como guía.

MODELO
el/la técnico/a / conectar / módem
Estudiante 1: Le pedí al técnico que conectara Internet, pero todavía no ha venido.
Estudiante 2: Yo también le pedí que fuera a su casa.

1. el/la electricista / poner / electricidad
2. el/la carpintero/a / construir / balcón
3. el/la diseñador(a) / escoger / muebles
4. el/la pintor(a) / pintar / paredes

trescientos sesenta y tres 363

Lección 16

Ampliación

Audio: Activity
Video: TV Clip

1 Escuchar

A Escucha la entrevista de la señora Sánchez y Rafael Ventura Romero. Antes de escucharla, prepara una lista de la información que esperas oír, según tu conocimiento previo (*prior knowledge*) del tema.

TIP Use background knowledge./Listen for specific information. Knowing the subject of what you are going to hear will help you use your background knowledge to anticipate words and phrases that you are likely to hear, and to determine important information that you should listen for.

Llena el formulario con la información necesaria. Si no oyes un dato (*piece of information*) que necesitas, escribe *Buscar en el currículum*. ¿Oíste toda la información de tu lista?

Puesto solicitado _____
Nombre y apellidos del solicitante _____
Dirección _____   Tel. _____
Educación _____
Experiencia profesional: Puesto _____
Empresa _____
¿Cuánto tiempo? _____
Referencias:
Nombre _____
Dirección _____   Tel. _____
Nombre _____
Dirección _____   Tel. _____

B ¿Cómo sabes si los resultados de la entrevista han sido positivos para Rafael Ventura?
_____

2 Conversar

Con un(a) compañero/a, conversen sobre sus planes para el futuro. Incluyan esta información en su conversación.

- ¿Qué profesión u oficio seguirás en el futuro?
- ¿Por qué te interesa esta carrera?
- ¿En qué compañía te gustaría trabajar?
- ¿Te gustaría tener un teletrabajo?
- ¿Qué se necesita hacer para tener éxito?
- ¿Te mudarías de país por un puesto excelente?
- ¿Crees que serás multimillonario?

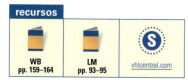

recursos
WB pp. 159–164
LM pp. 93–95
vhlcentral.com

El mundo del trabajo

3 Escribir Escribe una composición sobre tus planes para el futuro. Formula planes para tu vida personal, profesional y financiera. Termina tu composición con una lista de metas (*goals*).

TIP Use note cards. Note cards (**fichas**) can help you organize your information. Label the top of each card with a general subject, such as **lugar** or **empleo**. Number the cards so you can easily flip through them to find information.

Organízalo Utiliza fichas para apuntar cada plan o meta para el futuro. Asigna un año a cada meta.

Escríbelo Organiza tus fichas y escribe el primer borrador de tu composición.

Corrígelo Intercambia tu composición con un(a) compañero/a. Léela y anota sus mejores aspectos. ¿Habla de las metas específicas para su futuro? Ofrécele sugerencias para mejorar la organización. Si ves algunos errores, coméntaselos.

Compártelo Revisa el primer borrador de tu composición según las indicaciones de tu compañero/a. Incorpora nuevas ideas y/o más información si es necesario, antes de escribir la versión final.

4 Un paso más Imagina que en el futuro trabajarás para una empresa multinacional que tiene sus oficinas más importantes en algún país hispano. Crea una cronología con texto y fotos de tu futura carrera profesional y compártela con la clase.

- Escoge el país y busca información sobre las industrias y las compañías que operen allá.
- Describe la empresa y sus productos.
- Incluye fotos relacionadas con la empresa y con sus productos.
- Describe tu carrera, desde el comienzo hasta tu jubilación.
- Incluye los puestos que vas a tener en la empresa, y también fotos relacionadas con tu carrera.

CONEXIÓN INTERNET

Investiga estos temas en **vhlcentral.com**.
- Empresas en el mundo hispano
- Industrias en el mundo hispano
- Compañías multinacionales en el mundo hispano

Practice more at vhlcentral.com.

16 LECTURA

Antes de leer

**Audio: Reading
Additional Reading**

Summarizing a text in your own words can help you understand it better. Before you begin, you may find it helpful to skim the text and jot down a few notes about its general meaning. You can then read it again, writing down important details or noting special characteristics that occur in the text. Your notes will help you summarize what you have read.

The reading selection for this lesson consists of a short story by Augusto Monterroso. What special characteristics in this text could help you summarize it? Skim the story and jot down your ideas.

_____
_____
_____

Sobre el autor

Augusto Monterroso (1921–2003) fue un escritor guatemalteco. Sus textos son concisos, sencillos (*simple*) y accesibles. Su trabajo incluye la parodia, el humor negro, la fábula y el ensayo.

Imaginación y destino
Augusto Monterroso

En la calurosa° tarde de verano un hombre descansa acostado°, viendo° al cielo, bajo un árbol; una manzana cae sobre su cabeza; tiene imaginación, se va a su casa y escribe la **Oda a Eva**.

En la calurosa tarde de verano un hombre descansa acostado, viendo al cielo, bajo un árbol; una manzana cae sobre su cabeza; tiene imaginación, se va a su casa y establece la **Ley de la Gravitación Universal**.

366 *trescientos sesenta y seis*

El mundo del trabajo

En la calurosa tarde de verano un hombre descansa acostado, viendo al cielo, bajo un árbol; una manzana cae sobre su cabeza; tiene imaginación, observa que el árbol no es un manzano° sino una encina° y descubre, oculto° entre las ramas°, al muchacho travieso° del pueblo que se entretiene° arrojando° manzanas a los señores que descansan bajo los árboles, viendo al cielo, en las calurosas tardes del verano.

El primero era, o se convierte entonces para siempre en el poeta sir James Calisher; el segundo era, o se convierte entonces para siempre en el físico sir Isaac Newton[1]; el tercero pudo ser o convertirse entonces para siempre en el novelista sir Arthur Conan Doyle[2]; pero se convierte, o era ya irremediablemente desde niño, en el Jefe de Policía de San Blas, S.B.[3]

---

[1] Sir Isaac Newton (1642–1727), matemático y físico británico. Es considerado uno de los científicos más importantes de la historia. Formuló la Ley de la Gravitación Universal.
[2] Sir Arthur Conan Doyle (1859–1930), escritor británico. Sus más famosos protagonistas son Sherlock Holmes y su ayudante, el doctor Watson.
[3] S.B. Abreviatura para San Blas, una isla en Panamá. Una de las novelas de Monterroso tiene lugar en San Blas.

Después de leer

¿Comprendiste?

1. ¿Qué estación del año es y qué tiempo hace?

2. ¿Qué hace el primer hombre después de descansar?

3. ¿Qué hace el segundo hombre después de descansar?

4. ¿Qué encuentra el tercer hombre en el árbol?

5. ¿Cuáles son las profesiones de estos tres hombres al final del cuento?

Preguntas

Responde a estas preguntas con oraciones completas.

1. ¿Por qué lleva el cuento el título "Imaginación y destino"?

2. ¿Por qué utiliza el autor tanta repetición?

3. La misma cosa les ocurre a los tres hombres, pero tienen reacciones distintas. ¿Por qué?

4. El autor escribe "o era ya irremediablemente desde niño". ¿Qué significa esta frase en relación con el resto del cuento?

5. Imagina que hay una cuarta persona en la historia. Escribe un párrafo en el estilo del autor sobre qué le pasa a esta persona cuando "una manzana cae sobre su cabeza".

Coméntalo

En el cuento, tres personajes tienen la misma experiencia con distintos resultados. ¿Has tenido una experiencia así? Un ejemplo es la graduación: un grupo de personas se gradúa el mismo día, pero ¿qué pasa después? ¿Podemos controlar nuestros destinos? ¿Afectarán tus experiencias actuales tu futuro? ¿Cómo sabes qué profesión quieres ejercer (carry out) en el futuro?

---

calurosa *hot*　acostado *lying down*　viendo *looking up*　manzano *apple tree*　encina *oak tree*　oculto *hidden*　ramas *branches*　travieso *mischievous*　se entretiene *entertains himself*　arrojando *throwing*

trescientos sesenta y siete **367**

16 VOCABULARIO

Las ocupaciones

el/la abogado/a	lawyer
el actor	actor
la actriz	actress
el/la arqueólogo/a	archaeologist
el/la arquitecto/a	architect
el bailarín	dancer
la bailarina	dancer
el/la bombero/a	firefighter
el/la cantante	singer
el/la carpintero/a	carpenter
el/la científico/a	scientist
el/la cocinero/a	cook; chef
el/la consejero/a	counselor; advisor
el/la contador(a)	accountant
el/la corredor(a) de bolsa	stockbroker
el/la diseñador(a)	designer
el/la electricista	electrician
el/la escritor(a)	writer
el/la escultor(a)	sculptor
el/la gerente	manager
el hombre/la mujer de negocios	businessperson
el/la jefe/a	boss
el/la maestro/a	elementary school teacher
el/la peluquero/a	hairdresser
el/la pintor(a)	painter
el/la poeta	poet
el/la político/a	politician
el/la psicólogo/a	psychologist
el/la reportero/a	reporter
el/la secretario/a	secretary
el/la técnico/a	technician

Las entrevistas

el anuncio	advertisement
el/la aspirante	candidate; applicant
los beneficios	benefits
el currículum	résumé
la entrevista	interview
el/la entrevistador(a)	interviewer
el puesto	position; job
el salario	salary
la solicitud (de trabajo)	(job) application
el sueldo	salary
contratar	to hire
entrevistar	to interview
ganar	to earn
obtener	to obtain; to get
solicitar	to apply (for a job)

El mundo del trabajo

el ascenso	promotion
el aumento de sueldo	raise
la carrera	career
la compañía	company; firm
el empleo	job; employment
la empresa	company; firm
la especialización	field of study
los negocios	business; commerce
la ocupación	occupation
el oficio	trade
la profesión	profession
la reunión	meeting
el teletrabajo	telecommuting
el trabajo	job; work
la videoconferencia	videoconference
dejar	to quit; to leave behind
despedir (e:i)	to fire
invertir (e:ie)	to invest
renunciar (a)	to resign (from)
tener éxito	to be successful
comercial	commercial; business-related

¡VIVAN LOS PAÍSES HISPANOS!

Una mujer baila flamenco en Sevilla. El flamenco, el baile y su música expresan las pasiones de la gente de España. Tiene raíces (*roots*) judías (*Jewish*), árabes y africanas. Hoy es popular en todo el mundo. ¿Te gusta la música flamenca?

España

España

Área: 505.370 km^2 (195.124 millas^2), incluyendo las islas Baleares y las islas Canarias
Población: 47.043.000
Capital: Madrid–5.762.000
Ciudades principales: Barcelona, Valencia, Sevilla, Zaragoza
Moneda: euro

SOURCE: Population Division, UN Secretariat & CIA World Factbook

¡Vivan los países hispanos!

Interactive map
Video: *Países hispanos*

Lugares

Madrid: La Plaza Mayor

La Plaza Mayor de Madrid es uno de los lugares turísticos más importantes de la capital. Fue construida (*built*) en 1617 y está totalmente rodeada (*surrounded*) por edificios de tres pisos con balcones y pórticos antiguos. En la Plaza Mayor hay muchas cafeterías, donde la gente pasa el tiempo bebiendo café y hablando con amigos.

Celebraciones

La Tomatina

En Buñol, un pequeño pueblo de Valencia, la producción de tomates es un recurso económico muy importante. Cada año en agosto se celebra el festival de La Tomatina. Durante todo un día, miles de personas se tiran (*throw*) tomates. Llegan turistas de todo el mundo, y se usan varias toneladas (*tons*) de tomates.

370   trescientos setenta

España

FRANCIA

San Sebastián

ANDORRA

Pirineos

Zaragoza

Barcelona

Islas Baleares

Menorca

Valencia

Mallorca

Ibiza

Mar Mediterráneo

Artes

Velázquez y el Prado

El Prado, en Madrid, es uno de los museos más famosos del mundo. En el Prado hay miles de pinturas importantes, incluyendo obras (*works*) de Botticelli, El Greco y los españoles Goya y Velázquez. Diego Velázquez pintó (*painted*) *Las Meninas* en 1656 y es su obra más famosa. Actualmente, *Las Meninas* está en el Museo del Prado.

Lugares

La Universidad de Salamanca

La Universidad de Salamanca, fundada en 1218, es la universidad más antigua (*oldest*) de España. Más de 35.000 estudiantes toman clases en esta institución. La universidad está en la ciudad de Salamanca, famosa por sus edificios (*buildings*) históricos, sus puentes (*bridges*) romanos y sus catedrales góticas.

recursos		
WB pp. 165–166	**VM** pp. 91–92	vhlcentral.com

trescientos setenta y uno **371**

¡Vivan los países hispanos!

¿Qué aprendiste?

1 **¿Cierto o falso?** Indica si estas oraciones son **ciertas** o **falsas**.

Cierto	Falso	
_____	_____	1. La moneda de España es la peseta.
_____	_____	2. El flamenco es un instrumento musical.
_____	_____	3. El flamenco es hoy popular en todo el mundo.
_____	_____	4. En la Plaza Mayor no hay cafeterías.
_____	_____	5. La Plaza Mayor fue construida en 1617.
_____	_____	6. En Buñol, los tomates son un recurso importante.
_____	_____	7. Durante La Tomatina, se tiran pelotas.
_____	_____	8. En el Museo del Prado hay miles de pinturas importantes.
_____	_____	9. *Las meninas* es la obra más famosa de Botticelli.
_____	_____	10. En Salamanca se ve la influencia del imperio romano en la arquitectura.

2 **Preguntas** Contesta estas preguntas con oraciones completas.

1. ¿Alguna vez has visto bailar flamenco? ¿Te gustó?
2. ¿Sabes cuál es la capital de España? ¿Conoces algún dato interesante de esa ciudad?
3. ¿Te gustaría ir al festival de La Tomatina? ¿Conoces algún otro festival o celebración fuera de lo común (*out of the ordinary*)? ¿Cuál es y dónde se celebra?
4. ¿Cuál es tu museo favorito? ¿Recuerdas alguna obra de arte que se encuentra en ese museo? ¿Cuál?
5. ¿Cuál es la universidad más antigua que conoces? ¿Sabes en qué año fue fundada?

Investiga estos temas en el sitio vhlcentral.com.
- Gastronomía de España
- Españoles célebres

CONSULTA

Maps C2–C5

Glossary of Grammatical Terms C6–C9

Verb Conjugation Tables C10–C19

Vocabulario
Spanish-English C20-C35
English-Spanish C36–C51

Índice C52–C54

Credits C55-C57

About the Authors C58

MAPS

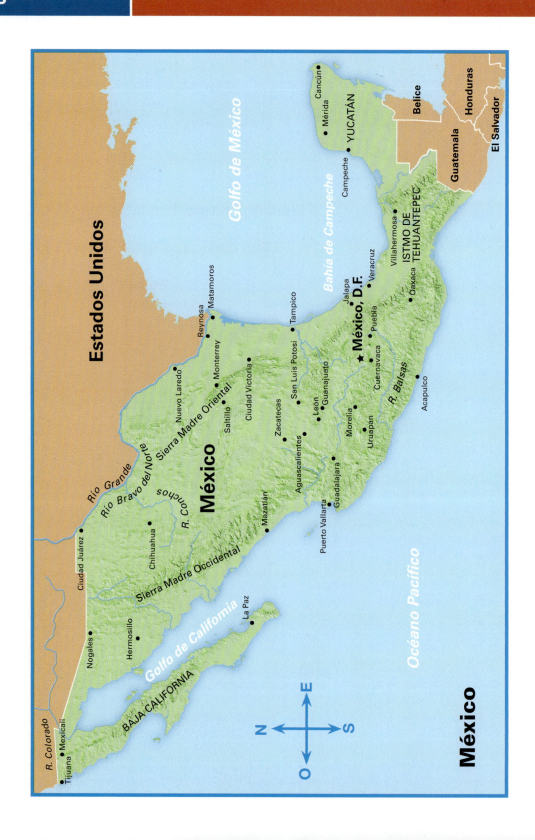

MAPS

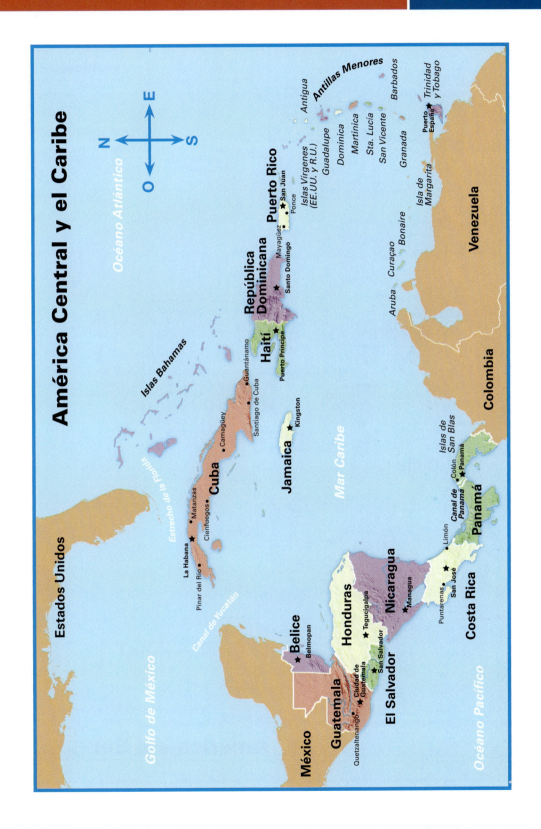

MAPS

MAPS

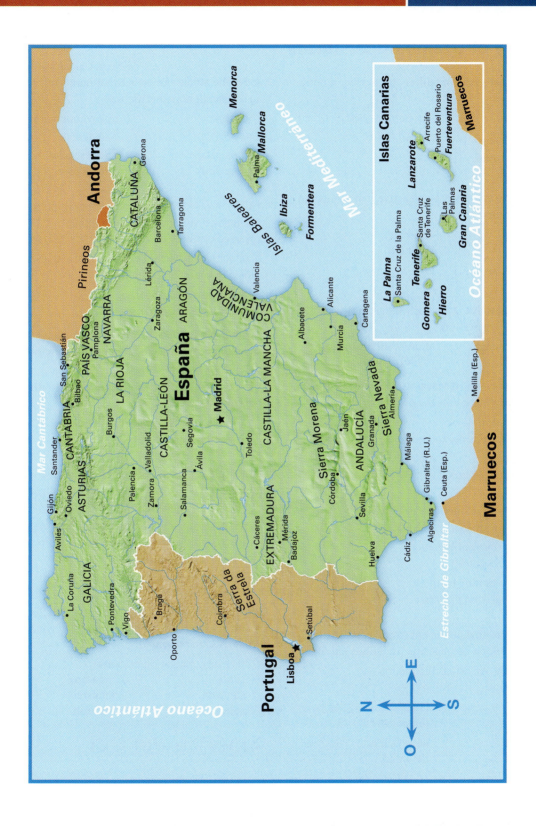

Glossary of Grammatical Terms

ADJECTIVE A word that modifies or describes a noun or pronoun.

muchos libros
many books

un hombre **rico**
*a **rich** man*

las mujeres **altas**
*the **tall** women*

Demonstrative adjective An adjective that points out a specific noun.

esta fiesta
***this** party*

ese chico
***that** boy*

aquellas flores
***those** flowers*

Possessive adjective An adjective that indicates ownership or possession.

tu mejor vestido
***your** best dress*

Éste es **mi** hermano.
*This is **my** brother.*

Stressed possessive adjective A possessive adjective that emphasizes the owner or possessor.

Es un libro **mío**.
*It's **my book**./It's a book **of mine**.*

Es amiga **tuya**; yo no la conozco.
*She's a friend **of yours**; I don't know her.*

ADVERB A word that modifies or describes a verb, adjective, or another adverb.

Pancho escribe **rápidamente**.
*Pancho writes **quickly**.*

Este cuadro es **muy** bonito.
*This painting is **very** pretty.*

ARTICLE A word that points out either a specific (definite) noun or a non-specific (indefinite) noun.

Definite article An article that points out a specific noun.

el libro
***the** book*

la maleta
***the** suitcase*

los diccionarios
***the** dictionaries*

las palabras
***the** words*

Indefinite article An article that points out a noun in a general, non-specific way.

un lápiz
***a** pencil*

una computadora
***a** computer*

unos pájaros
***some** birds*

unas escuelas
***some** schools*

CLAUSE A group of words that contains both a conjugated verb and a subject, either expressed or implied.

Main (or Independent) clause A clause that can stand alone as a complete sentence.

Pienso ir a cenar pronto.
I plan to go to dinner soon.

Subordinate (or Dependent) clause A clause that does not express a complete thought and therefore cannot stand alone as a sentence.

Trabajo en la cafetería **porque necesito dinero para la escuela**.

*I work in the cafeteria **because I need money for school**.*

COMPARATIVE A word or construction used with an adjective, adverb or noun to express a comparison between two people, places, or things.

Este programa es **más interesante que** el otro.
*This program is **more interesting than** the other one.*

Tomás no es **tan alto como** Alberto.
*Tomás is not **as tall as** Alberto.*

CONJUGATION A set of the forms of a verb for a specific tense or mood or the process by which these verb forms are presented.

Preterite conjugation of **cantar**:

cant**é**	cant**amos**
cant**aste**	cant**asteis**
cant**ó**	cant**aron**

C6

GLOSSARY OF GRAMMATICAL TERMS

CONJUNCTION A word or phrase used to connect words, clauses, or phrases.

> Susana es de Cuba **y** Pedro es de España.
> *Susana is from Cuba **and** Pedro is from Spain.*

> No quiero estudiar, **pero** tengo que hacerlo.
> *I don't want to study, **but** I have to do it.*

CONTRACTION The joining of two words into one. The only contractions in Spanish are **al** and **del**.

> Mi hermano fue **al** concierto ayer.
> *My brother went **to the** concert yesterday.*

> Saqué dinero **del** banco.
> *I took out money **from the** bank.*

DIRECT OBJECT A noun or pronoun that directly receives the action of the verb.

> Tomás lee **el libro**.   La pagó ayer.
> *Tomás reads **the book**.   She paid **it** yesterday.*

GENDER The grammatical categorizing of certain kinds of words, such as nouns and pronouns, as masculine, feminine, or neuter.

> **Masculine**
> *articles* **el**, l**o**s, un**o**, un**o**s
> *pronouns* **él**, l**o**, mí**o**, ést**e**, és**e**, aquél
> *adjective* simpátic**o**

> **Feminine**
> *articles* **la**, l**a**s, un**a**, un**a**s
> *pronouns* **ella**, l**a**, mí**a**, ést**a**, és**a**, aquéll**a**
> *adjective* simpátic**a**

IMPERSONAL EXPRESSION A third-person expression with no expressed or specific subject.

> **Es muy importante**.   **Llueve** mucho.
> *It's very important*.   *It's raining hard.*

INDIRECT OBJECT A noun or pronoun that receives the action of the verb indirectly; the object, often a living being, to or for whom an action is performed.

> Eduardo **le** dio un libro **a Linda**.
> *Eduardo gave a book **to Linda**.*
> Carlos **me** prestó cincuenta pesos.
> *Carlos lent **me** fifty pesos.*

INFINITIVE The basic form of a verb. Infinitives in Spanish end in **–ar**, **–er**, or **–ir**.

> **hablar**   **correr**   **abrir**
> *to speak*   *to run*   *to open*

INTERROGATIVE An adjective or pronoun used to ask a question.

> **¿Quién** habla?   **¿Cuántos** compraste?
> *Who is speaking?*   *How many did you buy?*

> **¿Qué** piensas hacer hoy?
> *What do you plan to do today?*

INVERSION Changing the word order of a sentence, often to form a question.

> *Statement:* Elena pagó la cuenta del restaurante.
> *Elena paid the restaurant bill.*

> *Inversion:* ¿Pagó Elena la cuenta del restaurante?
> *Did Elena pay the restaurant bill?*

MOOD A grammatical distinction of verbs that indicates whether the verb is intended to make a statement or command, or to express doubt, emotion, or a condition contrary to fact.

Imperative mood Verb forms used to make commands.

> **Di** la verdad.   **Caminen** ustedes conmigo.
> *Tell the truth.*   *Walk with me.*

> **¡Comamos** ahora!
> *Let's eat now!*

Indicative mood Verb forms used to state facts, actions, and states considered to be real.

> **Sé** que **tienes** el dinero.
> *I know that you have the money.*

Subjunctive mood Verb forms used principally in subordinate (or dependent) clauses to express wishes, desires, emotions, doubts, and certain conditions, such as contrary-to-fact situations.

> Prefieren que **hables** en español.
> *They prefer that **you speak** in Spanish.*

> Dudo que Luis **tenga** el dinero necesario.
> *I doubt that Luis **has** the necessary money.*

C7

GLOSSARY OF GRAMMATICAL TERMS

NOUN A word that identifies people, animals, places, things, and ideas.

hombre	gato	México
man	*cat*	*Mexico*
casa	libertad	libro
house	*freedom*	*book*

NUMBER A grammatical term that refers to singular or plural. Nouns in Spanish and English have number. Other parts of a sentence, such as adjectives, articles, and verbs, can also have number.

Singular	Plural
una cosa	**unas** cosas
a thing	*some things*
el profesor	**los** profesores
the professor	*the professors*

NUMBERS Words that represent amounts.

Cardinal numbers Words that show specific amounts.

cinco minutos	el año **dos mil quince**
five minutes	*the year 2015*

Ordinal numbers Words that indicate the order of a noun in a series.

el **cuarto** jugador	la **décima** hora
the fourth player	*the tenth hour*

PAST PARTICIPLE A past form of the verb used in compound tenses. The past participle may also be used as an adjective, but it must then agree in number and gender with the word it modifies.

Han **buscado** por todas partes.
They have searched everywhere.

Yo no había **estudiado** para el examen.
I hadn't studied for the exam.

Hay una **ventana rota** en la sala.
There is a broken window in the living room.

PERSON The form of the verb or pronoun that indicates the speaker, the one spoken to, or the one spoken about. In Spanish, as in English, there are three persons: first, second, and third.

Person	Singular	Plural
1st	**yo** *I*	**nosotros/as** *we*
2nd	**tú, Ud.** *you*	**vosotros/as, Uds.** *you*
3rd	**él, ella** *he/she*	**ellos, ellas** *they*

PREPOSITION A word that describes the relationship, most often in time or space, between two other words.

Anita es **de** California.
Anita is from California.

La chaqueta está **en** el carro.
The jacket is in the car.

¿Quieres hablar **con** ella?
Do you want to talk to her?

PRESENT PARTICIPLE In English, a verb form that ends in –ing. In Spanish, the present participle ends in **–ndo**, and is often used with **estar** to form a progressive tense.

Mi hermana está **hablando** por teléfono ahora mismo.
My sister is talking on the phone right now.

PRONOUN A word that takes the place of a noun or nouns.

Demonstrative pronoun A pronoun that takes the place of a specific noun.

Quiero **ésta**.
I want this one.

¿Vas a comprar **ése**?
Are you going to buy that one?

Juan prefirió **aquéllos**.
Juan preferred those (over there).

Object pronoun A pronoun that functions as a direct or indirect object of the verb.

Te digo la verdad.	**Me lo** trajo Juan.
I'm telling you the truth.	*Juan brought it to me.*

GLOSSARY OF GRAMMATICAL TERMS

Reflexive pronoun A pronoun that indicates that the action of a verb is performed by the subject on itself. These pronouns are often expressed in English with –self: *myself, yourself,* etc.

Yo **me bañé** antes de salir.
I bathed (myself) before going out.

Elena **se acostó** a las once y media.
Elena went to bed at eleven-thirty.

Relative pronoun A pronoun that connects a subordinate clause to a main clause.

El chico **que** nos escribió viene a visitarnos mañana.
The boy who wrote us is coming to visit us tomorrow.

Ya sé **lo que** tenemos que hacer.
I already know what we have to do.

Subject pronoun A pronoun that replaces the name or title of a person or thing and acts as the subject of a verb.

Tú debes estudiar más.   **Él** llegó primero.
You should study more.   *He arrived first.*

SUBJECT A noun or pronoun that performs the action of a verb and is often implied by the verb.

María va al supermercado.
María is going to the supermarket.

(Ellos) Trabajan mucho.
They work hard.

Esos **libros** son muy caros.
Those books are very expensive.

SUPERLATIVE A word or construction used with an adjective or adverb to express the highest or lowest degree of a specific quality among three or more people, places, or things.

Entre todas mis clases, ésta es la **más interesante**.
Among all my classes, this is the most interesting.

Raúl es el **menos simpático** de los chicos.
Raúl is the least pleasant of the boys.

TENSE A set of verb forms that indicates the time of an action or state: past, present, or future.

Compound tense A two-word tense made up of an auxiliary verb and a present or past participle. In Spanish, there are two auxiliary verbs: **estar** and **haber**.

En este momento, **estoy estudiando**.
At this time, I am studying.

El paquete no **ha llegado** todavía.
The package has not arrived yet.

Simple tense A tense expressed by a single verb form.

María **estaba** mal anoche.
María was ill last night.

Juana **hablará** con su mamá mañana.
Juana will speak with her mom tomorrow.

VERB A word that expresses actions or states of being.

Auxiliary verb A verb used with a present or past participle to form a compound tense. **Haber** is the most commonly used auxiliary verb in Spanish.

Los chicos **han** visto los elefantes.
The children have seen the elephants.

Espero que **hayas** comido.
I hope you have eaten.

Reflexive verb A verb that describes an action performed by the subject on itself and is always used with a reflexive pronoun.

Me compré un carro nuevo.
I bought myself a new car.

Pedro y Adela **se levantan** muy temprano.
Pedro and Adela get (themselves) up very early.

Spelling-change verb A verb that undergoes a predictable change in spelling in order to reflect its actual pronunciation in the various conjugations.

practicar	c → qu	practico	practi**qué**
dirigir	g → j	dirijo	diri**gí**
almorzar	z → c	almorzó	almor**cé**

Stem-changing verb A verb whose stem vowel undergoes one or more predictable changes in the various conjugations.

ent**e**nder (e:ie)	ent**ie**ndo
p**e**dir (e:i)	p**i**den
d**o**rmir (o:ue, u)	d**ue**rmo, d**u**rmieron

C9

VERB CONJUGATION TABLES

Verb Conjugation Tables

The verb lists

The list of verbs below and the model-verb tables that start on page 384 show you how to conjugate every verb taught in **¡VIVA!** Each verb on the list is followed by a model verb that is conjugated according to the same pattern. The number in parentheses indicates where in the tables you can find the conjugated forms of the model verb. If you want to find out how to conjugate **divertirse**, for example, look up number 33, **sentir**, the model for verbs that follow the **e:ie** stem-change pattern.

How to use the verb tables

In the tables you will find the infinitive, present and past participles, and all the simple forms of each model verb. The formation of the compound tenses of any verb can be inferred from the table of compound tenses, pages 384–391, either by combining the past participle of the verb with a conjugated form of **haber** or combining the present participle with a conjugated form of **estar**.

abrir like vivir (3) *except* past participle is **abierto**

aburrir(se) like vivir (3)

acabar de like hablar (1)

acampar like hablar (1)

aconsejar like hablar (1)

acordar(se) (o:ue) like contar (24)

acostar(se) (o:ue) like contar (24)

adelgazar (z:c) like cruzar (37)

afeitar(se) like hablar (1)

ahorrar like hablar (1)

alegrar(se) like hablar (1)

aliviar like hablar (1)

almorzar (o:ue) like contar (24) *except* (z:c)

alquilar like hablar (1)

apagar (g:gu) like llegar (41)

aprender like comer (2)

apurar(se) like hablar (1)

arrancar (c:qu) like tocar (43)

arreglar like hablar (1)

asistir like vivir (3)

aumentar like hablar (1)

bailar like hablar (1)

bajar(se) like hablar (1)

bañar(se) like hablar (1)

barrer like comer (2)

beber like comer (2)

brindar like hablar (1)

bucear like hablar (1)

buscar (c:qu) like tocar (43)

caer(se) (5)

calentarse (e:ie) like pensar (30)

cambiar like hablar (1)

caminar like hablar (1)

cantar like hablar (1)

casarse like hablar (1)

celebrar like hablar (1)

cenar like hablar (1)

cepillar(se) like hablar (1)

cerrar (e:ie) like pensar (30)

chocar (c:qu) like tocar (43)

cobrar like hablar (1)

cocinar like hablar (1)

comenzar (e:ie) (z:c) like empezar (26)

comer (2)

compartir like vivir (3)

comprar like hablar (1)

comprender like comer (2)

comprometerse like comer (2)

conducir (c:zc) (6)

confirmar like hablar (1)

conocer (c:zc) (35)

conseguir (e:i) like seguir (32)

conservar like hablar (1)

consumir like vivir (3)

contaminar like hablar (1)

contar (o:ue) (24)

controlar like hablar (1)

correr like comer (2)

costar (o:ue) like contar (24)

creer (y) (36)

cruzar (z:c) (37)

cuidar like hablar (1)

cumplir like vivir (3)

dañar like hablar (1)

dar(se) (7)

deber like comer (2)

decidir like vivir (3)

decir (e:i) (8)

dejar like hablar (1)

depositar like hablar (1)

desarrollar like hablar (1)

desayunar like hablar (1)

descansar like hablar (1)

describir like vivir (3) *except* past participle is **descrito**

descubrir like vivir (3) *except* past participle is **descubierto**

desear like hablar (1)

despedir (e:i) like pedir (29)

despertar(se) (e:ie) like pensar (30)

destruir (y) (38)

dibujar like hablar (1)

disfrutar like hablar (1)

divertirse (e:ie) like sentir (33)

divorciarse like hablar (1)

doblar like hablar (1)

doler (o:ue) like volver (34) *except* past participle is regular

dormir(se) (o:ue, u) (25)

duchar(se) like hablar (1)

dudar like hablar (1)

echar like hablar (1)

empezar (e:ie) (z:c) (26)

enamorarse like hablar (1)

encantar like hablar (1)

encontrar (o:ue) like contar (24)

enfermarse like hablar (1)

enojar(se) like hablar (1)

enseñar like hablar (1)

ensuciar like hablar (1)

entender (e:ie) (27)

entrenar(se) like hablar (1)

entrevistar like hablar (1)

enviar (envío) (39)

escalar like hablar (1)

escribir like vivir (3) *except* past participle is **escrito**

escuchar like hablar (1)

esperar like hablar (1)

esquiar (esquío) like enviar (39)

establecer (c:zc) like conocer (35)

estacionar like hablar (1)

C10

VERB CONJUGATION TABLES

estar (9)

estornudar like hablar (1)

estudiar like hablar (1)

evitar like hablar (1)

explicar (c:qu) like tocar (43)

faltar like hablar (1)

fascinar like hablar (1)

firmar like hablar (1)

fumar like hablar (1)

funcionar like hablar (1)

ganar like hablar (1)

gastar like hablar (1)

graduarse (gradúo) (40)

guardar like hablar (1)

gustar like hablar (1)

haber (hay) (10)

hablar (1)

hacer (11)

importar like hablar (1)

imprimir like vivir (3)

informar like hablar (1)

insistir like vivir (3)

interesar like hablar (1)

invertir (e:ie) like sentir (33)

invitar like hablar (1)

ir(se) (12)

jubilarse like hablar (1)

jugar (u:ue) (g:gu) (28)

lastimar(se) like hablar (1)

lavar(se) like hablar (1)

leer (y) like creer (36)

levantar(se) like hablar (1)

limpiar like hablar (1)

llamar(se) like hablar (1)

llegar (g:gu) (41)

llenar like hablar (1)

llevar(se) like hablar (1)

llover (o:ue) like volver (34)
  except past participle is regular

mandar like hablar (1)

manejar like hablar (1)

mantenerse (e:ie) like tener (20)

maquillar(se) like hablar (1)

mejorar like hablar (1)

merendar (e:ie) like pensar (30)

mirar like hablar (1)

molestar like hablar (1)

montar like hablar (1)

morir (o:ue) like dormir (25)
  except past participle is **muerto**

mostrar (o:ue) like contar (24)

mudarse like hablar (1)

nacer (c:zc) like conocer (35)

nadar like hablar (1)

navegar (g:gu) like llegar (41)

necesitar like hablar (1)

negar (e:ie) like pensar (30)
  except (g:gu)

nevar (e:ie) like pensar (30)

obtener (e:ie) like tener (20)

odiar like hablar (1)

ofrecer (c:zc) like conocer (35)

oír (y) (13)

olvidar like hablar (1)

pagar (g:gu) like llegar (41)

parar like hablar (1)

parecer (c:zc) like conocer (35)

pasar like hablar (1)

pasear like hablar (1)

patinar like hablar (1)

pedir (e:i) (29)

peinar(se) like hablar (1)

pensar (e:ie) (30)

perder (e:ie) like entender (27)

pescar (c:qu) like tocar (43)

pintar like hablar (1)

planchar like hablar (1)

poder (o:ue) (14)

poner(se) (15)

practicar (c:qu) like tocar (43)

preferir (e:ie) like sentir (33)

preguntar like hablar (1)

preocupar(se) like hablar (1)

preparar like hablar (1)

prestar like hablar (1)

probar(se) (o:ue) like contar (24)

prohibir like vivir (3)

proteger (g:j) (42)

quedar(se) like hablar (1)

querer (e:ie) (16)

quitar(se) like hablar (1)

recetar like hablar (1)

recibir like vivir (3)

reciclar like hablar (1)

recoger (g:j) like proteger (42)

recomendar (e:ie) like
  pensar (30)

recordar (o:ue) like contar (24)

reducir (c:zc) like conducir (6)

regalar like hablar (1)

regatear like hablar (1)

regresar like hablar (1)

reír(se) (e:i) (31)

relajarse like hablar (1)

renunciar like hablar (1)

repetir (e:i) like pedir (29)

resolver (o:ue) like volver (34)

respirar like hablar (1)

revisar like hablar (1)

rogar (o:ue) like contar (24)
  except (g:gu)

romper(se) like comer (2) *except*
  past participle is **roto**

saber (17)

sacar(se) (c:qu) like tocar (43)

sacudir like vivir (3)

salir (18)

seguir (e:i) (gu:g) (32)

sentarse (e:ie) like pensar (30)

sentir(se) (e:ie) (33)

separarse like hablar (1)

ser (19)

servir (e:i) like pedir (29)

solicitar like hablar (1)

sonar (o:ue) like contar (24)

sonreír (e:i) like reír(se) (31)

sorprender like comer (2)

subir like vivir (3)

sudar like hablar (1)

sufrir like vivir (3)

sugerir (e:ie) like sentir (33)

suponer like poner (15)

temer like comer (2)

tener (e:ie) (20)

terminar like hablar (1)

tomar like hablar (1)

torcerse (o:ue) like volver (34)
  except (c:z) and past participle is
  regular; e.g., **yo tuerzo**

toser like comer (2)

trabajar like hablar (1)

traducir (c:zc) like conducir (6)

traer (21)

transmitir like vivir (3)

tratar like hablar (1)

usar like hablar (1)

vender like comer (2)

venir (e:ie) (22)

ver (23)

vestir(se) (e:i) like pedir (29)

viajar like hablar (1)

visitar like hablar (1)

vivir (3)

volver (o:ue) (34)

VERB CONJUGATION TABLES

Regular verbs: simple tenses

Infinitive	INDICATIVE					SUBJUNCTIVE		IMPERATIVE
	Present	Imperfect	Preterite	Future	Conditional	Present	Past	
1 hablar	hablo	hablaba	hablé	hablaré	hablaría	hable	hablara	
Participles:	hablas	hablabas	hablaste	hablarás	hablarías	hables	hablaras	habla tú (no hables)
hablando	habla	hablaba	habló	hablará	hablaría	hable	hablara	hable Ud.
hablado	hablamos	hablábamos	hablamos	hablaremos	hablaríamos	hablemos	habláramos	hablemos
	habláis	hablabais	hablasteis	hablaréis	hablaríais	habléis	hablarais	hablad (no habléis)
	hablan	hablaban	hablaron	hablarán	hablarían	hablen	hablaran	hablen Uds.
2 comer	como	comía	comí	comeré	comería	coma	comiera	
Participles:	comes	comías	comiste	comerás	comerías	comas	comieras	come tú (no comas)
comiendo	come	comía	comió	comerá	comería	coma	comiera	coma Ud.
comido	comemos	comíamos	comimos	comeremos	comeríamos	comamos	comiéramos	comamos
	coméis	comíais	comisteis	comeréis	comeríais	comáis	comierais	comed (no comáis)
	comen	comían	comieron	comerán	comerían	coman	comieran	coman Uds.
3 vivir	vivo	vivía	viví	viviré	viviría	viva	viviera	
Participles:	vives	vivías	viviste	vivirás	vivirías	vivas	vivieras	vive tú (no vivas)
viviendo	vive	vivía	vivió	vivirá	viviría	viva	viviera	viva Ud.
vivido	vivimos	vivíamos	vivimos	viviremos	viviríamos	vivamos	viviéramos	vivamos
	vivís	vivíais	vivisteis	viviréis	viviríais	viváis	vivierais	vivid (no viváis)
	viven	vivían	vivieron	vivirán	vivirían	vivan	vivieran	vivan Uds.

All verbs: compound tenses

PERFECT TENSES

INDICATIVE								SUBJUNCTIVE			
Present Perfect		Past Perfect		Future Perfect		Conditional Perfect		Present Perfect		Past Perfect	
he	hablado	había	hablado	habré	hablado	habría	hablado	haya	hablado	hubiera	hablado
has	comido	habías	comido	habrás	comido	habrías	comido	hayas	comido	hubieras	comido
ha	vivido	había	vivido	habrá	vivido	habría	vivido	haya	vivido	hubiera	vivido
hemos		habíamos		habremos		habríamos		hayamos		hubiéramos	
habéis		habíais		habréis		habríais		hayáis		hubierais	
han		habían		habrán		habrían		hayan		hubieran	

C12

VERB CONJUGATION TABLES

PROGRESSIVE TENSES

INDICATIVE								SUBJUNCTIVE			
Present Progressive		**Past Progressive**		**Future Progressive**		**Conditional Progressive**		**Present Progressive**		**Past Progressive**	
estoy	hablando	estaba	hablando	estaré	hablando	estaría	hablando	esté	hablando	estuviera	hablando
estás	comiendo	estabas	comiendo	estarás	comiendo	estarías	comiendo	estés	comiendo	estuvieras	comiendo
está	viviendo	estaba	viviendo	estará	viviendo	estaría	viviendo	esté	viviendo	estuviera	viviendo
estamos		estábamos		estaremos		estaríamos		estemos		estuviéramos	
estáis		estabais		estaréis		estaríais		estéis		estuvierais	
están		estaban		estarán		estarían		estén		estuvieran	

Irregular verbs

Infinitive	INDICATIVE					SUBJUNCTIVE		IMPERATIVE
	Present	**Imperfect**	**Preterite**	**Future**	**Conditional**	**Present**	**Past**	
4 caber	**quepo**	cabía	**cupe**	**cabré**	**cabría**	**quepa**	**cupiera**	
	cabes	cabías	**cupiste**	**cabrás**	**cabrías**	**quepas**	**cupieras**	cabe tú (no **quepas**)
	cabe	cabía	**cupo**	**cabrá**	**cabría**	**quepa**	**cupiera**	**quepa** Ud.
Participles:	cabemos	cabíamos	**cupimos**	**cabremos**	**cabríamos**	**quepamos**	**cupiéramos**	**quepamos**
cabiendo	cabéis	cabíais	**cupisteis**	**cabréis**	**cabríais**	**quepáis**	**cupierais**	cabed (no **quepáis**)
cabido	caben	cabían	**cupieron**	**cabrán**	**cabrían**	**quepan**	**cupieran**	**quepan** Uds.
5 caer(se)	**caigo**	caía	caí	caeré	caería	**caiga**	**cayera**	
	caes	caías	**caíste**	caerás	caerías	**caigas**	**cayeras**	cae tú (no **caigas**)
	cae	caía	**cayó**	caerá	caería	**caiga**	**cayera**	**caiga** Ud. (no **caiga**)
Participles:	caemos	caíamos	**caímos**	caeremos	caeríamos	**caigamos**	**cayéramos**	**caigamos**
cayendo	caéis	caíais	**caísteis**	caeréis	caeríais	**caigáis**	**cayerais**	caed (no **caigáis**)
caído	caen	caían	**cayeron**	caerán	caerían	**caigan**	**cayeran**	**caigan** Uds.
6 conducir	**conduzco**	conducía	**conduje**	conduciré	conduciría	**conduzca**	**condujera**	
(c:zc)	conduces	conducías	**condujiste**	conducirás	conducirías	**conduzcas**	**condujeras**	conduce tú (no **conduzcas**)
Participles:	conduce	conducía	**condujo**	conducirá	conduciría	**conduzca**	**condujera**	**conduzca** Ud. (no **conduzca**)
conduciendo	conducimos	conducíamos	**condujimos**	conduciremos	conduciríamos	**conduzcamos**	**condujéramos**	**conduzcamos**
conducido	conducís	conducíais	**condujisteis**	conduciréis	conduciríais	**conduzcáis**	**condujerais**	conducid (no **conduzcáis**)
	conducen	conducían	**condujeron**	conducirán	conducirían	**conduzcan**	**condujeran**	**conduzcan** Uds.

C13

VERB CONJUGATION TABLES

7 dar

Infinitive: dar
Participles: dando, dado

	INDICATIVE					SUBJUNCTIVE		IMPERATIVE
	Present	Imperfect	Preterite	Future	Conditional	Present	Past	
	doy	daba	di	daré	daría	dé	diera	
	das	dabas	diste	darás	darías	des	dieras	da tú (no des)
	da	daba	dio	dará	daría	dé	diera	dé Ud.
	damos	dábamos	dimos	daremos	daríamos	demos	diéramos	demos
	dais	dabais	disteis	daréis	daríais	deis	dierais	dad (no deis)
	dan	daban	dieron	darán	darían	den	dieran	den Uds.

8 decir (e:i)

Infinitive: decir (e:i)
Participles: diciendo, dicho

	INDICATIVE					SUBJUNCTIVE		IMPERATIVE
	Present	Imperfect	Preterite	Future	Conditional	Present	Past	
	digo	decía	dije	diré	diría	diga	dijera	
	dices	decías	dijiste	dirás	dirías	digas	dijeras	di tú (no digas)
	dice	decía	dijo	dirá	diría	diga	dijera	diga Ud.
	decimos	decíamos	dijimos	diremos	diríamos	digamos	dijéramos	digamos
	decís	decíais	dijisteis	diréis	diríais	digáis	dijerais	decid (no digáis)
	dicen	decían	dijeron	dirán	dirían	digan	dijeran	digan Uds.

9 estar

Infinitive: estar
Participles: estando, estado

	INDICATIVE					SUBJUNCTIVE		IMPERATIVE
	Present	Imperfect	Preterite	Future	Conditional	Present	Past	
	estoy	estaba	estuve	estaré	estaría	esté	estuviera	
	estás	estabas	estuviste	estarás	estarías	estés	estuvieras	está tú (no estés)
	está	estaba	estuvo	estará	estaría	esté	estuviera	esté Ud.
	estamos	estábamos	estuvimos	estaremos	estaríamos	estemos	estuviéramos	estemos
	estáis	estabais	estuvisteis	estaréis	estaríais	estéis	estuvierais	estad (no estéis)
	están	estaban	estuvieron	estarán	estarían	estén	estuvieran	estén Uds.

10 haber

Infinitive: haber
Participles: habiendo, habido

	INDICATIVE					SUBJUNCTIVE		IMPERATIVE
	Present	Imperfect	Preterite	Future	Conditional	Present	Past	
	he	había	hube	habré	habría	haya	hubiera	
	has	habías	hubiste	habrás	habrías	hayas	hubieras	
	ha	había	hubo	habrá	habría	haya	hubiera	
	hemos	habíamos	hubimos	habremos	habríamos	hayamos	hubiéramos	
	habéis	habíais	hubisteis	habréis	habríais	hayáis	hubierais	
	han	habían	hubieron	habrán	habrían	hayan	hubieran	

11 hacer

Infinitive: hacer
Participles: haciendo, hecho

	INDICATIVE					SUBJUNCTIVE		IMPERATIVE
	Present	Imperfect	Preterite	Future	Conditional	Present	Past	
	hago	hacía	hice	haré	haría	haga	hiciera	
	haces	hacías	hiciste	harás	harías	hagas	hicieras	haz tú (no hagas)
	hace	hacía	hizo	hará	haría	haga	hiciera	haga Ud.
	hacemos	hacíamos	hicimos	haremos	haríamos	hagamos	hiciéramos	hagamos
	hacéis	hacíais	hicisteis	haréis	haríais	hagáis	hicierais	haced (no hagáis)
	hacen	hacían	hicieron	harán	harían	hagan	hicieran	hagan Uds.

12 ir

Infinitive: ir
Participles: yendo, ido

	INDICATIVE					SUBJUNCTIVE		IMPERATIVE
	Present	Imperfect	Preterite	Future	Conditional	Present	Past	
	voy	iba	fui	iré	iría	vaya	fuera	
	vas	ibas	fuiste	irás	irías	vayas	fueras	ve tú (no vayas)
	va	iba	fue	irá	iría	vaya	fuera	vaya Ud.
	vamos	íbamos	fuimos	iremos	iríamos	vayamos	fuéramos	vamos
	vais	ibais	fuisteis	iréis	iríais	vayáis	fuerais	id (no vayáis)
	van	iban	fueron	irán	irían	vayan	fueran	vayan Uds.

13 oír (y)

Infinitive: oír (y)
Participles: oyendo, oído

	INDICATIVE					SUBJUNCTIVE		IMPERATIVE
	Present	Imperfect	Preterite	Future	Conditional	Present	Past	
	oigo	oía	oí	oiré	oiría	oiga	oyera	
	oyes	oías	oíste	oirás	oirías	oigas	oyeras	oye tú (no oigas)
	oye	oía	oyó	oirá	oiría	oiga	oyera	oiga Ud.
	oímos	oíamos	oímos	oiremos	oiríamos	oigamos	oyéramos	oigamos
	oís	oíais	oísteis	oiréis	oiríais	oigáis	oyerais	oíd (no oigáis)
	oyen	oían	oyeron	oirán	oirían	oigan	oyeran	oigan Uds.

C14

VERB CONJUGATION TABLES

14 poder (o:ue) — Participles: pudiendo, podido

	Present	Imperfect	Preterite	Future	Conditional	Present (Subj.)	Past (Subj.)	Imperative
	puedo	podía	pude	podré	podría	pueda	pudiera	
	puedes	podías	pudiste	podrás	podrías	puedas	pudieras	puede tú (no puedas)
	puede	podía	pudo	podrá	podría	pueda	pudiera	pueda Ud.
	podemos	podíamos	pudimos	podremos	podríamos	podamos	pudiéramos	podamos
	podéis	podíais	pudisteis	podréis	podríais	podáis	pudierais	poded (no podáis)
	pueden	podían	pudieron	podrán	podrían	puedan	pudieran	puedan Uds.

15 poner — Participles: poniendo, puesto

	Present	Imperfect	Preterite	Future	Conditional	Present (Subj.)	Past (Subj.)	Imperative
	pongo	ponía	puse	pondré	pondría	ponga	pusiera	
	pones	ponías	pusiste	pondrás	pondrías	pongas	pusieras	pon tú (no pongas)
	pone	ponía	puso	pondrá	pondría	ponga	pusiera	ponga Ud.
	ponemos	poníamos	pusimos	pondremos	pondríamos	pongamos	pusiéramos	pongamos
	ponéis	poníais	pusisteis	pondréis	pondríais	pongáis	pusierais	poned (no pongáis)
	ponen	ponían	pusieron	pondrán	pondrían	pongan	pusieran	pongan Uds.

16 querer (e:ie) — Participles: queriendo, querido

	Present	Imperfect	Preterite	Future	Conditional	Present (Subj.)	Past (Subj.)	Imperative
	quiero	quería	quise	querré	querría	quiera	quisiera	
	quieres	querías	quisiste	querrás	querrías	quieras	quisieras	quiere tú (no quieras)
	quiere	quería	quiso	querrá	querría	quiera	quisiera	quiera Ud.
	queremos	queríamos	quisimos	querremos	querríamos	queramos	quisiéramos	queramos
	queréis	queríais	quisisteis	querréis	querríais	queráis	quisierais	quered (no queráis)
	quieren	querían	quisieron	querrán	querrían	quieran	quisieran	quieran Uds.

17 saber — Participles: sabiendo, sabido

	Present	Imperfect	Preterite	Future	Conditional	Present (Subj.)	Past (Subj.)	Imperative
	sé	sabía	supe	sabré	sabría	sepa	supiera	
	sabes	sabías	supiste	sabrás	sabrías	sepas	supieras	sabe tú (no sepas)
	sabe	sabía	supo	sabrá	sabría	sepa	supiera	sepa Ud.
	sabemos	sabíamos	supimos	sabremos	sabríamos	sepamos	supiéramos	sepamos
	sabéis	sabíais	supisteis	sabréis	sabríais	sepáis	supierais	sabed (no sepáis)
	saben	sabían	supieron	sabrán	sabrían	sepan	supieran	sepan Uds.

18 salir — Participles: saliendo, salido

	Present	Imperfect	Preterite	Future	Conditional	Present (Subj.)	Past (Subj.)	Imperative
	salgo	salía	salí	saldré	saldría	salga	saliera	
	sales	salías	saliste	saldrás	saldrías	salgas	salieras	sal tú (no salgas)
	sale	salía	salió	saldrá	saldría	salga	saliera	salga Ud.
	salimos	salíamos	salimos	saldremos	saldríamos	salgamos	saliéramos	salgamos
	salís	salíais	salisteis	saldréis	saldríais	salgáis	salierais	salid (no salgáis)
	salen	salían	salieron	saldrán	saldrían	salgan	salieran	salgan Uds.

19 ser — Participles: siendo, sido

	Present	Imperfect	Preterite	Future	Conditional	Present (Subj.)	Past (Subj.)	Imperative
	soy	era	fui	seré	sería	sea	fuera	
	eres	eras	fuiste	serás	serías	seas	fueras	sé tú (no seas)
	es	era	fue	será	sería	sea	fuera	sea Ud.
	somos	éramos	fuimos	seremos	seríamos	seamos	fuéramos	seamos
	sois	erais	fuisteis	seréis	seríais	seáis	fuerais	sed (no seáis)
	son	eran	fueron	serán	serían	sean	fueran	sean Uds.

20 tener (e:ie) — Participles: teniendo, tenido

	Present	Imperfect	Preterite	Future	Conditional	Present (Subj.)	Past (Subj.)	Imperative
	tengo	tenía	tuve	tendré	tendría	tenga	tuviera	
	tienes	tenías	tuviste	tendrás	tendrías	tengas	tuvieras	ten tú (no tengas)
	tiene	tenía	tuvo	tendrá	tendría	tenga	tuviera	tenga Ud.
	tenemos	teníamos	tuvimos	tendremos	tendríamos	tengamos	tuviéramos	tengamos
	tenéis	teníais	tuvisteis	tendréis	tendríais	tengáis	tuvierais	tened (no tengáis)
	tienen	tenían	tuvieron	tendrán	tendrían	tengan	tuvieran	tengan Uds.

C15

VERB CONJUGATION TABLES

21 traer
Participles: **trayendo**, **traído**

Infinitive	INDICATIVE					SUBJUNCTIVE		IMPERATIVE
	Present	Imperfect	Preterite	Future	Conditional	Present	Past	
traer	**traigo**	traía	**traje**	traeré	traería	**traiga**	**trajera**	
	traes	traías	**trajiste**	traerás	traerías	**traigas**	**trajeras**	trae tú (no **traigas**)
	trae	traía	**trajo**	traerá	traería	**traiga**	**trajera**	**traiga** Ud.
	traemos	traíamos	**trajimos**	traeremos	traeríamos	**traigamos**	**trajéramos**	**traigamos**
	traéis	traíais	**trajisteis**	traeréis	traeríais	**traigáis**	**trajerais**	traed (no **traigáis**)
	traen	traían	**trajeron**	traerán	traerían	**traigan**	**trajeran**	**traigan** Uds.

22 venir (e:ie)
Participles: **viniendo**, venido

Infinitive	INDICATIVE					SUBJUNCTIVE		IMPERATIVE
	Present	Imperfect	Preterite	Future	Conditional	Present	Past	
venir (e:ie)	**vengo**	venía	**vine**	**vendré**	**vendría**	**venga**	**viniera**	
	vienes	venías	**viniste**	**vendrás**	**vendrías**	**vengas**	**vinieras**	**ven** tú (no **vengas**)
	viene	venía	**vino**	**vendrá**	**vendría**	**venga**	**viniera**	**venga** Ud.
	venimos	veníamos	**vinimos**	**vendremos**	**vendríamos**	**vengamos**	**viniéramos**	**vengamos**
	venís	veníais	**vinisteis**	**vendréis**	**vendríais**	**vengáis**	**vinierais**	venid (no **vengáis**)
	vienen	venían	**vinieron**	**vendrán**	**vendrían**	**vengan**	**vinieran**	**vengan** Uds.

23 ver
Participles: viendo, **visto**

Infinitive	INDICATIVE					SUBJUNCTIVE		IMPERATIVE
	Present	Imperfect	Preterite	Future	Conditional	Present	Past	
ver	**veo**	**veía**	**vi**	veré	vería	**vea**	**viera**	
	ves	**veías**	**viste**	verás	verías	**veas**	**vieras**	**ve** tú (no **veas**)
	ve	**veía**	**vio**	verá	vería	**vea**	**viera**	**vea** Ud.
	vemos	**veíamos**	**vimos**	veremos	veríamos	**veamos**	**viéramos**	**veamos**
	veis	**veíais**	**visteis**	veréis	veríais	**veáis**	**vierais**	ved (no **veáis**)
	ven	**veían**	**vieron**	verán	verían	**vean**	**vieran**	**vean** Uds.

Stem-changing verbs

24 contar (o:ue)
Participles: contando, contado

Infinitive	INDICATIVE					SUBJUNCTIVE		IMPERATIVE
	Present	Imperfect	Preterite	Future	Conditional	Present	Past	
contar (o:ue)	**cuento**	contaba	conté	contaré	contaría	**cuente**	contara	
	cuentas	contabas	contaste	contarás	contarías	**cuentes**	contaras	**cuenta** tú (no **cuentes**)
	cuenta	contaba	contó	contará	contaría	**cuente**	contara	**cuente** Ud.
	contamos	contábamos	contamos	contaremos	contaríamos	contemos	contáramos	contemos
	contáis	contabais	contasteis	contaréis	contaríais	contéis	contarais	contad (no contéis)
	cuentan	contaban	contaron	contarán	contarían	**cuenten**	contaran	**cuenten** Uds.

25 dormir (o:ue)
Participles: **durmiendo**, dormido

Infinitive	INDICATIVE					SUBJUNCTIVE		IMPERATIVE
	Present	Imperfect	Preterite	Future	Conditional	Present	Past	
dormir (o:ue)	**duermo**	dormía	dormí	dormiré	dormiría	**duerma**	**durmiera**	
	duermes	dormías	dormiste	dormirás	dormirías	**duermas**	**durmieras**	**duerme** tú (no **duermas**)
	duerme	dormía	**durmió**	dormirá	dormiría	**duerma**	**durmiera**	**duerma** Ud.
	dormimos	dormíamos	dormimos	dormiremos	dormiríamos	**durmamos**	**durmiéramos**	**durmamos**
	dormís	dormíais	dormisteis	dormiréis	dormiríais	**durmáis**	**durmierais**	dormid (no **durmáis**)
	duermen	dormían	**durmieron**	dormirán	dormirían	**duerman**	**durmieran**	**duerman** Uds.

26 empezar (e:ie) (z:c)
Participles: empezando, empezado

Infinitive	INDICATIVE					SUBJUNCTIVE		IMPERATIVE
	Present	Imperfect	Preterite	Future	Conditional	Present	Past	
empezar (e:ie) (z:c)	**empiezo**	empezaba	**empecé**	empezaré	empezaría	**empiece**	empezara	
	empiezas	empezabas	empezaste	empezarás	empezarías	**empieces**	empezaras	**empieza** tú (no **empieces**)
	empieza	empezaba	empezó	empezará	empezaría	**empiece**	empezara	**empiece** Ud.
	empezamos	empezábamos	empezamos	empezaremos	empezaríamos	**empecemos**	empezáramos	**empecemos**
	empezáis	empezabais	empezasteis	empezaréis	empezaríais	**empecéis**	empezarais	empezad (no **empecéis**)
	empiezan	empezaban	empezaron	empezarán	empezarían	**empiecen**	empezaran	**empiecen** Uds.

C16

VERB CONJUGATION TABLES

27. entender (e:ie) — Participles: entendiendo, entendido

	INDICATIVE					SUBJUNCTIVE		IMPERATIVE
	Present	Imperfect	Preterite	Future	Conditional	Present	Past	
	entiendo	entendía	entendí	entenderé	entendería	entienda	entendiera	
	entiendes	entendías	entendiste	entenderás	entenderías	entiendas	entendieras	entiende tú (no entiendas)
	entiende	entendía	entendió	entenderá	entendería	entienda	entendiera	entienda Ud.
	entendemos	entendíamos	entendimos	entenderemos	entenderíamos	entendamos	entendiéramos	entendamos
	entendéis	entendíais	entendisteis	entenderéis	entenderíais	entendáis	entendierais	entended (no entendáis)
	entienden	entendían	entendieron	entenderán	entenderían	entiendan	entendieran	entiendan Uds.

28. jugar (u:ue) (g:gu) — Participles: jugando, jugado

	INDICATIVE					SUBJUNCTIVE		IMPERATIVE
	Present	Imperfect	Preterite	Future	Conditional	Present	Past	
	juego	jugaba	jugué	jugaré	jugaría	juegue	jugara	
	juegas	jugabas	jugaste	jugarás	jugarías	juegues	jugaras	juega tú (no juegues)
	juega	jugaba	jugó	jugará	jugaría	juegue	jugara	juegue Ud.
	jugamos	jugábamos	jugamos	jugaremos	jugaríamos	juguemos	jugáramos	juguemos
	jugáis	jugabais	jugasteis	jugaréis	jugaríais	juguéis	jugarais	jugad (no juguéis)
	juegan	jugaban	jugaron	jugarán	jugarían	jueguen	jugaran	jueguen Uds.

29. pedir (e:i) — Participles: pidiendo, pedido

	INDICATIVE					SUBJUNCTIVE		IMPERATIVE
	Present	Imperfect	Preterite	Future	Conditional	Present	Past	
	pido	pedía	pedí	pediré	pediría	pida	pidiera	
	pides	pedías	pediste	pedirás	pedirías	pidas	pidieras	pide tú (no pidas)
	pide	pedía	pidió	pedirá	pediría	pida	pidiera	pida Ud.
	pedimos	pedíamos	pedimos	pediremos	pediríamos	pidamos	pidiéramos	pidamos
	pedís	pedíais	pedisteis	pediréis	pediríais	pidáis	pidierais	pedid (no pidáis)
	piden	pedían	pidieron	pedirán	pedirían	pidan	pidieran	pidan Uds.

30. pensar (e:ie) — Participles: pensando, pensado

	INDICATIVE					SUBJUNCTIVE		IMPERATIVE
	Present	Imperfect	Preterite	Future	Conditional	Present	Past	
	pienso	pensaba	pensé	pensaré	pensaría	piense	pensara	
	piensas	pensabas	pensaste	pensarás	pensarías	pienses	pensaras	piensa tú (no pienses)
	piensa	pensaba	pensó	pensará	pensaría	piense	pensara	piense Ud.
	pensamos	pensábamos	pensamos	pensaremos	pensaríamos	pensemos	pensáramos	pensemos
	pensáis	pensabais	pensasteis	pensaréis	pensaríais	penséis	pensarais	pensad (no penséis)
	piensan	pensaban	pensaron	pensarán	pensarían	piensen	pensaran	piensen Uds.

31. reír(se) (e:i) — Participles: riendo, reído

	INDICATIVE					SUBJUNCTIVE		IMPERATIVE
	Present	Imperfect	Preterite	Future	Conditional	Present	Past	
	río	reía	reí	reiré	reiría	ría	riera	
	ríes	reías	reíste	reirás	reirías	rías	rieras	ríe tú (no rías)
	ríe	reía	rió	reirá	reiría	ría	riera	ría Ud.
	reímos	reíamos	reímos	reiremos	reiríamos	riamos	riéramos	riamos
	reís	reíais	reísteis	reiréis	reiríais	riáis	rierais	reíd (no riáis)
	ríen	reían	rieron	reirán	reirían	rían	rieran	rían Uds.

32. seguir (e:i) (gu:g) — Participles: siguiendo, seguido

	INDICATIVE					SUBJUNCTIVE		IMPERATIVE
	Present	Imperfect	Preterite	Future	Conditional	Present	Past	
	sigo	seguía	seguí	seguiré	seguiría	siga	siguiera	
	sigues	seguías	seguiste	seguirás	seguirías	sigas	siguieras	sigue tú (no sigas)
	sigue	seguía	siguió	seguirá	seguiría	siga	siguiera	siga Ud.
	seguimos	seguíamos	seguimos	seguiremos	seguiríamos	sigamos	siguiéramos	sigamos
	seguís	seguíais	seguisteis	seguiréis	seguiríais	sigáis	siguierais	seguid (no sigáis)
	siguen	seguían	siguieron	seguirán	seguirían	sigan	siguieran	sigan Uds.

33. sentir(se) (e:ie) — Participles: sintiendo, sentido

	INDICATIVE					SUBJUNCTIVE		IMPERATIVE
	Present	Imperfect	Preterite	Future	Conditional	Present	Past	
	siento	sentía	sentí	sentiré	sentiría	sienta	sintiera	
	sientes	sentías	sentiste	sentirás	sentirías	sientas	sintieras	siente tú (no sientas)
	siente	sentía	sintió	sentirá	sentiría	sienta	sintiera	sienta Ud.
	sentimos	sentíamos	sentimos	sentiremos	sentiríamos	sintamos	sintiéramos	sintamos
	sentís	sentíais	sentisteis	sentiréis	sentiríais	sintáis	sintierais	sentid (no sintáis)
	sienten	sentían	sintieron	sentirán	sentirían	sientan	sintieran	sientan Uds.

VERB CONJUGATION TABLES

34

Infinitive	INDICATIVE					SUBJUNCTIVE		IMPERATIVE
	Present	Imperfect	Preterite	Future	Conditional	Present	Past	
volver (o:ue)	**vuelvo**	volvía	volví	volveré	volvería	**vuelva**	volviera	
	vuelves	volvías	volviste	volverás	volverías	**vuelvas**	volvieras	**vuelve** tú (no **vuelvas**)
	vuelve	volvía	volvió	volverá	volvería	**vuelva**	volviera	**vuelva** Ud.
	volvemos	volvíamos	volvimos	volveremos	volveríamos	volvamos	volviéramos	volvamos
	volvéis	volvíais	volvisteis	volveréis	volveríais	volváis	volvierais	volved (no volváis)
Participles:	**vuelven**	volvían	volvieron	volverán	volverían	**vuelvan**	volvieran	**vuelvan** Uds.
volviendo								
vuelto								

Verbs with spelling changes only

35

Infinitive	INDICATIVE					SUBJUNCTIVE		IMPERATIVE
	Present	Imperfect	Preterite	Future	Conditional	Present	Past	
conocer (c:zc)	**conozco**	conocía	conocí	conoceré	conocería	**conozca**	conociera	
	conoces	conocías	conociste	conocerás	conocerías	**conozcas**	conocieras	conoce tú (no **conozcas**)
	conoce	conocía	conoció	conocerá	conocería	**conozca**	conociera	**conozca** Ud.
	conocemos	conocíamos	conocimos	conoceremos	conoceríamos	**conozcamos**	conociéramos	**conozcamos**
Participles:	conocéis	conocíais	conocisteis	conoceréis	conoceríais	**conozcáis**	conocierais	conoced (no **conozcáis**)
conociendo	conocen	conocían	conocieron	conocerán	conocerían	**conozcan**	conocieran	**conozcan** Uds.
conocido								

36

Infinitive	INDICATIVE					SUBJUNCTIVE		IMPERATIVE
	Present	Imperfect	Preterite	Future	Conditional	Present	Past	
creer (y)	creo	creía	creí	creeré	creería	crea	**creyera**	
	crees	creías	**creíste**	creerás	creerías	creas	**creyeras**	cree tú (no creas)
	cree	creía	**creyó**	creerá	creería	crea	**creyera**	crea Ud.
	creemos	creíamos	**creímos**	creeremos	creeríamos	creamos	**creyéramos**	creamos
Participles:	creéis	creíais	**creísteis**	creeréis	creeríais	creáis	**creyerais**	creed (no creáis)
creyendo	creen	creían	**creyeron**	creerán	creerían	crean	**creyeran**	crean Uds.
creído								

37

Infinitive	INDICATIVE					SUBJUNCTIVE		IMPERATIVE
	Present	Imperfect	Preterite	Future	Conditional	Present	Past	
cruzar (z:c)	cruzo	cruzaba	**crucé**	cruzaré	cruzaría	**cruce**	cruzara	
	cruzas	cruzabas	cruzaste	cruzarás	cruzarías	**cruces**	cruzaras	cruza tú (no **cruces**)
	cruza	cruzaba	cruzó	cruzará	cruzaría	**cruce**	cruzara	**cruce** Ud.
	cruzamos	cruzábamos	cruzamos	cruzaremos	cruzaríamos	**crucemos**	cruzáramos	**crucemos**
Participles:	cruzáis	cruzabais	cruzasteis	cruzaréis	cruzaríais	**crucéis**	cruzarais	cruzad (no **crucéis**)
cruzando	cruzan	cruzaban	cruzaron	cruzarán	cruzarían	**crucen**	cruzaran	**crucen** Uds.
cruzado								

38

Infinitive	INDICATIVE					SUBJUNCTIVE		IMPERATIVE
	Present	Imperfect	Preterite	Future	Conditional	Present	Past	
destruir (y)	**destruyo**	destruía	destruí	destruiré	destruiría	**destruya**	**destruyera**	
	destruyes	destruías	destruiste	destruirás	destruirías	**destruyas**	**destruyeras**	**destruye** tú (no **destruyas**)
	destruye	destruía	**destruyó**	destruirá	destruiría	**destruya**	**destruyera**	**destruya** Ud.
	destruimos	destruíamos	destruimos	destruiremos	destruiríamos	**destruyamos**	**destruyéramos**	**destruyamos**
Participles:	destruís	destruíais	destruisteis	destruiréis	destruiríais	**destruyáis**	**destruyerais**	destruid (no **destruyáis**)
destruyendo	**destruyen**	destruían	**destruyeron**	destruirán	destruirían	**destruyan**	**destruyeran**	**destruyan** Uds.
destruido								

39

Infinitive	INDICATIVE					SUBJUNCTIVE		IMPERATIVE
	Present	Imperfect	Preterite	Future	Conditional	Present	Past	
enviar (envío)	**envío**	enviaba	envié	enviaré	enviaría	**envíe**	enviara	
	envías	enviabas	enviaste	enviarás	enviarías	**envíes**	enviaras	**envía** tú (no **envíes**)
	envía	enviaba	envió	enviará	enviaría	**envíe**	enviara	**envíe** Ud.
	enviamos	enviábamos	enviamos	enviaremos	enviaríamos	**enviemos**	enviáramos	**enviemos**
Participles:	enviáis	enviabais	enviasteis	enviaréis	enviaríais	**enviéis**	enviarais	enviad (no **enviéis**)
enviando	**envían**	enviaban	enviaron	enviarán	enviarían	**envíen**	enviaran	**envíen** Uds.
enviado								

C18

VERB CONJUGATION TABLES

40

Infinitive	INDICATIVE					SUBJUNCTIVE		IMPERATIVE
	Present	Imperfect	Preterite	Future	Conditional	Present	Past	
graduarse (gradúo)	gradúo	graduaba	gradué	graduaré	graduaría	gradúe	graduara	
	gradúas	graduabas	graduaste	graduarás	graduarías	gradúes	graduaras	gradúa tú (no gradúes)
	gradúa	graduaba	graduó	graduará	graduaría	gradúe	graduara	gradúe Ud.
Participles:	graduamos	graduábamos	graduamos	graduaremos	graduaríamos	graduemos	graduáramos	graduemos
graduando	graduáis	graduabais	graduasteis	graduaréis	graduaríais	graduéis	graduarais	graduad (no graduéis)
graduado	gradúan	graduaban	graduaron	graduarán	graduarían	gradúen	graduaran	gradúen Uds.

41

Infinitive	INDICATIVE					SUBJUNCTIVE		IMPERATIVE
	Present	Imperfect	Preterite	Future	Conditional	Present	Past	
llegar (g:gu)	llego	llegaba	llegué	llegaré	llegaría	llegue	llegara	
	llegas	llegabas	llegaste	llegarás	llegarías	llegues	llegaras	llega tú (no llegues)
	llega	llegaba	llegó	llegará	llegaría	llegue	llegara	llegue Ud.
Participles:	llegamos	llegábamos	llegamos	llegaremos	llegaríamos	lleguemos	llegáramos	lleguemos
llegando	llegáis	llegabais	llegasteis	llegaréis	llegaríais	lleguéis	llegarais	llegad (no lleguéis)
llegado	llegan	llegaban	llegaron	llegarán	llegarían	lleguen	llegaran	lleguen Uds.

42

Infinitive	INDICATIVE					SUBJUNCTIVE		IMPERATIVE
	Present	Imperfect	Preterite	Future	Conditional	Present	Past	
proteger (g:j)	protejo	protegía	protegí	protegeré	protegería	proteja	protegiera	
	proteges	protegías	protegiste	protegerás	protegerías	protejas	protegieras	protege tú (no protejas)
	protege	protegía	protegió	protegerá	protegería	proteja	protegiera	proteja Ud.
Participles:	protegemos	protegíamos	protegimos	protegeremos	protegeríamos	protejamos	protegiéramos	protejamos
protegiendo	protegéis	protegíais	protegisteis	protegeréis	protegeríais	protejáis	protegierais	proteged (no protejáis)
protegido	protegen	protegían	protegieron	protegerán	protegerían	protejan	protegieran	protejan Uds.

43

Infinitive	INDICATIVE					SUBJUNCTIVE		IMPERATIVE
	Present	Imperfect	Preterite	Future	Conditional	Present	Past	
tocar (c:qu)	toco	tocaba	toqué	tocaré	tocaría	toque	tocara	
	tocas	tocabas	tocaste	tocarás	tocarías	toques	tocaras	toca tú (no toques)
	toca	tocaba	tocó	tocará	tocaría	toque	tocara	toque Ud.
Participles:	tocamos	tocábamos	tocamos	tocaremos	tocaríamos	toquemos	tocáramos	toquemos
tocando	tocáis	tocabais	tocasteis	tocaréis	tocaríais	toquéis	tocarais	tocad (no toquéis)
tocado	tocan	tocaban	tocaron	tocarán	tocarían	toquen	tocaran	toquen Uds.

VOCABULARIO

Guide to Vocabulary

Note on alphabetization

For purposes of alphabetization, **ch** and **ll** are not treated as separate letters, but **ñ** still follows **n**. Therefore, in this glossary you will find that **año**, for example, appears after **anuncio**.

Abbreviations used in this glossary

adj.	adjective	*form.*	formal	*pl.*	plural
adv.	adverb	*indef.*	indefinite	*poss.*	possessive
art.	article	*interj.*	interjection	*prep.*	preposition
conj.	conjunction	*i.o.*	indirect object	*pron.*	pronoun
def.	definite	*m.*	masculine	*ref.*	reflexive
d.o.	direct object	*n.*	noun	*sing.*	singular
f.	feminine	*obj.*	object	*sub.*	subject
fam.	familiar	*p.p.*	past participle	*v.*	verb

Spanish-English

A

a *prep.* at; to 1
  ¿A qué hora...? At what time...? 1, 9
  a bordo aboard 1
  a dieta on a diet 15
  a la derecha de to the right of 2
  a la izquierda de to the left of 2
  a la plancha grilled 8
  a la(s) + *time* at + *time* 1
  a menos que unless 13
  a menudo often 10
  a mi nombre in my name
  a nombre de in the name of
  a plazos in installments 14
  A sus órdenes. At your service.
  a tiempo on time 10
  a veces sometimes 10
  a ver let's see 2
abajo *adv.* down
abeja *f.* bee
abierto/a *adj.* open 5; *p.p.*
  opened 15
abogado/a *m., f.* lawyer 16
abrazar(se) *v.* to hug; to embrace
  (each other)
abrazo *m.* hug
abrigo *m.* coat 6
abril *m.* April 5
abrir *v.* to open 3
abuelo/a *m., f.* grandfather;
  grandmother 3
abuelos *pl.* grandparents 3
aburrido/a *adj.* bored; boring 5
aburrir *v.* to bore 7
aburrirse *v.* to get bored
acabar de (+ *inf.*) *v.* to have just (*done*

  something) 6
acampar *v.* to camp 5
accidente *m.* accident 10
acción *f.* action
aceite *m.* oil 8
ácido/a *adj.* acid 13
acompañar *v.* to go with; to accompany 14
aconsejar *v.* to advise 12
acontecimiento *m.* event
acordarse *v.* **(de) (o:ue)** to remember 7
acostarse (o:ue) *v.* to lie down;
  to go to bed 7
activo/a *adj.* active 15
actor *m.* actor 16
actriz *f.* actress 16
actualidades *f., pl.* news; current events
acuático/a *adj.* aquatic 4
adelgazar *v.* to lose weight; to slim
  down 15
además (de) *adv.* furthermore; besides 10;
  in addition (to)
adicional *adj.* additional
Adiós. *m.* Goodbye. 1
adjetivo *m.* adjective
administración *f.* **de empresas**
  business administration 2
adolescencia *f.* adolescence 9
¿adónde? *adv.* where (to)?
  (*destination*) 2, 9
aduana *f.* customs 5
aeróbico/a *adj.* aerobic 15
aeropuerto *m.* airport 5
afectado/a *adj.* affected 13
afeitarse *v.* to shave 7
aficionado/a *adj.* fan 4
afirmativo/a *adj.* affirmative
afueras *f., pl.* suburbs; outskirts 12
agencia *f.* **de bienes raíces** real estate
  agency 12
agencia de viajes *f.* travel agency 5

agente de viajes *m., f.* travel agent 5
agosto *m.* August 5
agradable *adj.* pleasant
agrio/a *adj.* sour 8
agua *f.* water 8
  agua mineral mineral water 8
ahora *adv.* now
  ahora mismo right now 5
ahorrar *v.* to save money 14
ahorros *m., pl.* savings 14
aire *m.* air 6
ajo *m.* garlic
al (*contraction of* **a + el**) 4
  al aire libre open-air 6
  al contado in cash 14
  (al) este (to the) east 14
  al fondo (de) at the end (of)
  al lado de next to; beside 2
  (al) norte (to the) north 14
  (al) oeste (to the) west 14
  (al) sur (to the) south 14
alcoba *f.* bedroom 12
alcohol *m.* alcohol 15
alcohólico/a *adj.* alcoholic 15
alegrarse *v.* **(de)** to be happy 13
alegre *adj.* happy; joyful 5
alegría *f.* happiness 9
alemán, alemana *adj.* German 3
alérgico/a *adj.* allergic 10
alfombra *f.* carpet; rug 12
algo *pron.* something; anything 7
algodón *m.* cotton 6
alguien *pron.* someone; anyone 7
algún, alguno/a(s) *adj.* any; some 7
aliviar *v.* to relieve 15
  aliviar el estrés/la tensión
    to relieve stress/tension 15
allí *adv.* there 5
  allí mismo right there 14
almacén *m.* department store 6

C20

Spanish-English

almohada *f.* pillow 12
almorzar (o:ue) *v.* to have lunch 8
almuerzo *m.* lunch 8
¿Aló? *interj.* Hello?
   (*on the telephone*) 11
alojamiento *m.* lodging 5
alquilar *v.* to rent 12
alquiler *m.* rent 12
alternador *m.* alternator
altillo *m.* attic 12
alto/a *adj.* tall 3
aluminio *m.* aluminum 13
amable *adj.* nice; friendly 5
ama *f.* **de casa** homemaker; housekeeper
   12; housewife
amarillo/a *adj.* yellow 6
amigo/a *m., f.* friend 3
amistad *f.* friendship 9
amor *m.* love 9
anaranjado/a *adj.* orange 6
animal *m.* animal 13
aniversario (de bodas) *m.* (wedding)
   anniversary 9
anoche *adv.* last night 6
anteayer *adv.* the day before yesterday 6
antes *adv.* before 7
   antes de *prep.* before 7
   antes (de) que *conj.* before 13
antibiótico *m.* antibiotic 10
antipático/a *adj.* unpleasant 3
anunciar *v.* to announce; to advertise
anuncio *m.* advertisement 16
año *m.* year 5
   el año pasado last year 6
apagar *v.* to turn off 11
aparato *m.* appliance 12
apartamento *m.* apartment 12
apellido *m.* last name 9
apenas *adv.* hardly; scarcely; just 10
aplaudir *v.* to applaud
apreciar *v.* to appreciate
aprender *v.* to learn 3
apurarse *v.* to hurry; to rush 15
aquel, aquella *adj.* that; those (over
   there) 6
aquél, aquélla *pron.* that; those (over
   there) 6
aquello *neuter, pron.* that; that thing;
   that fact 6
aquellos/as *pl. adj.* that; those
   (over there) 6
aquéllos/as *pl. pron.* those (ones)
   (over there) 6
aquí *adv.* here 1
   Aquí está... Here it is... 5
      Aquí estamos en... Here we are
         at/in... 2
      aquí mismo right here
árbol *m.* tree 13
archivo *m.* file 11
armario *m.* closet 12

arqueólogo/a *m., f.* archaeologist 16
arquitecto/a *m., f.* architect 16
arrancar *v.* to start (*a car*) 11
arreglar *v.* to fix; to arrange 11;
   to clean up 12
arriba *adv.* up
arroz *m.* rice 8
arte *m.* art 2
artes *f., pl.* arts
artesanía *f.* craftsmanship; crafts
artículo *m.* article
artista *m., f.* artist 3
artístico/a *adj.* artistic
arveja *m.* pea 8
asado/a *adj.* roasted 8
ascenso *m.* promotion 16
ascensor *m.* elevator 5
así *adj.* like this; so (*in such a way*) 10
   así así so-so
asistir (a) *v.* to attend 3
aspiradora *f.* vacuum cleaner 12
aspirante *m., f.* candidate; applicant 16
aspirina *f.* aspirin 10
atún *m.* tuna 8
aumentar *v.* **de peso** to gain weight 15
aumento *m.* increase 16
   aumento de sueldo pay raise 16
aunque *conj.* although
autobús *m.* bus 1
automático/a *adj.* automatic 14
auto(móvil) *m.* auto(mobile) 5
autopista *f.* highway
ave *f.* bird
avenida *f.* avenue
aventura *f.* adventure
avergonzado/a *adj.* embarrassed 5
avión *m.* airplane 5
¡Ay! *interj.* Oh!
   ¡Ay, qué dolor! Oh, what pain!
ayer *adv.* yesterday 6
ayudar *v.* to help 12
ayudarse *v.* to help each other
azúcar *m.* sugar 8
azul *adj.* blue 6

B

bailar *v.* to dance 2
bailarín/bailarina *m., f.* dancer 16
baile *m.* dance
bajar *v.* to go down 11
bajar(se) de *v.* to get off of/out of
   (a vehicle) 11
bajo/a *adj.* short (*in height*) 3
   bajo control under control
balcón *m.* balcony 12
ballena *f.* whale 13
ballet *m.* ballet
baloncesto *m.* basketball 4
banana *f.* banana 8

banco *m.* bank 14
banda *f.* band
bandera *f.* flag
bañarse *v.* to bathe; to take a bath 7
baño *m.* bathroom 7
barato/a *adj.* cheap 6
barco *m.* boat 5
barrer *v.* to sweep 12
   barrer el suelo to sweep the floor 12
barrio *m.* neighborhood 12
bastante *adv.* enough; quite 10; pretty
basura *f.* trash 12
baúl *m.* trunk 11
beber *v.* to drink 3
bebida *f.* drink 8
   bebida alcohólica alcoholic
      beverage 15
béisbol *m.* baseball 4
bellas artes *f., pl.* fine arts
belleza *f.* beauty 14
beneficio *m.* benefit 16
besar(se) *v.* to kiss (each other)
beso *m.* kiss 6
biblioteca *f.* library 2
bicicleta *f.* bicycle 4
bien *adj.* good; well 1
bienestar *m.* well-being 15
¡Bienvenido(s)/a(s)! *adj.* Welcome! 1
billete *m.* money (*paper*)
billón *m.* trillion 6
biología *f.* biology 2
bistec *m.* steak 8
bizcocho *m.* biscuit
blanco/a *adj.* white 6
bluejeans *m., pl.* jeans 6
blusa *f.* blouse 6
boca *f.* mouth 10
boda *f.* wedding 9
boleto *m.* ticket
bolsa *f.* bag; purse 6
bombero/a *m., f.* firefighter 16
bonito/a *adj.* pretty 3
borrador *m.* eraser 2
bosque *m.* forest 13
   bosque tropical tropical forest;
      rainforest 13
bota *f.* boot 6
botella *f.* bottle 9
   botella de vino bottle of wine 9
botones *m., f., sing.* bellhop 5
brazo *m.* arm 10
brindar *v.* to toast (*drink*) 9
bucear *v.* to scuba dive 4
bueno... *adv.* well...
buen, bueno/a *adj.* good 3, 6
   ¡Buen viaje! Have a good trip!
   buena forma good shape (*physical*) 15
   ¡Buena idea! Good idea! 4
   Buenas noches. Good evening;
      Good night. 1
   Buenas tardes. Good afternoon. 1

C21

VOCABULARIO

buenísimo extremely good
¿Bueno? Hello? (*on telephone*) 11
Buenos días. Good morning. 1
bulevar *m.* boulevard
buscar *v.* to look for 2
buzón *m.* mailbox 14
   buzón de voz voicemail 11

C

caballo *m.* horse 5
cabaña *f.* cabin 5
cabe: no cabe duda de there's no
   doubt 13
cabeza *f.* head 10
cada *adj.* each 6
caerse *v.* to fall (down) 10
café *m.* café 4; *adj.* brown 6; coffee 8
cafetera *f.* coffee maker
cafetería *f.* cafeteria 2
caído/a *p.p.* fallen 15
caja *f.* cash register 6
cajero/a *m., f.* cashier
   cajero automático automatic teller
     machine (ATM) 14
calcetín *m.* sock 6
calculadora *f.* calculator 11
caldo *m.* soup
   caldo de patas beef soup
calentamiento global *m.* global
   warming 13
calentarse (e:ie) *v.* to warm up 15
calidad *f.* quality 6
calle *f.* street 11
calor *m.* heat 3
caloría *f.* calorie 15
calzar *v.* to take size ... shoes 6
cama *f.* bed 5
cámara *f.* camera 11
   cámara de video videocamera 11
   cámara digital digital camera 11
camarero/a *m., f.* waiter 8
camarón *m.* shrimp 8
cambiar *v.* **(de)** to change 9
cambio *m.* **de moneda** currency exchange
caminar *v.* to walk 2
camino *m.* route 11
camión *m.* truck; bus
camisa *f.* shirt 6
camiseta *f.* t-shirt 6
campo *m.* countryside 5
canadiense *adj.* Canadian 3
canal *m.* channel (*TV*)
canción *f.* song
candidato/a *m., f.* candidate
cansado/a *adj.* tired 5
cantante *m., f.* singer 16
cantar *v.* to sing 2
capital *f.* capital city 1

capó *m.* (car) hood 11
cara *f.* face 7
caramelo *m.* caramel
carne *f.* meat 8
   carne de res beef 8
carnicería *f.* butcher's shop 14
caro/a *adj.* expensive 6
carpintero/a *m., f.* carpenter 16
carrera *f.* career 16
carretera *f.* highway
carro *m.* car 11
carta *f.* letter 4; (playing) card
cartel *m.* poster
cartera *f.* wallet 6
cartero *m.* mail carrier 14
casa *f.* house 4; home
casado/a *adj.* married 9
casarse *v.* **(con)** to get married (to) 9
casi *adv.* almost 10
catorce fourteen 1
caza *f.* hunting 13
cebolla *f.* onion 8
celebrar *v.* to celebrate 9
cena *f.* dinner 8
cenar *v.* to have dinner 8
centro *m.* downtown 4
   centro comercial shopping
     mall 6
cepillarse los dientes/el pelo *v.* to brush
   one's teeth/one's hair 7
cerámica *f.* pottery
cerca de *prep.* near 2
cerdo *m.* pork 8
cereales *m., pl.* cereal; grains 8
cero zero 1
cerrado/a *adj.* closed 5
cerrar (e:ie) *v.* to close 4
cerveza *f.* beer 8
césped *m.* grass 13
ceviche *m.* dish of lemon-marinated fish
   ceviche de camarón
     lemon-marinated shrimp
chaleco *m.* vest
champán *m.* champagne 9
champiñón *m.* mushroom 8
champú *m.* shampoo 7
chaqueta *f.* jacket 6
Chau. *fam., interj.* Bye. 1
cheque *m.* (bank) check 14
   cheque de viajero traveler's check 14
chévere *adj., fam.* terrific
chico/a *m., f.* boy/girl 1
chino/a *adj.* Chinese
chocar *v.* **(con)** to run into; to crash 11
chocolate *m.* chocolate
choque *m.* collision
chuleta *f.* chop (*food*) 8
   chuleta de cerdo pork chop 8
ciclismo *m.* cycling 4
cielo *m.* sky 13

cien(to) one hundred 2, 6
   por ciento percent
ciencia *f.* science
   ciencia ficción science fiction
científico/a *m., f.* scientist 16
cierto *m.* certain; true 13
   es cierto it's true/certain 13
   no es cierto it's not true/certain 13
cifra *f.* figure
cinco five 1
cincuenta fifty 2
cine *m.* movie theater 4
cinta *f.* (audio) tape
cinturón *m.* belt 6
circulación *f.* traffic
cita *f.* date; appointment 9
ciudad *f.* city 4
ciudadano/a *adj.* citizen
claro que sí *fam.* of course
clase *f.* class 2
   clase de ejercicios aeróbicos
     aerobics class 15
clásico/a *adj.* classical
cliente/a *m., f.* client 6
clínica *f.* clinic 10
cobrar *v.* to cash a check 14;
   to charge for a product or service 14
coche *m.* car 11
cocina *f.* kitchen 12; stove
cocinar *v.* to cook 12
cocinero/a *m., f.* cook, chef 16
cola *f.* line 14
colesterol *m.* cholesterol 15
color *m.* color 6
comedia *f.* comedy; play
comedor *m.* dining room 12
comenzar (e:ie) *v.* to begin 4
comer *v.* to eat 3
comercial *adj.* commercial;
   business-related 16
comida *f.* food; meal 8
como *adv.* like, as 8
¿cómo? *adv.* what?; how? 1, 9
   ¿Cómo es...? What's... like?
   ¿Cómo está usted? How are you?
     (*form.*) 1
   ¿Cómo estás? How are you?
     (*fam.*) 1
   ¿Cómo les fue...? *pl.* How did...
     go for you? 15
   ¿Cómo se llama usted?
     What's your name? (*form.*) 1
   ¿Cómo te llamas (tú)?
     What's your name? (*fam.*) 1
cómoda *f.* chest of drawers 12
cómodo/a *adj.* comfortable 5
compañero/a *m., f.* **de clase** classmate 2
compañero/a *m., f.* **de cuarto**
   roommate 2
compañía *f.* company; firm 16

C22

Spanish-English

compartir *v.* to share 3
completamente *adv.* completely
compositor(a) *m., f.* composer
comprar *v.* to buy 2
compras *f., pl.* purchases
   ir *v.* **de compras** to go shopping
comprender *v.* to understand 3
comprobar *v.* to check
comprometerse *v.* **(con)** to get engaged
   (to) 9
computación *f.* computer science 2
computadora *f.* computer 1, 11
   computadora portátil laptop 11
comunicación *f.* communication
comunicarse *v.* **(con)** to communicate
   (with)
comunidad *f.* community 1
con *prep.* with
   Con él/ella habla. This is
     he/she. *(on telephone)* 11
   con frecuencia *adv.* frequently 10
   Con permiso. Pardon me., Excuse me. 1
   con tal (de) que provided that 13
concierto *m.* concert
concordar *v.* to agree
concurso *m.* contest; game show
conducir *v.* to drive 8, 11
conductor(a) *m., f.* driver, chauffeur 1
conexión *f.* **inalámbrica** wireless
   (connection) 11
confirmar *v.* to confirm 5
   confirmar una reservación to confirm
     a reservation 5
congelador *m.* freezer
congestionado/a *adj.* congested;
   stuffed-up 10
conmigo *pron.* with me 4
conocer *v.* to know; to be acquainted
   with 8
conocido/a *adj.* known
conseguir (e:i) *v.* to get; to obtain 4
consejero/a *m., f.* counselor; advisor 16
consejo *m.* advice 9
conservación *f.* conservation 13
conservar *v.* to conserve 13
construir *v.* to build
consultorio *m.* doctor's office 10
consumir *v.* to consume 15
contabilidad *f.* accounting 2
contador(a) *m., f.* accountant 16
contaminación *f.* pollution 13;
   contamination
   contaminación del aire/del
     agua air/water pollution 13
contaminado/a *adj.* polluted 13
contaminar *v.* to pollute 13
contar *v.* **(con)** to count (on) 12
contento/a *adj.* happy; content 5
contestar *v.* to answer 2
contigo *pron.* with you

contratar *v.* to hire 16
control *m.* control
   control remoto remote control 11
controlar *v.* to control 13
conversación *f.* conversation 1
conversar *v.* to talk; to chat 2
copa *f.* wineglass; goblet 12
corazón *m.* heart 10
corbata *f.* tie 6
corredor(a) *m., f.* **de bolsa** stockbroker 16
correo *m.* post office; mail 14
   correo electrónico e-mail 4
correr *v.* to run 3
cortesía *f.* courtesy
cortinas *f., pl.* curtains 12
corto/a *adj.* short *(in length)* 6
cosa *f.* thing 1
costar (o:ue) *f.* to cost 6
cráter *m.* crater 13
creer *v.* to believe 13
   creer *v.* **(en)** to believe (in) 3
creído/a *p.p.* believed
crema *f.* **de afeitar** shaving cream 7
crimen *m.* crime; murder
cruzar *v.* to cross 14
cuaderno *m.* notebook 1
cuadra *f.* city block 14
cuadro *m.* picture 12
cuadros *m., pl.* plaid 6
¿cuál(es)? *adj., pron.* which?; which
   one(s)? 2; what? 9
   ¿Cuál es la fecha de hoy?
     What is today's date? 5
cuando *conj.* when 7
¿cuándo? *adv.* when? 2, 9
¿Cuántos/as? *pron.* How much?;
   How many? 1, 9
   ¿Cuánto cuesta…? How much
     does… cost? 6
   ¿Cuántos años tienes/tiene?
     How old are you? 3
cuarenta forty 2
cuarto *m.* room
cuarto/a *adj.* quarter 1; fourth 5
   menos cuarto quarter to (time) 1
   y cuarto quarter after (time) 1
cuarto de baño *m.* bathroom
cuatro four 1
cuatrocientos/as four hundred 6
cubiertos *m., pl.* silverware
cubierto/a *p.p.* covered
cubrir *v.* to cover
cuchara *f.* spoon 12
cuchillo *m.* knife 12
cuello *m.* neck 10
cuenta *f.* bill; account 14
   cuenta corriente checking account 14
   cuenta de ahorros savings account 14
cuento *m.* story
cuerpo *m.* body 10

cuidado *m.* care 3
cuidar *v.* to take care of 13
¡Cuídense! Take care!
cultura *f.* culture
cumpleaños *m., sing.* birthday 9
cumplir *v.* **años** to have a birthday 9
cuñado/a *m., f.* brother-in-law;
   sister-in-law 3
currículum *m.* résumé 16;
   curriculum vitae
curso *m.* course 2

D

danza *f.* dance
dañar *v.* to damage; to break down 10
dar *v.* to give 6
   dar un consejo to give advice
   darse *v.* **con** to bump into; to
     run into (something)
   darse prisa to hurry; to rush 15
de *prep.* of; from 1
   ¿de dónde? from where? 9
   ¿De dónde eres? *fam.* Where are
     you from? 1
   ¿De dónde es (usted)? *form.* Where
     are you from? 1
   ¿De parte de quién? Who is
     calling? *(on telephone)* 11
   ¿de quién…? *sing.* whose…? 1
   ¿de quiénes…? *pl.* whose…? 1
   de algodón (made of) cotton 6
   de aluminio (made of) aluminum 13
   de compras shopping
   de cuadros plaid 6
   de excursión hiking 4
   de hecho in fact
   de ida y vuelta round-trip 5
   de la mañana in the morning;
     A.M. 1
   de la noche in the evening; at
     night; P.M. 1
   de la tarde in the afternoon; in the
     early evening; P.M. 1
   de lana (made of) wool 6
   de lunares polka-dotted 6
   de mi vida of my life
   de moda in fashion 6
   De nada. You're welcome. 1
   de ninguna manera no way
   de niño/a as a child 10
   de parte de on behalf of
   de plástico (made of) plastic 13
   de rayas striped 6
   de repente suddenly 6
   de seda (made of) silk 6
   de vaqueros western (genre)
   de vez en cuando from time to time 10
   de vidrio (made of) glass 13

C23

VOCABULARIO

debajo de *prep.* below; under 2
deber (+ inf.) *v.* to have to (*do something*), should (*do something*) 3
    Debe ser… It must be… 6
deber *m.* responsibility; obligation
debido a due to; the fact that
débil *adj.* weak 15
decidido/a *p.p., adj.* decided
decidir *v.* to decide 3
décimo/a *adj.* tenth 5
decir *v.* to say; to tell 6
declarar *v.* to declare; to say
dedo *m.* finger 10
deforestación *f.* deforestation 13
dejar *v.* to let 12; to quit; to leave behind 16
    dejar de (+ inf.) to stop (*doing something*) 13
    dejar una propina to leave a tip
del (*contraction of* **de + el)** of the; from the
delante de *prep.* in front of 2
delgado/a *adj.* thin; slender 3
delicioso/a *adj.* delicious 8
demás *pron.* the rest
demasiado *adv.* too much 6
dentista *m., f.* dentist 10
dentro de *adv.* within
dependiente/a *m., f.* clerk 6
deporte *m.* sport 4
deportista *m.* sports person
deportivo/a *adj.* sports-related 4
depositar *v.* to deposit 14
derecha *f.* right 2
    a la derecha de to the right of 2
derecho *adj.* straight (ahead) 14
derechos *m., pl.* rights
desarrollar *v.* to develop 13
desastre natural *m.* natural disaster
desayunar *v.* to have breakfast 8
desayuno *m.* breakfast 8
descafeinado/a *adj.* decaffeinated 15
descansar *v.* to rest 2
descompuesto/a *adj.* not working; out of order 11
describir *v.* to describe 3
descrito/a *p.p.* described 15
descubierto/a *p.p.* discovered 15
descubrir *v.* to discover 13
desde *prep.* from 6
desear *v.* to want; to wish 2; to desire 12
desempleo *m.* unemployment
desierto *m.* desert 13
desigualdad *f.* inequality
desordenado/a *adj.* disorderly; messy 5
despacio *adj.* slowly
despedida *f.* farewell; goodbye
despedir (e:i) *v.* to fire 16
despedirse (e:i) *v.* (**de**) to say goodbye (to)
despejado/a *adj.* clear (*weather*)
despertador *m.* alarm clock 7

despertarse (e:ie) *v.* to wake up 7
después *adv.* afterwards; then 7
    después de after 7
    después (de) que *conj.* after 13
destruir *v.* to destroy 13
detrás de *prep.* behind 2
día *m.* day 1
    día de fiesta holiday 9
diario *m.* diary 1; newspaper
diario/a *adj.* daily 7
dibujar *v.* to draw 2
dibujo *m.* drawing
    dibujos animados *m., pl.* cartoons
diccionario *m.* dictionary 1
dicho/a *p.p.* said 15
diciembre *m.* December 5
dictadura *f.* dictatorship
diecinueve nineteen 1
dieciocho eighteen 1
dieciséis sixteen 1
diecisiete seventeen 1
diente *m.* tooth 7
dieta *f.* diet 15
    dieta equilibrada balanced diet 15
diez ten 1
difícil *adj.* difficult; hard 3
¿Diga? Hello? (*on telephone*) 11
diligencia *f.* errand 14
dinero *m.* money 6
dirección *f.* address 14
director(a) *m., f.* director; (*musical*) conductor
disco *m.* disk 11
disco compacto compact disc (CD) 11
discriminación *f.* discrimination
discurso *m.* speech
diseñador(a) *m., f.* designer 16
diseño *m.* design
disfrutar *v.* (**de**) to enjoy; to reap the benefits (of) 15
diversión *f.* entertainment; fun activity 4
divertido/a *adj.* fun
divertirse (e:ie) *v.* to have fun 9
divorciado/a *adj.* divorced 9
divorciarse *v.* (**de**) to get divorced (from) 9
divorcio *m.* divorce 9
doblar *v.* to turn 14
doble *adj.* double
doce twelve 1
doctor(a) *m., f.* doctor; physician 3, 10
documental *m.* documentary
documentos *m., pl.* **de viaje** travel documents
doler (o:ue) *v.* to hurt 10
dolor *m.* ache; pain 10
    dolor de cabeza *m.* headache 10
doméstico/a *adj.* domestic
domingo *m.* Sunday 2
don/doña title of respect used with a person's first name 1
donde *adv.* where

¿dónde? *adv.* where? 1, 9
    ¿Dónde está…? Where is…? 2
dormir (o:ue) *v.* to sleep 4
dormirse (o:ue) *v.* to go to sleep; to fall asleep 7
dos two 1
    dos veces twice; two times 6
doscientos/as two hundred 6
drama *m.* drama; play
dramático/a *adj.* dramatic
dramaturgo/a *m., f.* playwright
droga *f.* drug 15
drogadicto/a *m., f.* drug addict 15
ducha *f.* shower
ducharse *v.* to shower; to take a shower 7
duda *f.* doubt 13
dudar *v.* to doubt 13
dueño/a *m., f.* owner 8; landlord
dulce *adj.* sweet 8
dulces *m., pl.* sweets; candy 9
durante *prep.* during 7
durar *v.* to last

E

e *conj.* (*used instead of* **y** *before words beginning with* **i** *and* **hi**) and
echar *v.* to throw
    echar una carta al buzón to put a letter in the mailbox; to mail a letter 14
ecología *f.* ecology 13
ecologista *adj.* ecological; ecologist 13
economía *f.* economics
ecoturismo *m.* ecotourism 13
ecuatoriano/a *adj.* Ecuadorian 3
edad *f.* age
edificio *m.* building 12
    edificio de apartamentos apartment building 12
efectivo *m.* cash
ejercicio *m.* exercise 15
    ejercicios aeróbicos aerobic exercises 15
    ejercicios de estiramiento stretching exercises 15
ejército *m.* army
el *m., sing., def. art.* the 1
él *sub. pron.* he 1; *adj. pron.* him
elección *f.* election
electricista *m., f.* electrician 16
electrodoméstico *m.* electrical appliance 12
elegante *adj. m., f.* elegant 6
elegir *v.* to elect
ella *sub. pron.* she 1; *obj. pron.* her
ellos/as *sub. pron.* they 1; them
embarazada *adj.* pregnant 10
emergencia *f.* emergency 10
emitir *v.* to broadcast

C24

Spanish-English

emocionante *adj.* exciting
empezar (e:ie) *v.* to begin 4
empleado/a *m., f.* employee 5
empleo *m.* job; employment 16
empresa *f.* company; firm 16
en *prep.* in; on; at 2
  en casa at home 7
  en caso (de) que in case (that) 13
  en cuanto as soon as 13
  en efectivo in cash
  en exceso in excess; too much 15
  en línea in-line 4
  ¡En marcha! Let's get going!
  en mi nombre in my name
  en punto on the dot; exactly;
    sharp (*time*) 1
  en qué in which; in what; how 2
  ¿En qué puedo servirles?
    How can I help you? 5
enamorado/a *adj.* **(de)** in love (with) 5
enamorarse *v.* **(de)** to fall in love (with) 9
encantado/a *adj.* delighted; pleased to
  meet you 1
encantar *v.* to like very much; to love
  (*inanimate objects*) 7
encima de *prep.* on top of 2
encontrar (o:ue) *v.* to find 4
encontrar(se) *v.* to meet (each other);
  to find (each other)
encuesta *f.* poll; survey
energía *f.* energy 13
  energía nuclear nuclear
    energy 13
  energía solar solar energy 13
enero *m.* January 5
enfermarse *v.* to get sick 10
enfermedad *f.* illness; sickness 10
enfermero/a *m., f.* nurse 10
enfermo/a *adj.* sick 10
enfrente de *adv.* opposite; facing;
  in front of 14
engordar *v.* to gain weight 15
enojado/a *adj.* mad; angry 5
enojarse *v.* **(con)** to get angry (with) 7
ensalada *f.* salad 8
enseguida *adv.* right away
enseñar *v.* to teach 2
ensuciar *v.* to get (something) dirty 12;
  to dirty
entender (e:ie) *v.* to understand 4
entonces *adv.* then 7
entrada *f.* entrance 12; ticket
entre *prep.* between; among 2
entremeses *m., pl.* hors d'oeuvres 8;
  appetizers
entrenarse *v.* to practice; to train 15
entrevista *f.* interview 16
entrevistador(a) *m., f.* interviewer 16
entrevistar *v.* to interview 16
envase *m.* container 13
enviar *v.* to send 14; to mail

equilibrado/a *adj.* balanced 15
equipado/a *adj.* equipped
equipaje *m.* luggage 5
equipo *m.* team 4
equivocado/a *adj.* wrong; mistaken 5
eres you are *fam.* 1
es you are *form.*; he/she/it is 1
  Es a la una. Is at one o'clock. 1
  Es a las... Is at... 1
  Es una lástima... It's a shame... 13
  Es bueno que... It's good that... 12
  Es de... He/She is from . . . 1
  Es extraño... It's strange... 13
  Es importante que... It's
    important that . . . 12
  Es imposible... It's impossible... 13
  Es improbable... It's improbable... 13
  Es la una. It's one o'clock. 1
  Es malo que... It's bad that... 12
  Es mejor que... It's better that... 12
  Es necesario que... It's necessary
    that... 12
  Es obvio... It's obvious... 13
  Es ridículo... It's ridiculous... 13
  Es seguro... It's sure... 13
  Es terrible... It's terrible... 13
  Es triste... It's sad... 13
  Es urgente que... It's urgent
    that... 12
  Es verdad... It's true... 13
esa(s) *f., adj.* that; those 6
ésa(s) *f., pron.* those (ones) 6
escalar *v.* to climb 4
  escalar montañas *f., pl.* to climb
    mountains 4
escalera *f.* stairs; stairway 12
escoger *v.* choose
escribir *v.* to write 3
  escribir una carta to write a letter 4
  escribir un mensaje electrónico to write
    an e-mail message 4
  escribir una (tarjeta) postal
    to write a postcard 4
escrito/a *p.p.* written 15
escritor(a) *m., f.* writer 16
escritorio *m.* desk 2
escuchar *v.* to listen 2
  escuchar la radio to listen to
    the radio
  escuchar música to listen to music
escuela *f.* school 1
esculpir *v.* to sculpt
escultor(a) *m., f.* sculptor 16
escultura *f.* sculpture
ese *m., sing., adj.* that 6
ése *m., sing., pron.* that (one) 6
eso *neuter, pron.* that;
  that thing 6
esos *m., pl., adj.* those 6
ésos *m., pl., pron.* those (ones) 6
español *m.* Spanish (*language*) 2

español(a) *adj.* Spanish 3
espárragos *m., pl.* asparagus
especialización *f.* field of study 16;
  specialization
espectacular *adj.* spectacular
espectáculo *m.* show
espejo *m.* mirror 7
esperar *v.* to wait (for); to hope 2;
  to wish 13
esposo/a *m., f.* husband/wife;
  spouse 3
esquí *m.* **(acuático)** (water) skiing 4
esquiar *v.* to ski 4
esquina *m.* corner 14
está he/she/it is, you are *form.* 1
  Está despejado. It's clear.
    (*weather*) 5
  Está (muy) nublado. It's
    (very) cloudy. (*weather*) 5
  Está bien. That's fine.
esta(s) *f., adj.* this; these 6
  esta noche tonight 4
ésta(s) *f., pron.* this (one); these (ones) 6
  Ésta es... *f.* This is...
    (*introducing someone*) 1
establecer *v.* to establish
estación *f.* station; season 5
  estación de autobuses bus
    station 5
  estación del metro subway
    station 5
  estación del tren train station 5
estacionar *v.* to park 11
estadio *m.* stadium 2
estado civil *m.* marital status 9
estadounidense *adj.* from the United
  States 3
estampado/a *adj.* print
estampilla *f.* stamp 14
estante *m.* bookcase; bookshelf 12
estar *v.* to be 2
  estar a (veinte kilómetros)
    de aquí to be (20 kilometers)
    from here
  estar a dieta to be on a diet 15
  estar aburrido/a to be bored 5
  estar afectado/a (por) to be
    affected (by) 13
  estar bajo control to be under
    control
  estar cansado/a to be tired 5
  estar contaminado/a to be
    polluted 13
  estar de acuerdo to agree
  estar de moda to be in fashion 6
  estar de vacaciones to be on
    vacation 5
  estar en buena forma to be in
    good shape 15
  estar enfermo/a to be sick 10
  estar listo/a to be ready

C25

VOCABULARIO

estar perdido/a to be lost 14
estar roto/a to be broken
estar seguro/a (de) to be sure (of) 5, 13
estar torcido/a to be twisted;
    to be sprained 10
estatua *f.* statue
este *m.* east 14
este *m., sing., adj.* this 6; *interj.* umm
éste *m., sing., pron.* this (one) 6
    Éste es... *m.* This is...
    (*introducing someone*) 1
estéreo *m.* stereo 11
estilo *m.* style
estiramiento *m.* stretching 15
esto *neuter pron.* this; this thing 6
estómago *m.* stomach 10
estornudar *v.* to sneeze 10
estos *m., pl., adj.* these 6
éstos *m., pl., pron.* these (ones) 6
estrella *f.* star 13
    estrella de cine *m., f.* movie star
estrés *m.* stress 15
estudiante *m., f.* student 1, 2
estudiantil *adj. m., f.* student
estudiar *v.* to study 2
estufa *f.* stove 12
estupendo/a *adj.* stupendous 5
etapa *f.* stage 9; step
evitar *v.* to avoid 13
examen *m.* test; exam 2
    examen médico physical exam 10
excelente *adj.* excellent 5
exceso *m.* excess; too much 15
excursión *f.* hike; tour; excursion 4
excursionista *m., f.* hiker 4
éxito *m.* success 16
experiencia *f.* experience
explicar *v.* to explain 2
explorar *v.* to explore
    explorar un pueblo to explore a town
    explorar una ciudad to explore a city
expresión *f.* expression
extinción *f.* extinction 13
extranjero/a *adj.* foreign
extraño/a *adj.* strange 13

F

fábrica *f.* factory 13
fabuloso/a *adj* fabulous 5
fácil *adj.* easy 3
    facilísimo extremely easy 8
falda *f.* skirt 6
faltar *v.* to lack; to need 7
familia *f.* family 3
famoso/a *adj.* famous 16
farmacia *f.* pharmacy 10
fascinar *v.* to fascinate; to like very much 7

favorito/a *adj.* favorite 4
fax *m.* fax (machine) 11
febrero *m.* February 5
fecha *f.* date 5
feliz *adj.* happy 5
    ¡Felicidades! Congratulations!
    (*for an event such as a birthday*
    or anniversary)
    ¡Felicitaciones! Congratulations! (*for an*
    event such as an engagement or a good
    grade on a test)
    ¡Feliz cumpleaños! Happy birthday!
fenomenal *adj.* great 5; phenomenal
feo/a *adj.* ugly 3
festival *m.* festival
fiebre *f.* fever 10
fiesta *f.* party 9
fijo/a *adj.* set, fixed 6
fin *m.* end 4
    fin de semana weekend 4
finalmente *adv.* finally
firmar *v.* to sign (*a document*) 14
física *f.* physics 2
flan *m.* baked custard 9
flexible *adj.* flexible 15
flor *f.* flower 13
folclórico/a *adj.* folk; folkloric
folleto *m.* brochure
fondo *m.* end 12
forma *f.* shape 15
formulario *m.* form 14
foto(grafía) *f.* photograph 1
francés, francesa *adj.* French 3
frecuentemente *adv.* frequently 10
frenos *m., pl.* brakes 11
fresco/a *adj.* cool
frijoles *m., pl.* beans 8
frío *m.* cold 3
fritada *f.* fried dish (pork, fish, etc.)
frito/a *adj.* fried 8
fruta *f.* fruit 8
frutería *f.* fruit store 14
frutilla *f.* strawberry 8
fuente *f.* **de fritada** platter of fried food
fuera *adv.* outside
fuerte *adj.* strong 15
fumar *v.* to smoke 15
    no fumar not to smoke 15
funcionar *v.* to work 11; to function
fútbol *m.* soccer 4
    fútbol americano football 4
futuro/a *adj.* future 16
    en el futuro in the future

G

gafas (de sol) *f., pl.* (sun)glasses 6
gafas (oscuras) *f., pl.* (sun)glasses

galleta *f.* cookie 9
ganar *v.* to win 4; to earn (money) 16
ganga *f.* bargain 6
garaje *m.* garage; (mechanic's) repair
    shop 11; garage 12
garganta *f.* throat 10
gasolina *f.* gasoline 11
gasolinera *f.* gas station 11
gastar *v.* to spend (*money*) 6
gato/a *m., f.* cat 3
gente *f.* people 3
geografía *f.* geography 2
gerente *m., f.* manager 16
gimnasio *m.* gym, gymnasium 4
gobierno *m.* government 13
golf *m.* golf 4
gordo/a *adj.* fat 3
gracias *f., pl.* thank you; thanks 1
    Gracias por todo. Thanks for
    everything.
    Gracias una vez más. Thanks
    once again.
graduarse *v.* **(de)** to graduate (from) 9
gran; grande *adj.* great; big 3
grasa *f.* fat 15
gratis *adj.* free of charge 14
grave *adj.* grave; serious 10
    gravísimo/a *adj.* extremely serious 13
grillo *m.* cricket
gripe *f.* flu 10
gris *adj.* gray 6
gritar *v.* to scream
guantes *m., pl.* gloves 6
guapo/a *adj.* handsome;
    good-looking 3
guardar *v.* to save (on a computer) 11
guerra *f.* war
guía *m., f.* guide
gustar *v.* to be pleasing to; to like 2, 7
    Me gustaría(n)... I would like 7
gusto *m.* pleasure 1
    El gusto es mío. The pleasure
    is mine. 1
    Gusto de (+ *inf.*) It's a pleasure to...
    Mucho gusto. Pleased to meet you. 1

H

haber (*aux.*) *v.* to have (*done something*) 15
    ha sido un placer it's been a pleasure
habitación *f.* room 5
    habitación doble double room 5
    habitación individual single room 5
habitantes *m., pl.* inhabitants 13
hablar *v.* to talk; to speak 2
hacer *v.* to do; to make 4

Spanish-English

Hace buen tiempo. It's nice weather. 5; The weather is good.
Hace (mucho) calor. It's (very) hot. (*weather*) 5
Hace fresco. It's cool. (*weather*) 5
Hace (mucho) frío. It's (very) cold. (*weather*) 5
Hace mal tiempo. It's bad weather. 5; The weather is bad.
Hace (mucho) sol. It's (very) sunny. (*weather*) 5
Hace (mucho) viento. It's (very) windy. (*weather*) 5
hacer cola to stand in line 14
hacer diligencias to do errands; to run errands 14
hacer ejercicio to exercise 15
hacer ejercicios aeróbicos to do aerobics 15
hacer ejercicios de estiramiento to do stretching exercises 15
hacer un papel (de) to play a role (of)
hacer gimnasia to work out 15
hacer juego (con) to match 6
hacer la cama to make the bed 12
hacer las maletas to pack (one's suitcases) 5
hacer los quehaceres domésticos to do household chores 12
hacer turismo to go sightseeing 5
hacer un viaje to take a trip 5
hacer una excursión to go on a hike; to go on a tour 5
hacha *f.* ax
hacia *prep.* toward 14
hambre *f.* hunger 3
hamburguesa *f.* hamburger 8
hasta *prep.* until 6; toward
Hasta la vista. See you later. 1
Hasta luego. See you later. 1
Hasta mañana. See you tomorrow. 1
hasta que until 13
Hasta pronto. See you soon. 1
hay there is; there are 1
Hay (mucha) contaminación. It's (very) smoggy.
Hay (mucha) niebla. It's (very) foggy. 5
Hay que It is necessary that 14
No hay duda de There's no doubt 13
No hay de qué. You're welcome. 1
hecho/a *p.p.* done 15
heladería *f.* ice cream shop 14
helado/a *adj.* iced 8
helado *m.* ice cream 9
hermanastro/a *m., f.* stepbrother/stepsister 3
hermano/a *m., f.* brother/sister 3
hermano/a mayor/menor *m., f.* older/younger brother/sister 3

hermanos *m., pl.* siblings (brothers and sisters) 3
hermoso/a *adj.* beautiful 6
hierba *f.* grass 13
hijastro/a *m., f.* stepson/stepdaughter 3
hijo/a *m., f.* son/daughter 3
hijo/a único/a only child 3
hijos *m., pl.* children 3
historia *f.* history 2; story
hockey *m.* hockey 4
hogar *m.* home 12
Hola. *interj.* Hello; Hi. 1
hombre *m.* man 1
hombre de negocios businessman 16
hora *f.* hour 1
horario *m.* schedule 2
horno *m.* oven 12
horno de microondas microwave oven 12
hospital *m.* hospital 10
hotel *m.* hotel 5
hoy *adv.* today 2
hoy (en) día nowadays
Hoy es... Today is... 2
huelga *f.* strike (labor)
hueso *m.* bone 10
huésped *m., f.* guest 5
huevo *m.* egg 8
humanidades *f., pl.* humanities
huracán *m.* hurricane

I

ida *f.* one way (*travel*)
idea *f.* idea 4
iglesia *f.* church 4
igualdad *f.* equality
Igualmente. *adv.* Likewise. 1
impermeable *m.* raincoat 6
importante *adj.* important 3
importar *v.* to be important (to); to matter 7, 12
imposible *adj.* impossible 13
impresora *f.* printer 11
imprimir *v.* to print 11
improbable *adj.* improbable 13
impuesto *m.* tax
incendio *m.* fire
increíble *adj.* incredible 5
indicar *v.* **cómo llegar** to give directions 14
individual *adj.* private (*room*) 5
infección *f.* infection 10
informar *v.* to inform
informe *m.* report; paper (*written work*)
ingeniero/a *m., f.* engineer 3
inglés *m.* English (*language*) 2
inglés, inglesa *adj.* English 3
insistir *v.* **(en)** to insist (on) 12

inspector(a) *m., f.* **de aduanas** customs inspector 5
inteligente *adj.* intelligent 3
intercambiar *v.* exchange
interesante *adj.* interesting 3
interesar *v.* to be interesting to; to interest 7
internacional *adj.* international
Internet *m.* Internet 11
inundación *f.* flood
invertir (e:ie) *v.* to invest 16
invierno *m.* winter 5
invitado/a *m., f.* guest (*at a function*) 9
invitar *v.* to invite; to treat 9
inyección *f.* injection 10
ir *v.* to go 4
ir a (+ *inf.*) to be going to do something 4
ir a la playa to go to the beach 5
ir de compras to go shopping 6
ir de excursión (a las montañas) to go for a hike (in the mountains) 4
ir de pesca to go fishing 5
ir de vacaciones to go on vacation 5
ir en autobús to go by bus 5
ir en auto(móvil) to go by car 5; to go by auto(mobile)
ir en avión to go by plane 5
ir en barco to go by ship 5
ir en metro to go by subway
ir en motocicleta to go by motorcycle 5
ir en taxi to go by taxi 5
ir en tren to go by train
irse *v.* to go away; to leave 7
italiano/a *adj.* Italian 3
izquierdo/a *adj.* left 2
a la izquierda de to the left of 2

J

jabón *m.* soap 7
jamás *adv.* never; not ever 7
jamón *m.* ham 8
japonés, japonesa *adj.* Japanese 3
jardín *m.* garden; yard 12
jefe, jefa *m., f.* boss 16
joven *adj.* young 3
joven *m., f.* youth; young person 1
joyería *f.* jewelry store 14
jubilarse *v.* to retire (*from work*) 9
juego *m.* game
jueves *m., sing.* Thursday 2
jugador(a) *m., f.* player 4
jugar (u:ue) *v.* to play 4
jugar a las cartas to play cards
jugo *m.* juice 8

C27

VOCABULARIO

jugo de fruta fruit juice **8**
julio *m.* July **5**
jungla *f.* jungle
junio *m.* June **5**
juntos/as *adj.* together **9**
juventud *f.* youth **9**

K

kilómetro *m.* kilometer **11**

L

la *f., sing., def. art.* the **1**
la *f., sing., d.o. pron.* her, it,
  form. you **5**
laboratorio *m.* laboratory **2**
lago *m.* lake **13**
lámpara *f.* lamp **12**
lana *f.* wool **6**
langosta *f.* lobster **8**
lápiz *m.* pencil **1**
largo/a *m.* long (*in length*) **6**
las *f., pl., def. art.* the **1**
las *f., pl., d.o. pron.* them; *form.* you **5**
lástima *f.* shame **13**
lastimarse *v.* to injure oneself **10**
  lastimarse el pie to injure one's
    foot **10**
lata *f.* (*tin*) can **13**
lavabo *m.* sink
lavadora *f.* washing machine **12**
lavandería *f.* laundromat **14**
lavaplatos *m., sing.* dishwasher **12**
lavar *v.* to wash **12**
lavarse *v.* to wash oneself **7**
  lavarse la cara to wash one's
    face **7**
  lavarse las manos to wash one's
    hands **7**
le *sing., i.o. pron.* to/for him, her,
  you *form.* **6**
  Le presento a... I would like to
    introduce... to you. *form.* **1**
lección *f.* lesson **1**
leche *f.* milk **8**
lechuga *f.* lettuce **8**
leer *v.* to read **3**
  leer el correo electrónico
    to read e-mail **4**
  leer el periódico to read the
    newspaper **4**
  leer una revista to read a magazine **4**
leído/a *p.p.* read **15**
lejos de *prep.* far from **2**
lengua *f.* language **2**
  lenguas extranjeras *f., pl.*
    foreign languages **2**
lentes *m., pl.* **de contacto** contact lenses

lentes de sol sunglasses
lento/a *adj.* slow **11**
les *pl., i.o. pron.* to/for them, you *form.* **6**
letrero *m.* sign **14**
levantar *v.* to lift **15**
  levantar pesas to lift weights **15**
levantarse *v.* to get up **7**
ley *f.* law **13**
libertad *f.* liberty; freedom
libre *adj.* free **4**
librería *f.* bookstore **2**
libro *m.* book **2**
licencia *f.* **de conducir** driver's license **11**
limón *m.* lemon **8**
limpiar *v.* to clean **12**
  limpiar la casa to clean the house **12**
limpio/a *adj.* clean **5**
línea *f.* line **4**
listo/a *adj.* smart; ready **5**
literatura *f.* literature
llamar *v.* to call **11**
  llamar por teléfono to call on
    the phone
  llamarse to be called; to be named **7**
llanta *f.* tire **11**
llave *f.* key **5**
llegada *f.* arrival **5**
llegar *v.* to arrive **2**
llenar *v.* to fill
  llenar el tanque to fill up the tank **11**
  llenar un formulario to fill out
    a form **14**
lleno/a *adj.* full **11**
llevar *v.* to carry **2**; to take; to wear **6**
  llevar una vida sana to lead
    a healthy lifestyle **15**
  llevarse *v.* **bien/mal (con)** to
    get along well/badly (with) **9**
llover (o:ue) *v.* to rain **5**
  Llueve. It's raining. **5**
lluvia *f.* rain
lo *m., sing. d.o. pronoun.* him, it,
  you *form.* **5**
  lo mejor the best (thing)
  Lo pasamos de película. We had a
    great time.
  lo peor the worst (thing)
  lo que what; that; which **9**
  Lo siento. I'm sorry. **1**
  Lo siento muchísimo. I'm so sorry.
loco/a *adj.* crazy **6**
locutor(a) *m., f.* TV or radio announcer
lomo *m.* **a la plancha** grilled flank steak
los *m., pl., def. art.* the **1**
los *m., pl., do. pron.* them, you *form.* **5**
luchar *v.* **(contra), (por)** to fight; to struggle
  (against), (for)
luego *adv.* afterwards, then **7**; *adv.* later **1**
lugar *m.* place **4**
luna *f.* moon **13**
lunar *m.* polka dot **6**; mole

lunes *m., sing.* Monday **2**
luz *f.* light; electricity **12**

M

madrastra *f.* stepmother **3**
madre *f.* mother **3**
madurez *f.* maturity; middle age **9**
maestro/a *m., f.* teacher (*elementary
  school*) **16**
magnífico/a *adj.* magnificent **5**
maíz *m.* corn **8**
mal, malo/a *adj.* bad **3**; sick **5**
  malísimo very bad **8**
maleta *f.* suitcase **1**
mamá *f.* mom **3**
mandar *v.* to order **12**; to send **14**;
  to mail
manejar *v.* to drive **11**
manera *f.* way
mano *f.* hand **1**
  ¡Manos arriba! Hands up!
manta *f.* blanket **12**
mantener *v.* to maintain **15**
  mantenerse en forma to stay
    in shape **15**
mantequilla *f.* butter **8**
manzana *f.* apple **8**
mañana *f.* morning, A.M. **1**;
  tomorrow **1**
mapa *m.* map **1, 2**
maquillaje *m.* makeup **7**
maquillarse *v.* to put on makeup **7**
mar *m.* ocean; sea **5**
maravilloso/a *adj.* marvelous **5**
mareado/a *adj.* dizzy; nauseated **10**
margarina *f.* margarine **8**
mariscos *m., pl.* seafood **8**
marrón *adj. m., f.* brown
martes *m., sing.* Tuesday **2**
marzo *m.* March **5**
más *adj.* more **2**
  el/la/los/las más the most **8**
  más de (+ *number*) more
    than (+ *number*) **8**
  más tarde later (on) **7**
  más... que more... than **8**
masaje *m.* massage **15**
matemáticas *f., pl.* mathematics **2**
materia *f.* course
matrimonio *m.* marriage; married
  couple **9**
máximo/a *m., f.* maximum **11**
mayo *m.* May **5**
mayonesa *f.* mayonnaise **8**
mayor *adj.* older **3**; bigger **8**
  el/la mayor *adj.* the oldest; the biggest **8**
me *pron.* me **5**
  Me duele mucho. It hurts me a lot. **10**
  Me gusta(n)... I like... **2**

C28

Spanish-English

No me gusta(n)... I don't like... 2
Me gustaría(n)... I would like... 7
Me llamo... My name is... 1
Me muero por... I'm dying to (for)...
mecánico/a *m., f.* mechanic 11
mediano/a *adj.* medium
medianoche *f.* midnight 1
medias *f., pl.* pantyhose, stockings 6
medicamento *m.* medication 10
medicina *f.* medicine 10
médico/a *m., f.* doctor; physician 3;
  adj. medical 10
medio/a *m. adj.* half 3
  medio *m.* **ambiente** environment 13
  medio/a *adj.* **hermano/a**
    half-brother/half-sister 3
  medios de *m., pl.* **comunicación**
    means of communication; media
  y media thirty minutes past the
    hour (*time*) 1
mediodía *m.* noon 1
mejor *adj.* better 8
  el/la mejor *m., f.* the best 8
mejorar *v.* to improve 13
melocotón *m.* peach
menor *adj.* younger 3; smaller 8
  el/la menor *m., f.* the youngest;
    the smallest 8
menos *adv.* less 10
  el/la/los/las menos the least 8
  menos cuarto/menos quince
    quarter to (*time*) 1
  menos de (+ number) less
    than (+ *number*) 8
  menos... que less... than 8
mensaje *m.* **de texto** text message 11
mensaje *m.* **electrónico** e-mail message 4
mentira *f.* lie 6
menú *m.* menu 8
mercado *m.* market 6
  mercado al aire libre open-air
    market 6
merendar (e:ie) *v.* to snack in the
  afternoon; to have a(n) (afternoon)
  snack 15
merienda *f.* (afternoon) snack 15
mes *m.* month 5
mesa *f.* table 2
mesita *f.* end table 12
  mesita de noche night stand 12
metro *m.* subway 5
mexicano/a *adj.* Mexican 3
mí *pron. obj. of prep.* me
mi(s) *poss. adj.* my 3
microonda *f.* microwave 12
  horno de microondas
    microwave oven 12
miedo *m.* fear 3
mientras *adv.* while 10
miércoles *m., sing.* Wednesday 2
mil one thousand 6

mil millones billion 6
Mil perdones. I'm so sorry.
  (*lit.* A thousand pardons.)
milla *f.* mile 11
millón million 6
millones (de) millions (of) 6
mineral *m.* mineral 15
minuto *m.* minute 1
mío(s)/a(s) *poss.* my; (of) mine 11
mirar *v.* to look (at); to watch 2
  mirar (la) televisión to watch
    television 2
mismo/a *adj.* same
mochila *f.* backpack 1
moda *f.* fashion 6
moderno/a *adj.* modern
molestar *v.* to bother; to annoy 7
monitor *m.* monitor 11
mono *m.* monkey 13
montaña *f.* mountain 4
montar *v.* **a caballo** to ride a horse 5
monumento *m.* monument 4
mora *f.* blackberry 8
morado/a *adj.* purple 6
moreno/a *adj.* dark-haired 3
morir (o:ue) *v.* to die 8
mostrar (o:ue) *v.* to show 4
moto(cicleta) *f.* motorcycle 5
motor *m.* motor 11
muchacho/a *m., f.* boy; girl 3
mucho/a *adj., adv.* many; a lot of;
  much 2, 3
  muchas veces a lot; many
    times 10
  Muchísimas gracias. Thank you
    very, very much.
  muchísimo *adj., adv.* very much 8
  Mucho gusto. Pleased to meet
    you. 1
  (Muchas) gracias. Thank you
    (very much); Thanks (a lot). 1
mudarse *v.* to move (from one house
  to another) 12
muebles *m., pl.* furniture 12
muela *f.* tooth 10
muerte *f.* death 9
muerto/a *p.p.* died 15
mujer *f.* woman 1
  mujer de negocios business
    woman 16
  mujer policía female police
    officer 11
multa *f.* fine; ticket 11
mundial *adj.* worldwide
mundo *m.* world 13
municipal *adj.* municipal
músculo *m.* muscle 15
museo *m.* museum 4
música *f.* music
musical *adj.* musical
músico/a *m., f.* musician

muy *adv.* very 1
  Muy amable. That's very kind of you. 5
  (Muy) bien, gracias. (Very) well,
    thanks. 1

N

nacer *v.* to be born 9
nacimiento *m.* birth 9
nacional *adj.* national
nacionalidad *f.* nationality 1
nada *pron., adv.* nothing 1; not
  anything 7
  nada mal not bad at all 5
nadar *v.* to swim 4
nadie *pron.* no one, not anyone 7
naranja *m.* orange 8
nariz *f.* nose 10
natación *f.* swimming 4
natural *adj.* natural 13
naturaleza *f.* nature 13
navegador *m.* **GPS** GPS 11
navegar *v.* **en Internet** to surf the
  Internet 11
Navidad *f.* Christmas 9
necesario/a *adj.* necessary 12
necesitar *v.* to need 2, 12
negar (e:ie) *v.* to deny 13
negativo/a *m.* negative 7
negocios *m., pl.* business; commerce 16
negro/a *adj.* black 6
nervioso/a *adj.* nervous 5
nevar (e:ie) *v.* to snow 5
  Nieva. It's snowing. 5
ni... ni *conj.* neither... nor 7
niebla *f.* fog
nieto/a *m., f.* grandson/granddaughter 3
nieve *f.* snow
ningún, ninguno/a(s) *adj.* no; none;
  not any 7
  Ningún problema. No problem.
niñez *f.* childhood 9
niño/a *m., f.* child; boy/girl 3
no *adv.* no; not 1
  No cabe duda de There is no
    doubt 13
  No es así. That's not the way it is.
  No es para tanto. It's not a big deal.
  No es seguro... It's not sure... 13
  No es verdad... It's not true... 13
  No está. It's not here. 5
  No está nada mal. It's not bad
    at all. 5
  no estar de acuerdo to disagree
  no estar seguro/a (de) not to be
    sure (of) 13
  No estoy seguro. I'm not sure.
  no hay there is not; there are not 1
  No hay de qué. You're welcome. 1
  No hay duda de There is no doubt 13

VOCABULARIO

¡No me diga(s)! You don't say!
No me gustan nada. I don't
   like them at all.
no muy bien not very well 1
¿no? right? 1
no quiero I don't want to 4
no sé I don't know
No te/se preocupe(s). Don't
   worry. 7
no tener razón to be wrong 3
noche *f.* night 1
nombre *m.* name 5
norte *m.* north 14
norteamericano/a *adj.* (North)
   American 3
nos *pron.* us 5
Nos vemos. See you. 1
nosotros/as *sub. pron.* we 1;
   ob. pron. us 8
noticias *f., pl.* news
noticiero *m.* newscast
novecientos/as nine hundred 6
noveno/a *adj.* ninth 5
noventa ninety 2
noviembre *m.* November 5
novio/a *m., f.* boyfriend/girlfriend 3
nube *f.* cloud 13
nublado/a *adj.* cloudy
   Está (muy) nublado.
     It's (very) cloudy.
nuclear *adj.* nuclear 13
nuera *f.* daughter-in-law 3
nuestro(s)/a(s) *poss. adj.* our 3;
   of ours 11
nueve nine 1
nuevo/a *adj.* new 6
número *m.* number 1
   número (shoe) size 6
nunca *adj.* never; not ever 7
nutrición *f.* nutrition 15

O

o *conj.* or 7
o... o *conj.* either . . . or 7
obedecer (c:zc) *v.* to obey
obra *f.* work (*of art, literature, music, etc.*)
   obra maestra masterpiece
obtener *v.* to obtain; to get 16
obvio/a *adj.* obvious 13
océano *m.* ocean 13; sea
ochenta eighty 2
ocho eight 1
ochocientos/as eight hundred 6
octavo/a *adj.* eighth 5
octubre *m.* October 5
ocupación *f.* occupation 16
ocupado/a *adj.* busy 5
ocurrir *v.* to occur; to happen
odiar *v.* to hate 9

oeste *m.* west 14
oferta *f.* offer
oficina *f.* office 12
oficio *m.* trade 16
ofrecer (c:zc) *v.* to offer 8
oído *m.* sense of hearing; inner ear
oído *p.p.* heard 15
oír *v.* to hear 4
   oiga *form., sing.* listen (*in
     conversation*) 1
   oigan *fam., form., pl.* listen (*in
     conversation*) 1
   Oye. *fam., sing.* Listen. (*in
     conversation*) 1
ojalá (que) *interj.* I hope (that); I wish
   (that) 4
ojo *m.* eye 10
olvidar *v.* to forget 10
once eleven 1
ópera *f.* opera
operación *f.* operation 10
ordenado/a *adj.* orderly 5; well organized
ordinal *adj.* ordinal (*number*)
oreja *f.* (outer) ear 10
orquesta *f.* orchestra
ortográfico/a *adj.* spelling
os *fam., pl. pron.* you 5
otoño *m.* fall, autumn 5
otro/a *adj.* other; another 6
   otra vez again

P

paciente *m., f.* patient 10
padrastro *m.* stepfather 3
padre *m.* father 3
   padres *m., pl.* parents 3
pagar *v.* to pay 6
   pagar a plazos to pay in
     installments 14
   pagar al contado to pay in cash 14
   pagar con to pay with 6
   pagar en efectivo to pay in cash 14
   pagar la cuenta to pay the bill
página *f.* page 11
   página principal home page 11
país *m.* country 1
paisaje *m.* landscape 13; countryside
pájaro *m.* bird 13
palabra *f.* word 1
pan *m.* bread 8
   pan tostado toasted bread 8; toast
panadería *f.* bakery 14
pantalla *f.* screen 11
pantalones *m., pl.* pants 6
   pantalones cortos shorts 6
papa *f.* potato 8
   papas fritas *f., pl.* French fries 8
papá *m.* dad 3
   papás *m., pl.* parents 3

papel *m.* paper 2; role
paquete *m.* package 14
par *m.* pair 6
   par de zapatos pair of shoes 6
para *prep.* for; in order to; toward;
   in the direction of; by; used for;
   considering 11
   para que so that 13
parabrisas *m., sing.* windshield 11
parar *v.* to stop 11
parecer *v.* to seem; to appear 8
pared *f.* wall 12
pareja *f.* couple; partner 9
parientes *m., pl.* relatives 3
parque *m.* park 4
párrafo *m.* paragraph
parte: de parte de on behalf of
partido *m.* game 4; match (*sports*)
pasado/a *adj.* last; past 6
pasado *p.p.* passed
pasaje *m.* ticket 5
   pasaje de ida y vuelta *m.*
     round-trip ticket 5
pasajero/a *m., f.* passenger 1
pasaporte *m.* passport 5
pasar *v.* to go through 5; to pass
   pasar la aspiradora to vacuum 12
   pasar por el banco to go by
     the bank 14
   pasar por la aduana to go
     through customs 5
   pasar el tiempo to spend time 4
   pasarlo bien/mal to have a
     good/bad time 9
pasatiempo *m.* pastime, hobby 4
pasear *v.* to take a walk; to stroll 4
   pasear en bicicleta to ride a
     bicycle 4
   pasear por la ciudad/el pueblo to
     walk around the city/town 4
pasillo *m.* hallway 12
pastel *m.* cake 9
   pastel de chocolate chocolate cake
   pastel de cumpleaños birthday
     cake 9
pastelería *f.* pastry shop 14
pastilla *f.* pill; tablet 10
patata *f.* potato 8
   patatas fritas *f., pl.* French fries 8
patinar (en línea) *v.* to skate
   (in-line) 4
patio *m.* patio; yard 12
pavo *m.* turkey 8
paz *f.* peace
pedir (e:i) *v.* to ask for; to request 4, 12;
   to order (*food*) 8
   pedir prestado to borrow 14
   pedir un préstamo to apply for
     a loan 14
peinarse *v.* to comb one's hair 7
película *f.* movie 4

C30

Spanish-English

peligro *m.* danger 13
peligroso/a *adj.* dangerous
pelirrojo/a *adj.* red-haired 3
pelo *m.* hair 7
pelota *f.* ball 4
peluquería *f.* hairdressing salon 14
peluquero/a *m., f.* hairdresser 16
penicilina *f.* penicillin
pensar (e:ie) *v.* to think 4
   pensar (+ *inf.*) to intend;
      to plan (*to do something*) 4
   pensar en to think about 4
pensión *f.* boarding house 5
peor *adj.* worse 8
   el/la peor the worst 8
pequeño/a *adj.* small 3
pera *f.* pear
perder (e:ie) *v.* to lose; to miss 4
perdido/a *adj.* lost
Perdón. Pardon me.; Excuse me. 1
perezoso/a *adj.* lazy
perfecto/a *adj.* perfect 5
periódico *m.* newspaper 4
periodismo *m.* journalism 2
periodista *m., f.* journalist 3
permiso *m.* permission
pero *conf.* but 7
perro/a *m., f.* dog 3
persona *f.* person 3
personaje *m.* character
   personaje principal main character
pesas *f., pl.* weights 15
pesca *f.* fishing 5
pescadería *f.* fish market 14
pescado *m.* fish (*cooked*) 8
pescador(a) *m., f.* fisherman/fisherwoman
pescar *v.* to fish 5
peso *m.* weight 15
pez *m.* fish (*live*) 13
picante *adj.* hot, spicy 8
pie *m.* foot 10
piedra *f.* rock; stone 13
pierna *f.* leg 10
pimienta *f.* pepper 8
piña *f.* pineapple 8
pintar *v.* to paint
pintor(a) *m., f.* painter 16
pintura *f.* painting; picture 12
piscina *f.* swimming pool 4
piso *m.* floor (*of a building*) 5
pizarra *f.* blackboard 2
placer *m.* pleasure
   Ha sido un placer. It's been a pleasure.
planchar *v.* **la ropa** to iron clothes 12
planes *m., pl.* plans
planta *f.* plant 13
   planta baja ground floor 5
plástico *m.* plastic 13
plato *m.* dish (*in a meal*) 8; *m.* plate 12
   plato principal main dish 8
playa *f.* beach 5

plazos *m., pl.* periods; time
pluma *f.* pen 2
población *f.* population 13
pobre *m., f., adj.* poor 6
pobreza *f.* poverty
poco/a *adj.* little 5, 10; few
poder (o:ue) *v.* to be able to; can 4
poema *m.* poem
poesía *f.* poetry
poeta *m., f.* poet 16
policía *f.* police (force) 11; *m.* (male) police
   officer 11
política *f.* politics
político/a *m., f.* politician 16
pollo *m.* chicken 8
   pollo asado roast chicken 8
ponchar *v.* to deflate; to get a flat (*tire*)
poner *v.* to put; to place 4; to turn on
   (*electrical appliances*) 11
   poner la mesa to set the table 12
   poner una inyección to give an
      injection 10
ponerse (+ *adj.*) to become (+ *adj.*) 7;
   to put on 7
por *prep.* in exchange for; for; by; in;
   through; by means of; along; during;
   around; in search of; by way of; per 11
   por aquí around here 11
   por avión by plane
   por ciento percent
   por ejemplo for example 11
   por eso that's why; therefore 11
   Por favor. Please. 1
   por fin finally 11
   por la mañana in the morning 7
   por la noche at night 7
   por la tarde in the afternoon; in the
      (early) evening 7
   por lo menos at least 10
   ¿por qué? why? 2, 9
   por supuesto of course
   por teléfono by phone; on the phone
   por último finally 7
porque *conj.* because
portátil *adj.* portable 11
porvenir *m.* future
posesivo/a *adj.* possessive 3
posible *adj.* possible 13
   es posible it's possible 13
   no es posible it's not possible 13
postal *f.* postcard 4
postre *m.* dessert 9
practicar *v.* to practice 2
   practicar deportes *m., pl.* to play
      sports 4
precio (fijo) *m.* (fixed, set) price 6
preferir (e:ie) *v.* to prefer 4, 12
pregunta *f.* question
preguntar *v.* to ask (*a question*) 2
premio *m.* prize; award
prender *v.* to turn on 11

prensa *f.* press
preocupado/a (por) *adj.* worried (about) 5
preocuparse *v.* **(por)** to worry (about) 7
preparar *v.* to prepare 2
preposición *f.* preposition
presentación *f.* introduction
presentar *v.* to introduce; to put on
   (*a performance*)
presiones *f., pl.* pressure 15
prestado/a *adj.* borrowed
préstamo *m.* loan 14
prestar *v.* to loan 6
primavera *f.* spring 5
primer, primero/a *adj.* first 5
primo/a *m., f.* cousin 3
principal *adj.* main 8
prisa *f.* haste 3
probable *adj. m., f.* probable 13
   es probable it's probable 13
   no es probable it's not probable 13
probar (o:ue) *v.* to taste; to try 8
probarse (o:ue) *v.* to try on 7
problema *m.* problem 1
profesión *f.* profession 3, 16
profesor(a) *m., f.* teacher 1; professor 2
programa *m.* program 1
   programa de computación
      software 11
   programa de entrevistas talk show
programador(a) *m., f.* programmer 3
prohibir *v.* to prohibit 10, 12; to forbid
pronombre *m.* pronoun 8
pronto *adj.* soon 10
propina *f.* tip 9
propio/a *adj.* own
proteger *v.* to protect 13
proteína *f.* protein 15
próximo/a *adj.* next
prueba *f.* test; quiz 2
psicología *f.* psychology 2
psicólogo/a *m., f.* psychologist 16
publicar *v.* to publish
público *m.* audience
pueblo *m.* town 4
puerta *f.* door 2
puertorriqueño/a *adj.* Puerto Rican 3
pues *conj.* well; then
puesto *m.* position; job 16
puesto/a *p.p.* put 15
puro/a *adj.* pure 13

Q

que *conj. pron.* that; who; which 9
   ¡Qué…! How…! 3
   ¡Qué dolor! What pain!
   ¡Qué gusto (+ *inf.*)! What a
      pleasure to…!
   ¡Qué ropa más bonita!
      What pretty clothes! 6

VOCABULARIO

¡Qué sorpresa! What a surprise!
¿qué? what? 1; which? 9
¿Qué día es hoy? What day is it?
¿Qué es? What is it? 1
¿Qué hay de nuevo? What's
   new? 1
¿Qué hicieron ellos/ellas? What
   did they do? 6
¿Qué hicieron ustedes? What did
   you (*form., pl.*) do? 6
¿Qué hiciste? What did you
   (*fam., sing.*) do? 6
¿Qué hizo él/ella? What did
   he/she do? 6
¿Qué hizo usted? What did you
   (*form., sing.*) do? 6
¿Qué hora es? What time is it? 1
¿Qué les parece? What do
   you guys think? 9
¿Qué pasa? What's happening?;
   What's going on? 1
¿Qué pasó? What happened?;
   What's wrong?
¿Qué precio tiene? What is the
   price?
¿Qué tal? How are you?; How is it
   going? 1; How is/are…?
¿Qué talla lleva/usa usted? What
   size do you wear? 6
¿Qué tiempo hace? How's the
   weather?, What's the weather
   like? 5
quedar *v.* to be left over; to fit (*clothing*) 7;
   to be left behind 10; to be located 14
quedarse *v.* to stay; to remain 7
quehaceres *m., pl.* **domésticos** household
   chores 12
quemado/a *adj.* burned (out) 11
querer (e:ie) *v.* to want; to love 4
queso *m.* cheese 8
quien(es) *pron.* who 1; whom; that 9
   ¿Quién es...? Who is…? 1
   ¿Quién habla? Who is
      speaking? (*telephone*) 11
   ¿quién(es)? who?; whom? 1, 9
química *f.* chemistry 2
quince fifteen 1
   menos quince quarter to (*time*) 1
   y quince quarter after (*time*) 1
quinceañera *f.* young woman celebrating
   her fifteenth birthday 9
quinientos/as five hundred 6
quinto/a *adj.* fifth 5
quisiera *v.* I would like
quitar la mesa *v.* to clear the table 12
quitarse *v.* to take off 7
quizás *adv.* maybe 5

R

racismo *m.* racism
radio *f.* radio (*medium*)
radio *m.* radio (set) 11
radiografía *f.* X-ray 10
rápido/a *adj.* fast
ratón *m.* mouse 11
ratos libres *m., pl.* spare time 4
raya *f.* stripe 6
razón *f.* reason 3
rebaja *f.* sale 6
recado *m.* (*telephone*) message 11
receta *f.* prescription 10
recetar *v.* to prescribe 10
recibir *v.* to receive 3
reciclaje *m.* recycling 13
reciclar *v.* to recycle 13
recién casado/a *m., f.* newlywed 9
recoger *v.* to pick up 13
recomendar (e:ie) *v.* to recommend 8, 12
recordar (o:ue) *v.* to remember 4
recorrer *v.* to tour an area
recurso *m.* resource 13
   recurso natural natural resource 13
red *f.* network; Web 11
reducir *v.* to reduce 13
refresco *m.* soft drink 8
refrigerador *m.* refrigerator 12
regalar *v.* to give (*as a gift*) 9
regalo *m.* gift 6
regatear *v.* to bargain 6
región *f.* region; area 13
regresar *v.* to return 2
regular *adj. m., f.* so-so; OK 1
reído *p.p.* laughed 15
reírse (e:i) *v.* to laugh 9
relaciones *f., pl.* relationships
relajarse *v.* to relax 9
reloj *m.* clock; watch 2
renovable *adj.* renewable 13
renunciar *v.* **(a)** to resign (from) 16
repetir (e:i) *v.* to repeat 4
reportaje *m.* report
reportero/a *m., f.* reporter 16; journalist
representante *m., f.* representative
reproductor de CD *m.* CD player 11
reproductor de DVD *m.* DVD player 11
reproductor de MP3 *m.* MP3 player 11
resfriado *m.* cold (*illness*) 10
residencia estudiantil *f.* dormitory 2
resolver (o:ue) *v.* to resolve; to solve 13
respirar *v.* to breathe 13
respuesta *f.* answer 9
restaurante *m.* restaurant 4
resuelto/a *p.p.* resolved 15
reunión *f.* meeting 16
revisar *v.* to check 11

revisar el aceite to check the oil 11
revista *f.* magazine 4
rico/a *adj.* rich 6; *adj.* tasty; delicious 8
ridículo *adj.* ridiculous 13
río *m.* river 13
riquísimo/a *adj.* extremely delicious
rodilla *f.* knee 10
rogar (o:ue) *v.* to beg; to plead 12
rojo/a *adj.* red 6
romántico/a *adj.* romantic
romper *v.* **(con)** to break up (with) 9
romper(se) *v.* to break 10
   romperse la pierna to break one's leg 10
ropa *f.* clothing; clothes 6
   ropa interior underwear 6
rosado/a *adj.* pink 6
roto/a *adj.* broken; *p.p.* broken 15
rubio/a *adj.* blond(e) 3
ruso/a *adj.* Russian
rutina *f.* routine 7
   rutina diaria daily routine 7

S

sábado *m.* Saturday 2
saber *v.* to know; to know how 8
sabrosísimo/a *adj.* extremely delicious
sabroso/a *adj.* tasty; delicious 8
sacar *v.* to take out 12
   sacar fotos to take pictures 5
   sacar la basura to take out
      the trash 12
   sacar(se) una muela to have a
      tooth pulled 10
sacudir *v.* to dust 12
   sacudir los muebles dust the furniture 12
sal *f.* salt 8
sala *f.* living room 12; room
   sala de emergencia(s) emergency
      room 10
salado/a *adj.* salty 8
salario *m.* salary 16
salchicha *f.* sausage 8
salida *f.* departure; exit 5
salir *v.* to leave 4; to go out
   salir con to leave with; to go out
      with 4; to date (*someone*) 9
   salir de to leave from 4
   salir para to leave for (*a place*) 4
salmón *m.* salmon 8
salón *m.* **de belleza** beauty salon 14
salud *f.* health 10
saludable *adj.* healthy 10
saludar(se) *v.* to greet (each other)
saludo *m.* greeting 1
   saludos a... greetings to… 1
sandalia *f.* sandal 6
sándwich *m.* sandwich 8

C32

Spanish-English

sano/a *adj.* healthy 10
se *ref. pron.* himself, herself, itself, *form.* yourself, themselves, yourselves 7
se *impersonal* one 10
  Se nos dañó… The… broke down. 11
  Se hizo… He/she/it became…
  Se nos pinchó una llanta.
    We got a flat tire. 11
secadora *f.* clothes dryer 12
sección de (no) fumadores *f.* (non) smoking section 8
secretario/a *m., f.* secretary 16
secuencia *f.* sequence
sed *f.* thirst 3
seda *f.* silk 6
sedentario/a *adj.* sedentary 15; related to sitting
seguir (e:i) *v.* to follow; to continue; to keep (doing something) 4
  seguir una dieta equilibrada to eat a balanced diet 15
según *prep.* according to
segundo/a *adj.* second 5
seguro/a *adj.* sure; safe; confident 5
seis six 1
seiscientos/as six hundred 6
sello *m.* stamp 14
selva *f.* jungle 13
semáforo *m.* traffic light 11
semana *f.* week 2
  fin *m.* **de semana** weekend 4
  la semana pasada last week 6
semestre *m.* semester 2
sendero *m.* trail 13; trailhead
sentarse (e:ie) *v.* to sit down 7
sentir(se) (e:ie) *v.* to feel 7; to be sorry; to regret 13
señor (Sr.) *m.* Mr.; sir 1
señora (Sra.) *f.* Mrs.; ma'am 1
señorita (Srta.) *f.* Miss 1; young woman 1
separado/a *adj.* separated 9
separarse *v.* **(de)** to separate (from) 9
septiembre *m.* September 5
séptimo/a *adj.* seventh 5
ser *v.* to be 1
  ser aficionado/a (a) to be a fan (of) 4
  ser alérgico/a (a) to be allergic (to) 10
  ser gratis to be free of charge 14
serio/a *adj.* serious
servilleta *f.* napkin 12
servir (e:i) *v.* to help 5; to serve 8
sesenta sixty 2
setecientos/as seven hundred 6
setenta seventy 2
sexismo *m.* sexism
sexto/a *adj.* sixth 5
sí *adv.* yes 1
si *conj.* if 13
SIDA *m.* AIDS

sido *p.p.* been 15
siempre *adv.* always 7
siete seven 1
silla *f.* chair 2
sillón *m.* armchair 12
similar *adj. m., f.* similar
simpático/a *adj.* nice; likeable 3
sin *prep.* without 13, 15
  sin duda without a doubt
  sin embargo *adv.* however
  sin que *conj.* without 13
sino *conj.* but 7
síntoma *m.* symptom 10
sitio *m.* **web** website 11
situado/a *p.p.* located
sobre *m.* envelope 14; *prep.* on; over 2
sobrino/a *m., f.* nephew/niece 3
sociología *f.* sociology 2
sofá *m.* couch; sofa 12
sois *fam.* you are 1
sol *m.* sun 4, 5, 13
solar *adj.* solar 13
solicitar *v.* to apply (*for a job*) 16
solicitud (de trabajo) *f.* (job) application 16
sólo *adv.* only
soltero/a *adj.* single 9; unmarried
solución *f.* solution 13
sombrero *m.* hat 6
somos we are 1
son you/they are 1
  Son las… It's… o'clock. 1
sonar (o:ue) *v.* to ring 11
sonreído *p.p.* smiled 15
sonreír (e:i) *v.* to smile 9
sopa *f.* soup 8
sorprender *v.* to surprise 9
sorpresa *f.* surprise 9
sótano *m.* basement; cellar 12
soy I am 1
  Soy yo. That's me. 1
  soy de… I'm from… 1
su(s) *poss. adj.* his; her; its; *form.* your; their 3
subir *v.* to go up 11
subir(se) a to get on/into (a vehicle) 11
sucio/a *adj.* dirty 5
sucre *m.* former Ecuadorian currency 6
sudar *v.* to sweat 15
suegro/a *m., f.* father-in-law; mother-in-law 3
sueldo *m.* salary 16
suelo *m.* floor 12
sueño *m.* sleep 3
suerte *f.* luck 3
suéter *m.* sweater 6
sufrir *v.* to suffer 13
  sufrir muchas presiones to be under a lot of pressure 15
  sufrir una enfermedad to suffer (from) an illness 13

sugerir (e:ie) *v.* to suggest 12
supermercado *m.* supermarket 14
suponer *v.* to suppose 4
sur *m.* south 14
sustantivo *m.* noun
suyo(s)/a(s) *poss.* (of) his/her; (of) hers; (of) its; (of) *form.* your, (of) yours, (of) theirs; their 11

T

tal vez *adv.* maybe 5
talentoso/a *adj.* talented
talla *f.* size 6
  talla grande large 6
taller *m.* **(mecánico)** (mechanic's) repair shop 11
también *adv.* also; too 7
tampoco *adv.* neither; not either 7
tan *adv.* so 5
  tan pronto como as soon as 13
  tan… como as… as 8
tanque *m.* tank 11
tanto *adv.* so much
  tanto… como as much… as 8
  tantos/as… como as many… as 8
tarde *adv.* late 7
tarde *f.* afternoon; evening; P.M. 1
tarea *f.* homework 2
tarjeta *f.* card 4
  tarjeta de crédito credit card 6
  tarjeta postal postcard 4
taxi *m.* taxi(cab) 5
taza *f.* cup; mug 12
te *fam. pron.* you 5
  Te presento a… I would like to introduce… to you. (*fam.*) 1
  ¿Te gustaría? Would you like to?
  ¿Te gusta(n)…? Do you like…? 2
té *m.* tea 8
  té helado iced tea 8
teatro *m.* theater
teclado *m.* keyboard 11
técnico/a *m., f.* technician 16
tejido *m.* weaving
teleadicto/a *m., f.* couch potato 15
teléfono celular *m.* cell phone 11
telenovela *f.* soap opera
teletrabajo *m.* telecommuting 16
televisión *f.* television 11
  televisión por cable cable TV 11
televisor *m.* television set 11
temer *v.* to be afraid/concerned; to fear 13
temperatura *f.* temperature 10
temprano *adv.* early 7
tenedor *m.* fork 12
tener *v.* to have 3

C33

VOCABULARIO

tener... años to be... years old **3**
Tengo... años. I'm... years old. **3**
tener (mucho) calor to be (very) hot **3**
tener (mucho) cuidado to be (very) careful **3**
tener dolor de to have a pain in
tener éxito to be successful **16**
tener fiebre to have a fever **10**
tener (mucho) frío to be (very) cold **3**
tener ganas de (+ *inf.*) to feel like (*doing something*) **3**
tener (mucha) hambre *f.* to be (very) hungry **3**
tener (mucho) miedo to be (very) afraid/scared of **3**
tener miedo (de) que to be afraid that
tener planes to have plans **4**
tener (mucha) prisa to be in a (big) hurry **3**
tener que (+ *inf.*) *v.* to have to (*do something*) **3**
tener razón to be right **3**
tener (mucha) sed to be (very) thirsty **3**
tener (mucho) sueño to be (very) sleepy **3**
tener (mucha) suerte to be (very) lucky **3**
tener tiempo to have time
tener una cita to have a date; an appointment **9**
tenis *m.* tennis **4**
tensión *f.* tension
tercer, tercero/a *adj.* third **5**
terminar *v.* to end; to finish **2**
terminar de (+ *inf.*) to finish (*doing something*)
terremoto *m.* earthquake
terrible *adj.* terrible **13**
terror *m.* horror
ti *prep., obj. of prep., fam.* you
tiempo *m.* time **4**; weather
tiempo libre free time **4**
tienda *f.* shop; store **6**
tienda de campaña *f.* tent **5**
tierra *f.* land; soil **13**
tinto/a *adj.* red (wine) **8**
tío/a *m., f.* uncle/aunt **3**
tíos *m.* aunts and uncles **3**
título *m.* title
tiza *f.* chalk **2**
toalla *f.* towel **7**
tobillo *m.* ankle **10**
tocar *v.* to play (*a musical instrument*); to touch **13**
todavía *adv.* yet; still **5**
todo *m.* everything **5**
Todo está bajo control. Everything is under control.

todos/as *m., f., pl.* all of us; *m., pl.* everybody; everyone
¡Todos a bordo! All aboard!
todo(s)/a(s) *adj.* all **4**; whole; every; *adv.* completely
en todo el mundo throughout the world **13**
todos los días every day **10**
(todo) derecho straight ahead **14**
tomar *v.* to take; to drink **2**
tomar clases to take classes **2**
tomar el sol to sunbathe **4**
tomar en cuenta to take into account **8**
tomar fotos to take pictures **13**
tomar(le) la temperatura (a alguien) to take (someone's) temperature **10**
tomate *m.* tomato **8**
tonto/a *adj.* silly; foolish **3**
torcerse (el tobillo) *v.* to sprain (one's ankle) **10**
torcido/a *adj.* twisted; sprained **10**
tormenta *f.* storm
tornado *m.* tornado
tortilla *f.* tortilla **8**
tortillas de maíz tortilla made of corn flour
tortuga marina *f.* sea turtle **13**
tos *f., sing.* cough **10**
toser *v.* to cough **10**
tostado/a *adj.* toasted **8**
tostadora *f.* toaster
trabajador(a) *adj.* hard-working **3**
trabajar *v.* to work **2**
trabajo *m.* job; work **16**; written work
traducir *v.* to translate **8**
traer *v.* to bring **4**
tráfico *m.* traffic **11**
tragedia *f.* tragedy
traído/a *p.p.* brought **15**
traje *m.* suit **6**
traje de baño bathing suit **6**
tranquilo/a *adj.* calm; quiet **15**
¡Tranquilo! Stay calm!
transmitir to broadcast
tratar de (+ *inf.*) *v.* to try (*to do something*) **15**
Trato hecho. It's a deal.
trece thirteen **1**
treinta thirty **1**
y treinta thirty minutes past the hour (time) **1**
tren *m.* train **5**
tres three **1**
trescientos/as three hundred **6**
trimestre *m.* trimester; quarter **2**
triste *adj.* sad **5**
tú *fam. sing. sub. pron.* you **1**
Tú eres... You are... **1**
tu(s) *fam. poss. adj.* your **3**
turismo *m.* tourism **5**
turista *m., f.* tourist **1**

turístico/a *adj.* touristic
tuyo(s)/a(s) *fam. poss. pron.* your; (of) yours **11**

U

u *conj.* (*used instead of* **o** *before words beginning with* **o** *and* **ho**) or
Ud. *form., sing. sub. pron.* you **1**
Uds. *form., pl. sub. pron.* you **1**
último/a *adj.* last
un, uno/a *indef. art.* a; one **1**
una vez once; one time **6**
una vez más once again **9**
único/a *adj.* only **3**
universidad *f.* university **2**; college
unos/as *pron.* some **1**
urgente *adj.* urgent **12**
usar *v.* to wear; to use **6**
usted *form., sing. sub. pron.* you **1**
ustedes *form., pl. sub. pron.* you **1**
útil *adj.* useful
uva *f.* grape **8**

V

vaca *f.* cow
vacaciones *f., pl.* vacation **5**
valle *m.* valley **13**
Vamos. Let's go. **4**
vaquero *m.* cowboy
de vaqueros *m., pl.* western (*genre*)
varios/as *adj., pl.* several
vaso *m.* glass **12**
veces *f., pl.* times **6**
vecino/a *m., f.* neighbor **12**
veinte twenty **1**
veinticinco twenty-five **1**
veinticuatro twenty-four **1**
veintidós twenty-two **1**
veintinueve twenty-nine **1**
veintiocho twenty-eight **1**
veintiséis twenty-six **1**
veintisiete twenty-seven **1**
veintitrés twenty-three **1**
veintiún, veintiuno/a twenty-one **1**
vejez *f.* old age **9**
velocidad *f.* speed **11**
velocidad máxima speed limit **11**
vendedor(a) *m., f.* salesperson **6**
vender *v.* to sell **6**
venir *v.* to come **3**
ventana *f.* window **2**
ver *v.* to see **4**
ver películas *f., pl.* to watch movies **4**
a ver let's see **2**
verano *m.* summer **5**
verbo *m.* verbo
verdad *f.* truth **6**
¿verdad? right?

Spanish-English

verde *adj.*, green; not ripe **5**
verduras *pl., f.* vegetables **8**
vestido *m.* dress **6**
vestirse (e:i) *v.* to get dressed **7**
vez *f.* time **6**
viajar *v.* to travel **2**
viaje *m.* trip **5**
viajero/a *m., f.* traveler **5**
vida *f.* life **9**
video *m.* video **1**
videoconferencia *f.* video conference **16**
vidrio *m.* glass **13**
viejo/a *adj.* old **3**
viento *m.* wind
viernes *m., sing.* Friday **5**
vinagre *m.* vinegar **8**
vino *m.* wine **8**
   vino blanco white wine **8**
   vino tinto red wine **8**
violencia *f.* violence
visitar *v.* to visit **4**
   visitar un monumento to visit
     a monument **4**
visto/a *p.p.* seen **15**
vitamina *f.* vitamin **15**
viudo/a *adj.* widowed **9**
vivienda *f.* housing **12**
vivir *v.* to live **3**
vivo/a *adj.* clever; alive **5**; bright
volante *m.* steering wheel **11**
volcán *m.* volcano **13**
vóleibol *m.* volleyball **4**
volver (o:ue) *v.* to return **4**
   volver *v.* **a ver(te/lo/la)** to see (you/him/
     her) again
vos *pron.* you
vosotros/as *fam., pl. sub. pron.* you **1**
votar *v.* to vote
vuelta *f.* return trip
vuelto/a *p.p.* returned **15**
vuestro(s)/a(s) *poss. adj.* your **3**;
   (of) yours **11**

W

walkman *m.* Walkman

Y

y *conj.* and **1**
   y cuarto quarter after (*time*) **1**
   y media half-past (*time*) **1**
   y quince quarter after (*time*) **1**
   y treinta thirty (minutes past
     the hour) **1**
   ¿Y tú? *fam.* And you? **1**
   ¿Y usted? *form.* And you? **1**
ya *adv.* already **6**

yerno *m.* son-in-law **3**
yo *sub. pron.* I **1**
   Yo soy... I'm... **1**
yogur *m.* yogurt

Z

zanahoria *f.* carrot **8**
zapatería *f.* shoe store **14**
zapato *m.* shoe **6**
   par *m.* **de zapatos** pair of shoes **6**
   zapatos de tenis sneakers **6**

VOCABULARIO

English-Spanish

A

A.M. **mañana** *f.* 1
able: be able to **poder (o:ue)** *v.* 4
aboard **a bordo** 1
accident **accidente** *m.* 10
accompany **acompañar** *v.* 14
account **cuenta** *f.* 14
accountant **contador(a)** *m., f.* 16
accounting **contabilidad** *f.* 2
ache **dolor** *m.* 10
acquainted: be acquainted with
  conocer *v.* 8
action **acción** *f.*
active **activo/a** *adj.* 15
actor **actor** *m.* 16
actress **actriz** *f.* 16
addict (*drug*) **drogadicto/a** *adj.* 15
additional **adicional** *adj.*
address **dirección** *f.* 14
adjective **adjetivo** *m.*
adolescence **adolescencia** *f.* 9
adventure **aventura** *f.*
advertise **anunciar** *v.*
advertisement **anuncio** *m.* 16
advice **consejo** *m.* 9
  give advice **dar** *v.* **un consejo**
advise **aconsejar** *v.* 12
advisor **consejero/a** *m., f.* 16
aerobic **aeróbico/a** *adj.* 15
  aerobic exercises **ejercicios**
    aeróbicos 15
  aerobics class **clase de**
    ejercicios aeróbicos 15
affected **afectado/a** *adj.* 13
  be affected (by) **estar** *v.*
    afectado/a (por) 13
affirmative **afirmativo/a** *adj.*
afraid: be (very) afraid **tener (mucho)**
  miedo 3
  be afraid **temer** *v.* 13
after **después de** *prep.* 7; **después**
  (de) que *conj.* 13
afternoon **tarde** *f.* 1
afterward **después** *adv.* 7; **luego** *adv.* 7
again **otra vez** *adv.*
age **edad** *f.*
agree **concordar** *v.* agree; **estar** *v.* **de**
  acuerdo
agreement **acuerdo** *m.*
AIDS **SIDA** *m.*
air **aire** *m.* 6
  air pollution **contaminación del**
    aire 13
airplane **avión** *m.* 5
airport **aeropuerto** *m.* 5
alarm clock **despertador** *m.* 7

alcohol **alcohol** *m.* 15
alcoholic **alcohólico/a** *adj.* 15
  alcoholic beverage **bebida**
    alcohólica 15
all **todo(s)/toda(s)** *adj.* 4
  All aboard! **¡Todos a bordo!**
  all of us **todos/as** *m., f., pl.*
  all over the world **en todo el**
    mundo
allergic **alérgico/a** *adj.* 10
  be allergic (to) **ser alérgico/a (a)** 10
alleviate **aliviar** *v.*
almost **casi** *adv.* 10
alone **solo/a** *adj.*
along **por** *prep.* 11
already **ya** *adv.* 6
also **también** *adv.* 7
alternator **alternador** *m.*
although **aunque** *conj.*
aluminum **aluminio** *m.* 13
  (made of) aluminum **de aluminio** 13
always **siempre** *adv.* 7
American (*North*)
  norteamericano/a *adj.* 3
among **entre** *prep.* 2
amusement **diversión** *f.*
and **y** *conj.* 1; **e** *conj.* (*before words beginning*
  *with **i** or **hi***)
  And you? **¿Y tú?** *fam.* 1;
    ¿Y usted? *form.* 1
angry **enojado/a** *adj.* 5
  get angry (with) **enojarse** *v.* **(con)** 7
animal **animal** *m.* 13
ankle **tobillo** *m.* 10
anniversary **aniversario** *m.* 9
  wedding anniversary **aniversario**
    de bodas 9
announce **anunciar** *v.*
announcer (*TV/radio*) **locutor(a)** *m., f.*
annoy **molestar** *v.* 7
another **otro/a** *adj.* 6
answer **contestar** *v.* 2; **respuesta** *f.* 9
antibiotic **antibiótico** *m.* 10
any **algún, alguno/a(s)** *adj.* 7
anyone **alguien** *pron.* 7
anything **algo** *pron.* 7
apartment **apartamento** *m.* 12
apartment building **edificio de**
  apartamentos 12
appear **parecer** *v.* 8
appetizers **entremeses** *m., pl.*
applaud **aplaudir** *v.*
apple **manzana** *f.* 8
appliance (electrical) **electrodoméstico**
  m. 12
applicant **aspirante** *m., f.* 16
application **solicitud** *f.* 16
  job application **solicitud de**
    trabajo 16
apply (*for a job*) **solicitar** *v.* 16
  apply for a loan **pedir** *v.* **un**

    préstamo 14
appointment **cita** *f.* 9
  have an appointment **tener** *v.*
    una cita 9
appreciate **apreciar** *v.*
April **abril** *m.* 5
aquatic **acuático/a** *adj.* 4
archaeologist **arqueólogo/a** *m., f.* 16
architect **arquitecto/a** *m., f.* 16
area **región** *f.* 13
arm **brazo** *m.* 10
armchair **sillón** *m.* 12
army **ejército** *m.*
around **por** *prep.* 11
around here **por aquí** 11
arrange **arreglar** *v.* 11
arrival **llegada** *f.* 5
arrive **llegar** *v.* 2
art **arte** *m.* 2
  fine arts **bellas artes** *f., pl.*
article *m.* **artículo**
artist **artista** *m., f.* 3
artistic **artístico/a** *adj.*
arts **artes** *f., pl.*
as **como** *conj.* 8
  as… as **tan… como** 8
  as a child **de niño/a** 10
  as many… as **tantos/as… como** 8
  as much… as **tanto… como** 8
  as soon as **en cuanto** *conj.* 13;
    tan pronto como *conj.* 13
ask (*a question*) **preguntar** *v.* 2
  ask for **pedir (e:i)** *v.* 4, 12
asparagus **espárragos** *m., pl.*
aspirin **aspirina** *f.* 10
at **a** *prep.* 1; **en** *prep.* 2
  at + *time* **a la(s)** + *time* 1
  at home **en casa** 7
  at least **por lo menos** 10
  at night **por la noche** 7
  at the end (of) **al fondo (de)**
  At what time…? **¿A qué hora…?**
    1, 9
  At your service. **A sus órdenes.**
attend **asistir (a)** *v.* 3
attic **altillo** *m.* 12
attract **atraer** *v.*
audience **público** *m.*
August **agosto** *m.* 5
aunt **tía** *f.* 3
  aunts and uncles **tíos** *m., pl.* 3
automatic **automático/a** *adj.* 14
  automatic teller machine (ATM)
    cajero automático 14
automobile **automóvil** *m.* 5
autumn **otoño** *m.* 5
avenue **avenida** *f.*
avoid **evitar** *v.* 13
award **premio** *m.*

C36

English-Spanish

B

backpack **mochila** *f.* 1
bad **mal, malo/a** *adj.* 3
   It's bad that… **Es malo que…** 12
   It's not bad at all. **No está nada mal.** 5
bag **bolsa** *f.* 6
bakery **panadería** *f.* 14
balanced **equilibrado/a** *adj.* 15
   balanced diet **dieta equilibrada** 15
balcony **balcón** *m.* 12
ball **pelota** *f.* 4
ballet **ballet** *m.*
banana **banana** *f.* 8
band **banda** *f.*
bank **banco** *m.* 14
bargain **ganga** *f.* 6; **regatear** *v.* 6
baseball (*game*) **béisbol** *m.* 4
basement **sótano** *m.* 12
basketball (*game*) **baloncesto** *m.* 4
bath **baño** *m.*
   take a bath **bañarse** *v.* 7
bathe **bañarse** *v.* 7
bathing suit **traje** *m.* **de baño** 6
bathroom **baño** *m.* 7; **cuarto de baño** *m.*
be **ser** *v.* 1; **estar** *v.* 2
be… years old **tener… años** 3
beach **playa** *f.* 5
   go to the beach **ir a la playa** 5
beans **frijoles** *m., pl.* 8
beautiful **hermoso/a** *adj.* 6
beauty **belleza** *f.* 14
   beauty salon **peluquería** *f.*; **salón** *m.* **de belleza** 14
because **porque** *conj.*
   because of **por** *prep.*
become (+ *adj.*) **ponerse (+ *adj.*)** 7; **convertirse** *v.*
bed **cama** *f.* 5
   go to bed **acostarse (o:ue)** *v.* 7
bedroom **alcoba** *f.* 12; **cuarto** *m.*; **recámara** *f.*
beef **carne** *f.* **de res** 8
   beef soup **caldo** *m.* **de patas**
been **sido** *p.p.* 15
beer **cerveza** *f.* 8
before **antes** *adv.* 7; **antes de** *prep.* 7; **antes (de) que** *conj.* 13
beg **rogar (o:ue)** *v.* 12
begin **comenzar (e:ie)** *v.* 4; **empezar (e:ie)** *v.* 4
behalf: on behalf of **de parte de**
behind **detrás de** *prep.* 2
believe **creer** *v.* 13
   believe (in) **creer** *v.* **(en)** 3
   believed **creído** *p.p.* 15
bellhop **botones** *m., f., sing.* 5
beloved **enamorado/a** *adj.*
below **debajo de** *prep.* 2
belt **cinturón** *m.* 6

benefit **beneficio** *m.* 16
beside **al lado de** *prep.* 2
besides **además (de)** *adv.* 10
best **mejor** *adj.* 8
   the best **el/la mejor** *m., f.* 8; **lo mejor** *neuter*
better **mejor** *adj.* 8
   It's better that… **Es mejor que…** 12
between **entre** *prep.* 2
bicycle **bicicleta** *f.* 4
big **gran; grande** *adj.* 3
   bigger **mayor** *adj.* 8
   biggest, (the) **el/la mayor** *m., f.* 8
bill **cuenta** *f.*
billion **mil millones** 6
biology **biología** *f.* 2
bird **pájaro** *m.* 13; **ave** *f.*
birth **nacimiento** *m.* 9
birthday **cumpleaños** *m., sing.* 9
   birthday cake **pastel de cumpleaños** 9
   have a birthday **cumplir** *v.* **años** 9
biscuit **bizcocho** *m.*
black **negro/a** *adj.* 6
blackberry **mora** *f.* 8
blackboard **pizarra** *f.* 2
blanket **manta** *f.* 12
block (city) **cuadra** *f.* 14
blond(e) **rubio/a** *adj.* 3
blouse **blusa** *f.* 6
blue **azul** *adj.* 6
boarding house **pensión** *f.* 5
boat **barco** *m.* 5
body **cuerpo** *m.* 10
bone **hueso** *m.* 10
book **libro** *m.* 2
bookcase **estante** *m.* 12
bookshelves **estante** *m.* 12
bookstore **librería** *f.* 2
boot **bota** *f.* 6
bore **aburrir** *v.* 7
bored **aburrido/a** *adj.* 5
   be bored **estar** *v.* **aburrido/a** 5
   get bored **aburrirse** *v.*
boring **aburrido/a** *adj.* 5
born: be born **nacer** *v.* 9
borrow **pedir prestado** 14
borrowed **prestado/a** *adj.*
boss **jefe** *m.*, **jefa** *f.* 16
bother **molestar** *v.* 7
bottle **botella** *f.* 9
   bottle of wine **botella de vino** 9
bottom **fondo** *m.*
boulevard **bulevar** *m.*
boy **chico** *m.* 1; **muchacho; niño** *m.* 3
boyfriend **novio** *m.* 3
brakes **frenos** *m., pl.* 11
bread **pan** *m.* 8
break **romper(se)** *v.* 10
   break (one's leg) **romperse (la pierna)** 10

break down **dañar** *v.* 10
   The bus broke down. **Se nos dañó el autobús.**
break up (with) **romper** *v.* **(con)** 9
breakfast **desayuno** *m.* 8
   have breakfast **desayunar** *v.* 8
breathe **respirar** *v.* 13
bring **traer** *v.* 4
broadcast **transmitir** *v.*; **emitir** *v.*
brochure **folleto** *m.*
broken **roto/a** *adj.*; **roto/a** *p.p.* 15
   be broken **estar roto/a**
brother **hermano** *m.* 3
   brother-in-law **cuñado** *m., f.* 3
   brothers and sisters **hermanos** *m., pl.* 3
brought **traído/a** *p.p.* 15
brown **café** *adj.* 6; **marrón** *adj.*
brunet(te) **moreno/a** *adj.*
brush **cepillar** *v.* 7
   brush one's hair **cepillarse el pelo** 7
   brush one's teeth **cepillarse los dientes** 7
build **construir** *v.*
building **edificio** *m.* 12
bullfight **corrida** *f.* **de toros**
bump into (*something accidentally*) **darse con**
burned (out) **quemado/a** *adj.* 11
bus **autobús** *m.* 1
   bus station **estación** *f.* **de autobuses** 5
business **negocios** *m., pl.* 16
   business administration **administración** *f.* **de empresas** 2
   business-related **comercial** *adj.* 16
businessman **hombre** *m.* **de negocios** 16
businesswoman **mujer** *f.* **de negocios** 16
busy **ocupado/a** *adj.* 5
but **pero** *conj.* 2, 7; **sino** *conj.* (*in negative sentences*)
butcher's shop **carnicería** *f.* 14
butter **mantequilla** *f.* 8
buy **comprar** *v.* 2
by **por** *conj.* 11; **para** *prep.* 11
   by means of **por** *prep.* 11
   by phone **por teléfono**
   by plane **en avión** 5
   by way of **por** *prep.* 11
Bye. **Chau.** *interj. fam.* 1

C

cabin **cabaña** *f.* 5
cable TV **televisión** *f.* **por cable** *m.* 11
café **café** *m.* 4
cafeteria **cafetería** *f.* 2
cake **pastel** *m.* 9

C37

VOCABULARIO

calculator **calculadora** *f.* 11
call **llamar** *v.* 11
  call on the phone **llamar por teléfono**
  be called **llamarse** *v.* 7
calm **tranquilo/a** *adj.* 15
  Stay calm! **¡Tranquilo/a!**
calorie **caloría** *f.* 15
camera **cámara** *f.* 11
  digital camera **cámara digital** 11
camp **acampar** *v.* 5
can **lata** *f.* 13
can **poder (o:ue)** *v.* 4
Canadian **canadiense** *adj.* 3
candidate **aspirante** *m. f.* 16;
  candidate **candidato/a** *m., f.*
candy **dulces** *m., pl.* 9
capital city **capital** *f.* 1
car **coche** *m.* 11; **carro** *m.* 11;
  auto(móvil) *m.* 5
caramel **caramelo** *m.*
card **tarjeta** *f.* 4; *(playing)* **carta** *f.*
care **cuidado** *m.* 3
  take care of **cuidar** *v.* 13
career **carrera** *f.* 16
careful: be (very) careful **tener** *v.*
  (mucho) cuidado 3
caretaker **ama** *f.* **de casa** 12
carpenter **carpintero/a** *m., f.* 16
carpet **alfombra** *f.* 12
carrot **zanahoria** *f.* 8
carry **llevar** *v.* 2
cartoons **dibujos** *m., pl.* **animados**
case: in case (that) **en caso (de) que** 13
cash (a check) **cobrar** *v.* 14; **efectivo** *m.*
  cash register **caja** *f.* 6
  pay in cash **pagar** *v.* **al contado,**
  pagar en efectivo
cashier **cajero/a** *m., f.*
cat **gato/a** *m., f.* 3
CD player **reproductor** *m.* **de CD** 11
celebrate **celebrar** *v.* 9
cellar **sótano** *m.* 12
cell phone **teléfono** *m.* **celular** 11
cereal **cereales** *m., pl.* 8
certain **cierto** *m.*; **seguro** *m.* 13
  it's (not) certain **(no) es**
  seguro/cierto 13
chair **silla** *f.* 2
chalk **tiza** *f.* 2
champagne **champán** *m.* 9
change **cambiar** *v.* **(de)** 9
channel *(TV)* **canal** *m.*
character *(fictional)* **personaje** *m.*
  main character **personaje principal**
charge *(for a product or service)*
  cobrar *v.* 14
chauffeur **conductor(a)** *m., f.* 1
chat **conversar** *v.* 2
cheap **barato/a** *adj.* 6

check **comprobar** *v.*; **revisar** *v.* 11; *(bank)*
  cheque *m.* 14
  check the oil **revisar el aceite** 11
checking account **cuenta** *f.* **corriente** 14
cheese **queso** *m.* 8
chef **cocinero/a** *m., f.* 16
chemistry **química** *f.* 2
chest of drawers **cómoda** *f.* 12
chicken **pollo** *m.* 8
child **niño/a** *m., f.* 3
childhood **niñez** *f.* 9
children **hijos** *m., pl.* 3
Chinese **chino/a** *adj.*
chocolate **chocolate** *m.*
  chocolate cake **pastel** *m.* **de chocolate**
cholesterol **colesterol** *m.* 15
choose **escoger** *v.*
chop *(food)* **chuleta** *f.* 8
Christmas **Navidad** *f.* 9
church **iglesia** *f.* 4
citizen **ciudadano/a** *m., f.*
city **ciudad** *f.* 4
class **clase** *f.* 2
  take classes **tomar** *v.* **clases** 2
classical **clásico/a** *adj.*
classmate **compañero/a** *m., f.* **de clase** 2
clean **limpio/a** *adj.* 5; **limpiar** *v.* 12
  clean the house *v.* **limpiar la casa** 12
  clean up **arreglar** *v.* 12
clear *(weather)* **despejado/a** *adj.* 5
  clear the table **quitar** *v.* **la mesa** 12
  It's clear. *(weather)* **Está despejado.** 5
clerk **dependiente/a** *m., f.* 6
clever **vivo/a** *adj.* 5
client **cliente/a** *m., f.* 6
climb **escalar** *v.* 4
  climb mountains **escalar montañas** 4
clinic **clínica** *f.* 10
clock **reloj** *m.* 2
close **cerrar (e:ie)** *v.* 4
closed **cerrado/a** *adj.* 5
closet **armario** *m.* 12
clothes **ropa** *f.* 6
clothes dryer **secadora** *f.* 12
clothing **ropa** *f.* 6
cloud **nube** *f.* 13
cloudy **nublado/a** *adj.* 5
  It's (very) cloudy. **Está (muy) nublado.** 5
coat **abrigo** *m.* 6
coffee **café** *m.* 8
  coffee maker **cafetera** *f.*
cold **frío** *m.* 3; *(disease)* **resfriado** *m.* 10
  be (very) cold *(feel)* **tener (mucho) frío** 3
  It's (very) cold. *(weather)* **Hace (mucho) frío.** 5

college **universidad** *f.*
collision **choque** *m.*
color **color** *m.* 6
comb one's hair **peinarse** *v.* 7
come **venir** *v.* 3
comedy **comedia** *f.*
comfortable **cómodo/a** *adj.* 5
commerce **negocios** *m., pl.* 16
commercial **comercial** *adj.* 16
communicate (with) **comunicarse** *v.* **(con)**
communication **comunicación** *f.*
  means of communication
  medios *m., pl.* **de comunicación**
community **comunidad** *f.* 1
compact disc (CD) **disco** *m.* **compacto** 11
  compact disc player **reproductor** *m.* **de CD** 11
company **compañía** *f.* 16; **empresa** *f.* 16
comparison **comparación** *f.*
completely **completamente** *adv.*
composer **compositor(a)** *m., f.*
computer **computadora** *f.* 1, 11
  computer disc **disco** *m.* 11
  computer monitor **monitor** *m.* 11
  computer programmer
  programador(a) *m., f.* 3
  computer science **computación** *f.* 2
concerned: to be concerned **temer** *v.* 13
concert **concierto** *m.*
conductor *(musical)* **director(a)** *m., f.*
confirm **confirmar** *v.* 5
  confirm a reservation **confirmar una reservación** 5
congested **congestionado/a** *adj.* 10
Congratulations! **¡Felicidades!;**
  ¡Felicitaciones!
conservation **conservación** *f.* 13
conserve **conservar** *v.* 13
considering **para** *prep.* 11
consume **consumir** *v.* 15
contact lenses **lentes** *m., pl.* **de contacto**
container **envase** *m.* 13
contamination **contaminación** *f.*
content **contento/a** *adj.* 5
contest **concurso** *m.*
continue **seguir (e:i)** *v.* 4
control **control** *m.*; **controlar** *v.* 13
  be under control **estar bajo control**
conversation **conversación** *f.* 2
converse **conversar** *v.*
cook **cocinar** *v.* 12; **cocinero/a** *m., f.* 16
cookie **galleta** *f.* 9
cool **fresco/a** *adj.* 5
  It's cool. *(weather)* **Hace fresco.** 5
corn **maíz** *m.*
corner **esquina** *m.* 14
cost **costar (o:ue)** *v.* 6
cotton **algodón** *m.* 6
  (made of) cotton **de algodón** 6

C38

English-Spanish

couch **sofá** m. 12
couch potato **teleadicto/a** m., f. 15
cough **tos** f. 10; **toser** v. 10
counselor **consejero/a** m., f. 16
count (on) **contar** v. **(con)** 12
country (nation) **país** m. 1
countryside **campo** m. 5; **paisaje** m.
couple **pareja** f. 9
   couple (married) **matrimonio** m. 9
course **curso** m. 2; **materia** f.
courtesy **cortesía** f.
cousin **primo/a** m., f. 3
cover **cubrir** v.
covered **cubierto** p.p.
cowboy **vaquero** m.
crafts **artesanía** f.
craftsmanship **artesanía** f.
crash **chocar** v. **(con)** 11
crater **cráter** m. 13
crazy **loco/a** adj. 6
create **crear** v.
credit **crédito** m. 6
   credit card **tarjeta** f. **de crédito** 6
crime **crimen** m.
cross **cruzar** v. 14
culture **cultura** f.
cup **taza** f. 12
currency exchange **cambio** m. **de moneda**
current events **actualidades** f., pl.
curriculum vitae **currículum** m.
curtains **cortinas** f., pl. 12
custard (baked) **flan** m. 9
custom **costumbre** f.
customer **cliente/a** m., f.
customs **aduana** f. 5
   customs inspector **inspector(a)**
     m., f. **de aduanas** 5
cycling **ciclismo** m. 4

D

dad **papá** m. 3
daily **diario/a** adj. 7
   daily routine **rutina** f. **diaria** 7
damage **dañar** v. 10
dance **bailar** v. 2; **danza** f.; **baile** m.
dancer **bailarín/bailarina** m., f. 16
danger **peligro** m. 13
dangerous **peligroso/a** adj.
dark-haired **moreno/a** adj. 3
date (appointment) **cita** f. 9; (calendar)
   fecha f. 5; (someone) **salir** v. **con**
   (alguien) 9
   date: have a date **tener** v. **una cita** 9
daughter **hija** f. 3
   daughter-in-law **nuera** f. 3
day **día** m. 1
   day before yesterday **anteayer** adv. 6
deal **trato** m.

It's a deal. **Trato hecho.**
It's not a big deal. **No es para tanto.**
death **muerte** f. 9
decaffeinated **descafeinado/a** adj. 15
December **diciembre** m. 5
decide **decidir** v. 3
decided **decidido/a** p.p., adj.
declare **declarar** v.
deforestation **deforestación** f. 13
delicious **delicioso/a** adj. 8; **rico/a** adj. 8;
   sabroso/a adj. 8
delighted **encantado/a** adj. 1
dentist **dentista** m., f. 10
deny **negar (e: ie)** v. 13
department store **almacén** m. 6
departure **salida** f. 5
deposit **depositar** v. 14
describe **describir** v. 3
described **descrito/a** p.p. 15
desert **desierto** m. 13
design **diseño** m.
designer **diseñador(a)** m., f. 16
desire **desear** v. 12
desk **escritorio** m. 2
dessert **postre** m. 8
destroy **destruir** v. 13
develop **desarrollar** v. 13
diary **diario** m. 1
dictatorship **dictadura** f.
dictionary **diccionario** m. 1
die **morir (o:ue)** v. 8
died **muerto/a** p.p. 15
diet **dieta** f. 15
   balanced diet **dieta equilibrada** 15
   be on a diet **estar** v. **a dieta** 15
   eat a balanced diet **seguir una**
     dieta equilibrada 15
difficult **difícil** adj. 3
dining room **comedor** m. 12
dinner **cena** f. 8
   have dinner **cenar** v. 8
direction: in the direction of **para** prep. 11
directions: give directions **indicar cómo**
   llegar v. 14
director **director(a)** m., f.
dirty **ensuciar** v.; **sucio/a** adj. 5
   get (something) dirty **ensuciar** v. 12
disagree **no estar de acuerdo**
disaster **desastre** m.
discover **descubrir** v. 13
discovered **descubierto** p.p. 15
discrimination **discriminación** f.
dish **plato** m.
   main dish **plato principal** 8
dishwasher **lavaplatos** m., sing. 12
disk **disco** m. 11
disorderly **desordenado/a** adj. 5
dive **bucear** v. 4
divorce **divorcio** m. 9
divorced **divorciado/a** adj. 9

get divorced (from) **divorciarse** v. **(de)** 9
dizzy **mareado/a** adj. 10
do **hacer** v. 4
   do aerobics **hacer ejercicios**
     aeróbicos 15
   do errands **hacer diligencias**
   do household chores **hacer**
     quehaceres m., pl. **domésticos** 12
   do stretching exercises **hacer**
     ejercicios de estiramiento 15
doctor **médico/a** m., f. 3;
   doctor(a) m., f. 10
documentary (film) **documental** m.
dog **perro/a** m., f. 3
domestic **doméstico/a** adj.
done **hecho/a** p.p. 15
door **puerta** f. 2
dormitory **residencia** f. **estudiantil** 2
double **doble** adj. 5
   double room **habitación** f. **doble** 5
doubt **duda** f. 13; **dudar** v. 13
   There is no doubt… **No cabe duda**
     de… 13; **No hay duda de…** 13
down **abajo** adv.
downtown **centro** m. 4
drama **drama** m.
dramatic **dramático/a** adj.
draw **dibujar** v. 2
drawing **dibujo** m.
dress **vestido** m. 6
   get dressed **vestirse (e:i)** v. 7
drink **beber** v. 3; **bebida** f. 8; **tomar** v. 2
   Do you want something to drink?
     ¿Quieres algo de tomar?
drive **conducir** v. 8; **manejar** v. 11
driver **conductor(a)** m., f. 1
drug f. **droga** 15
   drug addict **drogadicto/a** adj. 15
due to **por** prep.
   due to the fact that **debido a**
during **durante** prep. 7; **por** prep. 11
dust **sacudir** v. 12
   dust the furniture **sacudir los**
     muebles 12
DVD player **reproductor de DVD** m. 11
dying: I'm dying to (for)… **me muero por…**

E

each **cada** adj. 6
eagle **águila** f.
ear (outer) **oreja** f. 10
early **temprano** adv. 7
earn **ganar** v. 16
earthquake **terremoto** m.
ease **aliviar** v.
east **este** m. 14
   to the east **al este** 14
easy **fácil** adj. 3

C39

VOCABULARIO

extremely easy **facilísimo** 8
eat **comer** v. 3
ecological **ecologista** adj. 13
ecologist **ecologista** adj. 13
ecology **ecología** f. 13
economics **economía** f.
ecotourism **ecoturismo** m. 13
Ecuadorian **ecuatoriano/a** adj. 3
effective **eficaz** adj. m., f.
egg **huevo** m. 8
eight **ocho** 1
eight hundred **ochocientos/as** 6
eighteen **dieciocho** 1
eighth **octavo/a** 5
eighty **ochenta** 2
either... or **o... o** conj. 7
elect **elegir** v.
election **elecciones** f., pl.
electrician **electricista** m., f. 16
electricity **luz** f. 12
elegant **elegante** adj. 6
elevator **ascensor** m. 5
eleven **once** 1
e-mail **correo** m. **electrónico** 4
　e-mail message **mensaje** m.
　　electrónico 4
　read e-mail **leer** v. **el correo**
　　electrónico 4
　write an e-mail **escribir** v. **un mensaje**
　　electrónico 4
embarrassed **avergonzado/a** adj. 5
embrace (each other) **abrazar(se)** v.
emergency **emergencia** f. 10
　emergency room **sala** f. **de**
　　emergencia(s) 10
employee **empleado/a** m., f. 5
employment **empleo** m. 16
end **fin** m. 4; **terminar** v. 2
　end table **mesita** f. 12
energy **energía** f. 13
engaged: get engaged (to)
　comprometerse v. **(con)** 9
engineer **ingeniero/a** m., f. 3
English (language) **inglés** m. 2; **inglés,**
　inglesa adj. 3
enjoy **disfrutar** v. **(de)** 15
enough **bastante** adj. 10
entertainment **diversión** f. 4
entrance **entrada** f. 12
envelope **sobre** m.14
environment **medio ambiente** m. 13
equality **igualdad** f.
equipped **equipado/a** adj.
eraser **borrador** m. 2
errand f. **diligencia** 14
establish **establecer** v.
evening **tarde** f. 1
event **acontecimiento** m.
every day **todos los días** 10
everybody **todos/as** m., f., pl.

everything **todo** m. 5
　Everything is under control. **Todo**
　　está bajo control.
exactly **en punto** adv. 1
exam **examen** m. 2
excellent **excelente** adj. 5
excess **exceso** m. 15
　in excess **en exceso** 15
exchange **intercambiar** v.
　in exchange for **por** 11
exciting **emocionante** adj. m., f.
excursion **excursión** f. 4
excuse **disculpar** v.
Excuse me. (May I?) **Con permiso.** 1;
　(I beg your pardon.) **Perdón.** 1
exercise **ejercicio** m. 15
　hacer v. **ejercicio** 15
exit **salida** f. 5
expensive **caro/a** adj. 6
experience **experiencia** f.
explain **explicar** v. 2
explore **explorar** v.
　explore a city/town **explorar una**
　　ciudad/pueblo
expression **expresión** f.
extinction **extinción** f. 13
eye **ojo** m. 10

F

fabulous **fabuloso/a** adj 5
face **cara** f. 7
facing **enfrente de** prep. 14
fact: in fact **de hecho**
factory **fábrica** f. 13
fall (down) **caerse** v. 10
　fall asleep **dormirse (o:ue)** v. 7
　fall in love (with) **enamorarse** v.
　　(de) 9
fall (season) **otoño** m. 5
fallen **caído/a** p.p. 15
family **familia** f. 3
famous **famoso/a** adj. 16
fan **aficionado/a** adj. 4
　be a fan (of) **ser aficionado/a (a)** 4
far from **lejos de** prep. 2
farewell **despedida** f.
fascinate **fascinar** v. 7
fashion **moda** f. 6
　be in fashion **estar** v. **de moda** 6
fast **rápido/a** adj.
fat **gordo/a** adj. 3; **grasa** f. 15
father **padre** m. 3
father-in-law **suegro** m. 3
favorite **favorito/a** adj. 4
fax (machine) **fax** m. 11
fear **miedo** m. 3; **temer** v. 13
February **febrero** m. 5
feel v. **sentir(se) (e:ie)** 7

feel like (doing something) **tener**
　ganas de (+ inf.**)** 3
festival **festival** m.
fever **fiebre** f. 10
　have a fever **tener** v. **fiebre** 10
few **pocos/as** adj. pl.
field: field of study **especialización** f. 16
fifteen **quince** 1
　young woman celebrating her
　　fifteenth birthday
　　quinceañera f. 9
fifth **quinto/a** adj. 5
fifty **cincuenta** 2
fight **luchar** v. **(por)**
figure (number) **cifra** f.
file **archivo** m. 11
fill **llenar** v.
　fill out a form **llenar un formulario** 14
　fill up the tank **llenar el tanque** 11
finally **finalmente** adv; **por último** 7;
　por fin 11
find **encontrar (o:ue)** v. 4
　find (each other) **encontrar(se)** v.
fine arts **bellas artes** f., pl.
fine **multa** f. 11
　That's fine. **Está bien.**
finger **dedo** m. 10
finish **terminar** v. 4
　finish (doing something)
　　terminar v. **de (+** inf.**)**
fire **incendio** m.; **despedir (e:i)** v. 16
firefighter **bombero/a** m., f. 16
firm **compañía** f. 16; **empresa** f. 16
first **primer, primero/a** adj. 5
fish (food) **pescado** m. 8; **pescar** v. 5;
　(live) **pez** m. 13
　fish market **pescadería** f. 14
fisherman **pescador** m.
fisherwoman **pescadora** f.
fishing **pesca** f. 5
fit (clothing) **quedar** v. 7
five **cinco** 1
five hundred **quinientos/as** 6
fix (put in working order) **arreglar** v. 11
fixed **fijo/a** adj. 6
flag **bandera** f.
flank steak **lomo** m. 8
flat tire: We got a flat tire. **Se nos**
　pinchó una llanta. 11
flexible **flexible** adj. 15
flood **inundación** f.
floor (story in a building) **piso** m. 5;
　suelo m.12
　ground floor **planta** f. **baja** 5
　top floor **planta** f. **alta**
flower **flor** f. 13
flu **gripe** f. 10
fog **niebla** f.
foggy: It's (very) foggy. **Hay (mucha) niebla.** 5
folk **folclórico/a** adj.

C40

English-Spanish

follow **seguir (e:i)** *v.* 4
food **comida** *f.* 8
foolish **tonto/a** *adj.* 3
foot **pie** *m.* 10
football **fútbol** *m.* **americano** 4
for **para** *prep.* 11; **por** *prep.* 11
   for example **por ejemplo** 11
   for me **para mí**
forbid **prohibir** *v.*
foreign **extranjero/a** *adj.*
   foreign languages **lenguas**
     f., pl. **extranjeras** 2
forest **bosque** *m.* 13
forget **olvidar** *v.* 10
fork **tenedor** *m.* 12
form **formulario** *m.* 14
forty **cuarenta** 2
forward **en marcha** *adv.*
four **cuatro** 1
four hundred **cuatrocientos/as** 6
fourteen **catorce** 1
fourth **cuarto/a** *adj.* 5
free **libre** *adj.* 4
   be free of charge **ser gratis** 14
   free time **tiempo** *m.* **libre** 4;
     ratos *m., pl.* **libres** 4
freedom **libertad** *f.*
freezer **congelador** *m.*
French **francés, francesa** *adj.* 3
   French fries **papas** *f., pl* **fritas** 8;
     patatas *f., pl* **fritas** 8
frequently **frecuentemente** *adv.* 10;
   con frecuencia 10
Friday **viernes** *m., sing.* 2
fried **frito/a** *adj.* 8
   fried potatoes **papas** *f., pl.* **fritas**;
     patatas *f., pl.* **fritas**
friend **amigo/a** *m., f.* 3
friendly **amable** *adj.* 5
friendship **amistad** *f.* 9
from **de** *prep.* 1; **desde** *prep.* 6
   from where? **¿de dónde?** 9
   from the United States
     estadounidense *adj.* 3
   from time to time **de vez en**
     cuando 10
   He/She/It is from… **Es de…** 1
   I'm from… **Soy de…** 1
fruit **fruta** *f.* 8
   fruit juice **jugo** *m.* **de fruta** 8
   fruit store **frutería** *f.* 14
full **lleno/a** *adj.* 11
fun **divertido/a** *adj.*
   fun activity **diversión** *f.* 4
   have fun **divertirse (e:ie)** *v.* 9
function **funcionar** *v.*
furniture **muebles** *m., pl.* 12
furthermore **además (de)** *adv.* 10
future **futuro** *m.* 16; **porvenir** *m.*
   in the future **en el futuro**

G

gain weight **aumentar** *v.* **de peso** 15;
   engordar *v.* 15
game (*match*) **partido** *m.* 4; **juego** *m.* 5
   game show **concurso** *m.*
garage **garaje** *m.* 11, 12
garden **jardín** *m.* 12
garlic **ajo** *m.* 8
gas station **gasolinera** *f.* 11
gasoline **gasolina** *f.* 11
geography **geografía** *f.* 2
German **alemán, alemana** *adj.* 3
get **conseguir (e:i)** *v.* 4; **obtener** *v.* 16
   get along well/badly (with)
     llevarse *v.* **bien/mal (con)** 9
   get bored **aburrirse** *v.*
   get off of/out of (a vehicle)
     bajar(se) *v.* **de** 11
   get on/into (a vehicle)
     subir(se) *v.* **a** 11
   get up **levantarse** *v.* 7
gift **regalo** *m.* 6
girl **chica** *f.* 1; **muchacha**; **niña** *f.* 3
girlfriend **novia** *f.* 3
give **dar** *v.* 6; (*as a gift*) **regalar** 9
   give directions **indicar cómo**
     llegar *v.* 14
glass (*drinking*) **vaso** *m.* 12; **vidrio** *m.* 13
   (made of) glass **de vidrio** 13
glasses **gafas** *f., pl.* 6
   sunglasses **gafas de sol** 6
global warming **calentamiento**
   global *m.* 13
gloves **guantes** *m., pl.* 6
go **ir** *v.* 4
   go away **irse** 7
   go by boat **ir en barco** 5
   go by bus **ir en autobús** 5
   go by car **ir en auto(móvil)** 5
   go by motorcycle **ir en**
     motocicleta 5
   go by plane **ir en avión** 5
   go by subway **ir en metro** 5
   go by taxi **ir en taxi** 5
   go by the bank **pasar por el banco** 14
   go by train **ir en tren** 5
   go by **pasar** *v.* **por**
   go down; **bajar** *v.* 11
   go fishing **ir de pesca** 5
   go for a hike (in the mountains) **ir de**
     excursión (a las montañas) 4
   go out **salir** *v.* 9
   go out with **salir con** 4, 9
   go through customs **pasar por la**
     aduana 5
   go up **subir** *v.* 11
   go with **acompañar** *v.* 14
   Let's get going. **En marcha.**
   Let's go. **Vamos.** 4

goblet **copa** *f.* 12
going to: be going to (*do something*) **ir a**
   (+ inf.) 4
golf **golf** *m.* 4
good **buen, bueno/a** *adj.* 1, 3
   Good afternoon. **Buenas tardes.** 1
   Good evening. **Buenas noches.** 1
   Good idea! **¡Buena idea!**
   Good morning. **Buenos días.** 1
   Good night. **Buenas noches.** 1
   I'm good, thanks. **Bien, gracias.**
   It's good that… **Es bueno que…** 12
Goodbye. **Adiós.** *m.* 1
   say goodbye (to) **despedirse** *v.*
     (de) (e:i)
good-looking **guapo/a** *adj.* 3
government **gobierno** *m.* 13
GPS **navegador** *m.* **GPS** 11
graduate (from) **graduarse** *v.* **(de)** 9
grains **cereales** *m., pl.* 8
granddaughter **nieta** *f.* 3
grandfather **abuelo** *m.* 3
grandmother **abuela** *f.* 3
grandparents **abuelos** *m., pl.* 3
grandson **nieto** *m.* 3
grape **uva** *f.* 8
grass **hierba** *f.*; **césped** *m.* 13
grave **grave** *adj.* 10
gray **gris** *adj. m., f.* 6
great **gran; grande** *adj.* 3;
   fenomenal *adj.* 5
green **verde** *adj. m., f.* 5
greet (each other) **saludar(se)** *v.*
greeting **saludo** *m.* 1
   Greetings to… **Saludos a…** 1
grilled (*food*) **a la plancha** 8
   grilled flank steak **lomo a la**
     plancha
ground floor **planta** *f.* **baja** 5
guest (*at a house/hotel*) **huésped** *m., f.* 5;
   (*invited to a function*) **invitado/a** *m., f.* 9
guide **guía** *m., f.*
gym **gimnasio** *m.* 4
gymnasium **gimnasio** *m.* 4

H

hair **pelo** *m.* 7
hairdresser **peluquero/a** *m., f.* 16
hairdressing salon **peluquería** *f.* 14
half **medio/a** *adj.* 3
   half-brother **medio hermano** 3;
   half-sister **media hermana** 3
   half-past (*time*) **y media** 1
hallway **pasillo** *m.* 12
ham **jamón** *m.* 8
hamburger **hamburguesa** *f.* 8
hand **mano** *f.* 1
Hands up! **¡Manos arriba!**

C41

VOCABULARIO

handsome **guapo/a** *adj.* 3
happen **ocurrir** *v.*
happiness **alegría** *f.* 9
Happy birthday! **¡Feliz cumpleaños!**
happy **alegre** *adj.* 5; **contento/a** *adj.* 5;
    feliz *adj.* 5
    be happy **alegrarse** *v.* **(de)** 13
hard **difícil** *adj.* 3
hard-working **trabajador(a)** *adj.* 3
hardly **apenas** *adv.* 10
haste **prisa** *f.* 3
hat **sombrero** *m.* 6
hate **odiar** *v.* 9
have **tener** *v.* 3
    Have a good trip! **¡Buen viaje!**
    have a tooth pulled **sacar(se) una**
        muela 10
    have to (*do something*) **tener**
        que (+ *inf.*) 3; **deber (+ *inf.*)** 3
he **él** *sub. pron.* 1
he is **él es** 1
he/she/it is, you (*form., sing.*) are **está** 2
head **cabeza** *f.* 10
headache **dolor de cabeza** *m.* 10
health **salud** *f.* 10
healthful **saludable** *adj.*
healthy **sano/a, saludable** *adj.* 10
    lead a healthy life **llevar** *v.* **una**
        vida sana 15
hear **oír** *v.* 4
heard **oído/a** *p.p.* 15
hearing: sense of hearing **oído** *m.*
heart **corazón** *m.* 10
heat **calor** *m.* 3
Hello. **Hola.** *interj.* 1; (*on the telephone*) **Aló.**
    11; **¿Bueno?** 11; **Diga.** 11
help **ayudar** *v.* 12
    help each other **ayudarse** *v.*
her **su(s)** *poss. adj.* 3; **la** *pron.* 5; **le** *pron.* 6;
    hers **suyo(s)/a(s)** *poss. pron.* 11
here **aquí** *adv.* 1
    Here it is… **Aquí está…** 5
    Here we are at/in… **Aquí estamos**
        en… 2
    It's not here. **No está.** 5
Hi. **Hola.** *interj.* 1
highway **autopista** *f.*; **carretera** *f.*
hike **excursión** *f.* 4
    go on a hike **hacer una excursión** 5;
    ir de excursión 4
hiker **excursionista** *m., f.* 4
hiking **de excursión** 4
him **lo** *pron.* 5; **le** *pron.* 6
hire **contratar** *v.* 16
his **su(s)** *poss. adj.* 3; **suyo(s)/a(s)**
    poss. pron. 11
history **historia** *f.* 2
hobby **pasatiempo** *m.* 4
hockey **hockey** *m.* 4

holiday **día** *m.* **de fiesta** 9
home **hogar** *m.* 12
    home page **página** *f.* **principal** 11
homemaker **ama** (*f.*) **de casa** 12
homework **tarea** *f.* 2
hood (car) **capó** *m.* 11
hope **esperar** *v.* 2, 13
    I hope (that) **ojalá (que)** *interj.* 13
horror **terror** *m.*
hors d'oeuvres **entremeses** *m., pl.* 8
horse **caballo** *m.* 5
hospital **hospital** *m.* 10
hot **picante** *adj.* 8
hot: be (very) hot (*feel*) **tener (mucho)**
    calor 3; (*weather*) **hacer (mucho)**
    calor 5
hotel **hotel** *m.* 5
hour **hora** *f.* 1
house **casa** *f.* 4
household chores **quehaceres** *m., pl.*
    domésticos 12
housekeeper **ama** *f.* **de casa** 12
housing **vivienda** *f.* 12
How…! **¡Qué…!** 3
    how **¿cómo?** *adv.* 1, 9
    How are you? **¿Qué tal?** 1
    How are you? **¿Cómo estás?**
        fam. 1
    How are you? **¿Cómo está usted?**
        form. 1
    How can I help you? **¿En qué**
        puedo servirles? 5
    How did… go for you? **¿Cómo les**
        fue…? 15
    How is it going? **¿Qué tal?** 1
    How is/are . . . ? **¿Qué tal…?**
    How much/many?
        ¿Cuántos/as? *pron.* 1, 9
    How much does… cost? **¿Cuánto**
        cuesta…? 6
    How old are you? **¿Cuántos**
        años tienes? *fam.* 3
    How's the weather? **¿Qué tiempo**
        hace? 5
however **sin embargo** *adv.*
hug (each other) **abrazar(se)** *v.*
humanities **humanidades** *f., pl.*
hunger **hambre** *f.* 3
hundred **cien, ciento** 2
hungry: be (very) hungry **tener** *v.*
    (mucha) hambre 3
hunting **caza** *f.* 13
hurricane **huracán** *m.*
hurry **apurarse; darse prisa** *v.* 15
    be in a (big) hurry **tener** *v.*
    (mucha) prisa 3
hurt **doler (o:ue)** *v.* 10
    It hurts me a lot. **Me duele mucho.** 10
husband **esposo** *m.* 3

I

I **yo** *sub. pron.* 1
    I am… **Yo soy…** 1
    I don't like them at all. **No me**
        gustan nada.
    I hope (that) **Ojalá (que)** *interj.* 13
    I wish (that) **Ojalá (que)** *interj.* 13
    I would like… **me gustaría(n)…** 7
    I would like to introduce… to you.
        Le presento a… *form.* 1;
        Te presento a… *fam.* 1
ice cream **helado** *m.* 9
    ice cream shop **heladería** *f.* 14
iced **helado/a** *adj.* 9
    iced tea **té helado** 8
idea **idea** *f.* 4
if **si** *conj.* 13
illness **enfermedad** *f.* 10
important **importante** *adj.* 3
    be important to **importar** *v.* 7, 12
    It's important that… **Es**
        importante que… 12
impossible **imposible** *adj.* 13
    It's impossible… **Es imposible…** 13
improbable **improbable** *adj.* 13
    It's improbable… **Es improbable…** 13
improve **mejorar** *v.* 13
in **en** *prep.* 2; **por** *prep.* 11
    in the afternoon **de la tarde** 1;
    por la tarde 7
    in the evening **de la noche** 1;
    (*early*) **por la tarde** 7
    in the morning **de la mañana** 1;
    por la mañana 7
    in love (with) **enamorado/a (de)** 5
    in which **en qué** 2
    in front of **delante de** *prep.* 2;
    enfrente 14
increase **aumento** *m.* 16
incredible **increíble** *adj.* 5
inequality **desigualdad** *f.*
infection **infección** *f.* 10
inform **informar** *v.*
inhabitants **habitantes** *m., pl* 13
injection **inyección** *f.* 10
    give an injection **poner** *v.* **una**
    inyección 10
injure (oneself) **lastimarse** *v.* 10
    injure (one's foot) **lastimarse**
    (el pie) 10
inner ear **oído** *m.*
insist (on) **insistir** *v.* **(en)** 12
installments: pay in installments
    pagar *v.* **a plazos** 14
intelligent **inteligente** *adj.* 3
intend **pensar** *v.* **(+ *inf.*)** 4
interest **interesar** *v.* 7

C42

English-Spanish

interesting **interesante** *adj.* 3
  be interesting to **interesar** *v.* 7
international **internacional** *adj. m., f.*
Internet **red** *f.*; **Internet** *m.* 11
interview **entrevista** *f.* 16; interview
  entrevistar *v.* 16
interviewer **entrevistador(a)** *m., f.* 16
introduction **presentación** *f.*
invest **invertir (e:ie)** *v.* 16
invite **invitar** *v.* 9
iron clothes **planchar** *v.* **la ropa** 12
it **lo/la** *pron.* 5
Italian **italiano/a** *adj.* 3
its **su(s)** *poss. adj.* 3, **suyo(s)/a(s)**
  poss. pron. 11

J

jacket **chaqueta** *f.* 6
January **enero** *m.* 5
Japanese **japonés, japonesa** *adj.* 3
jeans **bluejeans** *m., pl.* 6
jewelry store **joyería** *f.* 14
job **empleo** *m.* 16; **puesto** *m.* 16;
  trabajo *m.* 16
  job application **solicitud** *f.* **de**
  trabajo 16
jog **correr** *v.*
journalism **periodismo** *m.* 2
journalist **periodista** *m., f.* 3;
  reportero/a *m., f.*
joy **alegría** *f.*
  give joy **dar** *v.* **alegría**
joyful **alegre** *adj.* 5
juice **jugo** *m.* 8
July **julio** *m.* 5
June **junio** *m.* 5
jungle **selva** *f.* 13, **jungla** *f.*
just **apenas** *adv.* 10
  have just done something
  acabar de (+ *inf.***)** 6

K

keep (doing something) **seguir**
  (e:ie) *v.* 4
key **llave** *f.* 5
keyboard **teclado** *m.* 11
kilometer **kilómetro** *m.* 11
kind: That's very kind of you. **Muy**
  amable. *adj.* 5
kiss (each other) **besar(se)** *v.*; **beso** *m.* 6
kitchen **cocina** *f.* 12
knee **rodilla** *f.* 10
knife **cuchillo** *m.* 12
know **saber** *v.* 8; **conocer** *v.* 8
know how **saber** *v.* 8

L

laboratory **laboratorio** *m.* 2
lack **faltar** *v.* 7
lake **lago** *m.* 13
lamp **lámpara** *f.* 12
land **tierra** *f.* 13
landlord **dueño/a** *m., f.*
landscape **paisaje** *m.* 13
language **lengua** *f.* 2
laptop (computer) **computadora** *f.*
  portátil 11
large **gran, grande** *adj.* 3
large (*clothing size*) **talla** *f.* **grande** *adj.* 6
last **durar** *v.*; **pasado/a** *adj.* 6;
  último/a *adj.*
  last name **apellido** *m.* 9
  last night **anoche** *adv.* 6
  last week **la semana pasada** 6
  last year **el año pasado** 6
late **tarde** *adv.* 7
later (on) **más tarde** *adv.* 7
  See you later. **Hasta la vista.** 1;
  Hasta luego. 1
laugh **reírse (e:i)** *v.* 9
laughed **reído** *p.p.* 15
laundromat **lavandería** *f.* 14
law **ley** *f.* 13
lawyer **abogado/a** *m., f.* 16
lazy **perezoso/a** *adj.*
learn **aprender** *v.* 3
least, (the) **el/la/los/las menos** 8
leave **salir** *v.* 4; **irse** *v.* 7
  leave a tip **dejar una propina** 9
  leave for (*a place*) **salir para** 4
  leave from **salir de** 4
  leave behind **dejar** *v.* 16
left **izquierdo/a** *adj.* 2
  be left behind **quedar** *v.* 10
  be left over **quedar** *v.* 7
  to the left of **a la izquierda de** 2
leg **pierna** *f.* 10
lemon **limón** *m.* 8
lend **prestar** *v.*
less **menos** *adv.* 10
  less… than **menos… que** 8
  less than (+ *number*) **menos de**
  (+ *number***)** 8
lesson **lección** *f.* 1
let **dejar** *v.* 12
  let's see **a ver**
letter **carta** *f.* 4
lettuce **lechuga** *f.* 8
liberty **libertad** *f.*
library **biblioteca** *f.* 2
license (*driver's*) **licencia** *f.* **de conducir** 11
lie **mentira** *f.* 6
lie down **acostarse (o:ue)** *v.* 7

life **vida** *f.* 9
  of my life **de mi vida**
lifestyle: lead a healthy lifestyle
  llevar una vida sana 15
lift **levantar** *v.* 15
  lift weights **levantar pesas** 15
light **luz** *f.* 12
like **como** *adv.* 8; **gustar** *v.* 2, 7
  like this **así** *adv.* 10
  like very much **encantar** *v.*;
  fascinar *v.* 7
  I like… **me gusta(n)…** 2
  I like… very much *v.* **Me**
  encanta…
  Do you like… ? **¿Te gusta(n)…?** 2
likeable **simpático/a** *adj.* 3
likewise **igualmente** *adv.* 1
line **línea** *f.* 4; **cola** (*queue*) *f.* 14
listen to **escuchar** *v.* 2
  Listen! (*command*) **¡Oye!** *fam.,*
  *sing.*1; **¡Oiga!** *form., sing.*; **¡Oigan!**
  fam., form., pl.
  listen to music **escuchar música**
  listen to the radio **escuchar la radio**
literature **literatura** *f.*
little (*quantity*) **poco/a** *adj.* 5; **poco** *adv.* 10
live **vivir** *v.* 3
living room **sala** *f.* 12
loan **préstamo** *m.* 14; **prestar** *v.* 6
lobster **langosta** *f.* 8
located **situado/a** *adj.*
  be located **quedar** *v.* 14
lodging **alojamiento** *m.* 5
long **largo/a** *adj.* 6
look (at) **mirar** *v.* 2
look for **buscar** *v.* 2
lose **perder (e:ie)** *v.* 4
  lose weight **adelgazar** *v.* 15
lost **perdido/a** *adj.* 14
  be lost **estar perdido/a** 14
lot, a **muchas veces** 10
lot of, a **mucho/a** *adj.* 3
love (*another person*) **querer (e:ie)** *v.* 4;
  (*things*) **encantar** *v.* 7; **amor** *m.* 9;
  in love (with) **enamorado/a (de)** *adj.* 5
luck **suerte** *f.* 3
lucky: be (very) lucky **tener (mucha) suerte** 3
luggage **equipaje** *m.* 5
lunch **almuerzo** *m.* 8
  have lunch **almorzar (o:ue)** *v.* 8

M

ma'am **señora (Sra.)** *f.* 1
mad **enojado/a** *adj.* 5
magazine **revista** *f.* 4
  read a magazine **leer una revista** 4

C43

VOCABULARIO

magnificent **magnífico/a** *adj.* 5
mail **correo** *m.* 14; **enviar** *v.*, **mandar** *v.*
   mail a letter **echar una carta al buzón** 14
   mail carrier **cartero/a** *m.* 14
mailbox **buzón** *m.* 14
main **principal** *adj. m., f.* 8
maintain **mantener** *v.* 15
make **hacer** *v.* 4
   make the bed **hacer la cama** 12
makeup **maquillaje** *m.* 7
man **hombre** *m.* 1
manager **gerente** *m., f.* 16
many **mucho/a** *adj.* 3
   many times **muchas veces** 10
map **mapa** *m.* 1, 2
March **marzo** *m.* 5
margarine **margarina** *f.* 8
marinated fish **ceviche** *m.*
   lemon-marinated shrimp **ceviche de camarón**
marital status **estado** *m.* **civil** 9
market **mercado** *m.* 6
   open-air market **mercado al aire libre** 6
marriage **matrimonio** *m.* 9
married **casado/a** *adj.* 9
   get married (to) **casarse** *v.* **(con)** 9
marvelous **maravilloso/a** *adj.* 5
marvelously **maravillosamente** *adv.*
massage **masaje** *m.* 15
masterpiece **obra** *f.* **maestra**
match (*sports*) **partido** *m.*
   match **hacer** *v.* **juego (con)** 6
mathematics **matemáticas** *f., pl.* 2
matter **importar** *v.* 7, 12
maturity **madurez** *f.* 9
maximum **máximo/a** *m.* 11
May **mayo** *m.* 5
maybe **tal vez** *adv.* 5; **quizás** *adv.* 5
mayonnaise **mayonesa** *f.* 8
me **me** *pron.* 5
meal **comida** *f.* 8
means of communication **medios** *m., pl.* **de comunicación**
meat **carne** *f.* 8
mechanic **mecánico/a** *m., f.* 11
   (mechanic's) repair shop **taller** *m.* **mecánico** 11; **garaje** *m.* 11
media **medios** *m., pl.* **de comunicación**
medical **médico/a** *adj.* 10
medication **medicamento** *m.* 10
medicine **medicina** *f.* 10
medium **mediano/a** *adj.*
meet (each other) **encontrar(se)** *v.*
meeting **reunión** *f.* 16
menu **menú** *m.* 8
message (*telephone*) **recado** *m.* 11;
   (*text message*) **mensaje** *m.* **de texto** 11;

(*e-mail message*) **mensaje** *m.* **electrónico** 4
messy **desordenado/a** *adj.* 5
Mexican **mexicano/a** *adj.* 3
microwave **microonda** *f.* 12
   microwave oven **horno** *m.* **de microondas** 12
middle age **madurez** *f.* 9
midnight **medianoche** *f.* 1
mile **milla** *f.* 11
milk **leche** *f.* 8
million **millón** 6
   million of **millón de** 6
mine **mío/a(s)** *poss. pron.* 11
mineral **mineral** *m.* 15
   mineral water **agua** *f.* **mineral** 8
minute **minuto** *m.* 1
mirror **espejo** *m.* 7
Miss **señorita (Srta.)** *f.* 1
miss **perder (e:ie)** *v.* 4
mistaken **equivocado/a** *adj.* 5
modern **moderno/a** *adj.*
mom **mamá** *f.* 3
Monday **lunes** *m., sing.* 2
money **dinero** *m.* 6
monitor **monitor** *m.* 11
monkey **mono** *m.* 13
month **mes** *m.* 5
monument **monumento** *m.* 4
moon **luna** *f.* 13
more **más** *adj.* 2
   more... than **más... que** 8
   more than (+ *number*) **más de (+ number)** 8
morning **mañana** *f.* 1
most, (the) **el/la/los/las más** 8
mother **madre** *f.* 3
mother-in-law **suegra** *f.* 3
motor **motor** *m.* 11
motorcycle **moto(cicleta)** *f.* 5
mountain **montaña** *f.* 4
mouse **ratón** *m.* 11
mouth **boca** *f.* 10
move (*to another house/city/country*) **mudarse** *v.* 12
movie **película** *f.* 4
   movie star **estrella** *f.* **de cine**
   movie theater **cine** *m.* 4
MP3 player **reproductor** *m.* **de MP3** 11
Mr. **señor (Sr.)** *m.* 1
Mrs. **señora (Sra.)** *f.* 1
much **mucho/a** *adj.* 2, 3
mug **taza** *f.* 12
municipal **municipal** *adj.*
murder **crimen** *m.*
muscle **músculo** *m.* 15
museum **museo** *m.* 4
mushroom **champiñón** *m.* 8
music **música** *f.*
musical **musical** *adj.*
musician **músico/a** *m., f.*

must: It must be . . . **Debe ser...** 6
my **mi(s)** *poss. adj.* 3; **mío(s)/a(s)** *poss. pron.* 11

N

name **nombre** *m.* 5
   in my name **a mi nombre**
   in the name of **a nombre de**
   last name **apellido** *m.* 9
   My name is... **Me llamo...** 1
   be named **llamarse** *v.* 7
napkin **servilleta** *f.* 12
national **nacional** *adj., m., f.*
nationality **nacionalidad** *f.* 1
natural **natural** *adj., m., f.* 13
   natural disaster **desastre** *m.* **natural**
   natural resource **recurso** *m.* **natural** 13
nature **naturaleza** *f.* 13
nauseated **mareado/a** *adj.* 10
near **cerca de** *prep.* 2
necessary **necesario/a** *adj.* 12
   It's necessary that... **Es necesario que...** 12; **Hay que...** 14
neck **cuello** *m.* 10
need **faltar** *v.* 7; **necesitar** *v.* 2, 12
negative **negativo/a** *adj.*
neighbor **vecino/a** *m., f.* 12
neighborhood **barrio** *m.* 12
neither... nor **ni... ni** *conj.* 7; neither **tampoco** *adv.* 7
nephew **sobrino** *m.* 3
nervous **nervioso/a** *adj.* 5
network **red** *f.* 11
never **nunca** *adv.* 7; **jamás** *adv.* 7
new **nuevo/a** *adj.* 6
newlywed **recién casado/a** *m., f.* 9
news **noticias** *f., pl.*; **actualidades** *f., pl.*
newscast **noticiero** *m.*
newspaper **periódico** *m.* 4; **diario** *m.*
   read the newspaper **leer el periódico** 4
next **próximo/a** *adj.*
next to **al lado de** 2
nice **simpático/a** *adj.* 3; **amable** *adj.* 5
niece **sobrina** *f.* 3
night **noche** *f.* 1
   night stand **mesita** *f.* **de noche** 12
nine **nueve** 1
nine hundred **novecientos/as** 6
nineteen **diecinueve** 1
ninety **noventa** 2
ninth **noveno/a** 5
no **no** 1; **ningún, ninguno/a(s)** *adj.* 7
   no one **nadie** *pron.* 7
   No problem. **Ningún problema.**
   no way **de ninguna manera**
none **ningún, ninguno/a(s)** *pron.* 7
noon **mediodía** *m.* 1
nor **ni** *conj.* 7

C44

English-Spanish

north **norte** *m.* 14
  to the north **al norte** 14
nose **nariz** *f.* 10
not **no** 1
  not any **ningún, ninguno/a(s)** *adj.* 7
  not anyone **nadie** *pron.* 7
  not anything **nada** *pron.* 7
  not bad at all **nada mal** 5
  not either **tampoco** *adv.* 7
  not ever **nunca** *adv.* 7; **jamás** *adv.* 7
  Not very well. **No muy bien.** 1
  not working **descompuesto/a** *adj.* 11
notebook **cuaderno** *m.* 1
nothing **nada** *pron.* 1, 7
noun **sustantivo** *m.*
November **noviembre** *m.* 5
now **ahora** *adv.*
nowadays **hoy (en) día** *adv.*
nuclear energy **energía nuclear** 13
number **número** *m.* 1
nurse **enfermero/a** *m., f.* 10
nutrition **nutrición** *f.* 15

O

o'clock: It's… o'clock **Son las…** 1
  It's one o'clock. **Es la una.** 1
obey **obedecer (c:zc)** *v.*
obligation **deber** *m.*
obtain **conseguir (e:i)** *v.* 4; **obtener** *v.* 16
obvious **obvio** *adj.* 13
  it's obvious **es obvio** 13
occupation **ocupación** *f.* 16
occur **ocurrir** *v.*
ocean **mar** *m.* 5; **océano** *m.* 13
October **octubre** *m.* 5
of **de** *prep.* 1
  of course **claro que sí; por supuesto**
offer **oferta** *f.*; **ofrecer (c:zc)** *v.* 8
office **oficina** *f.* 12
  doctor's office **consultorio** *m.* 10
often **a menudo** *adv.* 10
Oh! **¡Ay!**
oil **aceite** *m.* 8
okay **regular** *adj.* 1
  It's okay. **Está bien.**
old **viejo/a** *adj.* 3; old age **vejez** *f.* 9
older **mayor** *adj., m., f.* 3
  older brother, sister **hermano/a mayor** *m., f.* 3
oldest **el/la mayor** 8
on **en** *prep.* 2; **sobre** *prep.* 2
  on behalf of **de parte de** *prep.*
  on the dot **en punto** *adv.* 1
  on time **a tiempo** *adv.* 10
  on top of **encima de** *prep.* 2
once **una vez** 6
once again **una vez más** 9
one **un, uno/a** 1

one hundred **cien(to)** 2
one million **un millón** 6
one thousand **mil** 6
one time **una vez** 6
one way (*travel*) **ida** *f.*
onion **cebolla** *f.* 8
only **sólo** *adv.*; **único/a** *adj.* 3
  only child **hijo/a único/a** *m., f.* 3
open **abrir** *v.* 3; **abierto/a** *adj.* 5
open-air **al aire libre** 6
opened **abierto/a** *p.p.* 15
opera **ópera** *f.*
operation **operación** *f.* 10
opposite **en frente de** *prep.* 14
or **o** *conj.* 7; **u** *conj.* (*before words beginning with o or ho*)
orange **anaranjado/a** *adj.* 6; **naranja** *f.* 8
orchestra **orquesta** *f.*
order **mandar** 12; (*food*) **pedir (e:i)** *v.* 8
  in order to **para** *prep.* 11
orderly **ordenado/a** *adj.* 5
ordinal (*numbers*) **ordinal** *adj.* 6
other **otro/a** *adj.* 6
our **nuestro(s)/a(s)** *poss. adj.* 3; *poss. pron.* 11
out of order **descompuesto/a** *adj.* 11
outside **fuera** *adv.*
outskirts **afueras** *f., pl.* 12
oven **horno** *m.* 12
over **sobre** *prep.* 2
own **propio/a** *adj.*
owner **dueño/a** *m., f.* 8

P

P.M. **tarde** *f.* 1
pack (one's suitcases) **hacer** *v.* **las maletas** 5
package **paquete** *m.* 14
page **página** *f.* 11
pain **dolor** *m.* 10
  have a pain in the (knee) **tener** *v.* **dolor de (rodilla)**
paint **pintar** *v.*
painter **pintor(a)** *m., f.* 16
painting **pintura** *f.* 12
pair **par** *m.* 6
  pair of shoes **par de zapatos** 6
pants **pantalones** *m., pl.* 6
pantyhose **medias** *f., pl.* 6
paper **papel** *m.* 2; (*report*) **informe** *m.*
  paper money **billete** *m.*
paragraph **párrafo** *m.*
Pardon me. (*May I?*) **Con permiso.** 1;
  (*Excuse me.*) Pardon me. **Perdón.** 1
parents **padres** *m., pl.* 3; **papás** *m., pl.* 3
park **parque** *m.* 4; **estacionar** *v.* 11
partner (*one of a couple*) **pareja** *f.* 9
party **fiesta** *f.* 9
pass **pasar** *v.*
passed **pasado/a** *p.p.*
passenger **pasajero/a** *m., f.* 1

passport **pasaporte** *m.* 5
past **pasado/a** *adj.* 6
pastime **pasatiempo** *m.* 4
pastry shop **pastelería** *f.* 14
patient **paciente** *m., f.* 10
patio **patio** *m.* 12
pay **pagar** *v.* 6
  pay with **pagar con** 6
  pay in cash **pagar al contado** 14; **pagar en efectivo**
  pay in installments **pagar a plazos** 14
  pay the bill **pagar la cuenta** 9
pea **arveja** *m.* 8
peace **paz** *f.*
peach **melocotón** *m.*
pear **pera** *f.*
pen **pluma** *f.* 2
pencil **lápiz** *m.* 1
penicillin **penicilina** *f.*
people **gente** *f.* 3
pepper **pimienta** *f.* 8
per **por** *prep.* 11
percent **por ciento**
perfect **perfecto/a** *adj.* 5
perhaps **quizás** *adv.*; **tal vez** *adv.*
periods **plazos** *m., pl.*
permission **permiso** *m.*
person **persona** *f.* 3
pharmacy **farmacia** *f.* 10
phenomenal **fenomenal** *adj.*
photograph **foto(grafía)** *f.* 1
physical (*exam*) **examen** *m.* **médico** 10
physician **médico/a** *m., f.* 3; **doctor(a)** *m., f.*
physics **física** *f., sing.* 2
pick up **recoger** *v.* 13
picture **foto** *f.* 5; **pintura** *f.*
pie **pastel** *m.*
pill (tablet) **pastilla** *f.* 10
pillow **almohada** *f.* 12
pineapple **piña** *f.* 8
pink **rosado/a** *adj.* 6
place **lugar** *m.* 4; **poner** *v.* 4
plaid **de cuadros** *adj.* 6
plan (*to do something*) **pensar** *v.* **(+ *inf.*)** 4
plane **avión** *m.* 5
plans **planes** *m., pl.*
  have plans **tener** *v.* **planes** 4
plant **planta** *f.* 13
plastic **plástico** *m.* 13
  (made of) plastic **de plástico** 13
plate **plato** *m.* 12
platter: platter of fried food **fuente** *f.* **de fritada**
play **drama** *m.*; **comedia** *f.*;
  jugar (u:ue) *v.* 4; (*a musical instrument*) **tocar** *v.*; (*a role*) **hacer** *v.* **un papel de**; (*cards*) **jugar** *v.* **a (las cartas)**; (*sports*) **practicar** *v.* **deportes** 4
player **jugador(a)** *m., f.* 4
playwright **dramaturgo/a** *m., f.*
plead **rogar (o:ue)** *v.* 12

C45

VOCABULARIO

pleasant **agradable** *adj.*
Please. **Por favor.** 1
Pleased to meet you. **Mucho gusto.** 1;
　Encantado/a. *adj.* 1
pleasing: be pleasing to **gustar** *v.* 7
pleasure **gusto** *m.* 1; **placer** *m.*
　It's a pleasure to… **Gusto de**
　　(+ *inf.*)
　It's been a pleasure. **Ha sido un**
　　placer.
　The pleasure is mine. **El gusto**
　　es mío. 1
poem **poema** *m.*
poet **poeta** *m., f.* 16
poetry **poesía** *f.*
police (force) **policía** *f.* 11
　police officer **policía** *m.*, **mujer** *f.*
　　policía 11
political **político/a** *adj.*
politician **político/a** *m., f.* 16
politics **política** *f.*
polka-dotted **de lunares** *adj.* 6
poll **encuesta** *f.*
pollute **contaminar** *v.* 13
polluted **contaminado/a** *adj.* 13
　be polluted **estar contaminado/a** 13
pollution **contaminación** *f.* 13
pool **piscina** *f.* 4
poor **pobre** *adj.* 6
population **población** *f.* 13
pork **cerdo** *m.* 8
　pork chop **chuleta** *f.* **de cerdo** 8
portable **portátil** *adj.* 11
　portable computer
　　computadora *f.* **portátil**
position **puesto** *m.* 16
possessive **posesivo/a** *adj.* 3
possible **posible** *adj.* 13
　it's (not) possible **(no) es posible** 13
post office **correo** *m.* 14
postcard **postal** *f.* 4; **tarjeta** *f.* **postal** 4
poster **cartel** *m.*
potato **papa** *f.* 8; **patata** *f.* 8
pottery **cerámica** *f.*
practice **entrenarse** *v.* 15; **practicar** *v.* 2
prefer **preferir (e:ie)** *v.* 4, 12
pregnant **embarazada** *adj. f.* 10
prepare **preparar** *v.* 2
preposition **preposición** *f.*
prescribe (*medicine*) **recetar** *v.* 10
prescription **receta** *f.* 10
present **regalo** *m.*; **presentar** *v.*
press **prensa** *f.*
pressure: be under a lot of pressure
　sufrir *v.* **muchas presiones** 15
pretty **bonito/a** *adj.* 3; **bastante** *adv.*
price **precio** *m.* 6
　fixed price **precio** *m.* **fijo** 6
print **estampado/a** *adj.*; **imprimir** *v.* 11
printer **impresora** *f.* 11
private (*room*) **individual** *adj.* 5

prize **premio** *m.*
probable **probable** *adj.* 13
　it's (not) probable **(no) es probable** 13
problem **problema** *m.* 1
profession **profesión** *f.* 3, 16
professor **profesor(a)** *m., f.* 1
program **programa** *m.* 1
programmer **programador(a)** *m., f.* 3
prohibit **prohibir** *v.* 10, 12
promotion (*career*) **ascenso** *m.* 16
pronoun **pronombre** *m.*
protect **proteger** *v.* 13
protein **proteína** *f.* 15
provided that **con tal (de) que** *conj.* 13
psychologist **psicólogo/a** *m., f.* 16
psychology **psicología** *f.* 2
publish **publicar** *v.*
Puerto Rican **puertorriqueño/a** *adj.* 3
pull a tooth **sacar** *v.* **una muela**
purchases **compras** *f., pl.*
pure **puro/a** *adj.* 13
purple **morado/a** *adj.* 6
purse **bolsa** *f.*
put **poner** *v.* 4; **puesto/a** *p.p.* 15
　put a letter in the mailbox **echar** *v.*
　　una carta al buzón 14
　put on (*a performance*) **presentar** *v.*
　put on (*clothing*) **ponerse** *v.* 7
　put on makeup **maquillarse** *v.* 7

Q

quality **calidad** *f.* 6
quarter **trimestre** *m.* 2
　quarter after (*time*) **y cuarto** 1;
　　y quince 1
　quarter to (*time*) **menos cuarto** 1;
　　menos quince 1
question **pregunta** *f.*
quickly **rápido** *adv.*
quiet **tranquilo/a** *adj.* 15
quit **dejar** *v.* 16
quite **bastante** *adv.* 10
quiz **prueba** *f.* 2

R

racism **racismo** *m.*
radio (*medium*) **radio** *f.*;
radio (*set*) **radio** *m.* 11
rain **llover (o:ue)** *v.* 5
　It's raining. **Llueve.** 5
raincoat **impermeable** *m.* 6
rainforest **bosque** *m.* **tropical** 13
raise (*salary*) **aumento** *m.* **de sueldo** 16
read **leer** *v.* 3; **leído/a** *p.p.* 15
ready **listo/a** *adj.* 15
real estate agency **agencia** *f.* **de bienes**
　raíces 12

reap the benefits (of) **disfrutar** *v.* **(de)** 15
reason **razón** *f.* 3
receive **recibir** *v.* 3
recommend **recomendar (e:ie)** *v.* 8, 12
recycle **reciclar** *v.* 13
recycling **reciclaje** *m.* 13
red **rojo/a** *adj.* 6
red-haired **pelirrojo/a** *adj.* 3
reduce **reducir** *v.* 13
　reduce stress/tension **aliviar** *v.* **el**
　　estrés/la tensión
refrigerator **refrigerador** *m.* 12
region **región** *f.* 13
regret **sentir (e:ie)** *v.* 13
related to sitting **sedentario/a** *adj.*
relationships **relaciones** *f., pl.*
relatives **parientes** *m., pl.* 3
relax **relajarse** *v.* 9
relieve stress/tension **aliviar el**
　estrés/la tensión 15
remain **quedarse** *v.* 7
remember **recordar (o:ue)** *v.* 4;
　acordarse (o:ue) *v.* **(de)** 7
remote control **control** *m.* **remoto** 11
renewable **renovable** *adj.* 13
rent **alquilar** *v.* 12; **alquiler** *m.* 12
repeat **repetir (e:i)** *v.* 4
report **informe** *m.*; **reportaje** *m.*
reporter **reportero/a** *m., f.* 16
representative **representante** *m., f.*
request **pedir (e:i)** *v.* 4
reservation **reservación** *f.* 5
resign (from) **renunciar** *v.* **(a)** 16
resolve **resolver (o:ue)** *v.* 13
resolved **resuelto/a** *p.p.* 15
resource **recurso** *m.* 13
responsibility **deber** *m.*; **responsabilidad** *f.*
rest **descansar** *v.* 2
　the rest **lo/los/las demás** *pron.*
restaurant **restaurante** *m.* 4
résumé **currículum** *m.* 16
retire (from work) **jubilarse** *v.* 9
return **regresar** *v.* 2; **volver (o:ue)** *v.* 4
　return trip **vuelta** *f.*
returned **vuelto/a** *p.p.* 15
rice **arroz** *m.* 8
rich **rico/a** *adj.* 6
ride **pasear** *v.* 4
　ride a bicycle **pasear en bicicleta** 4
　ride a horse **montar** *v.* **a caballo** 5
ridiculous **ridículo/a** *adj.* 13
　it's ridiculous **es ridículo** 13
right **derecha** *f.* 2
　right away **enseguida** *adv.*
　right here **aquí mismo**
　right now **ahora mismo** 5
　right there **allí mismo** 14
　be right **tener** *v.* **razón** 3
　to the right of **a la derecha de** 2
　right? (*question tag*) **¿no?** 1;
　　¿verdad?

C46

English-Spanish

rights **derechos** *m., pl.*
ring (*a doorbell*) **sonar (o:ue)** *v.* 11
river **río** *m.* 13
road **camino** *m.*
roast chicken **pollo** *m.* **asado** 8
roasted **asado/a** *adj.* 8
rock **piedra** *f.* 13
role **papel** *m.*
rollerblade **patinar** *v.* **en línea**
romantic **romántico/a** *adj.*
room **habitación** *f.* 5; **cuarto** *m.*;
  (*large, living*) **sala** *f.*
roommate **compañero/a** *m., f.*
  de cuarto 2
round-trip **de ida y vuelta** 5
  round-trip ticket **pasaje** *m.* **de**
    ida y vuelta 5
route **camino** *m.* 11
routine **rutina** *f.* 7
rug **alfombra** *f.* 12
run **correr** *v.* 3
  run errands **hacer** *v.* **diligencias** 14
  run into (*have an accident*)
    chocar *v.* **(con)** 11; (*run into*
    something) **darse con** *v.*
rush **apurarse; darse prisa** *v.* 15
Russian **ruso/a** *adj.*

S

sad **triste** *adj.* 5
  it's sad **es triste** 13
safe **seguro/a** *adj.* 5
said **dicho/a** *p.p.* 15
sake: for the sake of **por** *prep.*
salad **ensalada** *f.* 8
salary **salario** *m.* 16; **sueldo** *m.* 16
sale **rebaja** *f.* 6
salesperson **vendedor(a)** *m., f.* 6
salmon **salmón** *m.* 8
salt **sal** *f.* 8
salty **salado/a** *adj.* 8
same **mismo/a** *adj.*
sandal **sandalia** *f.* 6
sandwich **sándwich** *m.* 8
Saturday **sábado** *m.* 2
sausage **salchicha** *f.* 8
save (*on a computer*) **guardar** *v.* 11;
  save (*money*) **ahorrar** *v.* 14
savings **ahorros** *m., pl.* 14
  savings account **cuenta** *f.* **de ahorros** 14
say **decir** *v.* 6; **declarar** *v.*
scarcely **apenas** *adv.* 10
scared: be (very) scared **tener** *v.* **(mucho)**
  miedo 3
schedule **horario** *m.* 2
school **escuela** *f.* 1
science **ciencia** *f.*
  science fiction **ciencia ficción** *f.*
scientist **científico/a** *m., f.* 16

scream **gritar** *v.*
screen **pantalla** *f.* 11
scuba dive **bucear** *v.* 4
sculpt **esculpir** *v.*
sculptor **escultor(a)** *m., f.* 16
sculpture **escultura** *f.*
sea **mar** *m.* 5; **océano** *m.*
sea turtle **tortuga marina** *f.* 13
seafood **mariscos** *m., pl.* 8
search: in search of **por** *prep.* 11
season **estación** *f.* 5
seat **silla** *f.*
second **segundo/a** *adj.* 5
secretary **secretario/a** *m., f.* 16
sedentary **sedentario/a** *adj.* 15
see **ver** *v.* 4
  see (you/him/her) again **volver** *v.* **a**
    ver(te/lo/la)
  see movies **ver películas** 4
  See you. **Nos vemos.** 1
  See you later. **Hasta la vista.** 1;
    Hasta luego. 1
  See you soon. **Hasta pronto.** 1
  See you tomorrow. **Hasta**
    mañana. 1
seem **parecer** *v.* 8
seen **visto/a** *p.p.* 15
sell **vender** *v.* 6
semester **semestre** *m.* 2
send **enviar** *v.*; **mandar** *v.* 14
separate (from) **separarse** *v.* **(de)** 9
separated **separado/a** *adj.* 9
September **septiembre** *m.* 5
sequence **secuencia** *f.*
serious **grave** *adj.* 10
  extremely serious **gravísimo/a** *adj.* 13
serve **servir (e:i)** *v.* 8
set (*fixed*) **fijo** *adj.* 6
  set the table **poner** *v.* **la mesa** 12
seven **siete** 1
seven hundred **setecientos/as** 6
seventeen **diecisiete** 1
seventh **séptimo/a** *adj.* 5
seventy **setenta** 2
several **varios/as** *adj., pl.*
sexism **sexismo** *m.*
shame **lástima** *f.* 13
  It's a shame. **Es una lástima.** 13
shampoo **champú** *m.* 7
shape **forma** *f.* 15
  be in good shape **estar** *v.* **en**
    buena forma 15
share **compartir** *v.* 3
sharp (*time*) **en punto** 1
shave **afeitarse** *v.* 7
shaving cream **crema** *f.* **de afeitar** 7
she **ella** *sub. pron.* 1
  she is **ella es** 1
shellfish **mariscos** *m., pl.*
ship **barco** *m.*
shirt **camisa** *f.* 6

shoe **zapato** *m.* 6
  pair of shoes **par de zapatos** 6
  shoe size **número** *m.* **de zapato** 6
  shoe store **zapatería** *f.* 14
  tennis shoes **zapatos** *m., pl.*
    de tenis
shop **tienda** *f.* 6
shopping, to go **ir** *v.* **de compras** 6
  shopping mall **centro** *m.* **comercial** 6
short (*in height*) **bajo/a** *adj.* 3; (*in length*)
  corto/a *adj.* 6
short story **cuento** *m.*
shorts **pantalones cortos** *m., pl.* 6
should (*do something*) **deber** *v.*
  (+ inf.) 3
show **mostrar (o:ue)** *v.* 4; **espectáculo** *m.*
shower **ducha** *f.*; **ducharse** *v.* 7;
  bañarse *v.*
shrimp **camarón** *m.* 8
siblings **hermanos** *m., pl.* 3
sick **mal, malo/a** 5; **enfermo/a** *adj.* 10
  be sick **estar enfermo/a** 10
  get sick **enfermarse** *v.* 10
sickness **enfermedad** *f.* 10
sightseeing: go sightseeing **hacer** *v.*
  turismo 5
sign **firmar** *v.* 14; **letrero** *m.* 14
silk **seda** *f.* 6;
  (made of) **de seda** 6
silly **tonto/a** *adj.* 3
silverware **cubierto** *m.*
similar **similar** *adj. m., f.*
since **desde** *prep.*
sing **cantar** *v.* 2
singer **cantante** *m., f.* 16
single **soltero/a** *adj.* 9
  single room **habitación** *f.*
    individual 5
sink **lavabo** *m.*
sir **señor (Sr.)** *m.* 1
sister **hermana** *f.* 3
sister-in-law **cuñada** *f.* 3
sit down **sentarse (e:ie)** *v.* 7
six **seis** 1
six hundred **seiscientos/as** 6
sixteen **dieciséis** 1
sixth **sexto/a** *adj.* 5
sixty **sesenta** 2
size **talla** *f.* 6
  shoe size **número** *m.* **de zapato** 6
skate (in-line) **patinar** *v.* **(en línea)** 4
ski **esquiar** *v.* 4
skiing **esquí** *m.* 4
  water-skiing **esquí acuático** 4
skirt **falda** *f.* 6
sky **cielo** *m.* 13
sleep **dormir (o:ue)** *v.* 4; **sueño** *m.* 3
  go to sleep **dormirse (o:ue)** *v.* 7
sleepy: be (very) sleepy **tener** *v.* **(mucho)**
  sueño 3
slender **delgado/a** *adj.* 3

C47

VOCABULARIO

slim down **adelgazar** *v.* 15
slow **lento/a** *adj.* 11
slowly **despacio** *adv.*
small **pequeño/a** *adj.* 3
smaller **menor** *adj.* 8
smallest, (the) **el/la menor** *m., f.* 8
smart **listo/a** *adj.* 5
smile **sonreír (e:i)** *v.* 9
smiled **sonreído** *p.p.* 15
smoggy: It's (very) smoggy. **Hay
  (mucha) contaminación.**
smoke **fumar** *v.* 15
  not to smoke **no fumar** *v.* 15
smoking section **sección** *f.* **de fumadores** 8
  (non) smoking section **sección
  de (no) fumadores** 8
snack (in the afternoon) **merendar** *v.* 15;
  (afternoon snack) **merienda** *f.* 15
  have a snack **merendar** *v.* 15
sneakers **zapatos** *m., pl.* **de tenis** 6
sneeze **estornudar** *v.* 10
snow **nevar (e:ie)** *v.* 5; **nieve** *f.*
snowing: It's snowing. **Nieva.** 5
so (in such a way) **así** *adv.* 10; **tan** *adv.* 5
  so much **tanto** *adv.*
  so-so **regular** 1
  so that **para que** *conj.* 13
soap **jabón** *m.* 7
  soap opera **telenovela** *f.*
soccer **fútbol** *m.* 4
sociology **sociología** *f.* 2
sock **calcetín** *m.* 6
sofa **sofá** *m.* 12
soft drink **refresco** *m.* 8
software **programa** *m.* **de computación** 11
soil **tierra** *f.* 13
solar energy **energía solar** 13
solution **solución** *f.* 13
solve **resolver (o:ue)** *v.* 13
some **algún, alguno/a(s)** *adj.* 7; **unos/as**
  pron. 1; **unos/as** *m., f., pl. indef. art.* 1
somebody **alguien** *pron.*
someone **alguien** *pron.* 7
something **algo** *pron.* 7
sometimes **a veces** *adv.* 10
son **hijo** *m.* 3
song **canción** *f.*
son-in-law **yerno** *m.* 3
soon **pronto** *adj.* 10
  See you soon. **Hasta pronto.** 1
sorry: be sorry **sentir (e:ie)** *v.* 13
  I'm sorry. **Lo siento.** 1
  I'm so sorry. **Mil perdones.;
  Lo siento muchísimo.**
soup **caldo** *m.;* **sopa** *f.*
sour **agrio/a** *adj.* 8
south **sur** *m.* 14
  to the south **al sur** 14
Spanish (language) **español** *m.* 2;
  español(a) *adj.; m., f.* 3
spare time **ratos** *m., pl.* **libres** 4

speak **hablar** *v.* 2
specialization **especialización** *f.*
spectacular **espectacular** *adj.*
speech **discurso** *m.*
speed **velocidad** *f.* 11
  speed limit **velocidad máxima** 11
spelling **ortográfico/a** *adj.*
spend (money) **gastar** *v.* 6
  spend time **pasar** *v.* **el tiempo** 4
spicy **picante** *adj.* 8
spoon (table or large) **cuchara** *f.* 12
sport **deporte** *m.* 4
  sports-loving **deportivo/a** *adj.*
  sports-related **deportivo/a** *adj.* 4
spouse **esposo/a** *m., f.* 3
sprain (one's ankle) **torcerse** *v.*
  (el tobillo) 10
sprained **torcido/a** *adj.* 10
  be sprained **estar** *v.* **torcido/a** 10
spring **primavera** *f.* 5
stadium **estadio** *m.* 2
stage **etapa** *f.* 9
stairs **escalera** *f.* 12
stairway **escalera** *f.* 12
stamp **estampilla** *f.* 14; **sello** *m.* 14
stand in line **hacer** *v.* **cola** 14
star **estrella** *f.* 13
start (a vehicle) **arrancar** *v.* 11
state **estado** *m.*
station **estación** *f.* 5
statue **estatua** *f.*
status: marital status **estado** *m.*
  civil 9
stay **quedarse** *v.* 7
  Stay calm! **¡Tranquilo/a!** *adj.*
  stay in shape **mantenerse** *v.* **en
  forma** 15
steak **bistec** *m.* 8
steering wheel **volante** *m.* 11
step **etapa** *f.*
stepbrother **hermanastro** *m.* 3
stepdaughter **hijastra** *f.* 3
stepfather **padrastro** *m.* 3
stepmother **madrastra** *f.* 3
stepsister **hermanastra** *f.* 3
stepson **hijastro** *m.* 3
stereo **estéreo** *m.* 11
still **todavía** *adv.* 5
stock broker **corredor(a)** *m., f.* **de
  bolsa** 16
stockings **medias** *f., pl.* 6
stomach **estómago** *m.* 10
stone **piedra** *f.* 13
stop **parar** *v.* 11
  stop (doing something) **dejar** *v.* **de
  (+ inf.)** 13
store **tienda** *f.* 6
storm **tormenta** *f.*
story **cuento** *m.;* **historia** *f.*
stove **estufa** *f.* 12
straight (ahead) **derecho** *adj.* 14

straight ahead **(todo) derecho** 14
strange **extraño/a** *adj.* 13
  It's strange… **Es extraño…** 13
strawberry **frutilla** *f.;* **fresa** *f.* 8
street **calle** *f.* 11
stress **estrés** *m.* 15
stretching **estiramiento** *m.* 15
  stretching exercises **ejercicios
  m., pl. de estiramiento** 15
strike (labor) **huelga** *f.*
stripe **raya** *f.* 6
  striped **de rayas** *adj.* 6
stroll **pasear** *v.* 4
strong **fuerte** *adj.* 15
struggle (for) **luchar** *v.* **(por)**
student **estudiante** *m., f.* 1;
  estudiantil *adj.*
study **estudiar** *v.* 2
stuffed up (sinuses) **congestionado/a**
  adj. 10
stupendous **estupendo/a** *adj.* 5
style **estilo** *m.*
suburbs **afueras** *f., pl.* 12
subway **metro** *m.* 5
  subway station **estación** *f.* **del
  metro** 5
success **éxito** *m.* 16
successful: be successful **tener** *v.* **éxito** 16
such as **tales como**
suddenly **de repente** *adv.* 6
suffer **sufrir** *v.* 13
  suffer from an illness **sufrir una
  enfermedad** 13
sufficient **bastante** *adj.*
sugar **azúcar** *m.* 8
suggest **sugerir (e:ie)** *v.* 12
suit **traje** *m.* 6
suitcase **maleta** *f.* 1
summer **verano** *m.* 5
sun **sol** *m.* 4, 13
sunbathe **tomar** *v.* **el sol** 4
Sunday **domingo** *m.* 2
sunglasses **gafas** *f., pl.* **de sol** 6; **gafas
  oscuras; lentes** *m., pl.* **de sol**
sunny: It's (very) sunny.
  Hace (mucho) sol. 5
supermarket **supermercado** *m.* 14
suppose **suponer** *v.* 4
sure **seguro/a** *adj.* 5
  be sure (of) **estar** *v.* **seguro/a (de)**
  5, 13
surf the Internet **navegar
  v. en Internet**
surprise **sorprender** *v.* 9; **sorpresa** *f.* 9
survey **encuesta** *f.*
sweat **sudar** *v.* 15
sweater **suéter** *m.* 6
sweep the floor **barrer** *v.* **el suelo** 12
sweet **dulce** *adj.* 8
sweets **dulces** *m., pl.* 9
swim **nadar** *v.* 4

C48

English-Spanish

swimming **natación** *f.* 4
  swimming pool **piscina** *f.* 4
symptom **síntoma** *m.* 10

T

table **mesa** *f.* 2
tablespoon **cuchara** *f.* 12
tablet (*pill*) **pastilla** *f.* 10
take **tomar** *v.* 2, 8; **llevar** *v.*
  Take care! **¡Cuídense!**
  take care of **cuidar** *v.* 13
  take (someone's) temperature
    tomar(le) *v.* **la temperatura**
    (a alguien) 10
  take (*wear*) a shoe size **calzar** *v.* 6
  take a bath **bañarse** *v.* 7
  take a shower **ducharse** *v.* 7
  take into account **tomar** *v.* **en cuenta**
  take off **quitarse** *v.* 7
  take out the trash **sacar** *v.*
    la basura 12
  take pictures **sacar** *v.* **fotos** 5;
    tomar fotos 13
talented **talentoso/a** *adj.*
talk **hablar** *v.* 2; **conversar** *v.* 2
  talk show **programa** *m.*
    de entrevistas
tall **alto/a** *adj.* 3
tank **tanque** *m.* 11
tape (audio) **cinta** *f.*
taste **probar (o:ue)** *v.* 8
tasty **rico/a** *adj.* 8; **sabroso/a** *adj.* 8
tax **impuesto** *m.*
taxi(cab) **taxi** *m.* 5
tea **té** *m.* 8
teach **enseñar** *v.* 2
teacher **profesor(a)** *m., f.* 1;
  (*elementary school*) **maestro/a** *m., f.* 16
team **equipo** *m.* 4
technician **técnico/a** *m., f.* 16
telecommuting **teletrabajo** *m.* 16
teleconference **videoconferencia** *f.*
telephone **teléfono** *m.* 11
  cell phone **teléfono celular** 11
television **televisión** *f.* 11
  television set **televisor** *m.* 11
tell **decir** *v.* 6
temperature **temperatura** *f.* 10
ten **diez** 1
tennis **tenis** *m.* 4
  tennis shoes **zapatos** *m., pl.* **de tenis**
tension **tensión** *f.* 15
tent **tienda** *f.* **de campaña** 5
tenth **décimo/a** *adj.* 5
terrible **terrible** *adj. m., f.* 13
  it's terrible **es terrible** 13
terrific **chévere** *adj.*
test **prueba** *f.* 2; **examen** *m.* 2
text message **mensaje de texto** *m.* 11

Thank you. **Gracias.** *f., pl.* 1
  Thank you (very much).
    (Muchas) gracias. 1
  Thank you very, very much.
    Muchísimas gracias.
  Thanks (a lot). **(Muchas) gracias.** 1
  Thanks for everything. **Gracias**
    por todo.
  Thanks once again. **Gracias una**
    vez más.
that **que**; **quien(es)**; **lo que** *rel. pron.* 9
  that (one) **ése, ésa, eso** *pron.* 6;
    ese, esa, *adj.* 6
  that (*over there*) **aquél, aquélla,**
    aquello *pron.* 6;
    aquel, aquella *adj.* 6
  that which **lo que** *conj.* 9
  That's me. **Soy yo.**
  that's why **por eso** 11
the **el** *m.*, **la** *f. sing., def. art.*; **los** *m.*,
  las *f. pl., def. art.* 1
theater **teatro** *m.*
their **su(s)** *poss., adj.* 3; **suyo(s)/a(s)**
  poss., pron. 11
them **los/las** *pron.* 5; **les** *pron.* 6
then **después** (*afterward*) *adv.* 7;
  entonces (*as a result*) *adv.* 7;
  luego (*next*) *adv.* 7; **pues** *adv.* 15
there **allí** *adv.* 5
  There is/are… **Hay…** 1;
  There is/are not… **No hay…** 1
therefore **por eso** *adv.* 11
these **éstos, éstas** *pron.* 6;
  estos, estas *adj.* 6
they **ellos/as** *sub. pron.* 1
  they are **ellos/as son** 1
thin **delgado/a** *adj.* 3
thing **cosa** *f.* 1
think **pensar (e:ie)** *v.* 4; (believe)
  creer *v.*
  think about **pensar en** 4
third **tercer, tercero/a** *adj.* 5
thirst **sed** *f.* 3
thirsty: be (very) thirsty **tener** *v.*
  (mucha) sed 3
thirteen **trece** 1
thirty **treinta** 1; thirty (*minutes past
the hour*) **y treinta** 1; **y media** 1
this **este, esta** *adj.*;
  éste, ésta, esto *pron.* 6
  This is… (*introduction*) **Éste/a es…** 1
  This is he/she. (*on telephone*)
    Con él/ella habla. 11
those **ésos, ésas** *pron.* 6;
  esos, esas *adj.* 6
those (over there) **aquéllos, aquéllas** *pron.*
  6; **aquellos, aquellas** *adj.* 6
thousand **mil** *m.* 6
three **tres** 1
three hundred **trescientos/as** 6
throat **garganta** *f.* 10

through **por** *prep.* 11
throughout: throughout the world **en**
  todo el mundo 13
throw **echar** *v.*
Thursday **jueves** *m., sing.* 2
thus (*in such a way*) **así** *adj.*
ticket **boleto** *m.*; **entrada** *f.*; **pasaje** *m.* 5;
  (traffic) **multa** *f.* 11
tie **corbata** *f.* 6
time **vez** *f.* 6; **tiempo** *m.* 4
  buy on time **comprar** *v.* **a plazos** *m., pl.*
  have a good/bad time **pasarlo** *v.*
    bien/mal 9
  We had a great time. **Lo**
    pasamos de película.
times **veces** *f., pl.*
  many times **muchas veces** 10
tip **propina** *f.* 9
tire **llanta** *f.* 11
tired **cansado/a** *adj.* 5
  be tired **estar** *v.* **cansado/a** 5
title **título** *m.*
to **a** *prep.* 1
toast (*drink*) **brindar** *v.* 9
toast (*bread*) **pan** *m.* **tostado**
toasted **tostado/a** *adj.* 8
toaster **tostadora** *f.*
today **hoy** *adv.* 2
  Today is… **Hoy es…** 2, 5
together **juntos/as** *adj.* 9
tomato **tomate** *m.* 8
tomorrow **mañana** *adv.* 1
  See you tomorrow. **Hasta mañana.** 1
tonight **esta noche** *adv.* 4
too **también** *adv.* 7
  too much **demasiado** *adv.* 6;
    en exceso 15
tooth **diente** *m.* 7; tooth **muela** *f.* 10
tornado **tornado** *m.*
tortilla **tortilla** *f.* 8
touch **tocar** *v.* 13
tour an area **recorrer** *v.*; **excursión** *f.*
  go on a tour **hacer** *v.* **una**
    excursión 5
tourism **turismo** *m.* 5
tourist **turista** *m., f.* 1; **turístico/a** *adj.*
toward **para** *prep.* 11; **hacia** *prep.* 14
towel **toalla** *f.* 7
town **pueblo** *m.* 4
trade **oficio** *m.* 16
traffic **circulación** *f.*; **tráfico** *m.* 11
  traffic light **semáforo** *m.* 11
tragedy **tragedia** *f.*
trail **sendero** *m.* 13
  trailhead **sendero** *m.*
train **entrenarse** *v.* 15; **tren** *m.* 5
  train station **estación** *f.* **del tren**
    m. 5
translate **traducir** *v.* 8
trash **basura** *f.* 12
travel **viajar** *v.* 2

C49

VOCABULARIO

travel agency **agencia** *f.* **de viajes** 5
travel agent **agente** *m., f.* **de viajes** 5
travel documents **documentos** *m., pl.* **de viaje**
traveler **viajero/a** *m., f.* 5
traveler's check **cheque** *m.* **de viajero** 14
treat (entertain) **invitar** *v.* 9
tree **árbol** *m.* 13
trillion **billón** 6
trimester **trimestre** *m.* 2
trip **viaje** *m.* 5
take a trip **hacer** *v.* **un viaje** 5
tropical forest **bosque** *m.* **tropical** 13
truck **camión** *m.*
true **cierto/a**; **verdad** *adj.* 13
it's (not) true **(no) es cierto/verdad** 13
trunk **baúl** *m.* 11
truth **verdad** *f.* 6
try **intentar** *v.*; **probar (o:ue)** *v.* 8
try (*to do something*) **tratar** *v.* **de (+ inf.)** 15
try on **probarse (o:ue)** *v.* 7
t-shirt **camiseta** *f.* 6
Tuesday **martes** *m., sing.* 2
tuna **atún** *m.* 8
turkey **pavo** *m.* 8
turn **doblar** *v.* 14
turn off (*electricity/appliance*) **apagar** *v.* 11
turn on (*electricity/appliance*) **poner** *v.* 11; **prender** *v.* 11
turtle **tortuga** *f.* 13
sea turtle **tortuga marina** 13
twelve **doce** 1
twenty **veinte** 1
twenty-eight **veintiocho** 1
twenty-five **veinticinco** 1
twenty-four **veinticuatro** 1
twenty-nine **veintinueve** 1
twenty-one **veintiún, veintiuno/a** 1
twenty-seven **veintisiete** 1
twenty-six **veintiséis** 1
twenty-three **veintitrés** 1
twenty-two **veintidós** 1
twice **dos veces** 6
twisted **torcido/a** *adj.* 10
be twisted **estar** *v.* **torcido/a** 10
two **dos** 1
two hundred **doscientos/as** 6
two times **dos veces** 6

U

ugly **feo/a** *adj.* 3
uncle **tío** *m.* 3
under **debajo de** *prep.* 2; **bajo** *prep.*

understand **comprender** *v.* 3; **entender (e:ie)** *v.* 4
underwear **ropa** *f.* **interior** 6
unemployment **desempleo** *m.*
university **universidad** *f.* 2
unless **a menos que** *adv.* 13
unmarried **soltero/a** *adj.* 9
unpleasant **antipático/a** *adj.* 3
until **hasta** *prep.* 6; **hasta que** *conj.* 13
up **arriba** *adv.*
urgent **urgente** *adj.* 12
It's urgent that… **Es urgente que…** 12
us **nos** *pron.* 5
use **usar** *v.* 6
used for **para** *prep.* 11
useful **útil** *adj.*

V

vacation **vacaciones** *f., pl.* 5
be on vacation **estar** *v.* **de vacaciones** 5
go on vacation **ir** *v.* **de vacaciones** 5
vacuum **pasar** *v.* **la aspiradora** 12
vacuum cleaner **aspiradora** *f.* 12
valley **valle** *m.* 13
various **varios/as** *adj., pl.*
vegetables **verduras** *f., pl.* 8
verb **verbo** *m.*
very **muy** *adv.* 1
very bad **malísimo** 8
very much **muchísimo** *adv.*
Very good, thank you. **Muy bien, gracias.**
(Very) well, thanks. **(Muy) bien, gracias.** 1
vest **chaleco** *m.*
video **video** *m.* 1
video conference **videoconferencia** *f.* 16
videocamera **cámara** *f.* **de video** 11
vinegar **vinagre** *m.* 8
violence **violencia** *f.*
visit **visitar** *v.* 4
visit a monument **visitar un monumento** 4
vitamin **vitamina** *f.* 15
voicemail **buzón** *m.* **de voz** 11
volcano **volcán** *m.* 13
volleyball **vóleibol** *m.* 4
vote **votar** *v.*

W

wait (for) **esperar** *v.* 2
waiter **camarero/a** *m., f.* 8
wake up **despertarse (e:ie)** *v.* 7
walk **caminar** *v.* 2

take a walk **pasear** *v.* 4
walk around the city/town **pasear por la ciudad/el pueblo** 4
Walkman **walkman** *m.*
wall **pared** *f.* 12
wallet **cartera** *f.* 6
want **desear** *v.* 2; **querer (e:ie)** *v.* 4, 12
I don't want to **no quiero** 4
war **guerra** *f.*
warm (oneself) up **calentarse** *v.* 15
wash **lavar** *v.* 12
wash one's face/hands **lavarse** *v.* **la cara/las manos** 7
wash oneself **lavarse** 7
washing machine **lavadora** *f.* 12
watch **mirar** *v.* 2; **reloj** *m.*; **ver** *v.* 4
watch television **mirar (la) televisión** 2
watch movies **ver películas** 4
water **agua** *f.* 8
water pollution **contaminación** *f.* **del agua** 13
water-skiing **esquí** *m.* **acuático** 4
way **manera** *f.*
we **nosotros/as** *sub. pron.* 1
we are **nosotros/as somos** 1
weak **débil** *adj.* 15
wear **llevar** *v.* 6; **usar** *v.* 6; **calzar** *v.* (shoes) 6
weather **tiempo** *m.* 5
It's bad weather. **Hace mal tiempo.** 5
It's nice weather. **Hace buen tiempo.** 5
weaving **tejido** *m.*
Web **red** *f.* 11
website **sitio** *m.* **web** 11
wedding **boda** *f.* 9
Wednesday **miércoles** *m., sing.* 2
week **semana** *f.* 2
weekend **fin** *m.* **de semana** 4
weight **peso** *m.* 15
lift weights **levantar** *v.* **pesas** *f., pl.* 15
Welcome! **¡Bienvenido(s)/a(s)!** *adj.* 12
well **pues** *adv.*; **bueno** *adv.*
well-being **bienestar** *m.* 15
well organized **ordenado/a** *adj.*
west **oeste** *m.* 14
to the west **al oeste** 14
western (*genre*) **de vaqueros** *adj.*
whale **ballena** *f.* 13
what **lo que** 9
what? **¿qué?** *pron.* 1, 9; **¿cuál(es)?** *adj., pron.* 9
At what time…? **¿A qué hora…?** 1
What a…! **¡Qué…!**
What a pleasure to…! **¡Qué gusto (+ inf.)…**
What a surprise! **¡Qué sorpresa!**
What day is it? **¿Qué día es hoy?**
What did he/she do? **¿Qué hizo él/ella?** 6

C50

English-Spanish

What did they do? **¿Qué hicieron ellos/ellas?** 6

What did you do? **¿Qué hiciste?** *fam., sing.;* **¿Qué hizo usted?** *form., sing.;* **¿Qué hicieron ustedes?** *form., pl.* 6

What did you say? **¿Cómo?**

What do you guys think? **¿Qué les parece?** 9

What happened? **¿Qué pasó?**

What is it? **¿Qué es?** 1

What is the date (today)? **¿Cuál es la fecha (de hoy)?**

What is the price? **¿Qué precio tiene?**

What is today's date? **¿Cuál es la fecha de hoy?** 5

What pain! **¡Qué dolor!**

What pretty clothes! **¡Qué ropa más bonita!** 6

What size do you wear? **¿Qué talla lleva/usa?** 6

What time is it? **¿Qué hora es?** 1

What's going on? **¿Qué pasa?** 1

What's happening? **¿Qué pasa?** 1

What's… like? **¿Cómo es…?**

What's new? **¿Qué hay de nuevo?** 1

What's the weather like? **¿Qué tiempo hace?** 5

What's wrong? **¿Qué pasó?**

What's your name? **¿Cómo se llama usted?** *form.* 1

What's your name? **¿Cómo te llamas (tú)?** *fam.* 1

when **cuando** *conj.* 7

When? **¿Cuándo?** *adv.* 2, 9

where **donde** *adv., conj.*

where? (*destination*) **¿adónde?** 2, 9; (*location*) **¿dónde?** *adv.* 1, 9

Where are you from? **¿De dónde eres?** *fam.* 1; **¿De dónde es (usted)?** *form.* 1

Where is…? **¿Dónde está…?** 2

(to) where? **¿adónde?** 2

which **que; lo que** *rel. pron.* 9

which? **¿cuál(es)?** *adj., pron.;* **¿qué?** 2, 9

which one(s)? **¿cuál(es)?** 2

while **mientras** *adv.* 10

white **blanco/a** *adj.* 6

white wine **vino** *m.* **blanco** 8

who **que; quien(es)** *rel. pron.* 9

who? **¿quién(es)?** *pron.* 1, 9

Who is…? **¿Quién es…?** 1

Who is calling? (*on telephone*) **¿De parte de quién?**

Who is speaking? (*on telephone*) **¿Quién habla?** 11

whole **todo/a** *adj.*

whom **quien(es)** *rel. pron.* 9

whose…? **¿de quién(es)…?** *sing., pl.* 1

why? **¿por qué?** *adv.* 2, 9

widowed **viudo/a** *adj.* 9

wife **esposa** *f.* 3

win **ganar** *v.* 4

wind **viento** *m.*

window **ventana** *f.* 2

windshield **parabrisas** *m., sing.* 11

windy: It's (very) windy. **Hace (mucho) viento.** 5

wine **vino** *m.* 8

red wine **vino tinto** 8

white wine **vino blanco** 8

wineglass **copa** *f.* 12

winter **invierno** *m.* 5

wireless (connection) **conexión** *f.* **inalámbrica** 11

wish **desear** *v.* 2; **esperar** *v.* 13

I wish (that) **Ojalá que** 13

with **con** *prep.*

with me **conmigo** 4

with you **contigo** *fam.*

within **dentro de** *prep.*

without **sin** *prep.* 13, 15; **sin que** *conj.* 13

without a doubt **sin duda**

woman **mujer** *f.* 1

wool **lana** *f.* 6

(made of) wool **de lana** 6

word **palabra** *f.* 1

work **trabajar** *v.* 2; **funcionar** *v.* 11; **trabajo** *m.* 16

work (*of art, literature, music, etc.*) **obra** *f.*

work out **hacer** *v.* **gimnasia** 15

world **mundo** *m.* 13

worldwide **mundial** *adj. m., f.*

worried (about) **preocupado/a (por)** *adj.* 5

worry (about) **preocuparse** *v.* **(por)** 7

Don't worry. **No se preocupe.** *form.* 7; **No te preocupes.** *fam.* 7

worse **peor** *adj. m., f.* 8

worst **el/la peor** 8; **lo peor**

Would you like to? **¿Te gustaría?**

write **escribir** *v.* 3

write a letter/post card/e-mail message **escribir una carta/ (tarjeta) postal/un mensaje** *m.* **electrónico** 4

writer **escritor(a)** *m., f.* 16

written **escrito/a** *p.p.* 15

wrong **equivocado/a** *adj.* 5

be wrong **no tener** *v.* **razón** 3

X

X-ray **radiografía** *f.* 10

Y

yard **jardín** *m.* 12; **patio** *m.* 12

year **año** *m.* 5

be… years old **tener** *v.* **… años** 3

yellow **amarillo/a** *adj.* 6

yes **sí** *interj.* 1

yesterday **ayer** *adv.* 6

yet **todavía** *adv.* 5

yogurt **yogur** *m.*

you **tú** *sub. pron. fam. sing.* 1; **usted** *sub. pron. form. sing.* 1; **vosotros/ as** *sub. pron. fam. pl.* 1; **ustedes** *sub. pron. form. pl.* 1; **te** *d. o. pron. fam. sing.* 5; **lo** *d. o. pron. m. form. sing.* 5; **la** *d. o. pron. f. form. sing.* 5; **os** *d. o. pron. fam. pl.* 5; **los** *d. o. pron. m. form. pl.* 5; **las** *d. o. pron. f. form. pl.* 5; **le(s)** *i. o. pron. form.* 6

you are **tú eres** *fam. sing.* 1; **usted es** *form. sing.* 1; **vosotros/as sois** *fam. pl.* 1; **ustedes son** *form. pl.* 1

You don't say! **¡No me digas!** *fam.;* **¡No me diga!** *form.*

You're welcome. **De nada.** 1; **No hay de qué.** 1

young **joven** *adj.* 3

young person **joven** *m., f.* 3

young woman **señorita** *f.* 1

younger **menor** *adj. m., f.* 3

younger brother/sister **hermano/a menor** *m., f.* 3

youngest **el/la menor** *m., f.* 8

your **su(s)** *poss., adj., form.* 3

your **tu(s)** *poss., adj., fam. sing.* 3

your **vuestro(s)/a(s)** *poss., adj. form., pl.*

your(s) *form.* **suyo(s)/a(s)** *poss. pron., form.* 11

your(s) **tuyo(s)/a(s)** *poss., fam., sing.* 11

youth **juventud** *f.* 9; (*young person*) **joven** *m., f.* 1

Z

zero **cero** *m.* 1

C51

ÍNDICE

A

abbreviations (14) **309**
absolute superlative (8) **182**
acabar de + *infinitive* (6) **130**
academic courses (2) **24, 44**
accents (4), (10) **75, 219**
    on homonyms (11) **243**
accidental occurrences with **se** (10) **226**
adjectives
    demonstrative (6) **134**
    descriptive (3) **58**
    nationality (3) **58**
    past participles used as (15) **338**
    position (3) **58**
    possessive (3), (11) **60, 252**
    ser with adjectives (3) **58**
    stressed possessive (11) **252**
adverbs (10) **228**
age questions (3) **54, 64, 70**
al (contraction) (4) **80**
animals (3), (13) **51, 70, 287, 304**
appliances, household (12) **260, 280**
articles, definite and indefinite (1) **11**

B

b (5), (15) **101, 333**
Bajo la lupa
    ¡Los Andes se mueven! (13) **292**
    Beneficios en los empleos (16) **356**
    El Camino Inca (5) **104**
    Los cibercafés (11) **246**
    ¿Cómo te llamas? (3) **56**
    La elección de una carrera universitaria (2) **30**
    Frutas y verduras de América (8) **174**
    Los mercados al aire libre (6) **126**
    Paseando en metro (14) **312**
    El patio central (12) **266**
    Real Madrid y Barça: rivalidad total (4) **78**
    Saludos y besos en los países hispanos (1) **8**
    Semana Santa: vacaciones y tradición (9) **200**
    Servicios de salud (10) **222**
    La siesta (7) **152**
    Spas naturales (15) **336**
bank terms (14) **307, 324**
bathroom objects (7) **146, 166**
birthdays (9) **194, 214**
body parts (7), (10) **146, 166, 216, 234**

buildings
    campus (2) **24, 44**
    general (4) **73, 92**

C

c (8) **171**
campus buildings (2) **24, 44**
capitalization (12) **263**
car terms (11) **240, 244, 258**
celebrations (9) **194, 198, 214**
chores, household (12) **261, 280**
classroom objects and people (2) **24, 25, 44**
clothing (6) **121, 124, 140**
colors (6) **121, 140**
commands
    familiar (**tú**) (14) **316**
    with **nosotros** (14) **318**
    with **Ud.** and **Uds.** (12) **268**
comparatives and superlatives (8) **182**
computer terms (11) **241, 258**
conditional tense (16) **360**
conducir
    present tense (8) **180**
    preterite tense (9) **202**
conjunctions
    requiring subjunctive (13) **298, 304**
    requiring subjunctive or indicative (13) **298, 304**
conocer and **saber** (8) **180**
courses (academic) (2) **24, 44**
courtesy expressions (1) **3, 6, 22**

D

d (6) **123**
daily schedules (7) **147, 166**
dar
    present tense (6) **133**
    preterite tense (9) **203**
    with indirect object pronouns (6) **133**
dates (5) **99, 118**
days of the week (2) **25, 44**
decir
    present tense (6) **133**
    preterite tense (9) **202**
    with indirect object pronouns (6) **133**
definite articles (1) **11**
del (contraction) (1) **14**
demonstrative adjectives and pronouns (6) **134**
describing clothes (6) **121, 124, 140**

describing routines (7) **146, 150, 166**
descriptive adjectives (3) **58**
diphthongs and linking (3) **53**
direct object nouns and pronouns (5) **112**
directions, getting and giving (14) **307, 310, 324**
diversions, related verbs (4) **72, 92**
double object pronouns (8) **178**
downtown shops (14) **306, 324**

E

ecology terms (13) **286, 304**
emergencies, health-related (10) **216, 234**
entertainment, related verbs (9) **194, 214**
environmental terms (13) **286, 304**
estar
    present tense (2) **36**
    preterite tense (9) **202**
    comparing **ser** and **estar** (5) **110**
    with health conditions (2) **36**
    with location (2) **36**
    with conditions (5) **110**
    with emotions (5) **110**
exercise terms (15) **330, 348**

F

familiar (**tú**) commands (14) **316**
family members and relatives (3) **50, 70**
farewells (1) **2, 22**
fitness terms (15) **330, 348**
Flash cultura
    La casa de Frida (12) **267**
    La comida latina (8) **175**
    Comprar en los mercados (6) **127**
    Encuentros en la plaza (1) **9**
    ¿Estrés? ¿Qué estrés? (15) **337**
    Los estudios (2) **31**
    La familia (3) **57**
    Las fiestas (9) **201**
    ¡Fútbol en España! (4) **79**
    Maravillas de la tecnología (11) **247**
    El metro del D.F. (14) **313**
    El mundo del trabajo (16) **357**
    Naturaleza en Costa Rica (13) **293**
    La salud (10) **223**
    Tapas para todos los días (7) **153**
    ¡Vacaciones en Perú! (5) **105**
food and drink (8) **168, 172, 188**
    parties, related foods (9) **194, 214**
forming questions (2) **34**
furniture (12) **261, 280**
future tense (16) **358**

C52

ÍNDICE

G

g (9) **197**
greetings and introductions (1)
 2, 3, 6, 22
grooming, personal (7) **146, 150, 166**
gusta(n), me/te (2) **28**
gustar, gustaría, and verbs like **gustar**
 (7) **160, 166**

H

h (9), (16) **197, 353**
hacer
 present tense (4) **86**
 preterite tense (9) **202**
 with time expressions (10) **220, 234**
hay (1), (10) **12, 224**
health
 conditions with **estar** (5) **110**
 emergencies (10) **216, 234**
 fitness terms (15) **330, 348**
 questions (1), (10) **2, 22, 220**
 stress terms (15) **330, 348**
hotels (5) **98, 118**
housing
 appliances (12) **260, 280**
 chores (12) **261, 280**
 furniture (12) **261, 280**
 general terms (12) **260, 280**
 rooms (12) **260, 280**
 table settings (12) **260, 280**
 types (12) **261, 280**

I

imperfect and preterite contrasted (11)
 248
imperfect (*past*) subjunctive (16)
 362
imperfect tense, regular and irregular
 verbs (10) **224**
impersonal constructions with **se** (10)
 226
indefinite articles (1) **11**
indefinite words (7) **156**
indirect object pronouns (6) **132**
information questions (2) **34**
Internet terms (11) **241, 258**
interrogative words (2) **34**
intonation, for questions (2) **34**
introductions (1) **3, 7, 22**

ir
 present tense (4) **80**
 preterite tense (7) **158**
 ir a + *infinitive* (4) **80**
irregular verbs
 imperfect tense (10) **224**
 preterite tense (9) **202**

J

j (9) **197**
job terms (16) **351, 368**

L

life stages (9) **195, 214**
linking (3) **53**
ll (8), (16) **171, 353**
location with **estar** (2) **36**

M

mail terms (14) **306, 324**
meals (8) **168, 172, 188**
months of the year (5) **99, 118**

N

names of Spanish-speaking countries
 (1) **22**
nationalities (3) **58**
nature terms (13) **286, 304**
negation with **no** (2) **32**
negative words (7) **156**
nosotros/as commands (14) **318**
nouns (1) **10, 22**
numbers
 0–30 (1) **12**
 31–100 (2) **38**
 101 and higher (6) **128**

Ñ

ñ (8) **171**

O

object pronouns
 direct (5) **112**
 double (8) **178**
 indirect (6) **132**
 reflexive (7) **154**
occupations (16) **350, 368**
ofrecer, present tense (8) **180**
oír, present tense (4) **86**
ordinal numbers (5) **99**

P

participles
 past used as adjectives (15) **338**
 present with progressive tenses
 (5) **108**
parties, related people, items, foods (9)
 194, 198, 214
parts of the body (7), (10) **146, 166,
 216, 234**
past participles as adjectives (15) **338**
past perfect tense (15) **342**
past (*imperfect*) subjunctive (16) **362**
perfect tenses
 past perfect (15) **342**
 present perfect (15) **340**
pero vs. **sino** (7) **156**
personal **a** (5) **112**
place settings (12) **260, 280**
plural of nouns (1) **10**
poder, preterite tense (9) **202**
poner
 present tense (4) **86**
 preterite tense (9) **202**
por and **para,** uses (11) **250**
position of adjectives (3) **58**
possessive adjectives (3), (11)
 60, 252
possessive pronouns (11) **252**
post office terms (14) **306, 324**
present perfect tense (15) **340**
present progressive
 tense (5) **108**
prepositions of location (2) **36**
present subjunctive (12) **270**
preterite tense
 regular verbs (6) **130**
 irregular verbs (9) **202**
preterite vs. imperfect (11) **248**
professions (16) **350, 368**
pronouns
 demonstratives (6) **134**
 direct object (5) **112**
 double object (8) **178**
 indirect object (6) **132**
 possessive (11) **252**
 reflexive (7) **154**
 relative (9) **206**
 subject (1) **14**
 use and omission of subject (2) **32**
punctuation (13) **289**

C53

ÍNDICE

Q

¿**Qué?** and ¿**cuál?** (9) **208**
querer, preterite tense (9) **202**
questions, forming (2) **34**
    age (3) **55, 64, 70**
    information questions (2) **34**
    intonation for questions (2) **34**

R

r and **rr** (7) **149**
reflexive verbs (7) **146, 147,**
    154, 155, 166
regular verbs
    present tense
        –ar verbs (2) **32**
        –er and **–ir** verbs (3) **62**
    preterite (6) **130**
relative pronouns (9) **206**
restaurants (8) **168, 172, 188**
routines (7) **146, 150, 166**

S

saber
    and **conocer** (8) **180**
    preterite tense (9) **202**
salir, present tense (4) **86**
seasons of the year (5) **99, 118**
sequencing actions, words for (7)
    147, 166
se constructions
    accidental occurrences (10) **226**
    impersonal expressions (10) **226**
    reflexive verbs (7) **154**
    unplanned occurrences (10) **226**
ser
    comparing **ser** and **estar** (5) **110**
    present tense (1) **14**
    preterite tense (7) **158**
    to show identification (1) **14**
    to show origin (1) **15**
    to show possession (1) **14**
    with adjectives (3) **58**
    with nationalities (3) **58**
    with professions (1) **15**
shape, staying in (15) **330, 348**
shopping (6) **120, 124, 140**
shops downtown (14) **306, 324**
sickness vocabulary (10) **217, 234**
Spanish alphabet (1) **5**
Spanish speaking-countries, names
    of (1) **22**

sports and leisure activities (4)
    72, 73, 92
stages of life (9) **195, 214**
stem-changing verbs
    present tense (4) **82, 84**
    preterite tense (8) **176**
stress and accent marks (4) **75**
stressed possessive adjectives (11) **252**
stress (tension) terms (15) **330, 348**
subject pronouns (1) **14**
    use and omission (2) **32**
subjunctive
    following certain conjunctions
    (13) **298**
    past (*imperfect*) (16) **362**
    present (12) **270**
    to express indefiniteness and
    nonexistence (14) **314**
    with verbs and expressions of will
    and influence (12) **274**
    with verbs and expressions of doubt,
    disbelief, and denial (13) **296**
    with verbs and expressions of
    emotion (13) **294**
superlatives (8) **182**
    absolute superlatives (8) **182**

T

t (6) **123**
table settings (12) **260, 280**
technology terms (11) **241, 244, 258**
telephone, talking on (11) **244**
tener
    present tense (3) **64**
    preterite tense (9) **202**
    expressions with (3) **64**
telling time (1) **16**
time expressions with **hacer** (10)
    220, 234
town places (14) **306, 324**
traducir
    present tense (8) **180**
    preterite tense (9) **202**
traer
    present tense (4) **86**
    preterite tense (9) **202**
travel terms (5) **98, 118**

U

Ud. and **Uds.** commands (12) **268**
unplanned occurrences with **se** (10)
    226

V

v (5), (15) **101, 333**
venir
    present tense (3) **64**
    preterite tense (9) **202**
ver, present tense (4) **86**
verbs describing routines and personal
    grooming (7) **146, 150, 166**
verbs with irregular **yo** forms (**hacer,**
    oír, poner, salir, suponer,
    traer, and **ver**) (4) **86**
¡Vivan los países hispanos!
    Argentina (10) **235**
    Bolivia (10) **235**
    Canadá (2) **45**
    Chile (10) **235**
    Colombia (8) **189**
    Costa Rica (14) **325**
    Cuba (6) **141**
    Ecuador (8) **189**
    El Salvador (12) **281**
    España (16) **369**
    Estados Unidos, Los (2) **45**
    Guatemala (12) **281**
    Honduras (12) **281**
    México (4) **93**
    Nicaragua (14) **325**
    Panamá (14) **325**
    Paraguay (10) **235**
    Perú (8) **189**
    Puerto Rico (6) **141**
    República Dominicana (6) **141**
    Uruguay (10) **235**
    Venezuela (8) **189**

W

weather expressions (5) **98, 118**
work-related terms (16) **351, 368**
written accents (4), (10), (11)
    75, 219, 243

Y

y (16) **353**
years (e.g. 2015) (6) **128**
yes-no questions (2) **34**

Z

z (8) **171**

CREDITS

Text Credits

256–257 © TUTE.

322–323 © Denevi, Marco, *Cartas peligrosas y otros cuentos*. Obras completas, Tomo 5, Buenos Aires, Corregidor, 1999, págs. 192–193.

346–347 © EL VIAJE by CRISTINA PERI ROSSI

366–367 © Augusto Monterroso.

Photography and Art Credits

All images © Vista Higher Learning unless otherwise noted. Fotonovela photos provided by Carolina Zapata.

Cover: (full pg) © Cristina Llerena/Arcangel Images.

Front Matter (IAE): IAE-6 © INSADCO Photography/Alamy; **IAE-34** © Kevin Schafer/Corbis.

Front Matter (SE): iii Dario Eusse Tobon; **xxix** © Kevin Schafer/Corbis.

Lesson One: 1 (full pg) Carolina Zapata; **2** (l, tr) Martín Bernetti; (br) Darío Eusse Tobón; **3** (l, r) Martín Bernetti; **4** Martín Bernetti; **5** (l, m, r) Martín Bernetti; **8** (l) Rachel Distler; (r) Ali Burafi; **9** Paul Díez; **11** (left col: t, left col: mr, left col: bl, left col: br, right col: tm, right col: bl, right col: bm, right col: br) Martín Bernetti; (left col: ml) © Supertrooper/Shutterstock.com; (right col: tl) Darío Eusse Tobón; (right col: tr) © VibrantImage/Big Stock Photo; **12** Darío Eusse Tobón; **15** (t) © Fred Prouser/Reuters/Corbis; (ml) © s_bukley/Shutterstock.com; (mm) © Hector Mata/AFP/Getty Images; (mr) © Rafiqur Rahman/Reuters/Corbis; (b) © Reuters/CORBIS; **18** Martín Bernetti; **19** (t) Martín Bernetti; (b) © Philip Lange/123RF.

Lesson Two: 23 (full pg) Carolina Zapata; **24** (tr, br, tl) Martín Bernetti; (bl) © Moodboard/123RF; **25** (t, ml, mr, b) Martín Bernetti; **26** (l) © Bettmann/Corbis; (r) Carlos Arango; **30** (l) Mauricio Osorio; (r) © Pablo Corral V/Corbis; **31** © Damir Karan/iStockphoto; **33** (t, ml, br) Martín Bernetti; (mr) © LWA/Sharie Kennedy/Blend Images/Alamy; (bl) © Kenhurst/Dreamstime.com; **35** (t) © PNC/Media Bakery; (b) Martín Bernetti; **38** (l) Martín Bernetti; (r) © ADALBERTO ROQUE/AFP/Getty Images; **40** (tl, b) Martín Bernetti; (tr) Darío Eusse Tobón; **41** (t, b) Martín Bernetti; **42** Mauricio Osorio; **43** (t) José Blanco; (inset) Pascal Pernix; **45** © Schwarz Shaul/Corbis Sygma; **46** (tl) Janet Dracksdorf; (tr) © Patrick Ward/Corbis; (bl) © Scott Lituchy/Star Ledger/Corbis; (bml) © Lou Rocco/Disney ABC Television Group/Getty Images; (bmm) © Tina Gill/Shutterstock.com; (bmr) © spacephotos.com/Spacephotos/Age Fotostock; (br) © Alex Wong/Getty Images; **47** (tl) © BIG CHEESE/Age Fotostock; (tr) © Richard Cummins/Corbis; (b) Marta Mesa.

Lesson Three: 49 (full pg) Carolina Zapata; **50** Martín Bernetti; **51** (t, br) Martín Bernetti; (bl) Gloria Elena Restrepo; **52** (tl) Darío Eusse Tobón; (tm, bl, bm, br) Martín Bernetti; (tr) Carolina Zapata; **56** (tl) © David Cantor/ASSOCIATED PRESS; (tr) © Rafael Perez/Reuters/Corbis; (b) © Martial Trezzini/epa/Corbis; **57** © Media Bakery; **59** (left col: tl) © Chris Fertnig/iStockphoto; (left col: tm) © Juniors Bildarchiv/Alamy; (left col: tr, left col: bm, left col: br) Martín Bernetti; (left col: bl) © iofoto/Fotolia.com; (right col: t) © Larry Brownstein/Media Bakery; (right col: mtl) © Heribert Proepper/AP Images; (right col: mtr) © Shubroto Chattopadhyay/Corbis; (right col: mml) © Jon Kopaloff/Contributor/FilmMagic/Getty Images; (right col: mmr) © ZUMA Wire Service/Alamy; (right col: mbl) Ruben Varela; (right col: mbr) © Dennis Brack/Danita Delimont, Agent/Alamy; (right col: b) Gloria Elena Restrepo; **60** (l) © Melica/Dreamstime.com; (r) © Jupiterimages/Getty Images; **61** (left col, right col: m, right col: b) Martín Bernetti; (right col: t) Darío Eusse Tobón; **62** (t) © Design Pics Inc./Alamy; (b) Martín Bernetti; **63** (t) Darío Eusse Tobón; (ml, bl) Martín Bernetti; (mr) Alejandro Isaza Saldarriaga; (br) © Photodisc/Alamy; **66** (tl) Carolina Patiño Andrade; (tr) Martín Bernetti; (b) Darío Eusse Tobón; **67** (tl) Ventus Pictures; (tr, bl, br) Martín Bernetti; **68** (t, ml, bl) Martín Bernetti; (mr) © Chuck Savage/Corbis; **68–69** (b) Martín Bernetti; **69** (t) Nora y Susana © Fotocolombia.com.

Lesson Four: 71 (full pg) Carolina Zapata; **72** (tl) © PCN Photography/Alamy; (tr) Darío Eusse Tobón; (b) © Dirk-jan Mattaar/Dreamstime.com; **73** (tl) © Adventure_Photo/iStockphoto; (tm) Martín Bernetti; (tr) © Neal Preston/CORBIS; (bl) Linda Gee; (br) Darío Eusse Tobón; **74** (tl, tmr, tr, br) Martín Bernetti; (tml) Darío Eusse Tobón; (bl) © Image Source/Corbis; **78** (l) © Javier Soriano/AFP/Getty Images; (r) © AP Photo/Fernando Bustamante; **79** © Roberto Adrian/iStockphoto; **80** © Monkey Business Images/Dreamstime.com; **83** (tl) © Rolf

C55

CREDITS

Bodmer/iStockphoto; (tr) © Ana Abejon/iStockphoto; (b) © Curtis J. Morley/iStockphoto; **85** (left col) Martín Bernetti; (right col: t) © VojtechVlk/Shutterstock.com; (right col: b) © koh sze kiat/Shutterstock.com; **87** (left col: tl, left col: tr, left col: bl) Martín Bernetti; (left col: br, right col) Darío Eusse Tobón; **88** (tl, tr) Martín Bernetti; (b) Darío Eusse Tobón; **89** (t, b) Martín Bernetti; **90** (t) Janet Dracksdorf; (b) © Ghislain & Marie David de Lossy/2007 Cultura/Jupiterimages; **91** Lauren Krolick; **93** © Bill Ross/CORBIS; **94** (t) © jschultes/Big Stock Photo; (bl, br) © Corel/Corbis; **95** (tl) © Bettmann/CORBIS; (tr) Diego Rivera. (1866–1957) *Sugar Cane*, 1930. Fresco, 57 1/8 x 94 1/8 inches (145.1 x 239.1 cm). Gift of Mr. and Mrs. Herbert Cameron Morris, 1943. Location: Philadelphia Museum of Art, Philadelphia, U.S.A. © 2013 Banco de México Diego Rivera Frida Kahlo Museums Trust, Mexico, D.F./Artists Rights Society (ARS), New York. Photo credit: © Philadelphia Museum of Art/Corbis; (bl) Katie Wade; (br) Darío Eusse Tobón.

Lesson Five: 97 (full pg) Carolina Zapata; **98** (tl, tr, b) Martín Bernetti; **99** (t) Martín Bernetti; (b) Darío Eusse Tobón; **100** (l, m) Martín Bernetti; (r) Darío Eusse Tobón; **104** © Jeremy Horner/Corbis; **105** Paola Rios-Schaaf; **106** © Medioimages/Photodisc/Getty Images; **107** Martín Bernetti; **115** Martín Bernetti; **116** Carlos Gaudier; **117** (t) © Corel/Corbis; (mt, mb, b) Carlos Gaudier.

Lesson Six: 119 (full pg) Carolina Zapata; **120** (l, r) Martín Bernetti; **121** (l) Carolina Zapata; (r) Martín Bernetti; **122** (l) Martín Bernetti; (r) Darío Eusse Tobón; **126** (t) © Jose Caballero Digital Press Photos/Newscom; (b) © INSADCO Photography/Alamy; **127** © Sergey Ivanchenko/iStockphoto; **131** (all) Martín Bernetti; **133** © Javier Larrea/Age Fotostock; **134** (all) Martín Bernetti; **135** © Javier Larrea/Age Fotostock; **136** (all) Darío Eusse Tobón; **137** (t, b) Martín Bernetti; **138** Paula Díez; **139** Paula Díez; **141** © PictureLake/Fotolia.com; **142** (tl, tr) Doren Spinner; (bl) © Michael Kim/Corbis; (br) © Mike Segar/Reuters/Corbis; **143** (t) © Jeremy Horner/Corbis; (b) © R. Peterkin/Fotolia.com.

Lesson Seven: 145 (full pg) Carolina Zapata; **146** (l, r) Martín Bernetti; **147** (tl, b) Martín Bernetti; (tr) Darío Eusse Tobón; **148** (tl, tr, bml, br) Darío Eusse Tobón; (tml, tmr, bl, bmr) Martín Bernetti; **152** © Stewart Cohen/Getty Images; **153** © Ocean/Brand X/Corbis; **155** (tl, tr, bl) Martín Bernetti; (br) Darío Eusse Tobón; **157** (t, m) Martín Bernetti; (b) Darío Eusse Tobón; **158** © Masterfile (Royalty-Free Division); **159** Martín Bernetti; **162** Anne Loubet; **163** (t) © Corbis; (b) Jimena V.

Lesson Eight: 167 (full pg) Carolina Zapata; **168** (t) Martín Bernetti; (b) © Jack Puccio/iStockphoto; **169** (t, m, br) Martín Bernetti; (bl) © Barry Gregg/Corbis; **174** (t) Rachel Distler; (b) © Greg Elms/Lonely Planet Images/Getty Images; **175** María Eugenia Corbo; **176** (l) © Benitez, Rodolfo/Age Fotostock; (ml) Janet Dracksdorf; (mr) © StockFood/Gustavo Andrade - StockFood Munich; (r) José Blanco; **177** Darío Eusse Tobón; **180** © Jack Hollingsworth/Corbis; **181** (t) © Ben Blankenburg/Corbis; (ml) © Corbis; (mm, bm, br) Martín Bernetti; (mr, bl) Darío Eusse Tobón; **184** © Jack Hollingsworth/Getty Images; **185** Darío Eusse Tobón; **189** © Galen Rowell/Corbis; **190** (tl) © John Beatty/Getty Images; (tr) Martín Bernetti; (b) © Jeff Luckett/iStockphoto; **191** (t) © Piero Pomponi/Getty Images; (bl) Jimena V.; (br) © Marshall Bruce/iStockphoto.

Lesson Nine: 193 (full pg) Carolina Zapata; **194** (tl) © Susana/Fotocolombia.com; (tr, m) Martín Bernetti; (b) © Andrew Unangst/Corbis; **196** Martín Bernetti; **200** (l) © Sylwia Blaszczyszyn/Dreamstime.com; (r) © PictureNet/Corbis; **201** © Jeff Greenberg/Alamy; **204** (l) © Nikolai Sorokin/Dreamstime.com; (r) © ecliff6/iStockphoto; **205** (l) Anne Loubet; (m, r) Martín Bernetti; **208** (t) © Trouvail/Dreamstime.com; (b) © padnpen/iStockphoto; **209** (t) Darío Eusse Tobón; (ml, mr, br) Martín Bernetti; (bl) Gloria Elena Restrepo; **211** Darío Eusse Tobón; **212** (t) © Katrina Brown/123RF; (b) Esteban Corbo; **213** Armando Brito.

Lesson Ten: 215 (full pg) Carolina Zapata; **216** (t) Martín Bernetti; (b) José Blanco; **217** (t) © kmiragaya/Big Stock Photo; (b) © James Steidl/Dreamstime.com; **222** (l) © Ricardo Figueroa/AP Images; (r) José Blanco; **223** Janet Dracksdorf; **228** Martín Bernetti; **230** Darío Eusse Tobón; **231** © Media Bakery; **232** Martín Bernetti; **235** © Duomo/Corbis; **236** (t) Ali Burafi; (b) © gaelj/Fotolia.com; **237** (all) Ali Burafi.

Lesson Eleven: 239 (full pg) Carolina Zapata; **240** (t, br) Martín Bernetti; (bl) Celeste Avila; **241** (l) © Dmitry Kutlayev/iStockphoto; (r) © Julie Masson Deshaies/iStockphoto; **242** Darío Eusse Tobón; **246** (l) Esteban Andrés Corbo; (r) Carolina Zapata; **247** © Pictrough/Big Stock Photo; **249** Martín Bernetti; **253** (left col: t, left col: b, right

CREDITS

col: t) © Luca di Filippo/iStockphoto; (right col: mtl) © Fred De Bailliencourt/iStockphoto; (right col: mtr, right col: mbr, right col: bl) Martín Bernetti; (right col: mbl, right col: br) Liliana P. Bobadilla; **254** Martín Bernetti; **255** © frans lemmens/Alamy.

Lesson Twelve: 259 (full pg) Carolina Zapata; **260** (t, b) Martín Bernetti; **261** (tl, tr) Martín Bernetti; (b) © Comstock Images/Jupiterimages; **262** (l, r) Martín Bernetti; **266** (l) © Dusko Despotovic/Corbis; (r) Martín Bernetti; **267** © Iconotec/Alamy; **273** Martín Bernetti; **277** © Tony Arruza/Corbis; **278** © Chile DesConocido/Alamy; **281** © Owen Franken/Corbis; **282** (t) © Kato Inowe/Dreamstime.com; (bl) © Dave G. Houser/Corbis; (br) © Craig Lovell/Corbis; **283** (tl) © Kevin Schafer/Corbis; (tr) © Tony Arruza/Corbis; (b) © OSCAR RIVERA/Xinhua Press/Corbis.

Lesson Thirteen: 285 (full pg) Carolina Zapata; **286** (tl, b) Martín Bernetti; (tr) Rachel Distler; **287** (tl) © Ron Masessa/iStockphoto; (tm) © Wendy Boos/iStockphoto; (tr) © Simone van den Berg/iStockphoto; (b) © Darren Greenwood/Design Pics/Corbis; **288** (tl) Carlos Arango; (tml) © Daniel Stein/iStockphoto; (tmr, b) Martín Bernetti; (tr) © Dpenn/Dreamstime.com; **292** (t) © Clive Tully/Alamy; (b) © Fotosearch; **293** © Paul Springett 05/Alamy; **299** © Rick Rusing/Getty Images; **300** © Deron Rodehaver/123RF; **301** Doren Spinner.

Lesson Fourteen: 305 (full pg) Carolina Zapata; **306** (m, bl) Martín Bernetti; **307** (tl) Martín Bernetti; (tr) © skynesher/iStockphoto; (b) © bilge/iStockphoto; **308** (tl) Anne Loubet; (tm, tr, bl, bm, br) Martín Bernetti; **312** (t) José Blanco; (b) www.metro.df.gob.mx; **313** © meunierd/Shutterstock.com; **317** Darío Eusse Tobón; **319** Darío Eusse Tobón; **320** Martín Bernetti; **321** (t, b) Martín Bernetti; **323** © Radius Images/Alamy; **325** © Bettmann/Corbis; **326** (t) Oscar Artavia Solano; (bl) © John Nakata/Corbis; (br) © Bettmann/Corbis; **327** (t) © Bernard Bisson/Sygma/Corbis; (b) © Bill Gentile/Corbis.

Lesson Fifteen: 329 (full pg) Carolina Zapata; **330** (t, b) Martín Bernetti; (m) © Andrew Manley/iStockphoto; **331** (l) © Ints Vikmanis/iStockphoto; (r) Martín Bernetti; **336** (l) © Krzysztof Dydynski/Lonely Planet Images/Getty Images; (r) Oscar Artavia Solano; **337** © Ximagination/Big Stock Photo; **338** (t) Darío Eusse Tobón; (mt, mb, b) Martín Bernetti; **342** Martín Bernetti; **344** Martín Bernetti; **345** (t) Martín Bernetti; (b) Doren Spinner; **346** Martín Bernetti.

Lesson Sixteen: 349 (full pg) Carolina Zapata; **350** (tl) Darío Eusse Tobón; (tr, br) Martín Bernetti; (bl) © Glyn Jones/Corbis; **351** (t) © jeffwqc/Big Stock Photo; (m) © pressmaster/Fotolia.com; (b) Martín Bernetti; **356** (t) © PhotoAlto/Alamy; (b) © Rui Vale de Sousa/Fotolia.com; **357** © maigidesign/Big Stock Photo; **365** (t) Martín Bernetti; (b) Darío Eusse Tobón; **366** © Catherine Karnow/Corbis; **369** © Elke Stolzenberg/Corbis; **370** (t) © graficart.net/Alamy; (b) © Reuters/Corbis; **371** (tl) Velazquez, Diego Rodriguez (1599–1660) *Las Meninas* (with Velazquez' self-portrait) or the *Family of Philip IV*, 1656. Oil on canvas, 276 x 318 cm. Museo del Prado, Madrid, Spain. Photo credit: Ali Burafi; (tr) José Blanco;(b) © Paul Almasy/Corbis.

Television Credits

"Azucarlito Pedro" By permission of Azucarlito, Bokeh and CAMARA\TBWA.
"Balay" By permission of Jean Marie Boursicot.
"Cruzar la avenida 9 de Julio" By permission of Tango Films.
"Davivienda" By permission of Davivienda.
"Down Taxco" By permission of Univision.com.
"Edenor" By permission of Edenor S.A.
"Galerías" By permission of Jean Marie Boursicot.
"Jumbo mountainbike" By permission of Cencosud.
"Mastercard perrito" By permission of Edgardo Tettamanti.
"Personal - Hippie" By permission of Personal Argentina.
"Personal - Tres deseos" By permission of Personal Argentina.
"Sopas Roa" By permission of Andres Felipe Roa.
"Strepsils" By permission of Jean Marie Boursicot.
"Totofutbol" By permission of Diego Reves.
"Trivago" By permission of Trivago.
"Turismo a Suchitoto" By permission of La Prensa Gráfica.

About the Authors

José A. Blanco founded Vista Higher Learning in 1998. A native of Barranquilla, Colombia, Mr. Blanco holds a B.A. in literature from the University of California, Santa Cruz, and an M.A. in Hispanic studies from Brown University. He has worked as a writer, editor, and translator for Houghton Mifflin and D.C. Heath and Company, and has taught Spanish at the secondary and university levels. Mr. Blanco is also the co-author of several other Vista Higher Learning programs: **VISTAS, AVENTURAS** and **PANORAMA** at the introductory level, **IMAGINA, VENTANAS, FACETAS,** and **ENFOQUES** at the intermediate level, and **REVISTA** at the advanced conversation level.

Philip Redwine Donley received his M.A. in Hispanic Literature from the University of Texas at Austin in 1986 and his Ph.D. in Foreign Language Education from the University of Texas at Austin in 1997. Dr. Donley taught Spanish at Austin Community College, Southwestern University, and the University of Texas at Austin. He published articles and conducted workshops about language anxiety, language anxiety management, and the development of critical thinking skills, and was involved in research about teaching languages to the visually impaired. Dr. Donley was also the co-author of three other introductory college Spanish textbook programs published by Vista Higher Learning, **AVENTURAS, VISTAS,** and **PANORAMA.**